Play Your Best Nine Ball

Philip B. Capelle

First Edition
Billiards Press, Huntington Beach

Play Your Best Nine Ball

Philip B. Capelle

Publication Date: January, 2002

Published by: Billiards Press
P.O. Box 400
Midway City, CA 92655

First Printing

Printed in the United Stated of America

10 9 8 7 6 5 4 3 2 1

Library of Congress Control Number 2001118934

ISBN 0-9649204-3-3

Dedication

I dedicate this book to the late Jay Swanson. Watching "Swanee" play Nine Ball was one of the true joys of my pool career. He was a good friend, a genuinely nice guy, and an awesome player.

Acknowledgements

Working on this book was a true labor of love. Every day I looked forward to diagramming, writing, researching and learning something new about Nine Ball. Once again I was blessed with the support of friends and associates who share my passion for the game. I was fortunate to have them work with me, for there is no way the book would have turned nearly as well without their contributions.

Pat Fleming of Accu-Stats Video Productions and his team have toured the country for over a dozen years filming the very best professionals in tournament competition. He supported my efforts every step of the way and was kind enough to allow me to make use of shots and comments that appear on Accu-Stats extensive library of tapes.

Paul Harris was again the man at the computer, relentlessly turning my hand draw work into the splendid diagrams that are perhaps the most important feature of the book. He also laid out the book and he created the colorful cover that may have attracted you to this book in the first place. He was a constant source of positive energy for the project, and I thoroughly enjoyed our daily conversations on the book. Thanks again to the staff at *Pool & Billiard Magazine* for supporting my work.

Todd Fleitmann, a fellow BCA Certified Instructor, provided consulting and editing services. He provided numerous ideas for improving the quality of the book, and his keen eye for detail was instrumental in ensuring the accuracy of the illustrations.

Roy Yamane, a Master BCA instructor, and I spent several afternoons testing many of the shots in the book and discussing pool theory. He has the unique ability to take a good idea and expand and improve upon it.

Paul Gray and I conducted numerous research sessions at Danny Kuykendall's poolroom. He provided valuable assistance in running many of the tests that ensured the accuracy of the diagrams in the book.

Long time friends Rachel Brown and Regina Girardot as well as Melinda Bailey were very helpful in providing ideas for the women's perspective on pool. Thanks also go to any one who I may have failed to mention and to the hundreds of pool players I've met over the last 30+ years who are a part of the pages that follow.

Introduction

History

In the movie "The Hustler", which came out in 1961, Minnesota Fats and Eddie Felson were featured in two titanic duels of Straight Pool. When the "Color of Money" was released in 1986, the featured game had switched to Nine-Ball. While Eight Ball continues to be the most widely played game, Nine Ball has clearly emerged as the game of choice for the majority of serious pool players. Today Nine Ball is the game played at almost every major professional tournament around the world. In addition, Nine Ball at the amateur level has exploded as the number of weekly tournaments, regional events and leagues has grown tremendously over the last 10-15 years.

There were many great Nine Ball players prior to 1970 who avoided the limelight of tournament play, preferring instead to play high stakes games in relative obscurity. Because these great players avoided tournaments in years past, it is difficult to rank them with a high degree of accuracy. Most observers, however, are in agreement that Luther Lassiter was the greatest Nine Ball player in the era before the game achieved the widespread popularity it enjoys today. And many still feel he was the best ever.

While some would disagree, I personally feel the best test of a player's game is their performance in tournament competition. Tournaments demand that a player bring their best game to the table against a variety of opponents. This of course eliminates some of the great money players who seem to find their game only after several hours of uninterrupted competition against a solitary opponent.

The record book shows that from the 1970's on, the best players in tournament completion were, Jim Rempe, Mike Sigel, Earl Strickland, Buddy Hall, Nick Varner, Johnny Archer, and Efren Reyes. While most of these great champions are still active, Nine Ball has become a global game. It is now common for winners of major events to come from all over the globe.

While it would be great for fans of the sport to see the top men pros live on TV on a regular basis, such is not the case as this is being written. Serious students and fans of the game, however, can watch these marvels in tournament competition thanks to the efforts of Pat Fleming and his team at Accu-Stats, which has filmed pro events for over a dozen years.

On the women's side, Jean Balukas was dominant in Nine Ball in the 1980's before women's pool was televised on a regular basis. From the mid 1990's on, Allison Fisher has logged more TV time than any other player while dominating the ladies tour. Other fine players who have captured world titles or are well known to fans include Loree Jon Jones, Jeanette Lee, Robin Dodson, Ewa Mataya-Laurence and Karen Corr.

The Game of Nine Ball

Nine Ball is a fast paced game that provides a stern test of your skills. You need to shoot with great accuracy, play pin point position, play killer safeties and be able to kick or jump your way out of a jam. And at the higher levels of play, it helps to have a powerful and dependable break.

The object of Nine Ball is to sink the 9-ball In Nine Ball, you can win at any time as long as you hit the lowest numbered ball first. This unique feature brings in an element of luck and a degree of excitement to Nine Ball unlike no other game of pool.

The 500 Game Study

I conducted a study of 500 pro games as part of my research for this book. The study consisted largely of the exploits of the players whose names I mentioned a few moments ago. The purpose of the study was to shed some light on how the game is played at the very highest levels. My findings, several of which are sprinkled throughout the book, should be useful to players of all levels.

How to Use This Book

This book is intended to be your one stop reference guide to playing Nine Ball. It is for players of all levels of skill who have a sincere desire to play their best Nine Ball. The book is also designed to complement my previous books, *Play Your Best Pool* and *A Mind For Pool*, which give you a well-rounded course in pool and an extensive guide to the mental game.

I suggest you develop your own specific course of study based on your game and goals. You can design your curriculum by making extensive use of the detailed table of contents. Read through it and make a list of the things that you need to work on right now. Once you have mastered the subject matter, pick out your next course of study.

You certainly won't find a doctor or lawyer mastering their profession in a single semester. Similarly, it takes a long time to earn your degree in pool. I recommend that you take your time reading and implementing the material in the book. I also suggest that you view the book as a reference source and as a refresher course.

You can play a respectable game of Nine Ball by mastering 30-50% of the material in the book. But if you wish to play your very best Nine Ball, you eventually have to know everything in the book and more, for no book can cover everything. Keep in mind, however, that although there is much to learn, you have a lifetime to enjoy the fruits of your labor.

The ABC System

The wide range of player's skills dictates that players of varying levels should adopt strategies that correspond to their game. Average players, may see the same shot in several different ways because of their varying skills and levels of knowledge about what to do in a given situation. As a rule of thumb, the better you play Nine-Ball, the more your choices of shots will mirror other players at your level. At the pro level, there is usually a one single best shot in most positions, and the pros are capable of recognizing it and playing it in the most optimal fashion.

I have divided players into three broad categories that are based on your current level of skill. I refer to the rating in several places in the book as a means of tailoring the instruction to your current level of play. Below is a rough guide to rating your current level of play. For a more detailed explanation of my ABC rating system, please see pages 360-361.

Player Ratings

C is an average player. Your typical daily high run is 5-6 balls.

B is an advanced player: You can consistently run 5-7 balls, and are capable of running the easier layouts.

A is an expert player. You can run complete racks with consistency.

I mentioned a moment ago that you should design you course in Nine Ball based on your game and level of play. The suggestions that follow should be helpful for players at each of the levels mentioned above.

C Players Begin by brushing up on your fundamentals starting with the first 10 pages of Chapter 1. The most critical ingredient to Nine Ball is position play. Master the position routes labeled C in Chapter 3, then move on to the B's. Learn the basics of safety play as this can be an effective means of winning games against other C Players.

B Players Start by diagnosing your game. Pick out those areas you feel need work using the expanded table of contents. Include items that could use a refresher. Design your curriculum, and begin filling in the gaps in your game.

A Players– Evaluate your game to discover what still needs work. Look throughout the complete contents of the book for the fine points that can add an extra dimension to your game. Remember, the learning never stops if you want to reach your full potential as a player.

You can raise your winning percentage in competition right away with no increase in your skills by taking a more strategic approach to the game. Chapter 13, The ABC's of Strategy, gives you a game plan for competing successfully against opponents at all three levels of play.

The Illustrations

The illustrations are designed to compliment the text. The illustrations have been drawn perfectly to scale so that you can see exactly how the shots and strategies really work at the table. There are no balls that won't fit into the pockets or other techniques that detract from the realism of the shots. In fact, over 140 of the books' 470 illustrations are shots that have appeared in tournament competition by the world's best players. They were chosen primarily for their instructive value, but I think you will find the exploits of the great champions to be entertaining as well.

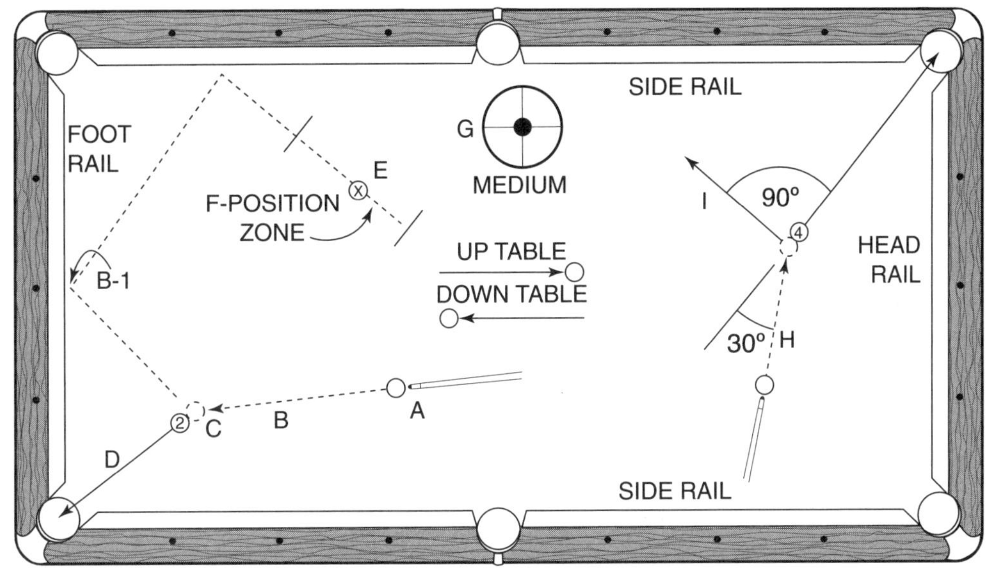

A The cue shows which direction the cue ball is being shot. When english is being applied, the cue will be positioned to either the left or right of center. You can gain the shooter's perspective by turning the book so you are looking straight down the cue stick, just as if you were playing the shot.
B The dashed line shows the path of the cue ball to the object ball, as well as its path after contact.
B-1 The cue ball's path is shown by where the center of the cue ball is traveling. As a result, the line will never touch the rail.
C The dashed circle shows the cue ball's position at contact with the object ball.
D The solid line shows the path of the object ball. In most, but not all cases, it will be to the pocket. On certain shots, the line into the pocket will be purposefully drawn to one side of the pocket or the other.
E The cue ball with an X inside shows where the cue ball has come to rest. When you see a series of cue balls with an X on one shot, they are illustrating several possible stopping points for the cue ball. On straight in shots when the cue ball stops dead at the point of contact, the X cue ball is used to show both contact and the cue ball's ending location.
F You will find descriptive text on the diagrams where appropriate throughout the book.
G Whenever the speed of stroke and cueing are particularly important to your understanding of a shot, you will find a box with a cue ball inside.
H It is important for you to understand the ideal cut angle for a wide variety of shots in Nine Ball. You will therefore find cut angles labeled throughout the book.
I You will find numerous references to the tangent line. It is simply a line that shows the cue balls path after contact at a 90-degree angle from the object ball's line to the pocket.

Pool Geometry Lesson 101

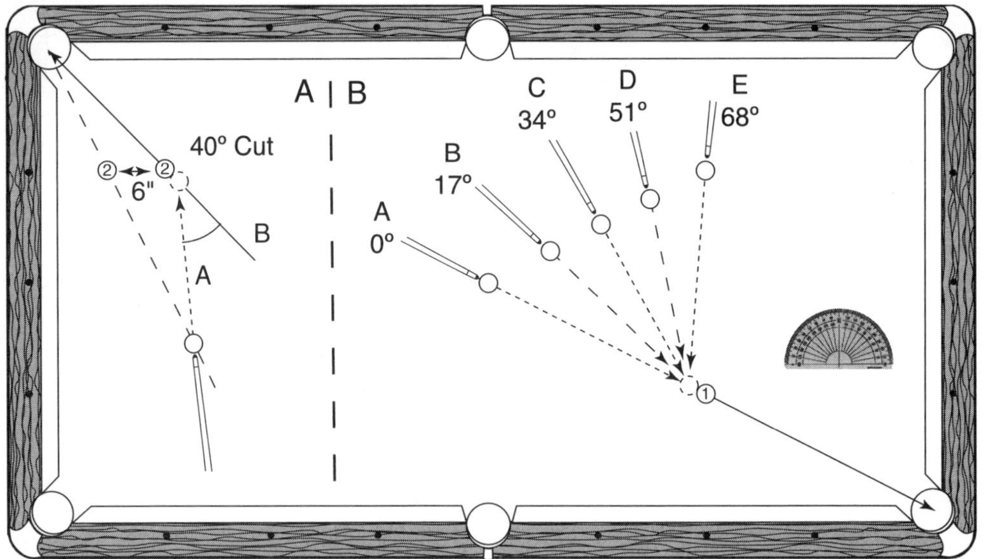

A working knowledge of angles is absolutely essential if you wish to play position with any degree of consistency in Nine Ball. Now I'm not suggesting that you carry a protractor (a device for measuring angles) to plot your position. But I am strongly recommending that you be able to tell the difference in angles within at least five degrees of accuracy. I will be referring to cut angles throughout the book, so those of you who are not totally comfortable with angles should take the lesson below.

For those of you who skipped geometry, an angle measures the relationship between two straight lines. Angles are measured in degrees. In Part A, the straight in shot has no cut angle (0-degrees). If you move the 2-ball 6" to the right, the shot now has a 40-degree cut angle. This angle is computed by comparing Line A, which is the cue ball's path to the 2-ball, to Line B, which is the path of the 2-ball to the pocket.

I suggest that you set up the shots in Part B so you can quickly become acquainted with five significantly different cut angles. The 1-ball is 1 diamond off the bottom side rail and two diamonds from the end rail. Cue Ball A is in the exact middle of the table. Cue Ball E is one diamond off the top side rail and two diamonds from the end rail. Cue Balls B, C, and D are spaced three balls apart between Cue Balls A and E. You can put them in the exact positions by placing two balls between each cue ball.

- Cue Ball A shows a straight in shot on the 1-ball (0-degrees angle).
- Cue Ball B shows a shallow 17-degree cut shot.
- Cue Ball C is at 34-degrees to the 1-ball line to the pocket. A good majority of your position play will use angles of 30-40 degrees.
- Cue Ball D shows a 51-degree cut angle. This angle is quite steep, and is almost never one that you would intentionally play for.
- Cue Ball E illustrates a cut shot that is at about the maximum angle that most players feel comfortable shooting.

Glossary
There are many terms that are used for pool in general, and many more that are specifically used in Nine Ball. If you have any question on the terminology used in the book, I suggest you look for the definition in the appendix.

Tips
There are a series of tips in the book. Each is designed to be a concise lesson related to the topic discussed just above it. Nevertheless, they can be read independently of the text. They provide you with a valuable piece of information to add to your game.

Using the Donuts
BCA Master Instructor Roy Yamane first gave me the idea for using the same hole reinforcements that you use for three ring binder paper as an inexpensive, but powerful training tool for pool. You can quickly and accurately mark the position of the balls when practicing so you can play the same shots over and over until they are mastered. Throughout the book, hole reinforcements are referred to simply as donuts.

Use of the Masculine Pronoun
I would like to make it perfectly clear that I am 100% in favor of women playing pool. For style purposes only, however, I chose to use the masculine pronoun throughout the book as I find it awkward to be constantly alternating between he and she. To women readers I ask that you understand that he really means he/she in the book.

A Word with Phil Capelle
Play Your Best Nine Ball is the culmination of my over 30 years of continuous involvement in pool. Along the way I learned by playing, watching players of all levels, reading books on pool, and from teaching.

I can honestly say that I looked forward to getting up every single day to work on this book, and that writing and producing it was indeed a labor of love. I hope you enjoy the book and that it helps you to play Nine Ball better than you perhaps ever imagined possible.

Reader Comments
I would like to hear your comments and suggestions for improving future editions. You can write to me at:

Billiards Press
P.O. Box 400
Midway City, CA 92655

Abridged Contents

(P) = Pro Diagram

Chapter 1 Shotmaking

Chapter 2 The Break

Chapter 3 Position Routes

CHAPTER 1

SHOTMAKING

"I think I am the best shotmaker."
***Jose Parica** on confidence*

It's been said that 9-ball is a shotmakers game, and that's true to a large degree. The game demands that you be able to consistently pocket tough shots. Even if you play position quite well, you will still have to play at least one or two moderately challenging shots in all but the easiest layouts.

One of your primary objectives, as a Nine-Ball player, is to make sure the tough shots arise primarily because of what your opponent leaves you or due to the inherent difficulty of the layout, not because you are failing to control the cue ball reasonably well. After studying over a thousand games by leading professionals, my research indicates that the best position players in the world still face an average of nearly one very difficult shot per rack. In fact, a fair percentage of the pros runouts consisted of at least two difficult shots. The typical amateur may face several challenging shots in an average rack due to errors in position. But as the top pros have shown, many of these shots can be eliminated through improved position play.

Position Play or Shotmaking ?

To excel at Nine-Ball you've got to be more of a position playing shotmaker than a shotmaking position player. No matter how accurate your shotmaking may become, you cannot consistently string together runs of more than 2-4 shots without playing at least adequate position. Nevertheless, even if you become an expert at cue ball control, you will still need to pocket a variety of challenging shots to initiate and sustain all but the simplest of layouts. You should therefore learn to enjoy the challenge each presents.

The Fundamentals

The upcoming sections discuss the fundamentals as they relate to Nine Ball. A complete discussion of the fundamentals is beyond the scope of this book, but can be found in my first book, *Play Your Best Pool*.

Stance

The stance, like the grip, is largely a matter of personal preference. Nevertheless, it should meet certain goals. Your stance should feel natural and comfortable, and provide stability. Some players prefer to have their dominant eye over the cue while others like to have the cue between their eyes underneath their chin. In any case, your head should be in a position where you can aim accurately. And lastly, a good stance will put your shooting arm in a position where you can swing it straight through contact with the cue ball and beyond.

There are three basic heights for the stance: low, medium, and high. A low stance, with your chin on or just above the cue, enables you to achieve a more consistent alignment, which is crucial in aiming. A low stance, however, can restrict your arm swing on power shots. This often leads to jumping up prematurely. Your chin will be roughly 6-8" above the cue with a medium height stance. This distance allows for a free arm swing for ample power, and it enables you to aim with accuracy. Your chin will be over a foot above the cue with a high stance. This stance promotes a very free arm swing with which you can apply plenty of power. It is not recommended for Nine Ball, however, because of the precise aiming that the game requires.

Variable Stance Height

You may wish to vary the height of your stance based on the requirements of each shot. For example, when the cue ball is very close to the object ball, a very high stance can improve depth perception and your aim of the shot. And when you have a long shot off the rail, a low stance enables you to look back and forth between the cue ball and object ball without having to move your head up and down to any great degree.

Your height and the height of your stance will naturally affect the distance of your grip hand from your bridge hand and the position of your grip hand relative to the cue. A tall player's hands will be further apart than are those of a shorter player. And players with a low stance will also have a longer distance between their two hands than those who use a more upright stance.

Grip

The grip is largely an individual matter, as can be seen by the grips of some of the world's top professionals and the many opponents you will encounter. If, however, you have neither the talent nor the time to master any of the non-textbook grips, I suggest that you stick to a grip that is at least somewhat closely related to the one I recommend in *Play Your Best Pool.*

The main requirement for the grip in Nine Ball is that it be loose and flexible. You need a supple wrist so you can whip the cue with authority. Any excess tension in your grip hand will reduce the action you can impart on the cue ball. Tension will lead to twisting the cue on the forward stroke. Remember, the lighter you grip the cue, the more you will feel the weight of the cue. A light grip creates the feeling that the cue is doing most of the work.

The Bridge

Bridge Length

Nine Ball is a full table game in which you must regularly play long shots, often using a powerful stroke. Because of the power required in Nine Ball, the average professional uses an 11" bridge according to a study conducted by *Pool & Billiard Magazine*. This is considerably longer than the 8" bridge length favored the great Straight Pool players. Eight Ball, which is much more closely related to Straight Pool, is also played with a shorter bridge. And those who play mostly on a bar table also tend to favor a shorter bridge as that version of Nine Ball is more about finesse than power.

Compromises Between Short and Long

Two of the primary requirements of Nine Ball are power and accuracy, which are at odds with one another. A long bridge gives you plenty of power, but at the expense of accuracy. A short bridge increases your accuracy, but limits your ability to generate power with a smooth delivery. Players who use an extremely short bridge tend to muscle the ball when they need extra power.

As a Nine Ball player, you need to strike the ideal balance between accuracy and power. In the beginning, I suggest you use a slightly shorter bridge than the pros. 9-10" is about right. As your stroke develops power and accuracy, you can lengthen your bridge to the 10-11" range. Since bridge length is largely a matter of personal preference, many of you with exceptional hand/eye coordination may be able to mimic the bridges of the pros who use a 12"+ bridge.

Benefits of a Long Bridge

A long bridge enables you to accelerate smoothly without having to force the action or make a conscious effort to apply extra power. This can help improve your touch and your speed control across a wider range of the Spectrum of Speeds. A long bridge can also improve your view down the cue and to the cue ball because the bridge loop does not interfere nearly as much with your line of sight.

On every shot the cue ball will be airborne for a short distance after contact even though its flight is rarely detectable to the human eye. A short bridge can cause an excessively downward hit, which will cause the cue ball to fly higher. In addition, any stroke errors will be magnified. A long bridge enables you to use a more level stroke, which reduces unwanted sidespin or stun caused by an error in your stroke.

You will always be hitting slightly down on the cue ball on draw shots due to the height of the rails. In addition, most players use a closed bridge on draw shots, which automatically raises the cue at their bridge to 1.5" or more above the cloth. Meanwhile, when you are using a full tip of draw, the middle of your tip is only 5/8" off the table. In other words, your cue is angled downward into the cue ball on draw shots. This creates a downward hit on the cue ball.

By using a longer bridge you can decrease the angle of your cue to the table, which reduces the amount the cue ball jumps after contact. This can be especially important if you have large hands, as they create a more elevated bridge. With an 8" bridge that is elevated 1.5" from the table, the cue will be at a 6.5-degree angle when 1 tip of draw is used. Using the same bridge elevation, an 11" bridge and 1 tip of draw would create a cue angle of only 4.5-degrees.

Those of you who favor a long bridge must make sure not to decelerate as you approach the cue ball. You can avoid this error by learning to use a shorter stroke on some shots. The long bridge will give you sighting accuracy, while a short stroke will minimize the impact of any errors in your stroke, such as unwanted deflection or sidespin.

Open Bridge

An open bridge has many advantages. Your line of sight to the cue ball is unobstructed, which makes aiming easier. There is also less friction between the cue and your bridge, which helps to promote a smoother stroke. You can bridge lower on draw shots, which decreases the cue's angle into the cue ball. On stretch shots it is easier to reach the cue ball. And finally, an open bridge will expose any errors in your technique, which may be disguised somewhat by a closed bridged. For example, if you twist your arm or wrist or rise up slightly, the cue will come flying off the "Vee" of your bridge hand. Even if you don't use an open bridge in competition, practicing with it will help groove a near flawless stroke.

Despite the many advantages of the open bridge, nearly all top players use a closed bridge for power shots and for other shots as well, for good reason: they like the feeling of stability and confidence that the closed bridge provides for them.

Variable Bridge Length

Golfers use a narrower stance for their short irons than they do for their driver. Similarly, you may wish to consider varying the length of your bridge to match the shot you are playing. On a finesse follow shot, a 6-7" bridge would provide more than enough length to smoothly generate the power you need. On a long draw shot, you might extend your bridge to

10-11". To use the variable bridge technique, you would have to either:

- Feel comfortable using strokes of varying lengths or,
- Use a backstroke on power shots that is no longer than the longest stroke you use when using a short bridge.

Changing Your Bridge Length

After evaluating your game, you may decide that a longer or shorter bridge would be better for your game. You can adjust your bridge by regulating the position of your grip hand. Both hands should move the same distance up or down the cue when you make the change. Lets say that you want to lengthen your bridge by 2". Here's how to do it:

- Take your normal shooting stance for a medium length shot.
- Take your bridge hand off the cue and grip the butt end of the cue next to your grip hand (at the side closest to the joint).
- Place a rubber band 2" towards the butt end of the cue.
- When you take your stance, your grip hand should be next to the rubber band.

The Stroke

Nine Ball, as I've said before, requires that you be able to play shots at all different speeds of stroke. At times you will need the touch of a surgeon, while, at other times you must be able to power the cue ball at speeds upwards of 10 MPH for position. Most new players like to hit the cue ball at high speeds, which seems to meet the requirements for Nine Ball. To play Nine Ball correctly, however, you need the kind of power that is generated by a fluid stroke, not the kind of power that is created by a muscular stab at the ball.

Graceful Power

A graceful swing of the arm and a snap of the wrist just prior to contact can produce all of the power that you will ever need in Nine Ball (with the exception of the break shot). And yet all too many players try to develop power by muscling the cue ball with their arm while freezing the wrist. This attempt to muscle the cue ball usually begins at the beginning of the transition of the backstroke to the forward stroke. The tensing of the arm and wrist actually slows down the arm, reducing power and accuracy. The real secret to power is to stay relaxed as you swing the arm forward and let your wrist accelerate the cue at the moment of contact. This timed release of the cue helps you to avoid steering the cue and it provides extra power precisely at the moment it is needed.

Become a Pool Shooting Machine

A smooth and powerful stroke is really a product of the various steps in your shooting routine that have preceded it. We've already discussed the stance, grip, bridge and stroke. Another important element is your preshot routine. Nine Ball requires precise shotmaking. Therefore, I strongly recommend that you make a habit of beginning your shooting routine by facing directly down the line of aim before assuming your stance. Try to land on the table with your bridge hand in the same way every time. Once you have mastered these steps, you will be well on your way to becoming a pool shooting machine. Two pros who especially embody this technique are Efren Reyes and Cory Deuel.

Warm Up Strokes

A whole chapter could be written on the various sequences of warm up strokes. Some players use the same back and forth motion on every warm up. Other prefer to mix things up with a series of short strokes. If you are not already completely comfortable with you warm up strokes, I suggest you watch the sequences of several top players. Experiment with the various techniques until you find the pattern that works best for you. There are several purposes for warm up strokes.

- You have enough time to lock in your aim.
- Make any last second adjustments in your position.
- Get a feel for the speed of stroke you will be using.
- Gain the feeling that your stroke in on track.
- Loosen up your arm and wrist.

The items on the list above will become instinctual after awhile.

The Transition

The make or break point of most players' strokes is the transition from the final backstroke (once the warm up strokes are over) to the forward stroke. A smooth and unhurried transition helps give you a longer look at the object ball. It also insures against a muscle bound jerk at the cue ball, and all of the attendant disasters. And yet it is amazing how so many players with a series of silky smooth warm-up strokes will end up making a spastic stab at the cue ball on the final stroke.

The culprit is the "hit impulse" that takes over during the transition from backstroke to forward stroke. To solve this problem, consciously slow the transition phase of the final stroke. Some top pros such as Buddy Hall and Allison Fisher have a very noticeable pause that separates the final swing back from the forward stroke through the cue ball. Try to accelerate smoothly so that you generate maximum power and speed at contact with the cue ball, not at the start of your forward stroke.

Finding "It", Losing "It", and Finding "It" Again

Sports like pool, tennis and golf, depend on the ability to repeat certain movements, at a very high level, for success. As a player, you will forever be finding your stroke, having it, losing it, and finding it again. It is a never-ending cycle. Your stroke will come and it will go. Hopefully, you'll spend most of the time in stroke instead of searching for the lost magic. Your cause for a consistent stroke that will stay with you for long periods of time will be greatly aided if you:

- Develop a fundamentally sound stroke in the first place.
- Know your game and your negative tendencies. This will allow you to quickly spot flaws and apply corrective measures before you head into an extended period of poor play.
- Visualize and imagine the feel of your stroke so you can utilize the benefits of muscle memory.

12 Keys for Getting in Stroke

You can quickly get back in the groove by focusing your attention on a specific fundamental. Your key thought may be a technique that has worked in the past, or it could be a new thought that does the trick.

1 Relax Your Grip - Let your shooting arm hang naturally at your side. Curl your fingers at the second joint. Then lay the cue across the middle pad of your fingers. Your little finger should hang freely. Your thumb merely acts as a support.

2 Set Up Correctly - Set up precisely for each shot to eliminate the need to shuffle around excessively in order to find your comfort zone.

3 Cue Perfectly - Try positioning your tip with extra care when setting up for your shots rather than simply putting your bridge hand down with the tip more or less where you want it.

4 Silky Smooth Stroke - As you settle into your shooting stance, think about making the smoothest stroke imaginable.

5 Swing Only Your Arm - Unwanted body movements, however small, can ruin your shots. To eliminate this fault, concentrate on moving only your shooting arm and wrist.

6 Use Extra Warm-up Strokes - If you have a tendency to rush your shots, try adding a couple of extra warm-up strokes into your shooting routine.

7 Slow the Transition –You can eliminate the tendency to tighten up at this critical stage by beginning your forward stroke in the same relaxed manner in which you make the transition during your warm up strokes.

8 Stare Intently At The Object Ball – Try to stare holes through the object ball on the final stroke and to lock in on the target.

9 Feel The Tip At Contact - You can learn about your stroke and the whys and hows of the cue ball's action by focusing on the feel of the tip at contact. Does the tip mesh with the cue ball in a crisp, satisfying manner?

10 Drop Your Elbow After Contact - After contact the elbow should drop as the arm swings forward and as it glides to a stop.

11 Follow Through Straight - Extend your cue directly down the line of aim. Hold your follow through as if posing for a picture and check to see if your cue is perfectly on line.

12 Stay Down - Try to stay down until the object ball is in the pocket. This will cure the dreaded Jack-in-the-Box syndrome, and it will keep you from taking your eyes off the target prematurely.

Shot Selection

When you are competing at Nine Ball, you must make very accurate assessments of your shotmaking capabilities. You must be able to gauge the difficulty of a shot so you can make correct decisions about playing offense or defense. As always, the question is whether the shot or the safety gives you the best odds of winning. You must know what is a go, and what is not. Your decision on any particular shot will vary depending on how you are playing, the equipment, and the pressure.

Difficult Shots

It is a common mistake for amateur players, and even pros, to at times give difficult shots their worst stroke. A poor effort results because of a lack of confidence in their ability to make the shot and because they are anticipating a poor result. Just ask yourself how many times have you seen someone jump towards the sky when playing a tough shot? Do you do it yourself? Unfortunately, this tendency towards poor execution happens on the kind of shots where you need to perform your fundamentals at your very best level.

You can take a big step towards solving this problem by first understanding that no one achieves perfection at pool. Everybody misses difficult shots. So while your goal on tough shots is to make the ball, you will still miss your share. Knowing that you can miss and will miss some of your tough shots should actually reduce the pressure as you prepare to shoot them. It's ok to miss. Everybody does. Once you believe that, you can now focus your efforts on giving difficult shots your very best effort. No jumping up or spasmodic arm-twisting is allowed. Aim carefully, use your very best, smoothest, and straightest stroke. And be sure to stay down as you follow through. If you can do this, you will have given yourself your very best chance of pocketing the shot. If you are now pocketing 40% of your difficult shots you could conceivably raise your average to 60%, or perhaps even higher.

In sum, understand that no matter how well you play, not all tough shots are destined for the pocket. So be willing to accept the results before you play the shot. Then go ahead and give them your very best stroke.

Extending Your Comfort Range

You've perhaps read stories of how leading pros will miss a shot in competition and then go shoot it a hundred times in a row in practice. There are a couple of reasons why they put themselves through such an exacting regime: 1) they don't want to miss that shot ever again for whatever the reason, 2) they don't want any routine shots to eat at their confidence, which must be extremely high to compete at the pro level.

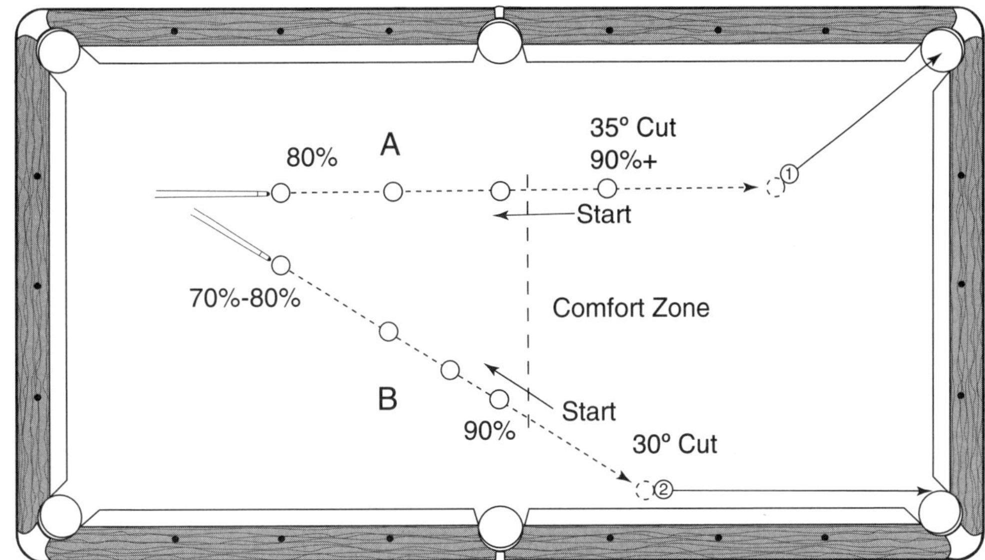

You are probably not as obsessive about your game as the pros, but you can employ a simple routine to discover where the hard shot syndrome starts to affect your shotmaking. The diagram shows two of the most commonly played shots in Nine-Ball. Shot A is a follow shot while Shot B is a draw shot. You may wish to add several other shots to this exercise, especially those that give you the most trouble.

Start the exercise with the cue ball closest to the object ball. Play the shot 10 times using a medium firm stroke. Observe your results. How many did you make? Did you stay down and execute the shot with a smooth stroke? Did you feel any apprehension about the shot or were you totally confident? You should make at least 9 out of 10 of each shot before moving the cue ball back for a longer version of the shot.

The idea is to discover the minimum distance at which you are no longer 90-100% sure you will pocket the shot. This is where your comfort zone ends. At this distance you should carefully assess the quality of your misses. How close are they to the pocket? If the misses are at the edge of the pocket that means your execution is still relatively good. If at some point your misses are several inches wide of the pocket, that indicates, your execution is faltering because of the perceived difficulty of the shot.

After a miss, evaluate your technique. Was it up to your usual standards, which you employ at shorter distances? If not, what did you do differently? Now try the shot again and this time give it your very best effort. Don't worry about whether it goes in or not. The objective is to give the longer versions of the shot the same quality of execution that you used, at the shorter ranges, where your confidence was high. This will enable you to extend your comfort zone and to improve your shotmaking on more difficult shots.

Use Feedback from Missed Shots

Missed shots don't just happen. There are reasons why the ball doesn't find the pocket. You can improve your shotmaking and reduce your misses by using your powers of awareness to discover the reason(s) for your missed shots. This is a much more productive exercise than simply cursing the fact that you are off your game or that you made a stupid mistake. After a miss, evaluate the shot using the checklist below. You may discover that:

- The feel of your stroke was off.
- Your sense of aim was incorrect, or you were just guessing where to aim.
- You took your eyes off the shot.
- You had a certain sense of uneasiness before you pulled the trigger. something wasn't right, perhaps with your stance or grip.
- You didn't feel comfortable over the shot, which led to a mechanical error in your stroke.
- You committed some combination of the above errors.
- You did not have a definite plan before executing the shot.

Your objective is to become aware of what you do so that you can initiate a self-corrective process to get your game back on track.

Missed Shot Tendencies

Nearly every shot can be missed to either side of the target. Nevertheless, on a great many shots most players have a tendency to miss the shot on the same side over and over again. There is just something about the shot that causes the same error to happen over and over again. Most players overcut shots using inside english at high speeds. The list below gives you some other shots for consideration. I suggest you evaluate your misses against those on the list. Do you miss where most other players do? Do your misses on a particular shot favor either side of the pocket? Or do you go completely against the norm by missing a particular shot on the list on the opposite side of the pocket?

Shot and the Error Tendency

- Inside english shots played with a hard stroke are almost always overcut, due to deflection.
- Thin cut banks are almost always undercut.
- Down the rail cut shots are overcut due to an optical illusion.
- Overcut combos.
- The tendency is to hit billiards too fully.
- There is a tendency to jump up on cut shots down the rail and overcut the shot.
- Undercut shots when you want to restrict the cue ball's traveling distance.

Diagnosing an error tendency is one thing. Doing something about it is a whole different matter. After all, there is a reason why the tendency exists in the first place: prior to playing the shot, in your minds eye you may feel as if your aim is correct. Otherwise you would adjust your aim. Right? Well, not always, and therein lies the problem. Shots with dominant error tendencies built into them just don't look right when you are, in fact, aiming correctly.

What's the solution? You need to single out the shots on the list and others that habitually give you trouble. Then you need to practice each one over and over again until you have discovered the correct line of aim. You may find one of a number of aim training devises to be useful. You must also convince your pool memory that the new point of aim is indeed correct so that when the shot comes up again in competition, you will knock it straight into the pocket.

Classifying Shots By Difficulty

The degree of difficulty of any shot that is not a relative hanger is largely an individual matter. A routine shot for Earl Strickland may be an extremely challenging shot for the average player. As a practical matter, it can help your efforts in competition if you have a reasonably good idea of where each shot rests on the degree of difficulty scale. Once armed with this self-knowledge, you will be able to fine-tune your shot selection. You will know which shots you are fully justified in taking, those that are on the borderline, and those where the odds favor a safety.

There are shots of above average difficulty that you must go for occasionally because there is no better choice available. I suggest, however, that you consider the probability of success for the "typical" shot. When you are figuring your percentages you must allow for the quality of competition you face on a regular basis. If you play with C players, then it is ok to go for shots in the 60-70% range and above. B players should play mostly shots in the 75-80%+ range. A players should attempt shots in the 85%+ range.

The chart below should help in giving you some perspective of where each shot belongs on the degree of difficulty scale.

- **Easy shot**. Always play these unless there is a better option.
- **Average difficulty**. Always play these unless there is a better option.
- **Above average in difficulty**. Play these some of the time. Your decision depends on how you are playing, the conditions, the situation, and what other options are available.
- **Very difficult shots**. Pass on these and play safe most of the time. Play these only when you have little or no choice.
- **Extremely difficult shots**. You should almost never play these as they are not a part of your game. Look for a safety no matter what the circumstances. Play only as a last resort.

Shots You Must Master

Since accurate shotmaking is such an important part of Nine-Ball, you should strive to raise your competency in all areas of this part of the game. The more shots you master, the more opportunities you give yourself to remain at the table and finish runouts. Your ability to consistently make a variety of shots can also enable you to avoid relying so heavily on your safeties when the outcome of the game is up for grabs. Below is a checklist of shots that, if largely mastered, can turn you into an offensive powerhouse.

____The long green	____Easier combos
____Thin cuts	____Rail first
____Off the rail shots	____Curve shots
____Jacked up	____Jump
____Basic short rail banks	____Power draw
____Basic long rail banks	____Power follow
____Billiards	____The break shot (see Chapter 2)
____Caroms	____Kick shots (see Chapter 12)

Maximum Practical Cut Angles

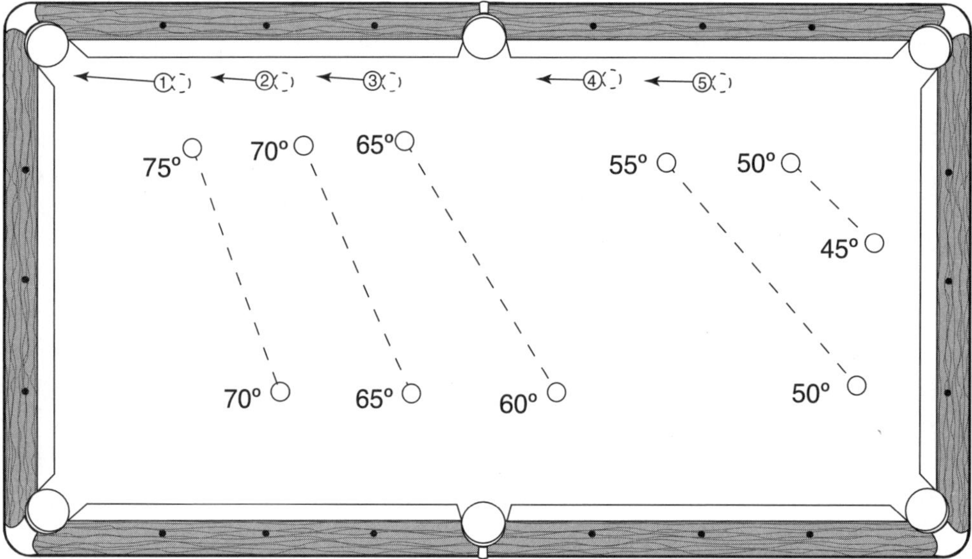

There comes a point for most players when a moderate cut angle quickly turns into a thin cut, and where the odds for making the shot begin to drop precipitously. The distance of the object ball from the pocket and the distance of the cue ball from the object ball largely determine the point at which a shot goes from very makeable to very missable. In the diagram above the 1-ball is close to the pocket, which makes this shot not so difficult even with a cut angle of 70-degrees. Notice how the recommended practical cut angle decreases as the object ball rests further from the pocket. With the 5-ball six diamonds from the pocket, the recommended maximum practical cut angle drops to about 45-degrees.

Side Pocket Cut Angles

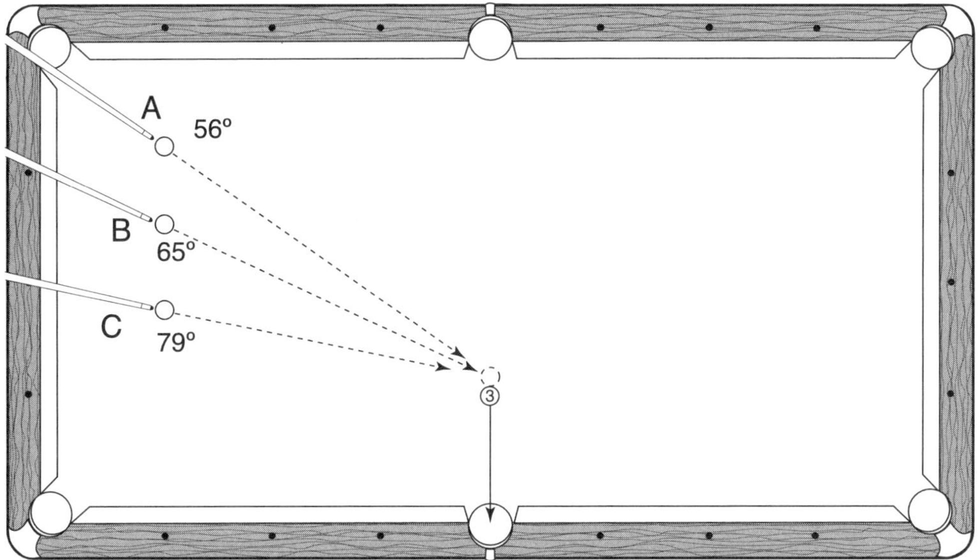

Most thin cut shots into the side are not exceedingly difficult because of the large opening of the pocket and due to the fact that most of the time the object ball is relatively close to the pocket. I suggest that you check out the cut angles from the shooters view by turning the book. The 56-degree cut is not difficult, and even the 65-degree cut is highly makeable. It is only above 70-degrees that the shot becomes a challenge.

Thin Cuts Rail First

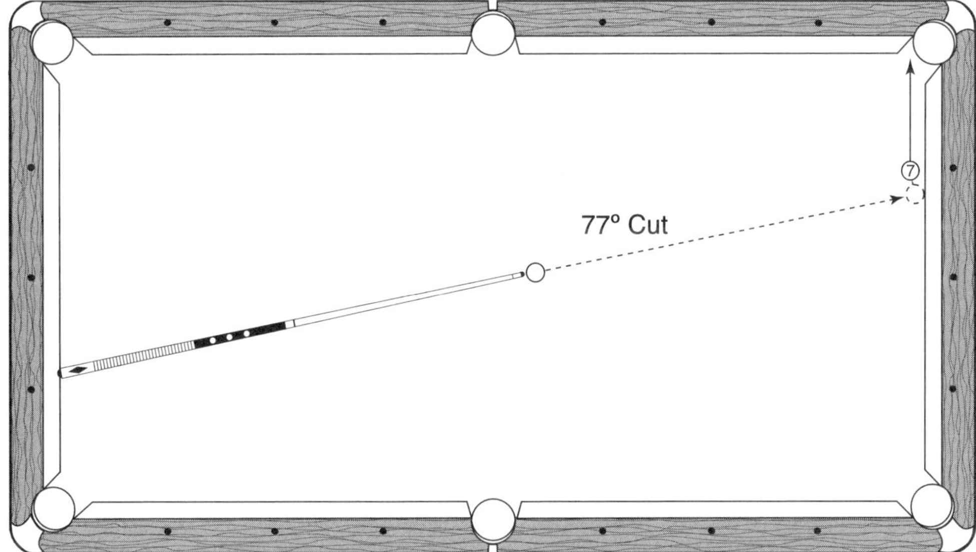

The diagram shows a 77-degree cut shot. This cut angle may be too much for most players if played directly into the edge of the 7-ball. Another highly effective technique for making this shot is to aim at the rail. Use inside english (left in this example).

Off the Rail

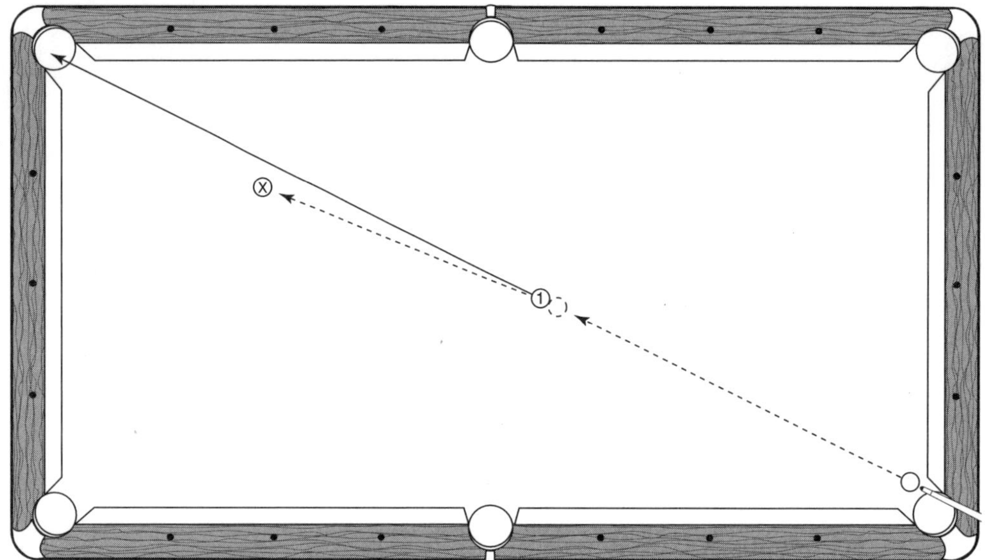

You will often find the cue ball on the rail or right next to it as a result of positional errors. These happen because it is difficult to precisely control cue ball speed when sending it long distances as you must often do in Nine-Ball. In addition, your opponent may push out to rail shots if they are good at them, or if they feel you are not. So even though I advise you to avoid the rail shots whenever possible, you will wind up shooting them quite often

When playing shots off the rail, hopefully you can meet your positional objective without having to elevate your cue. With your cue level to the rail your accuracy is much greater. Johnny Archer led Ismael Paez by the narrow margin of 7-6 racing to 11, in the 1997 U.S. Open when he was left with the table length shot shown in the diagram. He calmly rolled it into the pocket using a medium soft stroke. The cue ball rolled forward for excellent position and he went on to run the rack (not shown) and to win the match. The keys to making difficult, off the rail shots like this are to:

- Keep your cue as level as possible.
- If you normally have your head several inches above the cue, set up a little lower to the shot.
- Use a short stroke.
- Accelerate smoothly.
- Use a medium soft to medium speed stroke. Try to avoid using higher speeds unless absolutely necessary to send the cue ball a long distance.
- Stay down on the shot.

Jacked Up Near the Rail

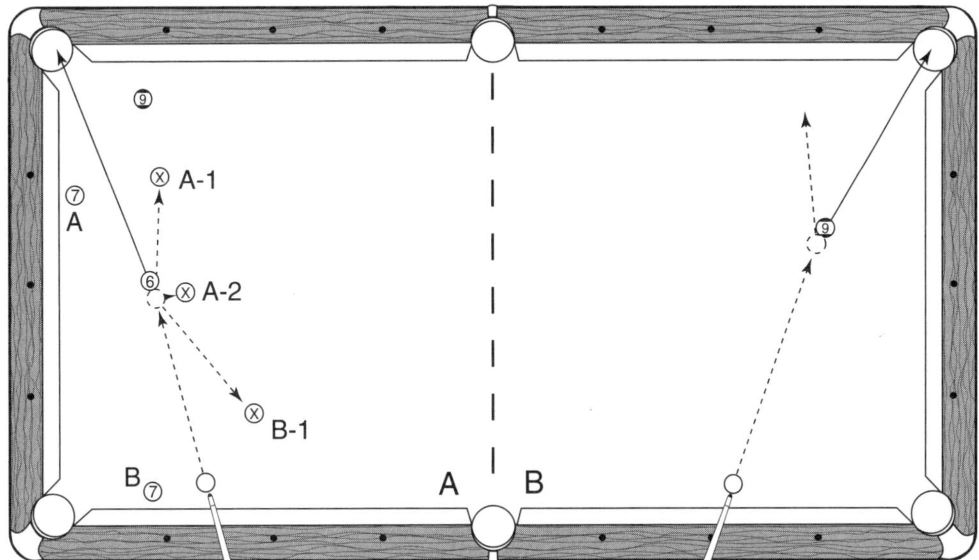

On a reasonably high percentage of shots with the cue ball near the rail, you will need to elevate your cue in order to get position on the next ball. The diagram above shows several of the most common uses of the jack up shot. In Part A, if you roll forward you will lose position on the 7-ball #A at A-1. The solution is to jack up and play a stop shot, which would leave the cue ball at A-2. If the 7-ball was at #B, you would need to jack up and draw the cue ball back to B-1. In Part B, the shot is on the 9-ball, which means you do not need to play position. Furthermore, the shot has a 10-degree cut angle, which eliminates the possibility of scratching with a follow shot. Even though there are no compelling reasons to play a jack up shot in this position, many players prefer to elevate the cue slightly and play the shot with a firm stroke, to avoid a roll off, rather than rolling the cue ball with a level cue.

When playing a jack up shot, you should avoid elevating the cue anymore than is needed to accomplish the objective of the shot. Excessive elevation will magnify any stroke errors at contact, resulting in an almost certain miss. I also advise you to take a little extra time in setting up for the shot so you can make the adjustments necessary to obtain the correct position over the shot. When playing the shot, be sure to choke up on the cue and use your smoothest stroke. This should keep you from employing a power jab as many players do on jack up shots. In sum, your fundamentals must be rock solid if you are to execute jack up shots successfully.

Jack up shots are one department where players with exceptional skills can gain a significant advantage over their opponents as they can execute position plays that others could only dream about. If you possess such skills, you are blessed with a powerful offensive weapon. If not, you may have another area of your game that can, with enough practice, lead to a meaningful gain in your overall level of play.

Basics of Banking

Bank shots are an integral part of a Nine Ball player's arsenal. Skill at banks can enable you to run out games that some of your opponents, when faced with a similar bank, would have to play safe or run the risk selling out. The majority of banks played in Nine-Ball are fairly routine, especially when compared to the kind that you must pocket regularly in Bank Pool or One-Pocket.

The bank shots you play in Nine-Ball should carry a success rate of at least 50-85%. If your pocketing percentage rests under this range, you are either playing overly difficult bank shots or you are missing the easy ones far too often. If the later is the case, the suggestions below and some time at the practice table could yield immediate and substantial results.

Short Rail Banks

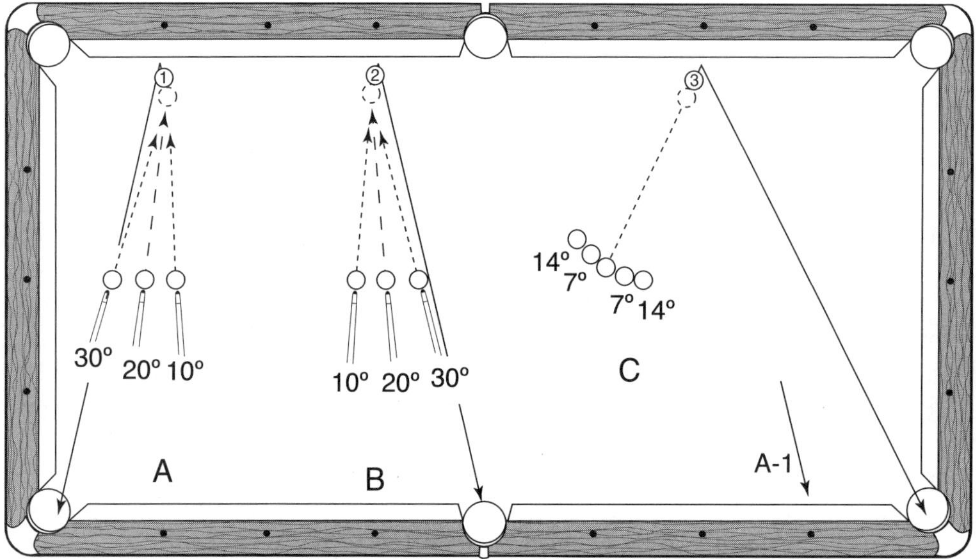

Our previous discussion on cut shots established that the difficulty factor rises quickly on cut shots beyond 60-70 degrees The maximum cut angles on banks shots are much shallower on than on shots played directly into the pocket. In other words, on most bank shots, you will be aiming to hit the object ball rather fully. And in no instances are you required to cut the paint off the ball in order to pocket a bank.

Parts A and B in the diagram above show two of the most common object ball locations for bank shots in Nine-Ball. In both positions are cut angles of 10, 20, and 30 degrees. Notice the fullness of the hit on cut angles of 10 or 20 degrees. With a cut angle of 30 degrees, you are still hitting a little more than half of the object ball. You will seldom cut a bank shot more than 30-degrees in game conditions. Keep in mind there is a tendency by most players to undercut bank shots with relatively thin cut angles (25 degrees+).

This discussion on bank shot cut angles is designed to demonstrate the narrow range on the object ball that needs to be considered when you are aiming at a bank shot. Since banking is largely a matter of making a successful educated guess, it may comfort you to know that you need only consider a very small part of the object ball's equator.

Part C shows the cut angles when the object ball is much further up the rail. Notice that the cut angles with a ball in this position normally range up to around 14 degrees on either side of the ball. With the object ball in this position, each degree your aim is off translates into an additional inch that the ball will travel off of the center of the pocket. As an example, if you hit the 4-ball fully from cue ball A, it would hit the opposite side rail at A-1.

Try this Bank for Fun

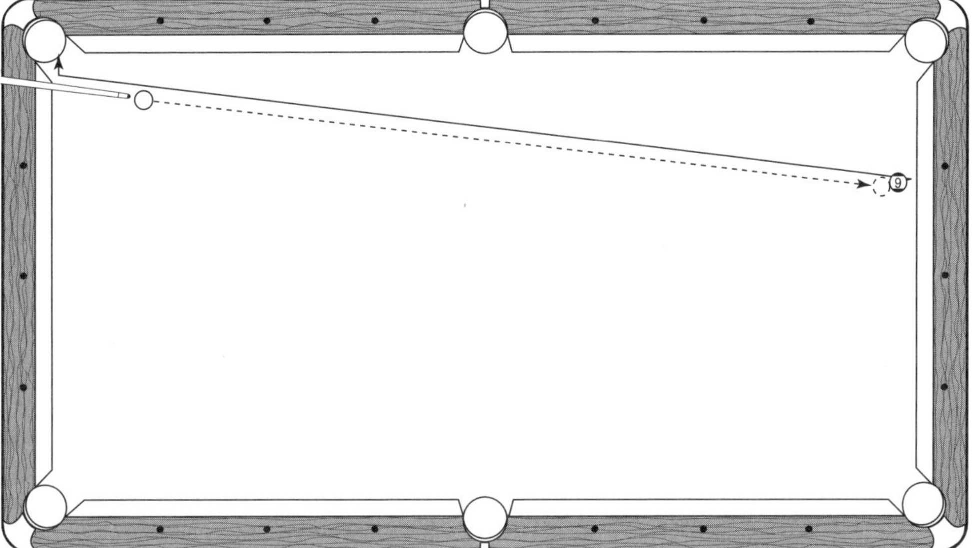

Mika Immonen and Jim Rempe were tied at 10 in a race to 11 late in the 1998 U.S. Open when Immonen stepped to the table to face this long rail bank on the 9-ball. He barely coaxed the shot into the far edge of the pocket as shown. This clutch shot helped him to a 3rd place finish. Rempe finished in the 5-6 slot. I suggest you set the balls up in the exact same positions and give yourself one shot. Imagine you are shooting this on double hill against a world-class competitor. Did you make it? Congratulations! I knew you would!

Long Rail Bank Cut Angles

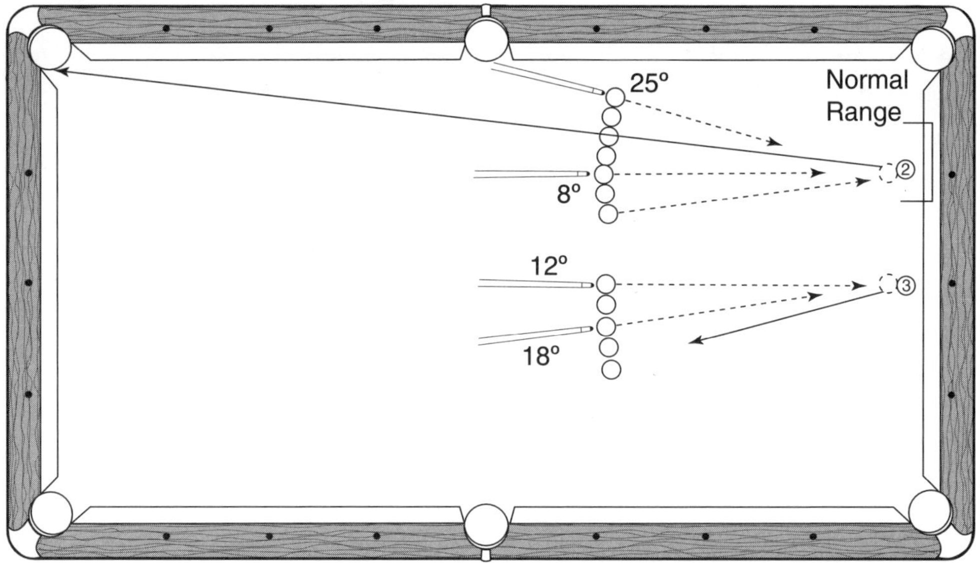

The cut angles on long rail bank shots are less severe than on short rail banks as they typically range from 8-25 degrees. On most long rail banks you need only aim for just a little less than a full ball. Just how much less than full, however, is the big challenge to making long rail banks. Most long rail banks are shot with the object ball between one-half diamond and one and a quarter diamonds up the rail from the opposite corner pocket.

One of the great joys of pool is the sight of a long rail bank whizzing towards the pocket. Table length banks take a long time to unfold, which raises your sense of anticipation as you wonder if your beautifully struck shot is about to split the pocket. When long rail banks are successful, they give you a certain sense of satisfaction that few other shots in the game can match.

Crossover Bank Shots

The diagram at the top of page 19 shows two common crossover bank shots. The cue ball will be traveling across the path that the object ball will be taking to the pocket after it rebounds off the cushion. On these two banks there is no risk of the cue ball hitting the object ball. Crossover banks must be played with a firm stroke since you are contacting only a small portion of the object ball. The cue ball will also travel a long distance on these shots so you need to plot your route with care.

You must allow for contact induced throw when aiming crossover bank shots. Both of the banks shown are normally shot from the other side of the ball. Because the cue ball will now be approaching from the opposite side of the object ball, you must allow for contact throw by aiming for a thinner hit than usual. The side pocket bank, for example, must be aimed about three degrees further to the left. You can also play the shot by aiming normally and using a hard stroke.

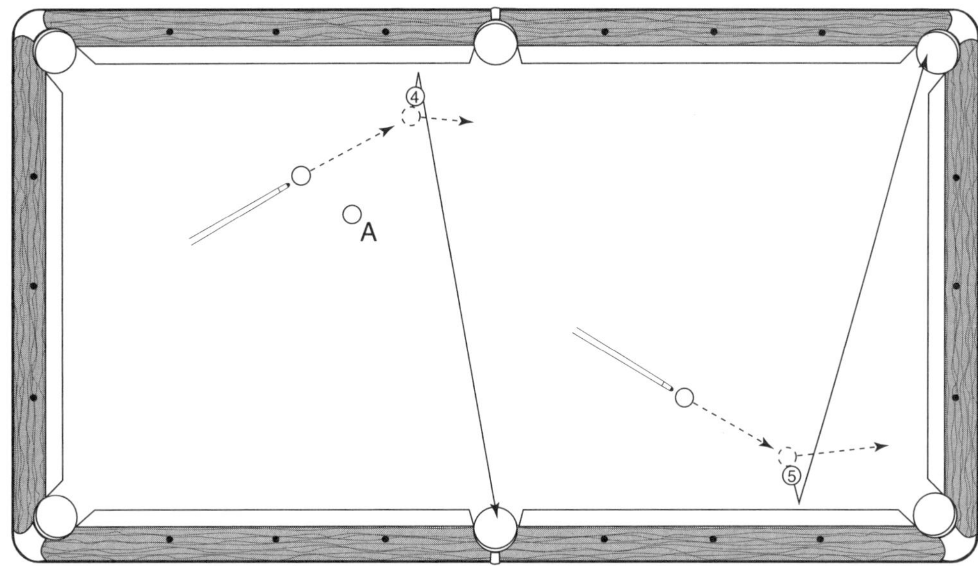

With the Position A for the side pocket bank, there would be a chance that cue ball would collide with the object ball after it rebound off the rail. I suggest you experiment with several positions for both the cue ball and object to determine when a crossover bank is possible and for when a collision with the cue ball cannot be avoided. A collision generally occurs when half or more of the cue ball strikes half or more of the object ball.

Bank Combos Offer a Big Target

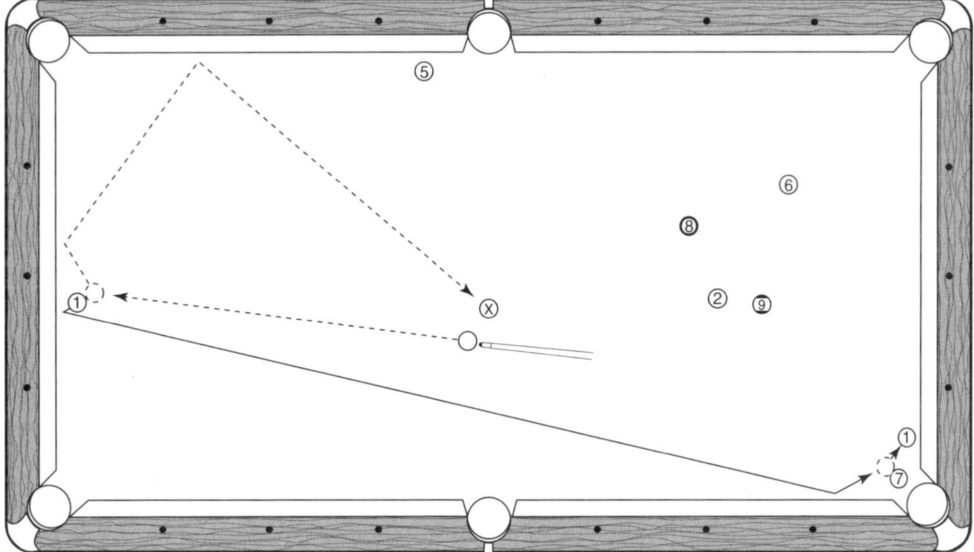

When an object ball is close to the corner pocket, it becomes an inviting target for a bank combination because the target is so large. Jeanette Lee played the long rail bank combo shown in the diagram below. Even though the 1-ball hit well up the cushion, she was still able to pocket the 7-ball. She ran this rack while on her way to winning the 1994 U.S. Open.

Aiming Factors

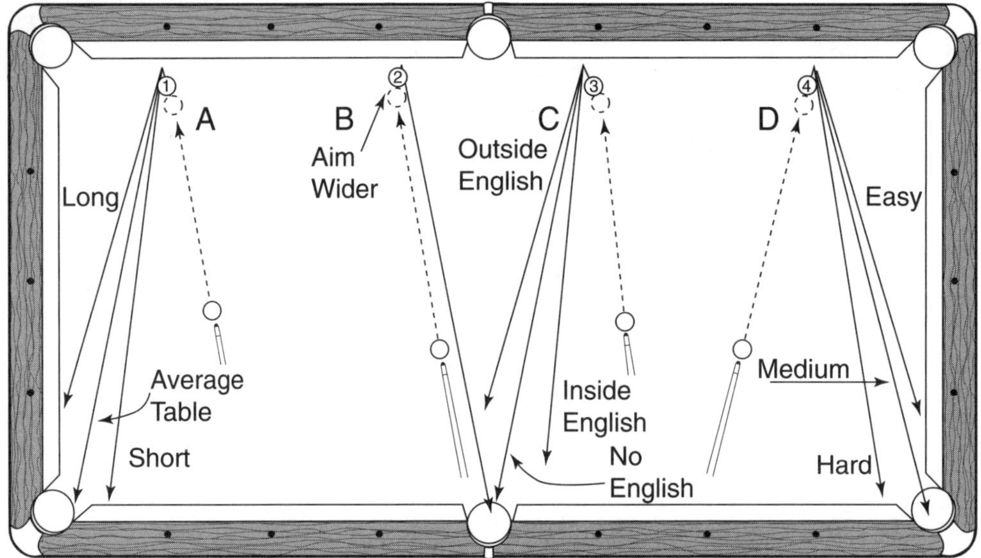

In an ideal world, we could pull out protractors, measure the angle to obtain the perfect point of aim, and subsequently split the pocket with our bank shots. If pool were only so easy, but of course it is not. There are four major factors that complicate the aiming equation. Each factor can, by itself, change your aim by a couple of degrees or more.

Factor #1 – The Table

Part A of the diagram shows three different scenarios for an identical bank that is struck with medium speed. If the table banks like the "average" table, it will split the pocket. If it banks "short" the ball will hit the bottom side rail. In this case you must cut the shot a little to the right to allow for the table, or hit the shot easier.. If the table banks "long", the ball object ball will strike the end rail. To offset this tendency, you must aim slightly to the left or hit the shot firmer.

Factor #2 – Contact Induced Throw

Part B is a simple crosside bank with a 15-degree cut angle. The shot is being played with a medium speed stroke. On banks with cut angles you must factor in contact throw, which can alter the path of the object ball by about 3- 6 degrees (see page 40, *Play Your Best Pool*). On this shot you must overcut the ball (aim to the left about 3 degrees more) to allow for contact throw.

Factor #3 English

Part C shows a relatively straight bank hit, once again, with a medium speed stroke. If you apply outside english(right in this example) to the shot, the bank will miss to the far side as shown. You can compensate for this by aiming for a fuller hit on the object ball and throwing it in the pocket. In fact, many excellent bankers prefer to shoot most of their banks shot with outside english. If you use inside english (left in this example), the bank will miss to the short side as shown. You can compensate for this by aiming for a slightly thinner hit on the object ball (a littler more to the right in this example).

Factor #4 Speed of Stroke

The bank in Part D is lined up perfectly straight. To pocket the shot, all you need do is hit the object ball fully with a medium speed stroke. If you were to lag the ball to the pocket, it could bank long and wind up hitting the end rail. If you hit the shot with a hard stroke, it would bank short as shown. Many of the top players prefer to hit banks with a hard stroke as they feel this helps with the accuracy of the shot. A firm stroke is typically used when they are confident of making the shot, and when the shot carries little or no defensive components to it. If you use this approach, be sure aim for a slightly thinner hit on the object ball to compensate for it's sharper rebound angle off the rail.

Using the Aiming Factors

There is nothing you can do to change the way a table plays. Using english or speed of stroke could reduce or eliminate the effects of contact throw. You can also use speed of stroke and/or english to create a successful shot. For example, you can hit the ball with a harder stroke to offset a table's tendency to bank long. And you could use outside english to throw a bank along a wider path if a table tends to bank short.

Combining Aiming Factors

It is possible to combine factors that will cancel each other out. This could be done by using outside english and a hard stroke. You can also change the point of aim greatly by combining factors to influence a bank in the same direction. For example, to open up the rebound angle of a bank as much as possible use a soft stroke with lots of outside english. And to create the sharpest rebound angle possible, you would use a hard stroke with a tip of inside english.

Aiming Factors

Influence	**Opens the angle**	**Closes the angle**
Speed of stroke	Easy stroke	Hard stroke
English	Outside english	Inside english
Table	Banks long	Banks short
Contact throw	Cut towards the shot	Cut away from the shot

Combining Aiming Factors

Goal Sought	**Action**
Open angle greatly	Outside english/soft stroke
Close angle greatly	Inside english/hard stroke
Avoid double kiss	Inside english/hard stroke

Billiards

A billiard in Nine Ball is a shot in which the cue ball strikes the lowest numbered ball first and glances off it and into the ball you wish to pocket. There are infinite uses for billiard shots in Nine-Ball, which naturally includes shots at the 9-ball.

Billiards Using the Tangent Line

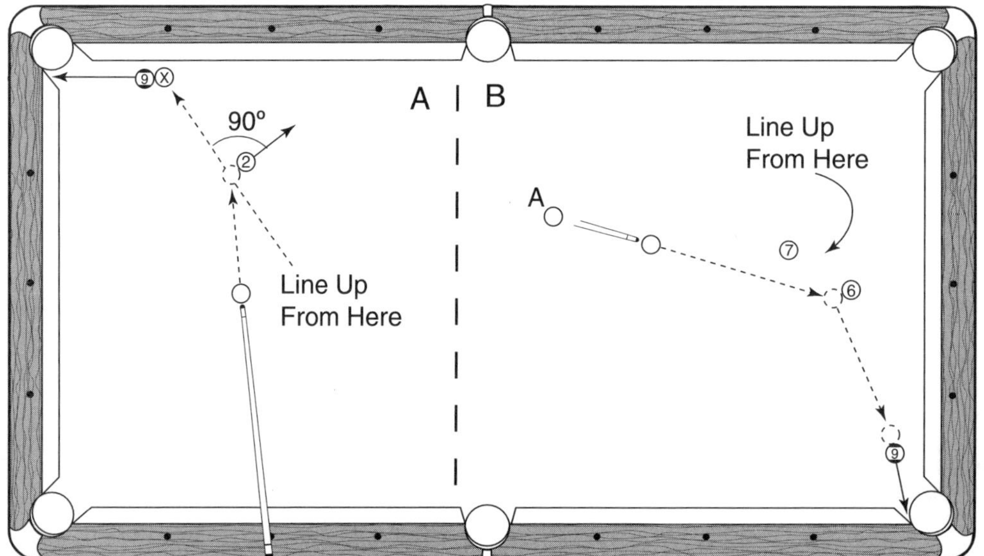

When the cue ball is struck firmly with centerball, it will travel at a 90-degree angle from the direction of the object ball. You can use this bit of pocket billiard physics to create the desired path for the cue ball into the ball you wish to pocket. In Part A of the diagram, the 2-9 combo is way too difficult to even think of playing. The billiard, however, is quite makeable. View the shot from the line that the cue ball must take after contacting the 2-ball in order to pocket the 9-ball. Your point of aim is the far left edge on the 2-ball when it is viewed from this position. Play the shot with centerball and a medium firm stroke.

Part B shows another billiard, only this time the 9-ball is much closer to the pocket. Walk over once again to view the direct line the cue ball must take into the 9-ball. This will help you to gauge where to send the cue ball into the 6-ball so that it will shoot off to the right and into the 9-ball. Use a medium firm stroke and centerball. This example shows the maximum distance you can play a centerball billiard with a good degree of accuracy. If the cue ball was further back, such as at Position A, you would need to use a very hard stroke or a little bit of draw to make the shot. In either case, the shot would become much less reliable.

The Draw Back Billiard

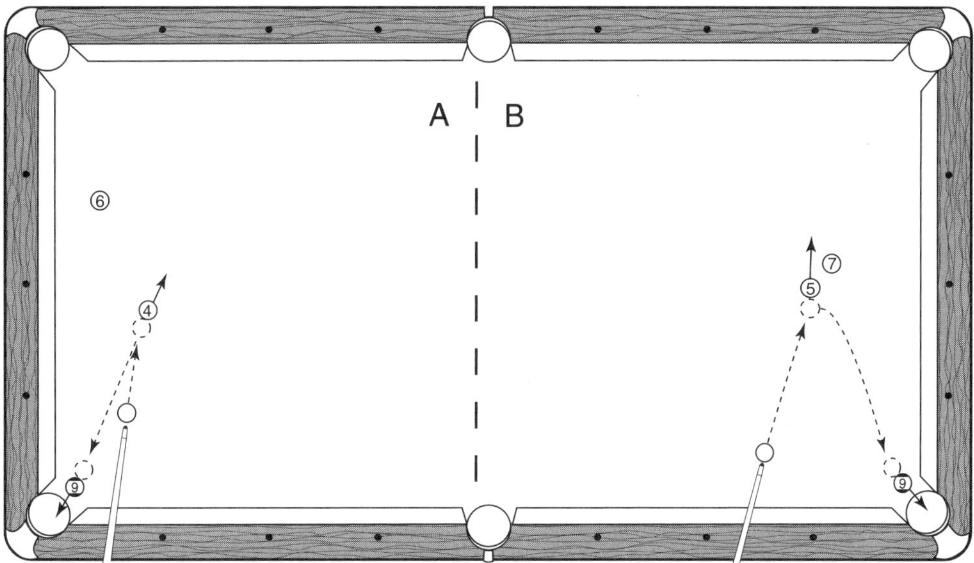

The draw back billiard is a very useful shot providing the circumstances are right. Look for the following conditions:

- The ball you wish to pocket is very close to the pocket.
- The ball you will be contacting first is within 2' of the ball you wish to pocket.
- The cue ball is on or not far from a line that runs from one object ball to the other.

In Part A of the example, you will notice that all of these conditions have been met. Now if the cue ball were on the dashed line that runs between the balls, you would simply shoot straight at the 4-ball and the cue ball would pull back into the 9-ball. However, the cue ball rests just to the right of the dashed line. Now you need to hit the 4-ball just slightly to the left of center. If you aim a hair too far to the left, the cue ball will travel just a fraction to the left before drawing back, which will cause the cue ball to strike the end rail instead of the 9-ball. The key to this shot is to hit the first ball just a fraction less than full.

The draw back shot in Part B is significantly more difficult than the one in Part A even though the 9-ball is hanging in the jaws. The problem is gauging the path of the cue ball after it makes contact with the object ball. In this case, a 15-degree cut on the 5-ball will result in about a 30-degree angle back. On this shot most players fail to compensate for the wide return angle by hitting the 5-ball too thinly. In our example, this aiming error would cause the cue ball to hit the end rail.

The Diversion Billiard

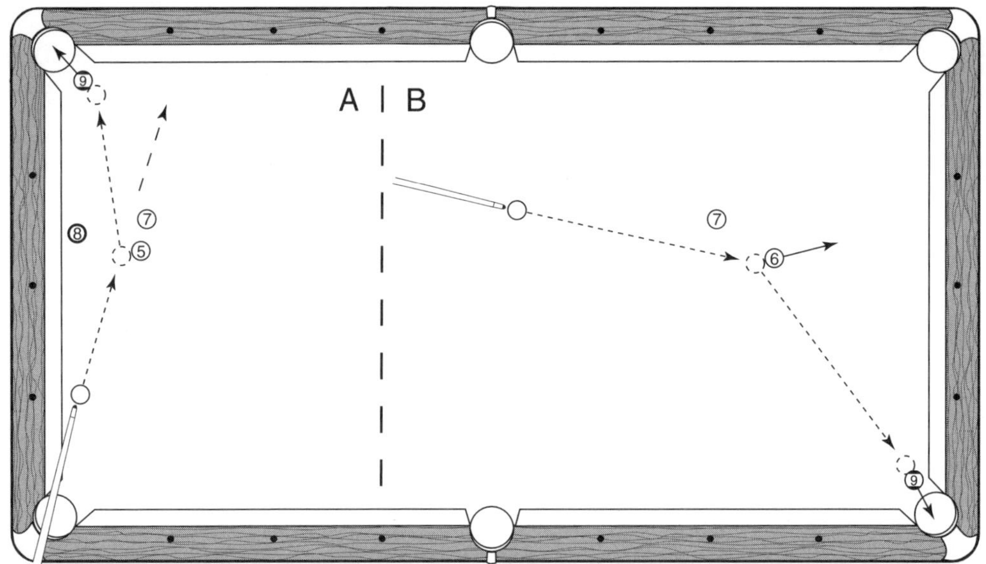

The diagram shows two examples of what I call the diversion billiard. Use a soft follow stroke to roll the cue ball into contact with the lowest numbered object ball. Rolling the cue ball eliminates nearly all of the bend in the cue balls path that occurs after contact, which simplifies aiming billiards. All you need is to figure how much of the object ball to hit in order to "divert" the cue ball into the ball you wish to pocket. A thin hit on the 5-ball in Part A will divert the cue ball slightly to the left and along a path into the 9-ball. In Part B a half ball hit on the 6-ball will send the cue ball to the right and towards the 9-ball.

A Long Distance Billiard

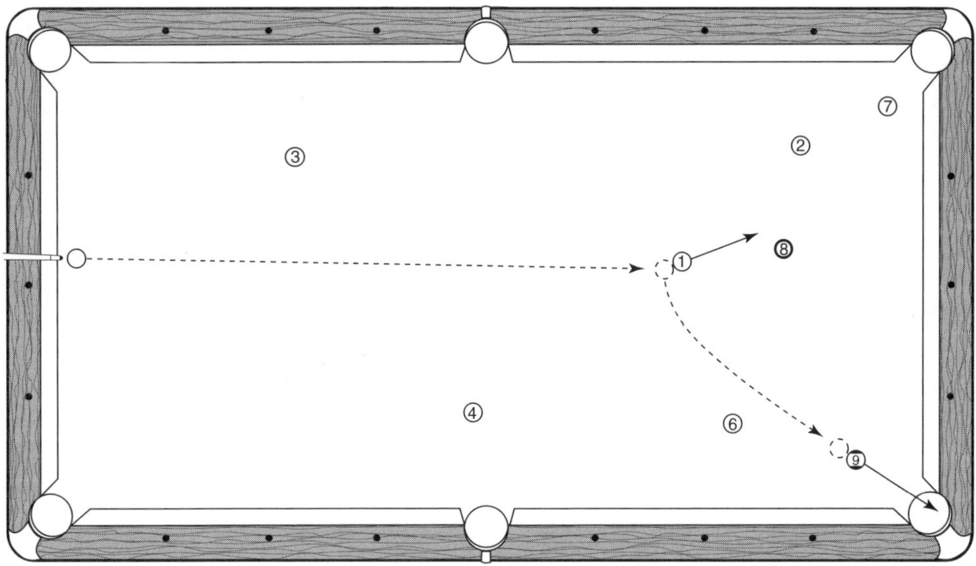

Sometimes it pays to throw caution to the wind when you are trailing in a match and need to build some momentum. This is especially true if you don't see a safety that is particularly appealing. Perhaps that was what Takeshi Okumura was feeling when he approached the table trailing Earl Strickland in the finals of the 2000 U.S. Open. Okumura used a hard follow stroke, aimed about 2/3 full on the 1-ball, and dazzled the crowd with the spectacular follow/curve billiard into the 9-ball on page 24.

Caroms

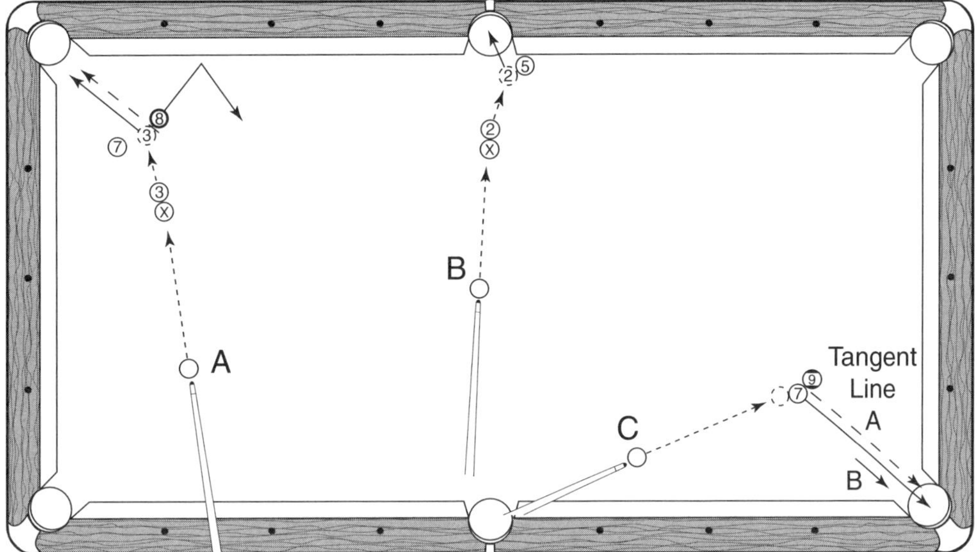

Carom shots are played by sending the cue ball into an object ball, which then glances off another ball and into the pocket. Carom shot can also be useful in playing safe. On a safety, your objective is to play the first ball into a second ball and have it continue to where your opponent has little or nothing with which to work (see carom safeties in chapter 11).

Part A shows a basic carom shot. The 7-ball prevents you from cutting the 3-ball into the corner. However, you can carom the 3-ball off the 8-ball, which is well positioned for this kind of shot. Use a medium firm stroke to keep the 3-ball on the correct line after it makes contact with the 8-ball. The 8-ball should be hit on the edge that lines up with the outside portion of the pocket as shown by the dashed line.

You could play the 2-ball directly into the pocket in Part B, but that would leave the 5-ball in the worst spot on the table. In this position, you are advised to get the 5-ball out of there by caroming the 2-ball off the 5-ball and into the side pocket.

In Part C shows a dead carom shot. The tangent line A that runs between the 7 and 9-balls points at the inside of the corner pocket. In this position you can pocket the 7-ball by using a soft follow stroke while hitting the left side of the 7-ball. Avoid using draw. Now if the tangent line was pointing down line B, you could pocket the 7-ball by hitting it about 2/3 full with a sharp draw stroke.

Combinations

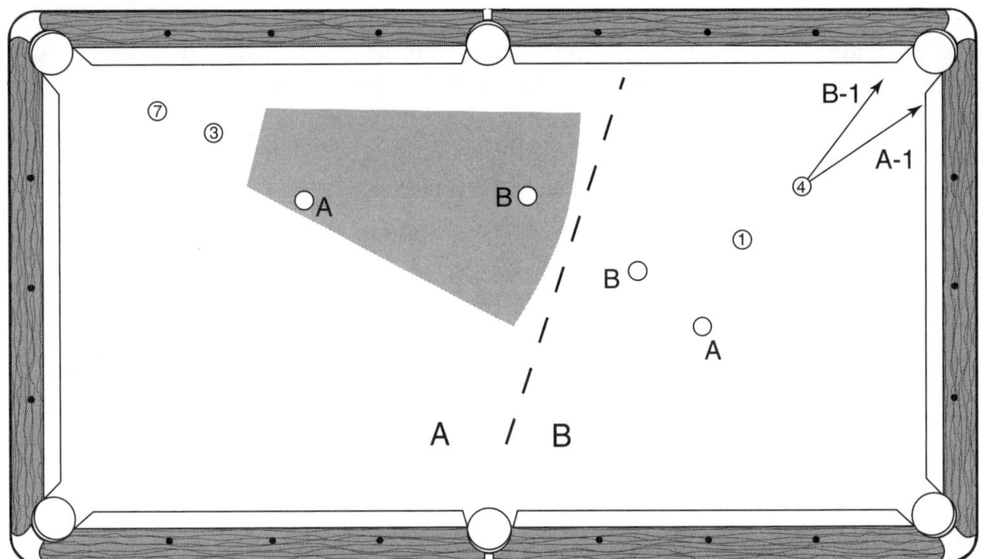

There are far fewer opportunities to play combos in Nine-Ball than in other pool games because there are only nine balls or less on the table after the break, and the balls are more widely spread than in other games. Combinations come into play most often when either or both players possess a weak break, which leads to congestion around the area of the rack Those who play on bar tables, where congestion is a way of life, will certainly encounter more chances to play combinations than those who play on the big table. Despite the shortage of combos in Nine-Ball, skill at them can provide you with a means for winning short racks and for completing your run outs.

I spent many hours studying the shot selection of the leading players in the world, who are almost all quite adept at combos. My findings indicate that the best players routinely avoid combos. That means most of you should also consider playing only the easiest kinds of combinations where the percentages are substantially in your favor. If a particular combo lies too difficult, you are almost always better off playing safe or choosing another offensive option.

Part A of the diagram shows a fairly easy combo as combos go. The 3-7 combo is lined up nearly straight at the pocket and the balls are only 4" apart. The 7-ball is a little less than a diamond from the pocket. Despite its apparent ease, this shot must still be played with great care. The position zone shows where the shot is not overly difficult. And yet I would guess that the odds of the average player pocketing the combo are about 60% with the cue ball in Position A, and about 50% with it in Position B.

You have certainly seen players line up combos from all angles. This includes pointing the cue carefully at the spot they hope to hit on the first ball. I would wager a guess that very few, however, have stopped to factor in contact throw in their calculations. Part B on page 26 shows a somewhat difficult 1-4 combo. If you fail to allow for contact throw, the 4-ball will be missed to the right of the pocket at A-1 when the cue ball is shot from Position A. The 4 would travel down B-1 if the cue ball was shot from Position B.

There seems to be a hypnotic lure that combos exert over a great many players, especially when they are on the 9-ball If you find that shooting anything but the easiest combos is costing you more games than they are winning for you, then your shot selection needs an overhaul.

Difficulty of Various Combos

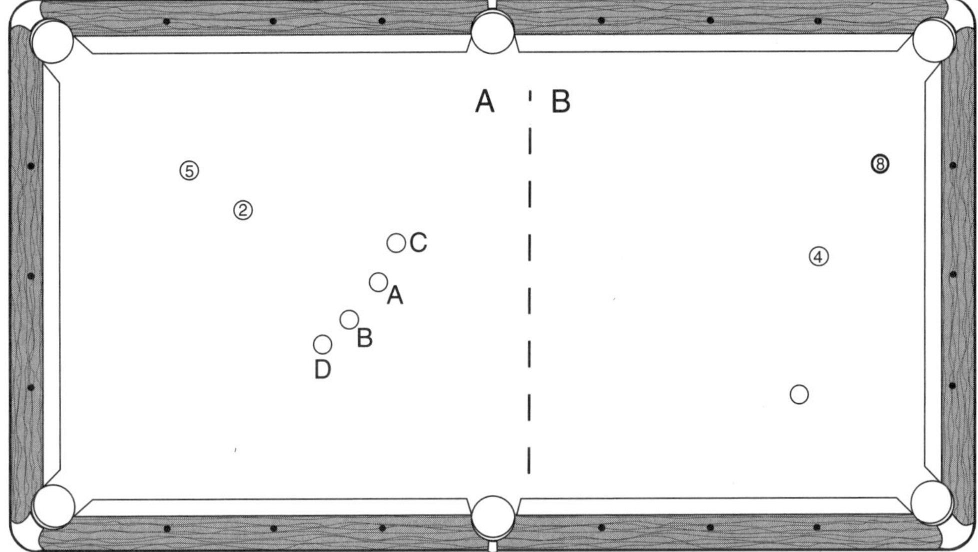

In Part A, the balls in the 2-5 combo are 5" apart. The 5-ball is about 18" from the pocket. The 2-ball is half of a ball's width to the right of lining up with the 5-ball and the pocket. Despite these seemingly minor differences, this combo lies much tougher than the one in the previous example. With the cue ball in Position A, you can shoot directly at the 2-ball. This is the easiest angle from which to play this combo. Position B is next in difficulty as you must cut the 2-ball slightly to the left to pocket the 5-ball. With the cue ball in Position C you are cutting the two in the direction of the 5-ball. Nevertheless, this is a very missable shot. From Position D you must backcut the 2-ball into the 5-ball, which is quite troublesome for most players. The shots in Part A of this diagram demonstrate combos with a degree of difficulty beyond which you should seldom stray. The combo in Part B is should carry a label "For Suckers Only". Hopefully this discussion has alerted you to the potential hazards of playing any but the easiest combos.

"You can miss a combo no matter how easy it looks." **Jim Rempe**

Combo or Partially Blocked Shot?

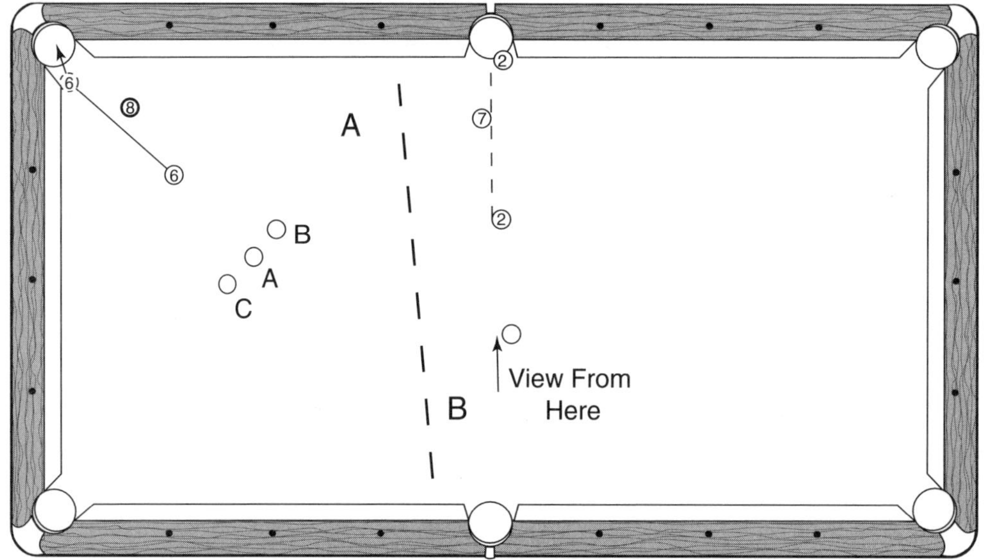

Part A of the diagram shows a tough decision: should you play the 6-ball directly into a partially blocked pocket or play a combo into a full pocket? When only about a third of the pocket is blocked, then you are better off shooting the ball directly into the pocket. When half the pocket is blocked (assuming a normal corner pocket of 4.75") then you only have a margin for error of about .25" on either side of the ball. When playing to a half pocket, don't forget that a half inch of the outside edge of the object ball can graze the point of the pocket and the shot will still fall.

The position of the cue ball can also affect your decision. When the cue ball is lined up straight with the pocket and the object ball, (see cue ball A) then you should play the ball straight into the pocket. When the cue ball is at Position B, you should also play the ball directly into the pocket as the combo is quite difficult. With the cue ball in Position C, the combo is probably the better choice.

Unless you check out the pocket opening with care, you may fall victim to a visual distortion that can trick you into believing that a ball won't go into a partially blocked pocket when in fact it will. In Part B, stand with your head at just above table level and imagine a line that runs from the inside of the ball you wish to pocket (in this case the 2-ball) and the outside edge of the obstructer (the 7-ball). Extend the line to the pocket opening. Is there at least enough room for the ball (2.5") with a little room to spare? If so, you can play the shot directly into the pocket.

Rail First Shots

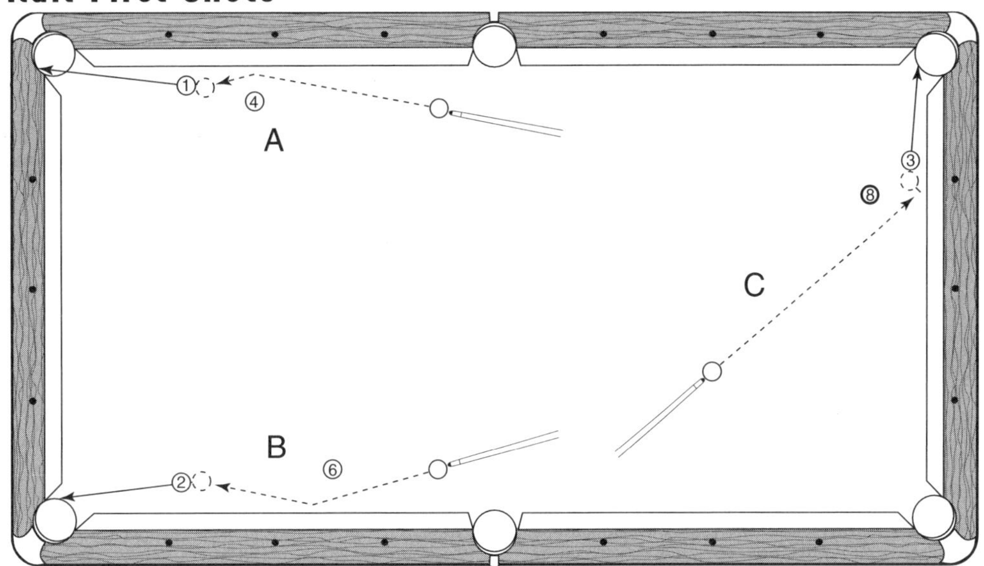

Rail first shots are used when the direct path to the object ball is blocked by an obstructer, the object ball is relatively close to the rail, and it is within a couple of diamonds of the pocket. In Part A, the 1-ball is blocked by the 4-ball. The 1-ball is also a little less than an inch from the rail and the cue ball is close to the rail. These factors add up to a comparatively easy rail first shot. Aim at the spot on the rail as indicated and avoid using english. I suggest you use a soft stroke on these shots when possible because it makes the pocket play bigger.

Even though I advise you to avoid english, some of you may discover that rail first shots work better when you apply some outside english. If you prefer this approach, you may need to adjust your aim to compensate for the throw that is applied to the object ball, and for the shallower rebound angle that the cue ball takes off the cushion. Take note, however, that the throw effect and the shallower angle of approach may largely offset each other.

In Part B, the 2-ball is significantly further from the rail than the 1-ball was in Part A. The cue ball is about the same distance from the rail as in Part A. Notice how much further up the rail you must aim to pocket the 2-ball. The 2-ball is about the maximum distance that a ball should rest from the rail for you to consider a rail first shot.

Notice the sharp angle of approach for the rail first shot in Part C. When you have an angle this steep, you should only consider playing a rail first shot if the object ball is very close to the rail as shown by the 3-ball. With a sharp angle of approach you will have to hit the rail very close to the object ball. I suggest that you use running english on this type of shot.

Curve Shots

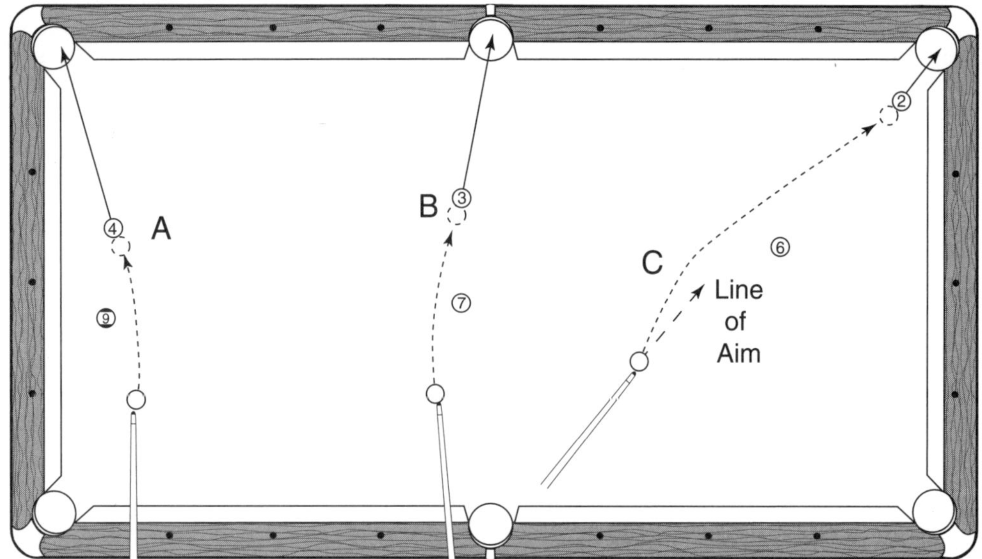

When an obstructer blocks part or the entire path of the cue ball to the object ball, conditions may be ripe for a curve shot. The curve has a couple of advantages over a jump shot when either is a possible choice: the cue ball never leaves the table on a curve shot, and it usually rolls only a short distance after contact, which makes position easier to predict.

Curve Shot Factors:

- The distance of the cue ball to the object ball.
- The amount of curve needed to avoid the obstructer with at least a little room to spare.
- The cue sticks angle of elevation.
- The force of the stroke.
- The amount of english you are applying.
- The distance the cue ball deflects to the side before it starts to curve back.
- The amount that the object ball will be thrown.

Wow! Now before you enlist a computer programmer to calculate the effects of these variables, or before you throw in the towel on curve shots, please understand that these shots are not nearly as complicated as you might imagine. For some mysterious reason, our minds are able to compute all of these variables and arrive at a reasonably accurate guesstimate of how to play the shot. That assumes, of course, you have spent some time at the practice table working on the shot.

It will perhaps improve your frame of mind towards curve shots if you realize that you will make some and miss some no matter what you do. But with some practice and a working knowledge of the factors that influence these shots, you should begin to start pocketing your share.

In Part A of the diagram on page 30, you can actually pocket the 4-ball without using a curve shot, but you only have 1/16" to spare. Under these conditions, the intervening ball seems to act like a magnet for the cue ball. The solution is to aim a half inch or so wide of the 9-ball and play a soft curve shot around it. A quarter tip of left english and a modest degree of elevation (10-degrees) should work.

The 7-ball blocks about a quarter of the cue ball's path to the 3-ball in Part B. Now you must aim a balls width to the left of the 7-ball. Elevate your cue to about 20-degrees and apply a half tip of right english. Use a medium soft stroke. The cue ball should curve around the 7-ball and into the 3-ball. Notice how the 3-ball was thrown to the left and into the pocket.

Part C shows a long distance curve shot in which you must bend the cue ball around the 6-ball to pocket the 2-ball. As a practical matter, long curve shots should only be played when the object ball is relatively close to the pocket. On this shot you should aim about 3.5" outside of the 6-ball. Elevate to about 25-degrees and use a tip of low right english. Use a firm stroke. You want the cue ball to squirt to the left beyond your line of aim and then curve back along the path shown.

A Masse/Curve Shot

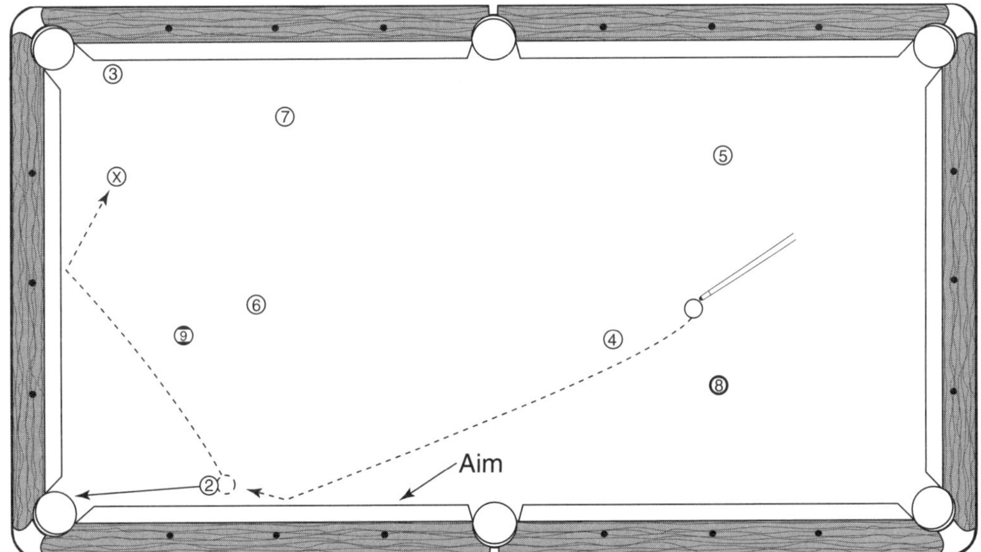

Fong-Pang Chao of Chinese Taipei really had no choice but to go for this difficult shot on his way to defeating Cory Deuel in the 2000 World Nine Ball championships. Chao elevated his cue to about a 50-degree angle and played a spectacular masse/curve shot that twisted the cue ball around the 4-ball and into a rail first shot on the 2-ball. The cue ball's path changed 12-degrees from the point of aim and its point of contact with the rail. As I mentioned earlier, curve shots like this are no sure thing, but they at least give you a fighting chance to stay at the table and continue your run.

Jump Shots

The jump shot has spiraled in popularity as more and more players view it as the best way to escape many of their opponent's safeties and bad leaves. A big for jump shots is that they give you a direct line to the object ball, which eliminates the guesswork that accompanies most kick shots. In addition, you have a much better chance of pocketing the ball than with a kick shot. On the negative side, are the high percentage of jump shots that fail to reach proper elevation then crash into the blocker and those that fly off the table and across the pool room floor, which can cause some embarrassing moments for the offender.

Amateur players tend to play more jump shots than the pros because they: lack their skills at kicking; face more hooks than the pros (because their games have more innings); feel it is the thing to do; have fallen in love with the shot and play it at every opportunity despite the risks involved. Nevertheless, before I continue to expound on the jump shot, it may be worth considering whether or not you want to master this skill, or instead spend your practice time on the kicking game.

The Pros Use of the Jump Shot

In a study I conducted of 500 pro games, the jump shot was used only 22 times in 20 games. Furthermore, the jumper won only 6 of the 20 games. Five of those wins came on run outs after making a ball. What this shows is that the pros are hesitant to pull out the short stick, and when they do they win only about 30% of the time. In sharp contrast, the pros played 241 kick shots in 159 games of the 500 studied.

Consider that Efren Reyes, the world's best kicker, almost never (if ever) plays a jump shot. But why should he with his kicking skills. On the other hand, Earl Strickland and Johnny Archer are extremely proficient at jump shots, but can't match Reyes kicking game.

Legal Jump Cues

The evidence above clearly demonstrates that it is vastly more important for you to first master the kicking game (see chapter 12). Nevertheless, jump shots do come up often enough in amateur competition that you will be well rewarded for your skill in this area, providing you pick your spots wisely. Your desire to go airborne has been aided by cue manufacturers, as there are a host of lightweight jump cues with special tips for jumping. There are even cues that serve the dual function of a jump cue and a break cue. If you haven't already purchased a jump cue or are not satisfied with your current make, I suggest you ask your friends and others, who seem to jump well, what brand they are using.

According to BCA rules, a cue must be at least 40" long. I advise that you stick to the rules, as this will avoid controversy. In addition, practicing legal jump shots will better prepare you for those events where the rules are strictly enforced.

Practicing the Jump Shot

Before you take to the airways to perfect your jump shot in the local poolroom for hour after hour, consider that the jump shot is probably not the most popular shot from the perspective of your poolroom owner or those on the tables nearby. After all, it doesn't take long for a series of constant explosions and flying cue balls to grate on anyone's nerves. In consideration of those around you, much less the beleaguered pooll room owner's fine slate, I suggest that you: practice it at home, in off hours at poolroom, with the manager's permission, and certainly not on the table(s) they reserve for big games.

Technique

Jump shots are played by elevating your cue and striking down on the cue ball. Aim below the center of the cue ball, when viewed from the angle at which your cue is pointing when elevated, as shown in the illustration. Use a sharp stroke with a definite snap of the wrist. While you need to use a firm stroke, you don't need to "kill the cue ball". You can achieve sufficient elevation for most jump shots by elevating the cue to about 30-40 degrees. However, when you must get the ball up quickly, you may go as far as 55-60 degrees of elevation.

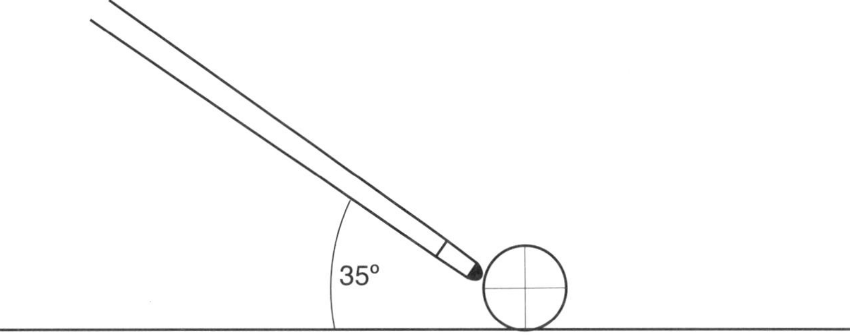

On most jump shots, your primary goals are to hit the ball and avoid fouling, which can be accomplished with no special attention to aiming. If however, you are intent on making every effort to pocket the ball, you will need to aim with even more care than on a regular shot. Some players seem to find it helps to line up the shot with the cue as level as possible, and then elevate the butt end to the desired angle.

When aiming to pocket a straight in shot, you can pocket the ball whether the cue ball is on or off the table at the moment of contact. On cut shots, the cue ball will most likely be in the air when it makes contact. Your accuracy will be determined by the cue ball's distance from the cloth at the moment of contact. You must compensate for this by aiming for a slightly fuller hit on the object ball than normal. The amount by which you must adjust your aim is a guessing game as it is impossible to predict exactly how far off the table the cue ball will be at contact.

The Cue Ball's Flight Pattern

The more you elevate your cue, the higher the cue ball will fly. This will cause the first bounce to be higher after it lands on the table. On most jump shots, the object ball will be hit after the initial bounce. When the landing strip is particularly long there is a chance the cue ball could bounce two or three times. Each successive bounce will naturally be lower, and the distance between each bounce will be considerable shorter. As a rule of thumb, you can expect the distance between the first and second bounces to be roughly 40-50% of the distance from where the cue ball was struck and first descended on the table.

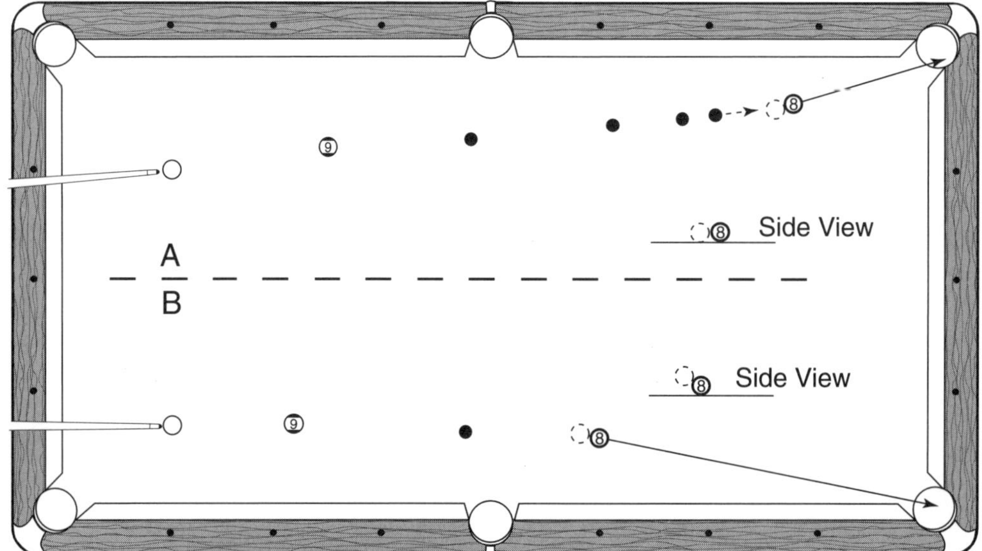

In Part A of the diagram, there is a long landing strip for the cue ball, which will enable it to bounce several times before contacting the 8-ball. This is the ideal scenario as the risk of the cue ball leaving the table is nil. In addition, the cut angle on the ball is much more predictable when it is being struck at table level. The ideal contact position is shown in the side view.

The 9-ball is much closer to the cue ball in Part B, which means that the cue must be elevated to produce more immediate elevation. The cue ball will bounce higher, which in this instance results in a downward hit on the 8-ball after the first bounce.

On short-range jumps shots, the big skill is to control the flight of the cue ball when there is little or no room for a bounce. You want to avoid having the cue ball hit close to the object ball on its first bounce, as there is a good chance it will glance off the object ball and fly off the table. This is especially true on cut shots. You can avoid fouling by having the cue ball fly down onto the object ball before it lands on the table. This requires expert technique and a precise knowledge of the cue ball's flight pattern.

Playing Position on Jump Shots

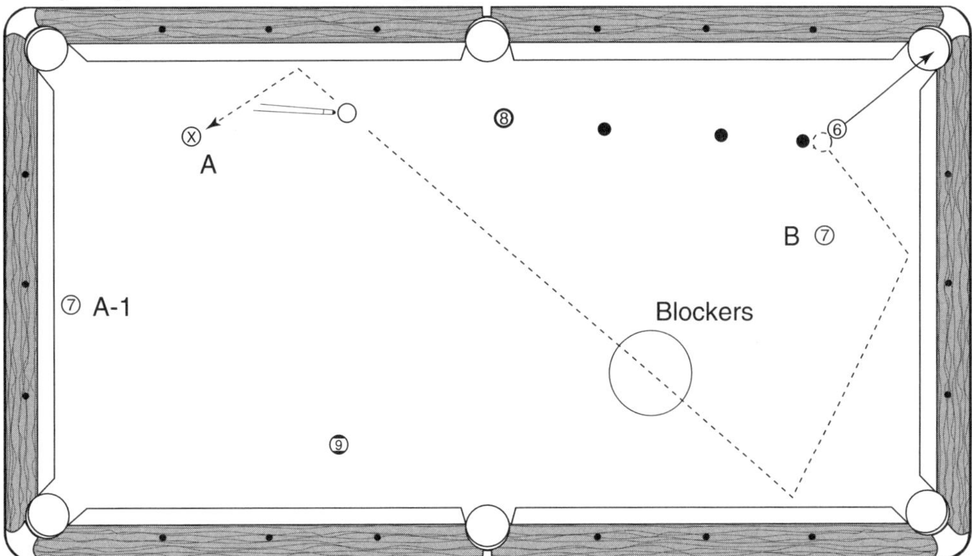

The ultimate goal on any jump shot is to make the ball and play position for either a shot or a safety. When you are cutting the object ball, be prepared for it to travel a long distance after contacting the object ball. In the illustration, the cue ball stopped at Position A for excellent shape on the 7-ball at A-1. If the 7-ball was at Position B, you would have a problem. Now let's assume the 7-ball was in Position B and there were one or more blockers around the area covered by the circle. They could be used to stop the cue ball for position on the 7-ball. In sum, your chances of playing position on jumps shots is linked to the position of the balls, and your options are limited.

If you are playing a straight or nearly straight in jump shot, you can bring the cue ball back as the draw spin that was applied at contact will still be on the cue ball when it contacts the object ball. It is difficult to apply follow unless you are jumping over an obstructer at a shallow angle, which allows you to hit higher on the cue ball.

When to Jump

A realistic appraisal of your jumping skills will go a long ways towards determining when you should go skywards as opposed to a ground attack via the kicking game. There are those who love jumping, those who hate it and never do it, and those in between who view jump shots as a necessary evil. In short, what is a kick shot for some is a jump for another, and vice versa. Below are the conditions when a jump shot, all things considered, may be your best bet:

- There is a long landing strip for the cue ball.
- The object ball that must be carried is in the ideal range (not to far or too close) from the cue ball so that there is no need for excessive elevation.

- The object ball is close to a pocket.
- You only have to clear the edge of the blocker.
- There is a good chance of making the ball and getting position on the next ball for a shot or safety.
- The cue ball will hit the object ball fully, which minimizes the risk of it flying off the table.
- The primary kicking lanes are blocked.
- There is a possible kick, but it requires you to use a difficult route to the object ball.
- The table is conducive to jump shots as some enable the cue ball to become elevated easier than others. Thicker slate generally leads to a higher bounce.

When Not to Jump

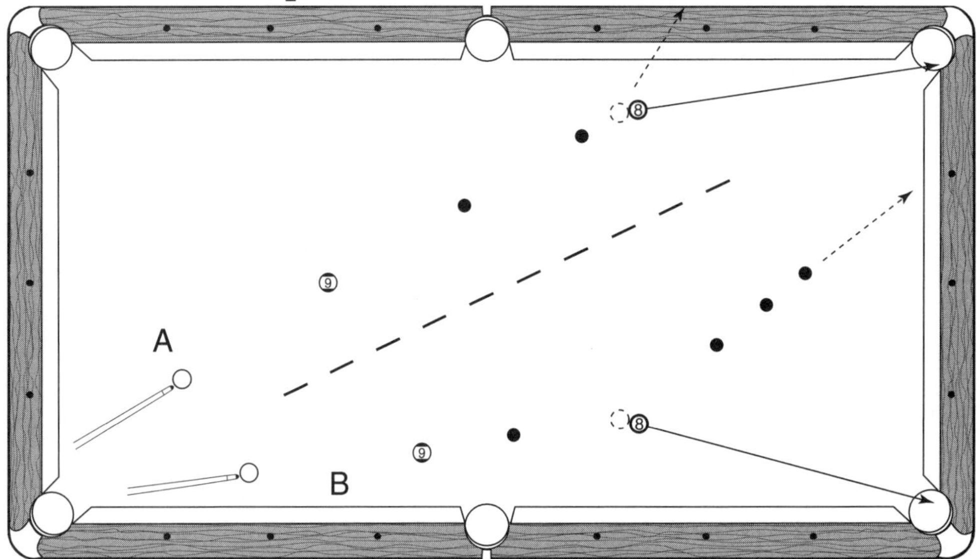

The conditions which make a jump shot a high risk venture are pretty much the opposite of those on the list above. If you have a short landing strip and the cue ball is likely to hit well up on the object ball or on the upswing after a short hop, you are likely to send the cue ball to the poolroom floor. In addition, you must pay special attention to the object ball's location.

Part A shows a partially successful jump shot: the 8-ball was pocketed (note the allowance for cutting the ball while the cue ball was still in the air). The cue ball flew off the table, however, because the object ball was close to the rail and the shot was being played towards the cushion. Notice that there was only a few inches for the cue ball to land.

In Part B, the cue ball flew into the upper half of the 8-ball, but it still stayed on the table thanks to the rather lengthy landing strip. Under ideal circumstances, you will have a sufficiently long area for the cue ball to land after it contacts the object ball. You can really view the landing zone after contact with the object ball as a secondary landing strip.

Shooting the Gamewinner

Here's some sobering news: in my 500 game study of tops pros, they missed only four 9-balls in the 426 games that went the distance, or less than 1%! This is certainly irrefutable evidence as to their ability to play position and to consistently pocket the gamewinner under tournament pressure. In sharp contrast, I can't recall how many zillions of times I've heard a novice complain that they can't make the 8-ball at the finish of a game of Eight Ball. Well, the same aversion to pocketing the gamewinner also holds true for many players who are relatively inexperienced at Nine Ball. But they are not alone, for even seasoned veterans have on occasion been known to cough up the 9-ball when on the verge of an important tile. In short, players at all levels have suffered from a disease called "9-ball-itis."

The 9-ball is usually a routine shot for A Players, but not always. This is especially true if they are competing against less skilled players who have a tendency to miss at the end of a game and leave long, tough shots. The 9-ball can be even more of an adventure for B Players who are more prone to positional errors. For C Players, the 9-ball is often a roller coaster ride into the unknown.

I can't offer you a 100% foolproof cure against "9-ball-itis". I will, however, provide you with some insights into playing the 9-ball that will help you cope successfully with the games most stressful shot. These ideas should save you a game or two here or there. And they could some day even spell the difference between winning and losing a double hill match.

Ideal Position on the 9-Ball

Let me begin by first stating the obvious: acceptable or excellent position is your best insurance against missing the money ball. The 9-ball should be the easiest ball on which to get shape because:

- You don't have to worry about setting up the correct angle or playing position for another shot.
- You needn't worry about getting hooked behind any other balls when playing position.
- You can play area position.

Your position on the 9-ball should be to a rather sizeable zone that enables you to pocket the 9-ball with little concern about the cue ball.

"I want to see the collision."
Nick Varner on watching the 9-ball go into the pocket.

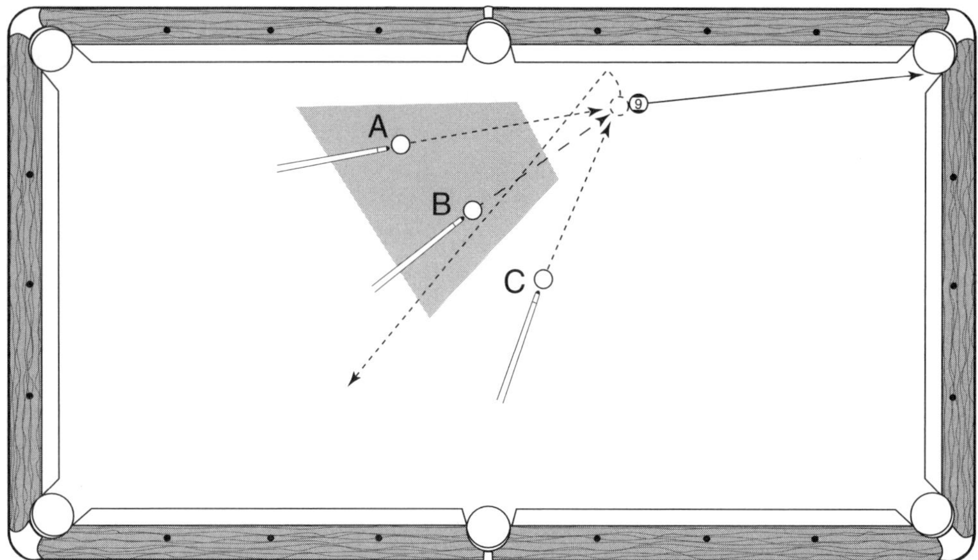

The diagram shows a typically large zone for the 9-ball. The cue ball in Position A presents you with the ideal scenario for shooting the 9-ball: a relatively easy shot with a small cut angle. In this position you can concentrate all of your energies on making the ball, since there is no chance of scratching. Play this shot with the speed of stroke that you feel gives you the best chance of making the ball. On this shot most players would use a medium soft stroke to a medium firm stroke.

When you have a little less than perfect shape, you must expend at least a little energy worrying about the cue ball. With the cue ball in Position B you must now control the direction of the cue ball to avoid scratching in the opposite side pocket. Some players prefer to play this shot with draw while others use follow Since you don't need shape, you should play this shot with the speed with which you are most comfortable. This also holds true for most shots on the 9-ball: try to play shape in a way that allows you to use the speed of stroke with which you are the most comfortable. The cue ball in Position C is well out of the ideal zone. The 60-degree cut angle makes this shot very missable. In addition, you must now apply either right or left english to avoid scratching in the opposite side pocket.

When you have a difficult shot on the money ball, be sure to complete your preshot routine. Take enough time to get comfortable over the shot. Then concentrate on giving it your best effort with the understanding that this will give you your best chance of making the ball.

CHAPTER 2

THE BREAK

"The cardinal rule of Nine-Ball is don't foul on the break."
Steve Mizerak

Breaking a rack of Nine-Ball is sort of like a golfer's putting or a basketball player's jump shot: sometimes you've got it and sometimes you don't. At times you'll consistently pocket balls and separate the pack across the table while on other occasions you can't buy a ball on the break. Often the conditions are breaker friendly while at other times the table is downright stingy.

In one pro match I witnessed the wing ball shoot straight into the corner pocket 21 straight games! In another match, the commentators at the 1992 Bicycle Club Invitational were reciting the super fast radar gun readings of Earl Strickland and Francisco Bustmante, as evidence of their breaking prowess, alerting viewers to the upcoming break and run show. So what happens? These two ball blasters failed to break and run one single rack in 23 games!

The pros probably work on their break as much as any other single shot, and yet, as these examples demonstrate, their results in this crucial area of performance are highly inconsistent. This is due to changing conditions and minor fluctuations in their technique. In the final analysis, you've got to perfect your break so you can wring as much from the table as possible, and so you won't be at a disadvantage when playing an opponent with a powerhouse buster.

When you posses a strong break, you always have a chance to stage a comeback providing the table is breaker friendly. A great break can also intimidate an opponent. If, however, you break poorly, your opponent will gain confidence because they know they will have a chance at winning most games.

The Importance of the Break

C Players

According to several studies, the 9-ball goes about once every 40-50 racks. If a new racking device gains widespread popularity, 9-balls on the break could occur far less often. At the C Player level, break and runs rarely happen. This means there are few opportunities for a C Player to win a game in the first inning. C Players, however, can easily wind up losing games by scratching. If they foul against a fellow C Player, their opponent may line up a combo on some other shot or on the 9-ball. And if they are playing a B Player or better, their opponent could run out. Therefore, a C Players main objective when breaking is to make a solid hit on the 1-ball and keep the cue ball on the table. This can be accomplished by employing a softer break. Ironically, many top players will go to a soft break under certain playing conditions. When a C Player is getting weight, however, they should consider using a power break, especially if they are being spotted two or more extra money balls.

B Players

B players can break and run the easier racks with a fair degree of consistency. And if a B Player is on their game, they are also fully capable of running tougher racks and making combos or other shots on the 9-ball. As a result, a B Player with an effective break can gain a significant advantage over an opponent with a comparatively poor break. A "B" Player who is breaking well can completely dominate a match with a C Player. Against an A Player, they will need their very best break working to have any chance of winning unless, of course, they are receiving weight. The last thing a B Player wants is for an A Player to go to the table with cue ball in hand after their break.

A Players

A Players are a threat to run out the majority of the time when they make a ball and have a reasonable shot at the lowest numbered ball, providing the layout has few, if any, complications. As a result, the break is an extremely valuable weapon at the A Player level. At the A level, many matches are won by the player whose break is working better during the match. Since A Players mostly compete with other A's, fouling on the break is perhaps the biggest single mistake they can make in Nine Ball. When their break is working an A Player will completely dominate C and B players even if they are giving them a sizeable spot.

In sum, the break becomes more of a factor the better you play. If you are a C Player, your practice time is better spent on other parts of your game. B Players can significantly raise their winning percentage by improving their break. Those who aspire to the A level and above must plan on developing a powerful break that allows them to run out consistently.

LAW: The greater the ability of the players, the more of a role the break plays in determining the outcome of the match, and vice versa.

The Pool & Billiard Study

Scientific evidence on the break shot was largely lacking until Pool & Billiard Magazine conducted a break speed contest at the 1996 BCA Trade Show. Karin Kaltofen, then the editor of the magazine, and engineer Steve Kasten measured the speed of the break shots of over 300 hundred amateurs and professionals using his "Laser Speed Meter". The 23 male pros averaged 24.9 MPH while the 15 women pros averaged 19.3 MPH. Sammy Jones recorded the fasted break with a speed of 31.1 MPH while Jeanette Lee lead the ladies with a speed of 23.8 MPH.

The most fundamental conclusion of the study was that high-speed hits with accuracy do produce more balls on the break. Imagine that! The test also revealed that going all out for speed creates a big variable in your results. A controlled, yet powerful break speed gives you consistency. The table below summarizes the results of their contest/study.

Summary of the Pool & Billiard Study

MPH/%	**MPH/%**	**MPH/%**
28 1.1	22 12.4	16 3.6
27 1.1	21 11.7	15 1.8
26 2.1	20 12.1	12-14 2.1
25 5.3	19 14.2	Under 12 1.1
24 5.3	18 13.5	
23 6.4	17 6.4	

All Breakers Approximate Ranges

16.0 – 25.8 MPH 90% 17.2 – 24.9 MPH 80%

Your Optimum Break Speed

Some people are born with bodies that allow them to run the 100 meters in under 10 seconds or throw a baseball at 90+MPH. Those lacking a certain muscle structure can never hope to become a Nolan Ryan. Similarly, you as pool player posses a certain strength, muscle structure and other elements of biomechanics that place natural limitations on the maximum speed that you can ever hope to obtain on the break.

Once you have come close to mastering the fundamental techniques of the power break, you will probably be within 1-2 MPH of the maximum you could ever hope to achieve. From that point forward, incremental improvement will come only from focusing extensively on a training regimen designed to enable you to reach your absolute maximum, period. Since you have so many other things to master in pool, your practice time is better spent elsewhere instead of trying to squeeze another mile or two per hour out of your break.

Earl Strickland, arguably the most feared Nine-Ball player on the planet, is the possessor of a powerhouse break and run game. And yet, according to the study by *Pool & Billiard Magazine* he has a top break speed about 3 MPH below the fastest breakers! Johnny Archer, who is also recognized for his awesome break and run game, has a break speed 5 MPH below the tops. Both of these players, however, have plenty of speed to scatter the balls effectively because they make such a consistently solid hit on the 1-ball. It is no coincidence that they are also excellent shotmakers, which enables them to hit the 1-ball precisely where intended.

The Strong Breakers Advantage

The break shot is the most crucial shot for the pros, when you consider that they break and run 28% of the time, according to a study I conducted of 500 games. The players with the two best tournament records in the 1990's were Johnny Archer and Earl Strickland. Each of their break and run percentages far exceeded the average pro. Earl Strickland broke and ran an astounding 32.7% of the time while Johnny Archer's average was nearly as good at 31.7%.

Even though the break is less important for amateurs, it can still provide you with the winning edge. Let's assume that you and your opponent are evenly matched in all other facets of the game. We're also going to assume, for the sake of argument, that you both have a 50% chance of winning any game that the breaker does not win on their first turn. Our final assumption is that you and your opponent played a race to 100, and that you broke and ran 10 times and your opponent broke and ran 6 times. All other games were split evenly. Your margin of victory would be 52-48. If you converted these results to a race to 11, your average margin of victory would be 11-10.15.

Goals for the Break Shot

Your goals for the break shot will vary somewhat, depending on your level of skill. The primary goal of C Players, as I mentioned earlier, is to avoiding a foul. B Players and above should be looking to accomplish the following objectives:

- Make at least one ball.
- Have the balls spread in such a way that the rack can be run.
- Have a reasonably makeable shot on the lowest numbered ball, which is usually the 1-ball or 2-ball.
- Park the cue ball in the center portion of the table.

The diagram at the top of the next page shows the ideal zone for the cue ball after the break. Let's assume that the cue ball parked in the dead center of the table. The 1-ball will almost always bank to the opposite end of the table when it does not go on the break. Notice the huge zone in which the 1-ball is a very makeable shot on the breaker's side of the table.

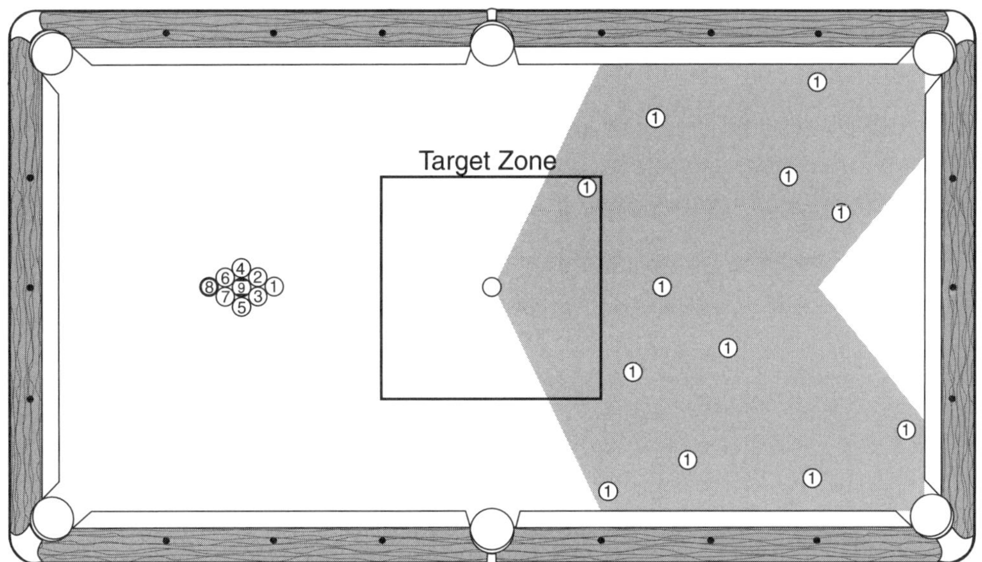

Where the Balls Go on the Break

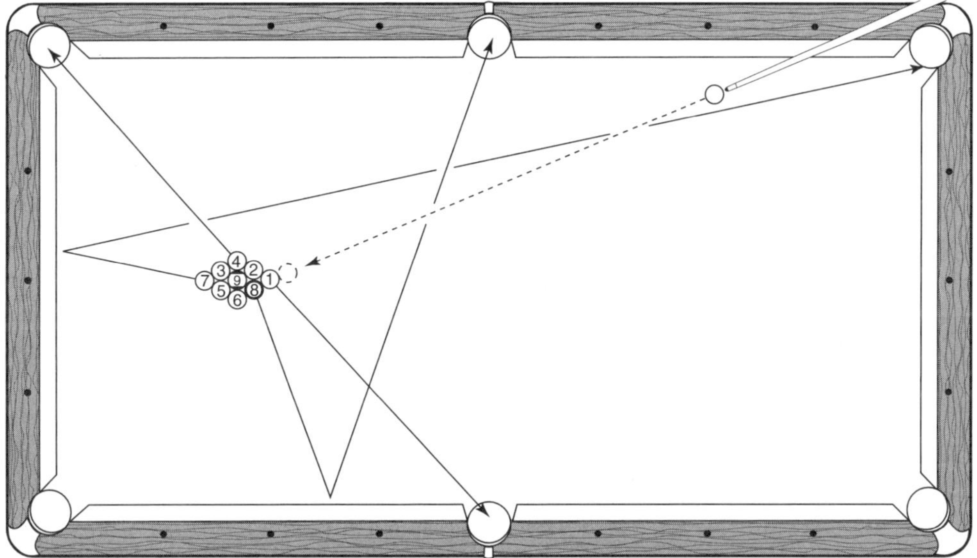

The majority of balls that fall on the break go into a few predictable destinations far more often than not. When the rack is broken from the right side, as in the example, the wing ball or corner ball (the 4-ball) will drop into the corner pocket on the same side of the breaker much more often than any other ball.

The 1-ball in the opposite side pocket is the second most pocketed ball on the break. The 8-ball in this rack will occasionally go cross side. If you are receiving a spot ball, you should break from the opposite side of the table. If you are giving up a spot and your opponent always breaks from the same side of the table, you should always place his money ball on the same side behind the 1-ball. The ball at the end of the rack (the 7-ball) occasionally banks into the far corner.

Playing Position After the Break

Your attempts to make a ball on the break should be focused on making either the wing ball or the 1-ball. Any other balls that fall are usually a result of the unpredictable collisions that take place. If the corner ball is going on nearly every break, you should really focus on controlling the cue ball. Try taking a little speed off the break. If the wing ball still goes with a softer break, you can hone in on position for the 1-ball.

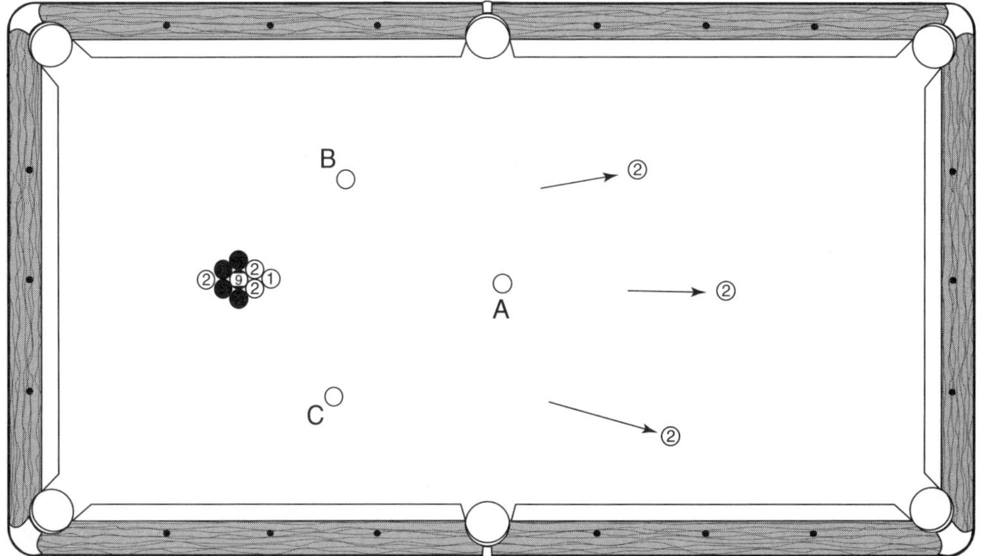

Many players prefer to go for the 1-ball in the side. If it is dropping regularly, begin to focus on how to play shape on the 2-ball. If the 2-ball is racked right behind the 1-ball or at the bottom of the rack, as in the example above, it should join Cue Ball A at the breakers end of the table. Your opponent may attempt to neutralize the effects of your strategy by placing the 2-ball in any of the positions shown by the solid balls. If that is the case, you may wish to send the cue ball to Positions B or C.

Losing the Cue Ball on the Break

A less than perfect hit on the cue ball and/or 1-ball can cause you to lose control of the cue ball. The cue ball in Position A in the diagram at the top of page 45 hit the 1-ball solidly, but continued forward because it was hit too high. To solve this problem, you need lower your tip at address. The cue ball scratched in Position B thanks to a less than perfect hit on the 1-ball combined with follow. Adjust your aim slightly to the right and hit the cue ball a bit lower.

The cue ball disappears into the opposite side pocket (Position C) on most scratches. Hitting to the right of the ideal line of aim caused the side pocket scratch. For some reason, many players have a very difficult time correcting this error. If this is a problem for you, you may have to overcompensate for a while until you slowly work your way back to the proper line. Hitting the cue ball too far below center caused the corner pocket scratch in Position D. Finally, the cue ball in Position E was

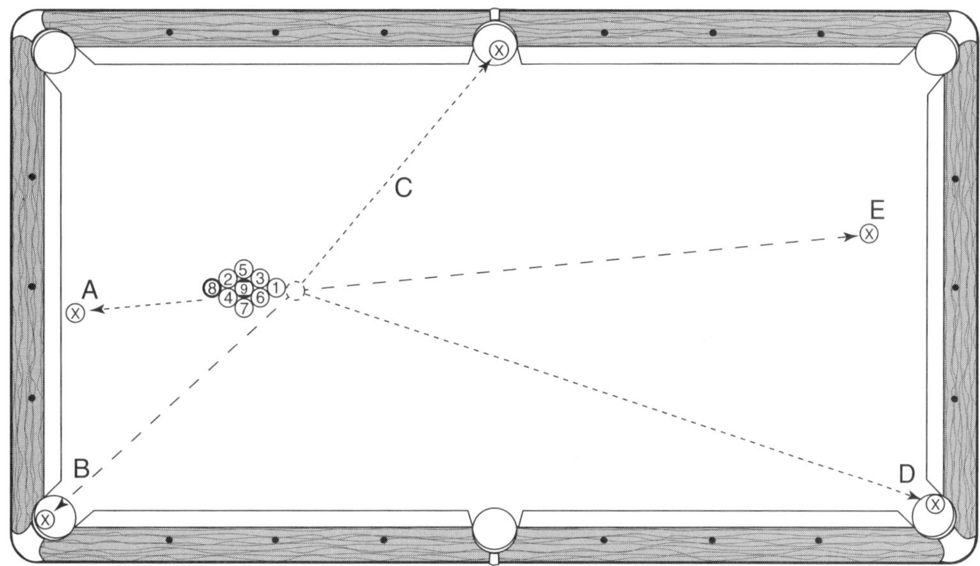

also caused by hitting the cue ball too low. This is the least damaging of all the errors since the cue ball is still on the table and there is an excellent chance the 1-ball could be in the same area of the table.

Where the Pros Scratch

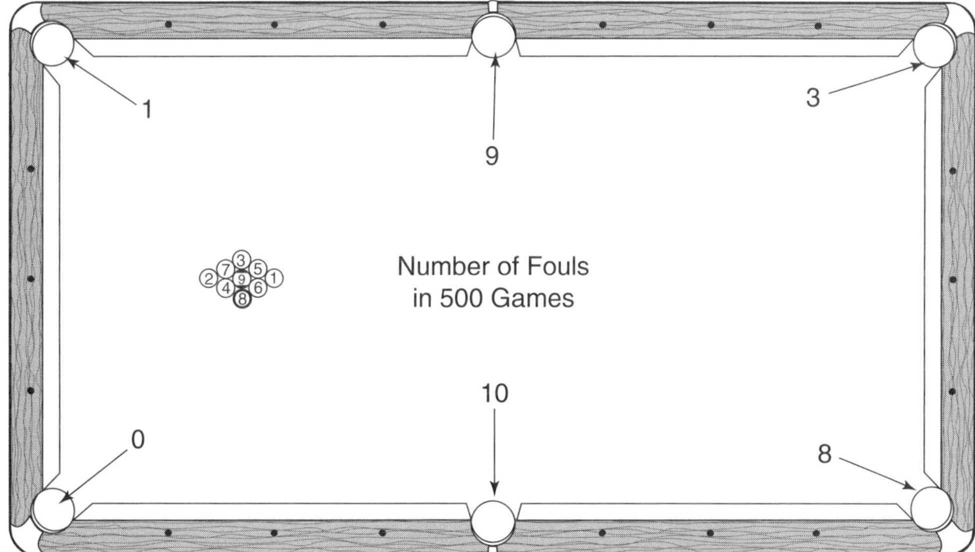

In a study I conducted of 500 games, the pros committed a foul on only 7.6% of their break shots, or once in every 13.2 breaks. The cue ball flew off the table 7 times, or once in every 71.4 breaks! The remaining 31 fouls were scratches into the various pockets shown above. The cue ball traveled directly into a pocket 21 times. The cue ball was kissed in 10 times. The study shows the pros remarkable skill at hitting the cue ball and 1-ball on target. The almost total absence of scratches at the foot end reveals that they almost never let the cue ball travel forward.

Cue Ball Location

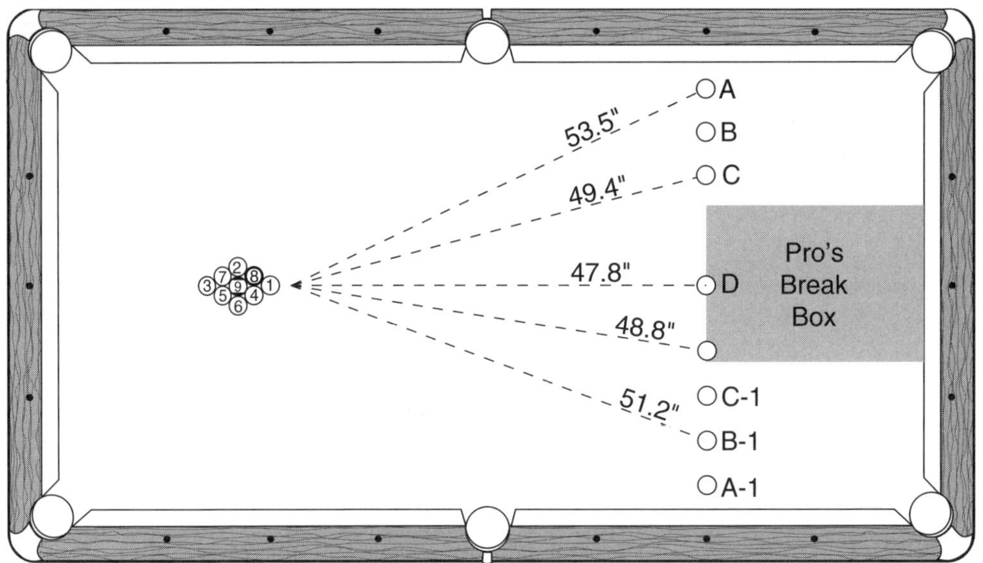

Most players feel more comfortable on one side of the table because they feel they can line up better with the rack. Positions A, B, C and their opposites on the other side of the table are the most popular cue ball locations for the break. Position D shows the seldom-used location with the cue ball in the center. There are two big advantages to Position D: it is the shortest distance to the rack; it is easier to aim directly at the 1-ball. This position is almost never used, however, because it yields the least number of balls on the break.

The cue balls in Positions A and A-1, next to the side rail, are furthest from the rack. Nevertheless, these are very popular locations from which to break because they raise your chances of making a wing ball. Many players also like bridging on the side rail. Positions B and B-1 are popular because they permit you to use a bridge on the bed of the table while still giving you a good chance to pocket the corner ball. Positions C and C-1 are good for control as they give you a more direct line on the 1-ball, plenty of room to use your normal bridge, and an even shorter distance to the 1-ball.

The rectangle shows the break box, which has been used at some of the pro events for several years. The idea behind the box is to create more balance in Nine Ball by reducing the number of balls on the break, thus increasing the value of the other components of the game. According to my study, the break box has cut the average number of balls made on the break from an average of 1.04 (in 350 games) to .75 (in 150 games).

Looking for the "Sweet Spot"

When you are evaluating a table before the start of a match, you should look for the track lines to the 1-ball, which show the spot from which other players have been breaking. This could be a good place to begin your quest for the "sweet spot."

When balls aren't falling, your mechanics may be to blame. Before you abandon a spot that has worked for you, evaluate your mechanics to make sure you don't give up on a productive spot prematurely. If you are certain your break stroke is working fine, then its time to go looking for a new location.

You should have at least two or more positions that you feel comfortable using. You should also consider the position your opponent is using if they are getting good results. When you switch locations, you need to monitor the hit on the 1-ball and make any adjustments if needed. Your break stroke mechanics should not be affected by switching locations. In sum, the ability break well from multiple locations is a valuable skill which must be learned if you are to compete at higher levels.

"A" Players simply cannot afford to come up empty on more than a couple of breaks in succession against opponents of their caliber, when their break is working. If you wait too long to figure out the break, your opponent could build a lead that will be hard to overcome. Remember, you need to avoid the scenario where you lose on your break as well as theirs, as that's too much "weight" to give any excellent player.

TIP: If you are pocketing balls other than the wing ball or 1-ball, you may wish to consider switching positions before the well runs dry.
TIP: When evaluating your opponents break, look for: 1) cue ball location; 2) contact with the 1-ball (full or partial); 3) where they are hitting the cue ball.

Looking for the "Sweet Speed"

When you have tried all of your favorite locations across the head string and the balls still aren't falling, you may wish to consider changing the speed of the break. If your soft break isn't making balls, increase the MPH. And if you have been using a power break, back off on the speed. A soft break can be especially successful in making the 1-ball in the side. If you plan on making the 1-ball as your break strategy, you need to know where the 2-ball is going, as we discussed in an earlier section. You should also pay close attention to the speed of your opponent's break, especially if they are consistently getting good results.

The Control Break

When you are having trouble making solid contact with the 1-ball, try reducing the speed of your break. Strive for solid contact with the 1-ball and cue ball control by using about 80% of your available power. You may be surprised at the power you generate. The control break can help you to loosen up and restore your timing. Once you are consistently making solid contact with the 1-ball, you can begin to apply more power if balls aren't yet falling.

Setting Up for the Break Shot

If you are a C Player, you should work on accurately hitting the 1-ball and using a controlled beak shot. Some of you, however, may be able to make consistent contact with the 1-ball using a power break. Those of you who play at the B level or above are ready to master the power break.

The power break shot is like no other shot in pool for the simple reason that you will be hitting the cue ball approximately twice as hard as on the most forceful of position plays. As you'll recall, the Pool & Billiard Magazine revealed that the average pro breaks at nearly 25 MPH. The hardest stroke I encountered on over 3,000 position plays was only a little over half that fast at 13 MPH.

You will obviously need to modify your shooting technique to achieve speeds of roughly double what you will use for the most powerfully struck of position plays. This begins with the set up.

The Break Stance

When your cue makes contact with the cue ball, your head will be considerably higher than it was at address. This is especially true if you use a low stance when setting up for the break. A low stance requires that you raise your head considerably as your arm begins to swing forward. I advise that you position your head several inches higher when setting up for the break shot. A higher head position will reduce the amount you will have to raise up during the forward stroke.

Your feet should be positioned several inches closer together than in your normal stance since you will be more upright at contact than with a normal shot. A narrower stance enables you to push off your back foot, which is an additional source of power. You should feel like you are in an explosive position, much like a sprinter who is ready to explode out of the blocks. I suggest you experiment with various stance widths until you find the right distance.

Front Arm

Some players bend their front arm considerably when taking their regular stance, but most players will keep it fairly straight. Some players even prefer to lock their front arm at the elbow. When taking your break stance, bend your front arm so that your forearm is at roughly a 40-degree angle to your upper arm. The bend in your front arm allows your body to move forward with the stroke. If you keep your front arm locked, you will block your body from moving into the shot, robbing your break of a big source of power.

Bridge Length

Your bridge for a break shot needs to be long enough so that you can smoothly accelerate to the moment of contact, at which point you want to experience an explosive burst of power that comes from whipping your wrist with perfect timing. The bridge length you use for position plays requiring a hard stroke may be sufficiently long. If you use an extra long bridge for the break, what little extra power that you gain could be more than offset by a unhealthy percentage of miss hits on the cue ball.

Grip

A major source of power come from whipping your cue through the cue ball with a perfectly timed snapping of the wrist a split second prior to contact. This kind of action can only be produced by a loose grip. Francisco Bustamante's break has been clocked at upwards of 30 MPH despite his slight stature. Bustamante uses a long bridge, but his primary source of power is the supplest wrist in pool. He uses a super light grip, which enables him to blast the balls all over the table.

Most players who fail to get the desired action on the balls have a tendency to tighten the muscles in their arm and wrist on the forward swing. Their attempt to muscle the balls and hit the rack with all their might accomplishes precisely the opposite effect. Remember, loose and relaxed muscles are fast muscles, and fast muscles equal power.

I hope that I've convinced you that a loose grip, perhaps even more relaxed than the one you use for your normal shots, is a must. Your relaxed grip hand should be placed a couple of inches further up the wrap of your cue than on normal shots. This is done to accommodate your more upright body position at contact. If you raise up on your forward swing (as you should) with your grip hand in it's normal position, it will be a few inches behind perpendicular at contact. With your grip hand too far "behind", it will be much harder, if not impossible, to achieve maximum power from the snapping of your wrist.

Cueing

In an earlier section I discussed how hitting the cue ball in the wrong spot can lead a to complete loss of control. It follows that one of your primary goals on the break shot is to hit the cue ball exactly where intended. You should observe the path of the cue ball after contact with great interest. If the cue ball is traveling forward after contact, you need to lower your bridge when setting up for the break. You will need to raise your bridge slightly if the cue ball is drawing back to the head of the table.

The cue ball will be ramming into a mass of balls, which provides much resistance. As a result, the cue ball will bounce back at least a foot or more when hit in the center. If you want the cue ball to return past the center of the table, strike the cue ball just a hair below center. You should understand that regulating the exact return distance of the cue ball on the break is one of the hardest things to accomplish in pool.

It is a common practice of many top players to set up with their tip well below center. As they swing forward, their arm drops and their cue strikes the cue ball near the center. Contacting the cue ball in the center will enable it to achieve its maximum speed.

The Break Shot Stroke

The break stroke is really more like a well-timed swing through the cue ball that in many ways resembles a golf swing. The break shot is played with a stroke that is approximately 3-5 times as hard as the stroke used for medium speed position plays. Since you will use it on just 7-10% of your shots, you should take a little extra time getting set for the shot. I suggest you use between 1.5 to 3 times as many warm up strokes as on a regular shot as this will give you ample time to lock in your aim on the 1-ball and get your arm nice and relaxed for the final stroke. The remainder of the fundamentals of the break stroke will be covered in the following break shot by Johnny Archer.

Johnny Archer's Break

Johnny Archer has arguably the best power break in pool. This sequence of photos captures his artistry while in the finals of the Sand Regency Open 20, December, 1994 against Rafael Martinez. We pick up the action after Archer has completed a lengthy series of warm up strokes.

1 In the address position prior to beginning the final stroke, Archer's head is about a foot above his cue, which is much higher than normal. His knees are flexed and ready to dive his body forward.

2 Archer's body starts to rise up in preparation for the transition. Rising up in the middle of the final backstroke is an important move.

3 As Archer nears the end of his backstroke, his lower body begins to shift forward. This transition is a critical move that sets the timing for his powerful release through the cue ball. You must avoid the impulse to crush the rack, which can cause you to tighten up.

4 Archer's cue explodes into the cue ball, sending it flying to the rack at over 25MPH in complete control. The stroke featured a powerful snap of the wrist. Notice that his head is much higher than at address, which allowed him to extend his shooting arm for power. The cue is slightly inclined, as it must be, because the rail is above his point of contact.

5 The cue tip brushes the cloth and Archer's body is going up. The cue ball is flying down the table.

6 His back foot is off the ground, which indicates how much forward momentum he puts into the break shot. His grip hand is about a foot above the table, so there is no chance of him ramming into the table.

7 Both of Archer's hands are now well above the table. His cue is extended to the center of the table, which is another sign of his tremendous forward momentum. The cue ball is now three quarters of the way to the rack.

8 The cue ball is smashing into the 1-ball and is about to reach an elevation of approximately 6" above the table. Archer's cue has now extended past the side pocket and he is hovering above the table. A full follow through is a must for maximum power.

The Result: Archer watches as the balls roll around the table for 5.7 seconds. The cue ball is a few inches from dead center. Archer had an easy shot on the 1-ball, and he proceeded to run out.

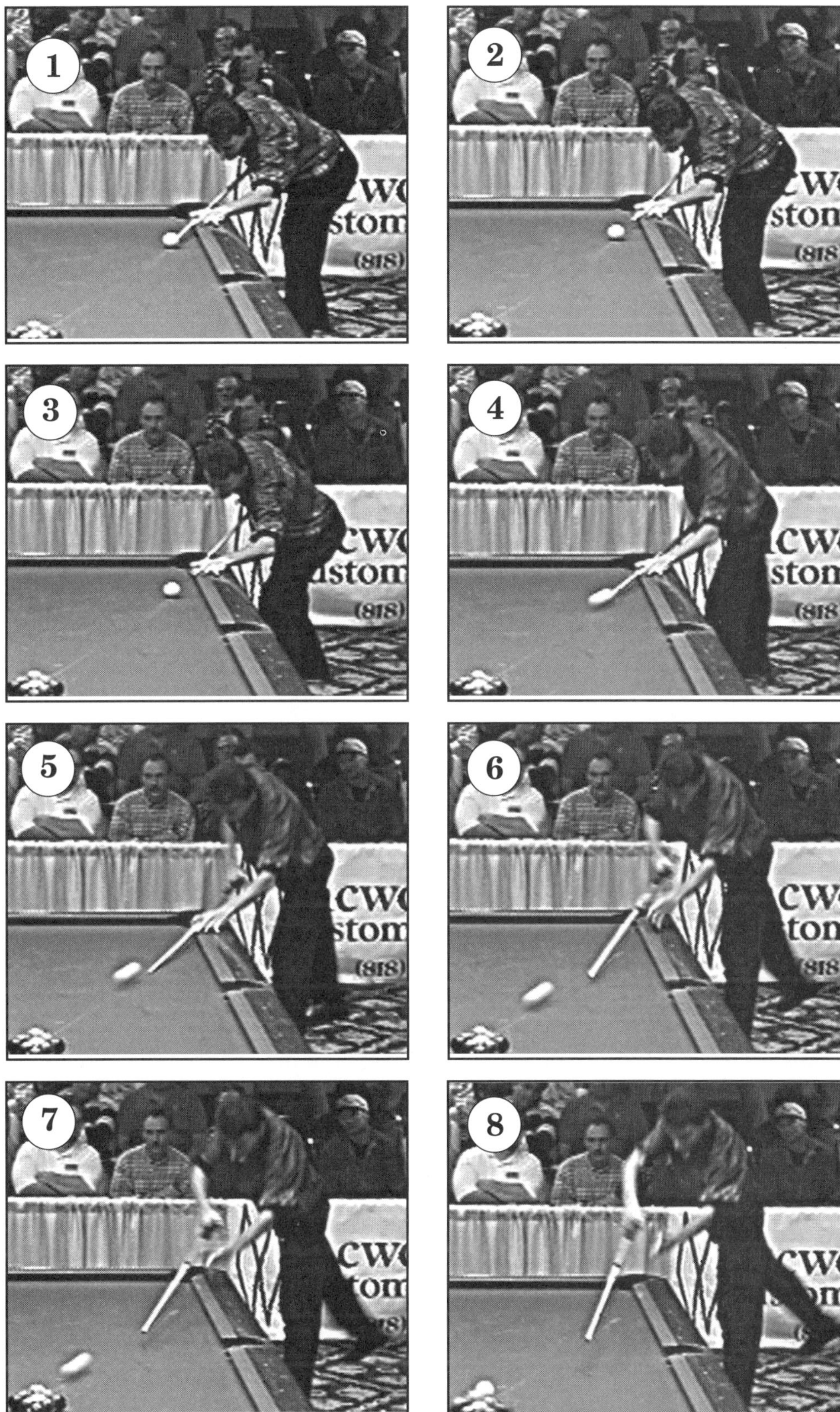

Photos courtesy of Accu-Stats Video Productions

The Cue Balls Flight Pattern

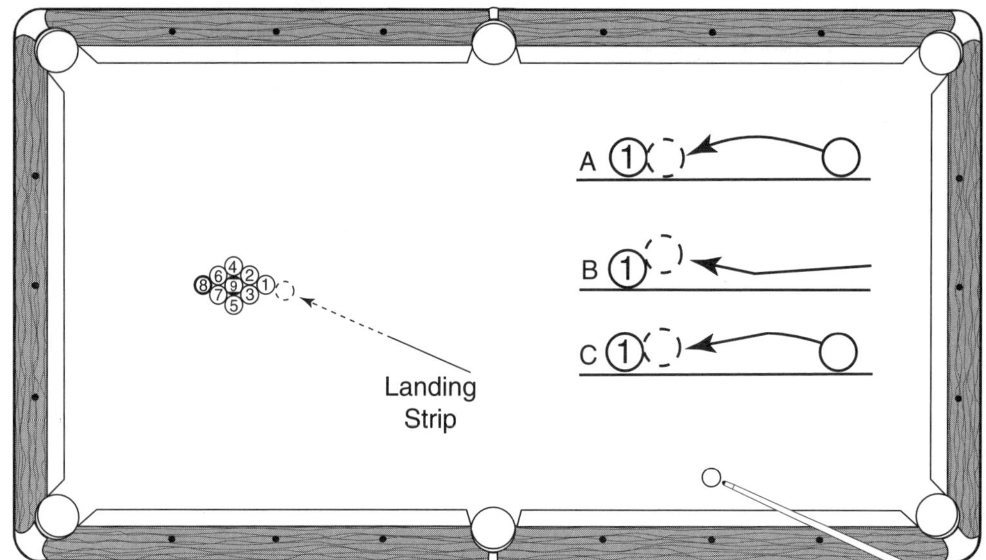

The cue ball should be struck in either the dead center or just a hair below center to keep it from rolling forward after the break. The center of your tip will be about 1 1/8" above the playing surface at contact. Since the rail is higher than the center of the cue ball, the butt end of the cue will be slightly higher than the tip at contact. The cue ball will therefore be struck with a slightly descending blow, which will send it flying down the table.

The flight pattern is very visible on tables where the break is being played from the same spot, as can be seen at any pro event. The diagram shows the landing strip for the cue ball when a power break is employed. After its first bounce, the cue ball will either fly the rest of the way into the 1-ball or take one more bounce before initiating contact.

Position A shows the cue ball hitting the 1-ball and the table at the exact same moment. This kind of contact allows the cue ball to impart maximum energy into the rack. There is no risk of the cue ball leaving the table.

The cue ball in Position B has struck the 1-ball with an uppercut after bouncing in front of the rack. This type of contact minimizes the transfer of the cue ball's energy to the rack and also causes the cue ball to fly off the table, especially if the 1-ball is hit off center. Hitting the cue ball with an excessively downward blow causes this flight pattern.

The cue ball in Position C struck the 1-ball with a downward blow after bouncing well down the table. The less than pure contact with the 1-ball will result in a loss of power, but there is little chance of the cue ball flying off the table. Hitting the cue ball at an overly steep angle causes this error. It is very difficult to regulate the flight of the cue ball into the rack when your cue is at an overly steep angle at contact. Your best bet for solid contact is to minimize the altitude of the cue ball's flight by hitting it with the cue as close to level as possible.

The Sardo Rack

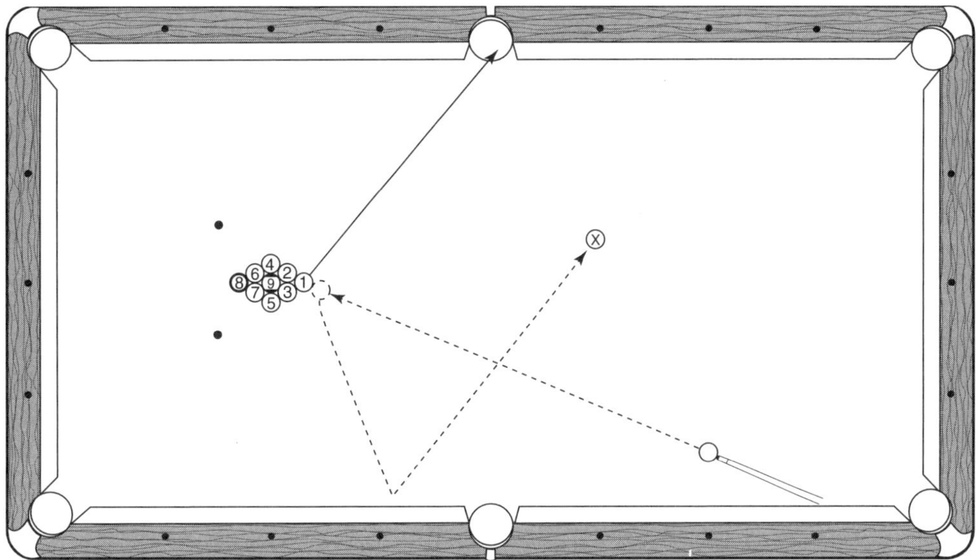

Lou Sardo is the inventor of a racking device called the Sardo Tight Rack. The idea behind his invention is to solve, once and for all, the problems and controversies that surround the racking process by providing Nine Ball players with consistently tight racks. The first step in using the device is to mark the table with two small dots as shown in the illustration. The dots enable the user to place the rack in the same place over and over again. The balls are then placed in the appropriate locations within the rack. The next step is to squeeze the two levers on either side, which presses the balls tightly together, creating a perfectly tight rack. The rack is then carefully lifted from the table. Perhaps the big key to the rack is that it be used from the moment a table is recovered, as this allows the table to be properly trained. If the rack is used on a table that has an irregular series of pit marks, as most do, it is much more difficult to train the cloth properly. It also helps if the balls are fairly new and are the same size.

The Sardo Tight Rack has been used in pro events for some time now. Initially the perfect racks led to the corner ball being pocketed consistently on the break. This problem was solved by racking the 9-ball on the spot, which moved the 1-ball 3 7/8" closer to the center of the table. Many pros changed to a softer break with the goal of pocketing the 1-ball in the side pocket, as shown in the illustration. The 1-ball is hit slightly off center (to the left in the example) and the cue ball is hit a hair below center. The cue ball typically follows a very predictable path to the side rail and out to the center of the table.

This new break is another form of the soft cut break, which has been used for several years. The break allows you to maintain excellent control over the cue ball, thanks in part to the soft hit, which keeps the cue ball much closer to the table on its way to the 1-ball.

It is quite possible that the Sardo Tight Rack will become a regular feature of tournament play across the country, in which case you will need to become accustomed to breaking a perfect rack, which may be a foreign experience to many players.

Racking is as Easy as 1-2-3

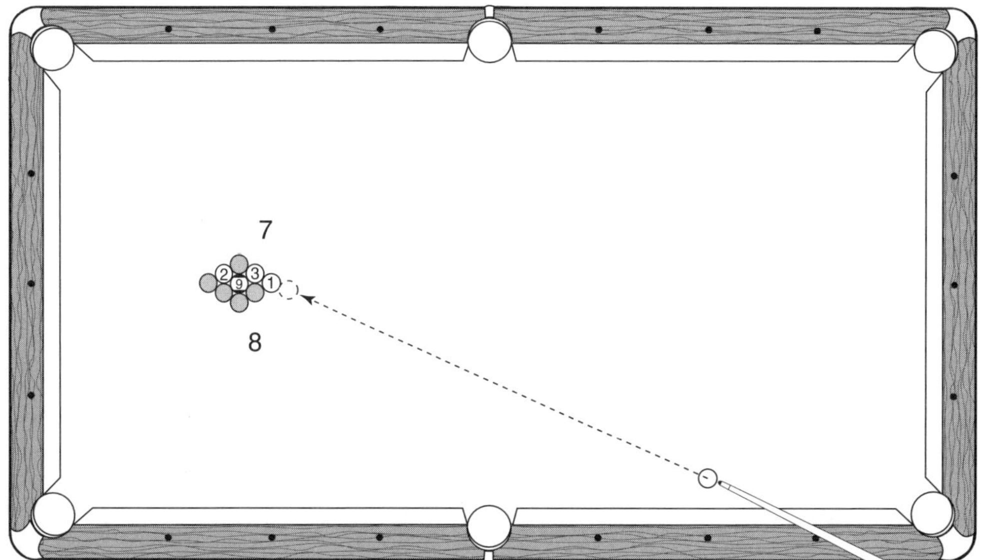

You can make life a little tougher for your opponent by placing the balls in the positions shown in the diagram above. When your opponent is breaking from the left side, place the 2 and 3-balls where shown. With the balls in these positions, they will have a tendency to spread across the table, possibly making your opponent play long distance position through traffic on his first couple of shots. If your opponent breaks from the other side of the table, switch the 2 and 3-balls to the other side of the rack.

Reading a Table for Tendencies

The playing conditions and you and/or your opponent's breaking skill, at any particular moment, can lead to a variety of layouts. I suggest you watch how the balls are breaking on the first few games of a match. This can help you to manage your expectations and adopt the appropriate strategy.

Wide Open Layout and Balls Are Falling

When you see this happening, you must gear up for an offensive match. You should really bear down on the break and adopt a mindset that you are ready to run out. And don't be too surprised if your opponent also plays well and runs out under these conditions.

The Table is Stingy and the Balls Are Clustering

Sometime you and/or your opponent's break is not working or perhaps the playing conditions are simply not conducive to making ball. When this happens and the balls are clustering towards the rack end of the table, you should be set to play a defensive game. Take advantage of the many opportunities to hook your opponent and look for combos and billiards when you get ball in hand, especially if there is a safety that can be built into the shot.

Racking Technique

Before pushing the rack into place, you may wish to occasionally rub the cloth in the area of the rack to remove unwanted particles of chalk or other small specks of debris that could keep the balls from settling nicely into place. This procedure can also condition the cloth. The next step is to put the balls in the proper places within the rack. Obviously the 1-ball goes up front and the 9-ball in the middle.

You should consider where you place the other balls, especially if you are playing someone who runs out regularly. With proper ball placement you can make it as difficult as possible for your opponent to run out should they be so lucky as to make a ball or two on your 100% tight and honest racks. If you are getting a spot and you are racking for your opponent, be sure to place your "money balls" in the row adjacent to the 1-ball.

The worst offense in racking Nine-Ball is a 1-ball that has broken loose from the rest of the rack. A gap between the 1-ball and the rest of the rack will lead to a marshmallow break accompanied by a sickening thud. You can largely avoid this "mistake" by following the proper racking technique. Once you have positioned the balls in the rack, put the 1-ball on the spot and let it settle into place. Next, carefully slide the top edge of the rack up against the 1-ball. Then push the second row of balls and the remainder of the rack carefully into place. While doing so, keep your eyes on the 1-ball to make sure it hasn't moved. If the 1-ball gets moved out of place, you will have to start over. Press the rack together and observe the results. If they are satisfactory, push the rack slightly forward and lift it from the table.

Accept Imperfection

The pros play with new sets of balls that are nearly perfectly round on brand new cloth from the world's finest manufacturers. At many tournaments the balls are also being racked with a new device that bonds them together. In your poolroom, the balls will probably not all be of exactly the same size due to wear and tear. In addition, the cloth will be pitted in several locations because the balls are not always racked in the exact same spot. As a result, it is impossible to get all nine balls to fit completely together. This means that you can't give your opponent a perfect rack, nor should they expect one from you. In fact, both you and your opponent can save each other a lot of grief by agreeing where the balls should be racked and on the acceptable standard of quality.

The Racker – It Takes All Kinds

The wide variance in the quality of racks demonstrates differences in equipment as well as the spectrum of character in humans. The people racking the balls for you will range from the 100% honest good citizen to the petty larcenist to the outright crook. The good citizen is a true sportsman who makes a legitimate effort to give you the best rack possible. Most players probably fall somewhere in the middle: they will make a fair attempt to give you a decent rack, but do not like to spend much time fiddling with the balls. And then there are the slug artists, who take pride in their craft. They view their ability to slip their opponent bad racks as an integral part of their strategy.

"With some people you don't really have to worry about the slug so you can just play pool." **Bill Incardona**

"I come to a tournament to play pool, not to rack balls."
Grady Mathews

If the truth were told, most pool players might admit to having a little devilish streak that comes out most often when racking the balls. Many players at least occasionally seem to take a special delight in watching their opponent blast away at their carefully crafted slug racks with no favorable results. Many slug artists may even find it hard to keep from chuckling at the sound of the cue ball going splat upon contact with the 1-ball.

When to Play Rack Inspector

Less than perfect racks can be the fault of imperfect equipment, which keeps all the balls from touching snugly into place. Poor racks can also be caused by your opponent, who may be may be an inherently honest person who is simply careless or unskilled at racking the balls. Still, you must insist on your right to a reasonably tight rack if winning is important to you. I recommend that you check the rack periodically, especially if you are breaking well but balls aren't falling.

In baseball, a brush back pitch is used to keep a hitter, who has homered in their last at bat, back from the plate. The slug rack is pool's answer to the brush back pitch. It's like saying you're not going to break and run forever against me. Here is a set of circumstances in which you are ripe for receiving a slug rack:

- When your opponent is mad after losing a game and takes little time racking.
- When you've been breaking and running regularly.
- When you've just made the 9-Ball.

"I find it kind of insulting to have someone eyeballing every little bit of space in the balls. It is kind of degrading." **Grady Mathews**

I strongly recommend that you occasionally inspect the rack, especially if you suspect your opponent is a blatant slug artist. In most other cases, however, a spot inspection should be all that is necessary. But I certainly don't advise you to slow down the game to a snails pace by making your opponent rack the balls over and over again. In fact, those who inspect every rack and force their beleaguered opponent to rerack the balls constantly are probably a bigger nuisance than all but the dastardliest of slug artists.

TIP: Conduct spot inspections to keep the racker honest.

Rack Classifications

You can lump a rack's quality into one of four categories. You should factor in the conditions when determining the minimum standard of quality that you are willing to accept.

1 Perfect All balls are frozen. The 1-ball is on the spot. The rack is perfectly straight. It is not realistic to expect this unless you are playing under perfect conditions, which include a new set of balls and a table that's just been recovered.

2 Near Perfect There is a small gap in a non critical location or in a place that could actually help you make a ball. This rack is the best either you or your opponent can expect under normal playing conditions.

3 Satisfactory An acceptable rack under the conditions, but it could be slightly better. When your opponent is giving you less than the best rack possible under the conditions, they must also be willing to accept the same quality.

4 Unacceptable This is a slug or a close cousin. There is one, or more gaps that will severely limit your ability to make a ball and get a good spread.

You Come Up Empty Over and Over Again

If you are hitting the break perfectly time and again, and nothing is going, you should change your break spot and/or speed, as we discussed earlier. Now it could be that the table is just plain stingy. But if your opponent is consistently making balls, and you are getting a good spread but are not making anything, it's possible your opponent is a true master of the racking arts. You are advised to take a closer look at their handiwork. Make sure that the 1-ball is touching the second row, but also make sure the second row is touching the 9-ball on at least one side.

The Rack Is Not Straight

A rack artist may take advantage of your propensity to always break from the same side by slightly tilting the rack. You can take advantage of this by changing sides. If you discover the rack is pointing to the right (from your vantage point at the head of the table), break from the right side as this will give you a good chance to make the wing ball. Of course you will want to break from the left side if the rack is tilted to the left.

Bad Sound on the Break

When your break lacks that crack and pop that you expect to hear when you hit the 1-ball just right, there is a good chance that one or more balls were loose.

High and Low Racks

When the balls have been racked above the spot, your chances of making a corner ball have been severely reduced or eliminated. However, you now have a better chance of making the 1-ball in the side pocket. Sometimes it is possible to see a good portion of the spot after the balls have been racked, which indicates that the balls have been racked low. When this happens, the chances of making the wing ball have gone up, so you are well advised to leave this "bad rack" alone. You may even be wise to use a medium speed for control if the corner ball is going every time.

Pounding the Balls

According to BCA rule 1.16.5, you and your opponent must "refrain from tapping the object balls more than is absolutely necessary." If your opponent is pounding the balls into the slate, you are within your rights to ask them to refrain from this objectionable practice.

Beware the Slow Rackers

It may be more than a little disconcerting if your opponent seems to throw together the rack while giving you barely any time to revel in your victory. Fast rackers are generally either very good or very careless. Let the quality of your break or an occasional inspection be your guide.

You should not be fooled by those who seem to be exercising the care of a diamond cutter in assembling the rack. They may be pretending to take all of the time necessary to make sure they give you a perfect rack In fact, they could be trying to arrange a slug rack that may possibly pass your inspection should you wander up the table to check it out. I get a kick out of the ones that peer at the rack from all angles to make sure they are giving you a gap free experience. If the racker is honest, but slow, you should walk away and start your break shot routine over again.

CHAPTER 3

POSITION ROUTES

"If you are playing with confidence you can control the cue ball within inches."
Jim Rempe

Superior shotmaking skills by themselves can only take you so far in Nine Ball. After 2-3 tough shots in succession, even the most talented ball pocketers will succumb to the pressure or the odds of having to make several tough shots in a row. In fact, all but the easiest runouts will quickly terminate due to lack of position after 1-3 tough shots. While position play is important in all pool games, it is extremely critical in Nine Ball because you must play shape on a specific ball. This requires that you master a variety of routes that can take the cue ball just about anywhere on the table.

Since you are using only nine balls and they are usually spread across the table, a typical Nine Ball rack is far less congested than in other pool games. As a result, you don't always have to be as precise with your position. But you do have to fall within certain well-described boundaries or zones on most shots if you want to simplify matters and entertain any hopes of consistently running out. And you must pay particular attention to the size of the cut angles you leave yourself.

In this chapter we'll discuss playing position from one ball to the next. If you master the basic Nine-Ball routes and have a working knowledge of several of the advanced routes as well, you will have the tools to play patterns and to consistently run out. If you then add a number of the expert routes to your arsenal and learn to recognize a variety of patterns, you'll be able to run racks that most players only dream about running.

The Run Out Game Plan

Position Play (this chapter) is how you get on the next ball. This includes the route, the target zone, and measures to reduce risk.

Patterns (chapter 6) are recognizable sequences of shots that tend to repeat themselves.

Run Outs (chapter 7) are the end result of stringing position plays and patterns together.

The Sequence for Learning Position

One of the great mysteries of pool to the casual observer is the ease and beauty with which a master makes the game appear. In reality, position play is deceptively difficult. There is, however, a logical sequence to learning the art and science of cue ball control. If you follow the sequence in order you can learn the necessary skills to proceed to each successive level. As long as you keep learning, perfecting and expanding your skills, you will be on the path to mastering control of the cue ball. To play position well you need to follow these steps:

- Become proficient in the fundamentals of the game.
- Learn basic stroking with fairly straight shots.
- Learn to pocket cut shots.
- Learn to hit the cue ball above and below center.
- Learn to feel comfortable using different speeds of stroke.
- Learn to recognize the various position routes. This includes the speed and cueing that a route requires.
- Learn to execute the position route.
- Learn variations of the position route.

Cueing - Learn to Become Multi Dimensional

The cue ball's ending location results from cueing (where your tip strikes the cue ball) and the speed with which you stroke the shot. In other words, cueing + speed of stroke = position. You can play adequate shape for most shots by cueing on the center axis and by using a few basic speeds of stroke. You will extend your position play repertoire by adding english and by using an even wider variety of speeds of stroke.

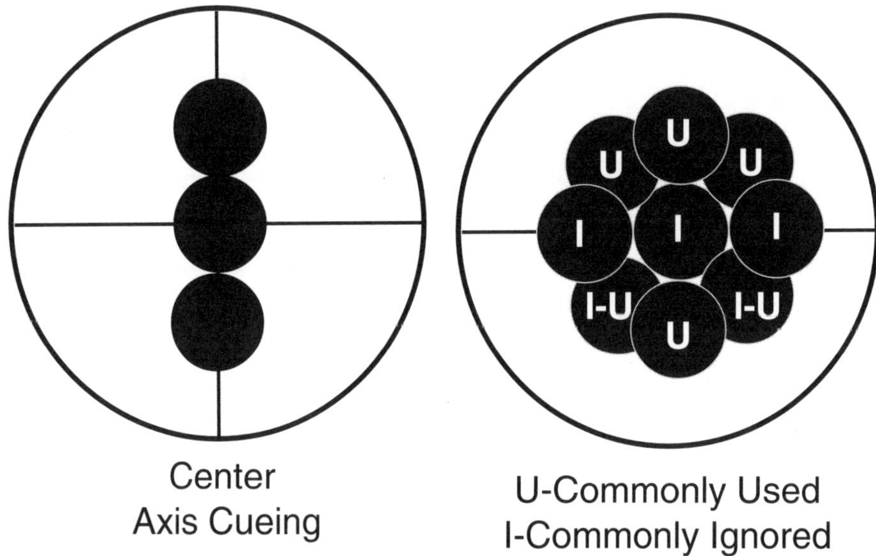

Center Axis Cueing

U-Commonly Used
I-Commonly Ignored

The cue ball on the right shows the nine points of contact. Those labeled with a U are the most commonly used spots on the cue ball. The areas labeled with an I are intentionally avoided by a great number of players. The locations labeled I-U indicate low inside english and low outside english. For example, Low right english is commonly used when it is outside english, but not when it is inside english.

Many players unwittingly fall into the trap of using only a limited number of cueing options. These players may use draw on shots where a follow shot is the better choice. Or they may avoid inside english even when it is essential to the success of the shot. If you restrict your cueing to a few pet favorite shots, you will not have routes available to you that you could be playing. To truly master position play you will need to expand your skills to the point where you feel confident cueing on any of the 9 basic locations on the cue ball (and variations of these locations) with a wide range of speeds of stroke.

English and Position Play

In Nine Ball there is a high priority on shotmaking because of the challenging shots you'll routinely encounter. Using english increases the challenge, but it must be used regularly to play position. Therefore, the big challenge is to use english effectively in a game where shotmaking accuracy is at a premium. You must use it, but not abuse it.

Too many players make the big mistake of using english as a crutch. This tendency becomes exaggerated when these players are out of stroke. Should you fall out of stroke, I advise that you play as many shots as possible on the center axis. Don't make the mistake of using side spin to make up for deficiencies in your stroke. In the final analysis, you should strive for the perfect balance between shotmaking accuracy and cue ball control. The following rules will help guide your use of english:

Rules for Using English:

- Avoid english on long shots unless it is absolutely necessary. An exception is long shots when the object ball is close to the pocket.
- On long shots, try to use no more than one half tip, if possible. Try experimenting with a quarter tip or even less.
- On short shots, avoid the temptation to apply extreme english just because the shot is relatively easy.
- On short shots, use what you need, but go no further than a tip off center.
- If you tend to use a firm stroke, you should use less english.
- You may wish to spin balls in with english as a matter of personal preference, but don't over do it.
- A smooth stroke enables you to hit closer to center axis and still get the required action on the cue ball.

TIP: Remember: center axis and speed of stroke = shotmaking accuracy and cue ball control, which is all that is needed on most position plays.

How English Affects the Cue Ball

English is essential to the success of the shot on many position plays. On others, english adds that subtle difference that enables you to fine tune a position route. English has a small affect on the cue ball's path prior to contact with the rail. The major influence of english on the cue ball's path is felt after it contacts one or more cushions. After contacting the rail, english can:

- Add speed to the cue ball
- Slow down the cue ball
- Open up the rebound angle
- Close the rebound angle

How English Affects the Rebound Angle

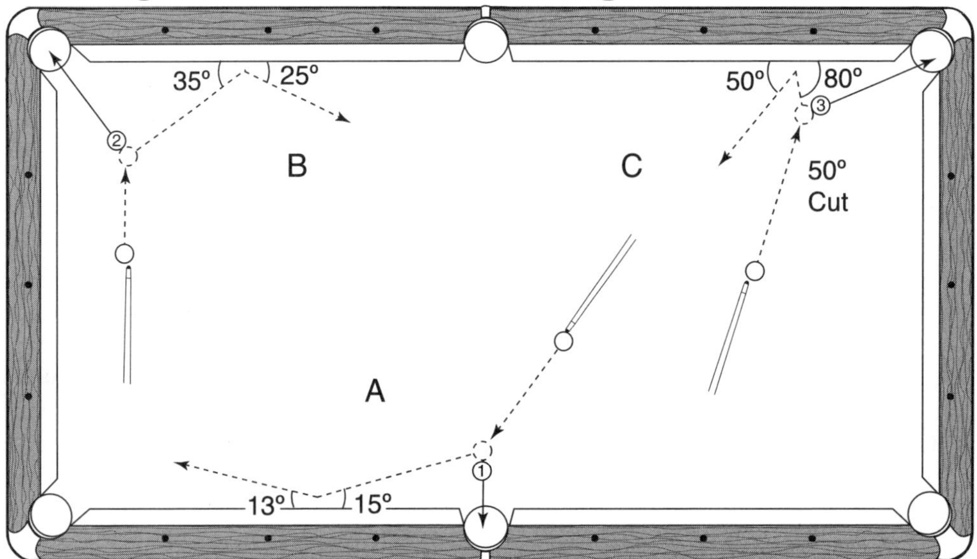

The diagram shows three typical examples of how english affects the rebound angle. When the approach angle is shallow as in Position A, then there is little affect on the rebound angle. In this case, right (outside) english is used to speed up the cue ball. In Position B the cue ball entered the rail at 35-degrees and exited at only 25-degress thanks to the outside english. Position C shows how english can radically affect the rebound angle when the cue ball enters at a steep angle. Notice how the rebound angle was a full 30-degrees shallower than the entrance angle. It is important to have a working knowledge of how english affects the cue ball's path after it strikes the rail.

Entrance Angles		Impact of English
Very Shallow	1-18	Very Little
Shallow	19-36	Some change in direction
Medium	37-54	A fair amount of change in direction
Sharp	55-72	Pronounced
Very Sharp	73-90	Very Pronounced

The Cue Ball's Traveling Distance

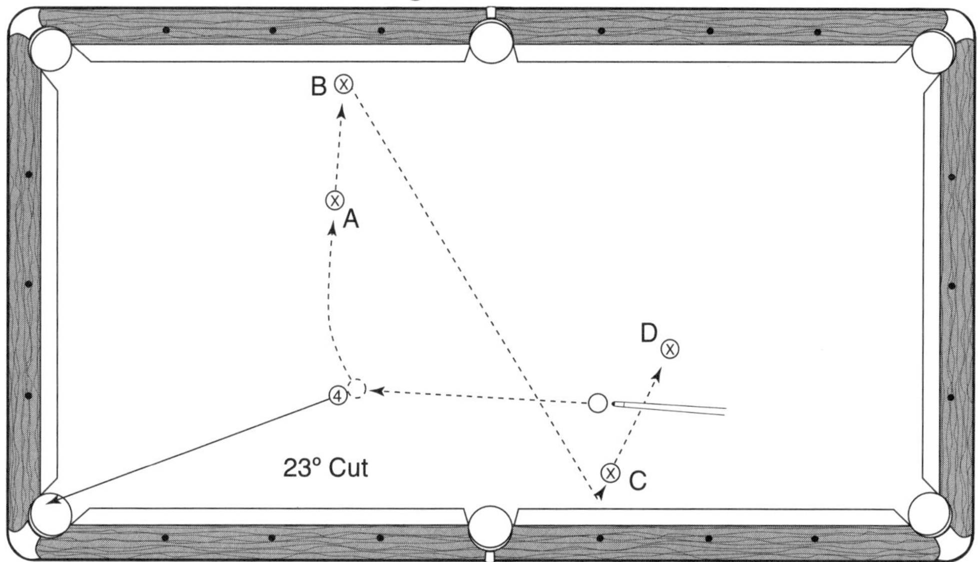

In Nine Ball, angles are used extensively to facilitate position play. On every position route involving a cut angle you need to learn the cue ball's range of traveling distances for that particular shot. The example shows a medium long 23-degree cut shot. Let's assume we're going to play the shot with draw and a half tip of right english. The cue ball in Position A shows the Minimum Traveling Distance it will travel when hit with low right english along this path. This shot takes great finesse and is not a practical shot for most players. When the cue ball is struck with the slowest speed that most players feel comfortable using, it will stop at Position B, which is the Minimum Practical Traveling Distance.

The cue ball at Position C shows the Longest Practical Traveling Distance for this shot. While you could send the cue ball to Position D with an extremely hard stroke, which is the Longest Traveling Distance, this is beyond the capabilities of most players. The normal range for playing this route is the line that stretches from the cue ball at Position B to the one at Position C.

The minimum and longest traveling distances for a particular position play such as the one in the example will be affected by the playing conditions. Lively rails or a slow table are just a couple of factors that could add or subtract from the length of the position route.

Mixing the Right Ingredients for Position

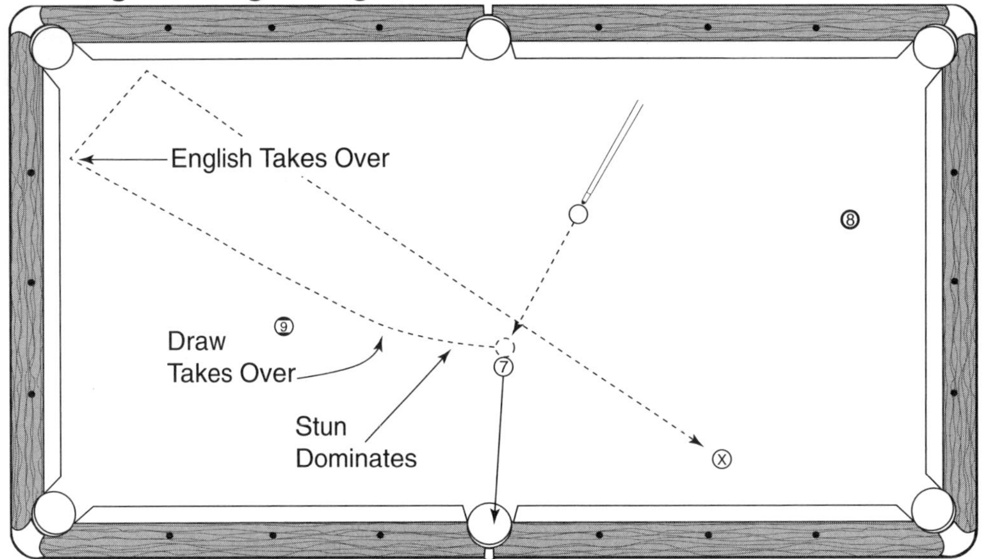

Planning an effective position route is like creating a perfect recipe. When planning a route that involves contact with one or more rails, you must map out the cue ball's route to the first rail, and its subsequent path after it strikes the rail(s). If you fail to mix the ingredients correctly, disasters could result such as scratches or hooks.

The first step is to select the desired location for the cue ball, which is at Position X. Then you must concoct the correct mixture of ingredients. In this case, mix a hard stroke with stun, a half tip draw and a half tip of right english to produce the route shown. The route to the first rail was initially controlled by the stun. After the cue ball traveled a short distance, the draw spin took over, causing the cue ball to curve to the right. The right english took over when the cue ball hit the rail. Notice that three forces took turns dominating the action of the cue ball. Understanding the timing and magnitude of each component force is a big key to position play.

In our example, all three components exerted their influence in during the cue ball's journey to Position X. On other shots, one component (such as draw or english) may exert a significantly larger influence than the other(s) in order for the shot to be successful. Even so, all components are needed to make the shot work. For example, a shot might require a hard stroke, a tip of follow, but only one quarter tip of english. While the english is the smallest ingredient, it is still vital to the success of the shot. Some very fine players are able to regulate their use of english in increments as small as one eighth of a tip.

The Primary Emphasis

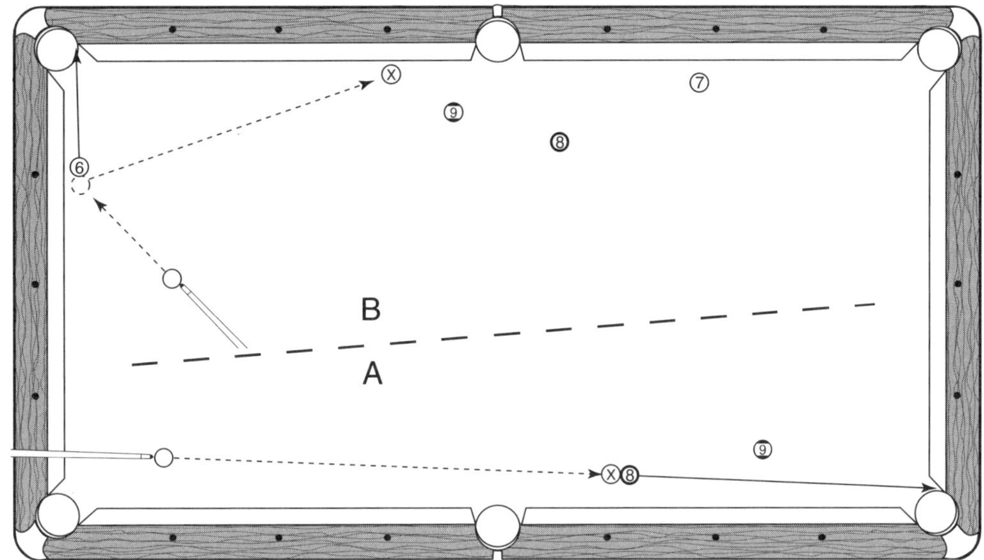

Successful position plays in Nine Ball are a combination of:

- Shotmaking accuracy.
- Directional control.
- Speed control.

On any position play there may be one element that is particularly crucial to the success of the shot. That element then becomes the primary emphasis of the shot. It is always important, of course, to pocket the ball. But when a shot is easy to pocket, the primary emphasis could be on:

- Directional control (to avoid an obstacle or a scratch).
- Speed control (to perhaps get the best angle for the next ball).
- Strategy (two way shot).

The success of the shot could rest on the precise execution of two or three challenging components. As a Nine Ball player, you must learn which component(s) needs to be emphasized on any given shot.

The position play in Part A of the diagram is pretty self-explanatory: your emphasis should be 99% on pocketing the ball and 1% on shape. Make the 8-ball with a stop shot and the game is essentially over. In Part B the primary emphasis is split evenly between speed control and directional control. Both are needed to avoid getting hooked behind the 9-ball. For the sake of argument, lets say 45% each. The shot is a hanger, so about 10% of your attention is on making the ball. I give pocketing the shot 10% because you must always give enough attention to making the ball.

On the toughest shots the primary emphasis is split between two or more components, each of which has to be executed to near perfection. An example would be a long shot using english, which must be hit three rails with perfect speed. The ability to accomplish several challenging objectives on a single position play is the stuff of champions.

Don't Fight the Physics of Pool

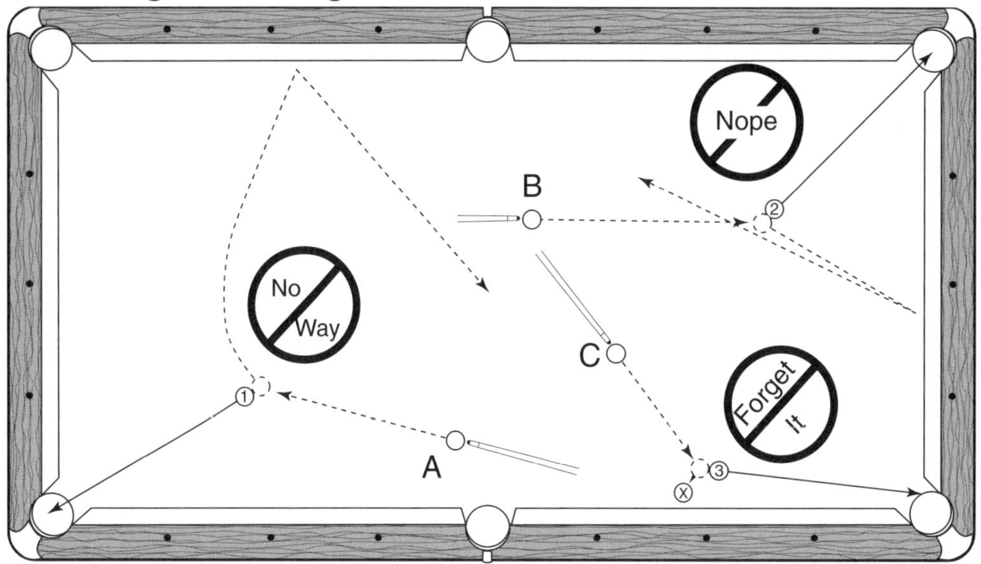

Your best efforts to send the cue ball from Point A to Point B will meet with frustration and failure if you insist on fighting the balls and the physics of the game. The three shots in the diagram are slightly exaggerated, but they serve to illustrate the ways in which you can wage a losing battle with the balls. The 45–degree cut angle in Position A completely rules out any possibility of drawing back down the table off the side rail. Inside english can be used to work some eye popping miracles, but none like reversing the cue ball's direction off the end rail as shown in Position C. The 50-degree cut angle in Position C means that there is no chance of killing the stone at Position X as indicated.

It takes a while to learn to distinguish between what is possible and those routes that are 100% unrealistic. I advise that you pay very close attention to what the balls can and can't do when you are playing position. The idea is to: 1) learn what the balls can do and what routes are natural and very reliable based on the position of the balls; 2) learn what routes, such as those in the diagram, have absolutely no chance of working.

A Few Shots Where You Can't Fight the Physics of Pool

- Holding the cue ball close to the rail on thin cuts.
- Trying to play routes that aren't available when the object ball is frozen to the rail.
- Attempting to draw the cue ball 2.5 table lengths.
- Expecting the cue ball to change the rebound angle by an unreasonable amount.
- Expecting the cue ball to follow an impossible route immediately after contact.

ABC's of Position Plays

The sections ahead cover the basic position routes and advanced position plays that can enable you to send the cue ball to almost any part of the table. The learning starts with the basic routes (C Routes), which provide the foundation for position play. Skill at the basic routes will enable you to run the easiest racks with little difficulty. The typical rack, however, consists of at least a couple of advanced position plays (B Routes). When you have learned a good number of C's and B's, you will be able to consistently run at least 5-6 balls, or more. The toughest position plays are the A Routes. These usually appear at the start of a run or in the middle of a run out due to positional errors. They can also appear in the middle of a runout when the balls are lying tough.

There are a number of factors that can influence the difficulty of a position route, which are listed below.

Degree of Difficulty Factors

The Shot
- Cut angle
- Distance
- Jacked up, on the rail

Cueing
- Draw, follow, stun
- English, inside english
- Extreme english

Speed of Stroke
- A comfortable speed
- A finesse stroke
- A hard or very hard stroke

The Position Route
- The difficulty of the route
- Pocketing correctly
- Dealing with obstructions
- Avoiding scratches

The Conditions
- The table
- The pressure of a match

Recovery Shape

In an ideal world you would play nothing but routine position routes as a result of your expert cue ball control. In the real world, however, you will quite often miss position by several inches or more. The players call this getting out of line. You can get back in line and in sync with the layout by playing what I call a recovery position route. These are not the position routes you would employ if given a choice, but are instead those that can enable you to get back in line with a challenging shot. Recovery routes will be labeled by a RR throughout the upcoming sections on position routes.

Setting Your Positional Goals

I suggest that you put aside any illusions about your ability and instead make a serious attempt to grade your current level of play. By objectively placing yourself in a category of skill you will have taken a big step in evaluating your game. This will enable you to select the position routes for practice that coincide with your current level of skill.

The position routes in the sections that follow have all been graded. Your rate of success with each shot and the various categories (draw or follow, for example) will tell you which position plays deserve your valuable practice time. The table below gives you some very general guidelines as to the expected success ratio.

Success Rates

Player/Route	**C Route**	**B Route**	**A Route**
C Player	70%	50%	10%
B Player	85%	70%	40%
A Players	98%	85%	70%

The table below will help you create a practice regimen for your game.

Average Players

C- Players should work exclusively on the C's.
C Players should work on the C and easier B's.
C+ Players work on the C's and easy to moderately difficult B's.

Advanced Players

B-Players should master the C's and become very familiar with a wide variety of the B's.
B Players should maintain their mastery the C's. In addition, they should become familiar with most of the B's. They may also begin learning a few of the easier A's.
B+Players should continue practicing the easier routes they have mastered while gaining proficiency at the tougher B's and easier A's.

Expert Players

A-Players should spend as much time as necessary maintaining their mastery of the routes they already know. They should also be perfecting the tougher B's and adding to their list of A's.
A Players should spend time perfecting the tougher routes they already know while adding additional A's to their arsenal. They should also spend as much time as necessary maintaining their mastery of a wide range of routes.
A+Players have mastered all but the very toughest position routes. Their goal is to maintain their level of skill across the board while continuing to add additional routes and fine points to their game.

Learn Both Sides of the Shot

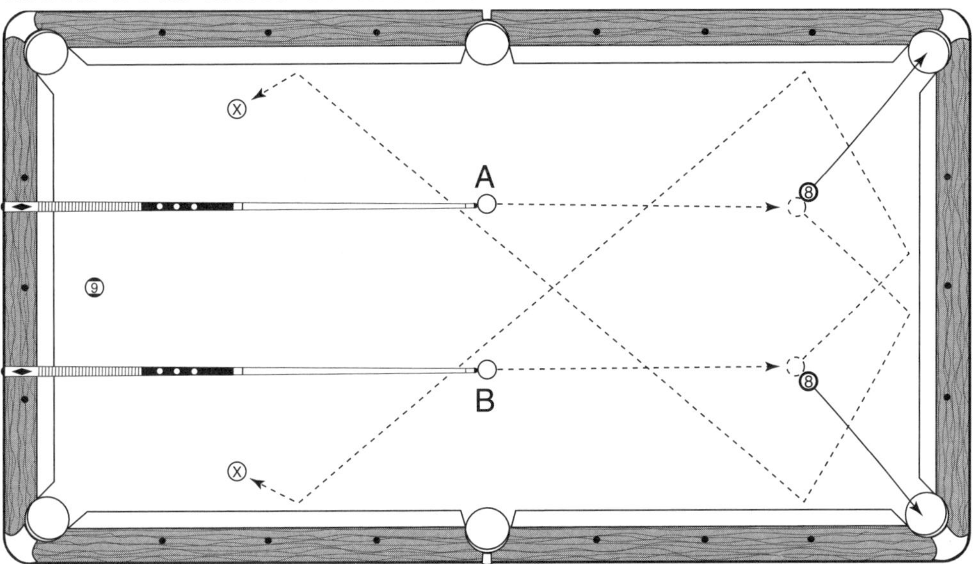

The position routes in the sections that follow are diagrammed in one specific direction. However, you should learn both sides of the same shot. For example, the illustration shows a cut shot to the left with the cue ball at Position A. The mirror image of this route is shown with the cue ball in Position B.

Many players are more comfortable using left english as opposed to right english on a particular shot. Others prefer to cut to the right versus cutting to the left. To master each route, you must know both "sides" of the shot.

Practice tips:

- Set up both versions with the donuts.
- Play each route 5 times from each side.
- Note which side is your good side, and which side of the shot gives you trouble (if any).

Formulas for Position Play

Before we venture into the wonderful world of position play diagrams, it may help for you to ingrain these simple formulas for position play, for they embody the essence of cue ball control. Once you have chosen the correct route for a particular position play, you must simply hit the cue ball in the right location with the correct speed to send the cue ball where intended. Hence, formula #1:

#1) Cueing + Speed of Stroke = Position

In order for the cue ball to arrive at the desired location it must be sent along the correct path with the right speed. This gives us formula #2:

#2) Directional Control + Distance Control = Position

No-Rail Position Routes

Introduction

Nine Ball is a traveling game in which the rails are used extensively for position. Nevertheless, according to my research, nearly 24% of the position plays of the top pros are routes in which the cue ball does not strike a single cushion. No-rail position routes are fairly straightforward. But while many of them are among the easiest position plays, there are those that require expert handling of the cue ball. These include draw shots in which good speed control is essential and position plays that incorporate stun. Since the cue ball is not going to a cushion on a no-rail route, you rarely need to use english. This should lead to accurate shotmaking.

Stop Shots (C)

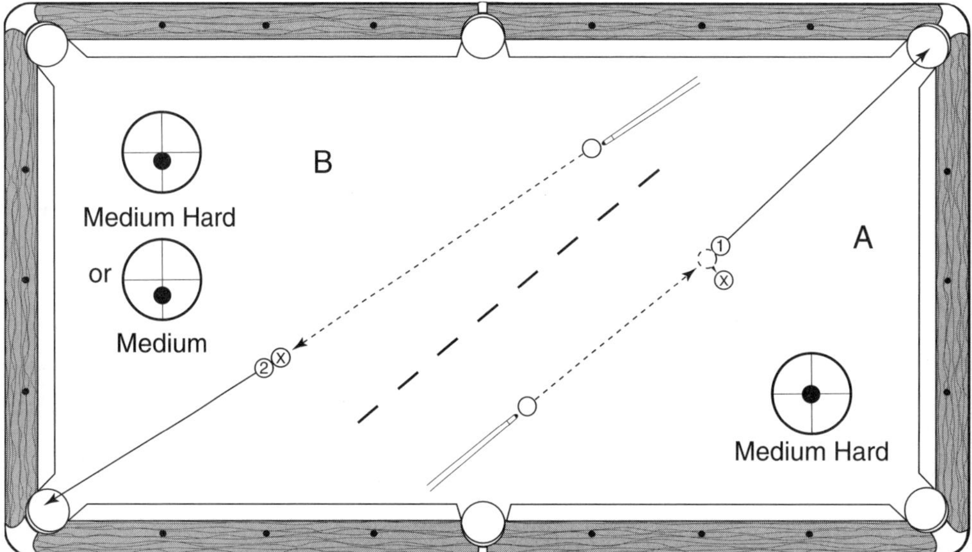

The stop shot is the most basic position play. When you have a dead straight in shot and you execute a stop shot to perfection, you know exactly where the cue ball will reside for the next shot. If the cue ball is within 3' or less of the object ball, you can make the cue ball stop dead in its tracks by using centerball and a medium hard stroke.

Shots with very small cut angles in which the cue ball is going to travel only a few inches sideways are also commonly referred to as stop shots. Part A shows a "stop shot" with a 3-degree cut angle. Part B is a long-range stop shot. Shots like this must be played with varying combinations of draw and speed in order for the cue ball to stop dead. The lower you hit the cue ball, the less speed you need, and vice versa.

Soft Follow Shots (C)

The soft follow shot is one of the easiest and yet most valuable positional weapons. Soft follow shots enable you to control the rolling distance of the cue ball with great accuracy. On the typical follow shots shown in Parts A

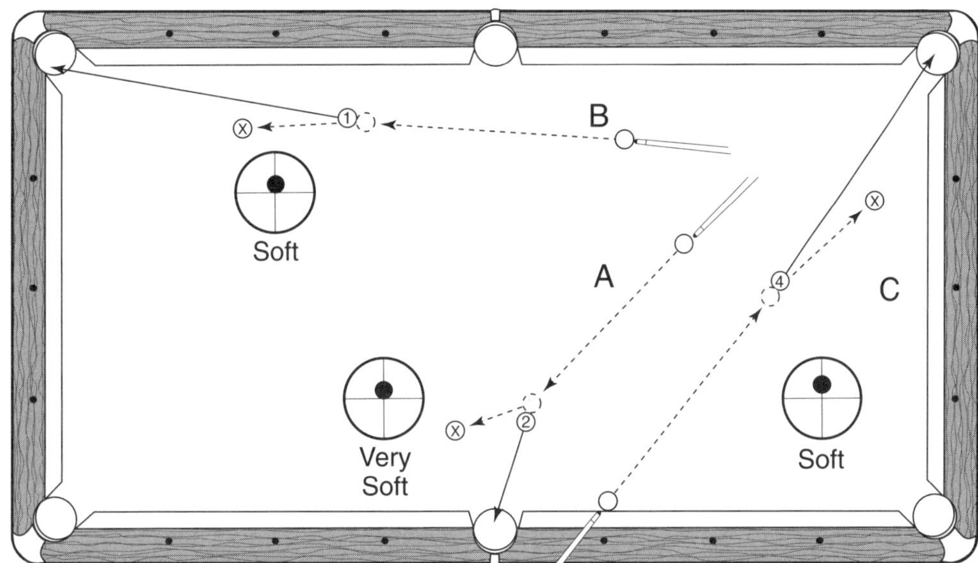

and B, you should be able to send the cue ball to within 2-3" of the bulls eye. Play soft follow shot with a shorter stroke than normal and be sure to accelerate smoothly. When the cue ball is on the rail as in Part C, use a 3-4" backstroke and a very smooth stroke.

Power Floaters (A)

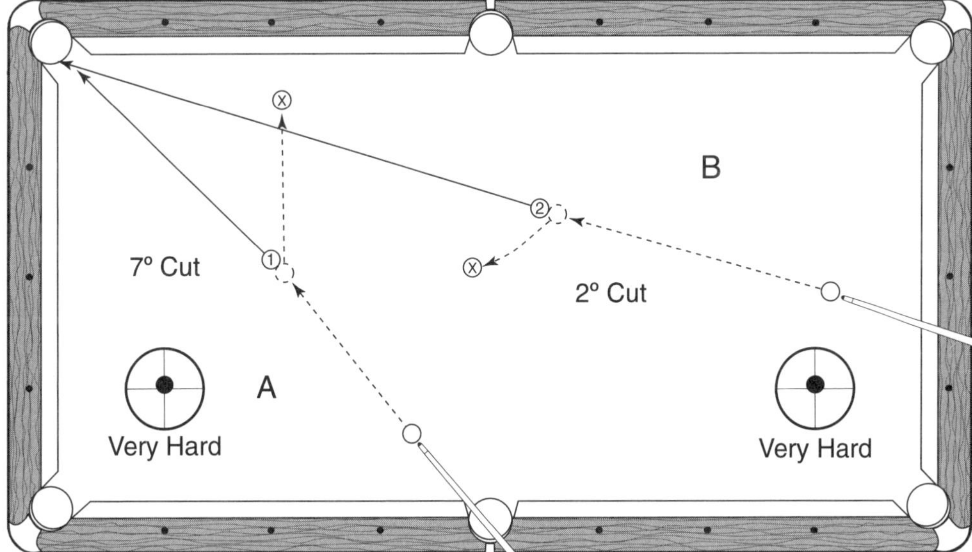

The power follow floater is an advanced position play that requires a very hard stroke. The idea is to squeeze the cue ball sideways and forward on shots with very little cut angle. You are, in essence, creating something out of almost nothing. Both shots were played with a very hard stroke. Notice how much further the cue ball slid sideways with a cut angle of 7-degrees (Part A) compared to the 2-degree cut angle in Part B.

Follow Stun (Part 1 is a B, Part 2 is an A)

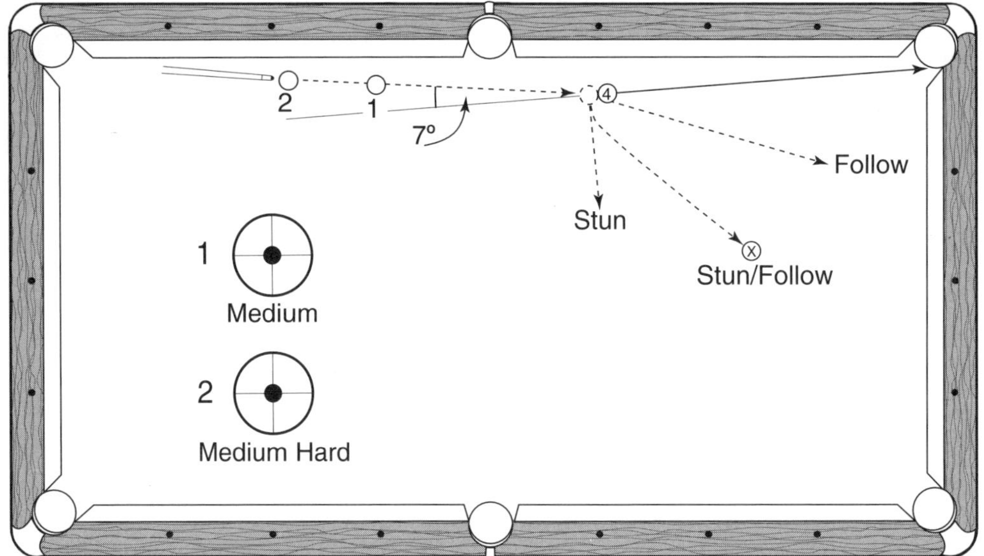

The follow/stun is one of the trickiest position plays. The goal is to send the cue ball to a location in between where it would go if the shot was played with straight follow or a stun shot. This is a feel shot that takes much practice. With the cue ball in Position 1 (rated B), use a medium stroke with a half tip of follow. With the cue ball further back at Position 2 (rated A), use a medium hard stroke one eighth of a tip above center. While you are practicing this shot, note how small adjustments in cueing and speed of stroke affect the outcome of the shot.

Basic Short Range Draw Shots (C)

Precise short-range draw control is one of the hallmarks of fine players. Making the shot at the top of page 73 is the easy part. Regulating your cueing and speed of stroke to get the desired return distance requires great touch. The draw shot in Part A is played with a medium soft stroke. It pays to become very familiar with the cue ball's path on angled draw shots where the rail is not used. In Part B, a medium speed draw stroke will pull the cue ball back about a foot on this near straight in shot.

Part C shows a pinch shot. The goal is to minimize the cue ball's sideways movement. Play this shot a tip or more below center with the softest stroke that will keep the cue ball from rolling forward.

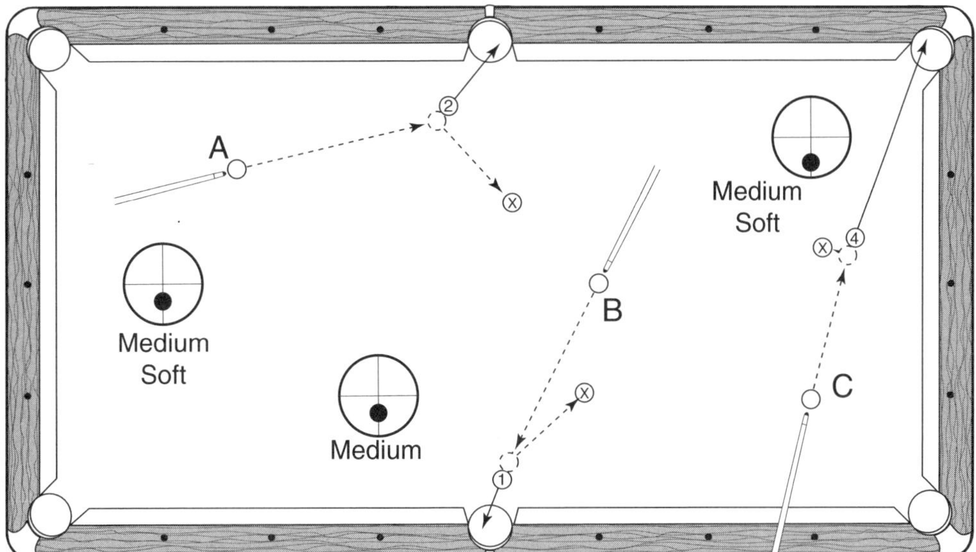

Long Draw Shots (Part A is an A, Part B is a B)

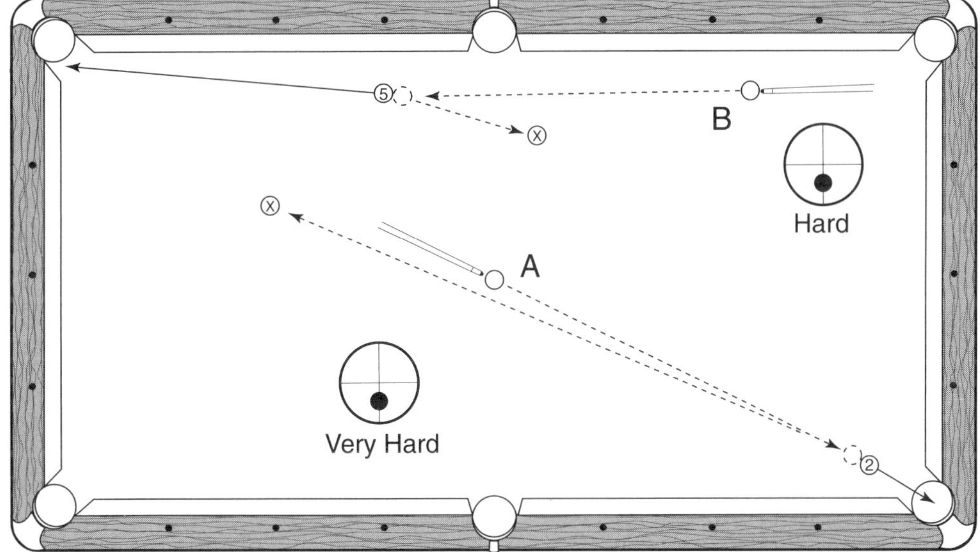

Long draw shots require great technique. And yet the difficulty of these position plays often causes many players to give them their worst effort. Long draw shots must be played with a smooth, but authoritative stroke. You can't baby the shot and still create decisive draw action. At the same time, a powerful poke at the ball is likely to result in the cue ball dribbling back a few inches, or worse yet, a stop shot.

The solution is to keep your arm and wrist relaxed and to whip the cue smoothly through the cue ball. When playing long draw shots, remember to stay down and follow through completely. The draw shot in Part A requires a very hard stroke to create sufficient backspin to take the cue ball 6' backwards. The long-range draw shot in Part B is played with a hard stroke.

The Return Path on Draw Shots Widens (B)

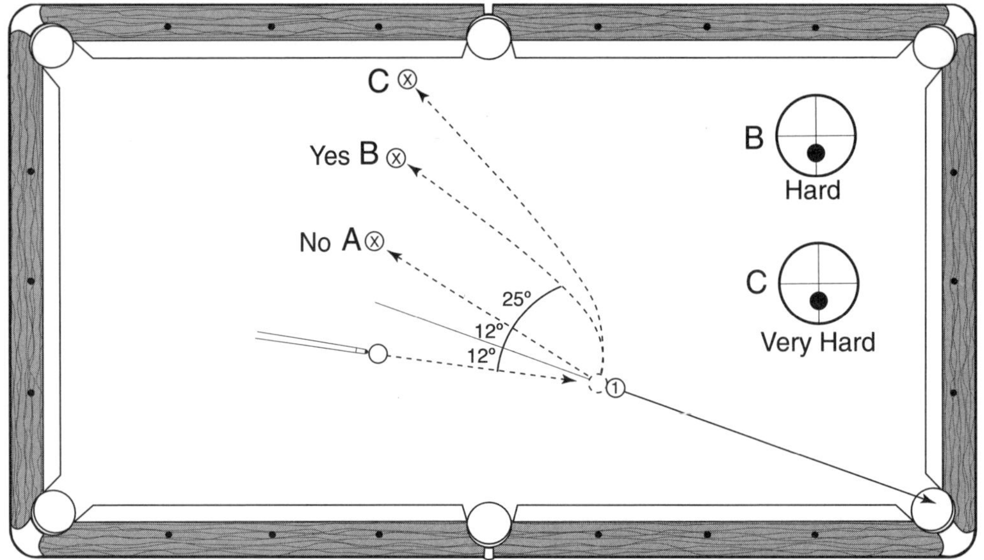

Many players are surprised at how wide the cue ball travels when coming back on draw shots with a relatively small cut angle. The example shows a 12-degree cut shot. If the cue ball's return path mirrored its original cut angle, it would have retreated to Position A. In fact, the cue ball will draw back on a much wider angle.

A medium hard draw stroke will send the cue ball to Position B down a line that is about 25-degress on the other side of the line that runs straight to the pocket. When you hit draw shots with a harder stroke, the cue ball will travel even further down the tangent line before coming back, creating an even wider return angle as shown by the cue ball in Position C.

Draw Floater (B)

The illustration at the top of page 75 shows the path for three commonly played routes: the follow shot, the stun shot, and the draw shot. In addition, it shows a path between the follow and stun shot that can be accessed via what I call a draw floater shot, also known as a drag shot. The draw floater is another one of those "in between" shots that many players fail to use, but that can help you to access position routes your competition couldn't dream of reaching. A medium soft stroke and a tip of draw will cause the cue ball to act like a quasi follow shot as it rolls between the paths that would be created by using a follow shot and a stun shot.

Even though the draw floater is not difficult, it seems to be used mostly by advanced players. Ten or fifteen minutes of practice should be sufficient time to enable you to get the hang of this useful tool.

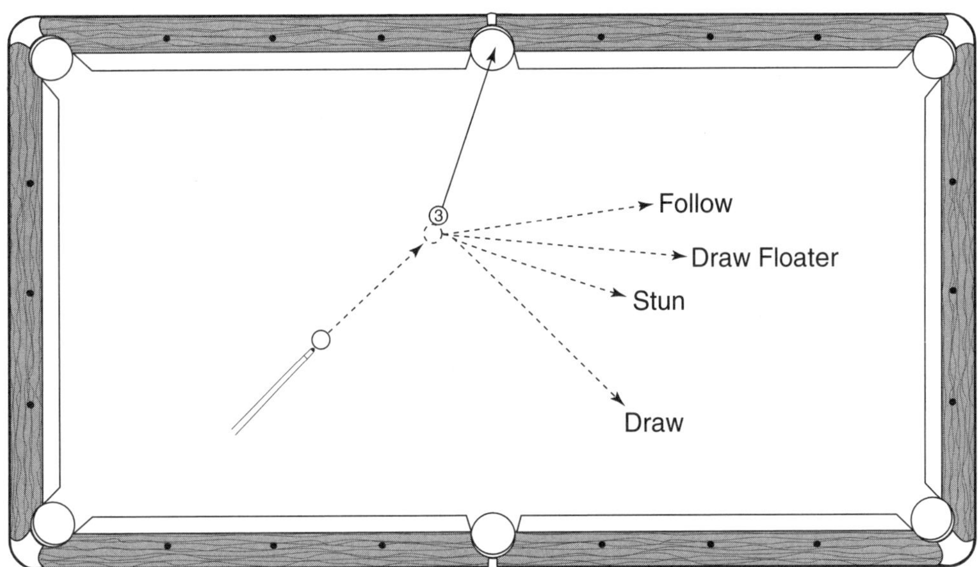

Draw Stun (B)

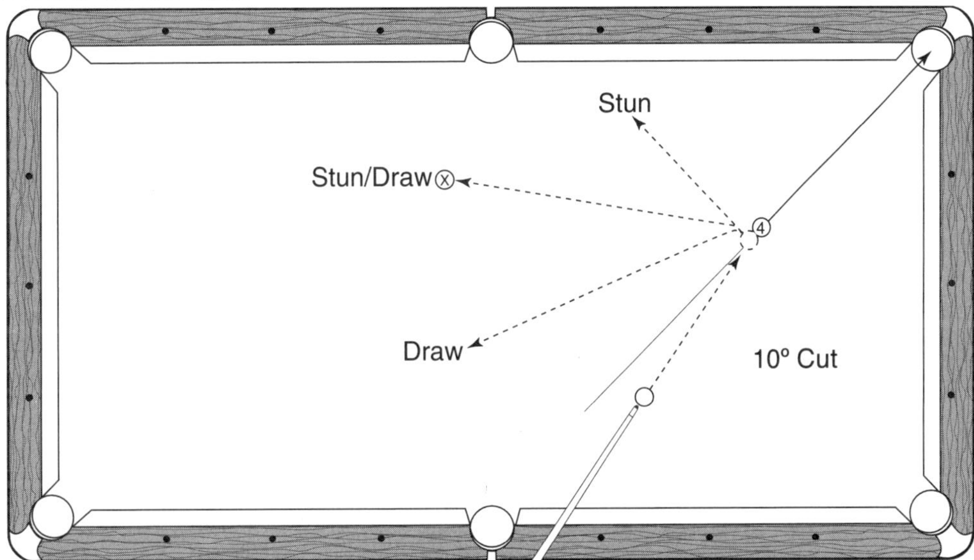

The draw/stun shot is another difficult but necessary position play if you wish to rise far up in the ranks of Nine Ball players. The diagram shows the expected path of the cue ball on a 10-degree cut when played with stun and with straight draw. There is a large gap between the two directional lines. The area between these two pathways can be accessed with a draw/stun shot. The draw/stun shot is played with varying amounts of draw and speed. How much you use of either depends on where you need to send the cue ball. Again, this is a feel shot that takes much practice, so be patient while you experiment with the different variables.

One-Rail Position Routes

According to my research, the tops pros play one-rail position on nearly half (48.5% to be exact) of their position plays. This clearly shows the ability to control the cue ball off one rail is the foundation of position play in Nine Ball. In the pages that follow you'll learn one-rail routes from the most basic to the advanced techniques that can save your run outs. I advise that you completely master the basic routes (the C's) before tackling the more difficult position routes. Don't let the apparent simplicity of the basic routes cause you to pass lightly over them.

Basic Follow Routes (C)

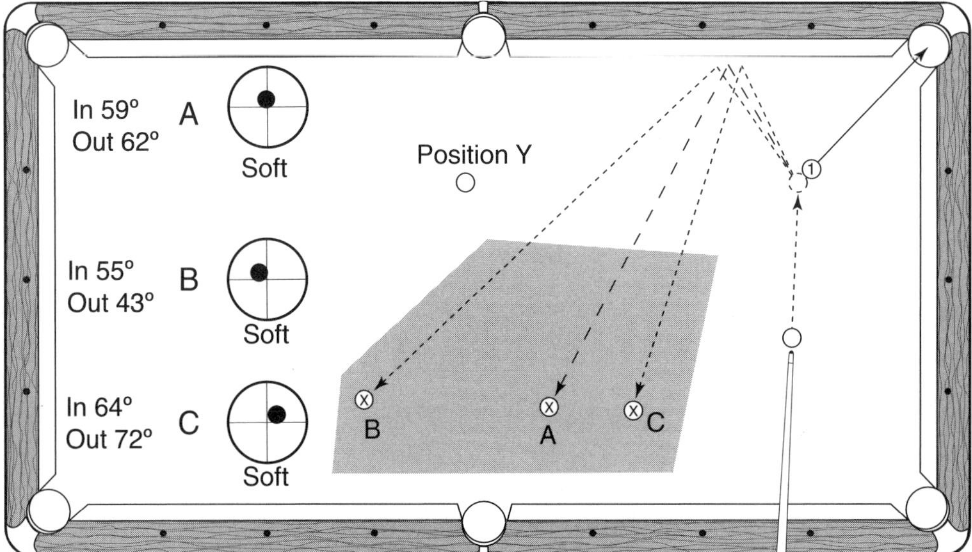

This is one of the most basic position routes as it requires a soft follow stroke, which is one of the easiest shots to control. Route A shows the cue ball's path when follow is used without english. Note how the rebound angle is just a shade wider than the angle of entry. The primary reasons for using english in Nine Ball is to adjust the cue ball's rebound angle after it contacts a rail. Outside english (left in this case) was applied to create Route B. Observe how the cue ball rebounded at a shallower angle, which caused it to travel further up the table as shown. Route C shows how inside english (right in the example) causes the cue ball to rebound at a steeper angle. You can use varying amounts of english to fine tune the cue ball's path of the cushion. When you combine cueing with expert speed control, you can begin to pinpoint the cue ball anywhere in the position zone.

TIP: You can maximize the effects of english on shots like this by cueing on the horizontal axis.

Balls Near a Pocket (C)

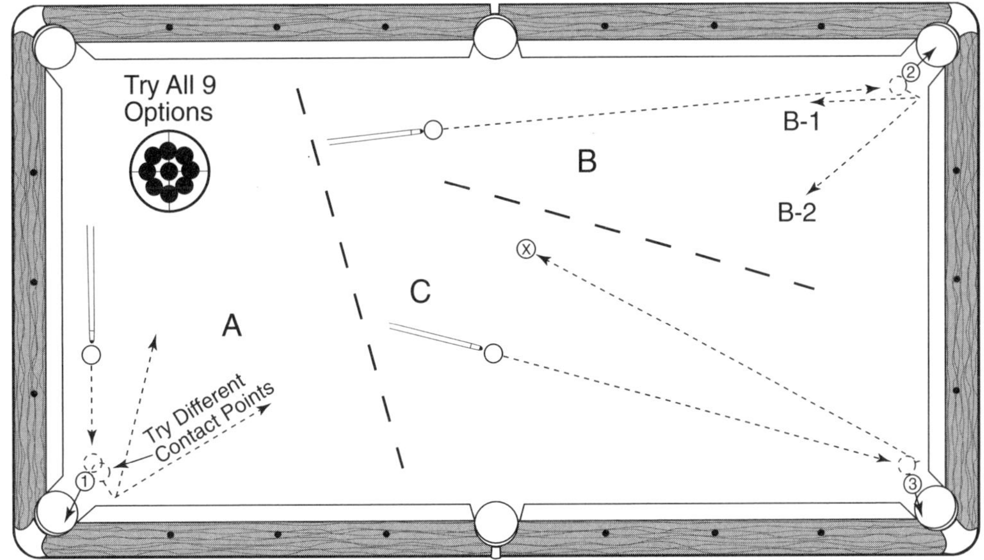

Experienced players have learned to treat pocket hangers with the utmost of care and respect. Even though pocketing is a cinch, they know that position is tricky The major emphasis is on controlling the direction and speed of the cue ball. There are nearly a zillion possible ways to play pocket hangers thanks to the fact that you can hit so many places on the ball and still make the shot, and because you have so much latitude in cueing.

You can begin to learn shape on pocket hangers by setting up the balls is Position A. (Note: you can also try this exercise with the cue ball next to the side rail.) With the balls this close together you can accurately hit the contact point on the object ball. When you combine different points of contact on the object ball with a wide range of cueing options and speeds of stroke, you will begin to discover more ways to play position on these shots than you would have imagined possible. Once you have learned some of the more practical variations of this shot at close range, try playing them from longer distances. I think you will quickly discover that distance adds an unexpected degree of difficulty to the shot. This is especially true when english is used.

Position B shows a longer-range version where you need to exert maximum control. You could send the cue ball down Route B-1 by either hitting the 2-ball very full, or by hitting a third of the 2-ball with left english. Route B-2 shows the natural path on a half ball hit with no english. Position C demonstrates the best way for creating an exact route when you must bring the cue ball a long distance back down the table. Use a thin hit with no english. Let the contact with the object ball control the direction. If you fool with english on this shot and hit the object ball too fully, it will die well short of the position zone.

Pocket Speed Position and the Lag Shot (B, B, C, B)

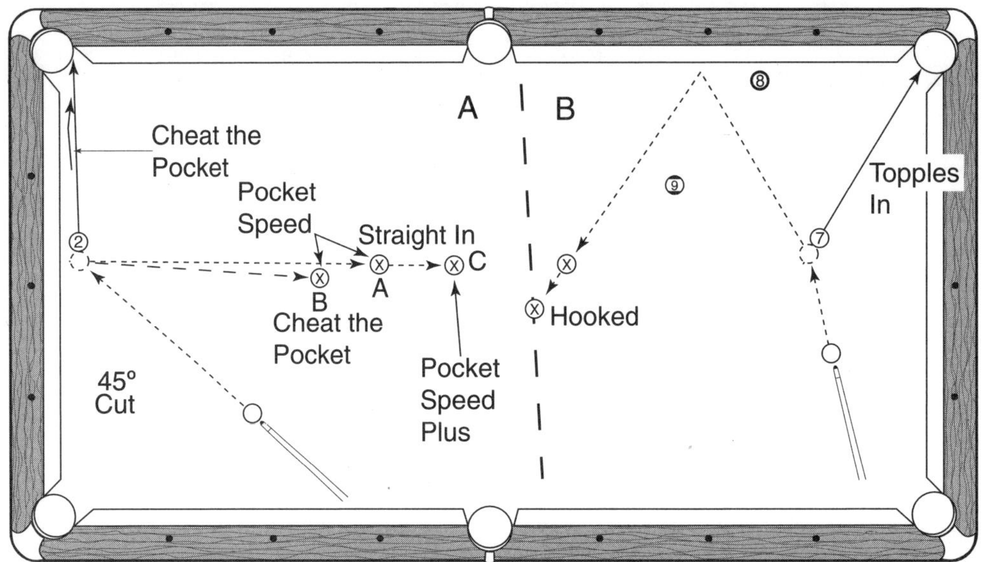

There will be ample opportunities for you to display your soft touch when playing Nine-Ball. In Part A, a 45-degree cut was played with just enough force to get the 2-ball over the lip of the pocket. The cue ball drifted lazily to Position A (this is rated B). When the object ball barely gets to the pocket, this is called pocket speed. You can reduce the distance the cue ball will travel up the table even further by playing the shot with pocket speed and by cheating the pocket, which effectively reduces the cut angle. The cue ball will then stop at Position B (also rated B).

It takes a very fine touch and nerves of steel to play a shot at pocket speed. If rolling balls in at very slows speeds is not your forte, you may wish to use what I call pocket speed plus, which is pocket speed with 6-8" to spare. In the example, a shot hit with pocket speed plus would send the cue ball to Position C (rated C). When using this speed, the shot is hit hard enough so that the object ball would hit the back of the pocket if the slate extended that far. Pocket speed plus also helps avoid roll offs, which are typically a problem when the ball nears the pocket on softly hit shots.

Part B shows a lag shot on a 40-degree cut, which is for rated B despite it apparent simplicity. The hard part on cut shots where you are lagging the ball into the pocket at pocket speed is gauging the speed so it topples into the pocket. If the shot in this example was hit a whisker harder, the cue ball would have rolled a few inches further, resulting in a hook.

One-Rail Follow on 30-Degree Cut (C)

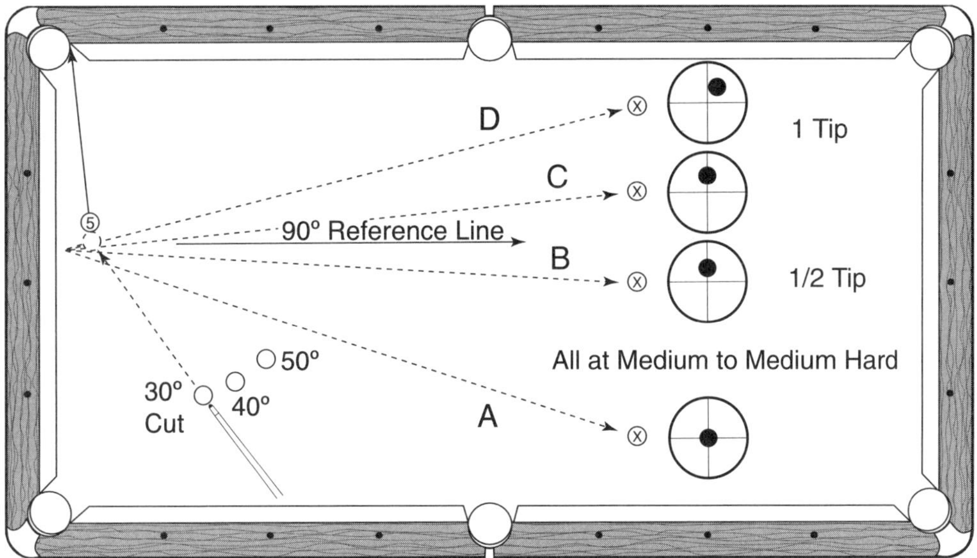

The cue ball must often travel a long distance after rebounding off either end rail, such as on the 30-degree cut shot in the example.. When the object ball is even a couple of inches from the rail you must take active measures to control its direction off the cushion. Start by mentally constructing the 90-degree reference line off the rail. The next step is to determine how far the cue ball needs to travel on either side of the line, if at all. Then choose the cueing and speed that will create the desired direction. With a medium to medium hard stroke and centerball, the cue ball will travel down Route A. Route C resulted from using follow. Route D required the use of right english.

It is quite a bit easier to control the direction of the shot when the cut angle is a little sharper, such as at 40 or 50-dgrees. I suggest you experiment with different cut angles and with the object ball at various distances from the rail. A practice session or two devoted to learning all variations of this valuable route will pay big dividends.

Once you get proficient at these routes, try adding a little speed and note carefully the additional routes you have created. You will discover many two and three rails routes are merely extensions of these basic one-rail routes. For example, if the cue ball traveling down Route A continued to the side rail and then off end rail, you would have a three-rail route that is a natural extension of the one-rail route in the diagram.

Inside English and the 90-Degree Reference Line (B)

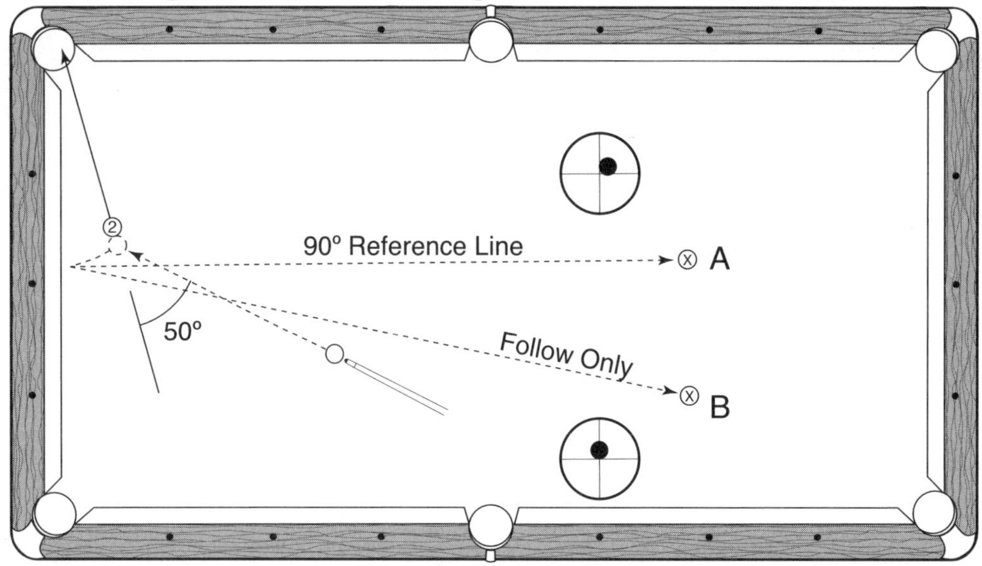

When the object ball is several inches from the rail, you must apply inside english to have it travel down the 90-degree reference to Position A. Long distance inside english one-rail follow shots with large cut angles require a fairly soft stroke, which keeps deflection to a minimum. Try aiming at first with no allowance for english. Then try a quarter tip and a half tip.

How the Angle Naturally Widens (B)

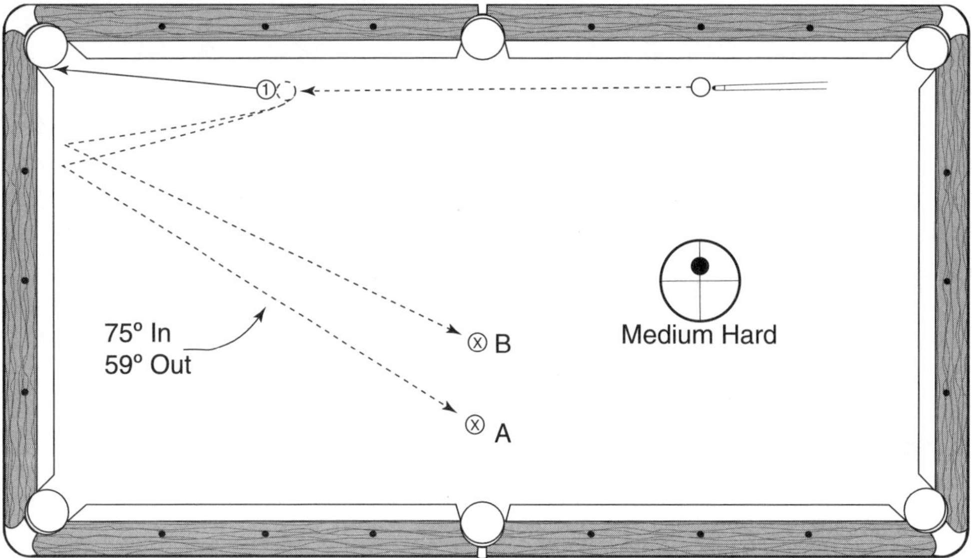

This position play catches many players by surprise as they are expecting a much sharper rebound of the end rail. Notice that the angle opens significantly even though the shot was played without english. The two ending locations demonstrate the difference that pocketing makes on this shot. Position A resulted from cutting the shot slightly more than in Position B.

Long Distance 1 Rail Follow (B)

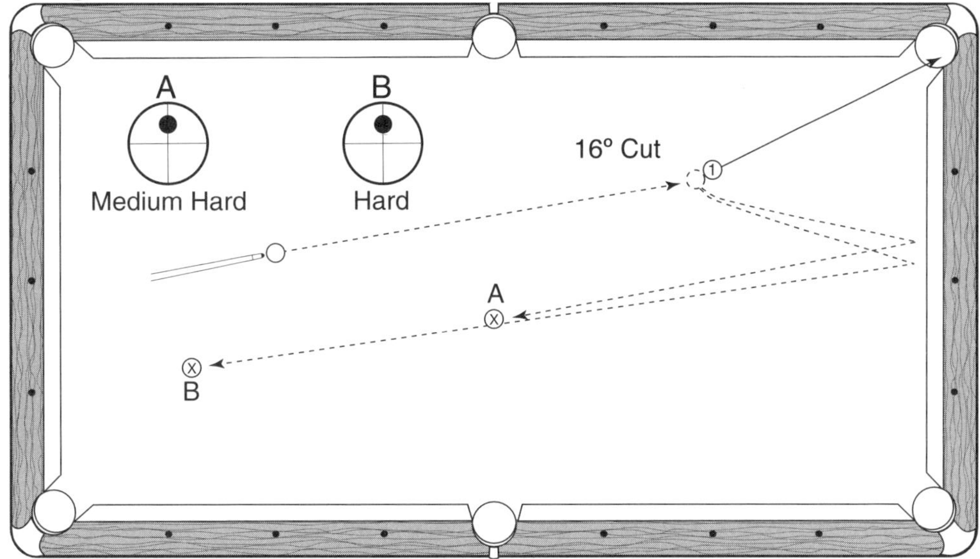

Long distance follow shots require an extra smooth stroke with a full follow through. Try practicing both the short range (Position A) and long-range (Position B) versions in the illustration. The smooth and authoritative stroke you develop with these position plays will come in handy when a powerful stroke is required on other shots.

Targeting the Contact Point (B)

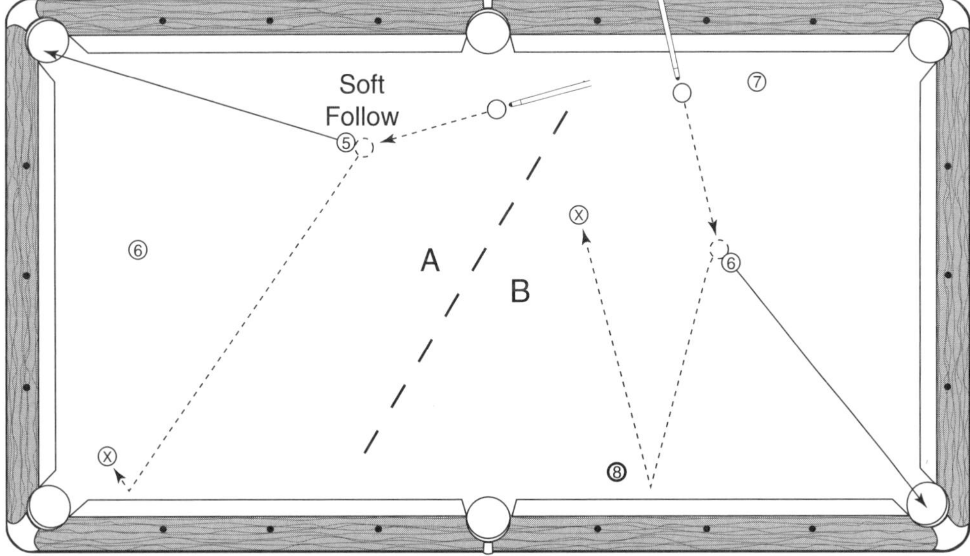

When the cue ball will be traveling a long distance across the table to the rail after contacting the cue ball, it is often very important for you to accurately gauge where it will strike the rail. This can enable you to play the shot with the assurance that you won't scratch, as in Part A, or that you won't run into an obstacle, as shown in Part B.

Long Distance Finesse Stun Follow (A)

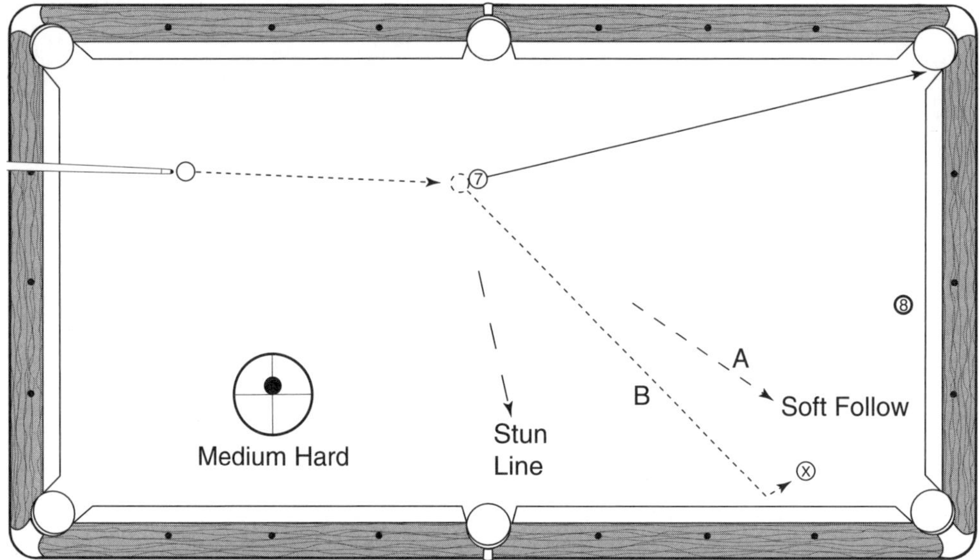

If the shot was hit with a soft follow stroke, the cue ball would travel down Route A directly towards a scratch. You can avoid a scratch on this long distance follow shot by using just enough stun so the cue ball follows Route B. Try setting up the balls in the position shown and play the soft follow shot. Then use a little less follow and a medium hard stroke.

Basic Side Pocket 1 Railers (C)

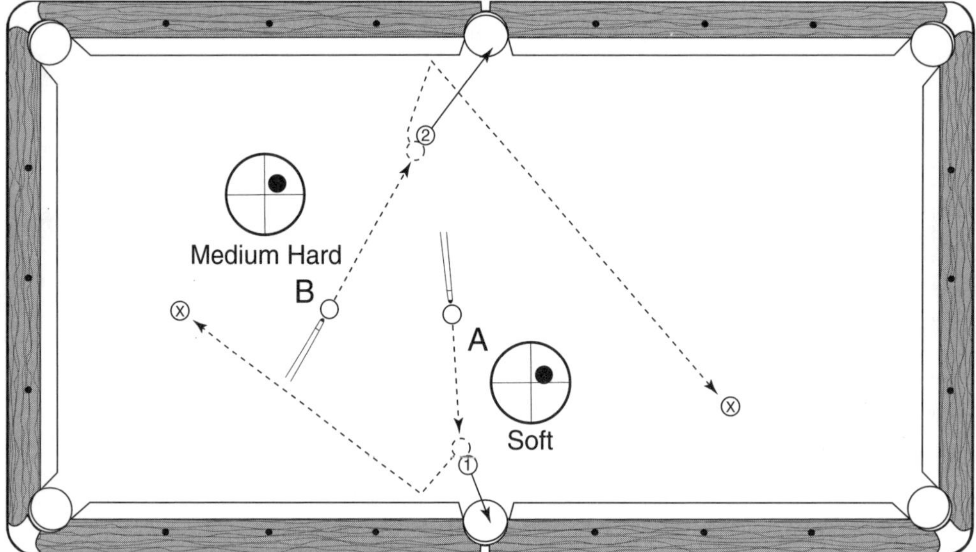

The diagram shows two of the most basic side pocket one-rail position plays. Route A is played with a soft stroke and outside english. Route B takes a medium hard stroke with inside english and follow. The side pockets allow for an extremely wide ranges of possible routes, especially when the object ball is opposite the pocket.

Creeper Follow (B)

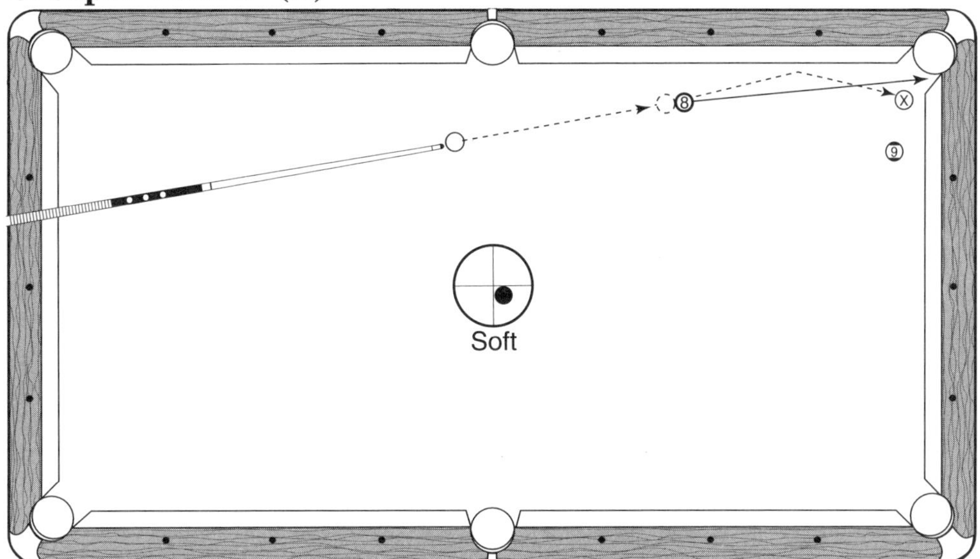

Francisco Bustamante played short side shape on the 9-ball using this finesse follow shot in a match against Earl Strickland at the Bicycle Club in 1992. This follow shot is struck with low inside english and a very soft stroke. The draw helps keep the cue ball close to the rail, but does not act as "normal" draw.

Inside Power Follow (A)

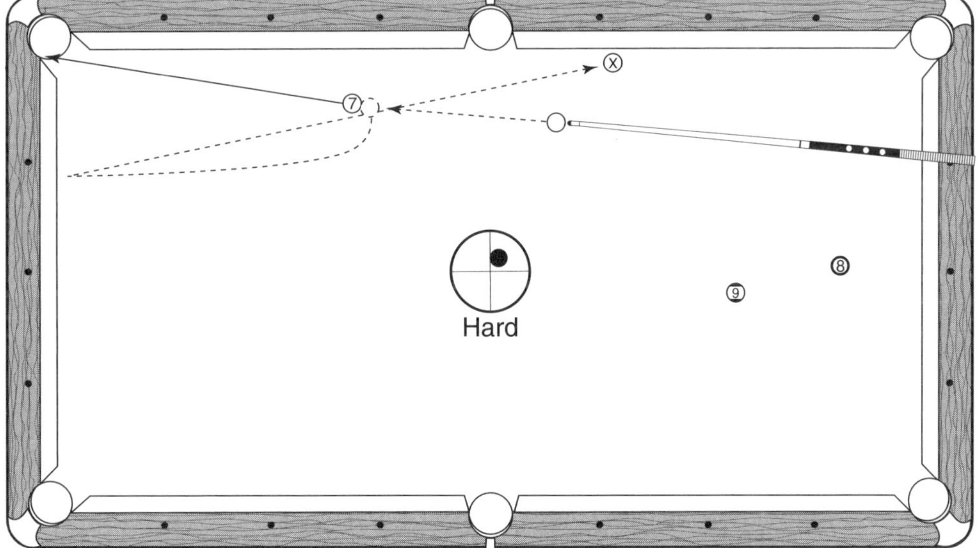

Jeremy Jones used a hard stroke with inside follow to get back down table for the 8-ball in the finals of the 1999 U.S. Open against Johnny Archer. Notice how the cue ball bent back towards the end rail and how the right english took over upon contact with the cushion. If you can execute this shot, it indicates you possess great fundamentals.

1-Rail and Out (C & A)

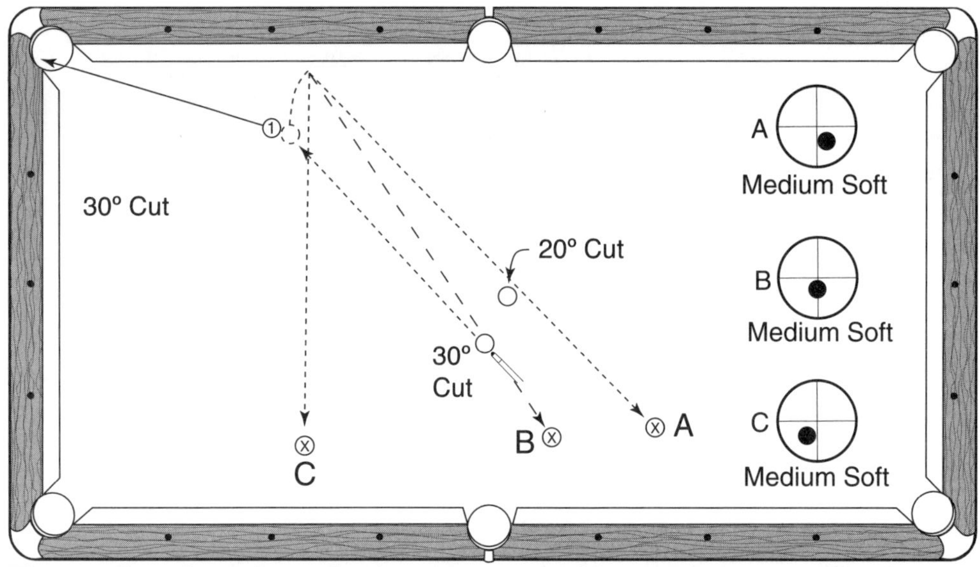

The 1-rail and out draw shot is a most valuable position route. The illustration shows a 30-degree cut angle with the object ball about 7" off the rail. Master Routes A and B first as they are rated C. Practice the shot with a cut angle of 30-degrees (as shown) and from 20-degrees. When the ball is close to the rail, it's return path falls within more well confined limits. Route C (rated A) is for advanced players.

Draw Across Table and Out (B)

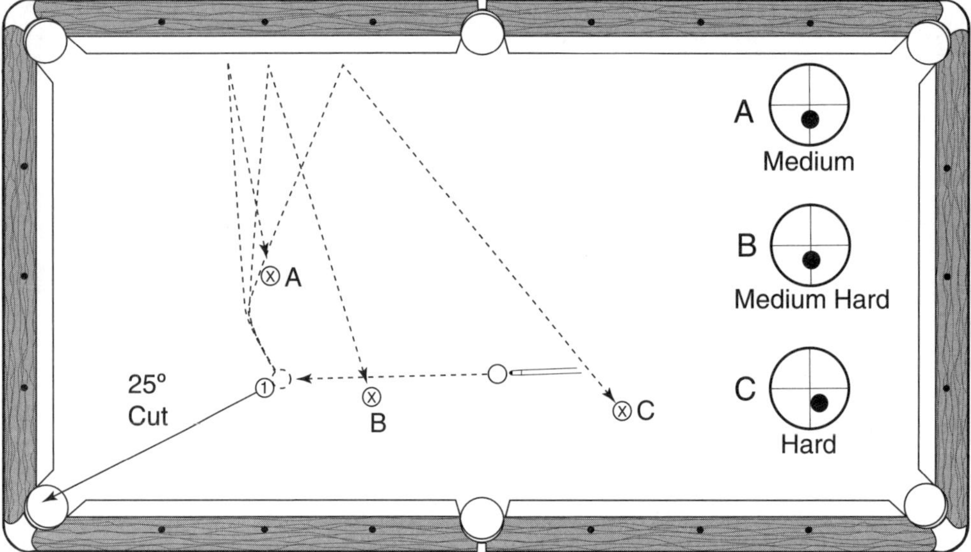

The cue ball must travel a long distance to the side rail after contacting the object ball, which makes this a challenging position play. Route A is designed to send the cue ball straight back across the table. Route B, which requires a firm stroke, will bring the cue ball a little up table. Draw combined with outside english and a hard stroke will create Route C. This requires a very solid stroke.

Draw Across Table and Out on Backcut (B)

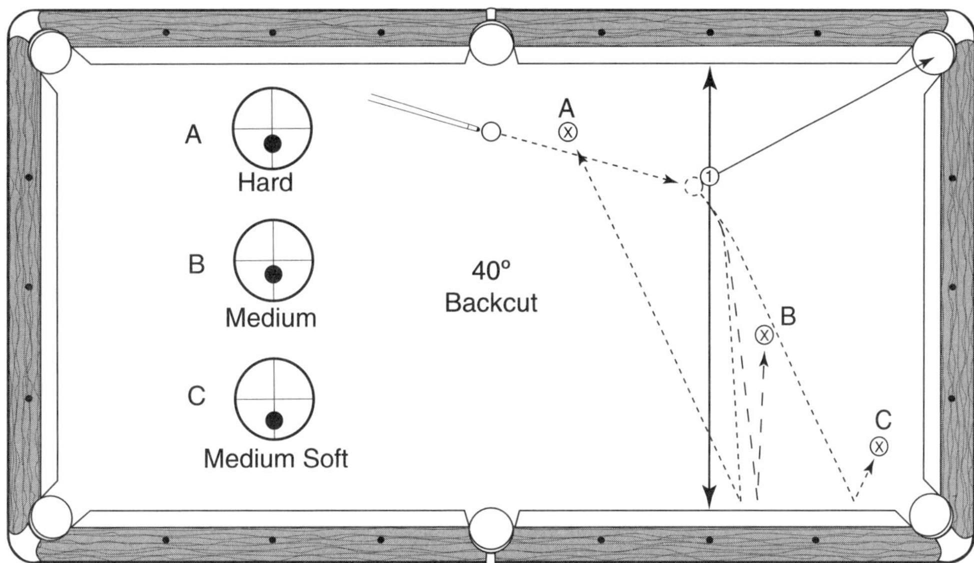

This shot is a variation of the previous position play. This time, however, you are playing a 40-degree back cut, which limits the "comeback" distance to Position A. Observe that the cue ball is further down the table in Positions B and C as it rests beneath the line that runs from side rail to side rail through the 1-ball.

Draw to the Rail and Out (B)

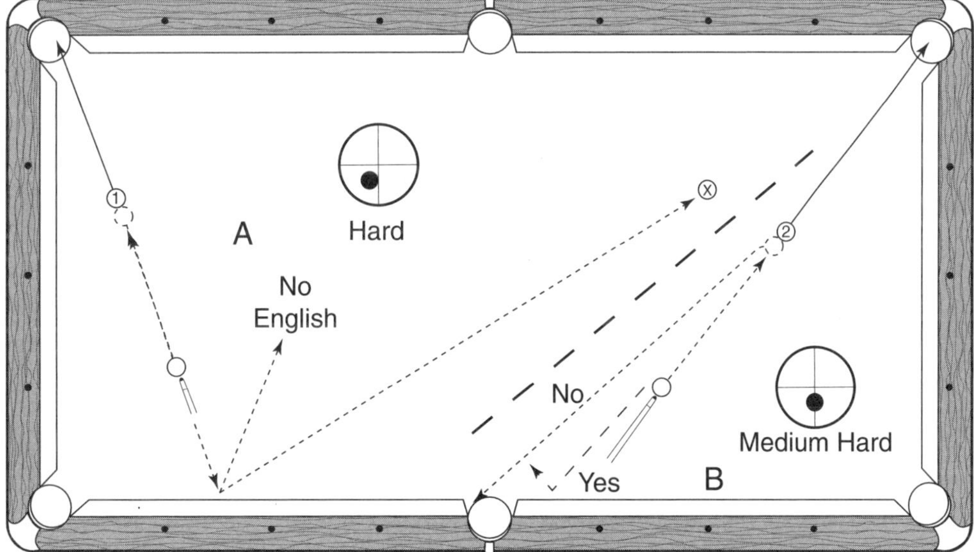

When you make an error and get straight in as in Part A, you can still send the cue ball well down the table by using draw and outside english. Use a very smooth stroke. The english will shoot the cue ball down the table. Part B shows that it is possible to make a straight in shot and still scratch even though the shot was not lined up to the side pocket. To avoid a scratch, you must make an extra effort to hit the 2-ball squarely.

Draw Up the Side Rail (C)

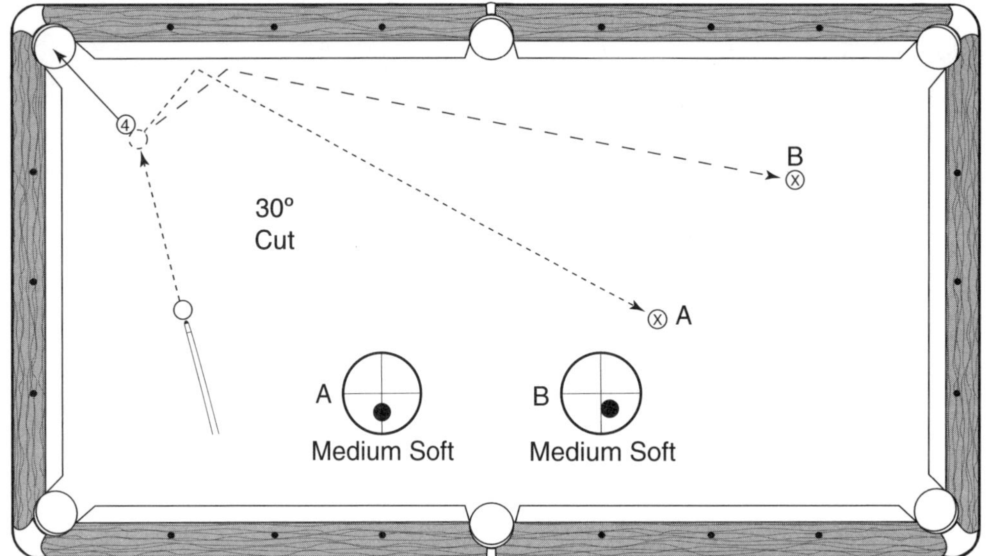

Route A is quite tricky as there is a tendency among most players to overshoot the position zone. This is especially true when using outside (running) english, as in Route B. When you practice this route, mark 3-4 targets along the two routes. Observe carefully where the cue ball stops and make any necessary adjustments in speed.

Finesse Draw Outside English (B)

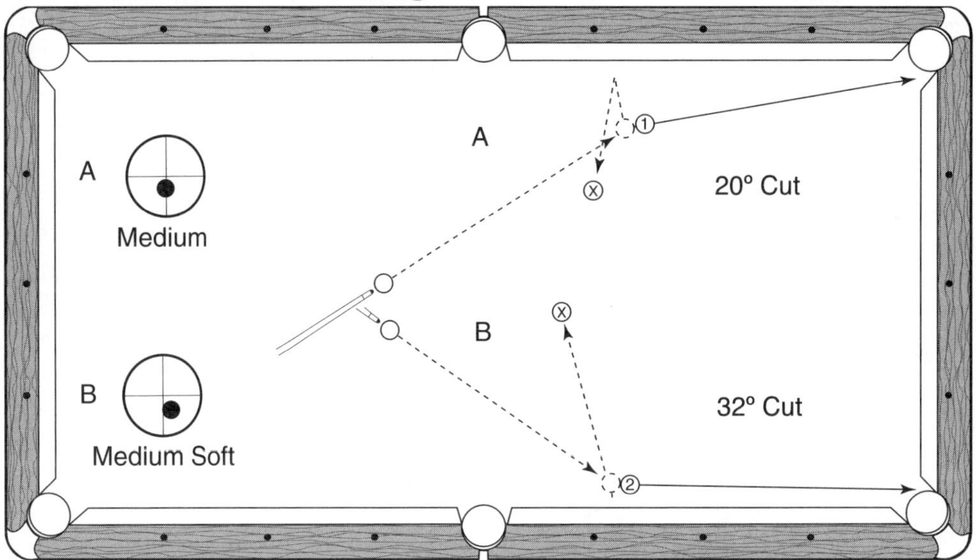

These examples show how to use a finesse draw stroke with outside english to float the cue ball gently into the middle of the table. Route A is played with a medium speed and a half tip of left english. Route B requires a medium soft stroke and a half tip of right english. In both cases, the draw is not used to bring the cue ball back up table, but it enables you to shoot with greater authority.

Draw Kill Shot (B) and (A)

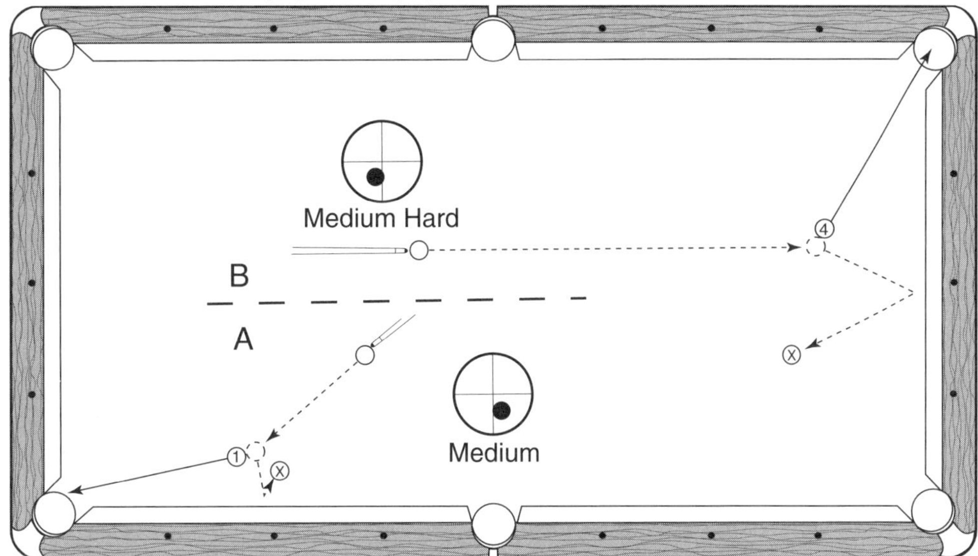

The draw kill shot seemingly defies the physics of the game since the cue ball travels such a short distance after a cut shot. Part A is rated (B) since it is played from short range. Use inside english and draw with a definite wrist snap to impart extra spin. Part B (rated A) takes expert technique because aiming with low inside english is difficult at this distance. Make sure to use a smooth stroke and with a snap of the wrist at contact.

Side Pocket to the End Rail (C)

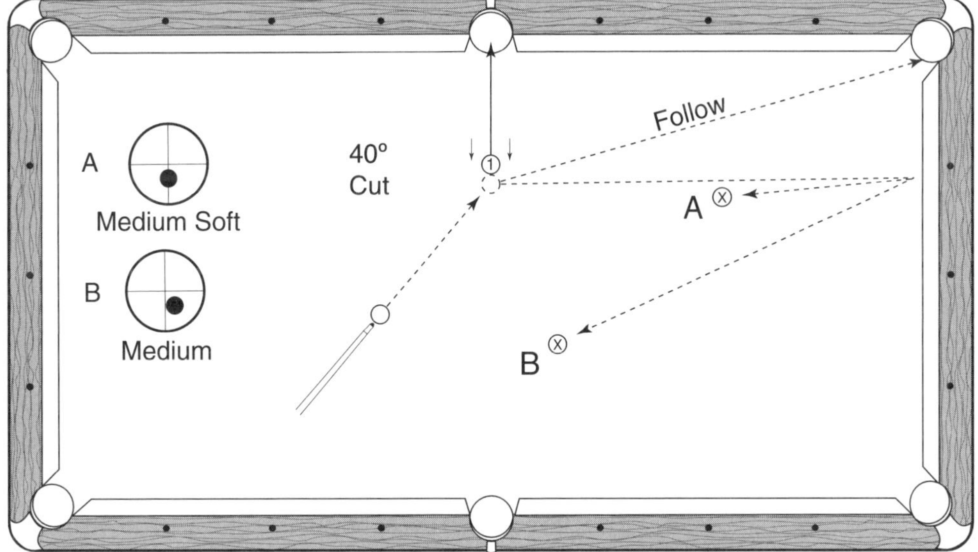

A soft follow stroke would lead to scratch in the corner pocket. Now use the same speed of stroke with draw. The draw will hold it on a straight line to the end rail, resulting in Position A. Draw with outside english will pull the cue ball across the table to Position B. After practicing this shot, try it with the object ball over a balls width to either side as shown.

The Pound Shot (A) (RR)

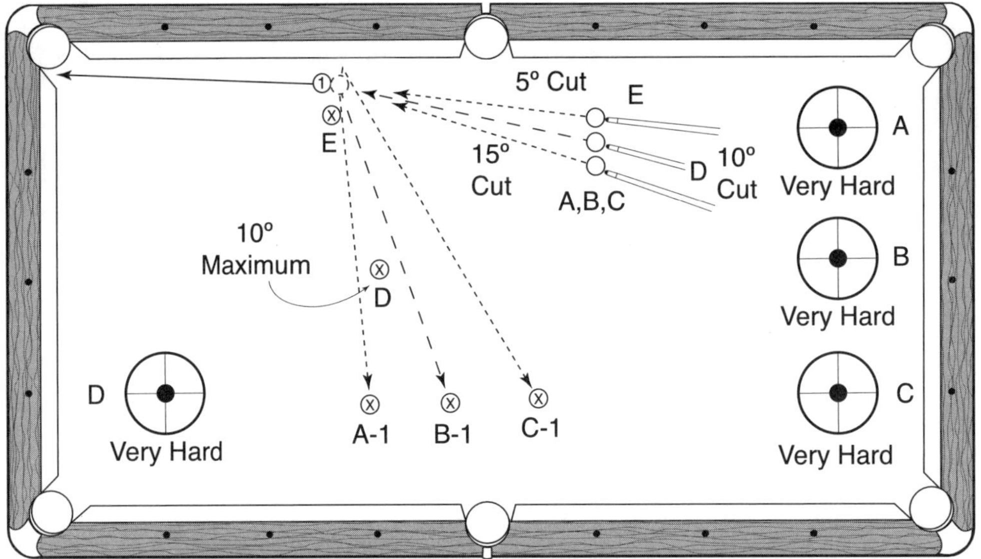

The pound shot is a recovery route that is used to get whitey back in line when you have left yourself an overly shallow cut angle. Pound shots are normally played when the object ball is close to the rail, but they can also be used when the ball is several inches or more from the cushion. The pound shot is played with very forceful, high-speed stroke. When you combine a high speed with the smaller effective pocket opening for shots down the rail, you have a shot that requires both power and a high degree of accuracy.

The diagram shows a 15-degree cut shot. A very hard stroke with a quarter to a half tip of follow will send the cue ball to A-1. A centerball hit will result in Position B-1. A very hard stroke with a half tip of draw will send the cue ball to Position C-1. When you first practice this shot, try using a medium hard speed to get your stroke loosened up and in the groove. Gradually add speed as long as you are continuing to pocket the ball. Keep adding speed until the cue ball reaches the three locations. You want to avoid slamming into the shot at the start, which could lead to frustration.

When the cut angle is reduced to 10-degrees, the maximum distance that you can realistically expect to send the cue ball off the rail is shown by the cue ball in Position D. With a cut angle of only 5-degrees, Position E is about the best you can hope for. When the cut angle ranges from 7-12 degrees, your results are subject to a fair amount of variation. What may seem like the same stroke could result in about 6-12" difference in position.

Super Hard Pound & Draw (A) (RR)

Part A shows a pound draw shot using an extremely hard stroke. Pocketing the 1-ball is a challenge because of the high speed of stroke.

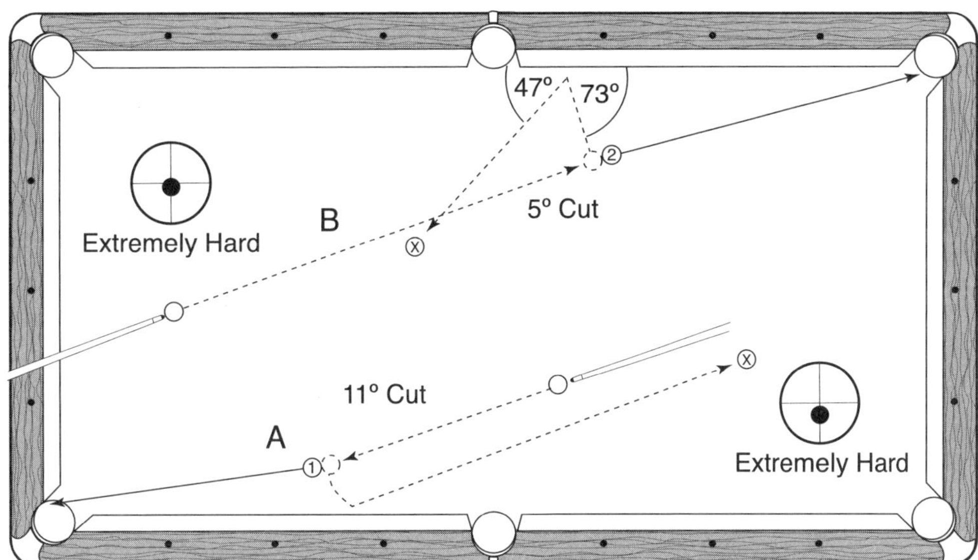

The pound and draw shot in Part B takes about the hardest stroke you will ever use for any shot other than a break shot. The shot is hit with a quarter tip of draw. Notice how the rebound angle is much shallower than the entrance angle, which indicates how the cue ball picks up english at contact on high speed shots with a nearly full hit. This monster of a shot is rated A++.

Creating an Angle (B) (RR)

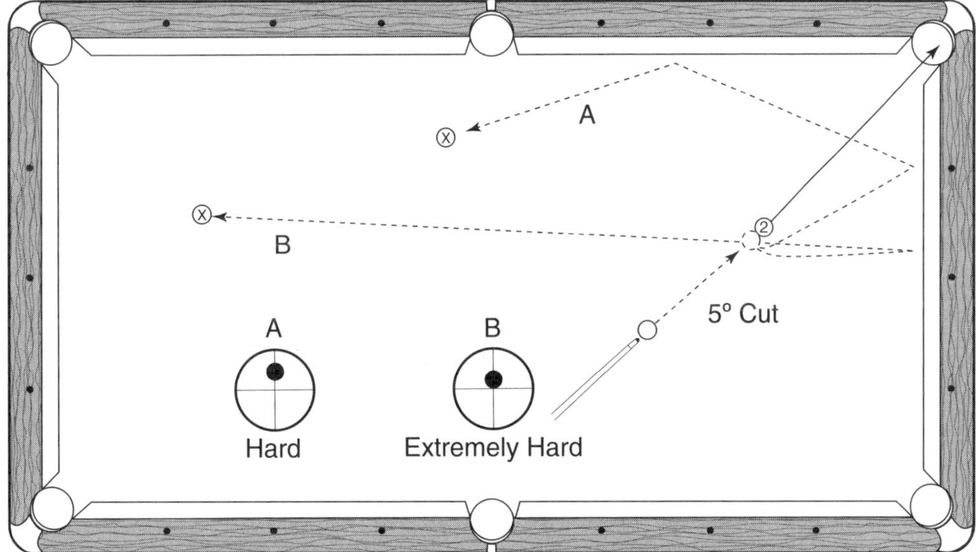

The cue ball would normally follow the two-rail route to Position A when struck with a hard follow stroke. If this route is not available, you can create a new angle of departure from the rail by playing the shot with an extremely hard stroke and a half tip of follow, which will take the cue ball to Position B.

Two-Rail Position Routes

Two-rail position plays are the third most commonly use routes by the top pros as they are used on 22% of their position plays. The majority of two-rail position plays are end rail first, side rail second and out towards the center portion of the table. The ability to fine tune your two-rail routes is a huge asset to your game. In addition, many of the two-rail routes can easily be extended to create three rail position plays. So when you are learning two-rail shape you are, in many instances, also adding three-rail routes to your arsenal.

Two Rails with Follow (C)

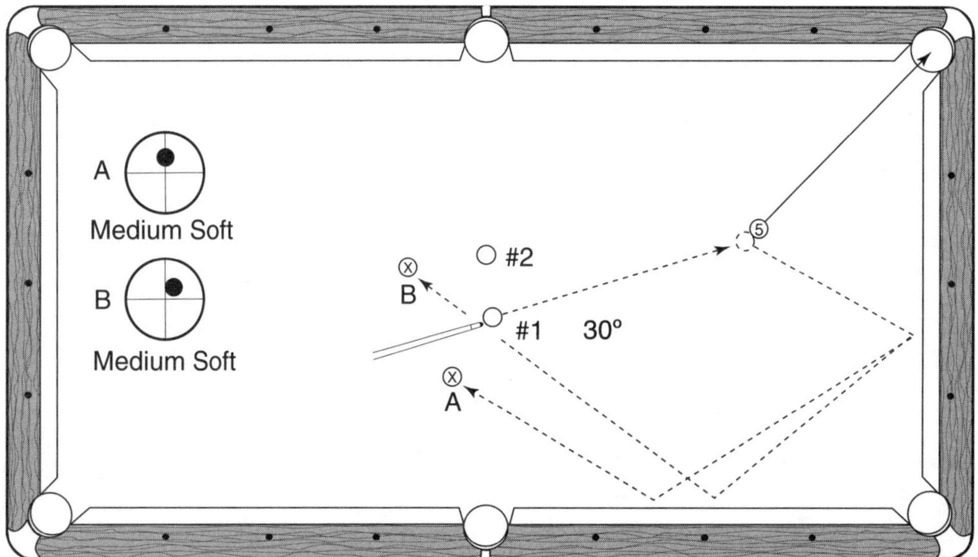

This useful position route allows you to easily access a large portion of the center of the table. The shot is a natural route that, when played with follow and a medium soft stroke, will result in Position A. If you add a half tip of outside english, the cue ball will follow a shallower path off the first rail, resulting in Position B. When practicing this shot, set up the balls as in the positions in the diagram, which is a 30-degree cut.

When you can consistently send the cue ball to Positions A and B, add and then subtract a foot from the target to develop a feel for other distances. After you complete this exercise, repeat the same steps with the cue ball at #2, which is a 40-degree cut. This will teach you how small differences in the position of the balls can influence a position route.

Cueing and Speed Affects the Follow Route (B)

Your choice of cueing and speed can have a significant impact on the direction of the cue ball as shown by the two-rail position play at the top of page 90. All three routes were hit with a medium hard stroke. Position A resulted from using follow and a half tip of right english. A half tip of follow on

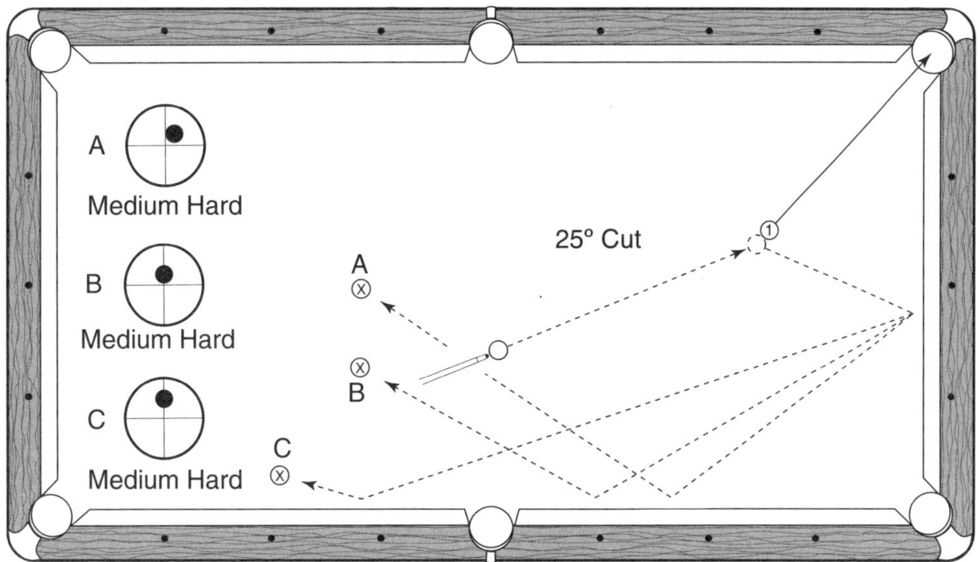

the vertical axis (no english) was used to send the cue ball to Position B. A full tip of straight follow was the ticket to Position C. Notice that the difference between Positions A and C, which is almost half a table width, was a result of slight modifications in cueing.

Two Rails with Inside Follow (B)

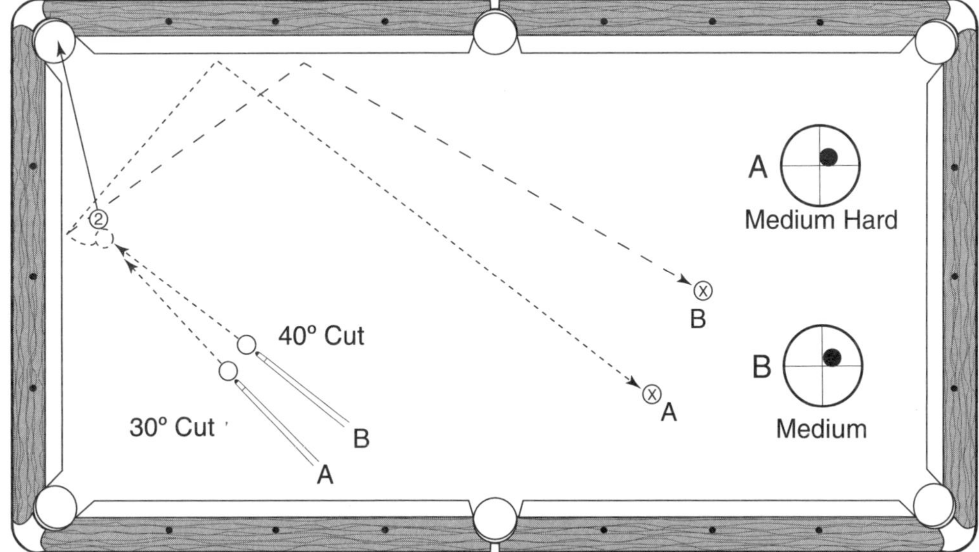

The big key to the position plays in this diagram is adjusting your aim for inside english. You must aim for a rather full hit on the 2-ball since deflection will cause the cue ball to squirt to the left. A smooth stroke (I know you've heard this before) will create additional inside spin with less force, hence less deflection. Notice how the 30-degree cut angle in Position A required a firmer stroke than the 40-degree cut in Position B to propel the cue ball about the same distance.

Shallow Angle Two Railer (B, B, & A) (RR)

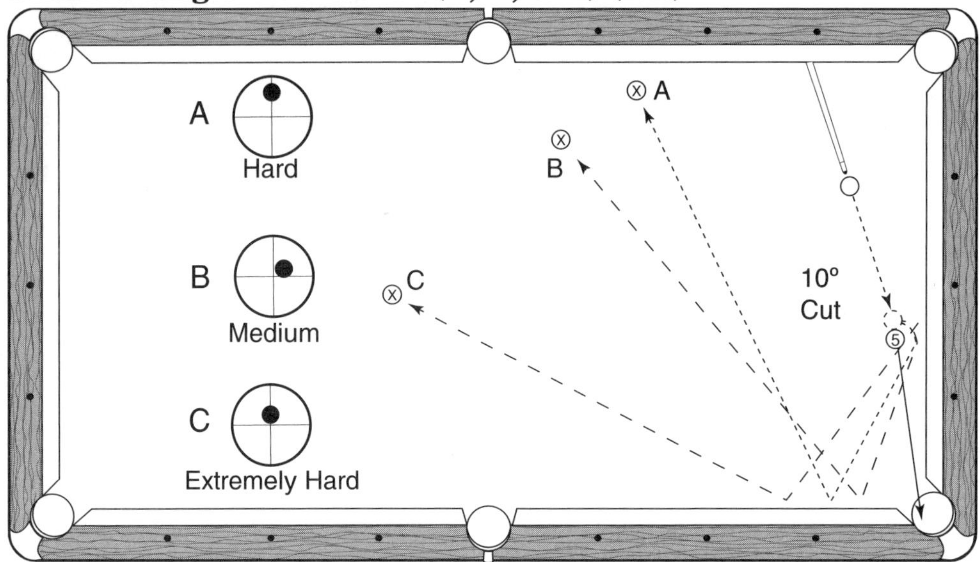

These position plays show you several ways to escape the end rail when you have left yourself an overly shallow cut angle. The recovery routes once again demonstrate how cueing and speed of stroke can exert a huge influence on the direction of the shot. Position A is obtained by using a hard stroke with a full tip of follow. No english is needed. This route requires a hard stroke to send the cue ball a relatively short distance, which leads to a tendency to come up short.

The cue ball Position B is not far from the one at Position A, but this shot takes a radically different approach. Play this route with a medium speed. Use a half tip of inside (running) english as this will add velocity to the cue ball after it strikes each cushion. You should also use a shorter bridge to prevent misses and to insure the proper stun effect.

Now for the fun part, which is getting the cue ball over half way down table to Position C. This A rated route takes a full tip of follow and an extremely hard stroke. The extra power produces a stun like effect to the first rail, at which point the follow takes over. The cue ball will strike much further up the side rail than on Routes A and B.

Small Cut Angle Two Railer (A, A, & B) (RR)

You can reach a number of destinations on the relatively straight in shot at the top of page 92. thanks to the magic of cueing and speed of stroke. Route A (rated A) is created by using a hard follow stroke. No english is needed. It is important to know where the cue ball will strike each cushion as this can help you to avoid obstructers. In this case, the cue ball hit the end rail opposite the first diamond.

A hard follow stroke with a full tip of follow will send the cue ball further up table to Position B (rated A). This time the cue ball hit the end rail 1.25' from the corner pocket. This is a dangerous route, as the cue ball must flirt with the side pocket.

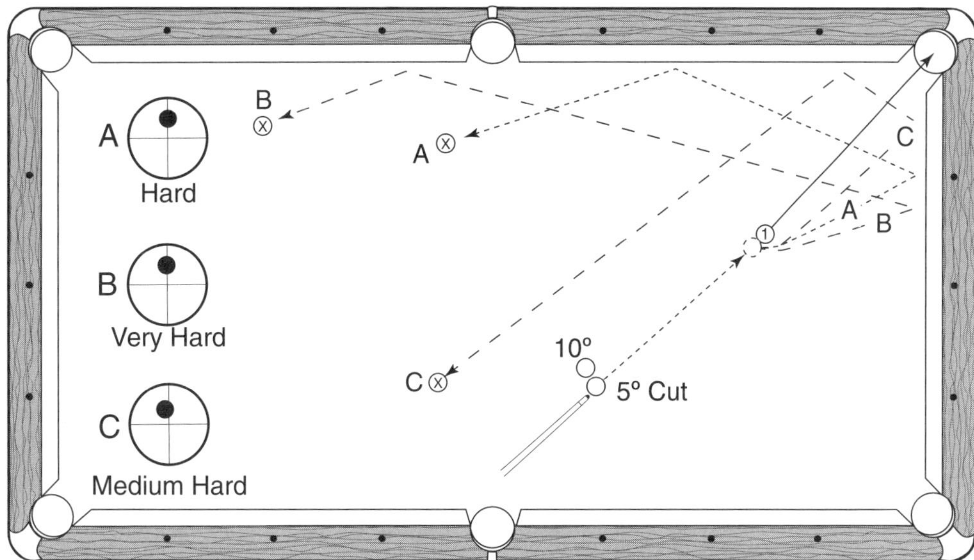

A half tip of inside english and a medium hard follow stroke combine to create a wildly different path that results in Position C (rated B). Now the cue ball is almost all of the way across the table. Try practicing this shot with the balls in the position shown. Use a shallow 5-degree cut angle. Then move the cue ball over about 2.5" to Position D, which is a 10-degree cut. The dynamics of this shot are about the same, but they begin to change radically once the cut angle exceeds about 12-degrees.

Crossing the Table with English

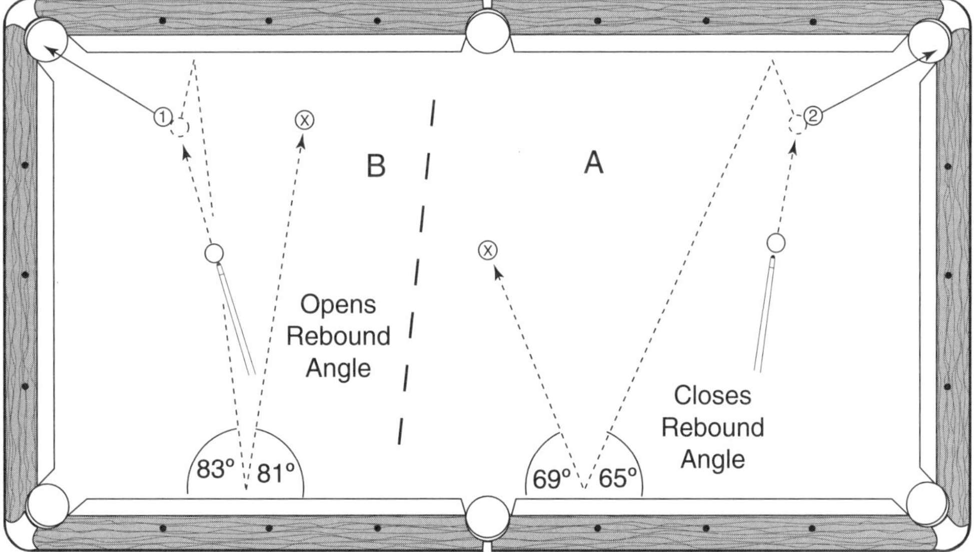

When you apply sufficient sidespin to the cue ball and it is traveling back and forth across the table, it will retain the sidespin from one cushion to the next. When outside english is applied, as in Part A, the rebound angle will open up off the first side rail and close slightly off the opposite side rail. The opposite is true in Part B where inside english was employed.

Long Distance Side Rail Follow Shots (A) (RR)

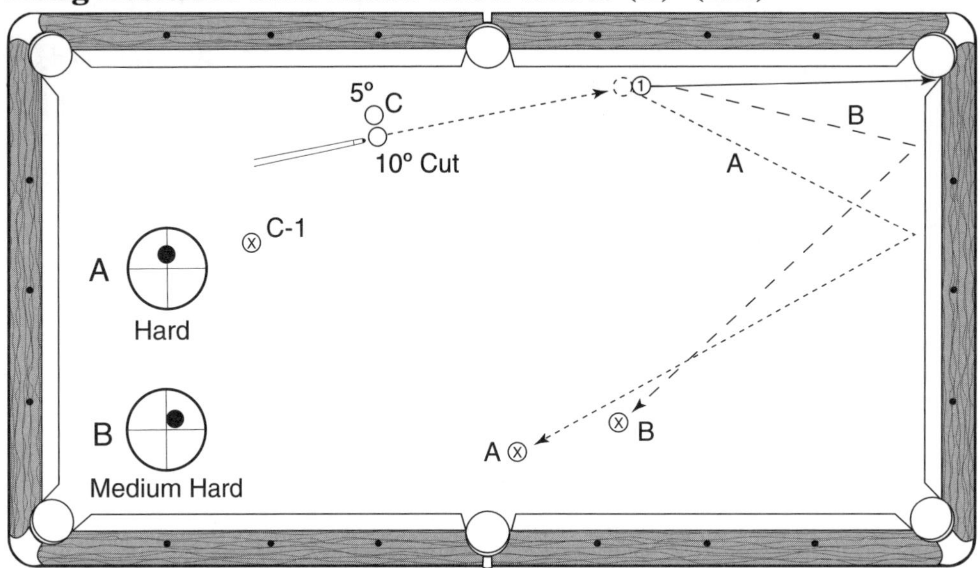

These challenging recovery routes are both rated A. Route A shows the cue ball's path when the shot is played with follow, but no english. Route B shows how the cue ball will swing across the table with inside english. You can send the cue ball a relatively long distance with a medium hard stroke. If the cue ball was in Position C at 5-degrees, a hard follow stroke would take it to Position C-1.

Avoiding a Common Scratch (C)

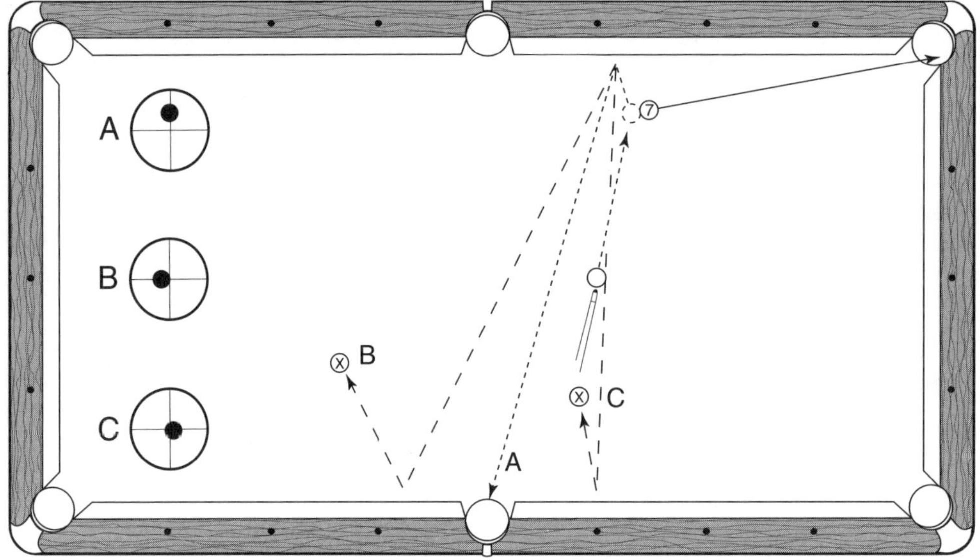

The cue ball always follows a path up the table from the point where it strikes the cushion on shots like the 7-ball when played straight follow, as in Route A. You can avoid this common scratch by using outside english, which will send the cue ball along Route B above the side pocket. Inside english was used in Route C to keep the cue ball below the side pocket.

A Natural Centerball Two Railer (A)

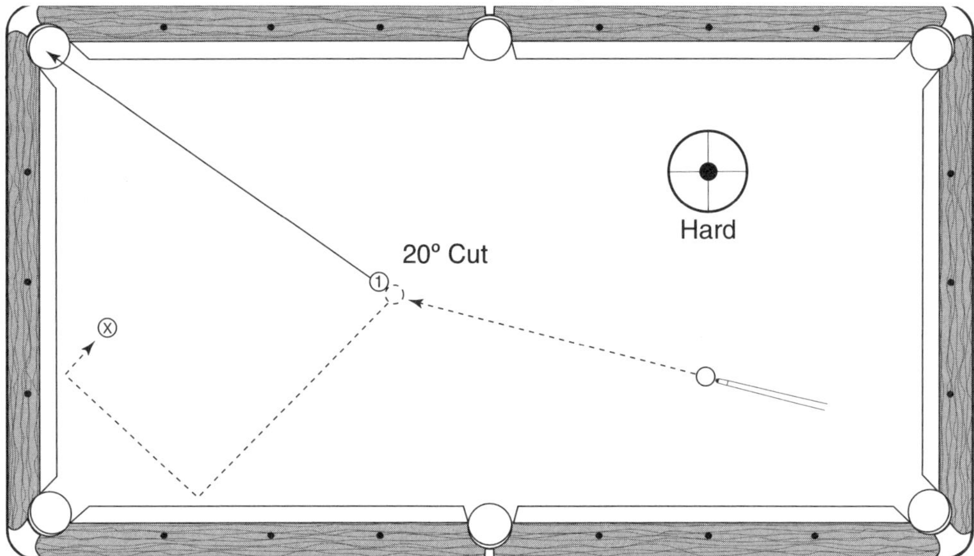

This shot is played with centerball and a hard stroke buy the cue ball will take a path that looks very similar to a follow shot. The cue ball will pick up a little bit of topspin because of the distance of the cue ball to the object ball. The length of the shot and the use of centerball, which is foreign to many players, conspire to make this a challenging position play.

Going Deep into the Corners (A)

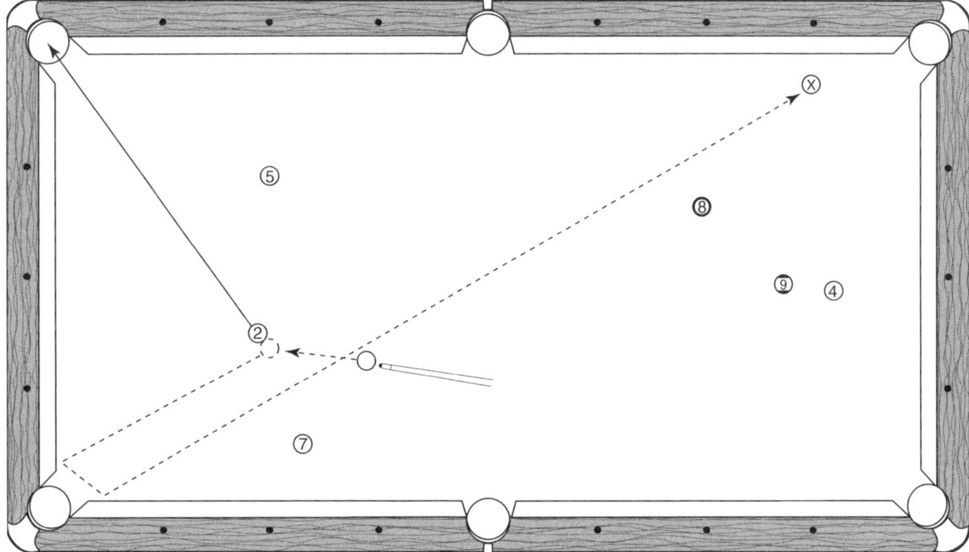

Nick Varner demonstrated exceptional cue ball control on this two-rail position play in a match with Mike Sigel at the 1990 U.S. Open. Varner had almost no margin for error as he barely avoided scratching. You will have a strong indicator that your positional skills are at a very high level when you can purposefully play this close to a pocket without scratching.

Reversing with Outside English (A)

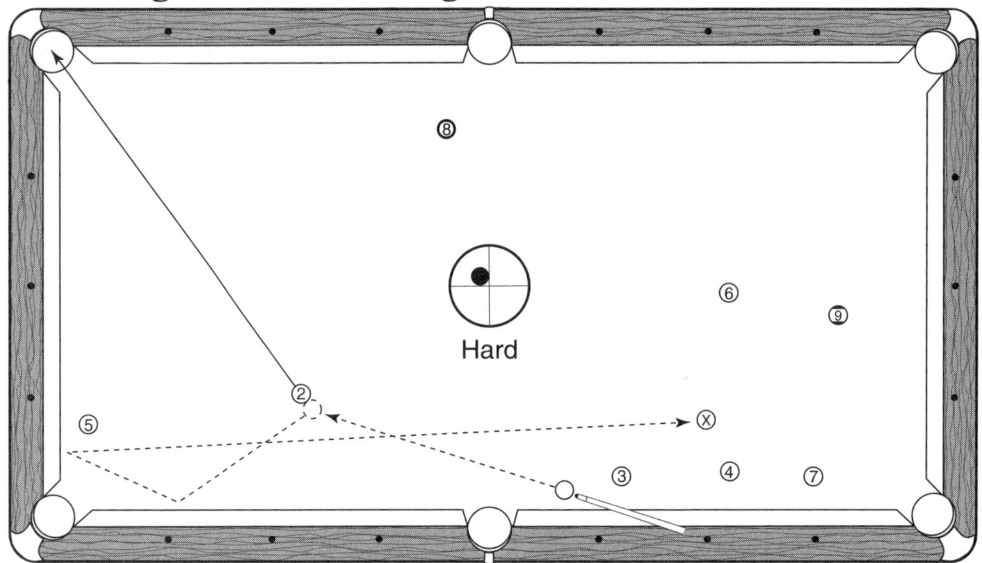

This brilliant position play was executed by Earl Strickland in the 1997 U.S. Open, while on his way to his forth Open title against Efren Reyes. This unusual position play clearly demonstrates the possibilities when you learn to "think out of the box". Outside (left) english is used to reverse the cue ball's path off the second rail.

Across and Down with Inside English (A)

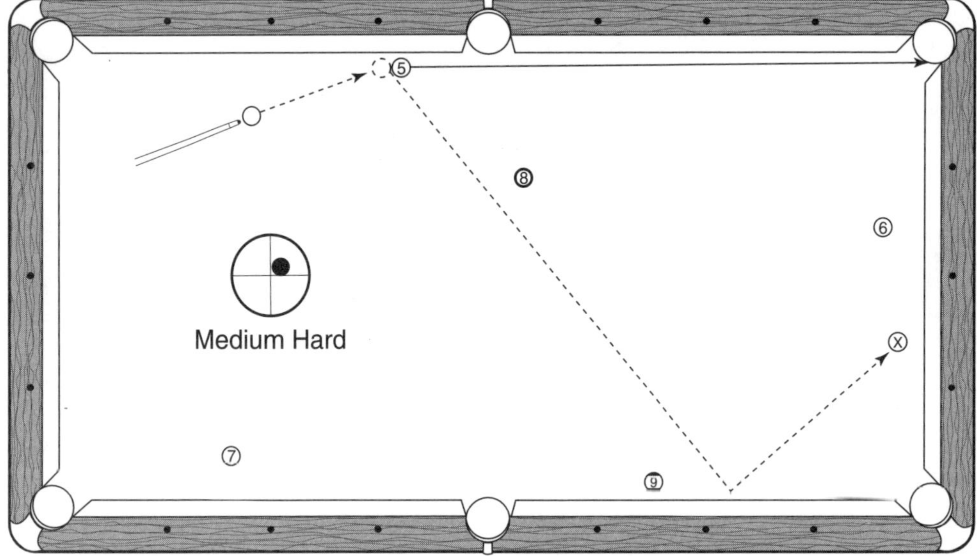

Here's another gem from the talented hands of Earl Strickland that occurred in a match with Buddy Hall at the Sands Regency Open 12, 1990. He routed the cue ball perfectly past both the 8 and 9-balls. Too much spin and the cue ball would have hit the 8-ball. If he had not applied sufficient english, the cue ball could have run into the 9-ball.

Two Rails with Draw (C & B)

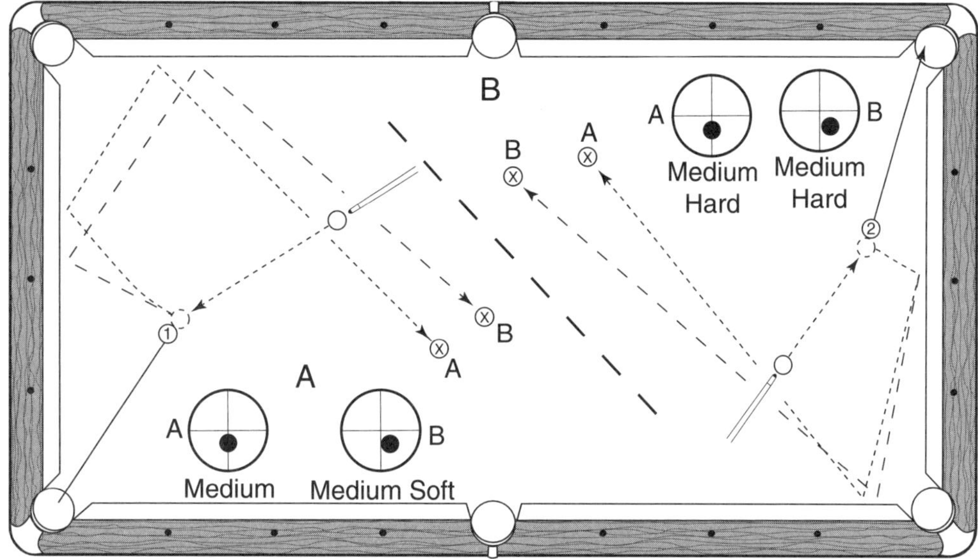

The two-rail draw shot is one of the most commonly played position routes in Nine-Ball, which makes it a must for your arsenal. Part A shows a two rail route off a 30-degree cut shot. Route A (rated C) was played with a medium speed draw stroke without english. A medium soft stroke with outside running english lead to Route B (rated C). Notice that the cue ball ended up in almost the same place using either route, but that it's path was slightly different in each case.

You can change your routes on two-rail position plays to avoid obstacles while sending the cue ball to essentially the same location. You can also fine-tune your routes to play pinpoint position. You may develop a preference for using only draw. Or perhaps you can achieve better speed control by using outside english, which enables you to play this route with a softer stroke.

The two-rail routes in Part A are excellent vehicles for sending the cue ball to the central portion of the table, from which you can play balls in a wide variety of locations. Two-rail draw routes can also be extended to three rail routes which, of course, can enable you to play position on balls at the opposite end of the table. For example, imagine that the cue ball in either Routes A or B had continued to the bottom side rail and out.

Part B gives you a somewhat different version of the two-rail draw shot. This time the cut angle is only 20-degrees and the object ball is much closer to the rail. Now you must use a firmer stroke to bring the cue ball out to the center of the table. Route A (rated B) was played with draw, Route B (rated B) was played using draw and outside english. Notice that the main difference in their paths occurred after the cue ball exited the second rail.

Stun Draw Two Railer (B) (RR)

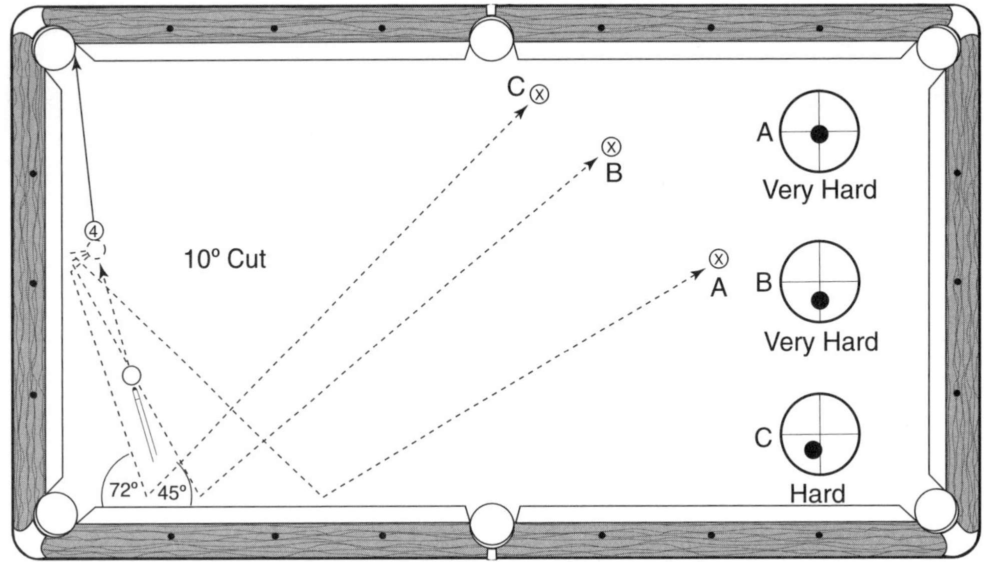

When you have a small angled cut shot, such at the 10-degree cut in the illustration, you can employ one of the recovery routes in the diagram to propel the cue ball far up the table. You can send the cue ball down Route A by using a very hard stroke and a quarter tip of draw. Notice that the cue ball hit the side rail 2.5 diamonds up from the corner pocket.

A stun/draw shot is used to send the cue ball to Position B. Use a very hard stroke and a full tip of draw. Observe how the cue ball struck the side rail much closer to the corner pocket compared to Route A.

Getting the cue ball to Position C requires a hard stun/draw stroke with a half tip of outside english. You must aim this shot with extra care as it is always difficult to use english with the higher speeds of stroke. Be Use a slightly shorter bridge, and make sure your bridge is firm. Notice that the cue ball entered the rail at a 72-degree angle and departed at 45-degrees thanks to the hard hit and the outside english.

Two Rails Across with Draw Outside (B)

Drawing the cue ball across and down the table is seldom easy. The task becomes even more difficult when you must contend with the side pocket. The key is to know when you can draw past the side and when you must play to the near side to be sure of avoiding a scratch.

The object ball's distance from the rail and the cut angle are the major factors in determining how far you can bring the cue ball back down the table. When the object ball is close to the rail and the cut angle is sharp, you are limited to how far you can bring the cue ball down the table.

The 2-ball is a half of a ball's width off the rail in all of the position plays. Position A shows a 20-degree cut shot. A medium hard draw stroke with a half tip of outside english will send the cue ball four diamonds down the table, or well past the side pocket. In sharp contrast,

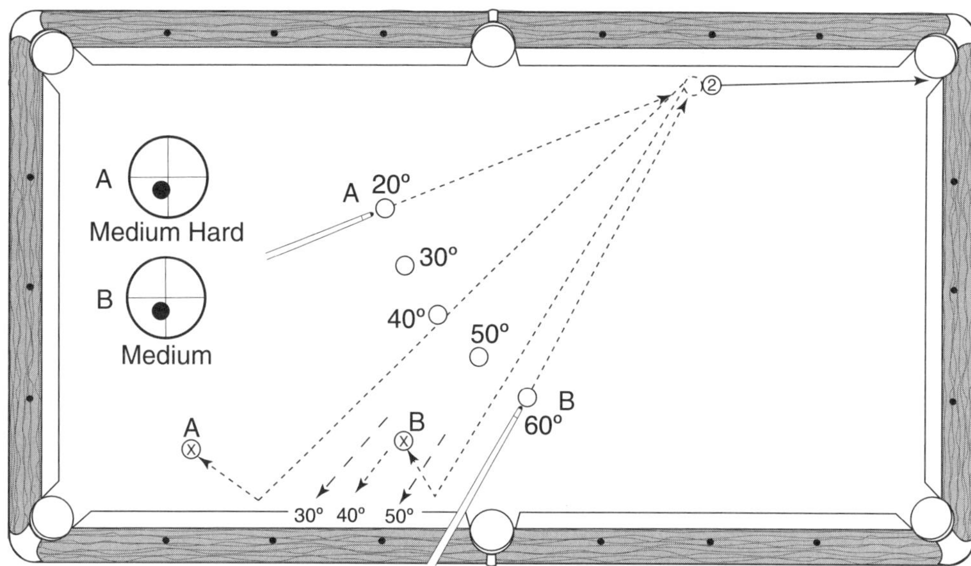

when the cue ball is in Position B, you have a 60-degree cut, which makes it much more difficult to avoid the side pocket. This route is played with low left english and a medium speed stroke. You must really spin the cue ball to get past the side, which means that english (and not draw) is the key to this position play. Practice this shot from all five angles in the diagram and take note of how far you can bring the cue ball down table.all down table.

Stun Across and Down the Table (B)

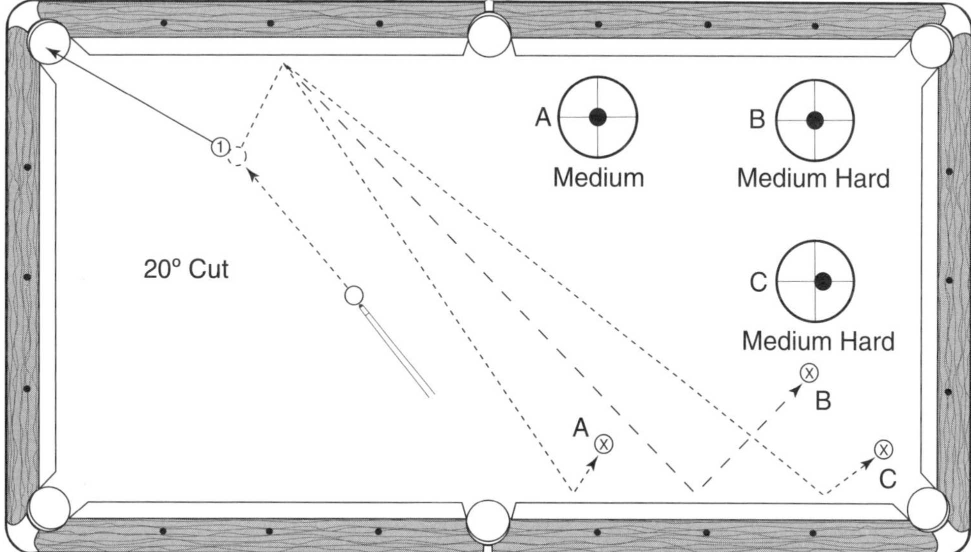

This extremely valuable position play gives you a very effective method for sending the cue ball across and down the table. The key ingredients are: a firm stroke, centerball, and a relatively small cut angle, such as the 20-degree angle shown. The route is created by the predictable path down the tangent line and the running english that comes from contact with the object ball. Route C was created with a half tip of outside english.

Basic Side Pocket Two-Railer (B)

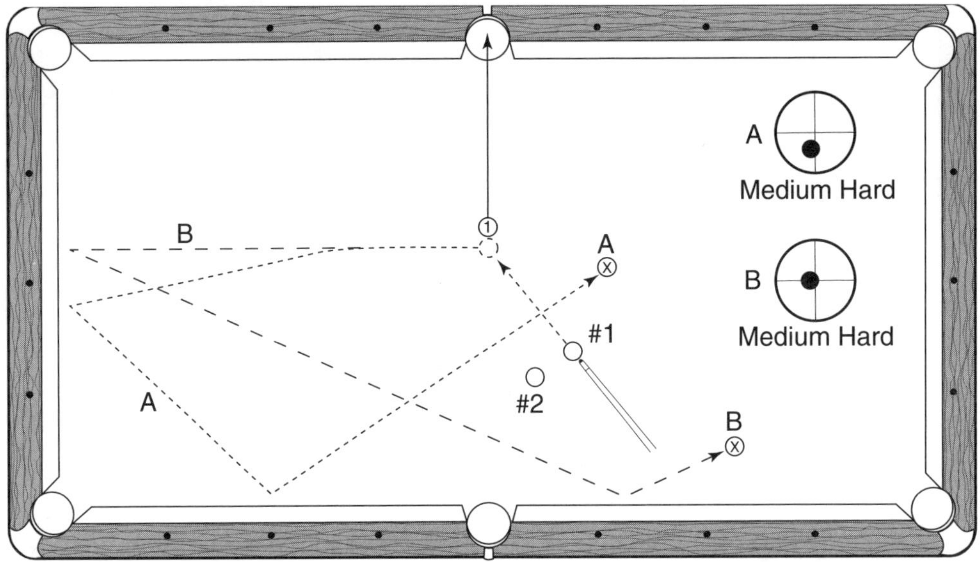

One nice thing about the side pocket routes in this illustration is that the object ball is directly opposite the side pocket, which makes pocketing the ball a cinch. Controlling the cue ball is a whole other matter.

Route A is played with a draw stroke and outside english when the cue ball is Position #1. This position play is not nearly as challenging as it appears since there is no risk of scratching. In addition, it is not difficult to create the route to Position A with a 40-degree cut since the path to the end rail is fairly predictable. Move the cue ball over to Position #2, which is a 20-degree cut, and the draw becomes much less predictable. If you make even a small error, it will be greatly magnified by the time the cue ball reaches the other end of the table. It is even possible to scratch in the lower left corner pocket if you use too much draw! With the cue ball in Position #2, use a quarter tip of draw, and a shorter bridge than normal.

The path to the end rail is very predictable in Route B since the shot is being played on the horizontal axis with outside english. The trick in Route B is to regulate the english so you strike the side rail safely past the side pocket.

Side Pocket Inside English Two-Railers (B)

You can achieve a variety of positional objectives when playing into the side pocket by adjusting your cueing. The illustration at the top of the next page shows two underused, but valuable position plays. In Part A, a medium speed stroke with inside (right) english will send the cue ball to the end rail first, then off the side rail and down table. The key is to play the shot with enough force so that the stun does not convert into follow, which could lead to a scratch. The route in Part B was created by using a medium speed stroke with follow and inside (right) english. The cue ball will strike the side rail first, then the end rail. Notice how the english straightened out the cue ball's rebound angle off the end rail.

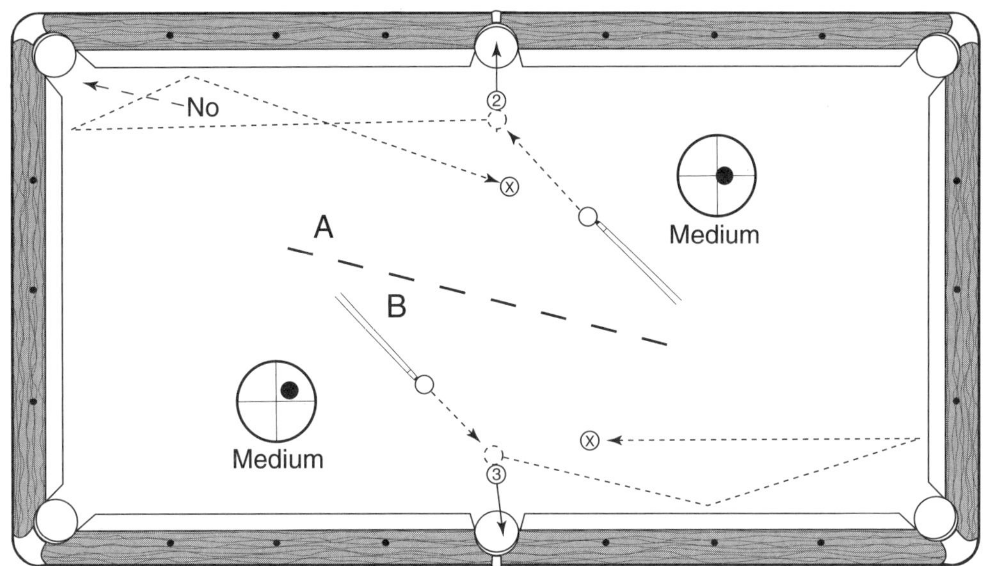

Inside Draw 2 Rails (A)

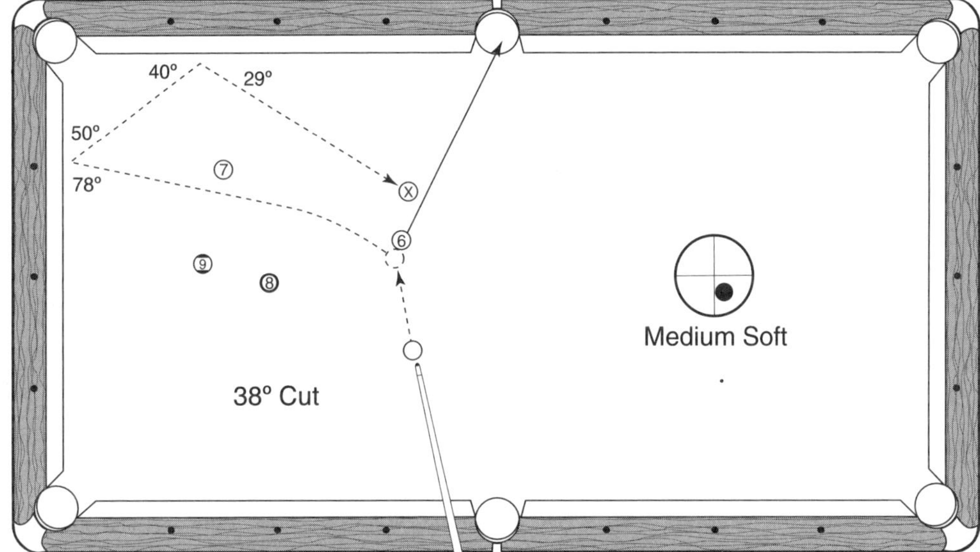

The artistry of Efren Reyes was on full display in the finals of the 1994 U.S. Open in a match with Nick Varner. The Magician was facing a rather awkward situation when he concocted the route in the illustration. A medium soft draw stroke put enough bend on the cue ball to barely avoid running into the 7-ball. If Reyes had hit the shot a tad harder, the draw would not have taken in time and the cue ball would have crashed into the 7-ball. When the cue ball struck the end rail, the inside english took over as it widened the rebound angle by a full 28 degrees (78 in – 50 out). The english off the side rail propelled the cue ball to excellent position on the 7-ball. The lesson: inside draw is a very valuable positional tool that experts use to give an added dimension to their game.

Three-Rail Position Routes

The professionals use three-rail position routes on a little over 5% of their position plays, or about 1 shot in 20. This means you will need to employ one roughly once every 4 games, assuming you shoot about half of the time. While three-rail routes are certainly not the mainstay of a Nine Ball player's game, they do come up often enough that you need to become quite capable of playing the ones we'll cover in this section

Many, but not all three-rail routes, are natural extensions of the one and two-rail routes we've covered earlier. The cue ball will usually be traveling a long distance on three-rail routes, so you should use rail targets whenever possible to help plan your route. In addition, you should guard against scratching, especially when the cue ball is heading towards the second or third rail.

Power Three-Railer (B & A)

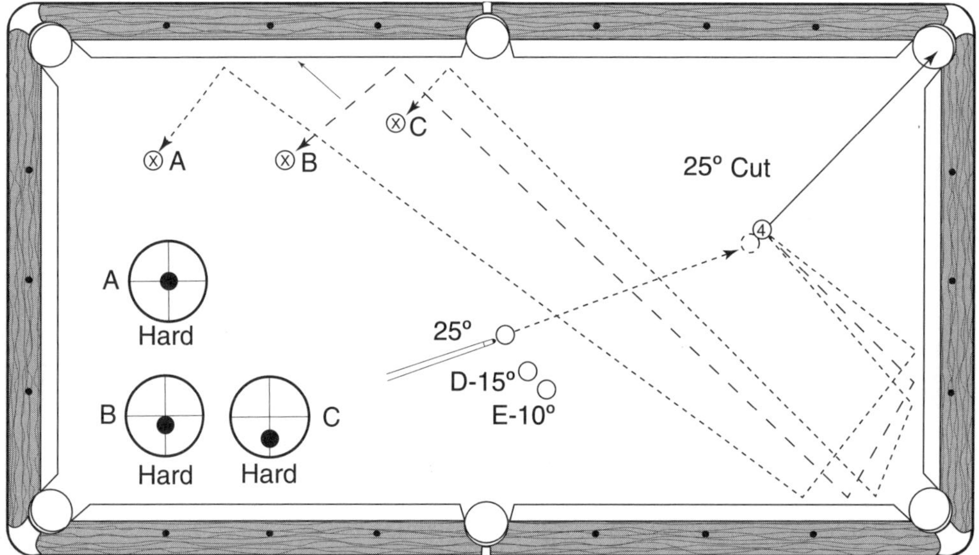

The rather modest 25-degree cut angle fools many players into believing that you can only use a one or two rail position route to get to the opposite end of the table. A dead centerball hit with a hard stroke will send the cue ball down Route A (rated B). Variations of this route with larger cut angles are among the most commonly used three rail routes. You can adjust the contact point on the third rail by applying a half tip of draw and a hard stroke, which will produce Route B (rated B). Cue one full tip below center with a hard stroke produces Route C (rated B).

After practicing the routes above, move the cue ball to Position D. Centerball and a very hard stroke will send the cue ball to the third rail where shown. Now try the shot with the cue ball at Position E, which is only a 10-degree cut! A centerball hit with an extremely hard stroke will send cue ball into the third rail at about the same place as in the previous shot. The routes from Positions D and E are rated A.

Off Side Rail Three-Railer (B)

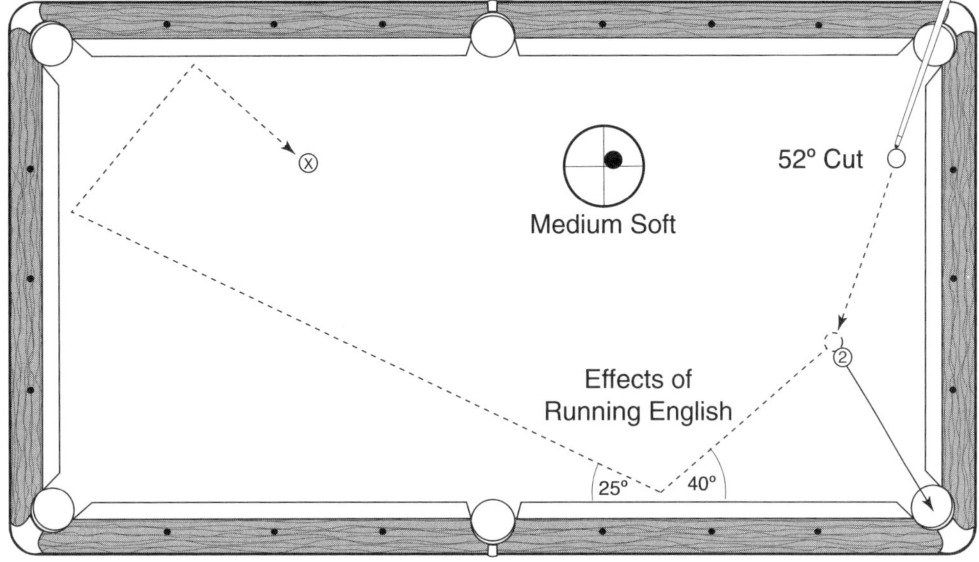

The cue ball will travel a long distance on this shot despite the fact it only takes a medium soft stroke with a half tip of outside english, thanks to the thin 52-degree cut angle. It is somewhat difficult to play pinpoint shape on a route this long, but your efforts are enhanced by the fact that the cue ball will slow down quickly off the last rail.

Three Rails Across (A)

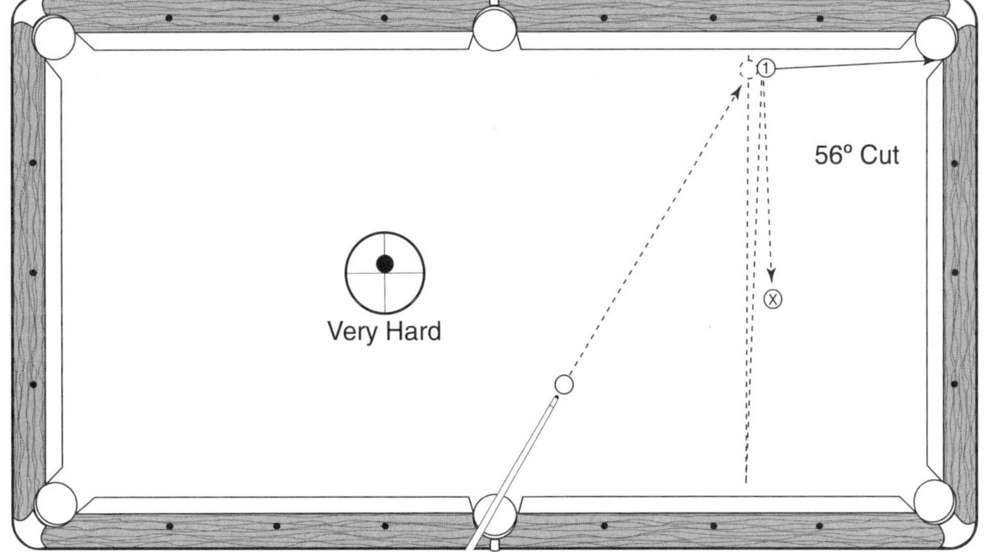

Three rail routes can take you across as well as around the table, as this demanding position play demonstrates. The 56-degree cut requires that you hit the shot with a very hard stroke. Although a high-speed cut shot is never easy, what really makes this shot difficult is estimating where the cue ball will finally come to rest.

Three Rails After a Thin Cut (A)

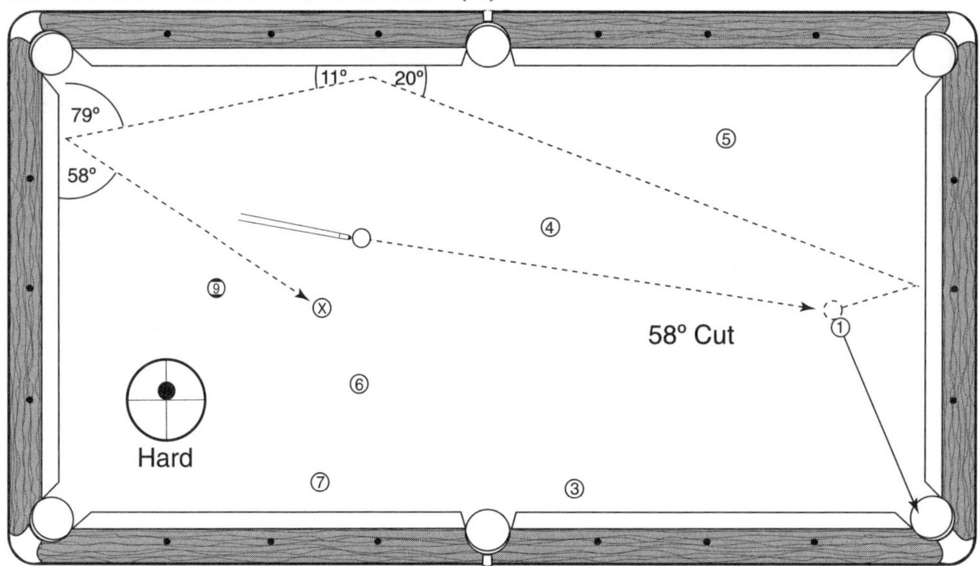

This masterpiece was executed by Mike Sigel against Johnny Archer at the 1993 U.S. Open. The thin 58-degree cut was played with straight follow and a hard stroke. Even though no english was used, plenty was picked up by contact with the rails, as evidenced by the opening of the rebound off the last rail. This A+ rated route required accurate long-range shotmaking with a hard stroke and incredibly precise routing through a mine field.

Power Three Rail Position (A)

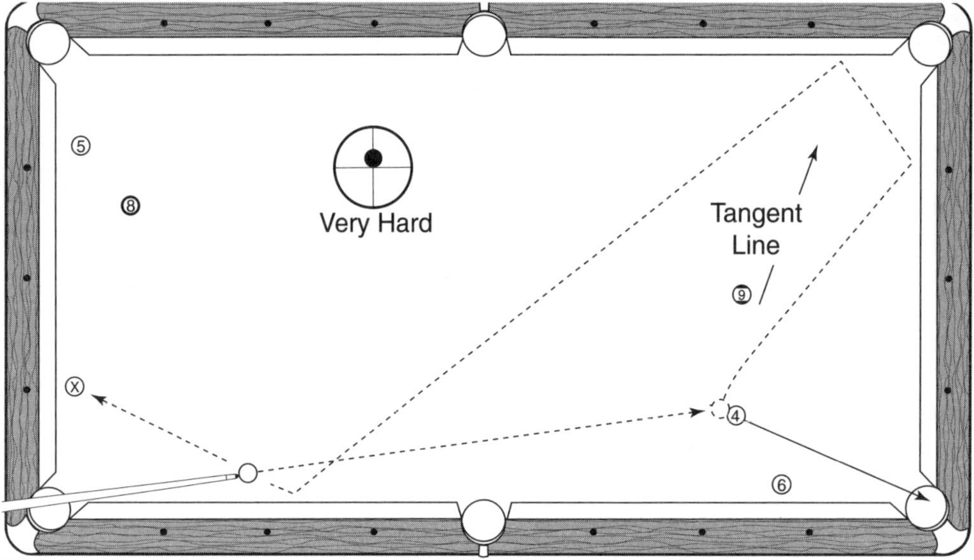

This powerful three-railer was drilled home by Chuck Altomare at the 1999 U.S. Open against Kunihiko Takahashi. When the cue ball is hit hard with follow, and it must travel across the table, is has plenty of time to bend forward to contact with the end rail and avoid a scratch.

Side Pocket Three Railer (C)

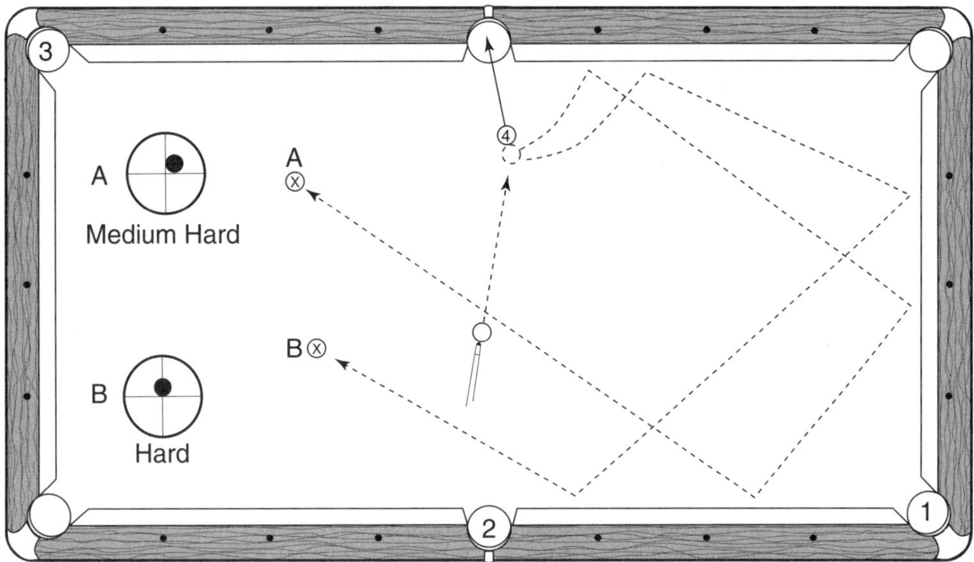

Three-rail side pocket position plays are used frequently as a recovery route when you have missed position and are on the wrong side of the ball. The diagram shows two of many possible fight patterns. The short shot to a big side pocket gives you much flexibility in planning your route. Your main considerations are obstacles in route, and scratching in pockets 1, 2 or 3. The scratch risk depends on the route you have chosen and the position of the balls.

Inside English Side Rail Three Railer (A)

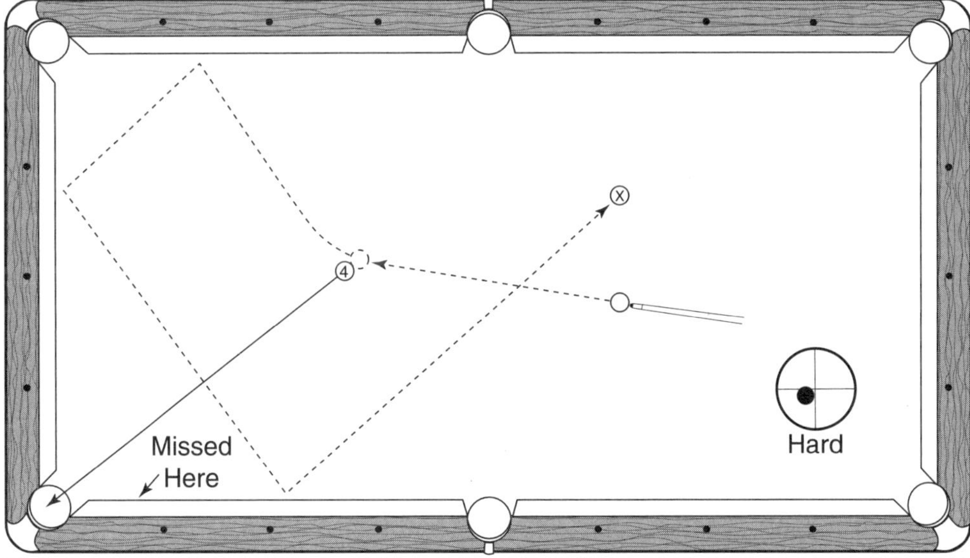

This is a very demanding position play. The shot requires a hard stroke with inside english. The tendency among 99.9% of all players is to overcut the shot, due to deflection. To master this rascal, you must aim for a fuller hit than you may be comfortable doing at first. The big secret is practice.

Inside English Three-Railer (B)

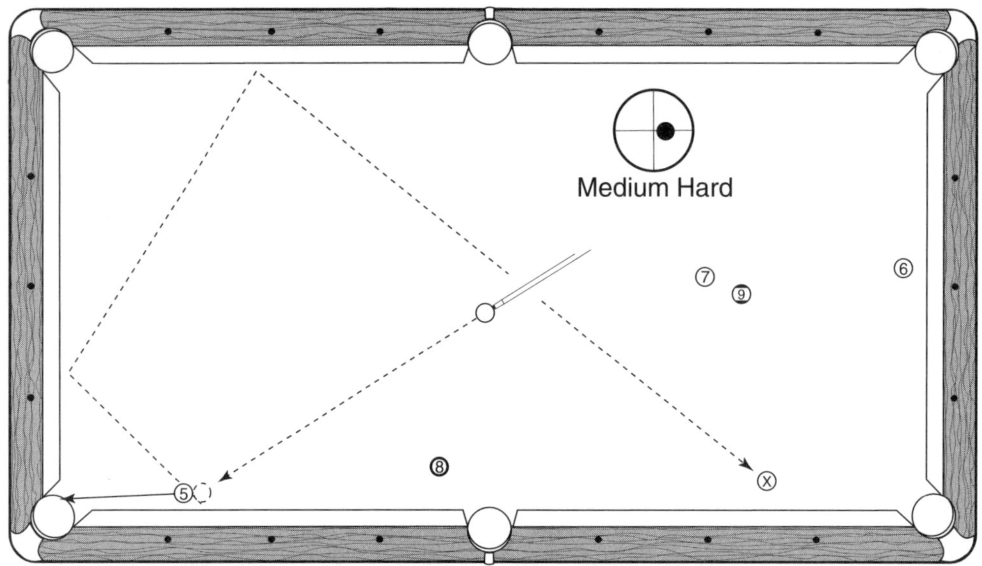

German wizard Ralf Souquet played this challenging three-rail position play against Efren Reyes on his way to capturing the Sands Regency Open 27 in 1998. The shot is played with a medium hard stroke on the center axis with inside english. Again, the main challenge is to allow sufficiently for deflection, which often causes this shot to be overcut.

Inside Draw off the Side Rail (A)

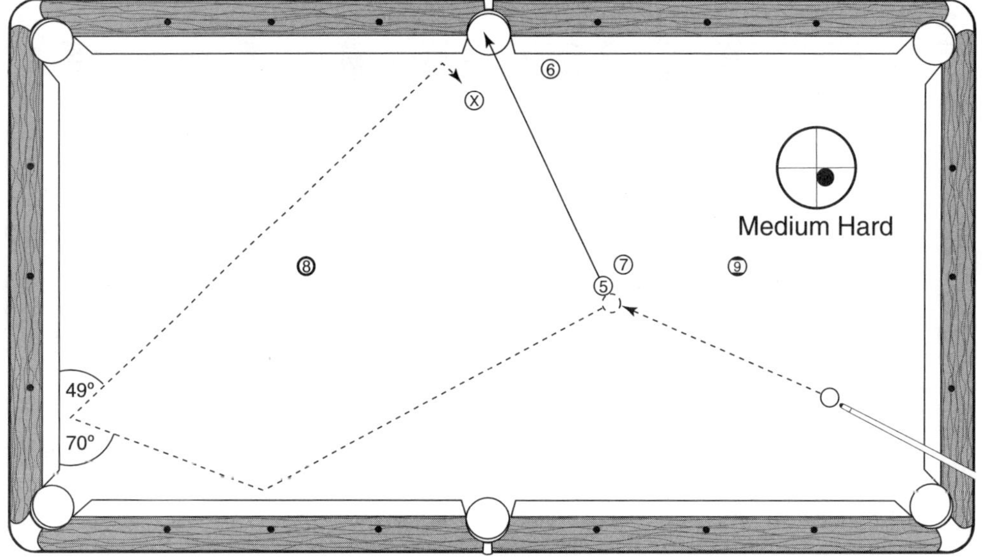

Nick Varner uncorked this gem on Johnny Archer on his way to winning the Sands Regency Open 23, 1996. Draw was used to avoid a corner pocket scratch and so the cue ball would strike far enough up the side rail to avoid the opposite side pocket. The inside english kicked in on the second rail. Varner's perfect execution lead to fine position on the 6-ball.

Cross Table Twice (A)

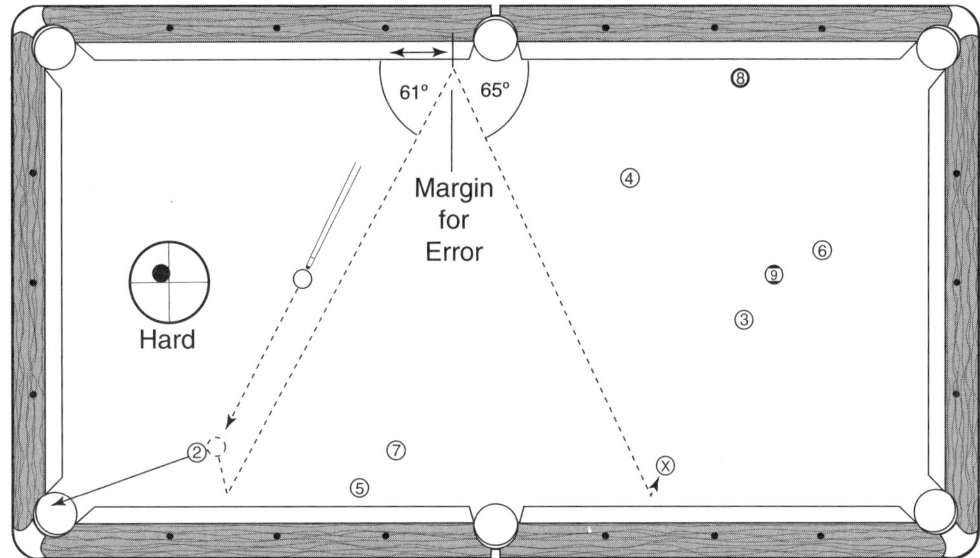

Loree Jon Jones set up a 3-9-ball combination with this twice across and out route against Allison Fisher at the 1999 Prescott Resort Classic. Jones probably came a little closer to the side than she had planned, but with a player of her caliber, this represented her margin for error. A hard stroke with left english opened up the rebound angle off the bottom rail and closed it slightly off the second rail.

Massive Three Rail Draw (A)

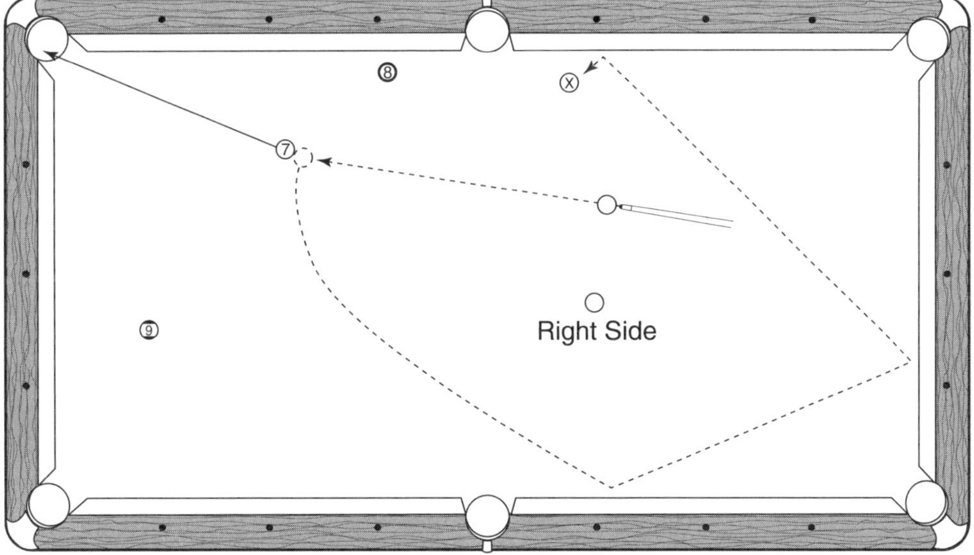

Efren Reyes would no doubt have preferred to have the cue ball on the right side. No problem when you're a Magician! Just cue low and let her go with a massive three-rail position play. Notice the huge arc as the forces of stun and draw battled it out until draw won out. This action took place at the Sands Regency Open 23, 1996, against Johnny Archer.

Four-Rail Position Routes

In the pro game four-rail routes appear once in every 150 position plays (.7% of the time). This means that a four-rail route will only come up about once every 35-40 games, once again assuming you shoot about half of the time. Even though four rail routes are rather uncommon, there is a time and place for everything in pool, so it is necessary to know the routes in this section and others for when they make an appearance.

Four rail position plays are typically very exacting as the cue ball will be traveling a long distance around the table, so you must be very precise in your planning and execution. While I don't recommend that you spend a great deal of time perfecting four rail position plays, you should consider playing the shots in this section a few times each to familiarize yourself with these routes.

Draw Four-Railer (A)

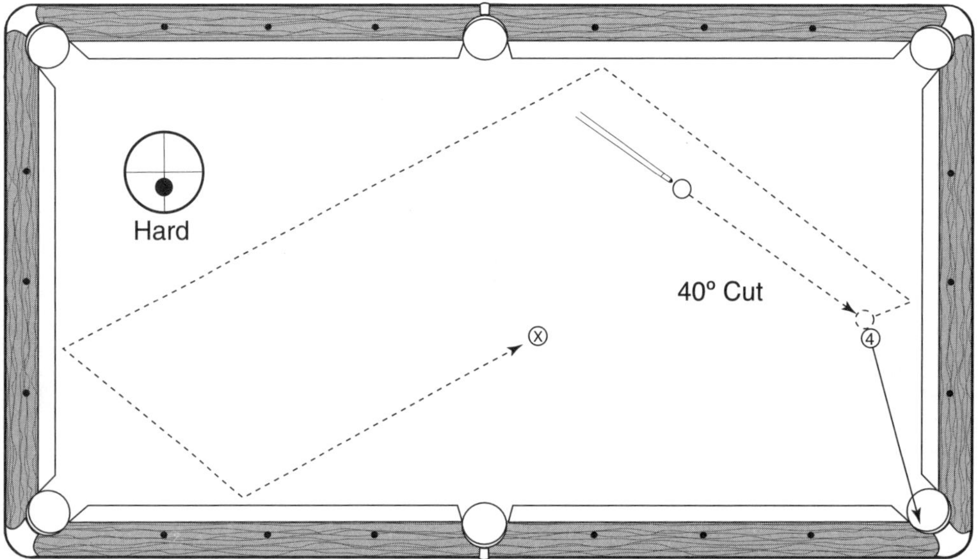

A hard stroke a half tip below center will produce the four-rail route above. The big key is to hit the second rail below the side pocket, thus avoiding a scratch. When plotting your course for a four-rail route, there is very often at least one pocket that presents the risk of a scratch. If you can avoid that pocket, the rest of the route will take care of itself.

Four Rails to the Short Side (A)

Mike Sigel was playing Earl Strickland at the Sands Regency Open 17, 1993 when he came up against this challenging position play on the 4-ball. Four rail routes like this are largely used when you are facing a thin cut that prevents you from playing a more conventional route. If the cue ball were in Position B, Sigel would have perhaps chosen to play a conventional two-rail route to the 6-ball. This could have left him with a shot on the 6-ball from Position B-1.

With the cue ball in Position A, the 67-degree cut angle prevented

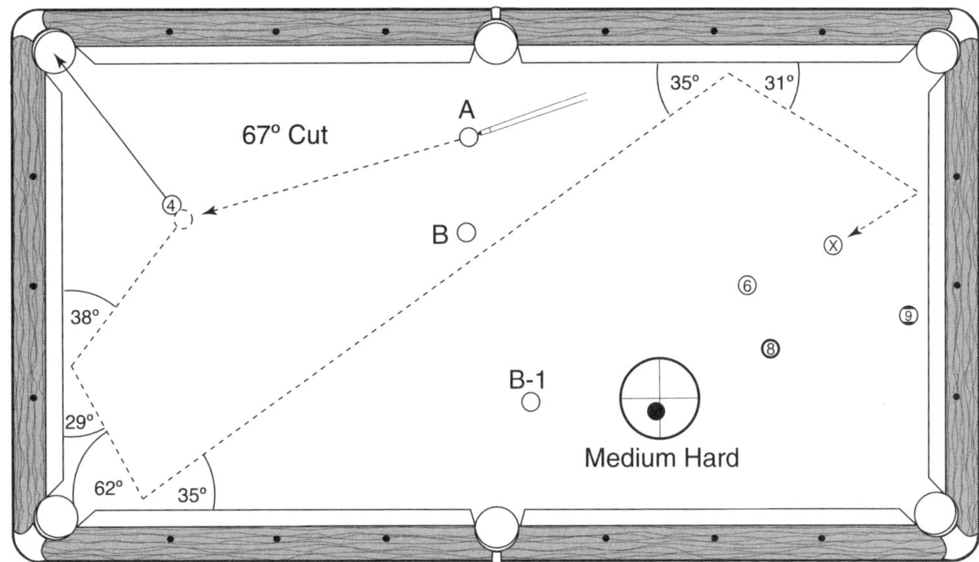

Sigel from playing to Position B-1. He chose to play to the short side of the 6-ball via the precise and imaginative route shown in the diagram. The shot was played with draw and a half tip of outside english. The running english opened the rebound angle considerably off the second rail and accelerated the cue ball down table. Even though the cue ball traveled over 13' to its final destination at Position X, this shot was all about precision, not power.

Inside English Four Rails to the Short Side (A)

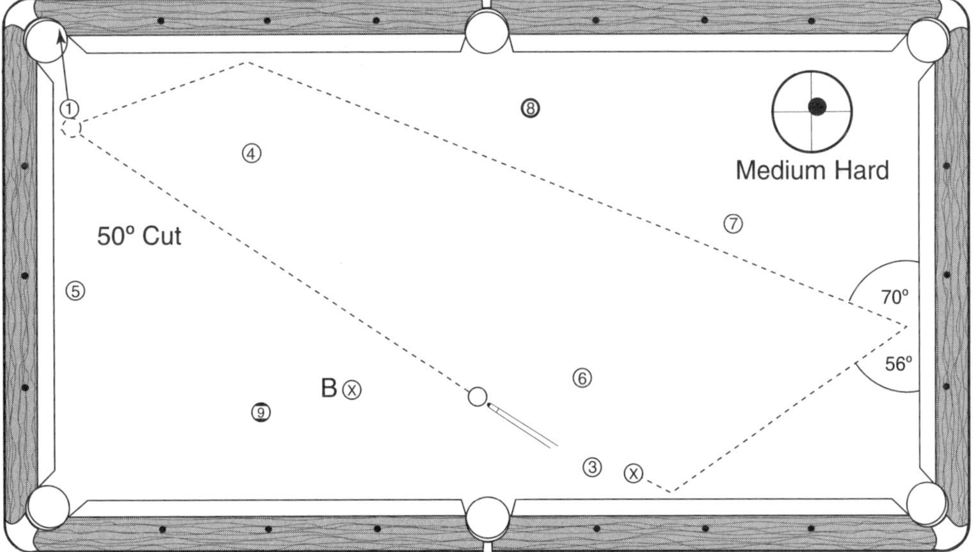

Earl Strickland used high inside english and a medium hard stroke in playing this creative four-railer against Efren Reyes at the Sand Regency Open 21, 1995. The english really took off the third rail as the cue ball was losing speed. The long distance and the thin cut on the 1-ball kept him from playing a more conventional route to the long side at Position B.

Four Rails with Inside Spin (2) (A)

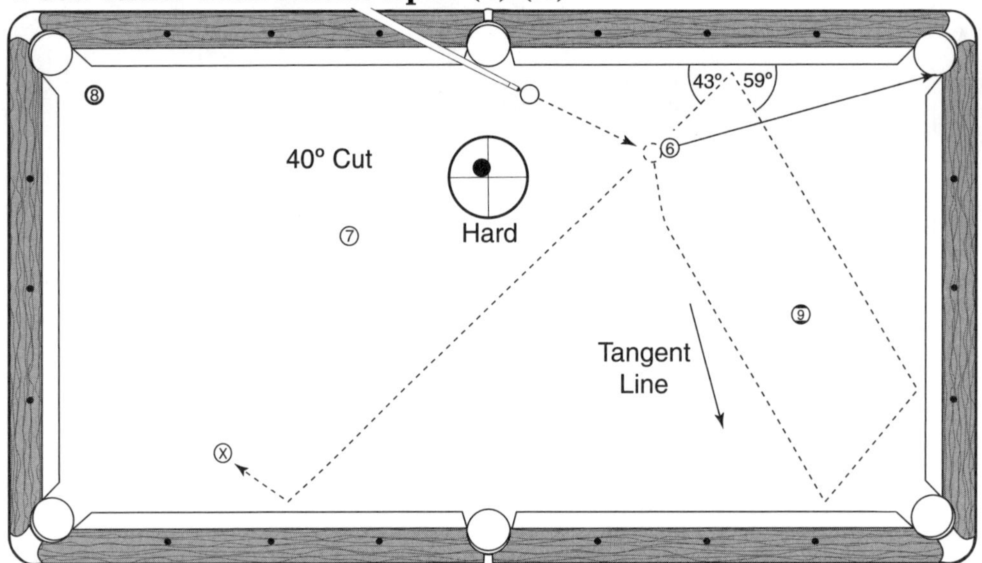

Allison Fisher masterminded this beautiful four-railer in a match against Loree Jon Jones at the 1999 Prescott Resort Classic. The shot was played with a hard stroke and high left english. The follow turned the cue ball towards a lower hit on the bottom rail while the inside running english shot the cue ball down table off the third rail.

Long Distance Four-Railer (A)

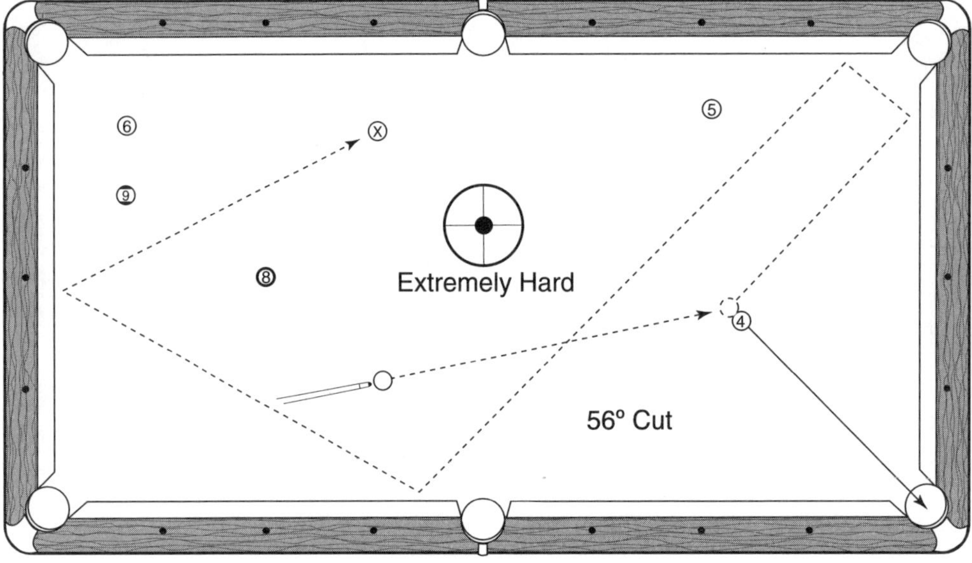

Cory Deuel showed exceptional planning and skill in executing this powerhouse four-railer against Fong-Pang Chao at the 1999 World 9-Ball Championships. The cue ball traveled over 16' while narrowly avoiding two pockets. The shot was played with an extremely hard stroke, which enabled the cue ball to bounce so far out off the fourth rail.

Follow/Pound Around the Table (A)

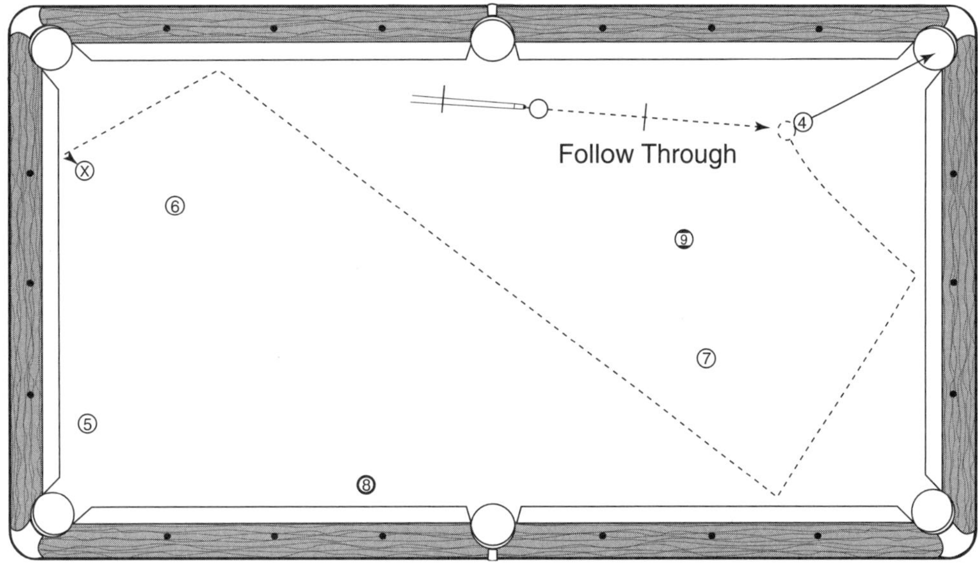

Rodney Morris employed a 10" bridge and a 13" follow through in powering the cue ball four-rails for position on the 5-ball. The cue ball was never in danger of scratching as it struck the third rail in the ideal position, 1 2/3 diamonds up from the corner pocket. This shot took place in the finals of the 1996 U.S. Open against Efren Reyes.

Thin Cut Four Rail Route (A)

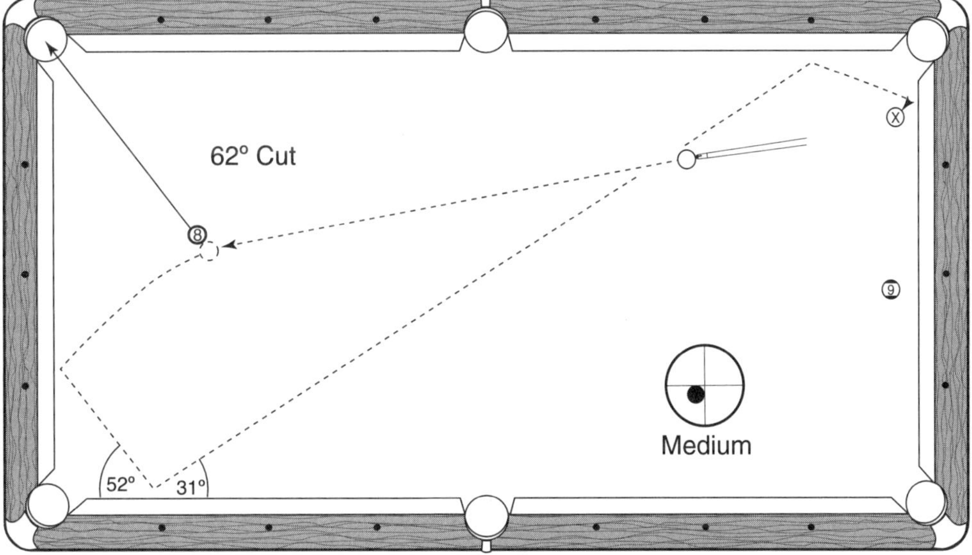

The cut angle to pocket #1 was 62-degrees while the cut angle to pocket #2 was 55-degrees. Nevertheless, it is sometimes better to play a thinner cut to control the cue ball as Steve Mizerak demonstrated with this four-rail position play at the 1994 U.S. Open against Earl Strickland.

Position off of Bank Shots

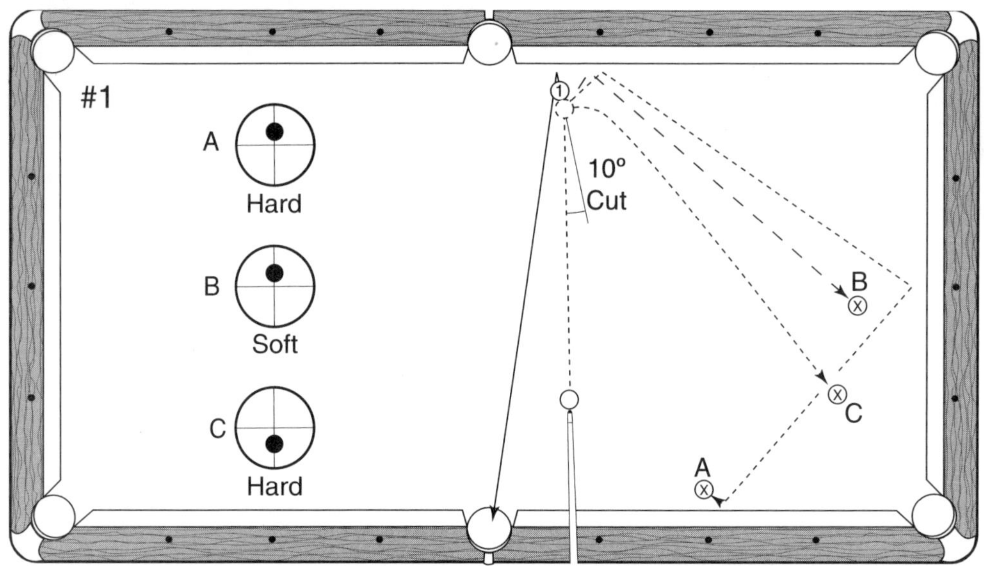

Most of the banks you'll normally play in Nine-Ball are the easy ones. You should assume you're going to make the ball and plan carefully for position. Diagram #1 shows three of the many ways you can play shape on this routine crosside bank. A hard follow stroke will send the cue ball three rails to Position A. A soft follow stroke will send the cue ball to Position B, giving you shape for a ball on the end rail. You can also get to the end rail by using a hard draw stroke to send the cue ball to Position C.

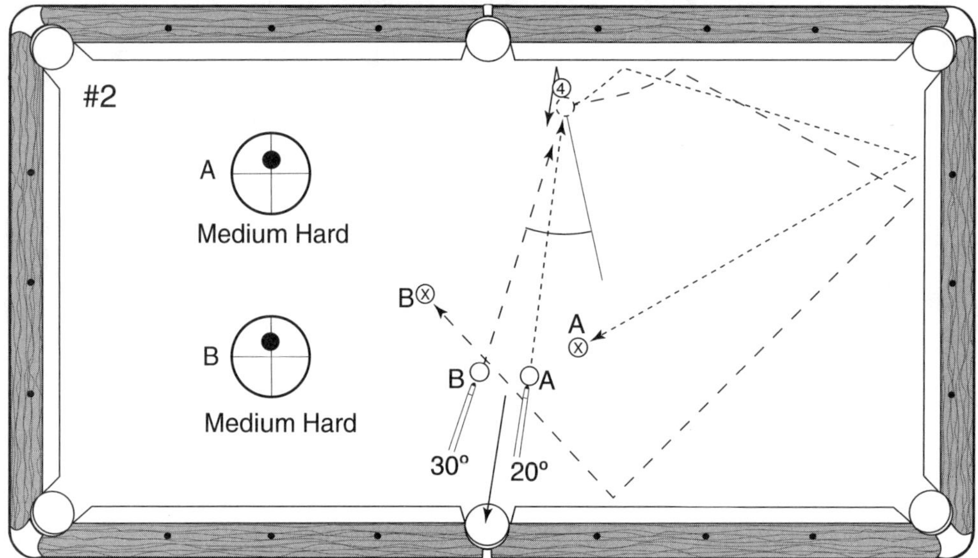

Diagram #2 demonstrates two routes for banks with thinner cut angles. A medium hard follow stroke will send the cue ball to Position A. When the cue ball is at B, which is a 30-degree cut, the cue ball will run to Position B when hit with a medium hard follow stroke.

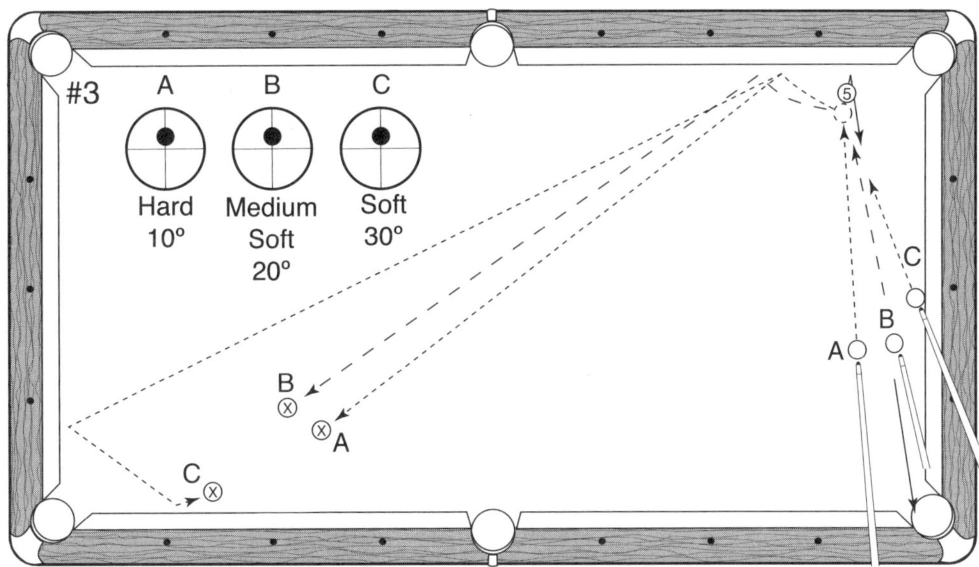

You must be prepared for the cue ball to travel well up the table when you are playing a backcut bank into the corner, as shown by diagram #3. Notice that the cue ball ended up in about the same location on all three shots which were played from varying cut angles. Each, however, was hit at a different speed.

Long Rail Bank Routes

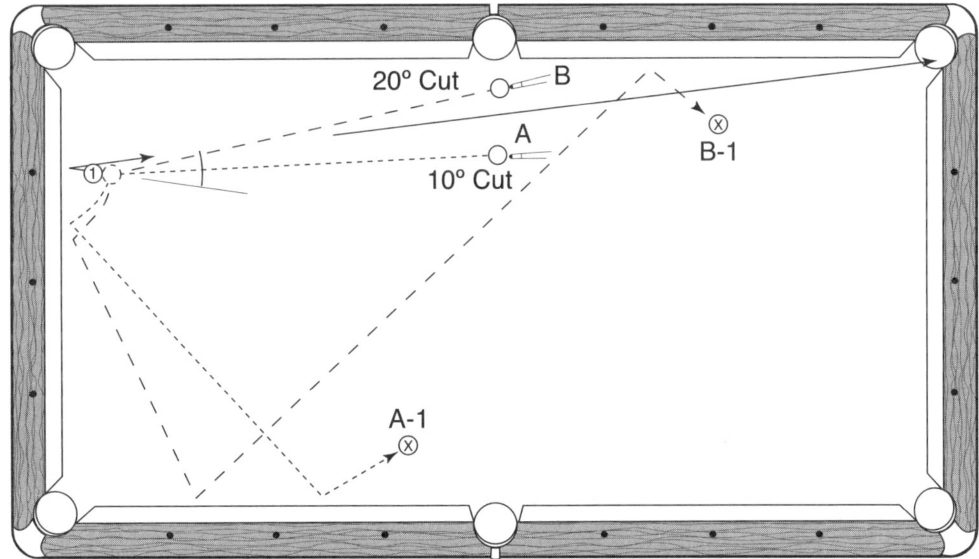

The long rail banks that are normally played in Nine-Ball have very small cut angles, typically no more than 20-degrees. The cut angle is only 10-degrees with the cue ball in Position A. It takes a hard stroke just to advance the cue ball to A-1. The cut angle is 20-degrees in Position B. Now you can send whitey to B-1 with a hard follow stroke.

Crossover Side Pocket Bank

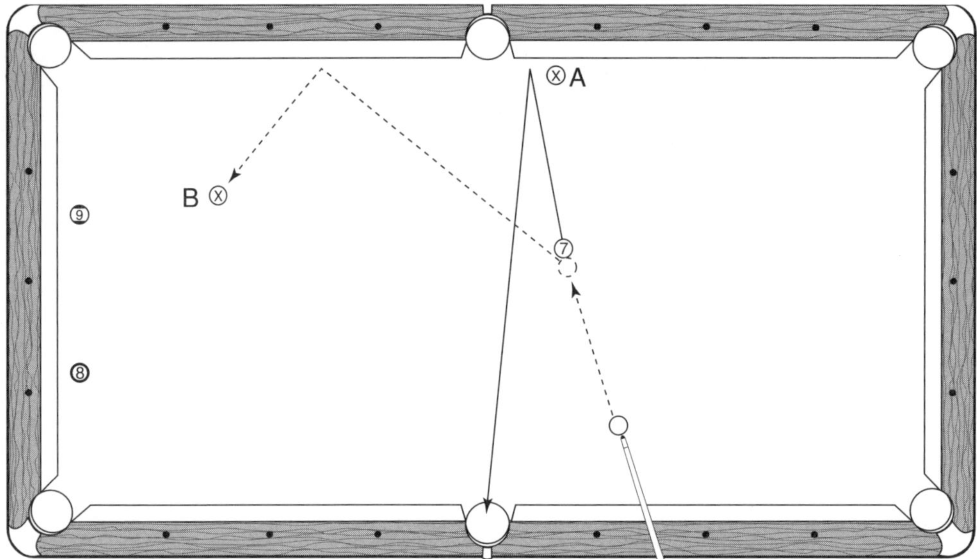

You could play a soft follow shot to Position A for the 8-ball. But then you would have to send the cue ball to the distant end rail and back for position on the 9-ball. A better choice is to play the simple crossover bank in the illustration The cue ball will end up at Position B, allowing you to play shape on the 9-ball with a soft follow shot.

Intentionally Banking for Shape

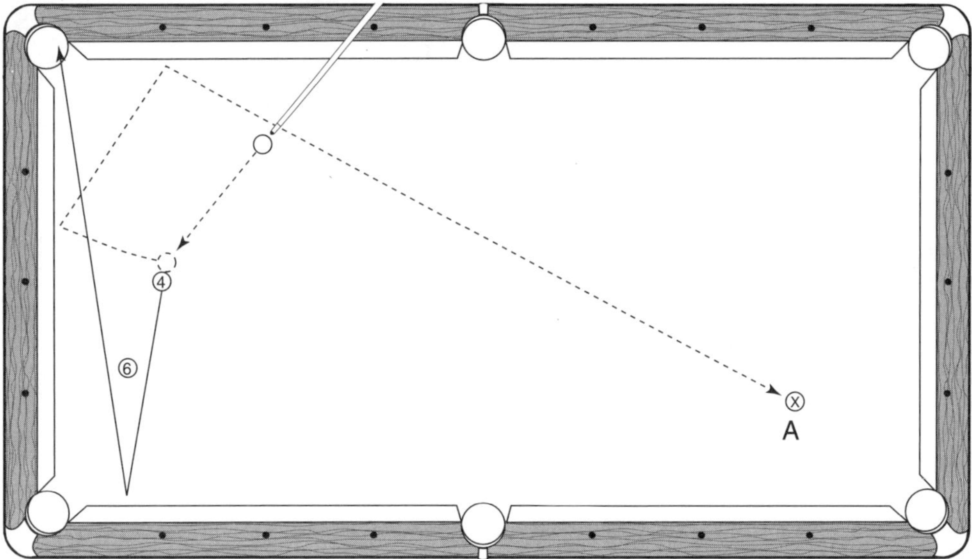

The 6-ball is blocking the pocket, but you can still send the cue ball to the opposite end to Position A by intentionally banking the 4-ball cross corner. This increases the cue angle to 30-degrees, which adds tremendous speed to the cue ball. Play this shot only when you are feeling confident in your banking or you need to make something happen.

Around the Table Bank Shape

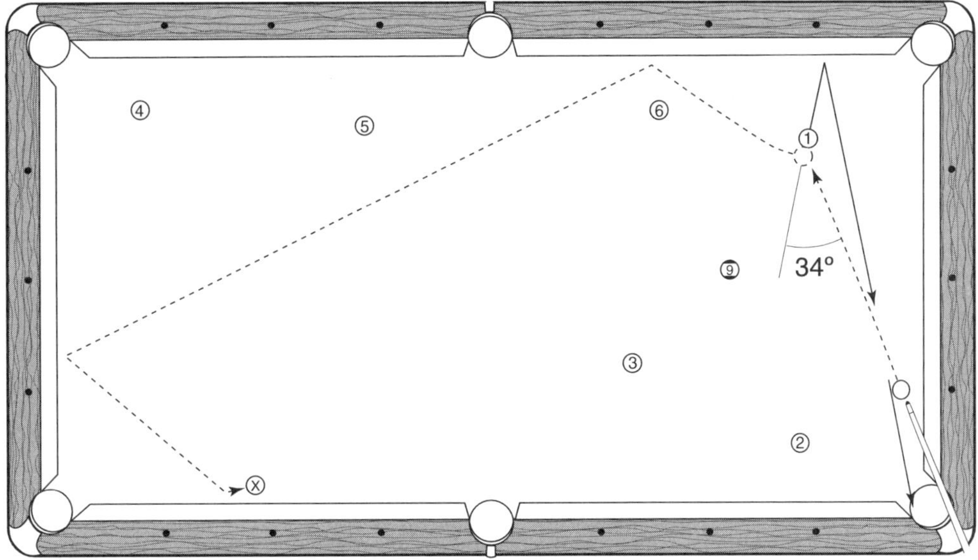

Mike Sigel sent the cue ball three rails for position on the 2-ball following this difficult cross corner bank shot. While the cut angle on the bank was a healthy 34-degrees, the thin cut enabled Sigel to send the cue ball a long distance with only a medium soft stroke. This shot took place at the 1990 U.S. Open against Nick Varner.

Draw to Rail and Out off a Cut Bank

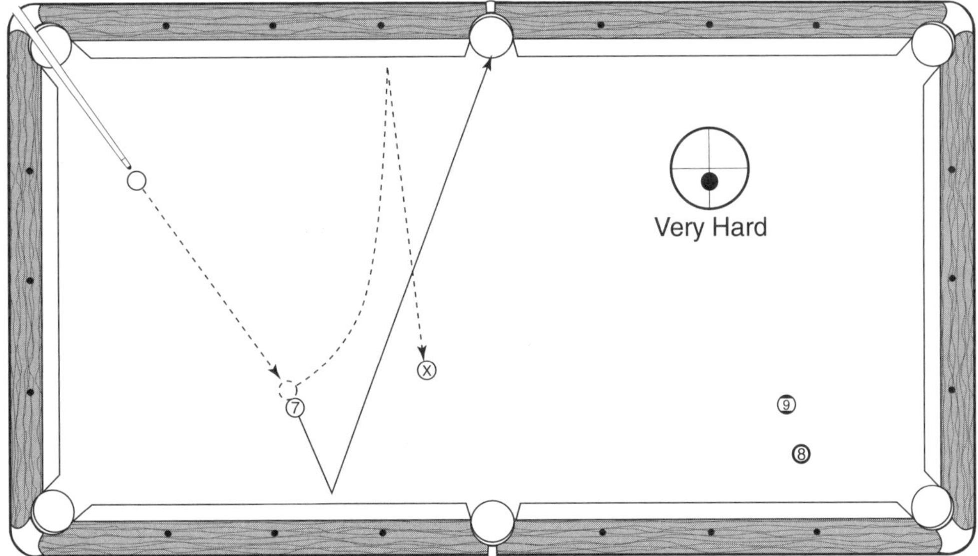

Earl Strickland hammered home this cross side bank on 7-ball while drawing to the top side rail and back across the table for position in the 8-ball against Takeshi Okumura at the 2000 U.S. Open. He used a very hard draw stroke, which bent the cue ball away from the side pocket and gave it enough steam to bounce back across the table.

Draw for Shape off the End Rail

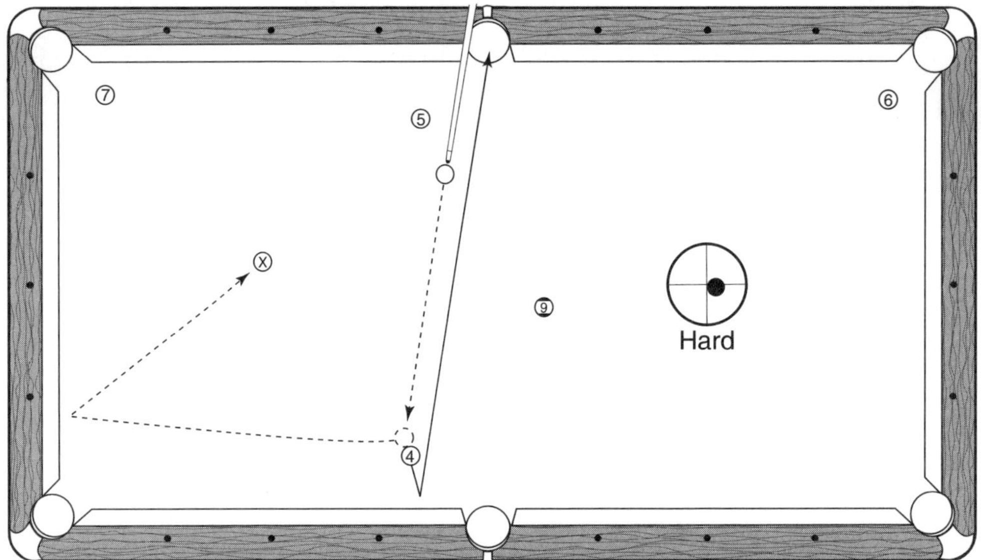

Jeremy Jones could have cut the 4-ball into the near side pocket but he might have overrun the position zone on the 5-ball. He instead chose to bank the 4-ball, which enabled him to maintain better control of the cue ball. The shot was played with a hard stroke just a hair below center with outside english. The shot occurred in the finals of the1999 U.S. Open against Johnny Archer.

Bank and Go Three Rails

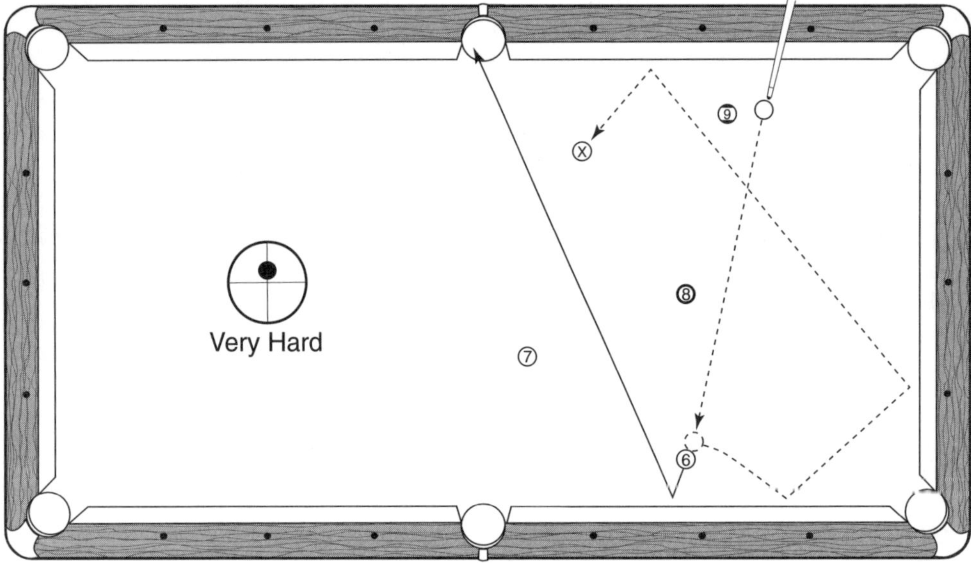

Even though a safety was readily available, Efren Reyes chose to slam home this cross side bank and send the cue ball three rails for shape on the 7-ball. Sometimes an aggressive shot like this can loosen you up and build momentum. This shot was played at the Sands Regency Open 23, 1996, in a match against Johnny Archer.

Position Play Errors

Nine-Ball is unlike other games where you could be playing position on any of several balls at the same time. Because you are playing shape on one specific ball, Nine Ball really illuminates your mistakes. You either get position on the next ball or you don't. Since your mistakes are so obvious, you should have a clear indication of the position plays that need work. For example, if you overrun your position zones, you must quell your urge to use an excessively forceful stroke.

Why Errors Happen

Poor Execution

You planned the right shot, but executed it poorly. This happens because:

- Your execution skills are deficient.
- You don't know where to hit the cue ball or the correct speed for the particular shot.

Poor Planning

You select the wrong routes. The sad part here is that your execution could be perfect, but you still end up with a poor result. Worse yet is the mistake of taking little if any time to plan properly for position. Planning errors happen because:

- You do not yet know the correct route for the particular shot.
- You know where you want the cue ball, but you don't know the route required to get it there.
- You know where you want the cue ball and the route it must take, but you didn't figure out the cueing and speed for the shot.

Poor Planning and Poor Execution

The worst of all worlds is when you combine poor planning with poor execution. Strangely enough, however, you may sometimes luck out by planning the wrong shot, executing it poorly, and yet winding up with the position you would have gotten with proper planning and execution! Don't count on accidents like this happening too often.

Poor Planning and Poor Execution

The worst of all worlds is when you combine poor planning with poor execution. Strangely enough, however, you may sometimes you luck out by planning the wrong shot, executing it poorly, and yet you wind up with the position you would have gotten with proper planning and execution! Don't count on accidents like this happening too often.

The Corrective Cycle

It is crucial for you to learn from your mistakes in order to play consistent run out Nine-Ball. You can correct errors by simply following these simple steps:

1 **Recognize the mistake**. This is no place for denial or lack of attention.

2 **Adjust how you play the shot**. Adjust your cueing and/or routing.

3 **Learn the shot, and commit it to memory**. Practice the shot until you own it.

4 **Play the shot correctly from now on**. Have the confidence to play the shot correctly when it comes up in competition.

Specific Error Tendencies

There are certain shots on which almost all players tend to make the same errors. These are position plays where it is difficult to compensate sufficiently, on a consistent basis, for the predominant error factor that is built into the shot. One example would be coming up short of the position zone when using inside english to reverse the direction of the cue ball. Player's at all levels also have their individual list of position plays that give them the most trouble.

Error tendencies on specific position plays occur because:

- You don't really know the shot or you are unable to execute the shot consistently, even though you know what you want to do.
- The shot encourages errors, by almost all Nine-Ball players, because of the degree of difficulty in the shot.
- Errors occur because there is something troublesome about the shot even though it does not appear too difficult.

General Error Tendencies

These are errors are typically made on a variety of position plays. These would include the tendency too:

Repeatedly overshoot position. This could be a result of a tendency to stroke excessively hard and/or a tendency to play position on shots with excessively thin cut angles.

Repeatedly come up short of the position zone. This could happen because your angles may be too shallow, or because you are stroking too timidly.

Shots with High Error Potential

Some position plays are simply riskier than others. When planning some shots, you must take into account several possible things that could go wrong. The shot at the top of the next page is loaded with danger. Position A is ideal, but to send the cue ball there you must flirt with a side pocket scratch (B). If the cue ball stops near the rail, you could be jacked up over the 8-ball (C). Should you use too much left english, you could get hooked behind the 8-ball (D). Another mistake would be to run into the 9-ball (E). And finally, you could wind up with the 9-ball in your way if you came up short at Position F and had to cross the table and back for the 8-ball.

This example may seem a little extreme, but you will face even more demanding position plays in Nine Ball that will require you to take all of the necessary precautions in order to avoid a needless mistake.

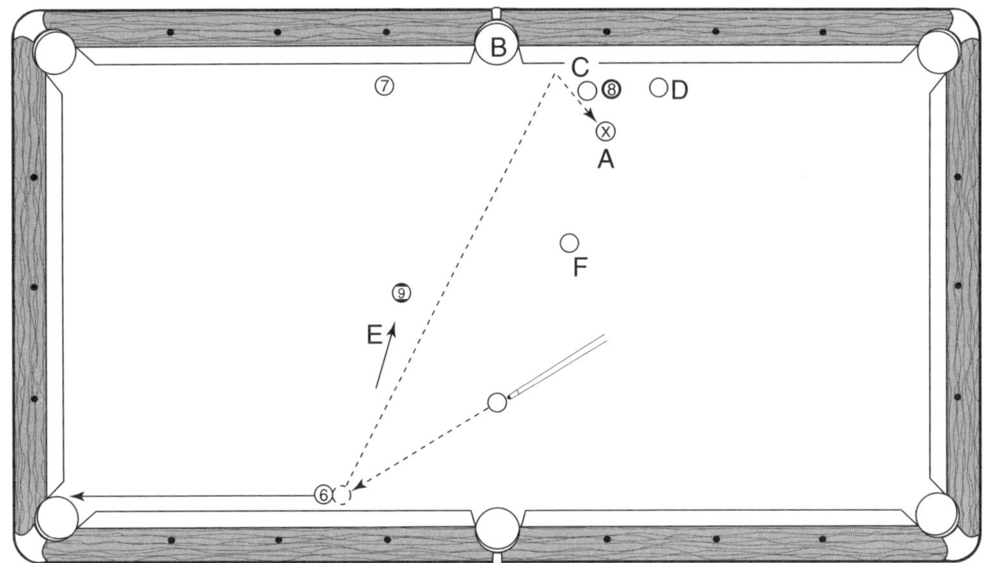

Landing Behind the Big Ball

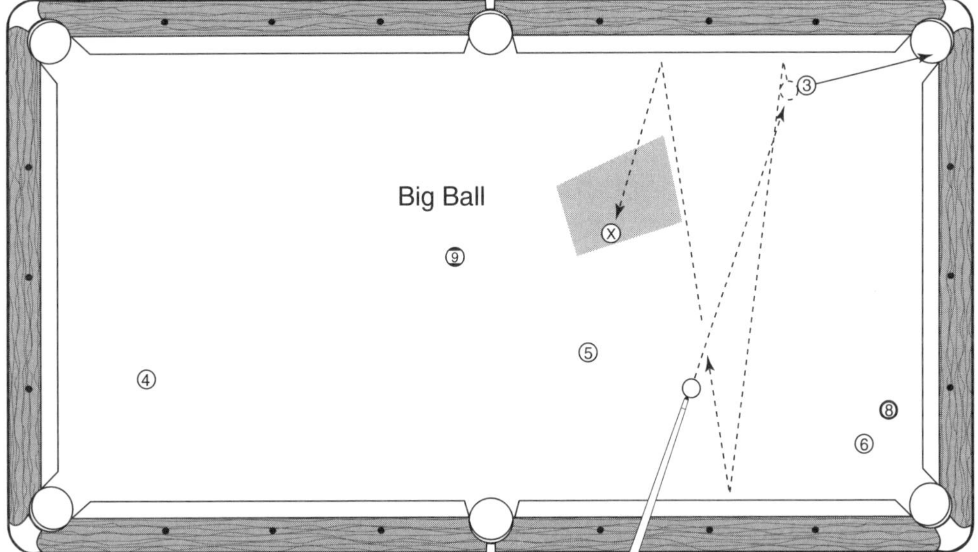

A solitary ball stationed in the middle of the table can wreck havoc with your position. Speed control is not easy when you are crossing the table over two times. When you combine this with the large 9-ball which is blocking 9" of the table, you have the makings for a positional disaster. When you are faced with a situation like this, try to overplay the shot to either side of the potential obstructer.

Other Instances When a Hook Is Likely

- You run into a ball and then get stuck behind it.
- Obstructers near your position zone cause you to play safe on yourself.
- You make a ball in the wrong side of the pocket, which changes the cue ball's path, creating a hook.

Undercutting for Position

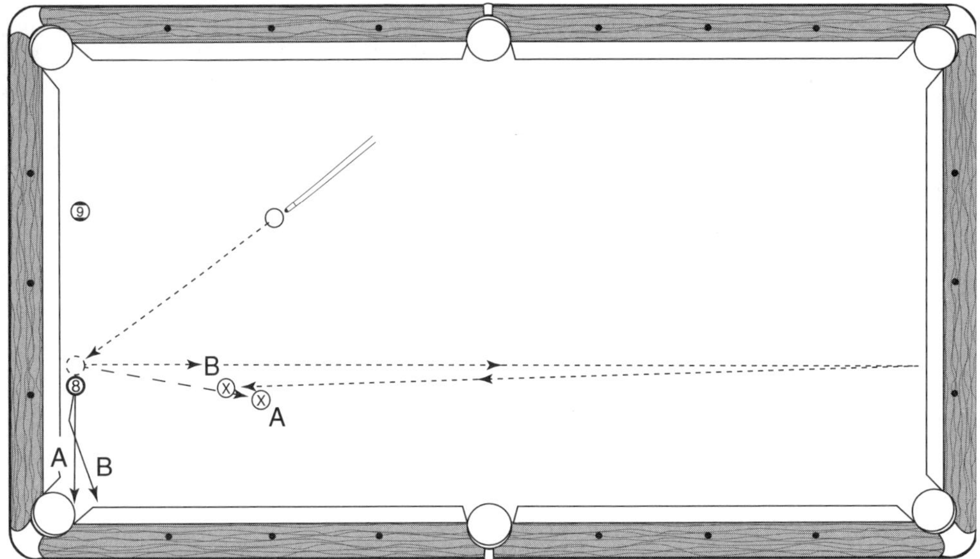

When you have a thin cut angle and you need to minimize the cue ball's rolling distance after contact with the rail, there is a tendency to undercut the shot for position. The illustration shows a 50-degree cut angle. If you miss the shot by undercutting the shot the cue ball will stop at Position A, which is great shape for the 9-ball except that you will be sitting in your chair. Often you will hear a player who has missed exclaim, "at least I got my shape". The truth is that they probably wouldn't have gotten anywhere close to the same position if they had made the ball. Shape and position are linked together, so don't make the mistake of thinking you "at least played shape" when you miss. The correct play is to send the cue ball to the opposite end rail and back to Position A.

Overcutting for Position

The opposite mistake of the one discussed above is to overcut a shot for position. This is done to create additional speed when you have left yourself an overly shallow cut angel.

Hitting Another Ball

The diagram shows two of the biggest positional errors, each of which involves running into the next ball. In Part A, the cue ball clipped the 8-ball after bouncing off the side rail, which turned a fairly easy cut shot into a razor thin slice. The solution to this mistake is to allow for a sufficiently wide margin for error when passing by the next ball, or to play for the next shot in a different pocket if possible.

The blunder in Part B is far worse because the cue ball is frozen against the 8-ball. When this happens you sometimes get lucky as the balls may be lined up towards a pocket. But 9 times out of 10 you will have to play safe. You can prevent errors such as this by having a definite plan for position (as opposed to playing random shape) and by playing area shape well back from the ball.

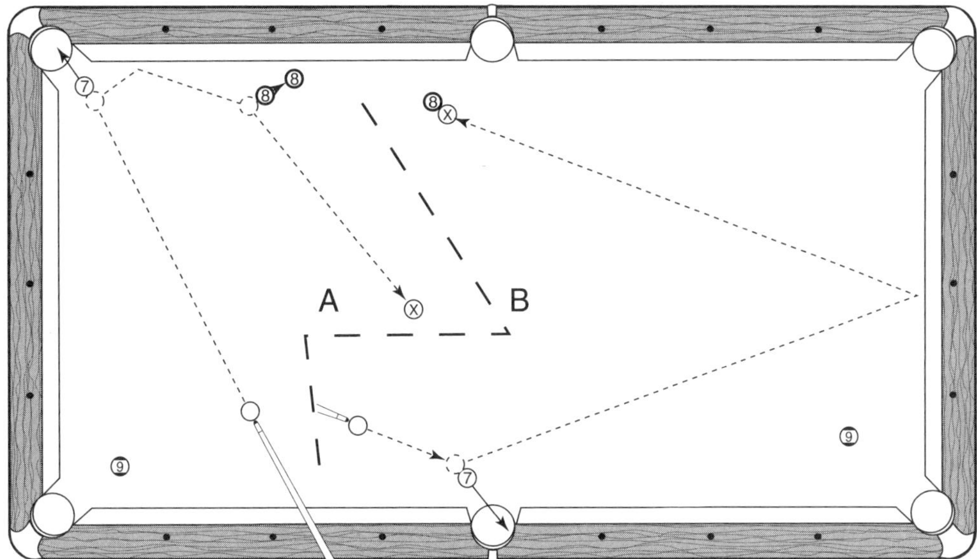

Choosing the Wrong Route

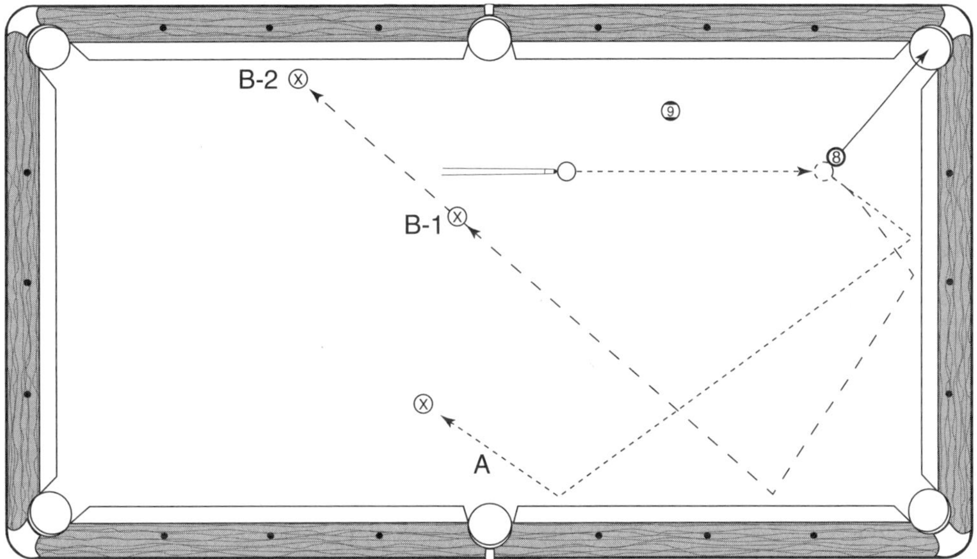

Either lack of knowledge or poor execution could be the reason for the cue ball winding up at Position A, which results in a missable cut on the 9-ball. The correct route will take the cue ball to anywhere between B-1 and B-2. The player could have intended to send the cue ball down Route B, but failed to apply the necessary draw. A less experienced player might have executed their chosen route correctly, but made the mistake of playing Route A.

Some Other Routing Mistakes

- The cue ball has a tendency to die off the last rail on several multi-rail routes, which can keep it from reaching the position zone.
- When you are playing to the short side you must guard against coming up with an overly steep cut angle.

Speed Control

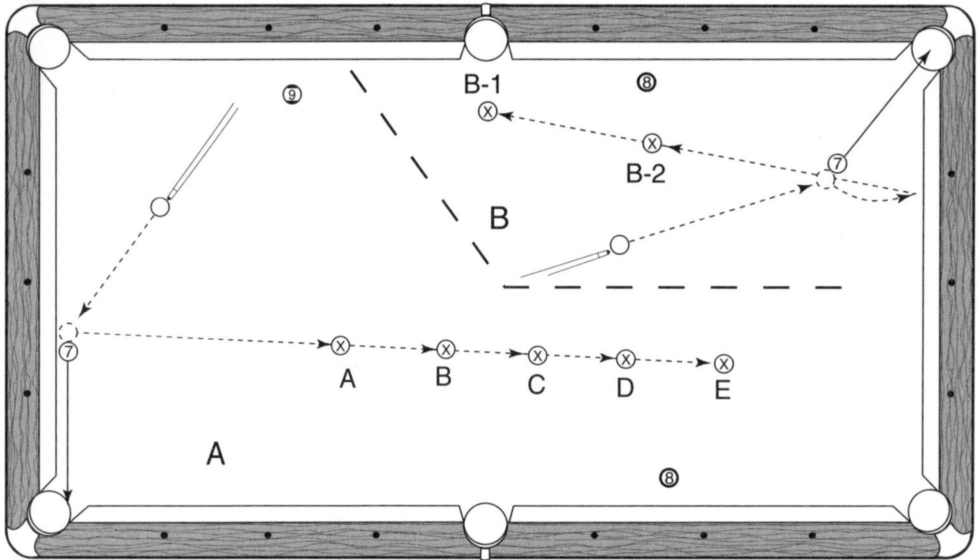

Perhaps the biggest cause of position play errors is poor speed control. This can be unfortunate when it happens because the player may have chosen the correct route and struck the cue ball in the right location with a straight and authoritative stroke, but the net result is no position for the next ball. In Part A good speed control will send the cue ball anywhere between Positions A and C. It is a very common error among amateurs to overrun their shape zone to Position D or E.

In contrast, Part B shows a position play that gives even experienced players trouble on occasion. The cue ball must reverse course with inside english, which creates a tendency to come up short of B-1, at B-2.

CHAPTER 4

FINE POINTS OF POSITION PLAY

"In 9-ball there are a lot of little percentage moves that come into play."
Bill Incardona

In Chapter 3 we covered routes that you can use to send the cue ball from Point A to B under "normal" circumstances. Nine Ball layouts, however, do not always lend themselves to the conventional means of playing position. Things like combinations, awkward layouts, billiards and a host of other offbeat positions may conspire to add to the challenge of running out. Knowledge, as you might have suspected, is once again the key. When you are facing a position play that does not lend itself to the standard techniques of position play, you must dig a little deeper for a solution or face the prospects of a stalled run out.

The fine points you'll learn in this chapter should stimulate your thinking towards additional methods for handling atypical positions. These fine points, tricks of the trade, inside stuff or whatever you want to call them are techniques used by top players to maintain absolute control of the table. When you have searched for a regular position route or a fine point solution and have come up empty, it is probably time to consider playing safe.

Hitting Balls for Position

The physics of the game largely dictate what routes are possible and those that aren't on regular position plays from Point A to B. For example, if a cut angle is very steep, the cue ball is going to travel a long distance after contact. In pool, however, you are not always encumbered by physics. You can quite often bring a runaway cue ball under control and bring it to a quick halt by means of contact with a second object ball.

Hit the 9-Ball for Shape

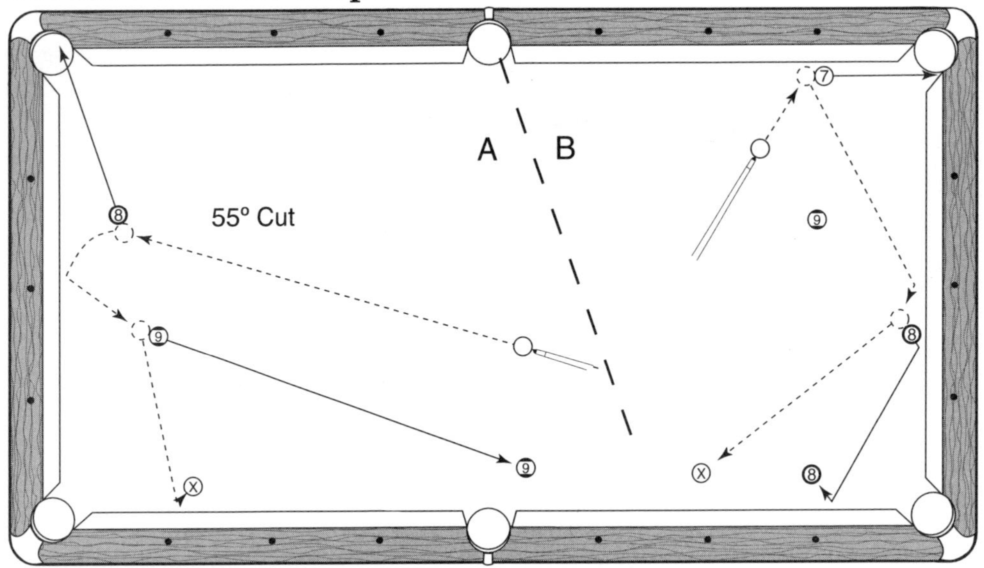

In Part A, Francisco Bustamante was facing a 55-degree cut shot on the 8-ball, which kept him from holding the cue ball at the same end of the table for the 9-ball. He chose to pass on a risky around the table route and instead ran into the 9-ball for shape. This shot occurred at the Bicycle Club Invitational, 1992 in a match with Earl Strickland. Part B is another position where you can make your shape by running into the next ball.

Using a Backstop

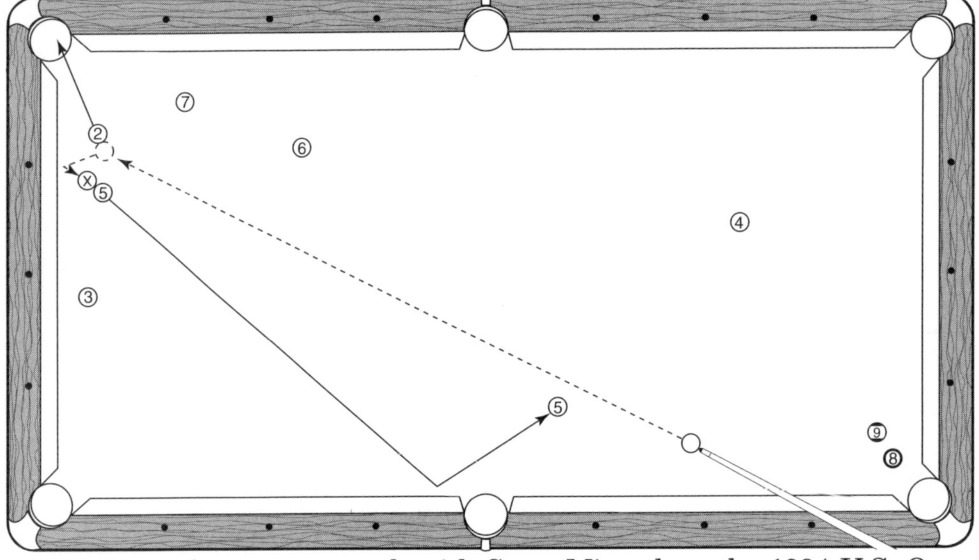

Earl Strickland was in a match with Steve Mizerak at the 1994 U.S. Open when he came across a long cut shot on the 2-ball with the 3-ball on the same rail. Normally this would spell trouble, but Strickland wisely employed the 5-ball as a backstop, thereby holding the cue ball in check for position on the 3-ball. Notice the precise full ball hit on the 5-ball.

Using a Backstop (2)

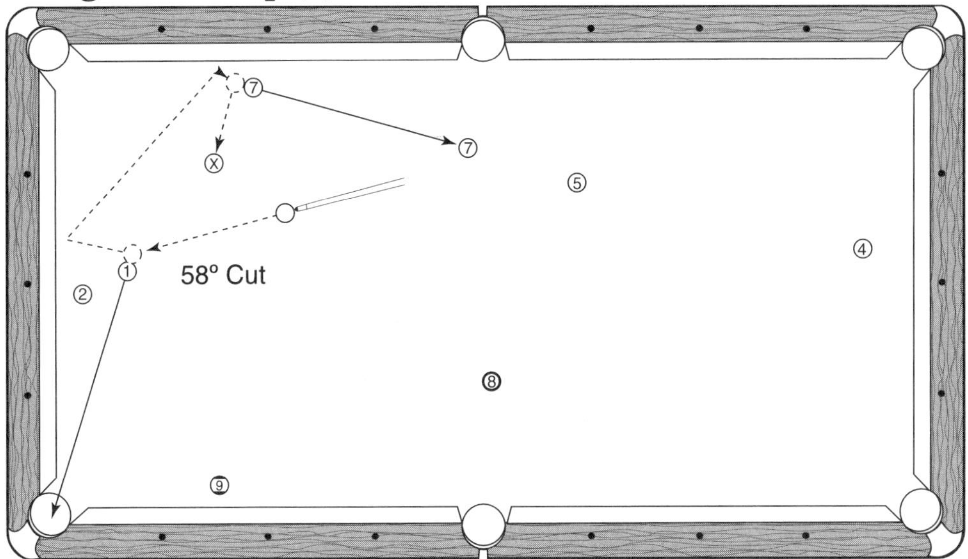

When you are in the early stages of a rack, congestion may keep you from playing a multi-rail route. If you can't hold the cue ball, then hitting a backstop is a useful tactic for controlling the cue ball. When the ball you must hit is some distance away, as in the example, be as precise as possible in planning and executing your point of contact with the backstop. It would be a mistake to hit the outside half of the 7-ball.

The Kiss of Death (to your opponent)

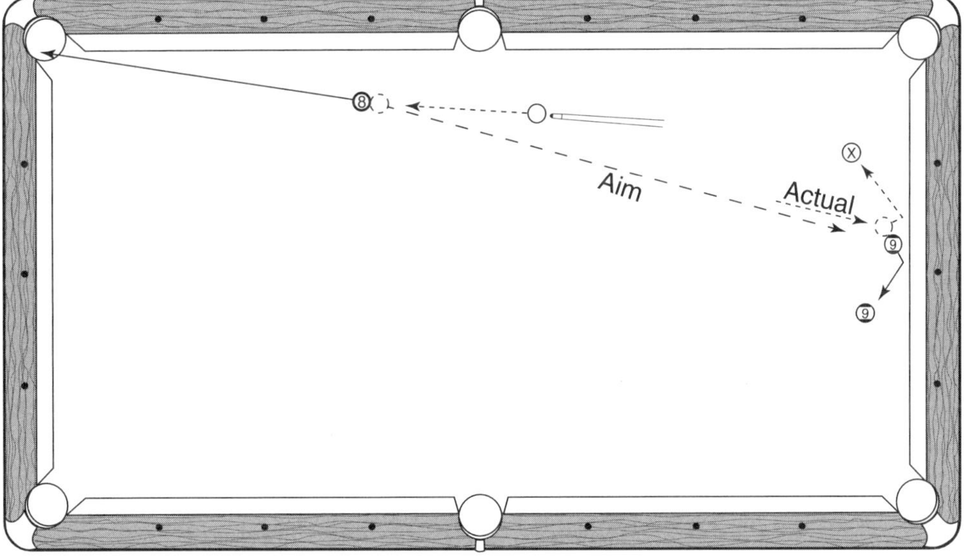

On long distance draw shots it is hard to predict the return path of the cue ball. In this position you could easily wind up with a steep cut angle on either side of the 9-ball if the cue ball bounced very far off the rail after missing the 9-ball. An offbeat solution is to try to hit the 9-ball fully. If you hit one side or the other, you will have position like that shown.

Billiards for Position

At times there is no way you can avoid having the cue ball run into another ball immediately after contact with the first ball. You can choose to depend on luck for position, or you can take matters into your own hands. I suggest you opt for the later approach by using the techniques in the following sections.

Billiards for Shape – Takahashi

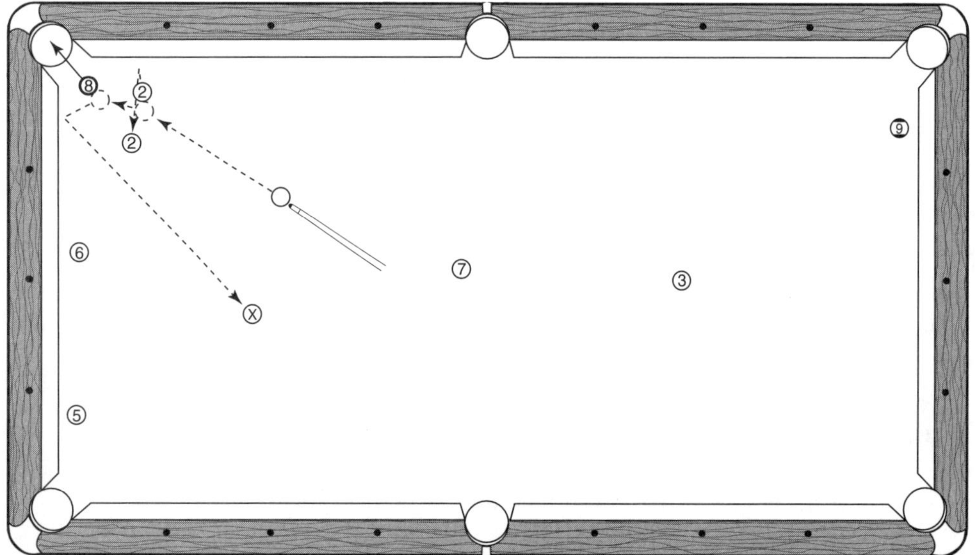

Kunihiko Takahashi played position off the 1-ball for shape on a billiard in a match with Chuck Altomare at the 1999 U.S. Open. Many factors went into making this shot a success. Takahashi had to clip the 2-ball thinly enough that he would not only hit the 8-ball, but hit enough so that the cue ball would be forced slightly to the left after contact. The thin hit on the 2-ball kept it out of the cue ball's path off the end rail. And finally, left english was used open up the cue balls rebound angle so it would avoid running into the 2-ball. Lots of little details went into producing this winner, as is often the case when you are using billiards to play position.

Draw/Billiard for Shape

You could play a soft draw shot on the 6-ball and use the 9-ball to stop the cue ball near where the 9 is now. But that would leave you with a table length draw shot for position on the 8-ball. A better choice is to draw off the 9-ball to the side rail and out for a much shorter shot on the 7-ball. With the cue ball in Position X, it will be much easier to send the cue ball back down table for the 8-ball. The key is to make a third to a half full hit on the 9-ball. When the second ball (the 9-ball in this example) is going to be traveling towards the cue ball's new location, you must make sure it doesn't interfere with your position.

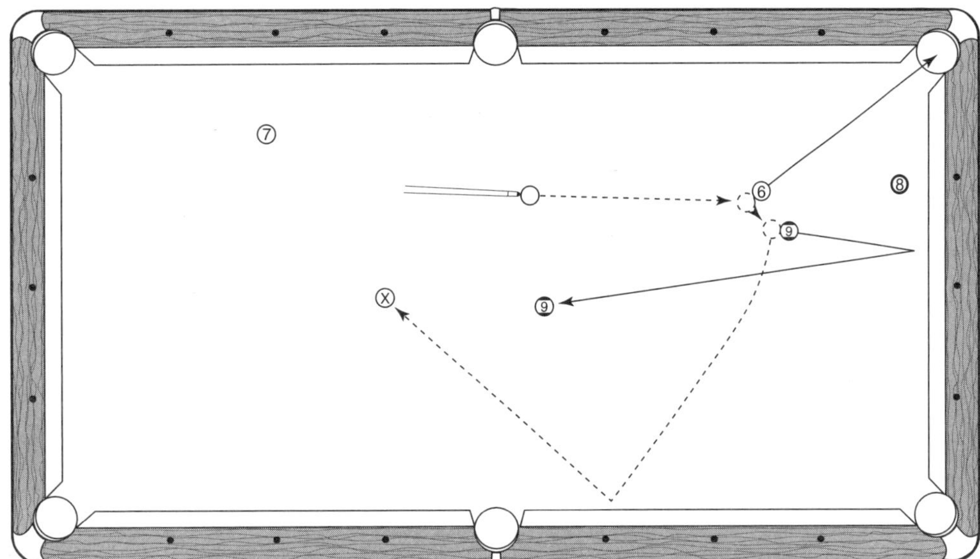

Bouncing off an Obstructer for Shape

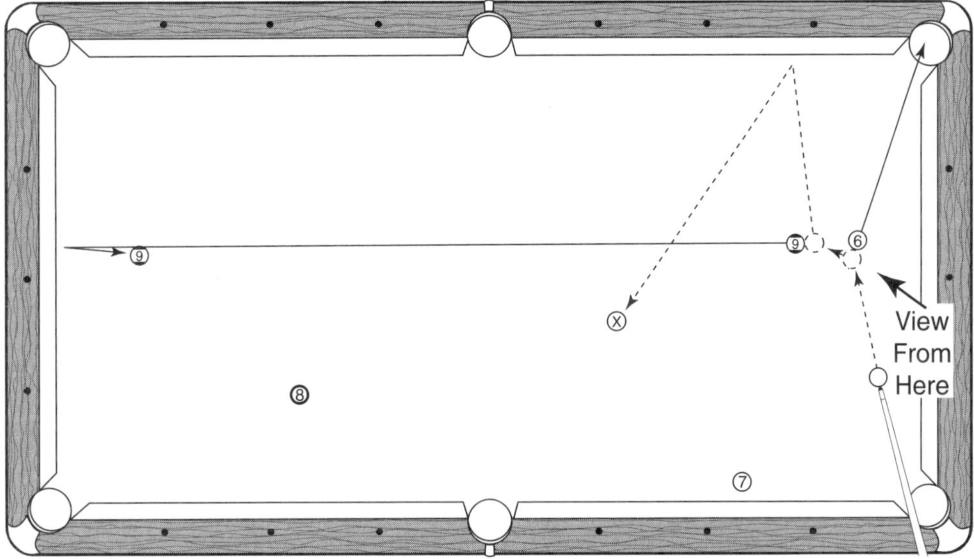

The 9-ball appears to be in the way of the cue ball's path to the 7-ball. However, the opportunity for position off a billiard may be present if you can strike the correct portion of the 9-ball. The first step is to walk over to where indicated and view the cue ball's path down the stun line after contact. A full hit will kill the cue ball, but since it will be hitting the right side of the 9-ball, it will follow the path to the side rail and out. Outside english (left) was used to open the rebound angle off the side rail. The 9-ball was be long gone before the cue ball crosses its path.

Position after a Combination

Pocketing combinations is tough enough, but often the major challenge with a combo is planning position for the next ball. When you are playing position on the first ball of the combo, you are playing shape on a moving target. This means that you have to figure out where the first ball is likely to end up and match your position route to correspond to its new location.

Controlling Both Balls on a Combo

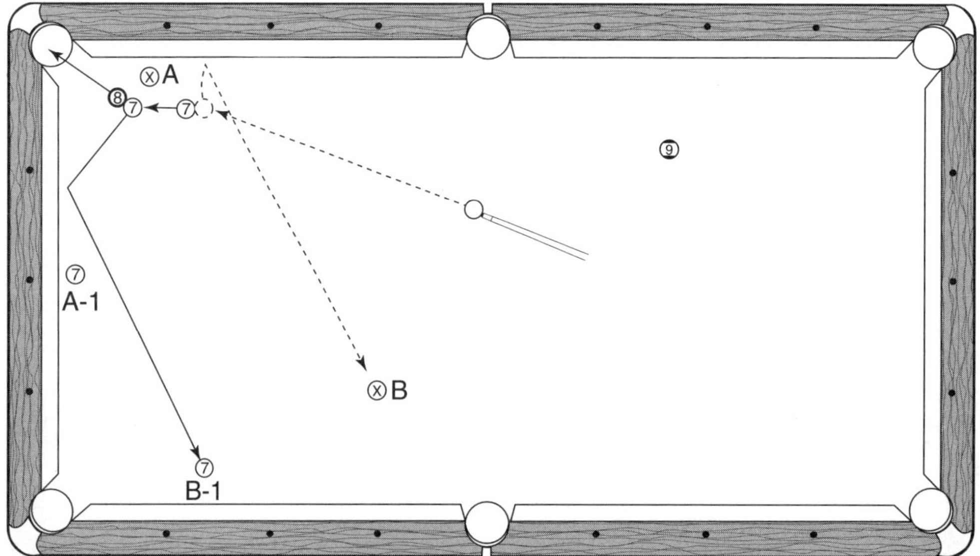

This combination is not difficult as combos go, but you must still aim with the utmost of care. Before pulling the trigger, take a couple of moments to figure out where the 7-ball is going. Its new location is related to the speed you play the shot. If you use a soft follow stroke, the cue ball could wind up at Position A with the 7-ball at A-1. If you dislike using such a soft stroke at this distance, then you will have to plan on the 7-ball traveling much further. A medium hard draw stroke will bring the cue ball out to Position B. Meanwhile, the 7-ball will relocate to Position B-1. The lesson: you must match your position on the first ball of a combo to the speed of stroke you are using.

Rail First Combo Guarantees Position

Most players facing the 6-7 combination above would instinctively play the 6-ball directly into the 7-ball while assuming they will emerge with shape because the 7-ball is close to the pocket. But not Efren Reyes, who shows great attention to the kind of details that ensure position and that keep him out of trouble. Reyes chose to play this creative rail first combo shape against Buddy Hall at the 2000 U.S. Open. The 6-ball crept slightly to the right after contact. Meanwhile, the cue ball continued to Position X thanks to the increased cut angle on the 6-ball that was created by playing the shot rail first.

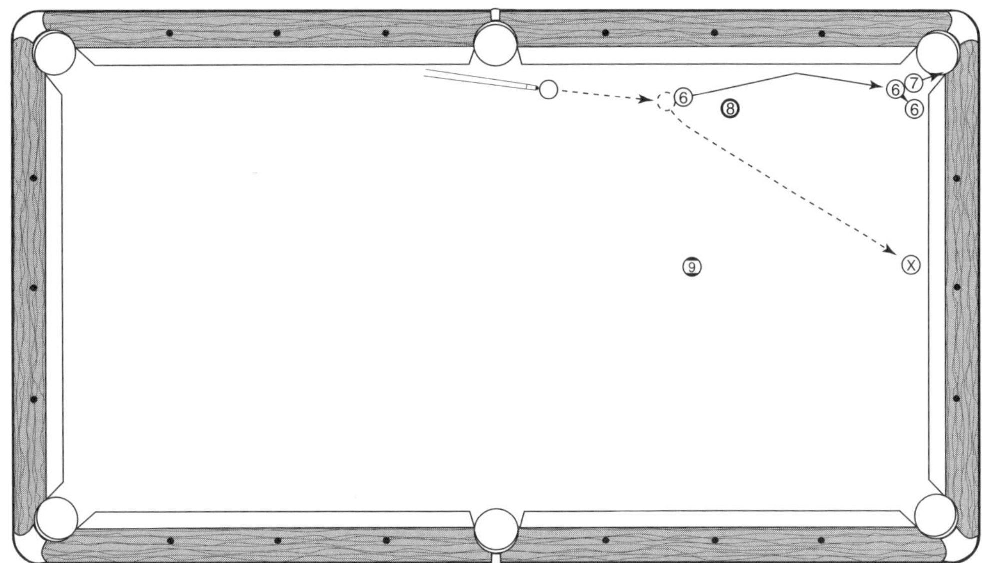

Shape After a Combo

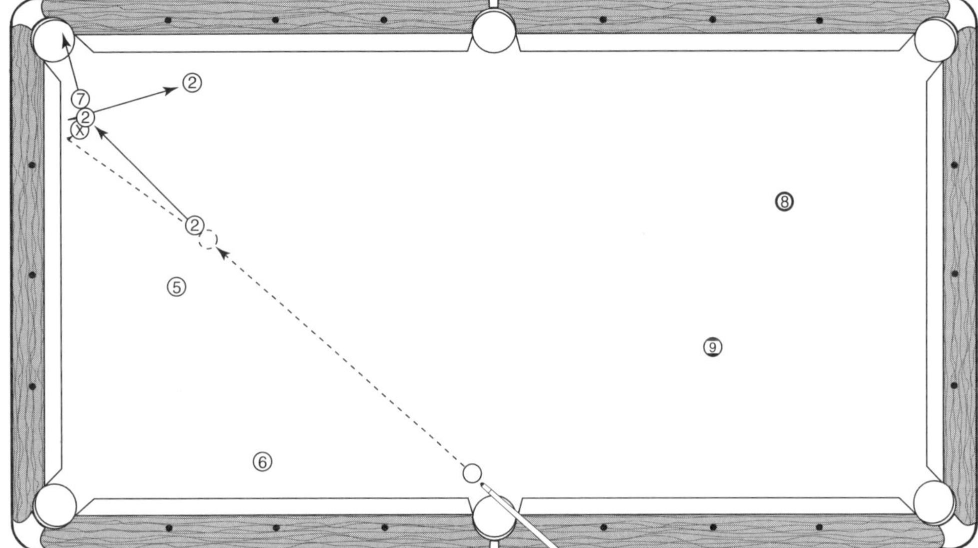

Efren Reyes was also the architect of this insightful combo shape, which took place at the Sands Regency Open 23, 1996 in competition with Johnny Archer. Reyes was well aware of the fact that the 2-ball was going up the side rail after knocking in the 7-ball. He took advantage of this by using a soft stroke, which positioned the cue ball on the short side of the 2-ball. Since the path to the 2-ball was nearly straight on, it would have taken a much harder stroke to send the cue ball off the end rail. Besides, with the cue ball and 2-ball in their new positions, Reyes was in excellent shape to make the 2-ball and get on the 5-ball nearby.

The Angle Of Departure

Angle of Departure on Soft Follow Shots

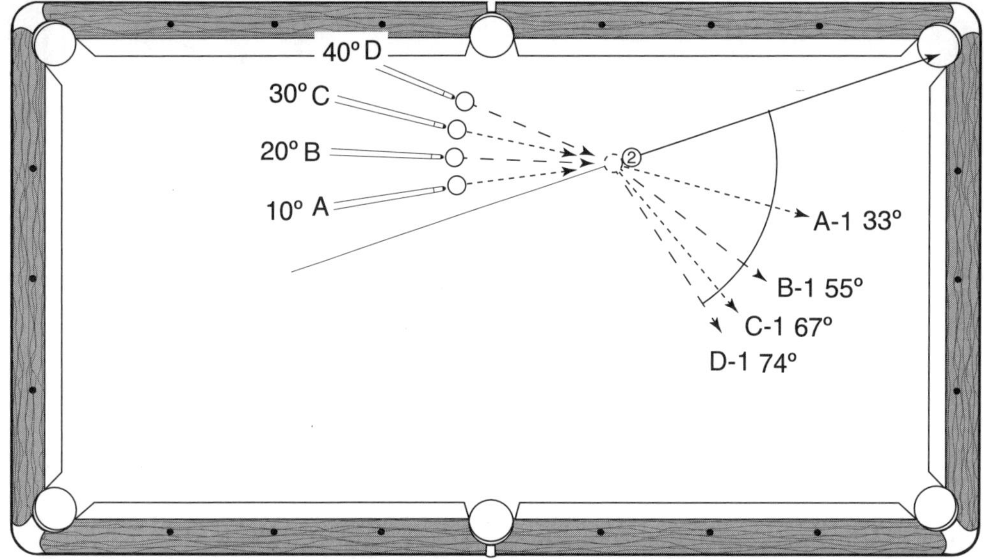

When the cue ball is struck softly on follow shots, it will follow a path that corresponds precisely to the cut angle of the shot. This occurs largely because the cue ball rolls directly forward after a soft shot without spending hardly any time traveling down the tangent line.

The angle of departure is shown for four different cut angles. When the cue ball approaches the object ball at a 10-degree angle as shown by Position A, it will depart at a 33-degree angle to the line to the pocket along Path A-1. And when the cut angle is 40-degrees (Position D), it will depart at a 74-degree angle (D-1). This bit of pocket billiard physics has many uses, including planning your position routes, as we'll see below.

I know you are not going to carry and use a protractor to measure cut angles. You should, however, develop a keen eye for the magnitude of various angles now that you know what they look like, and now that you know how important they can be to your game.

Playing Position Using the Path of Departure

In Part A you have a 20-degree cut angle on the 5-ball and your goal is to play position on the 6-ball. A soft follow stroke will result in the path to Position X, safely avoiding the 8-ball. If you were unaware of the true angle of departure on this shot, you could be like many players who arc fooled into thinking you have to do something special to get around the 8-ball when you don't. Remember when playing pool that simpler is generally much better.

In Part B you have a 30-degree cut shot on the 7-ball. The 67-degree angle of departure means that the cue ball will run into the 9-ball if you use a soft follow stroke. With this bit of knowledge, you can now avoid the 9-ball by using a soft stroke with a tip of draw, which will send the cue ball past the 9-ball to Position X.

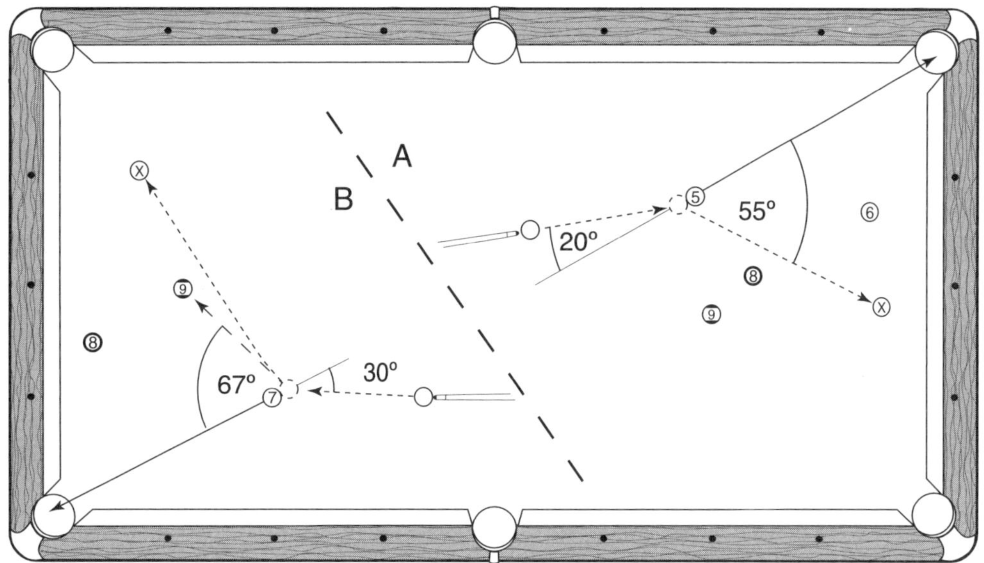

Cut Angle Dictates Angle Out

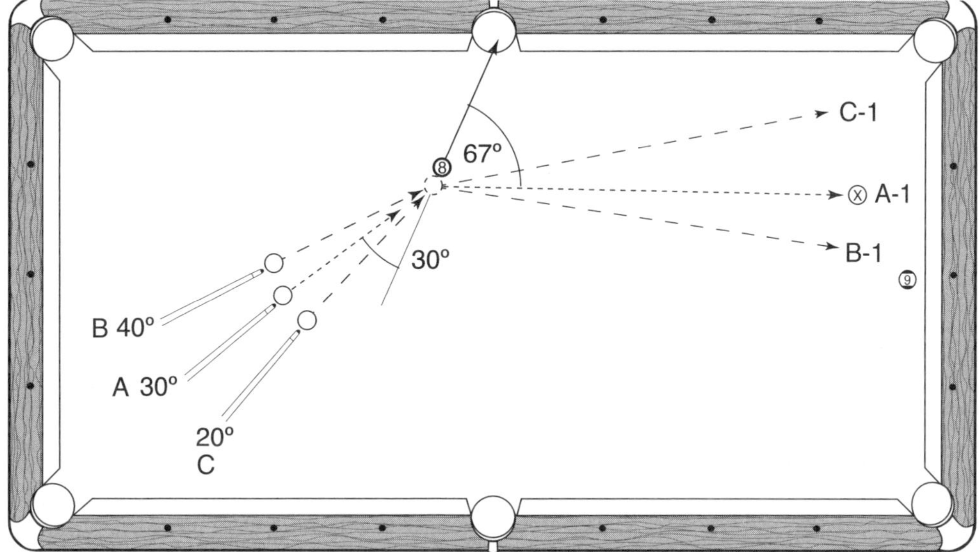

There is almost always an ideal angle that can enable you to play position on the next ball in the absolute easiest manner possible with the least amount of risk. The 30-degree cut angle in Position A enables you to play a soft follow shot to A-1 for ideal position on the 9-ball. A soft follow shot, as you'll recall, is one of the easiest position plays in pool.

In Position B the cue ball is at a 40-degree cut angle so it will travel just inside the 9-ball along line B-1 when a soft follow shot is used. Now you must do something to play shape. One option is to draw to the opposite side of the 9-ball. When the cue ball is in Position C, you must guard against a scratch since the cue ball will be traveling down Path C-1.

Frozen Balls

When the object ball is frozen to the rail, you must take special measures when planning and executing your position route as these shots severely restrict what you can do with the cue ball.

Angle In Dictates the Angle Out

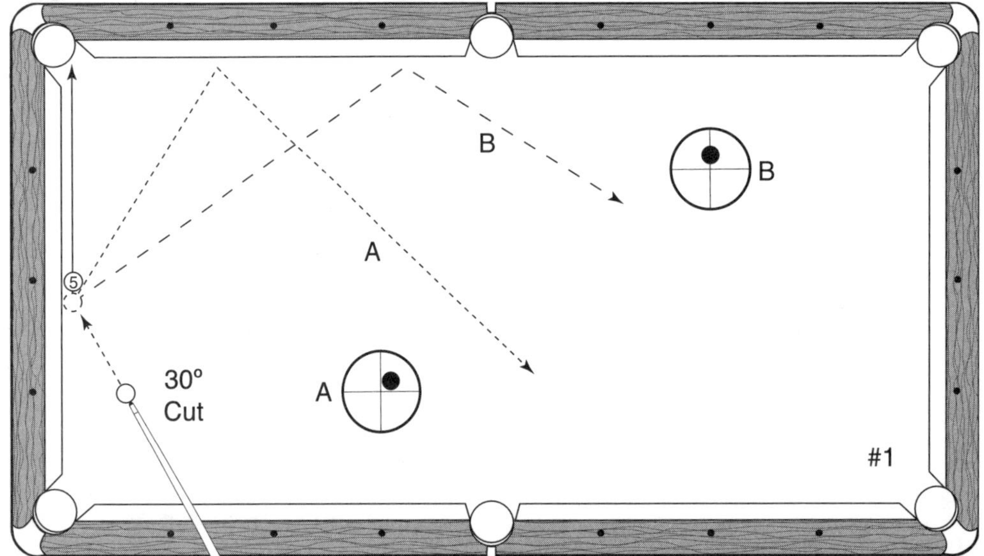

The cut angle of the shot largely determines the cue ball's route when the object ball is frozen because your options for "working" the cue ball off the rail are severely restricted. For example, you cannot use outside english when a ball is frozen to the rail unless it is within a diamond or so of the pocket. Diagram #1 shows two possible routes on a 30-degree cut shot. Route A was played with follow and a half tip of inside (right) english. Route B was played with follow, but no english. Diagram #2 show a similar shot, only now the cut angle is 50-degrees.

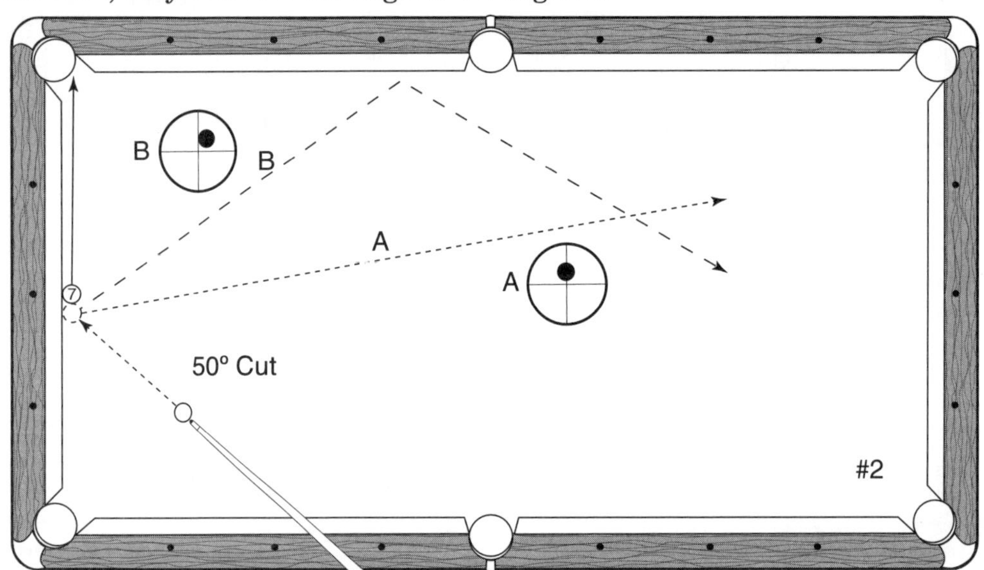

The Cue Ball Tends to Run Wild

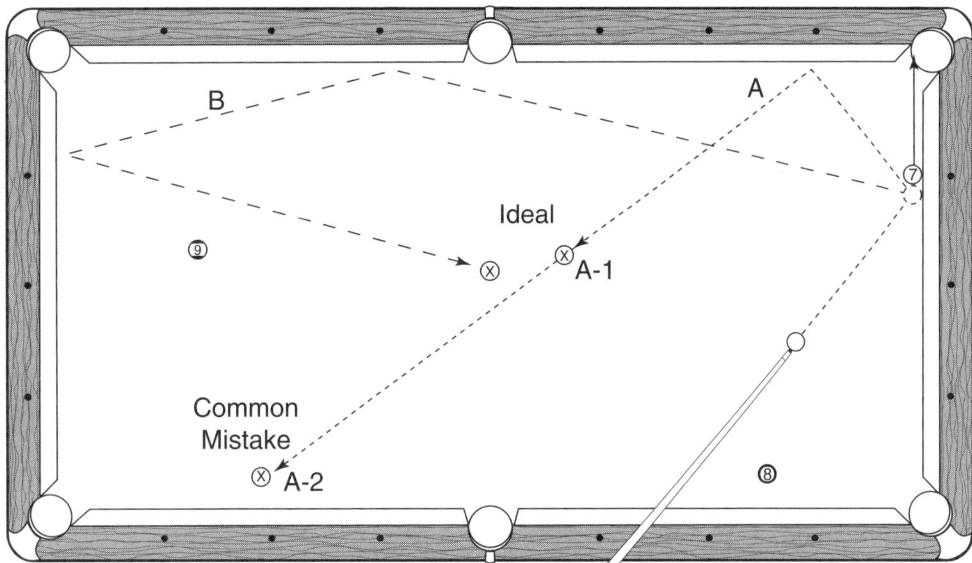

The 7-ball, which is frozen to the rail, is a bomb ready to go off as there is a tendency among 99.99% of all pool players to greatly over shoot their position route on a frozen shots like this. The goal on Route A is to arrive at A-1 However, more often than not, the cue ball will run towards A-2 far down the table. Sometimes the best (or only) play is to take the long way to the position zone as shown by Route B.

Big Danger on Frozen Balls (A Near Dead Scratch)

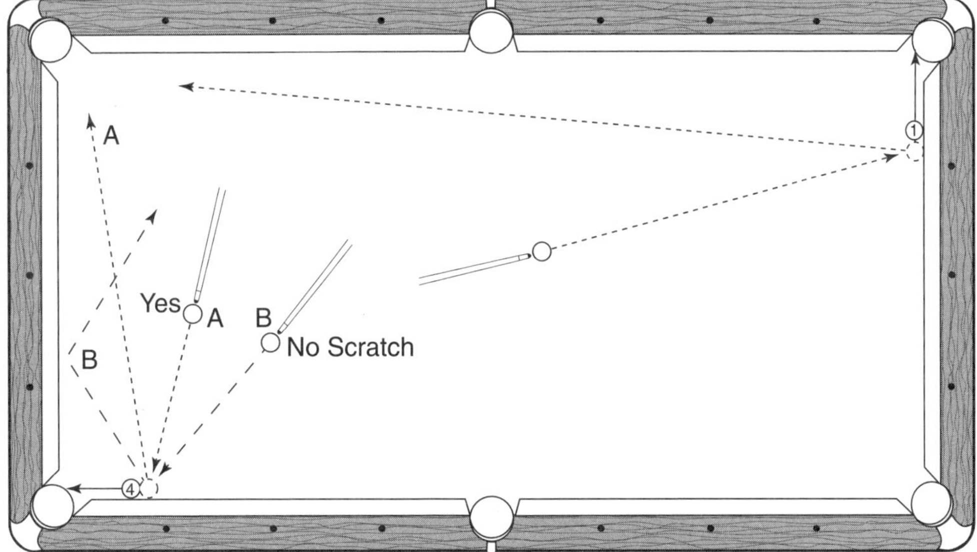

The example shows two of the most deadly scratches in pool. You need to use inside english to pocket the ball. But when the ball is within a diamond of the corner pocket, a scratch in the opposite corner is almost dead because the inside english at this angle does little to change the cue ball's rebound angle. Now that you've been warned, plan accordingly!

Various Concepts

Peripheral Vision

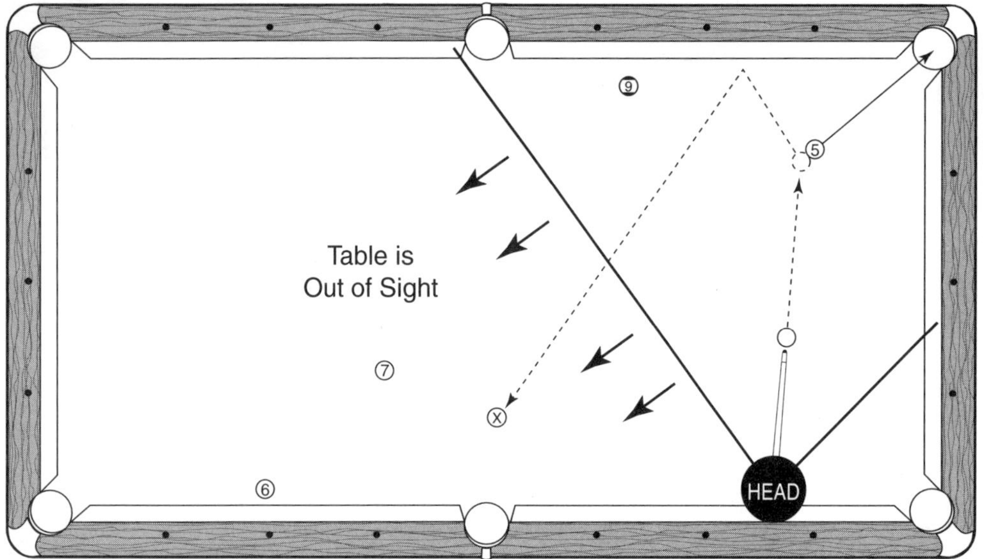

Normally it is easier to play position when, as a part of your preshot routine, you can look over the table in front of you to get your bearings. In many positions you are not afforded this luxury. The typical field of vision is about 40-degress left and right of the target line. The diagram shows a shot in which you would have to twist your body out of alignment to do any last second planning. When the shot will largely be unfolding out of your initial line of sight, make a positive plan prior to addressing the cue ball, execute it with confidence, and hope for the best.

Take the Long Way Home

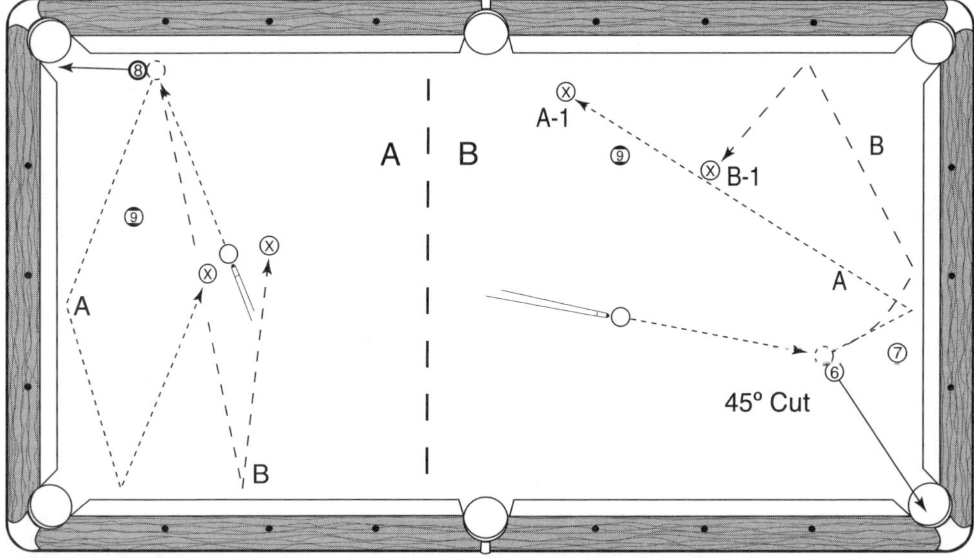

It takes a certain amount of the cue ball's energy to drive the object ball to the pocket. In Part A you must make sure to use sufficient speed to pocket this 60-degree cut. The cue ball traveled the same distance down Routes A and B but Route A left the cue ball in a better position for the 9-ball.

On the thin 45-degree cut shot in Part B, the cue ball will hit only about a third of the object ball, again retaining much of its energy after contact with the object ball. If you play the shot with straight follow the cue ball will travel down Route A, possibly leaving you hooked behind the 9-ball at A-1. Route B is played with a draw stroke that will send the cue ball to B-1. The cue ball traveled the same distance as in Route A, but wound up much closer to the object ball! By using this tactic you are, in effect, letting the cue ball exhaust its energy by making it take a longer route to the same place.

Using Balls as Targets And Landmarks

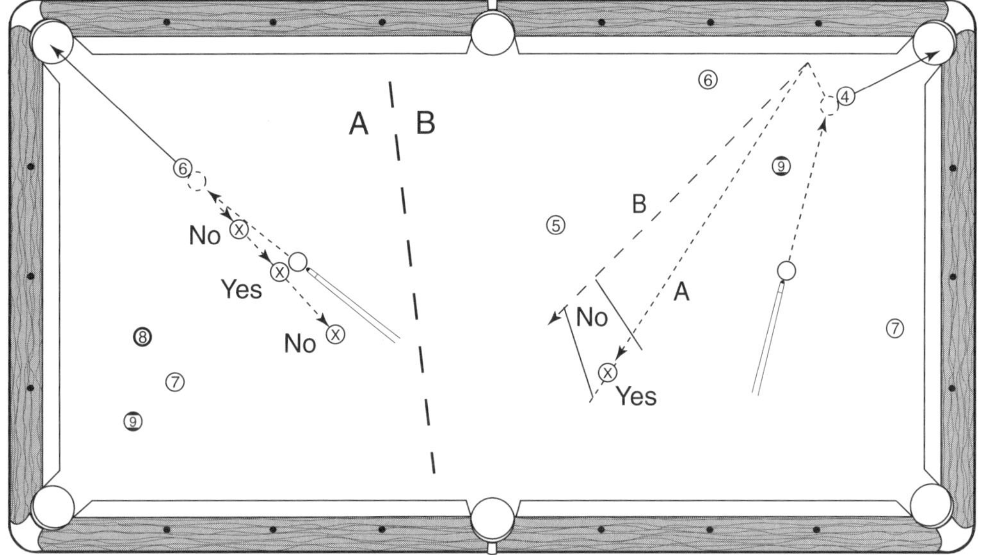

In Part A you really have little choice except to draw back for the 7-9 combo. If you fall short or go past the ideal position, the combo will be much tougher. The cue ball's original position can be used in positions like this to give you a concrete target for the cue ball. Instead of having to draw the cue ball back to an unmarked spot on table, you have a very handy frame of reference. If the cue ball stops at or next to the cue ball's original location, you will have great shape for the combo. Should you miss position, you can always play a safety.

Part B shows a demanding position play in which the cue ball will be traveling across the position zone. You can add a few precious inches to the zone by entering the wide side down Route A. In this case, the 9-ball can be used as a landmark for playing position. The idea is to send the cue ball down a line that's slightly above the 9-ball. If you played it too safe by using Route B, the position zone would shrink dramatically.

Cheat the Pocket

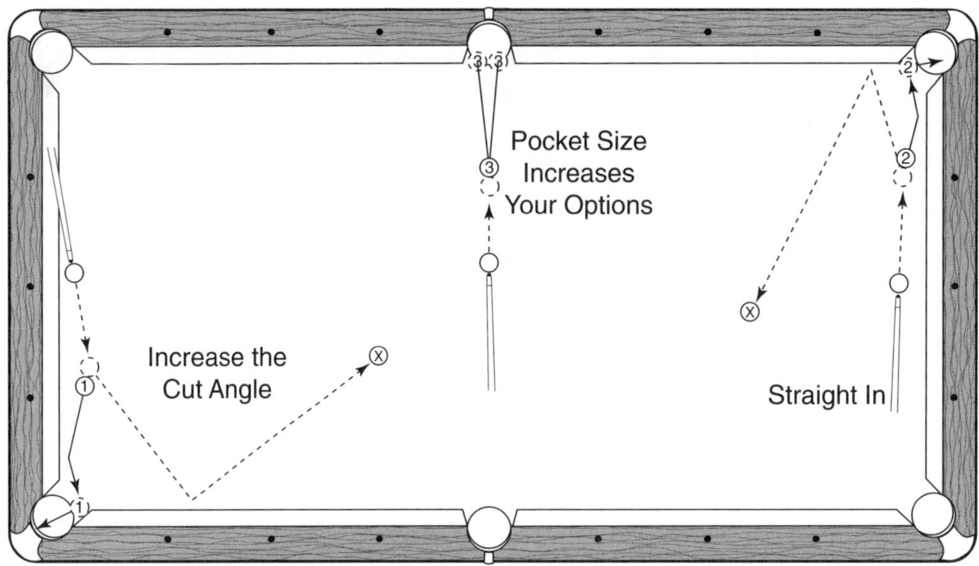

You can exit the end rails, play a huge variety of routes into the side pockets and otherwise accomplish a number of positional objectives by shooting into the side of the pocket, otherwise known as cheating the pocket. These shots are most effective when: the ball is close to the pocket; the pockets are generous; a soft stroke is used; or you are on a bar table.

Rail First Position

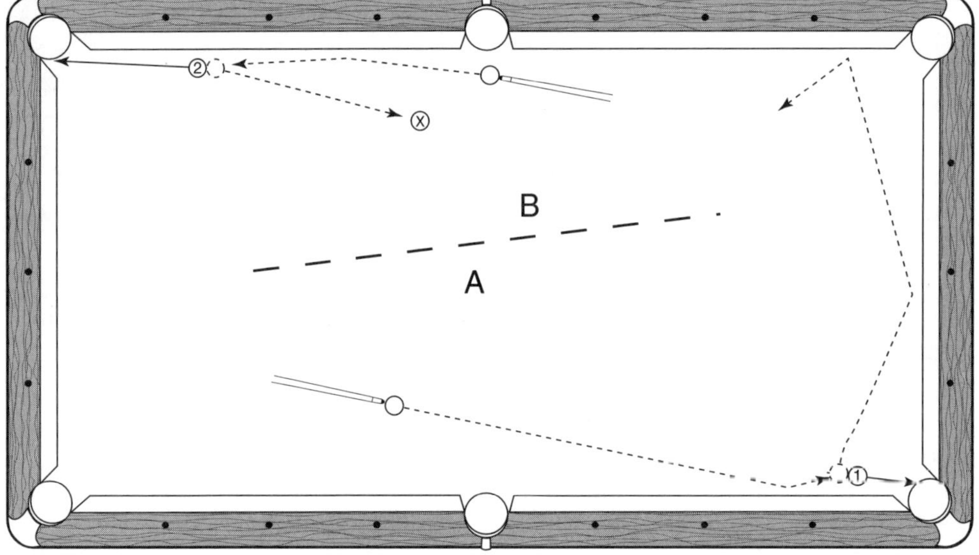

When you have left yourself a straight in (or near straight in) and the object ball is near the rail, you may be able to escape the rail by playing position rail first. Part A shows a way to send the cue ball across the table. Part B is a draw shot that will take the cue ball away from the side rail. Rail first shots should be confined to when the object ball is close to the rail and the object ball is within about 1.5 diamonds of the pocket.

CHAPTER 5

PRINCIPLES OF POSITION PLAY

On two-rail shape: "As soon as you hit the second rail you're in line."
Buddy Hall

The Principles of Position Play, which first appeared in Play Your Best Pool, apply to most of the popular pool games. Position play in each game varies somewhat, so in the pages that follow, I have adapted the principles to the special needs of the Nine Ball player.

You may already be applying many of the principles to your game. Others with which you are not yet familiar, could add a whole new dimension to your play. I advise that you take your time in learning the principles. Concentrate on applying one or two principles at a time while you are playing until it becomes an automatic part of your planning process. In time you will learn to quickly evaluate the table and plan your shots by using the principles that apply to that particular shot.

There will usually be several that apply to each position play. Furthermore, the principles are designed to complement one another. There will, however, be exceptions to the principles. At times one principle will clearly take precedence over another. In sum, the main purpose of the principles is to teach you how to think pool correctly.

#1 Speed Control

The Importance of Speed Control

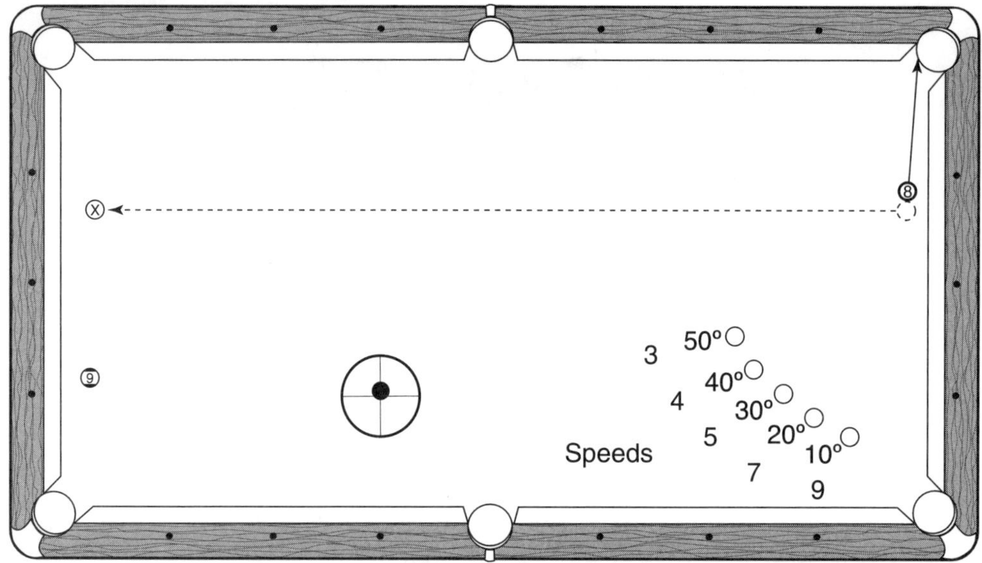

There is perhaps no more valuable skill in pool than the ability to consistently stroke the cue ball with the correct speed. When you combine proper speed with expert directional control, you largely have what it takes to play pinpoint position.

Nine Ball is played over the entire table, which means that you will routinely face a wide variety of position plays, from the softest bunt, to ultra hard pound shots, and all points in between. This means that you must become comfortable playing shots all across the Spectrum of Speeds, which I developed to quantify speed of stroke. The softest shots are a 1, while the break is a 10. Break shots are hit anywhere from about 14-30+ miles per hour (MPH). Position plays, which are the subject of this chapter, range from a stroke speed of 1.5 MPH for extremely soft shots (1 on the scale) to speeds of 10-12+ MPH for shots that require an extremely hard stroke (9 on the scale). Most position plays fall in the 4-7 range. Nevertheless, you need be able to play position at either end of the spectrum for your game to be complete.

The Spectrum of Speeds

Speed	MPH	Speed	MPH
1 Extremely Soft	1.5	**6** Medium Hard	6.0
2 Very Soft	2.0	**7** Hard	7.0
3 Soft	3.0	**8** Very Hard	8.0
4 Medium Soft	4.0	**9** Extremely Hard	10.0
5 Medium	5.0	**10** The Break	15.0-30.0+

The diagram on the previous page gives an example of the Spectrum of Speed. The play is to send the cue ball straight down the table for position on the 9-ball. Each cut angle corresponds to one of 5 different speeds of stroke. I suggest you start with the 50-degree cut angle and work your way to 10-degrees. Play the shot as close to centerball as possible. Don't be too concerned if you come up short from 10-degrees as it takes time to develop a stroke powerful enough to cover this distance. I advise you to first learn the basic speeds of stroke including soft (3), medium (5) and hard (7). Once you've got these mastered, gradually start filling in the gaps.

Importance of Speed Control Varies from Shot to Shot

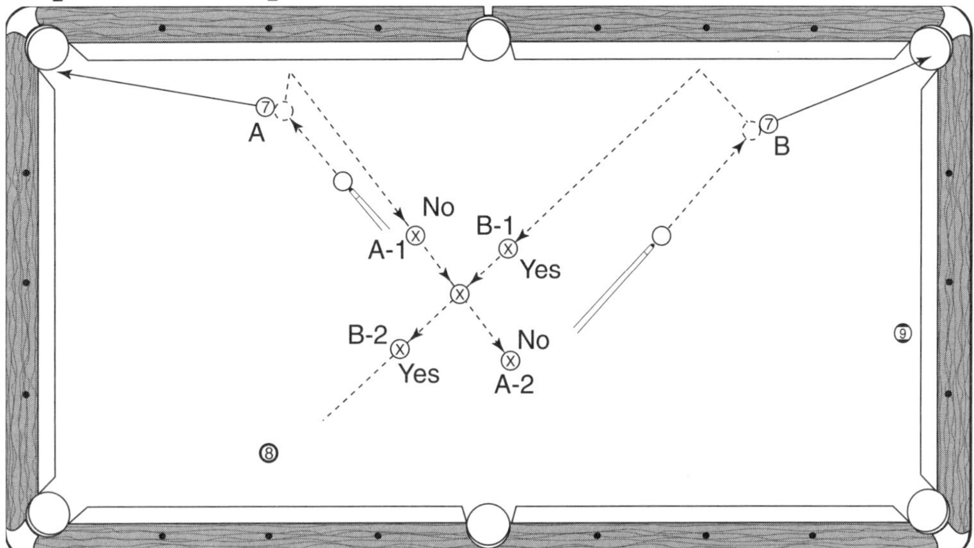

The importance of speed control varies from shot to shot. The diagram shows two different shots on the 7-ball. The objective in each case is to get the correct angle on the 8-ball. With the 7-ball in Position A, speed is the critical element to the shot. If the cue ball comes up short at A-1 or long at A-2, it will be much tougher to get from the 8-ball to the 9-ball. With the 7-ball in Position B, speed control is not nearly as important. Anywhere from B-1 to B-2 will work just fine.

Speed Control versus Pocketing the Shot

Perfect speed control is of great value in playing position, but you must not obsess on speed control to the point where you miss shots for the sake of position. On soft shots, you must be careful to use the minimum speed to get the object ball to the pocket. A little extra force can eliminate roll offs and ensure stroking accuracy, especially when the object ball is over a foot from the pocket. On firmly stroked shots, you must balance positional requirements with the need to pocket the shot.

#2 The Correct Cut Angle Optimizes Position

The correct angle is vital to position play in Nine-Ball because of the distances you must send the cue ball across and around the table. The correct angle will give you the high percentage position route. In addition, the correct angle will enable you to use the speed of stroke that maximizes the accuracy of the shot. In fact, consistently arriving in the position zone with a workable cut angle is perhaps the most important thing that you need to do to run out regularly in Nine-Ball. At the same time, you also want the cue ball to be a comfortable distance from the object ball.

Table Speed and Preferences Affect Cut Angles

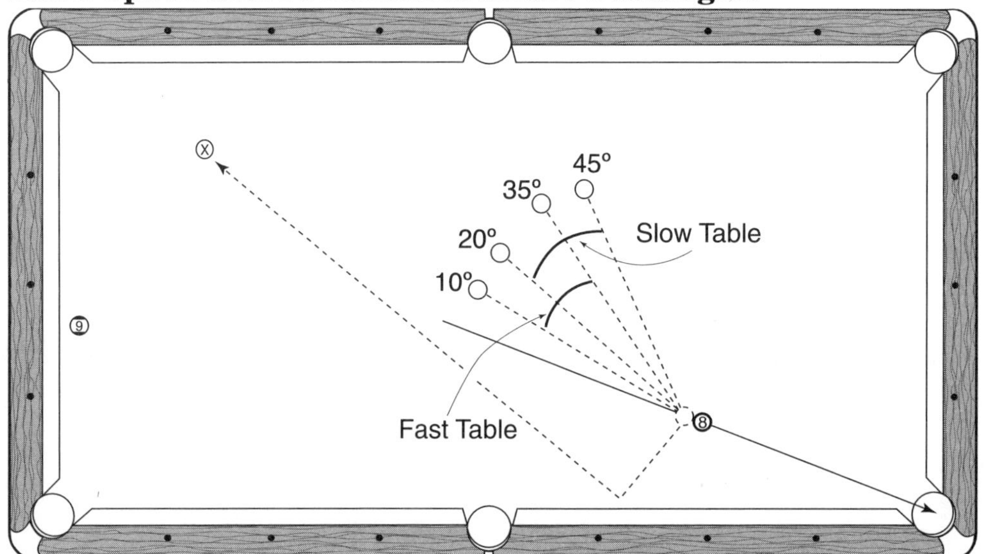

There are several ways to accomplish the same objective on any given position play. The correct choice depends largely on your style of play and the conditions. The diagram shows several cut angles for a typical position play. You must send the cue ball off the side rail and down table for the 9-ball to around Position X.

- If you use a hard stroke, you'll generally play for a shallow angle (20-degrees in this position).
- If you use an easy stroke, you'll normally play for a steeper angle (35-degrees in this position).
- If you like to use running english, you'll need less angle on some shots.
- If you prefer to cue on the vertical center axis, you'll need a slightly greater angle.

Your Ideal Angles are also determined by your preference for using center axis cueing or for using english.

- Small angles go with a hard stroke and running english.
- Medium angles go with a softer stroke and running english.
- Medium angles go with a harder stroke and no english.
- Large angles go with a soft stroke and no english.

The conditions also have a significant influence on the ideal angle.

- On a fast table, play for a smaller cut angle.
- On a slow table leave yourself larger cut angles.
- Lively rail require less of a cut angle while spongy rails require a larger cut angle than normal.

Ideal Angle for Speed Control

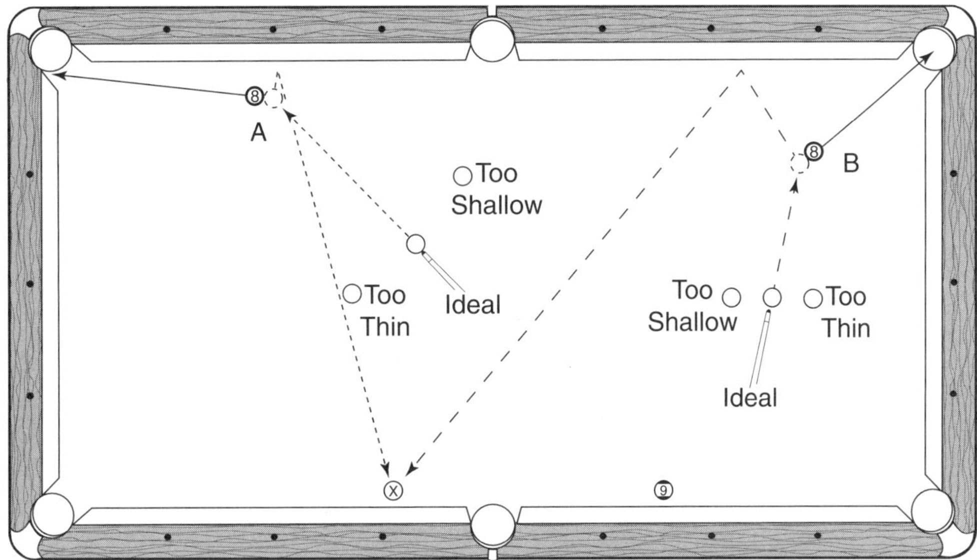

If you obtain the correct cut angle, you can play the shot at a speed of stroke that maximizes your chances of pocketing the ball. The correct angle will also make it easier to send the cue ball to within a few inches or less of the bulls eye for shape. The objective in Parts and A and B is to send the cue ball across table for position on the 9-ball. In each case there is an ideal angle that creates the ideal speed without compromising the accuracy of the shot. In Position A, pocketing and speed will be much more difficult than from the ideal angle. In Position B, pocketing is not a problem, but speed control will not be nearly as easy as with ideal shape.

Low Risk and High Risk Cut Angles

Low-risk angles fall between the extremes of being either too sharp or too shallow. They enable you to use a speed of stroke with which you are comfortable. They also can help you to easily arrive in the position zone.

High-risk angles require you to use an extra firm stroke when the cut angle is shallow. You will be forced into using an exceptionally soft stroke when the angle is too sharp.

Ideal Crossing Angles

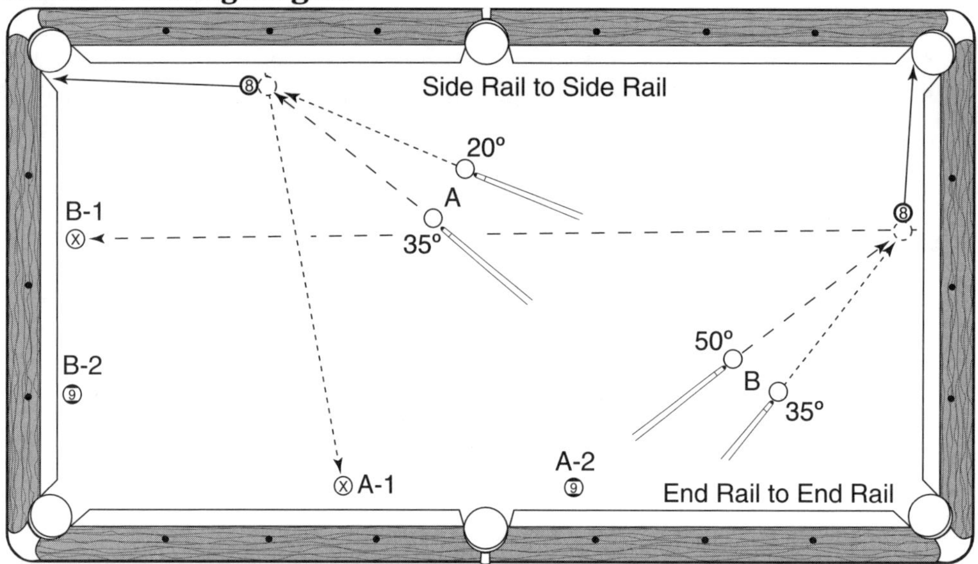

It will help your position play tremendously if you become familiar with the ideal cut angle for each position play. The diagram shows two of the most common routes. With the cue ball in Position A, a cut angle of 20-35 degrees makes it easier to send the cue ball across the table to A-1 for the 9-ball at A-2. A 35-50 degree cut angle is optimal for sending the cue ball from Position B to B-1 for position on the 9-ball at B-2.

#3 Know the Boundaries of a Position Zone

Speed and Direction Create the Zone

Part A of the diagram at the top of the next page shows how the size of a position zone is created. Direction establishes the width of the zone while speed is responsible for the length. Amateurs have wider margins for error than pros, hence their position zones are quite a bit larger. Part B shows a soft follow shot where speed is the primary ingredient in establishing the zone. As a result, the zone is quite narrow.

The boundaries you set for a position zone should be based on the requirements for the shot. You need to also factor in your level of skill when setting practical boundaries for any given position play.

The maximum size of any zone, is one that enables you to make the second ball and proceed to the third ball. I recommend you play for zones that you are capable of hitting consistently with what, for you, is an average to above average shot. I advise that you strive to consistently upgrade position play no matter what your level of skill. Your goal is to consistently send the cue ball within zones that enable you to continue your run.

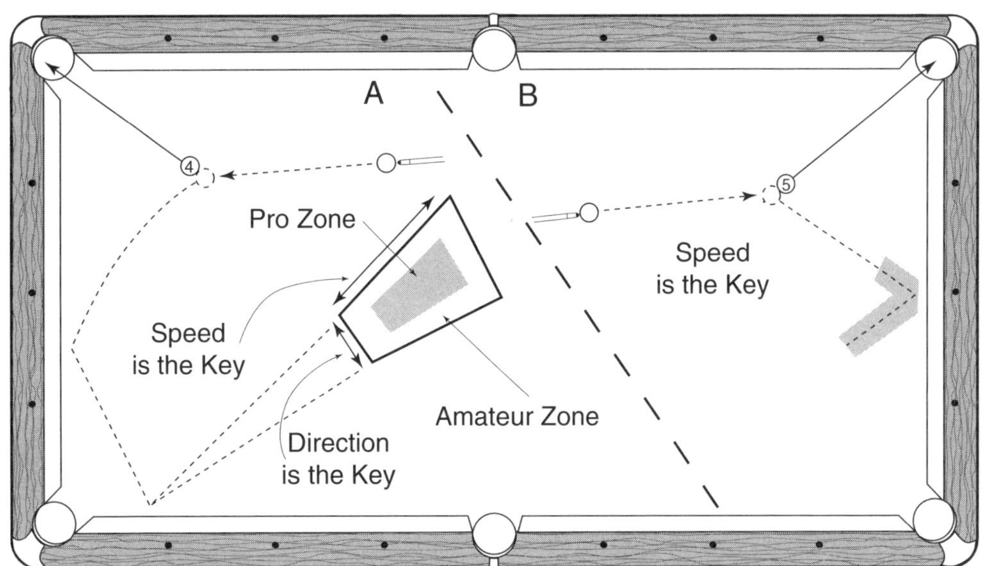

Ideal Distance

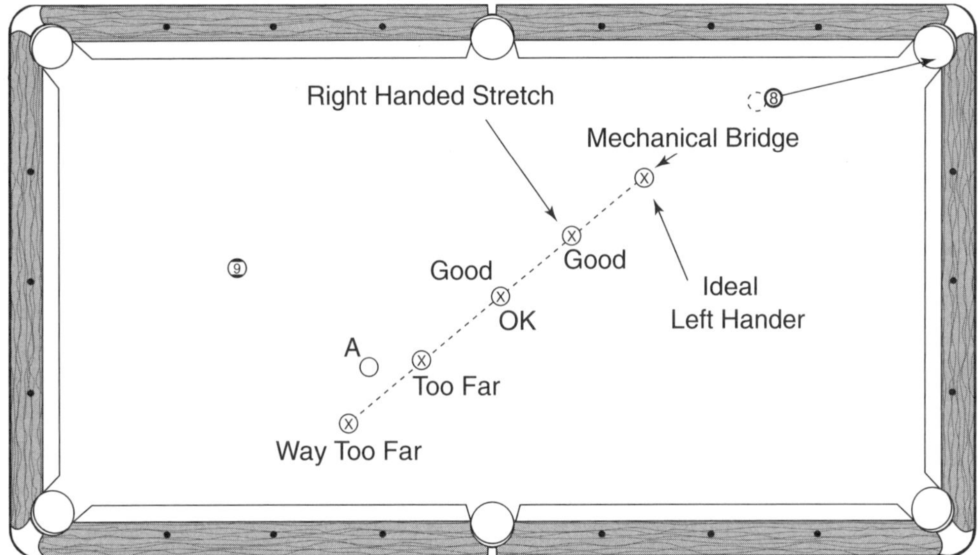

You must develop a consciousness for distance when playing position in Nine Ball. The diagram above shows position on the 8-ball for cross table shape on the 9-ball to Position A. Notice that the right-hander has a much more limited zone for playing this shot than a left-hander. When planning shape you must:

- Take into account the stretch factor. This often means that you must purposefully play for longer shots.
- You need to consider the distance you feel comfortable shooting before your accuracy begins to drop significantly.
- Calculate the minimum distance you want the cue ball from the object ball.

Long and Narrow Zones

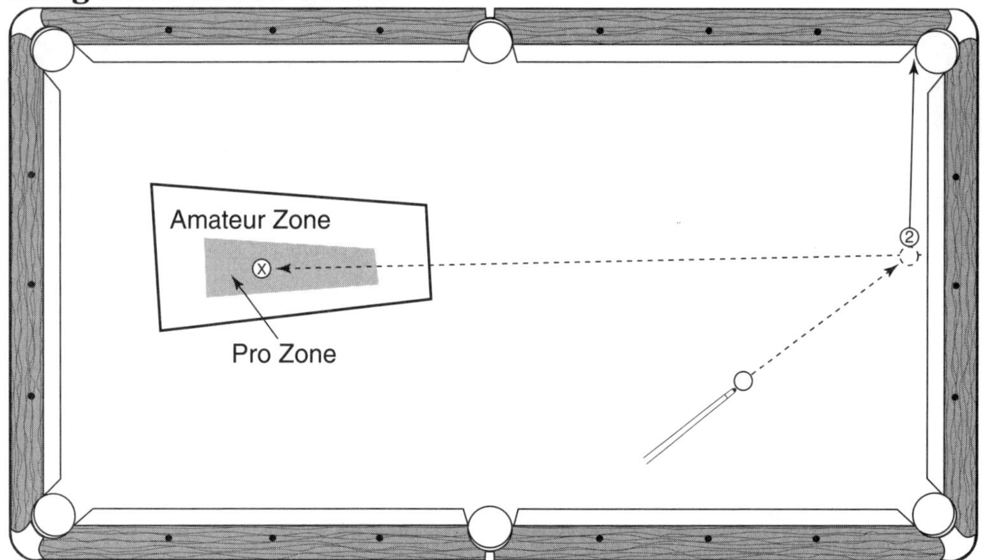

The width and length of a position zone are determined by the difficulty in controlling both speed and direction When it is easy to control the direction, the zone will be narrow, and vice versa. And when speed is easy to control, the length of the zone will be short, and vice versa. When the object ball is close to the rail as shown, then direction is relatively easy to control. Speed then becomes the critical element to this shots success. As a result, the position zone is long and narrow.

Unusually Shaped Position Zones

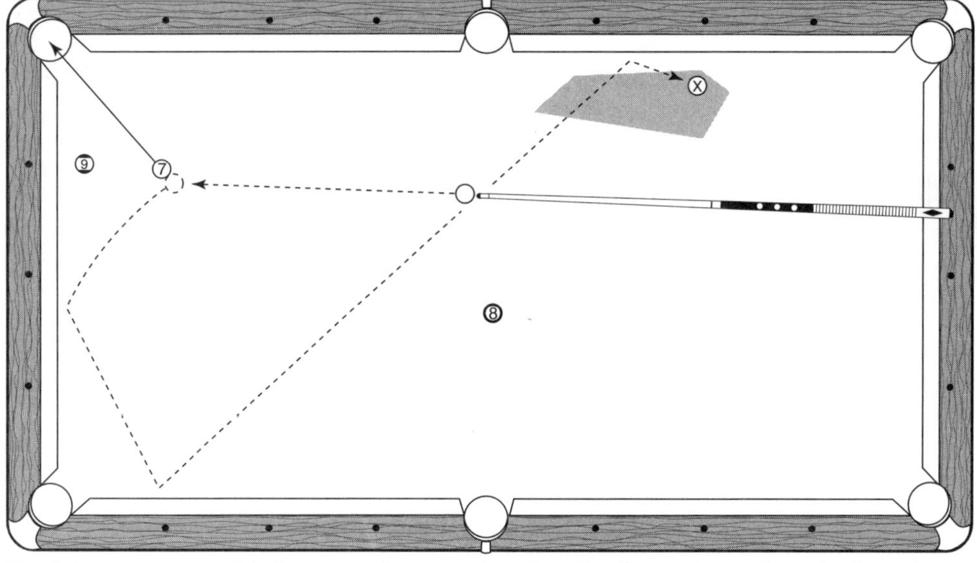

Position zones, which many have mistakenly thought to be circles or triangles, actually come in all shapes and sizes. Their shape depends on the layout. The diagram shows an unusually shaped zone for the playing position on the 8-ball.

#4 Margin for Error

If you possessed perfect cue ball control, you wouldn't need to worry about playing for a margin for error. But since we all make mistakes, factoring a margin for error into your position plays gives you an insurance policy against disaster. The policy protects you from scratching, getting hooked or otherwise missing shape. The "premium" for this kind of insurance is a slightly more difficult shot than the one you might have if you played for perfect position. The size of the margin you leave on any particular shot is dependent on:

- The dangers surrounding the shot.
- Your skill as a position player.
- Your skill as a shotmaker.

If you are a skillful shotmaker, you can play further away from danger because you're not too worried about a moderately tougher shot. If you have great cue ball control, then you can, of course, allow for a smaller margin for error.

Know When to Go Short or Long

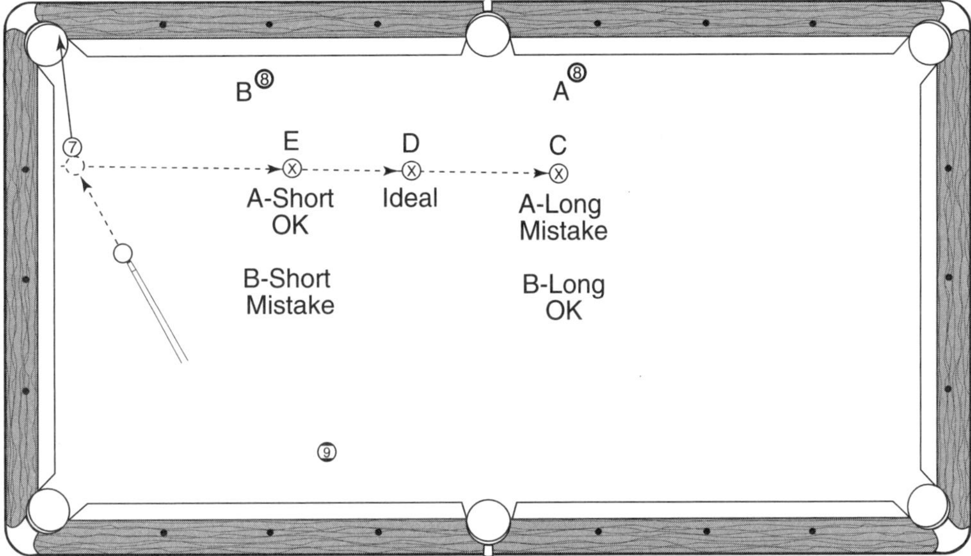

This three-ball run out presents no special problems as long as you play it with a reasonable amount of care and by building a safety net into your position on the 8-ball. With the 8-ball in Position A, the big mistake would be to send the cue ball past ideal position (D) to Position C. Now you would have to bank the 8-ball. The smart play is to send the cue ball to Position E. If you hit the shot a little too hard, you could wind up with perfect shape at Position D.

Now let's assume the 8-ball is in Position B. In this case, the smart play is to go long to Position C. If you hit the shot to easy, you could once again end up with perfect shape at Position D. The pros call this strategy dog proofing the layout.

Allowing for a Margin for Error

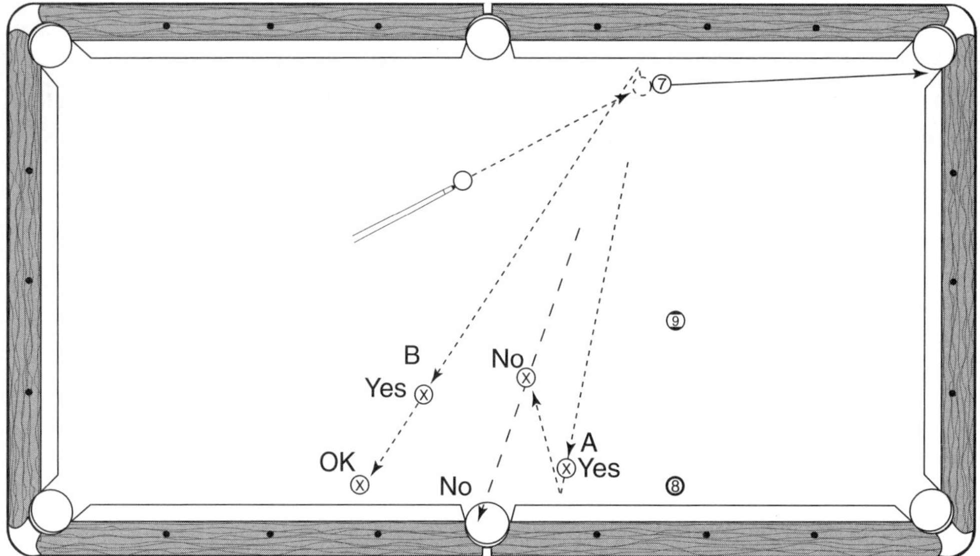

Here is a classic case of using a margin for error to avoid a scratch in the side pocket. Those who possess superb cue ball control may play for a closer shot on the 8-ball down Route A. This shot, however, requires expert speed and directional control. Route B is better for most players as it gives you a much larger margin for error. The price for the larger safety net is a shot on the 8-ball that is roughly 1.5' longer.

Low Risk Position on the 9-Ball

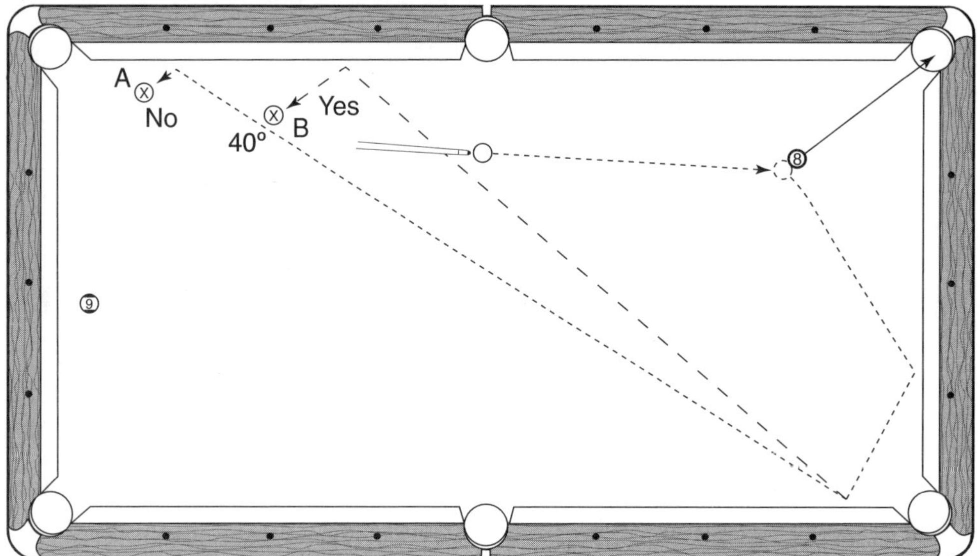

The only thing that can go wrong on this three-rail position route is a scratch in the upper left cornet pocket. The near straight in shot from Position A is just not worth the risk of scratching. The high percentage play is to aim higher up on the third rail and accept a modest 40-degree cut shot on the 9-ball at Position B.

#5 When to Play Area Shape

When the position zone to which you will be sending the cue ball is substantial and you only need adequate position, you should take aim in the center of the zone. This will give you the largest margin for error and should provide you with a 100% guarantee that you will complete the next sequence of shots. The goal of area shape is to completely eliminate the risk of not having a shot, or of having to play a difficult recovery shot to make up for poor position.

When Conditions Favor Area Shape

- The next ball is close to a pocket.
- There are very few balls on the table.
- Trying to get close to the next ball could result in a scratch, a hook, a difficult shot or a difficult position play.

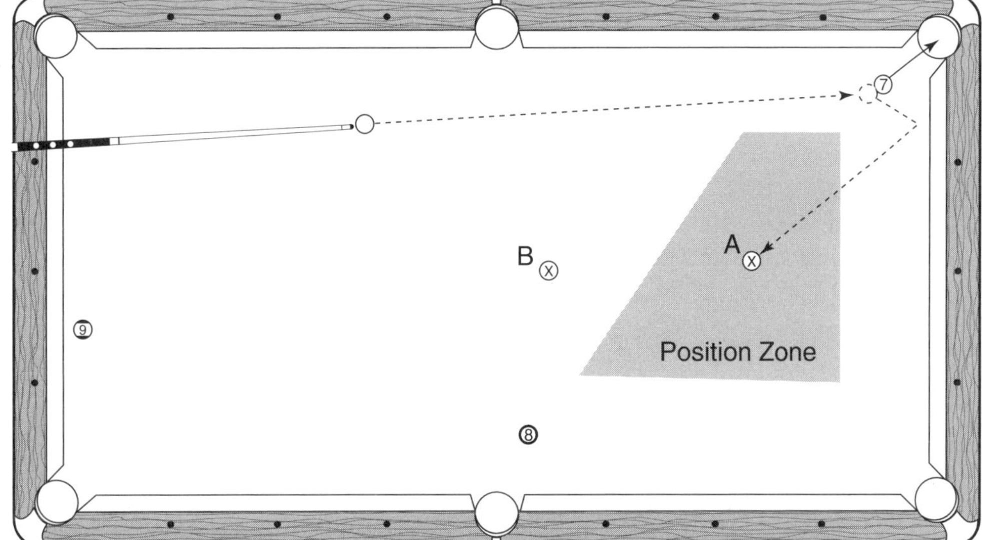

When the object ball is close to the pocket and the cue ball is a long distance away, as in the example, then it is difficult to play pinpoint position. In this position you can complete your run by playing area shape. Just make sure the cue ball lands anywhere within the sizeable position zone. From Position A it will be easy to play shape on the 9-ball. Now if you got greedy or careless with your position and the cue ball rolled to Position B, you would now be faced with a difficult 4-rail route to the 9-ball.

Going with the Flow

When your game is "on" you can get away with larger position zones) than you might normally play for, providing they don't endanger the shot. The idea is to let your better than average shotmaking carry a larger part of the burden. You must, however, guard against venturing outside of the limits of a larger zone due to sloppy play. When your game is in top gear, you may discover that your position play is on target with no special effort.

#6 Survey the Table Before Shooting

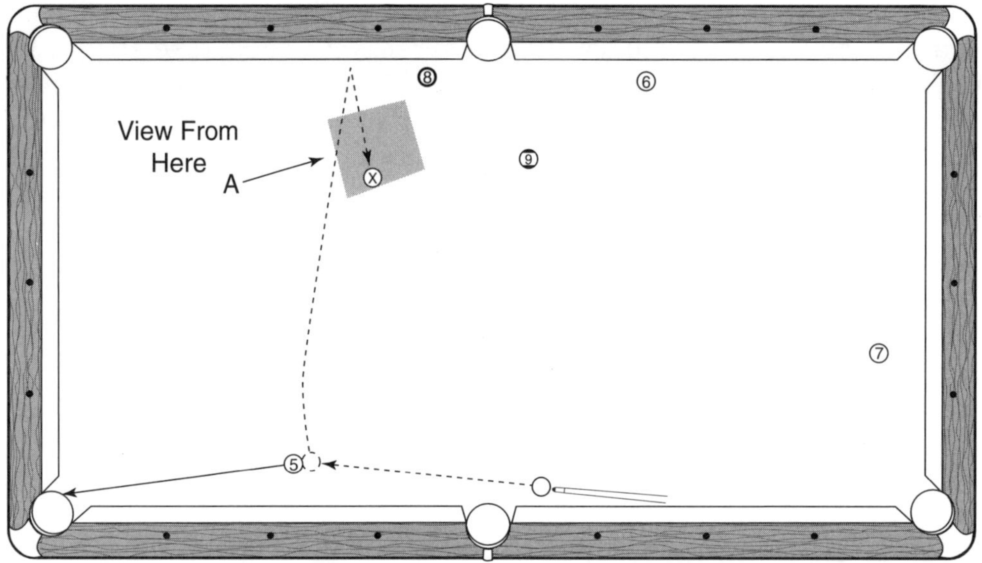

You can often get all the information you need for a shot by looking around the table from the position where you will be taking your stance. If so, go right ahead with your routine from that position. Don't, however, commit a blunder just because you were too lazy to check things out by walking to another vantage point or two. As a word of caution, laziness is one of the biggest reasons why a player stops advancing to higher levels of play.

The best view of a shot is from straight above the table. Since that area is inaccessible, the next best thing is to view your shots from whatever positions around the table are necessary to give you the information you need to plan the shot and play it correctly. Below is a list of possible things to look for while conducting your survey:

- When the next ball is close to other balls, you'll discover whether or not it will go into the pocket.
- You may discover unseen dangers, such a scratch off another ball.
- You could confirm that the shot you were considering is, in fact, the correct shot, or that it only needs a small modification.
- You can identify the rail targets more precisely for your position route. (There will be a discussion on rail targets later in the chapter).
- You can size up the exact dimensions of your position zone and the ideal angle for the next shot.
- You can reduce misses by getting the answers to all other possible questions prior to playing the shot.

Before playing the 5-ball it is a great idea to walk over to Position A to get a better look at exactly where the position zone lies. This information will give you a crystal clear picture of where you need to send the cue ball. This is a much better approach than playing the shot first, and then walking over to your shot on the 6-ball, only to discover you are hooked. Remember this sequence: survey, plan, execute.

#7 Playing for Three Balls (or more) at a Time

The principle of playing for three balls at a time is really the heart and soul of pattern play in Nine Ball. When you have mastered this concept and you will have taken a quantum leap in your ability to run racks. The key is to carefully plan your shape on the second ball. The shape you play on the second ball must enable you to continue to the third ball. The process is continually rolled forward until you arrive at the last two balls. Planning and playing for three balls at a time must become ingrained in your mental computer until you can do it easily and effortlessly on almost every shot.

To recap the process: before shooting the first ball determine:

- What options are available for playing position on the second ball?
- What route among those possible choices will enable you to then play position on the third ball?
- After the first ball, the process repeats itself.

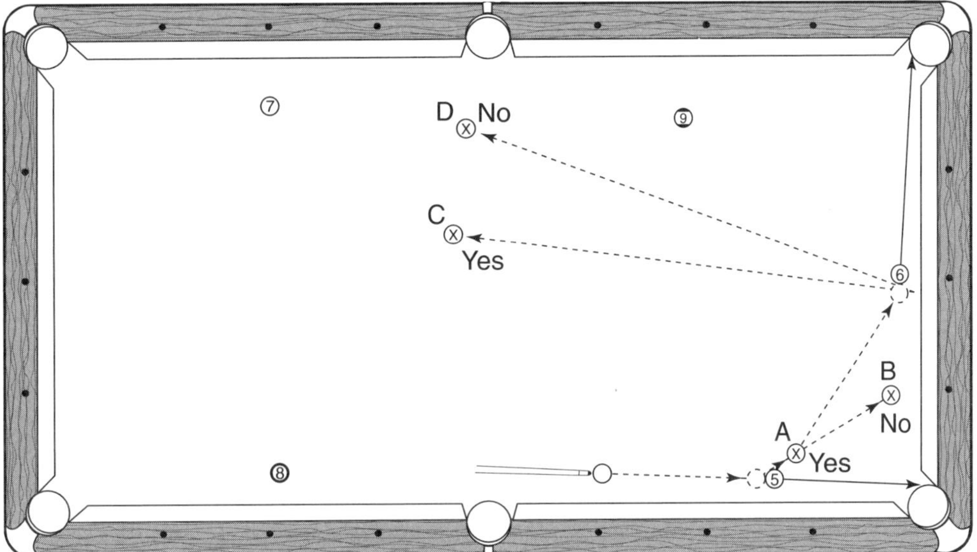

A soft follow shot on the 5-ball will leave the cue ball at Position A for the 6-ball. With a modest cut angle on the 6-ball it will be easy to escape the end rail and send the cue ball up table for the 7-ball. Notice what a big mistake it would have been to plan for only the 6-ball. With the cue ball in Position B the run out could quickly grind to a halt.

Again, when playing the 5-ball we were planning how we could get on the 7-ball! Now the process rolls forward. When playing the 6-ball you must now plan on how you are going to get from the 7-ball to the 8-ball. The example shows both the correct and incorrect position. Take a moment to figure out why Position C is preferable to Position D.

There will many more examples of this principle in Chapter 7. In that chapter you'll also learn those not so rare occasions when you must plan for 4 balls at a time.

#8 Play the High Percentage Sequence

Playing the high percentage sequence is all about balancing the difficulty of your shots. If you apply this principle correctly, you will optimize your chances of successfully completing any given sequence of shots. The following table is strictly for purposes of illustration. It breaks down the three possible sequences into cold, hard percentages. The ideal sequence gives you two fairly high percentage shots in a row. The worst sequence is to play a very simple shot followed by a very difficult shot, which lowers your overall odds of running out from 72% to 50%.

Sequence Rating	#1 Shot Difficulty(%)	#2 Shot Difficulty(%)	Cumulative Percentage
Ideal	90%	80%	72%
Fair	95%	70%	67%
Poor	100%	50%	50%

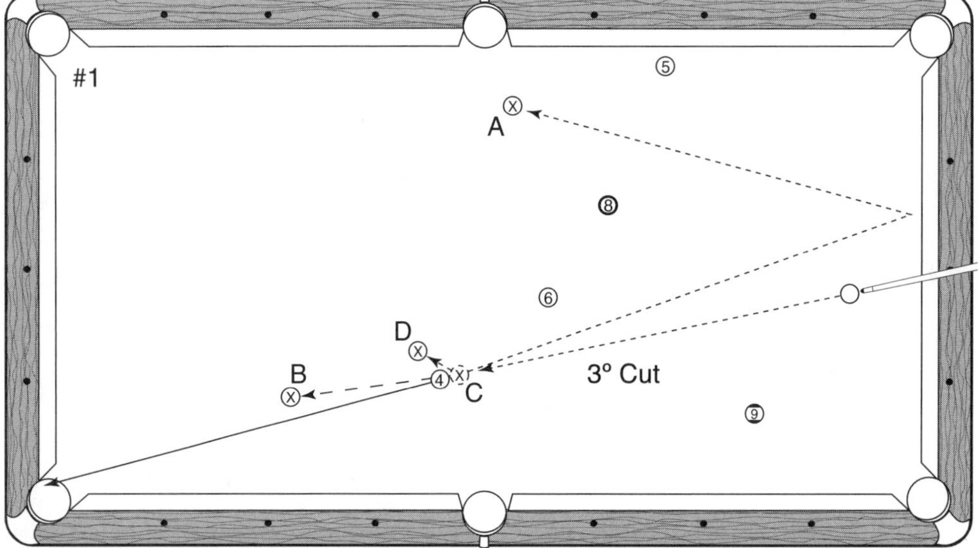

Mike Sigel, a member of the BCA Hall of Fame, was pitted against fellow hall member Nick Varner in the 1990 U.S. Open. Sigel was faced with the challenging position play in Diagram #1. He first considered drawing to the end rail and back out as shown. Accu-Stats commentator Buddy Hall knew better, however, as he kept insisting Sigel would avoid shooting a power draw shot when it was unnecessary. A power draw off the end rail and out could have left Sigel with an easy 10-15 degree cut on the 5-ball at Position A. Furthermore, completing the run from Position A would have been a cinch. But playing the power draw would have necessitated shooting a long and very difficult draw shot to make the next shot extremely simple. This choice would have violated the principle of playing the high percentage sequence.

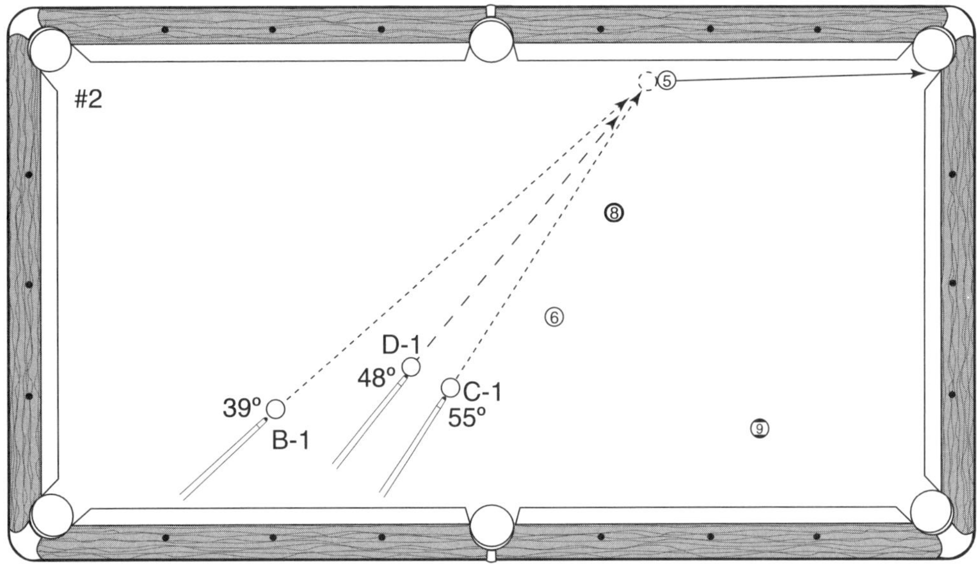

Another possibility would be to roll forward 1.5 diamonds to Position B. This would have left a longer 37-degree cut shot on the 5-ball. This option, however, increases the chances of missing the 4-ball as it is difficult to slow roll the cue ball with great accuracy over long distances.

If Sigel played a medium speed stop shot, the cue ball would have come to rest at Position C. This choice would give him the highest probability of pocketing the 4-ball. It also would have left him with a 55- degree cut on the 5-ball. Instead, he choose to lower the odds slightly of making the 4-ball by pounding it with an extremely hard stroke. The cue ball crawled a few precious inches forward and to the right to Position D. The pound shot raised his odds of pocketing the 5-ball by reducing the cut angle to 48-degrees.

Diagram #2 shows the shot that correspond to three of Sigel's options. C-1 was the position that resulted after the stop shot while B-1 is the position on the 5-ball after a soft follow shot. D-1 was the place from which Sigel played the 5-ball.

At the highest levels of play, balancing a sequence of shots is a sophisticated shifting of percentage points from one shot to the other. While I can't presume to know Sigel's pocketing percentages, I will, for purposes of illustration, guess that he lowered his pocketing percentage 2% with the pound shot so he could raise the odds of making the cut shot 5%. For a B player, the percentages on this shot may have been a loss of 5% on the pound shot, which would be more than offset by a gain of 15% on the cut shot. A C Player might actually be better off playing the softer stop shot and accepting the thinner cut.

Pros are very sophisticated in the way they balance shots. They are experts at adding and subtracting a few % points. They know the percentage points add up over time. Remember, when choosing the first shot, keep in mind that your goal is to select the shot that gives you the maximum probability of successfully completing the entire sequence.

#9 Right Side/Wrong Side

One of the master keys to position play is the principle of right side/wrong side. Positioning the cue ball on the right side makes playing shape on the next ball an easy and natural process. When the cue ball is on the wrong side, position on the next ball becomes more difficult, if not impossible. You can incorporate this concept into your game by deciding which side of the next ball you want the cue ball for each position play.

When the object ball is within an inch or so of the rail, there is essentially only one side of the ball on which the cue ball can be positioned. Furthermore, as a rule of thumb, you'll almost always want to be shooting towards the rail when the object ball is within about 6" or less of the rail. There are exceptions, of course.

Draw to the Right Side

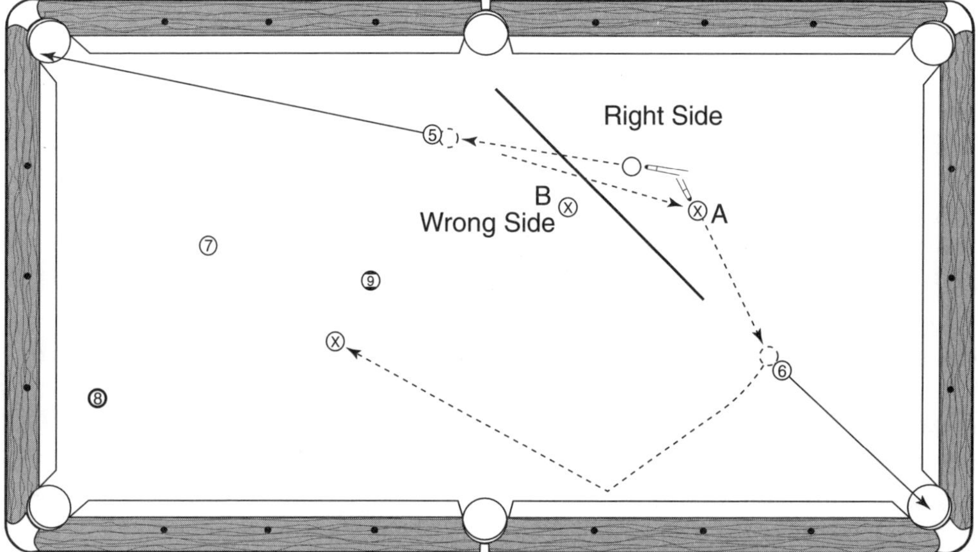

Our first example shows a typical position play in which you must draw nearly straight back down table. The heavy line is an extension of the line that goes directly from the 6-ball to the pocket. When playing the 5-ball, it is better to draw the cue ball back to Position A, which is the right side of the line. Now it will be easy to play shape on the 7-ball by sending the cue ball off the side rail and up the table as shown.

If the cue ball had stopped at Position B, it would be on the wrong side of the heavy solid line. With the cue ball in this position you would have to use a hard follow stroke with inside english, which would greatly increase the chances of missing the 6-ball. In addition, it would not be nearly as easy to get the correct angle on the 7-ball.

The Wrong Side Leaves a Long Shot

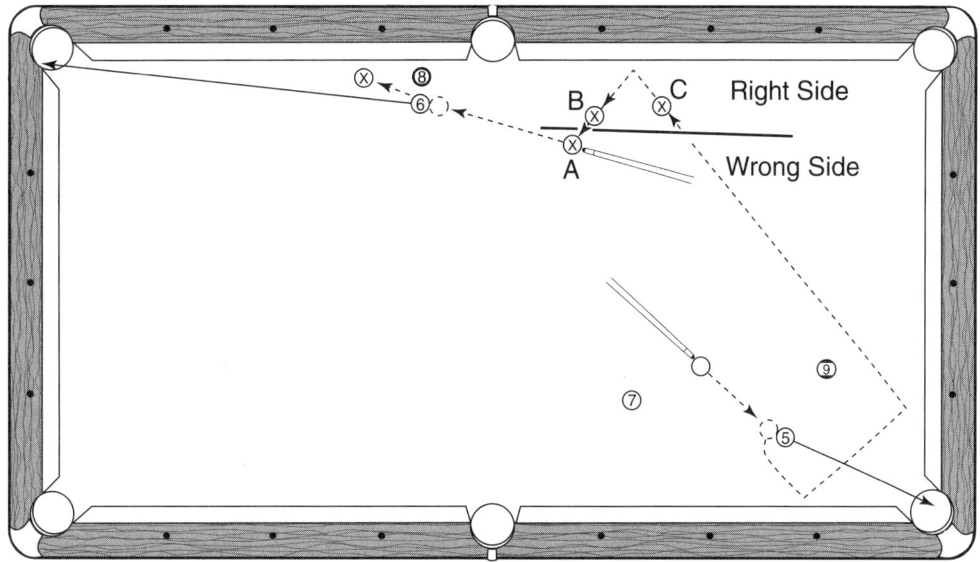

Efren Reyes picked the correct route but struck the cue ball a little firmly, sending it to the wrong side at Position A. Anywhere on the other side of the line such as at Positions B or C would have been ideal. Notice that the cue ball entered on the right side, was briefly the ideal zone, and then reemerged on the wrong side. Reyes recovered from this shot and ran out against Earl Strickland at the Sands Regency Open, June, 1995.

One Foot or Eighteen Feet?

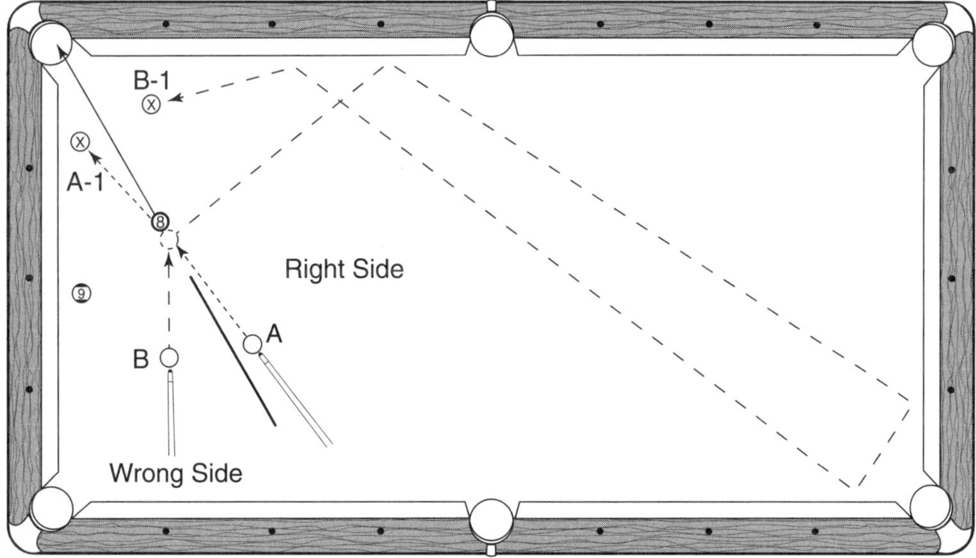

The position play error in this illustration comes up quite often, usually as a result of poor planning or execution. With the cue ball on the correct side at Position A, shape on the 9-ball at A-1 is easy. With the cue ball on the wrong side at Position B, it must now embark on an 18' long journey around the table to arrive at B-1 for the 9-ball.

An Exception Rule

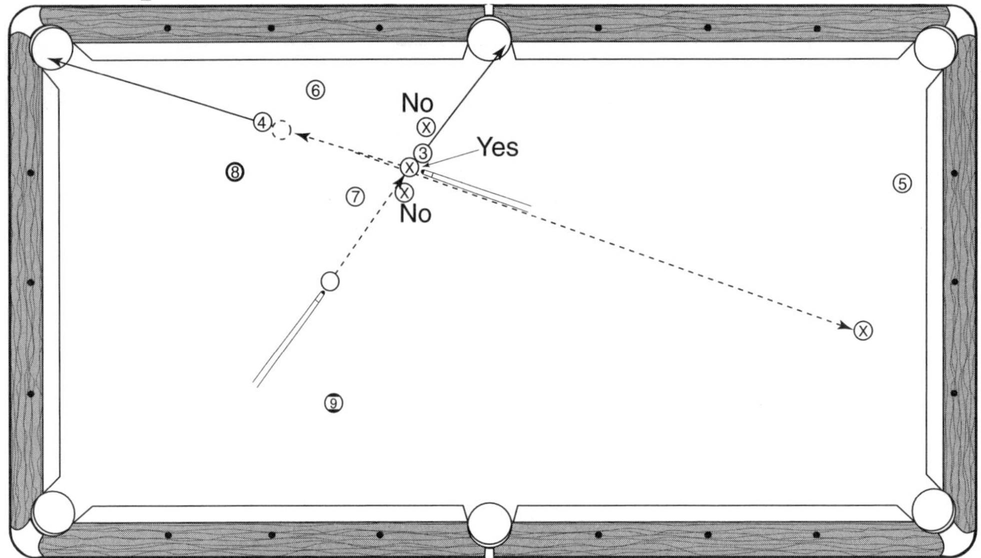

When balls are stationed on either side of the ball you are about to play, they could easily block the position route to the next ball. The 6, 7 and 8-balls are all conspiring to prevent you from getting back up table for the 5-ball. A stop shot on the 3-ball into the side pocket will leave you with a straight in shot on the 4-ball With the cue ball in this position you can draw straight back past the obstructers to the 5-ball.

#10 Play to the Long Side When Possible and Practical

In Nine Ball you will quite often be required to send the cue ball on a rather lengthy journey to the position zone. As a result, it behooves you to play for the largest zones that can provide you with workable position. This means that you will typically want to send the cue ball to the long side of the object ball. This usually gives you a bigger zone and a shorter distance for the object ball to the pocket.

In Part A of the diagram at the top of the next page, the 2-ball is well past the mid point towards the upper right cornet pocket. The position zone is considerably larger on the long side as shown. It will be much easier to send the cue ball into the long side on most occasions. You will discover, however, that there are many exceptions to this rule.

Part B gives you an exception to the long side principle. Notice that the 6-ball has effectively shrunk the size of the long side position zone. In addition, playing shape on this side now creates the risk of a hook. In this case, the short side is preferable.

In Part C the 1-ball is stationed directly opposite the side pockets, and it is much closer to the top side pocket. The short and long side position zones on a side pocket shot typically don't extend to either side of the ball, which is why the zones in this example stop on line between the two side pockets.

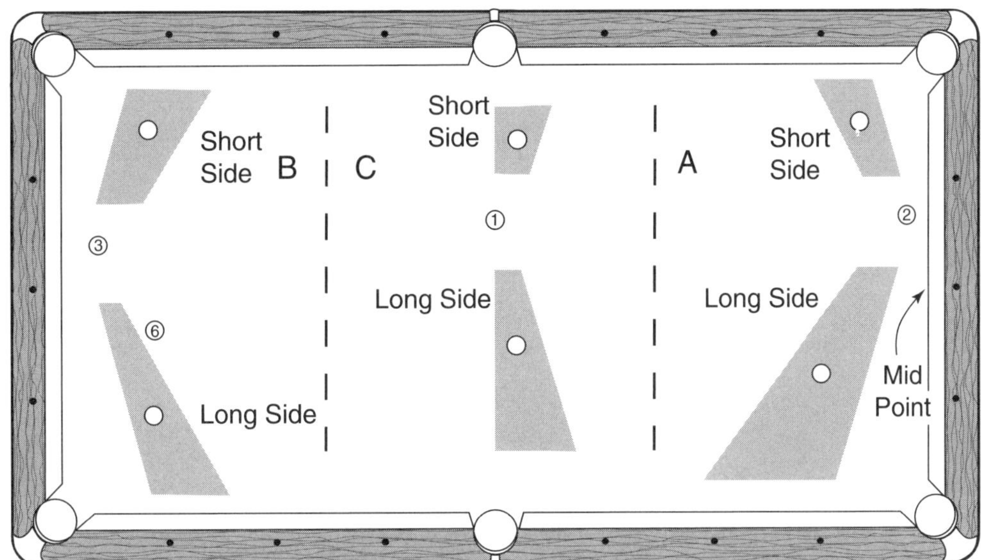

Short Side Ensures the Angle

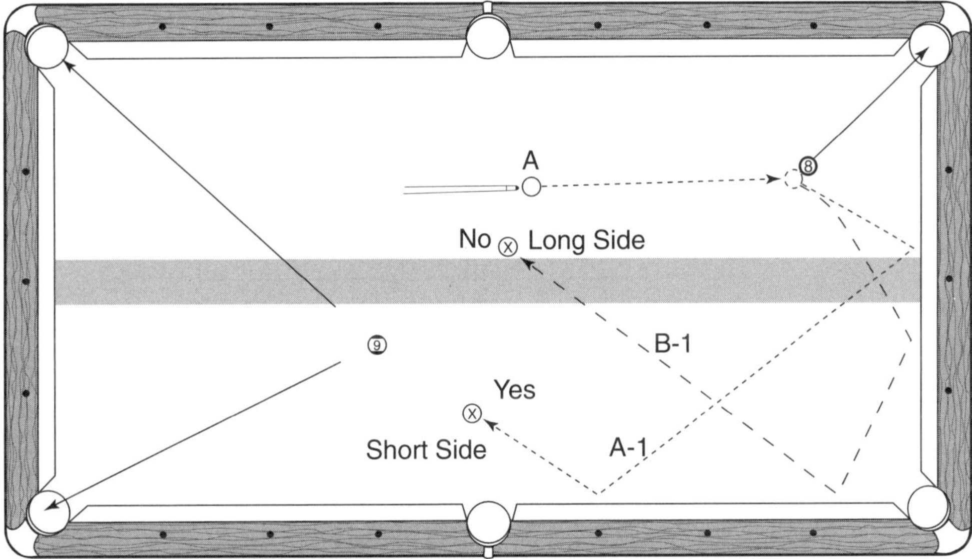

The channel that runs down the middle of the table is a neutral zone when the object ball rests in this zone, there is no great advantage to playing on the long side versus the short. When the next ball rests outside this zone, then the long side if generally preferable, but not always. In the example, you need only pocket the 8 and 9-balls. When the cue ball is in Position A, then you should play to the short side down Route A-1. It would be a mistake to send the cue ball on Route B-1 to the long side as you would be crossing through the position zone (see principle 12).

Other Principles Override the Long Side

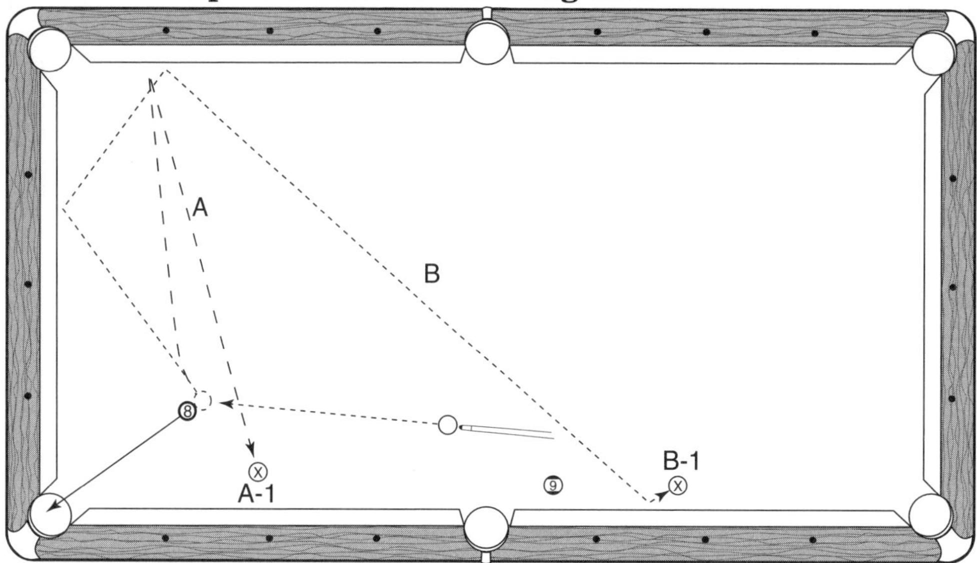

The principles of position play usually work together to create a successful position play. At times, however, one principle will take precedence over another. You could play a draw shot across the table and back along Route A to the long side at A-1, but this would require a perfect stroke. It is much easier to send the cue ball to the short side by using Route B, which is the natural path (See principle 14) to B-1.

Avoiding a Combo

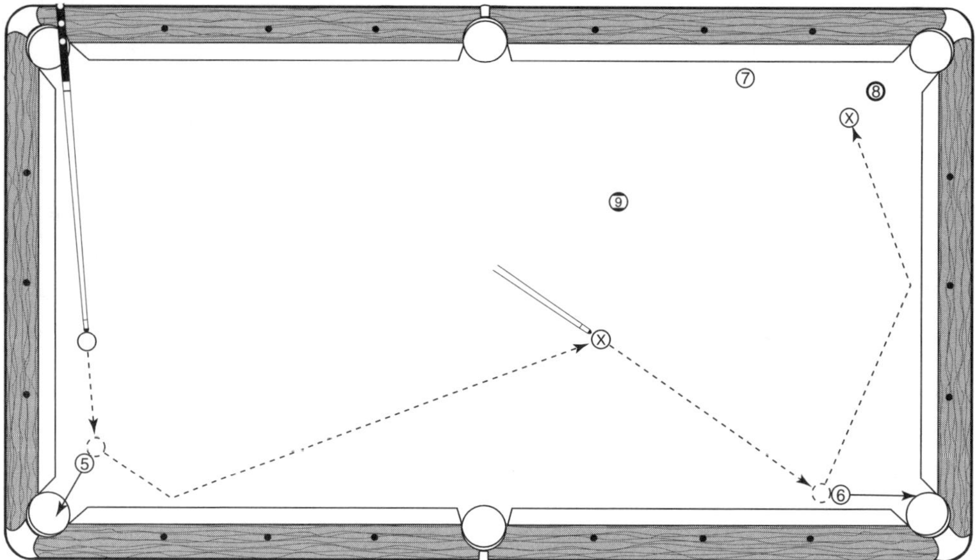

The 7-ball won't go past the 8-ball, and the 7-8 combo is quite difficult. The alternative is to play the pattern shown in the diagram, which results in short side shape on the 7-ball for the upper left cornet pocket. The key is to execute two fairly easy position plays to near perfection in consecutive order.

#11 Ball in Hand Shape

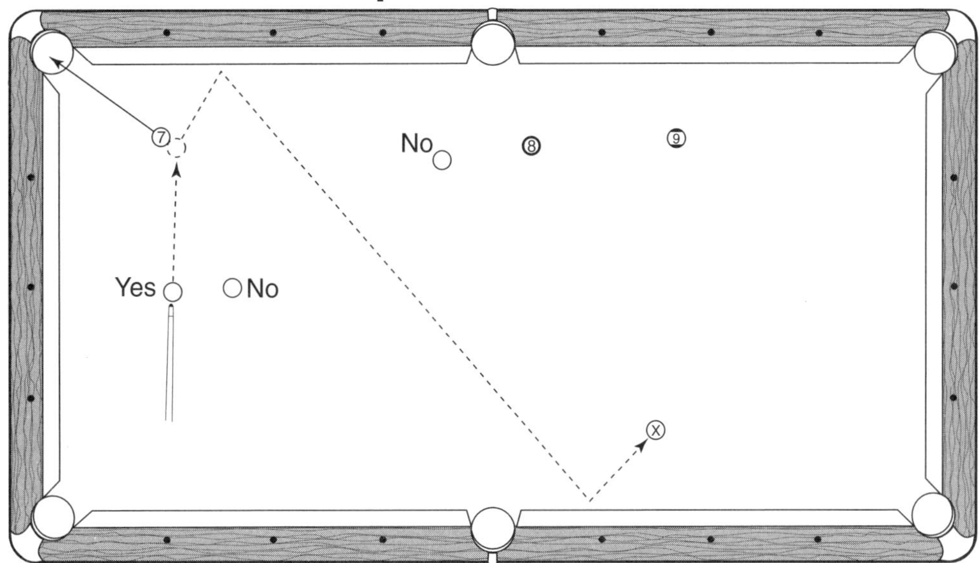

Nine Ball position is largely about making longer shots and getting the correct angle on the next ball. When you are awarded ball in hand, for at least one shot you don't have to worry about making the ball or playing for the correct angle. When "playing shape" with ball in hand, you should put the cue ball as close to the object ball as you can without losing your line or having to stretch. As a rule of thumb, 6"-18" is the right distance.

You have much more latitude in choosing your cut angle with ball in hand. In the position above, a 50-degree cut angle will give you the perfect speed and direction when the shot is played with a soft stroke. In essence, the position you create with ball in hand almost plays the shot for you before the cue ball has even been struck.

When playing certain routes with ball in hand, you can be more exacting in your position. You can set the angle to precisely match the requirements of the route. In doing so, you can avoid having to apply excess english or use a stroke with which you are not totally comfortable. You can also play closer to obstacles and hazards when you are completely certain of the direction the cue ball will be traveling.

You can quickly learn position routes by watching where excellent players place the cue ball with ball in hand. Did they get good position on the next ball? What route did they take? After watching good players, you will learn many of the best routes, which you will hopefully remember when you encounter them. If you can't consistently get shape on the next shot with ball in hand, you have a strong indicator that your ball placement and/or execution needs work.

TIP: The size of the ideal position zone with ball in hand is not much larger than the cue ball Be a perfectionist. Perfect shape on the first ball should enable you to get excellent shape on the next ball, which could kick start a run out through the 9-ball.

#12 Playing Down the Line of a Position Zone when Possible

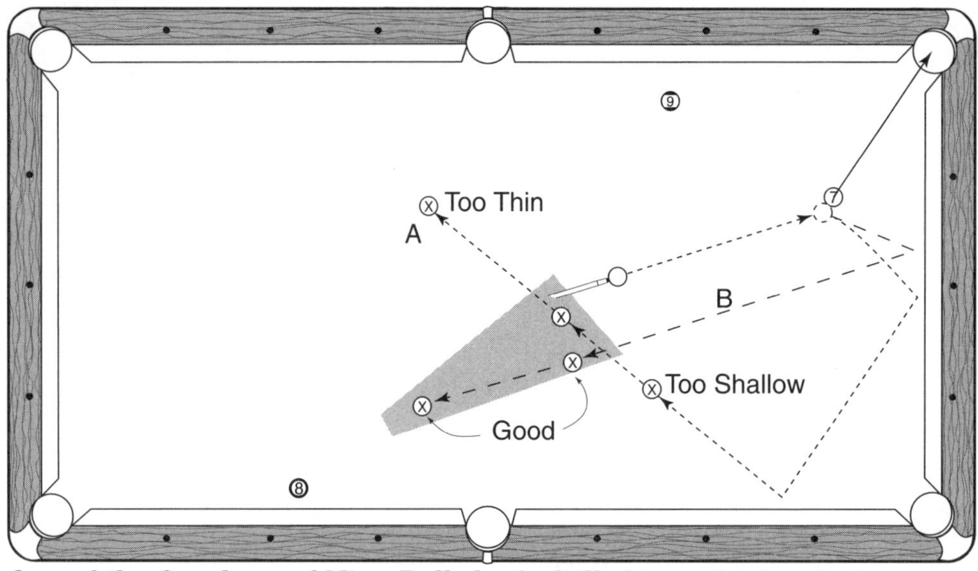

One of the first laws of Nine Ball that's drilled into the head of any new player is that you've got to leave yourself an angle. If you adhere to the principle of Playing Down the Line When Possible, you will go a long ways towards creating and maintaining the correct angle.

There are three balls remaining in the diagram above. All you need is the correct angle on the 8-ball after playing the 7-ball and the game should be over. Players who believe that two-rail position is the big secret to Nine Ball may chose Route A. The problem with this route is that the cue ball will be in the position zone for only a short distance. If your speed is not near perfect, you could easily wind up with a cut that is either too shallow or too thin. The high percentage route is play 1-rail shape by sending whitey down Route B. Notice that the cut angle remains almost the same no matter where it stops in the zone.

Maintaining a Constant Angle

In the diagram at the top of the next page, the ideal cut angle for the 8-ball is 30-degrees. By extending the 30-degree cut line to the side rail you can discover where the cue ball must hit the side rail. If the cue ball hits the designated spot on the rail, at the right angle, it will maintain a constant 30-degree cut angle as it travels across the position zone directly towards the ghost ball adjacent to the 8-ball. The cue ball must also rebound at the appropriate angle in order to travel at a constant angle. In our example, the cue ball entered at 54-degrees and rebounded at 40-degrees. Notice that ideal position lies all the way from Point A to Point C. Point B is the bulls eye.

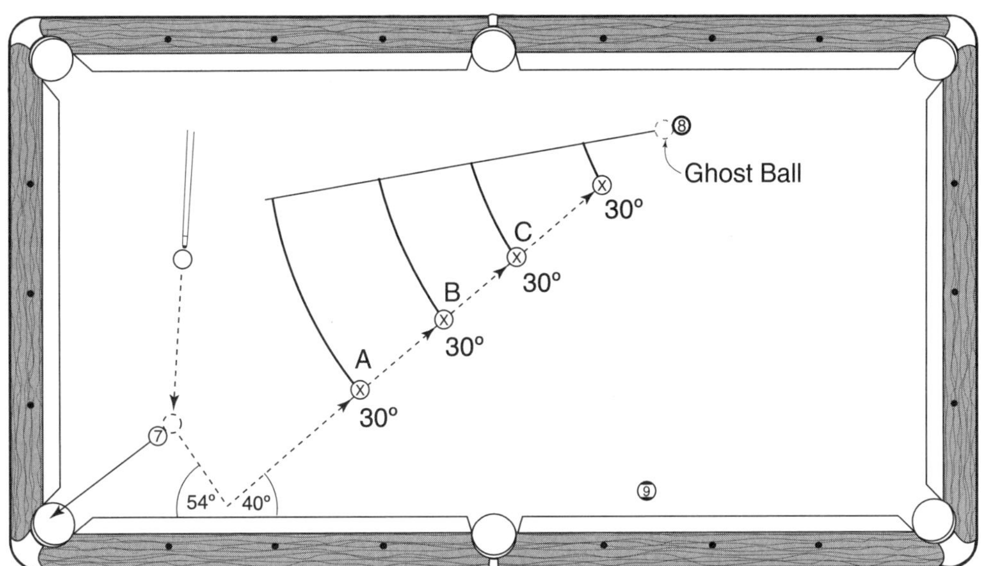

Gradually Changing Angles

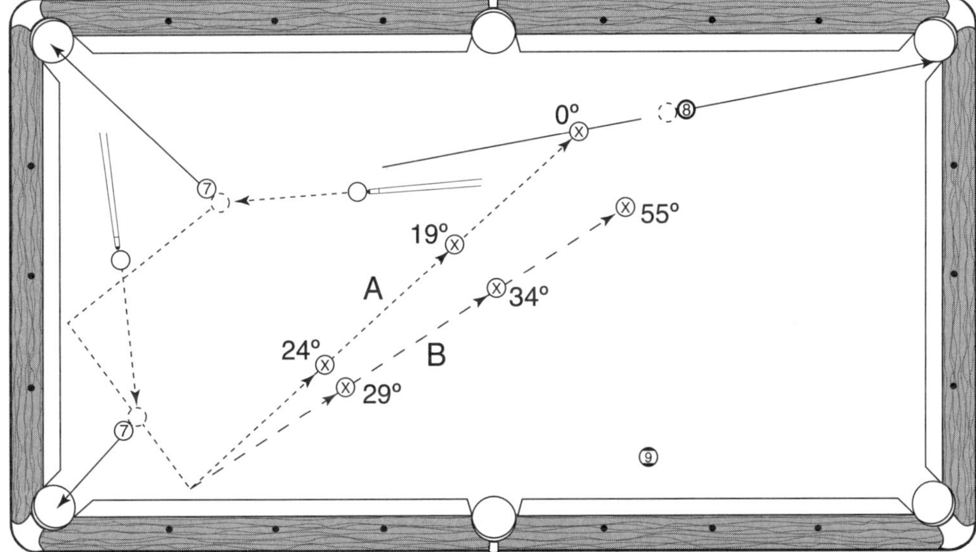

Most of the time it will not be possible to set up an angle that does not change as the cue ball travels down the position zone. The next best thing is a line of travel in which the cut angle changes little in route. Route A shows a cut angle that is slowly decreasing while the cue ball travels across the table. Route B demonstrates a cut angle that is slowly growing in size as the cue ball rolls toward the 8-ball. When you have a choice, as in this position, you should opt for either Route A or B. If you don't mind a longer shot or might have trouble stretching for the shot (assuming you are right handed) then Route A would be better. If you are left-handed or are a tall player with a long reach, then Route B is preferable.

Rapidly Changing Angles

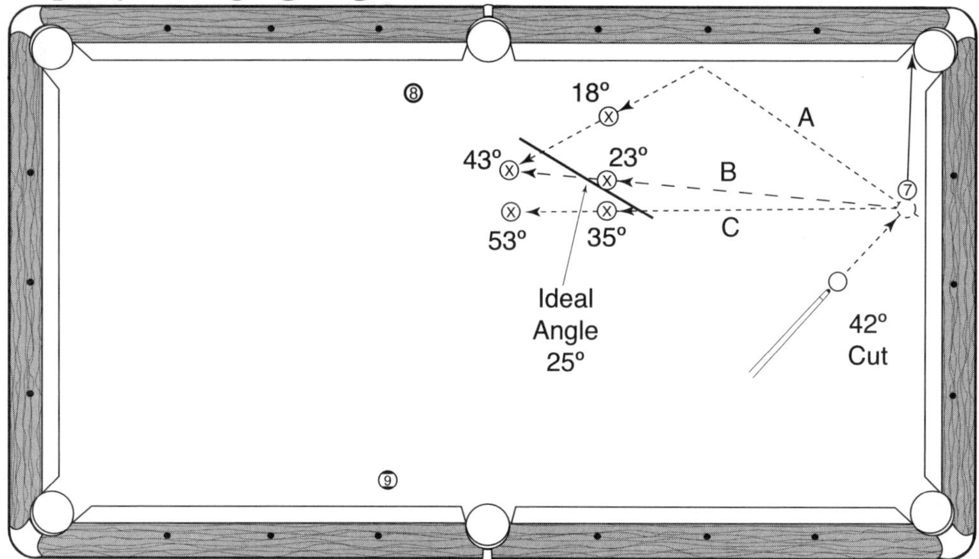

The diagram shows three routes to the 8-ball. The ideal angle on the 8-ball is about 25-30 degrees. Route A carries the most risk of missing the ideal zone as the cut angle changes rapidly from 12 to 43-degrees within about one foot. The angle on Route B changes quickly, but nearly as fast as Route A. In the space of a foot it changes from 23 to 43 degrees.

Players who prefer a soft stroke might choose Route C, in which the cut angle changes by 18 degrees within about a foot. When you are playing position in a similar situation, you must plot your position route with great care to optimize your chances of having a workable angle.

#13 Enter the Wide Part of a Position Zone

When you have to send the cue ball across a position zone, you have far less margin for error than if you are able to play down the line, as we discussed in the previous section. Playing across a zone can be a disaster waiting to happen if you don't plan carefully, or if speed control is not your forte.

When crossing the zone, speed control is crucial. You can improve your odds of landing within a position zone by entering its widest part. The widest part is always further from the object ball. You are, in essence, giving up a little accuracy on the next shot in exchange for making sure you wind up with a workable cut angle. The keys to playing across the line position are:

- Recognize the danger in the first place.
- Plan to play to the wide side.
- Execute the shot as precisely as possible. Speed control is crucial.

Enter the Wide Side

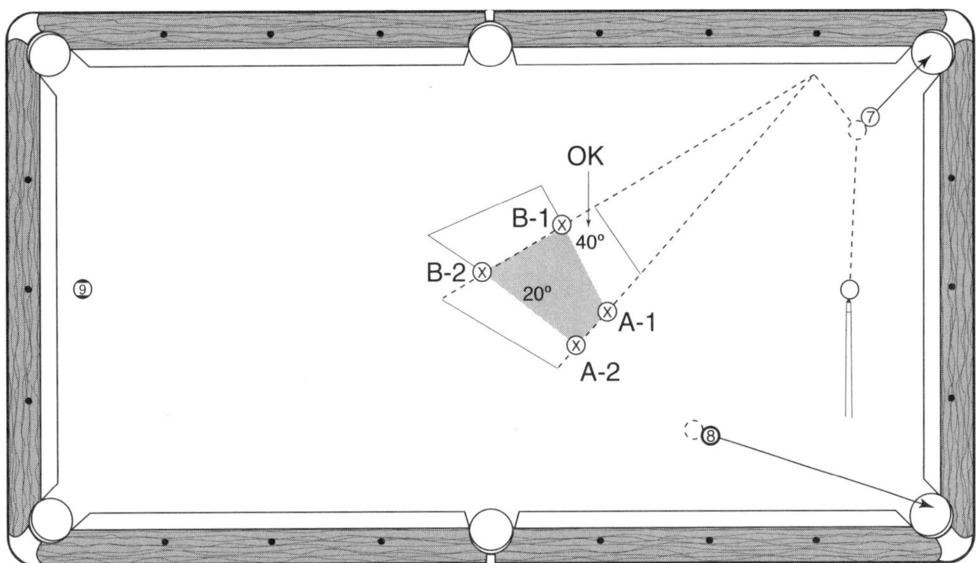

The position play from the 7-ball to the 8-ball gives you no choice but to send the cue ball across the width of the position zone. The ideal cut angle on the 8-ball is between 20 and 40-degrees. The zone is only about 6" wide from A-1 to A-2. By entering the wide side, you have an 11" long zone from B-1 to B-2. This extra 5" gives you approximately an 80% larger target.

The Wide Side Lowers the Risk

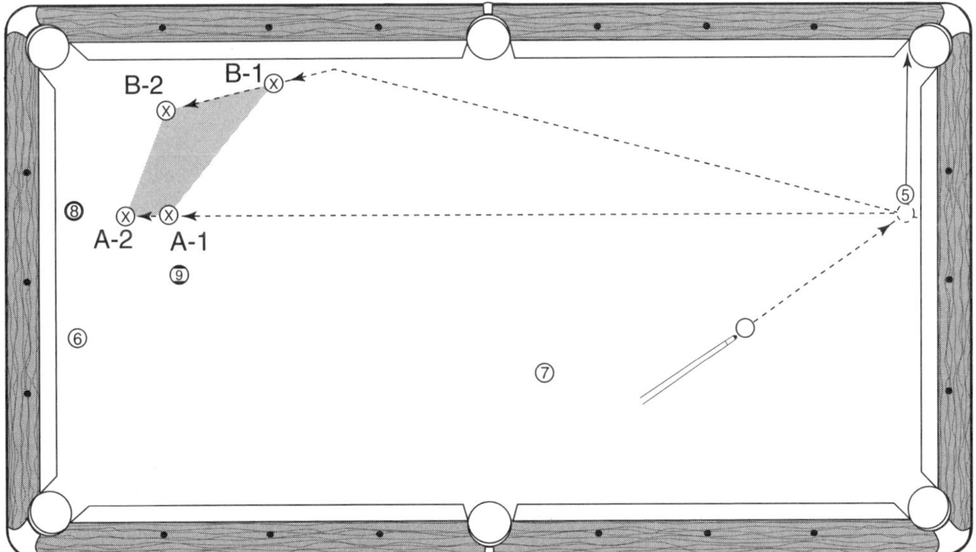

This position play is fraught with danger as you could easily get hooked behind either the 8 or 9-ball. Normally it is much easier to control the cue ball by sending it straight down the table, but not here as the position zone from A-1 to A-2 is a scant 5" long. Sending the cue ball off the side rail nearly triples the zone to 13.5" from B-1 to B-2.

#14 Play Natural Shape as Often as Possible

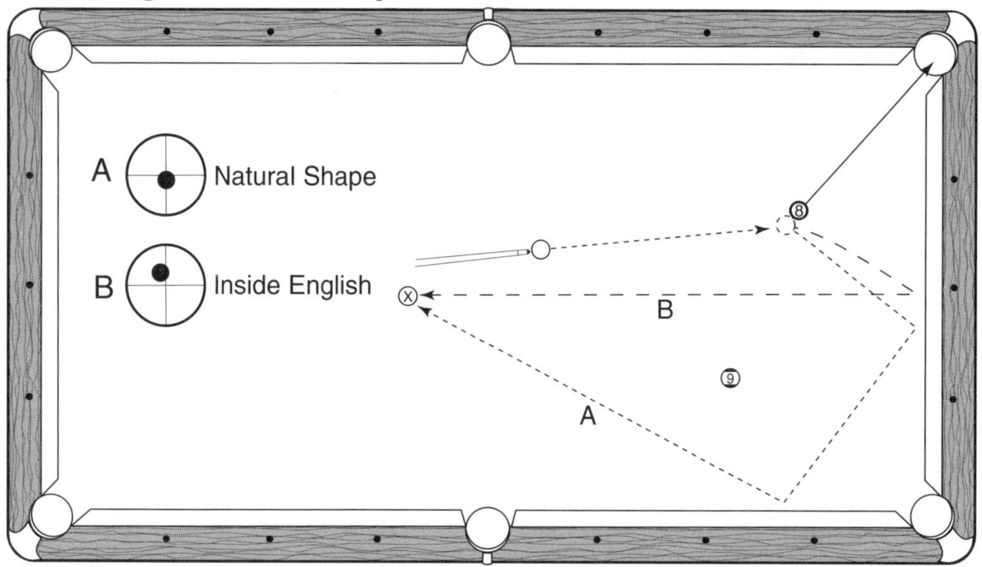

Nine Ball requires you to shoot with great accuracy while sending the cue ball long distances for position. To ensure the accuracy of each shot, you should play natural shape whenever possible. You can discover natural shape for a variety of routes by playing the shots using a speed with which you are comfortable, and by cueing on the vertical axis (no sidespin).

Route A in the illustration above is a natural two-rail path to the 9-ball. The shot was played with a half tip of draw, a medium soft stroke and no english. To play Route B, you have to force the cue ball to go against its natural inclination by using high inside english. This shot is much tougher to pocket that the one in Route A.

#15 Plan Your Route and Avoid Obstructions

Nine Ball is a traveling game. When you consider that the balls are spread randomly across the entire length of the table, you have the makings of an obstacle course. Other balls are obviously obstacles. A possible scratch can also be an obstacle. Obstacles appear most often in the early stages of a game. This is especially true among players who have a weak break, as the balls tend to cluster at the foot end of the table. However, obstacles can also appear with only a few balls left on the table.

If there were no obstacles, you could get by most of the time with just a few common position routes. Obstacles do exist, however, which is partly why I covered such a wide variety of position routes in Chapter 3. Your ability to carefully plan your route and adapt your cueing and speed to the situation will go along ways towards helping send the cue ball untouched through obstacle courses. Your skill at avoiding obstacles will also go a long ways towards building your run out power.

Tips for Running the Obstacle Course

The following is a list of items that will stimulate your thinking on how to best plan your way through an obstacle course.

- The obstacle is easy to deal with, as it only requires only a slight modification from the ideal route.
- There is only one obstacle, but it is a major hurdle.
- There are multiple obstacles. These could be two balls en route, or a ball and a possible scratch.
- You might have to choose a very difficult route because a simple position play is simply not available.
- The obstacle is such a big challenge that a safety is a better percentage play.

Rate Your Chances of Avoiding the Obstacle

Before forging ahead with a questionable position play, you should weigh the alternatives. Your possible choices include:

- Playing a position route with which you are comfortable, but which has an obstacle that you could possibly encounter.
- Play a slightly less familiar route that allows you to completely avoid any obstacles. You may have to compromise your shotmaking accuracy with this choice.

Going Through Traffic

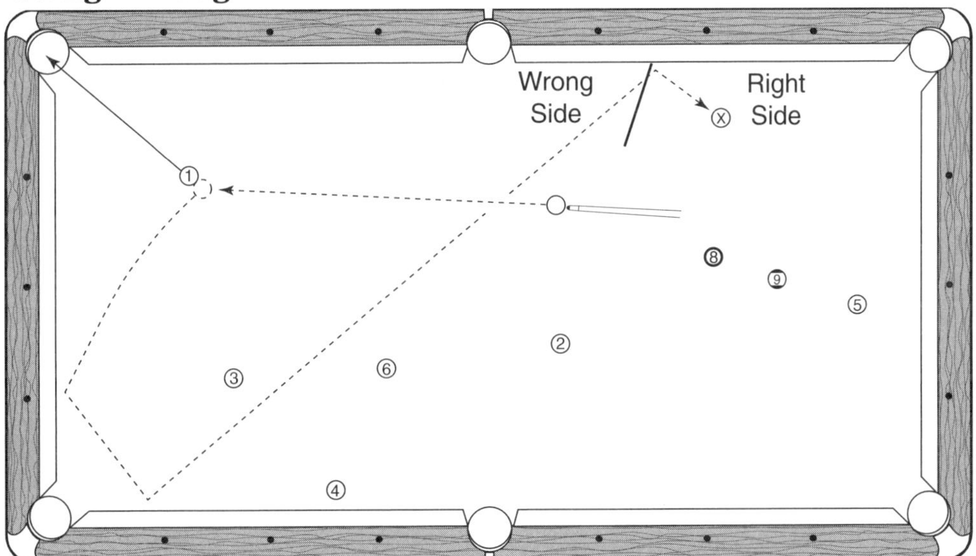

Nick Varner successfully negotiated this obstacle course to land on the correct side of the 2-ball (remember Principle # 9). His cueing and speed were perfect. If he had used a little more draw he would have run into the 3-ball. If he used follow, the cue ball would have run into the 6-ball. When you posses the skills of a Nick Varner, you can cut things pretty close with the assurance that the cue ball will emerge unharmed. This action took place in a match against Mike Sigel at the 1990 U.S. Open.

#16 Use Rail Targets

Before the cue ball arrives at its final destination, it could contact one or more rails. Each rail the cue ball contacts en route can provide a useful intermediate target. You can pinpoint these rail targets by using the diamonds. When planning multi rail routes, try to hit the first rail target precisely where intended, as this will establish the direction for the rest of the cue ball's path to the position zone.

When playing, and especially in practice, take careful note of where you want to hit the rail. Carefully observe your results. File the information away for future reference. Eventually you will become very proficient at hitting these intermediate targets, which will improve your shape while keeping you out of trouble.

Setting Rail Targets

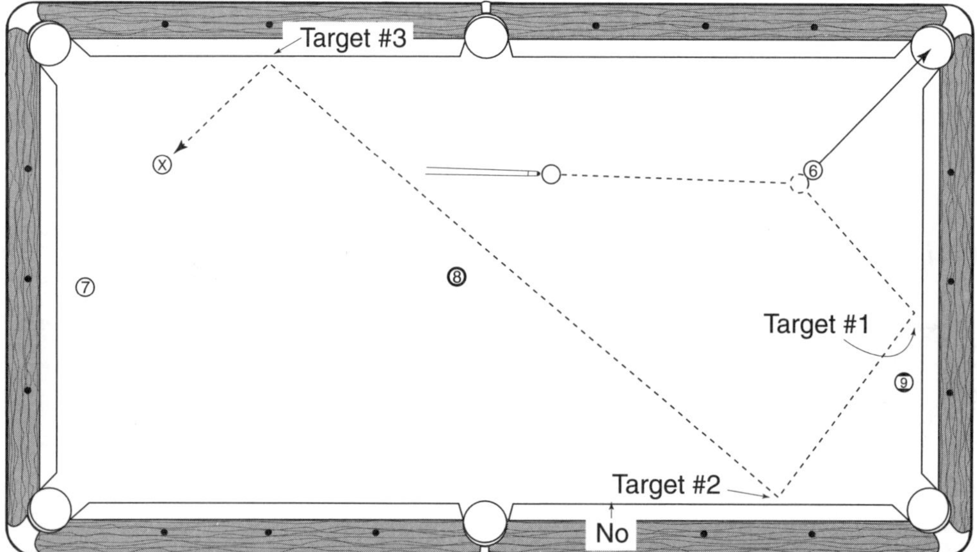

Rail targets can help you play this common three-rail route with precision. Target #1 is key because it establishes the direction of the shot. You must avoid the 9-ball on your way to the first rail. If the cue ball hits too far up the second rail, it could easily run into the 8-ball up table. The third rail target is two diamonds up from the corner, which gives you ample protection against scratching in the upper left corner pocket.

Rail Targets in Small Increments

In the example at the top of the next page, the cue ball must weave past the 9 and 8-balls for position on the 7-ball. Now is the time to divide the area between the diamonds into small increments. This will give you a precise rail target that, if hit, will guarantee the cue ball arrives safely at Position X. If the cue ball had struck the rail one quarter diamond (3 1/8") above or before the target, it would have run into the 8-ball. The cue ball would have hit the 9-ball if you had aimed one quarter diamond below the ideal target.

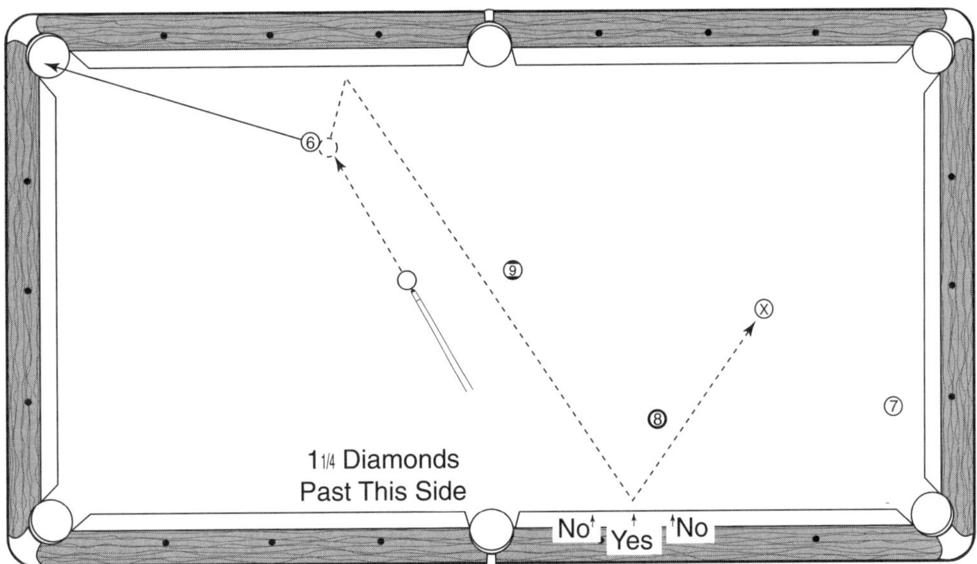

#17 Avoid Scratching

The biggest mistake in Nine Ball is to commit a foul, which gives your opponent ball in hand anywhere on the table. Fouls that follow a tough safety by your opponent are understandable. Bad fouls are the silly scratches that occur on position plays where things are largely under your control. While many players feel the pool gods are conspiring against them when they scratch, on most fouls, it is the player's fault. Bad luck has little to do with the vast majority of scratches that come on position plays. The true culprits are lack of knowledge and/or faulty execution. The diagram below shows three of the most common scratches, each of which can be avoided with proper planning and execution.

Common Scratches

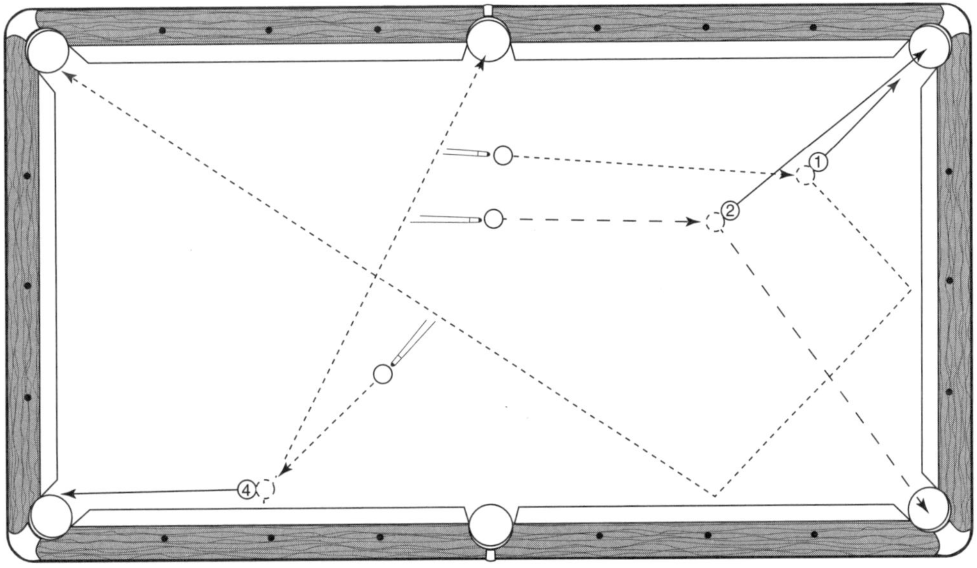

How Scratches Happen

- Natural scratches – the cue ball is going towards the pocket and there is sometimes little you can do to avoid the scratch.
- Poor execution – you can avoid these with proper execution.
- Poor planning – these scratches result from choosing a high-risk route that places the cue ball in danger.
- The conditions – while you are adjusting to an unfamiliar table, you may be vulnerable to scratching because the cue ball follows an unexpected path off one or more cushions.
- Bad luck – difficult position plays may involve an element of risk. For example, the cue ball must narrowly miss a pocket or two by design. A very slight miscalculation or a bad table roll could result in a scratch.

If you are scratching far too often, I suggest that you learn from each one so you won't repeat the scratch again. Also pay attention to other player's scratches. How do they unfold? What can be learned from them so you can avoid a similar mistake? Your powers of observation can enable you to soon become familiar with the shots that carry the highest risk of a scratch. At the same time, you will know the preventive measures.

When Scratches are "On" or "Off"

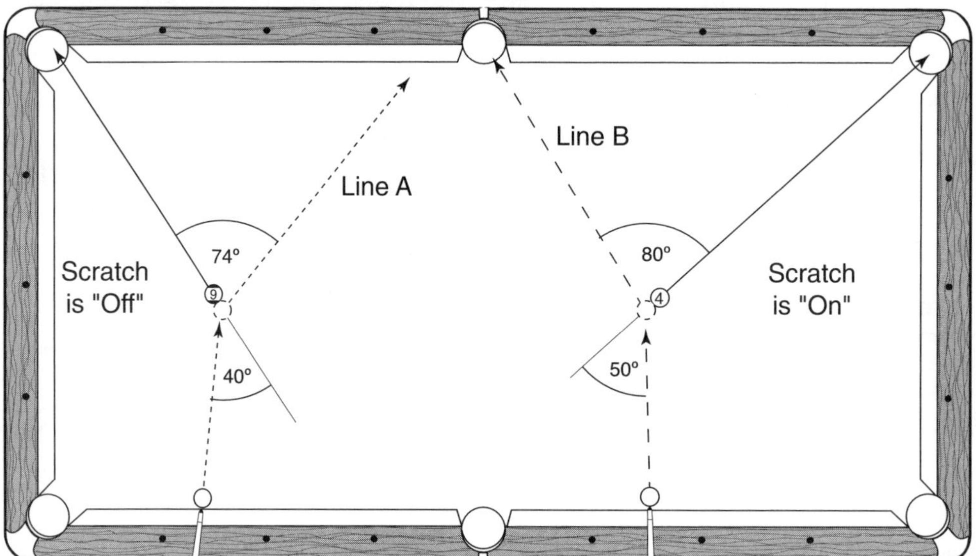

Some scratches are "on" and there is little you can do to avoid them. One of the most common types are thin cuts where you can do little to alter the course of the cue ball. Another type are shots off the rail, which limit your choice of cueing. Part A shows a rail shot where the scratch is "off". It pays to know when a scratch is off so you can shoot the shot with confidence, and not pass on the shot because you think there is a scratch when there isn't. Part B shows a thin cut off the rail in which a scratch is "on."

Close But no Scratch with Pro Like Control

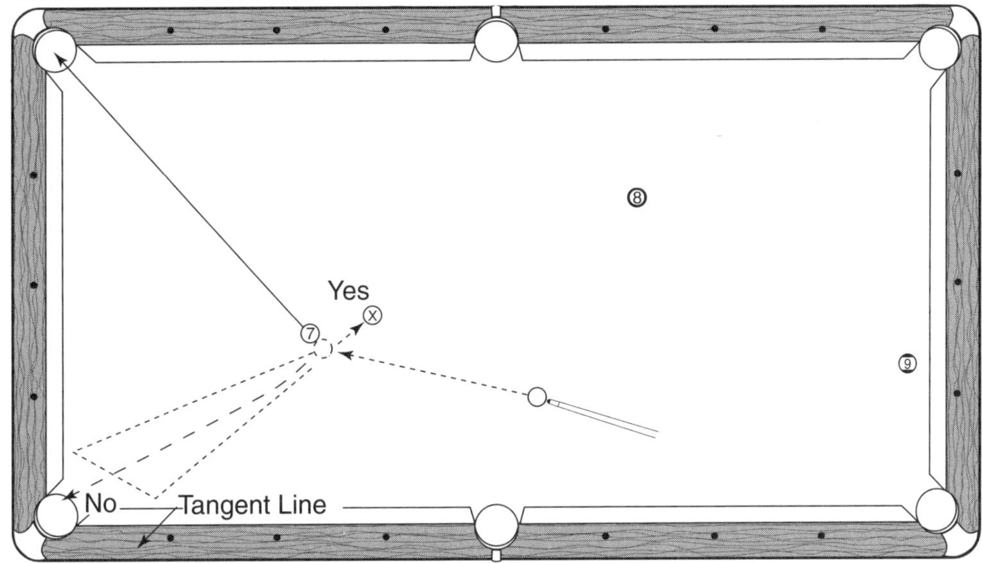

Earl Strickland narrowly avoided a scratch while playing this two-rail beauty against Buddy Hall, at the Sands Regency 12 Open, in December 1990. Turn the book so you can look at the shot from Strickland's perspective. Does it look like a scratch shot to you? Notice that the tangent line is actually pointing at the opposite side of the pocket The shot was played with follow, so the cue ball curved to avoid the scratch.

Avoiding an Obvious Scratch

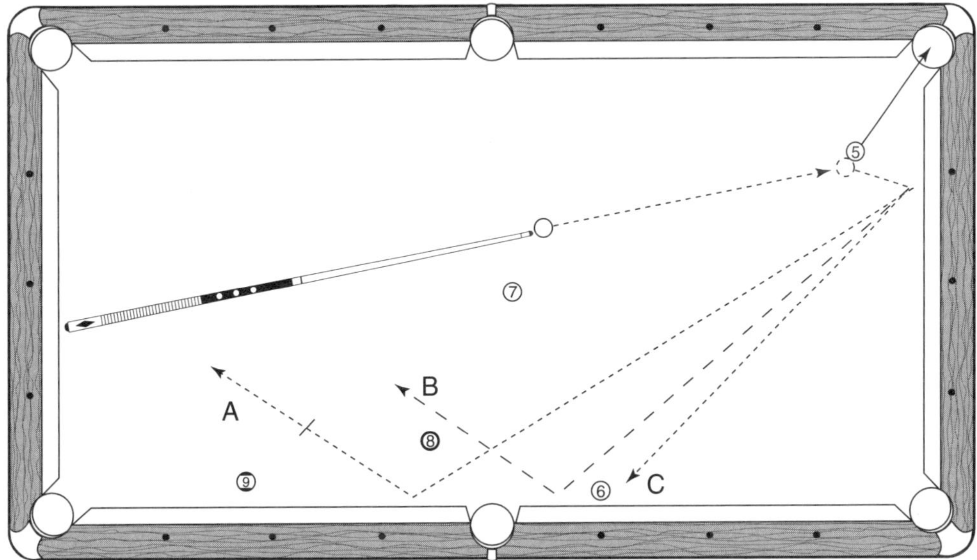

This shot is loaded with danger no matter which route you choose. If you go long down Route A, you could get hooked. Route B could easily result in a side pocket scratch. Route C eliminates these dangers, but you may not have a shot on the 6-ball after running into it. You must pick your poison and hopefully avoid a disaster with superlative execution.

#18 Keep the Cue Ball Away from the Rails and Other Balls

The vast majority of position plays in Nine-Ball require at least a fair amount of power. You will severely limit your ability to apply needed power if you make a habit of leaving the cue ball close to or against the rails. The worst mistakes are to leave the cue ball on the rail when:

- You will need english on the next shot.
- You need to send the cue ball a long distance on the next shot.
- You need to draw the next shot.
- The next shot is a long shot.

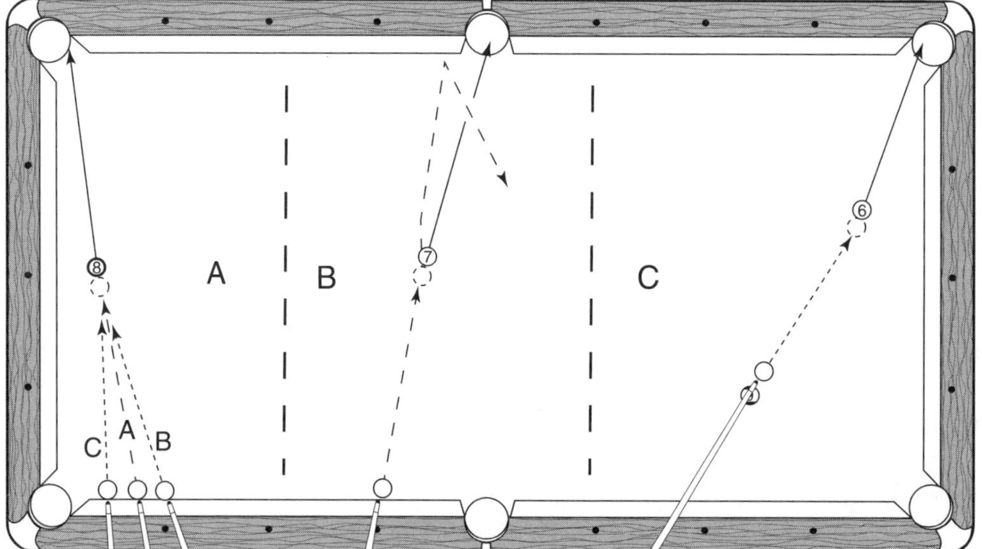

Part A shows one of the worst positions in Nine Ball: you are stuck with a straight shot or with a small cut angle with the cue ball frozen to the rail. With the cue ball in Position A many players are, strangely enough, better off than with a slight cut angle as in Positions B and C. The reason is they will accept their fate by rolling in the shot and then play the next ball with the cue ball a few inches off the end rail. With the cue ball in either Position B or C, many players will attempt to use the cut angle for all it is worth by trying to power the cue ball up table. The result is very often a missed shot. When you have a small cut angle, by all means use it to escape the end rail, but don't get greedy when playing position by trying to muscle the cue ball several feet up table.

It is very tempting to use english to send the cue ball further down the route shown in Part B. Once again I advise that you stay within the limitations of the shot. You should use very little if any sidespin when the cue ball is on the rail because english may cause the cue ball to curve, which could easily lead to a missed shot.

In Part C, the cue ball is next to the 9-ball, which means that you will have to jack up to play the 6-ball. Once again, you must accept your fate and use a speed of stroke that does not compromise your accuracy.

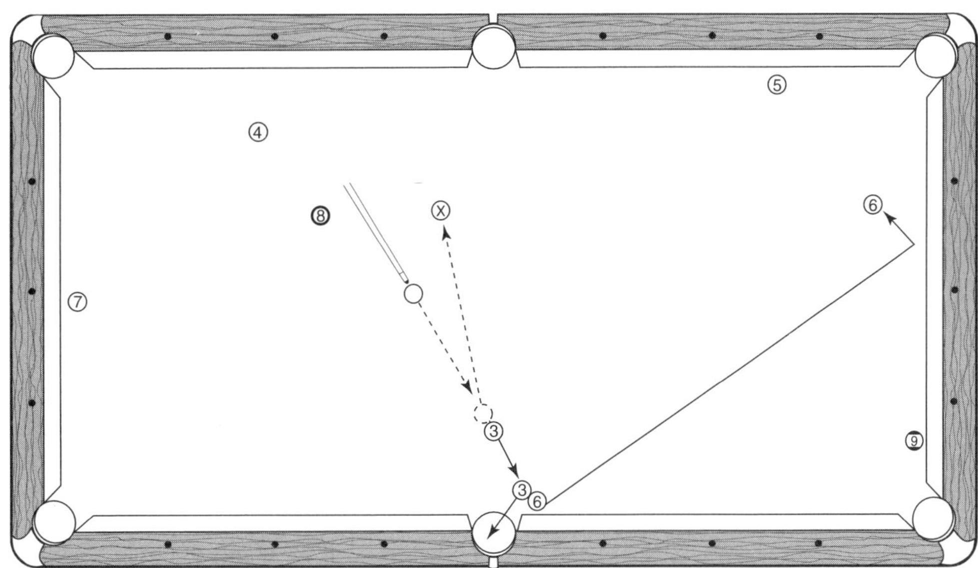

#19 Pay Attention to Details

Seemingly small details often spell the difference between success and failure. They can also be your insurance policy against disaster. I once saw Joe Salazar, a very fine player, adjust the position of the cue ball (with ball in hand) 6-7 times within a 1-2" circle until he got it just where his instincts told him it needed to be.

When you have an easy rack, what can guarantee you will finish it off, with little trouble, is your attention to detail. When you have easy shots, you have a chance to hone your execution. The position play skills that you develop while playing easy layouts will be useful when you have to play longer and tougher versions of the same position routes.

The 3-ball is in a perfect position to be played off the 6-ball into the side pocket, which would get the 6-ball away from the worst spot on the table. I would hope that most players would grasp this opportunity. A player who adheres to the principle of paying attention to details will, however, look for even more ways to improve the layout. The first thing is to make sure the draw shot is played with good speed control for position on the 4-ball.

A player with an attention for the fine points will notice the 9-ball is slightly off the rail and near the pocket, which makes it an ideal candidate for a combo. . If the 6-ball is hit with the correct speed, you could wind up with a 6-9 combo. Astute observers will also notice that the 5-ball is in ideal position to play shape on the combo. Finally, playing the easy 6-9 combo can save you from having to play shape from the 6-ball to the 7-ball, which is on the middle of the opposite end rail. The lesson: littlie things very often make a big difference, so make a habit of looking for them

TIP: Look for the little things you can do to make shots and position just that much better. Try to raise 80-85% shots into 90-95% shots.

#20 Play Your Game

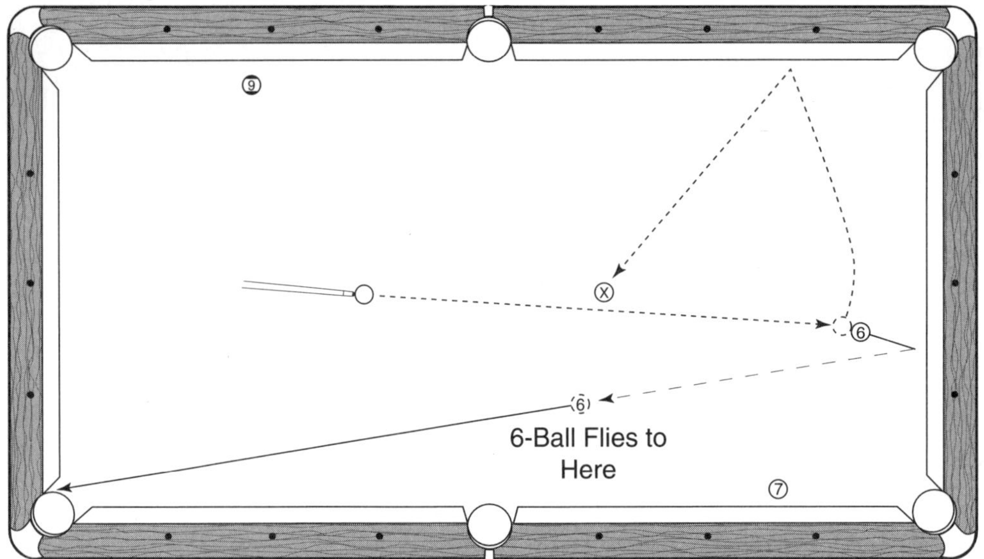

Earlier in the chapter we discussed how players who prefer to use a firm stroke will play for smaller cut angles than those who like to use a softer stroke. Some players prefer to play on the center axis while others prefer to spin cut balls whenever possible. And then there are the shotmakers who prefer playing for larger zones while other players strive for pinpoint shape. The list goes on but the point is the same: after you have gained ample experience playing Nine Ball, you will develop a certain style that largely dictates how you go about playing position.

When it comes to playing your game, you've got to know your limitations. If you don't like limitations (Who does? I know I don't.), then you must work to expand your skills on the practice table. Just because you play one style right now doesn't mean "your game" can't change. The more variety in "your game", the greater will be your ability to handle any situation that comes up.

One of the most dramatic examples of a person playing their game came at the 1992 U.S. Open in the finals between Tommy Kennedy and Johnny Archer. The 62-degree cut angle on the 6-ball was a thin but very makeable shot into the lower right corner pocket. The cue ball could have then be sent on a natural 4-rail route to the 7-ball. Kennedy, however, chose to play his game, which favored playing shape for the 7-ball off of a long rail bank. He slammed the 6-ball home with the highest speed of stroke on a non-break shot that I have witnessed in 1,000 games on tape. The cue ball flew into the 6-ball at over 13 MPH! The 6-ball was airborne for nearly half of its journey down the table as shown. The shot enabled Kennedy to grab a 2-1 advantage on his way to the title.

#21 Use Your Imagination

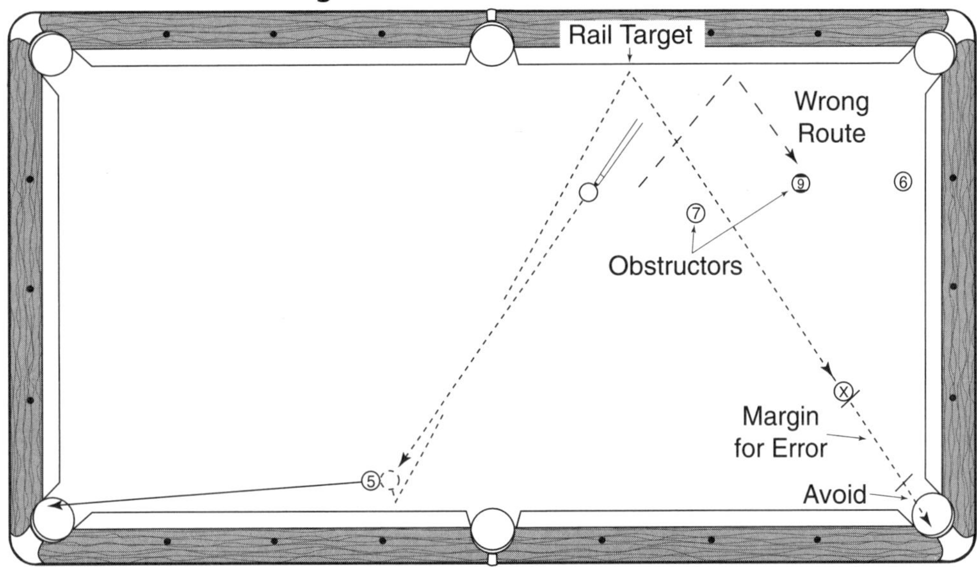

There is no way that this book or any book can cover every possible position play. You've therefore got to use your imagination and knowledge of how the balls behave to fill in the gaps and to construct position plays that are out of the ordinary. Imaginative shots take superior planning and execution. A super shot will often incorporate a half dozen or more of the 20 other principles we've covered in this chapter.

Finnish star Mika Immonen masterminded the position play in the illustration above in a match against Keith McCready at the Crystal Park Casino near Los Angeles. He was faced with the challenge of getting back down table from the 5-ball to the 6-ball. Immonen had to contend with the obstructing 7 and 9-balls. Should the cue ball run into either ball, he could very easily fail to get shape on the 6-ball. In this position many amateurs will hit and hope to get past the 7 and 9-balls. Immonen, on the other hand, began to **survey the table** from several vantage points (Note: The Principles of Position are in bold type). At first he considered the route labeled "wrong".

He then checked out the shot from several angles, all the while using his imagination to plan a route that would avoid the obstructers. You could see the wheels turning as he calculated the angle of departure off the first rail. He then carefully set a **rail target** that, if hit precisely with just the right amount of spin off the top rail, would enable the cue ball to **avoid the obstructers**.

The route past the obstructers meant that the cue ball would be rolling straight towards the corner pocket. To **avoid scratching** he would have to calculate the **correct speed control** for the shot. And since nobody's perfect, and since the shot required a very powerful stroke, he was wise to allow for a **margin for error**. After all of this planning Immonen executed the shot perfectly as shown. He was rewarded with a warm ovation from the knowledgeable crowd of pool enthusiasts.

#22 Know the Exceptions to the First 21 Principles

The vast majority of layouts contain a series of familiar positions in which the 21 Principles of Position should be applied. But you will soon discover, if you haven't already, that pool is a game full of exceptions the rules. Principle #22 is to know the exceptions to the first 21 Principles. Experience and a fair degree of pool sense will tell you when to ignore one or more of the not always sacred principles in this chapter. At various times, for example, you may have to:

- Risk what appears to be an obvious scratch.
- Play shape on a shot that allows virtually no margin for error.
- Turn the cue ball loose and hope for the best because there is no safety and the position route is very unfamiliar or difficult to control.

The principles are designed to work with each other to produce a successful position play. We identified six of the principles that went into producing Mika Immonen's superlative position play on the previous page. Quite often, however, the principles may be at odds with one another. On page 162 we learned that the Principle of Playing Natural Shape took precedence over the principle of Playing to the Long Side Whenever Possible. Below are some additional instances where one principle may override another.

- You may have to play Area Shape on a difficult shot, which may be at odds with playing for the Right Side.
- Ball in hand shape can enable you to violate several of the principles on one shot, because you can very accurately control the path of the cue ball, such as allowing for a sizeable margin for error.
- The principles of Playing Down the Line and Entering the Wide Side are always in conflict with one another.

CHAPTER 6

PATTERN PLAY

"I've always got a plan. I'm not shooting without thinking."
Nick Varner

The ultimate compliment for any pool player is that he plays his patterns well. Good pattern players have refined the ability to make sense out the seemingly complex jumble that is typical of a Nine Ball layout. Good pattern players make the game look easy. They always seem to be moving in concert with the layout. There is a certain flow to the runouts of good pattern players. This is in sharp contrast to those players who always seem to be awkwardly fighting for position ball after ball. A good pattern player's ability to run out easily and effortlessly stems from their skills at position play (see Chapter 3), their skills at pattern recognition (this chapter) and their ability to combine patterns to create runouts (Chapter 7).

The Run Out Game Plan

Position Play (chapter 3) is how you get on the next ball. This includes the route, the target zone, and measures to reduce risk.
Patterns (this chapter) are recognizable sequences of shots that tend to repeat themselves.
Run Outs (chapter 7) are the end result of stringing position plays and patterns together.

Pattern Recognition

Even though there are an infinite number of ball positions, a number of highly recognizable configurations appear repeatedly. These typically consist of two or three consecutive balls that present a special problem or opportunity. One pattern may require you to handle two consecutive balls on the same rail. On another pattern the key may be choosing whether to play a ball in the corner or side pocket. In the pages that follow you will be shown how to plan and execute the most commonly recurring patterns. As you learn to recognize these patterns, you will begin to say things to yourself like "If I play the 5-ball using a natural two-rail route to the end rail, I will have the correct angle on the 6-ball to send the cue ball back up table for the 7-ball."

The Primary Skill of Pattern Play

The primary skill of pattern play is the ability to construct a plan comprised of a series of position routes that enables you to run several balls in succession with the minimum degree of difficulty. These patterns are linked together with connecting balls to form a complete run out. Running a complete rack will be covered in Chapter 7.

Position Routes as Tools

In Chapter 4 we covered a wide variety of position routes that can enable you to play position from one ball to the next. These position plays give you the tools to execute patterns, which are a series of position plays. When planning the first shot of a pattern, you will often have to choose between two or more position routes for the next ball. Your choice of routes must give you position on the next ball. Your position route must also fit the pattern of the layout, which requires that you plan for two or more successive shots at a time.

Choosing the correct route will:

- Create a pattern and a run that flows.
- Give you the high percentage route.
- Avoid trouble (scratching, hooked, hitting balls into bad locations).
- Ensure that the cue ball lands on the right side of the next ball.
- Result in the optimal angle for the next ball.
- Provide a recovery route just in case it is needed.
- Largely enable you to avoid having to play recovery routes.
- Solve problems with difficult balls.

Key Principles of Position for Planning Patterns

All of the 21 Principles of Position Play covered in Chapter 5 are vital to playing top caliber position. Nevertheless, the following are crucial to planning and executing your patterns successfully:

#1 Speed Control (see page 138)
#2 The Correct Cut Angle Optimizes Position (see page 140)
#3 Know the Boundaries of a Position Zone (see page 142)
#7 Playing for Three Balls (or more) at a Time (see page 149)
#8 Play the High Percentage Sequence (see page 150)
#9 Right Side/Wrong Side (see page 152)
#12 Playing Down the Line of a Position Zone (see page 158)
#15 Plan Your Route and Avoid Obstructions (see page 162)

A Tale of Two Players

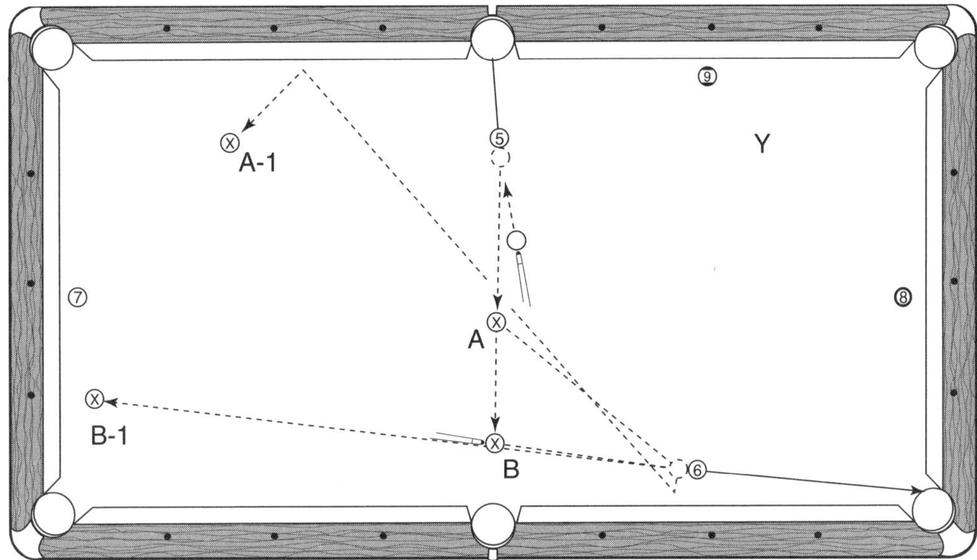

Good pattern players make the game look easy, while others have to struggle to complete their runs. This example is a contrast in styles, which shows the essence of good and poor pattern play. The 5-ball is played with a draw shot. Player A brought the cue ball to Position A, leaving a 30-degree cut on the 6-ball. Player B drew back to Position B for a straight in shot on the 6-ball. To the novice this appears to be better position since the shot on the 6-ball is easier. But patterns are a series of shots, not one shot in isolation. Player B now must draw back to the short side for position on the 7-ball. Player B's speed was off a little on the 6-ball, which is often the case when playing a long straight in draw shot. With a miniscule 10-degree cut angle on the 7-ball, Player B is now facing a very difficult recovery route to Position Y for the 8-ball.

Now back to Player A. From Position A, he can easily bring the cue ball across and up the table for excellent position on the 7-ball at Position A-1. The angle on the 7-ball will make it easy for Player A to then bring the cue ball down table to Position Y for excellent shape on the 8-ball.

When you are finished with this book I hope that you have become Player A, and that Player B is a distant memory.

Become a Skillful Navigator

The biggest mistakes in pattern play usually happen in the planning process. You can largely avoid them by learning to enjoy the challenge of navigating your way past the obstacles and hazards that appear in nearly every rack of Nine-Ball. A Nine-Ball rack is really nothing more than a big puzzle that needs solving. If you plough ahead without a plan, your runs are destined for failure. But if you map your course with care, the cue ball will arrive safely at all of its series of ports of call until your voyage is complete.

Choosing the Optimal Route

Choosing the correct position routes time after time enables you to execute your patterns in the simplest and most effective manner. Your choice of routes should be based on: 1) the chances for playing the route successfully and 2) how the route fits into the pattern or sequence of shots that follows.

Distance Affects Your Choice of Routes

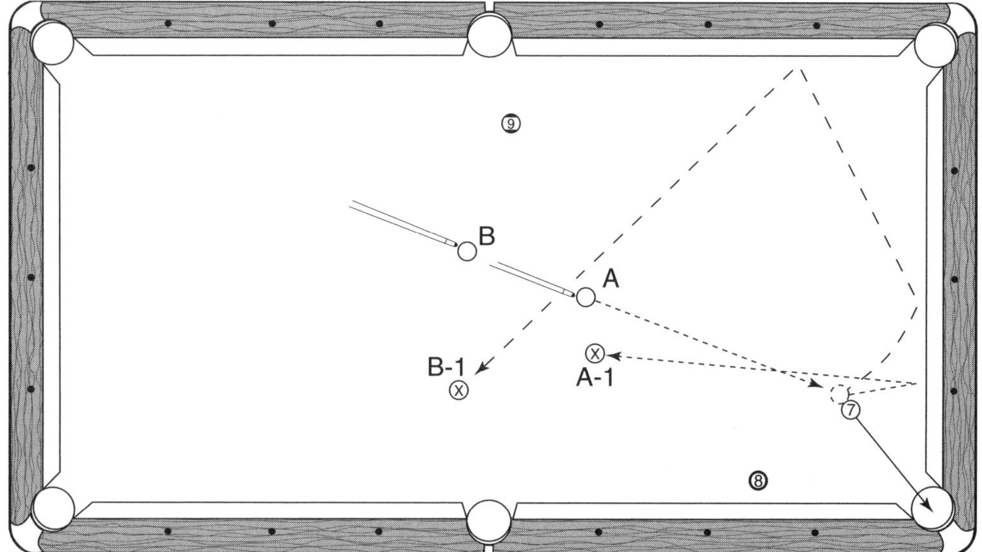

The distance of the cue ball from the object ball can be the deciding factor in which route to play. With the cue ball in Position A, a soft follow stroke with a half tip of inside english (right) is all that's needed to send the cue ball to Position A-1 for the 8-ball. Using inside english at this distance is not hard because the soft stroke minimizes the effects of deflection.

The cue ball is only 15" further away from the 7-ball in Position B, but far enough to alter the complexion of the shot. Using inside english would dramatically increase the chances of missing the 7-ball. The correct choice from Position B is to use draw to send the cue ball two rails to Position B-1. The remainder of the rack is a breeze from either A-1 or B-1, which indicates that the pattern was played correctly in both cases.

Obstruction Creates a Gap in Position Zones

Obstructing balls can have a huge bearing on your choice of possible routes. The 8-ball is blocking a very attractive two-rail route from the 6-ball to the 7-ball that could have taken the cue ball to Position A. You still, however, can play position on either side of the gap. Route B is the logical choice since it gives you a much larger position zone, and therefore a larger margin for error.

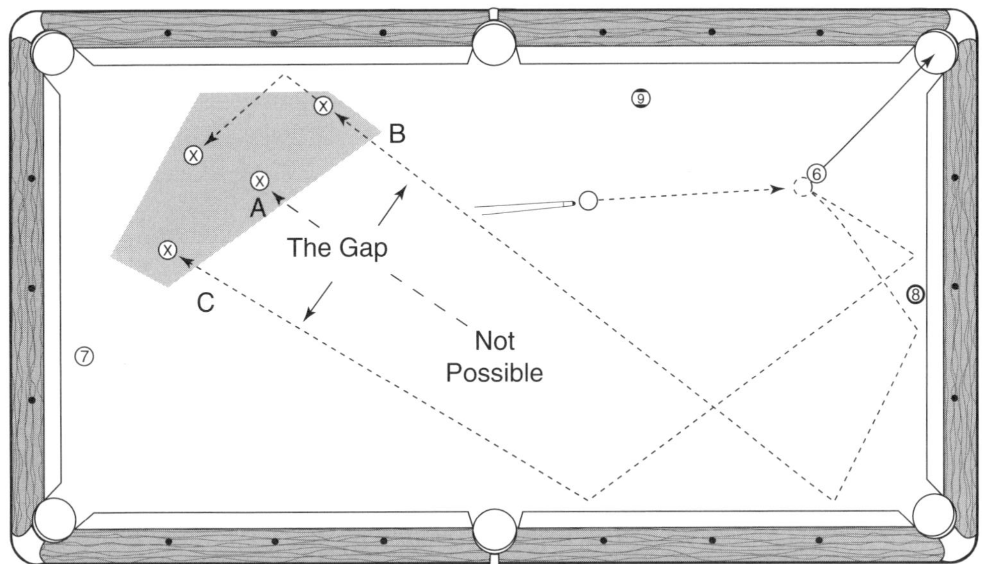

You can get much closer to your work using Route C. This advantage is offset by the damage that would be incurred if you came up short or long of the position zone. The lesson: when a blocker is preventing you from playing the ideal route, you must choose the next best one, all things, including the pattern, considered.

Connecting Naturally to the Next Ball

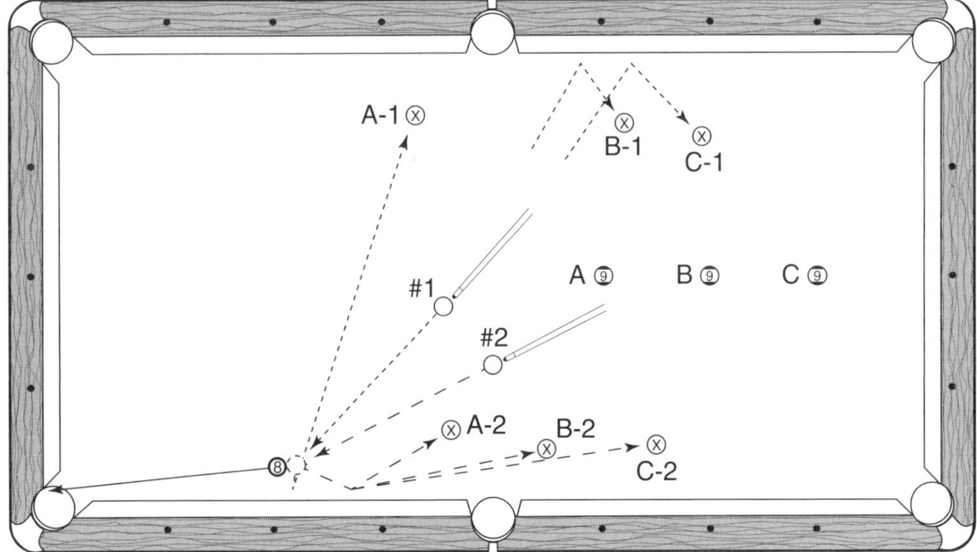

Your patterns will begin to flow when you understand how the balls are connected to one another. When the cue ball is in Position #1, the logical position for 9-ball A is at A-1. When the 9-ball is at B, Position B-1 is best. And with the 9-ball at C, position C-1 is best. Now take note of ending cue ball locations that match up with the cue ball in Position #2. Problems arise when you play a route that does not correspond to the object ball's-position. Route C-1, for example, doesn't match up with 9-ball B.

Using a Natural Route to Avoid a Combo

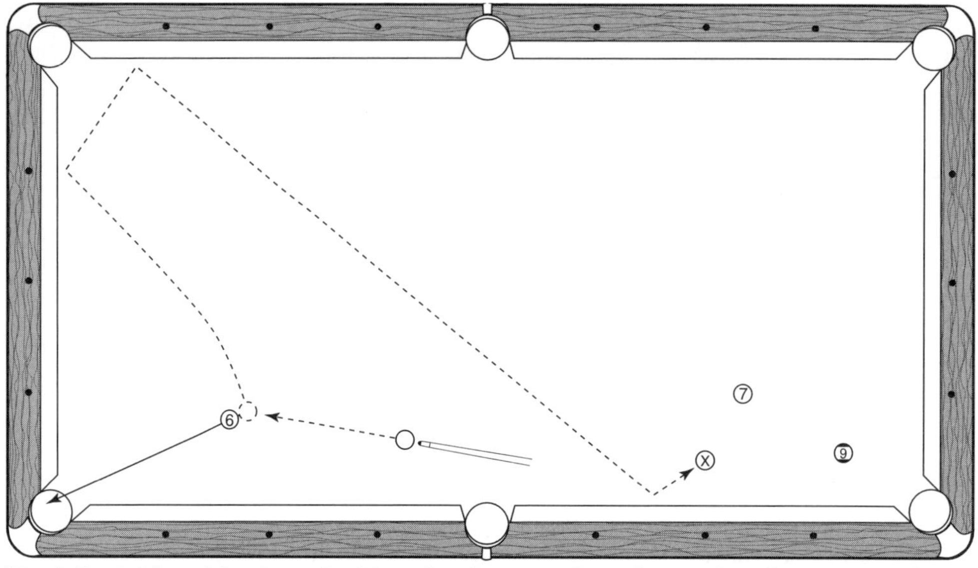

Earl Strickland had to decide whether to play shape for the 7-9 combo or run out in the 1999 U.S. Open against Cliff Joyner. In most cases combo shape would have been the better choice, but not here thanks to the natural three-rail route to the short side of the 7-ball. The lesson: long distance shape is not necessarily difficult when you can play a natural route, so use it when it can help you avoid a missable shot.

Drawing to the Right Side

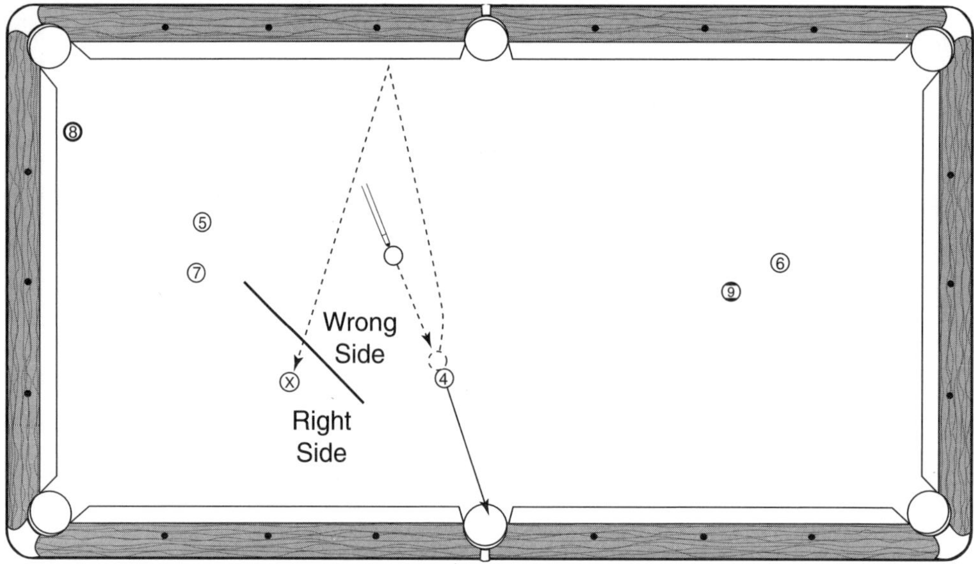

Buddy Hall, a master of pattern play, exhibited great table sense in playing this off the rail draw shot to the right side of the 5-ball. The correct side allowed him to avoid hitting the 7-ball it enabled him to send the cue ball down table for the 6-ball. This shot was played at the Sands Regency Open 15 against Grady Mathews.

Setting Up the Zorro Shot

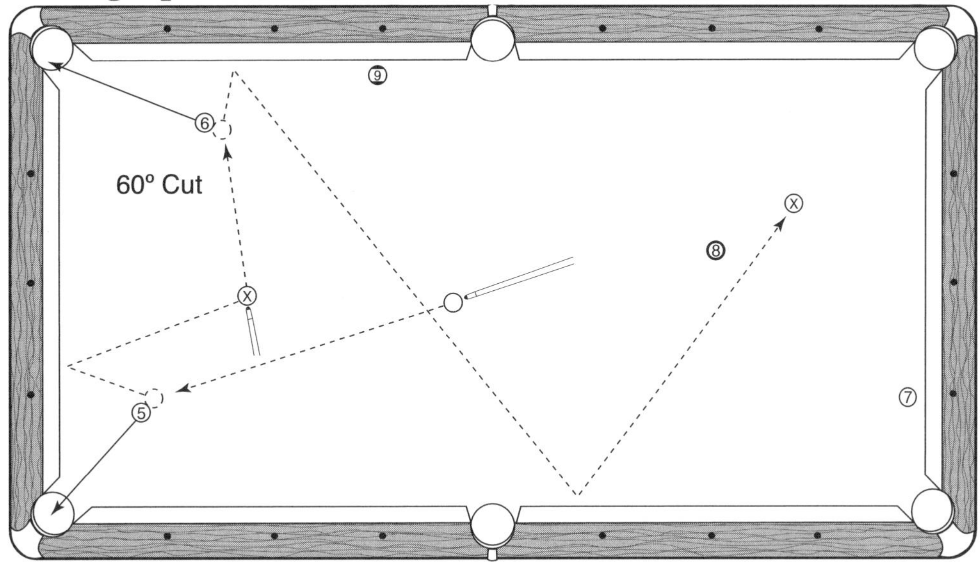

Zorro was one of my favorite TV shows, and the Big Z is also one of the most useful position routes. Kunihiko Takahashi meticulously set up the optimal angle for the zorro shot by obtaining a 60-degree cut on the 6-ball. This enabled him to play shape on the 7-ball with precision. This pattern and the one in the following illustration occurred at the 1999 U.S. Open in a match with Chuck Altomare.

Setting Up a 1-Rail Route

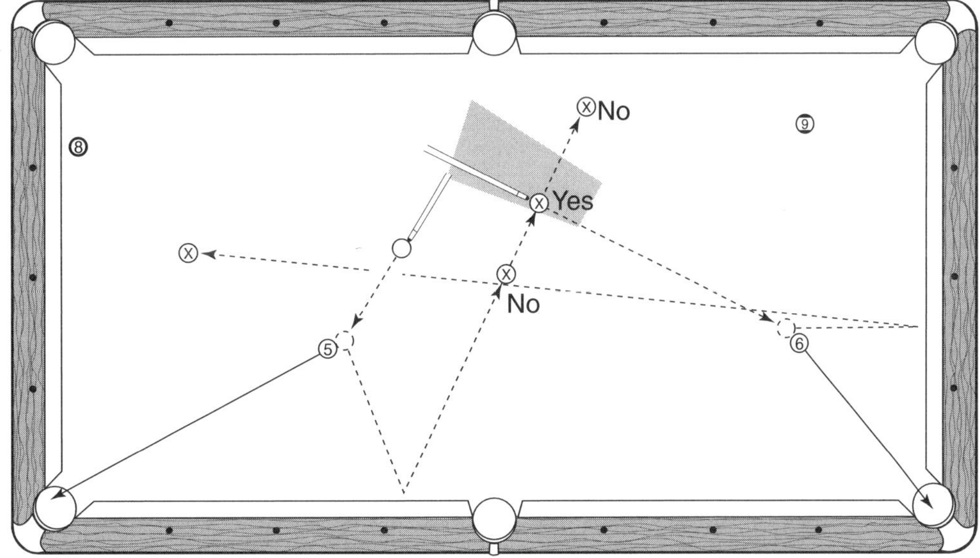

The 9-ball was right in the middle of a possible three-rail route from the 6-ball to the 8-ball. Realizing this, Takahashi once again showed his knowledge of pattern play by setting up the ideal angle for one-rail shape from the 6-ball to the 8-ball. His speed control on the 5-ball was perfect as it needed to be since he was crossing through a narrow position zone.

Three Ball Patterns

Three-ball patterns, which we covered briefly in Chapter 5 (see Principles of Position Play #7, page 149), are at the heart of pattern play. Once again, when playing for three balls at a time, before shooting the first ball you must determine:

- What options are available for playing position on the second ball?
- What route among those possible choices will enable you to then play position on the third ball?
- After playing the first ball, the process repeats itself.

Three ball patterns are so vital to running racks of Nine Ball that if you learn nothing else from this book, at least master this concept.

Good Speed to Get on the Right Side

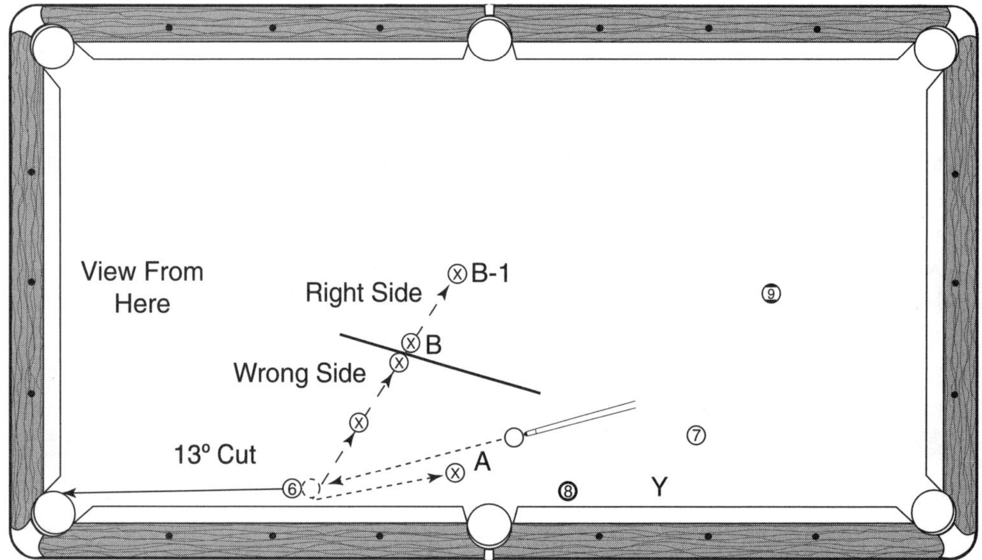

The 7 and 8-balls are close to the same rail, which makes pattern play a challenge. You could draw to Position A for the 7-ball. However, you would have to send the cue ball across the table and back for the 8-ball.

An easier 3-ball pattern is to use a hard stroke and force the cue ball away from the rail to the zone between Positions B and B-1.This would place the cue ball on the right side of the 7-ball. Therefore you would be able to float the cue ball over to Position Y when playing the 7-ball. If you came up short of the right side, you would be forced to play a recovery route to get good position on the 8-ball. The big key to this pattern is playing the 6-ball with enough speed that you wind up on the right side.

Setting up Two Way Position

The big challenge in this run out is to get back up table for the 9-ball when playing the 8-ball. The thin 50-degree cut on the 7-ball makes speed control difficult. Add to this the fact that the cue ball will be crossing the position zone and you have one tough pattern. In this position, however, you have an opportunity to play two-way position, which significantly

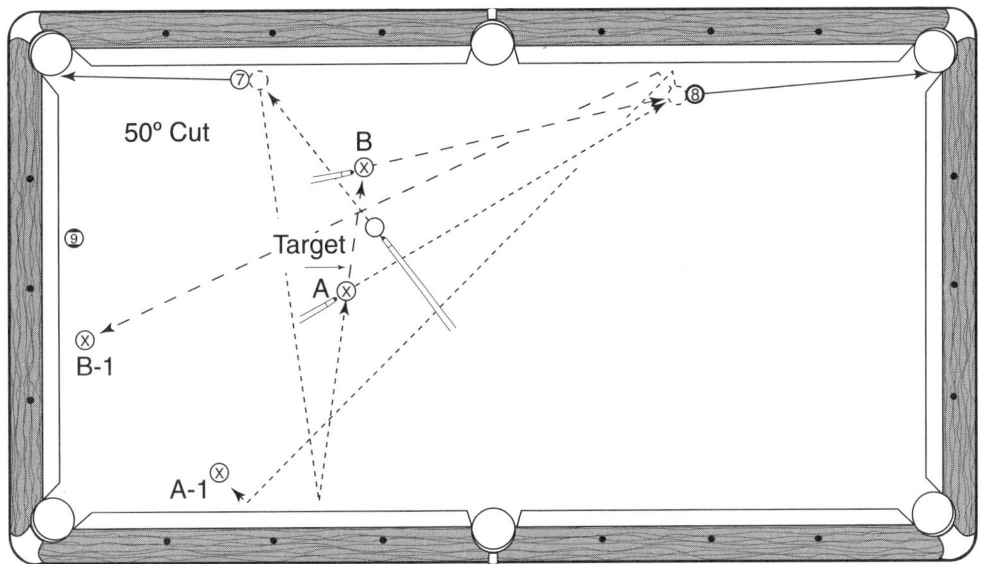

widens the position zone. If the cue ball stops at Position A, you can use Route A-1 to get on the 9-ball. And if the cue ball continues to Position B, you can use Route B-1 when playing the 8-ball. The positional bulls eye should be set in the middle so you have a little room for error to either side.

When A Sharper Angle Works Better

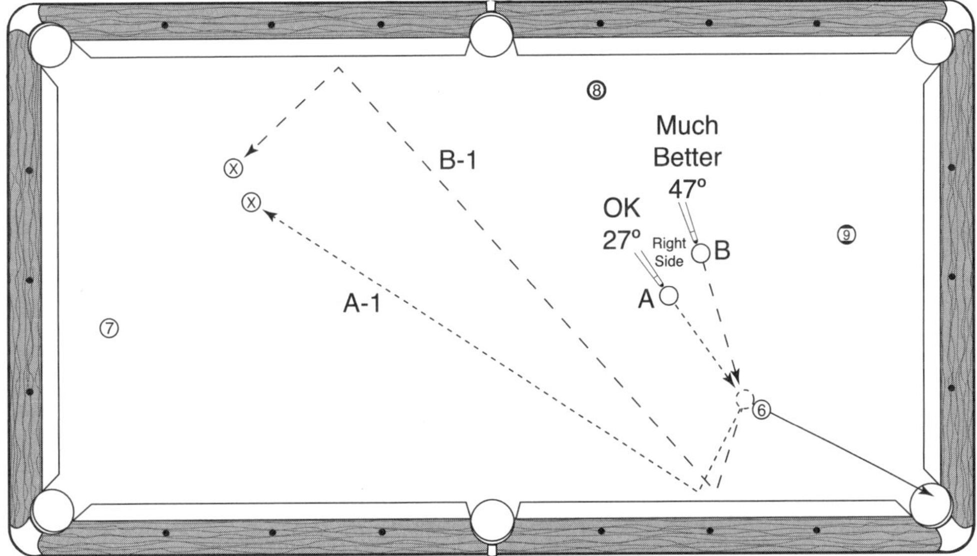

Placing the cue ball on the right side of the ball is vital, but that is not always enough as Nine Ball is largely a game of angles. The cut angle in Position A dictates that the most natural path to the 7-ball is down Route A-1. But this route means the cue ball will be crossing through the zone. The natural path to the 7-ball from the steeper angle at Position B is Route B-1, which allows you to play down the line shape on the 7-ball.

A Multiple Option Pattern - Two Way Position

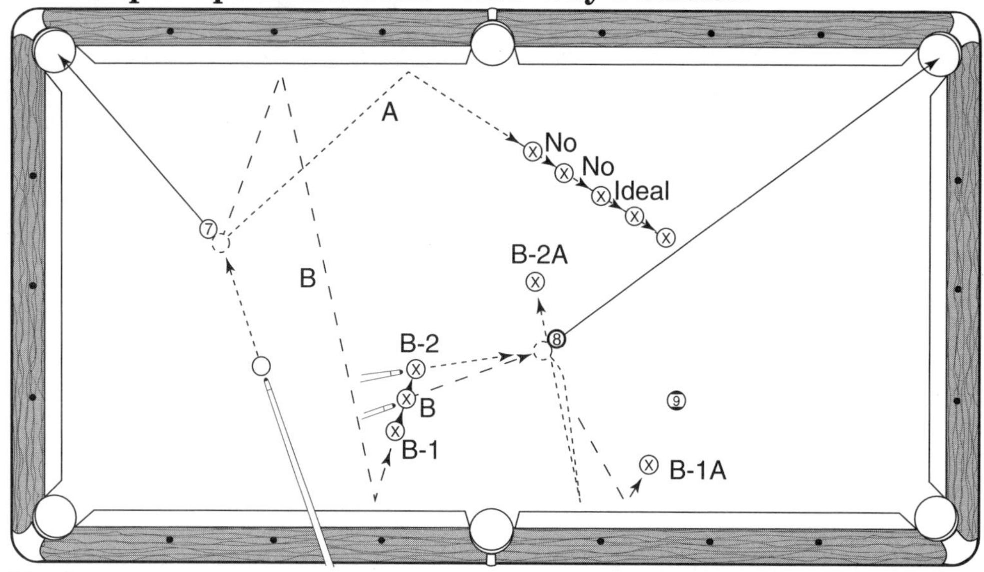

You have two routes to the 8-ball at your disposal. The problem is that you must play across the line shape no matter which way you go. If you employed Route A, you would have a very awkward position play on the 8-ball if the cue ball stopped short of ideal. Should the cue ball go past the ideal, you will have to send whitey to the end rail and back for the 9-ball. Route B also requires that you play across the line, but it offers much better routes from the 8-ball to the 9-ball were you to miss ideal shape at Position B. From B-1 you can easily draw to the short side at B-1A. From B-2 you could play off the rail to B-2A. Both of these alternative routes are much preferable to those available on Route A.

End to End

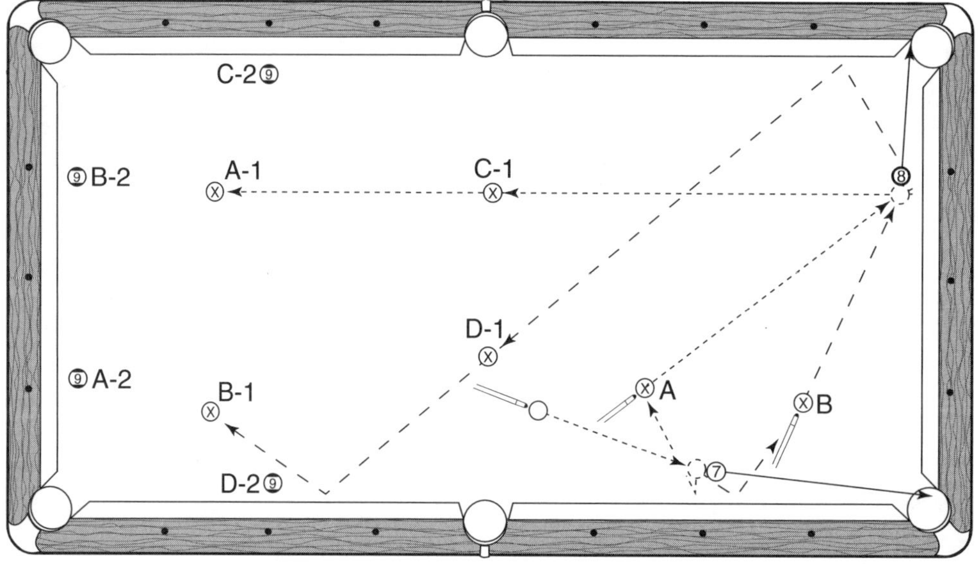

The 9-ball has been placed in four locations. The key to getting on each 9-ball is to carefully plan your position from the 7-ball to the 8-ball. Drawing off the rail to Position A will set up a sharper angle on the 8-ball. This will make it easier to send the cue ball straight down the table to A-1 for the 9-ball at A-2, or to C-1 for the 9-ball at C-2. A soft follow shot to Position B will set up the two-rail position route to B-1 for the 9-ball at B-2, or to D-1 for the 9-ball at D-2. Notice that the position played on the 8-ball was dictated by the need to get on the 9-ball in the best way possible.

Four Ball Patterns

Planning for three balls is essential, but often you must take the planning process one step further. At times you must play shape on the second ball that will enable you to get position on the third ball, and that allows you to get on the third ball in a way that ensures you'll be able to continue to the fourth ball. This may sound a bit complex, but hopefully the concept will become much clearer in the diagrams that follow.

Second Ball Cut Angle

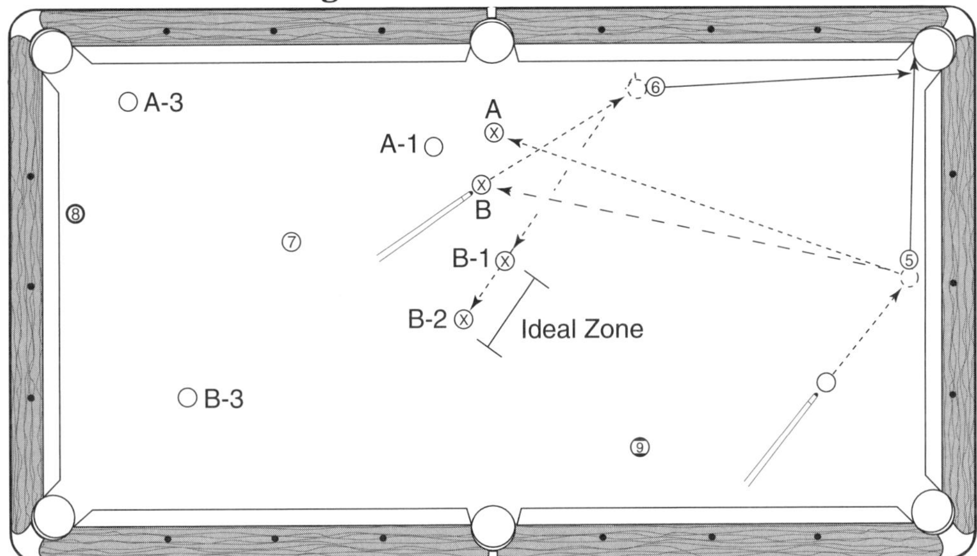

Position from the 5-ball to the 6-ball is no problem. If the cue ball stops at Position A, you will have no trouble making the 7-ball. That takes care of three balls, but what about the 8-ball? With the shallow angle on the 6-ball, you will likely wind up at Position A-1 for the 7-ball. Now you must flirt with the upper left corner while playing short side position to A-3.

Now let's assume you had sent the cue ball to Position B for the 6-ball. With a larger cut angle on the 6-ball, you can easily float the cue ball across the table to the position zone at B-1 to B-2. From here you can now play to the long side of the 8-ball somewhere around B-3. To recap, the cut angle on the second ball (the 6-ball) ensured that you could easily get the correct position on the third ball (the 7-ball) that could, in turn, get you to the fourth ball (the 8-ball).

The Second Ball's Cut Angle is Key

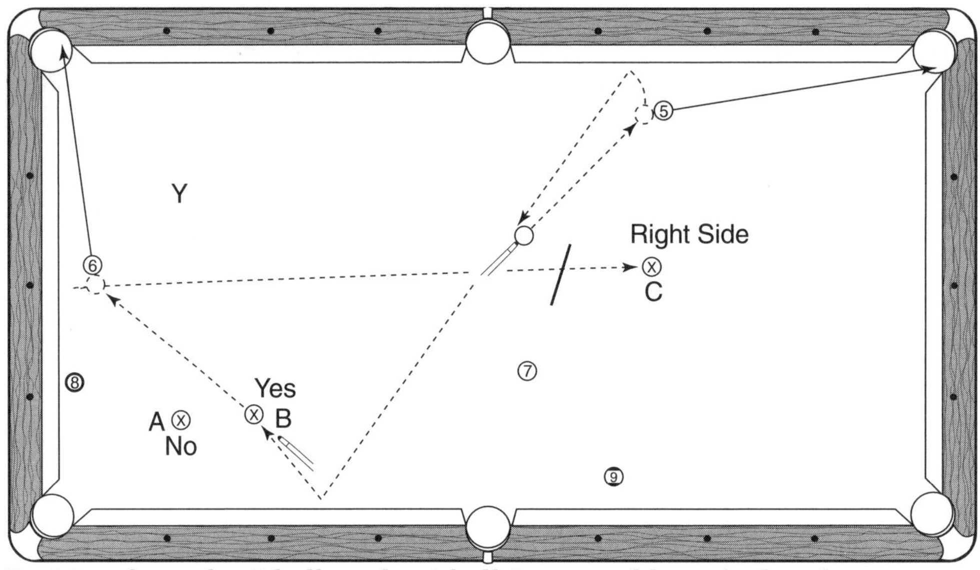

Position from the 5-ball to the 6-ball is no problem. And as long as you have an angle on the 6-ball you can escape the end rail and send the cue ball down table for the 7-ball. If you were originally planning for only three balls, the cut angle on the 6-ball at Position A would work just fine. This plan is ok as far as it goes, but in this case, that's not far enough. The real key to this run is getting from the 7-ball to the 8-ball. The first step is to leave a sufficiently large cut angle on the 6-ball as shown by Position B. This angle will allow you to use a speed of stroke you can control with precision. When playing the 6-ball you must get to the right side of the 7-ball. Position C is ideal. From there it will be easy to follow down to Position Y for the 8-ball.

Setting Up Down the Line Shape

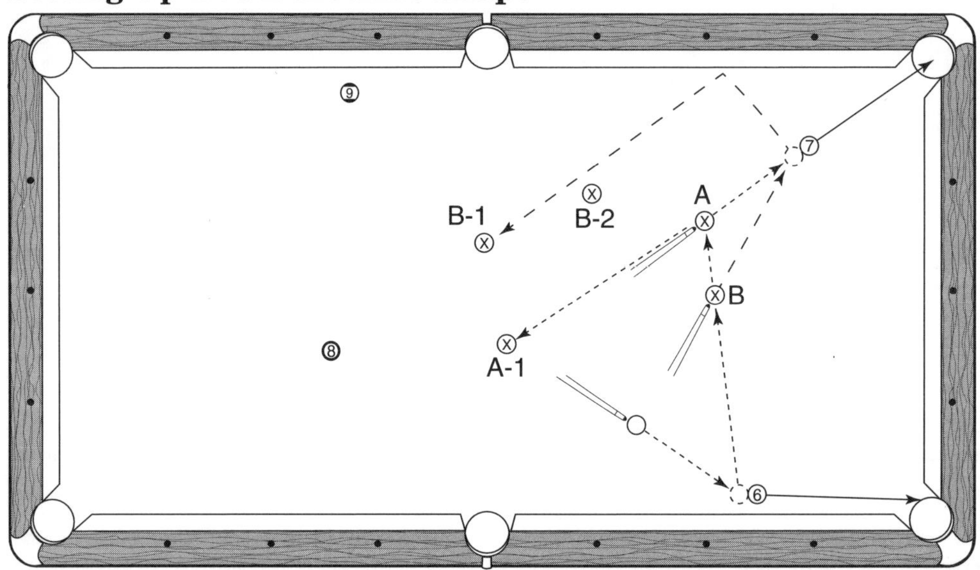

The 8-ball is in the middle of the table and the 9-ball is high up on the side rail, which should alert you to the need to play this pattern with great care. If the cue ball landed at Position A for the 7-ball, you could then draw back to A-1 for the 8-ball. With the cue ball at A-1, however, it will be very difficult to get good shape on the 9-ball. Once again the answer is to plan for four balls. Sending the cue ball to Position B will give you an angle on the 7-ball. Now you can draw off the side rail and play down the line shape on the 8-ball to B-1. From B-1 you can draw straight back to B-3 for excellent shape on the 9-ball. The angle on the second ball (the 7-ball) was the key to the pattern.

One Good Angle Leads to Another

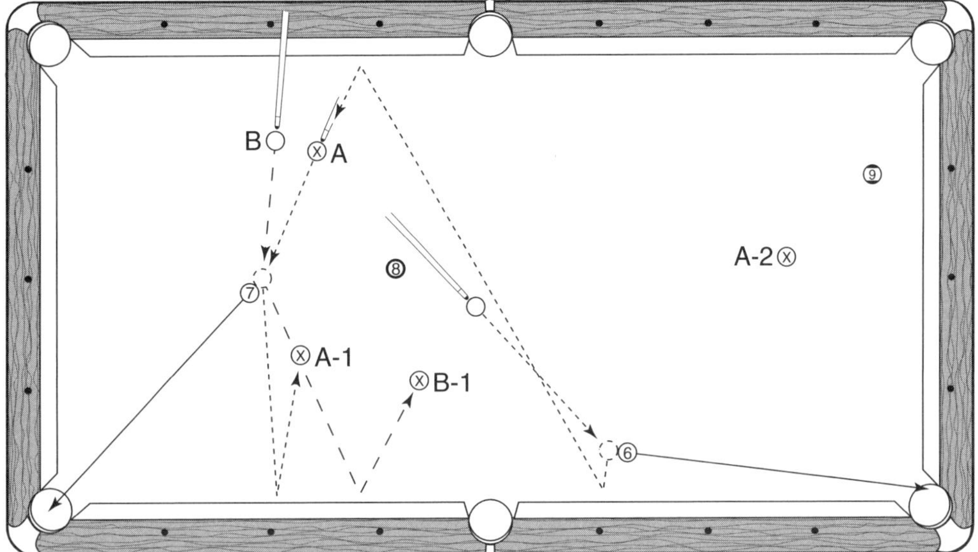

When you play one good angle followed by another, running out can seem ridiculously easy. Good angles eliminate the need for recovery shots and other heroics that may be entertaining to onlookers, but are sheer nonsense to the trained observer. This example is a case in point.

After playing the 6-ball the cue ball crossed the table and out to Position A for a perfect angle on the 7-ball. A soft follow shot on the 7-ball took the cue ball to Position A-1 for fine position on the 8-ball. One more soft follow shot and the cue ball will land at A-2 for a simple shot on the 9-ball. Observe how the ideal angle turned every shot into a hanger. The key to this pattern, as in the previous examples in this section, was to play the correct position on the second ball so you could get to the forth ball with little trouble.

Now let's assume when the 6-ball was played that the cue ball traveled past our ideal angle to Position B. A soft follow shot on the 7-ball will result in Position B-1 or somewhere even worse. Now it will be a struggle to get on the 9-ball. The lesson: planning for three balls at a time works most of the time but occasionally you must plan for four ball for positioning the cue ball in the ideal place for the second ball.

Don't Fight the Table

One of the biggest mistakes in pattern play is the failure to accept what the table gives you. When the layout is not completely to your liking, you must play the hand you've been dealt, as card players would say. That means that you shouldn't force the situation or try to make something out of nothing. Play the table and make your decisions based on the layout as is, not as you would have preferred it to be.

Accept what the Table Gives You

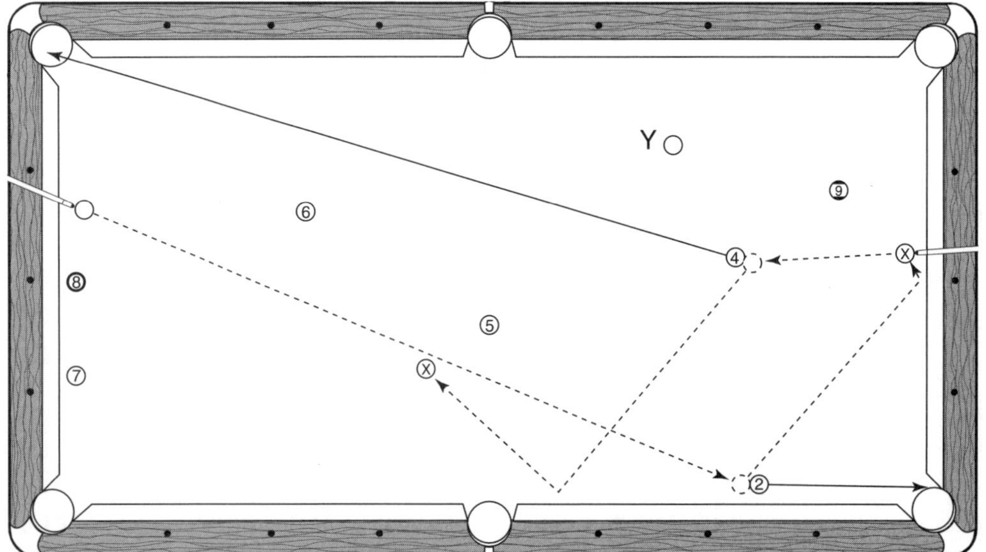

Earl Strickland was faced with a table length shot on the 2-ball off the rail in a match with Johnny Archer at the Sands Regency Open 16, 1992. Now if there is one player who can pocket a long tough shot and send the cue ball to any other location on the table, Strickland, who is the ultimate sharpshooter, is the man.

Strickland could have powered in the 2-ball and sent the cue ball two rails to Position Y. He knew, however, that this would be forcing the issue, and that his pocketing percentage would drop significantly playing the shot in this manner. He chose instead to use a medium speed of stroke off the rail, which insured the accuracy of the shot. Playing the shot this way also meant that he would next be looking at a table length shot on the 4-ball. So be it. The high percentage sequence was to play two moderately difficult shot in succession rather than overplaying the 2-ball in the hopes of having a hanger on the 4-ball.

Cinching Position with a Long Shot

The hard part of this layout is getting from the 4-ball to the 5-ball, thanks to the 9-ball, which severely reduces the size of the position zone for the 5-ball. Efren Reyes could have drawn back to Position A when playing the 3-ball. This would have made the 4-ball much easier. But Reyes would then have to send the cue ball through traffic to get on the 5-ball. Reyes recog-

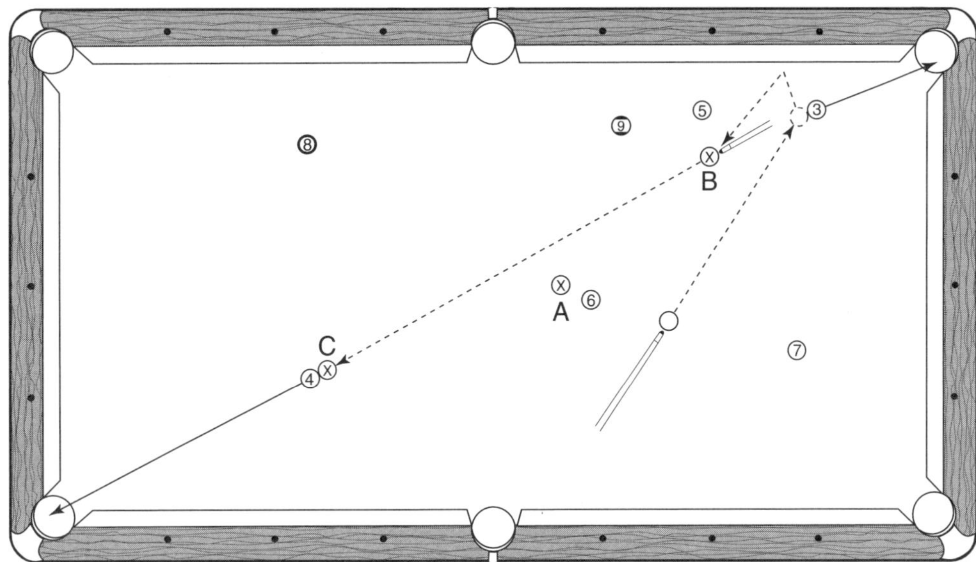

nized the danger in this position. He decided not to fight the table and instead chose to play a short-range draw shot on the 3-ball. This left him with a long stop shot on the 4-ball from Position B. After the 4-ball, Reyes had a clear shot on the 5-ball from Position C. This took place in the finals with Ralf Souquet at the Sands Regency Open 27, 1998.

Play Shape for a Combo

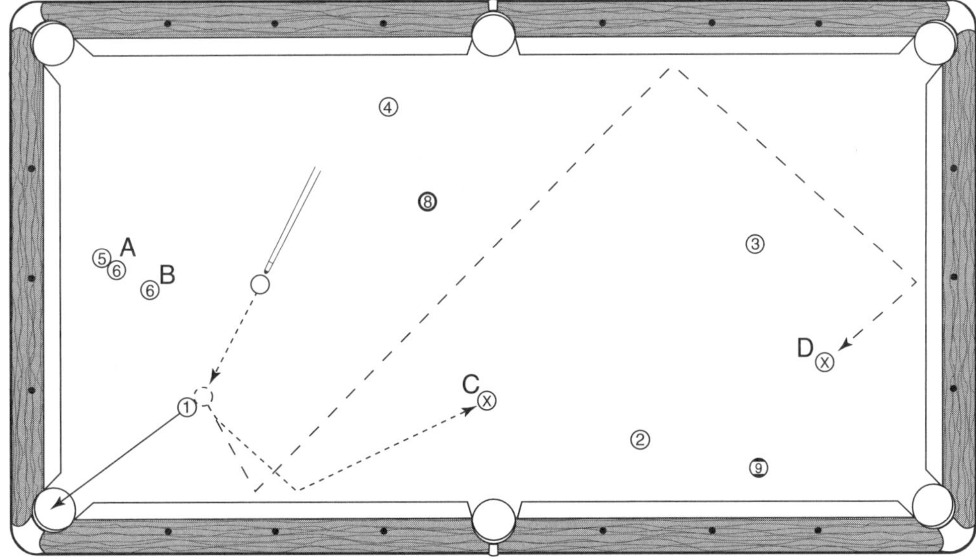

The 5 and 6-balls are clustered in Position A. This makes a runout unlikely. The smart choice for many players in this position is to send the cue ball to Position C for the 2-9 combo. Now if the 6-ball was in Position B, then the best strategy is to play for the run out by sending the cue ball three rails to Position D for position on the 2-ball. In both positions, strategy was dictated by the layout. Remember: don't fight the table. Play what you're given and go with the flow.

Simple is Often Best

There is a tendency by many players to unnecessarily complicate matters when playing position. Often the best approach is the simplest one. No frills routes or patterns may not look impressive, but they can be very, very, very effective.

Don't Needlessly Play Shape When You Have Shape

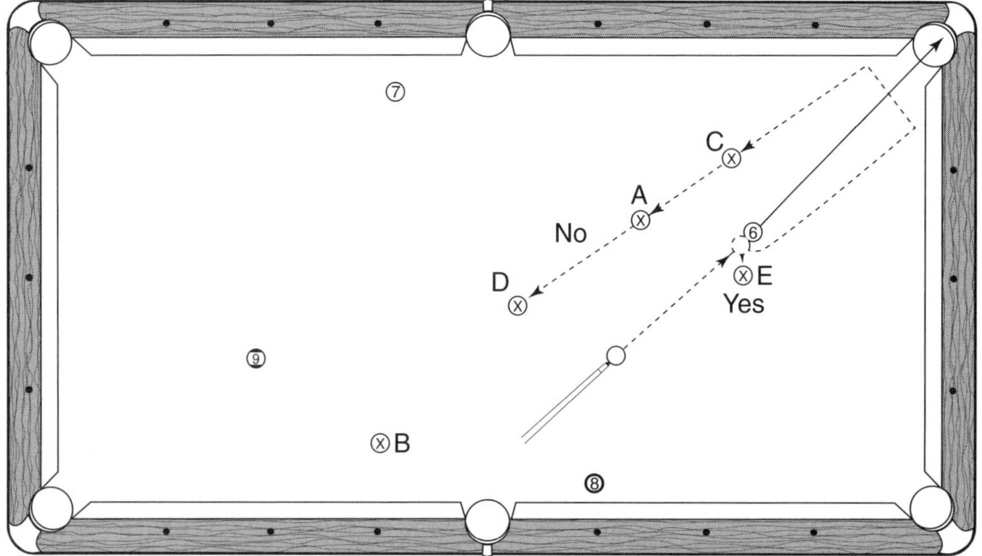

The most important rule of the no frills, keep it simple method of pattern play is to not play position when you already have position. This sounds kind of funny when you first hear it, but the concept will become crystal clear in a moment.

The key to completing the run out above is to get an angle on the 7-ball that allows you to send the cue ball across the table for the 8-ball. You could use top left (inside) english to send the cue ball two rails to Position A. This would leave you with a 25-degree cut on the 7-ball, which is ideal for sending the cue ball to Position B for the 8-ball. If the cue ball stopped short at Position C, you would have to play a difficult two-rail recovery route to the 8-ball. This would require a hard follow stroke with left english. You would be in even worse shape if you hit the cue ball too firmly. With the cue ball in Position D, you will likely have to play safe. As you can see, "playing" shape is very risky in this situation.

Now let's go back to our original position. A 3" draw shot to Position E would give you the same cut angle as in Position A. Although the shot on the 7-ball is about a foot longer, you have completely eliminated the risk of not having good shape on the 7-ball. You didn't have to play position for the 7-ball because it was sitting there right next to the 6-ball.

Keep it Simple to Avoid Trouble

The position route chosen by Ismael "Morro" Paez in this illustration is a single shot clinic in keeping things simple. Paez could have chosen to

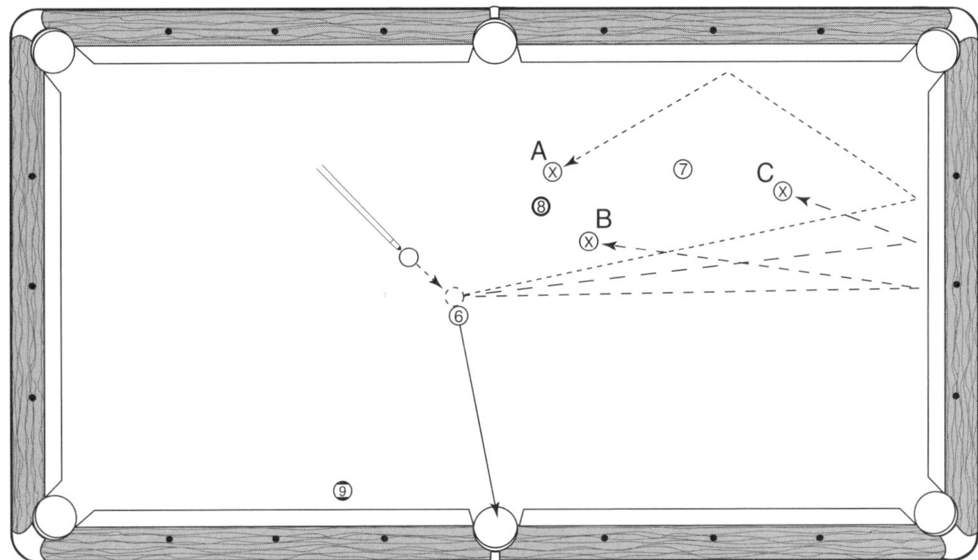

leave himself a shorter shot on the 7-ball by using either Route A or B. Each of these choices, however, brought a hook behind the 8-ball into play. Instead he chose to keep things simple by following Route C for short side position on the 7-ball. This shot took place in a match with Johnny Archer at the 1997 U.S. Open. Archer, who did a player review for Accu-Stats of this match, totally agreed with Paez' shot selection.

A Sensible but Overlooked Pattern

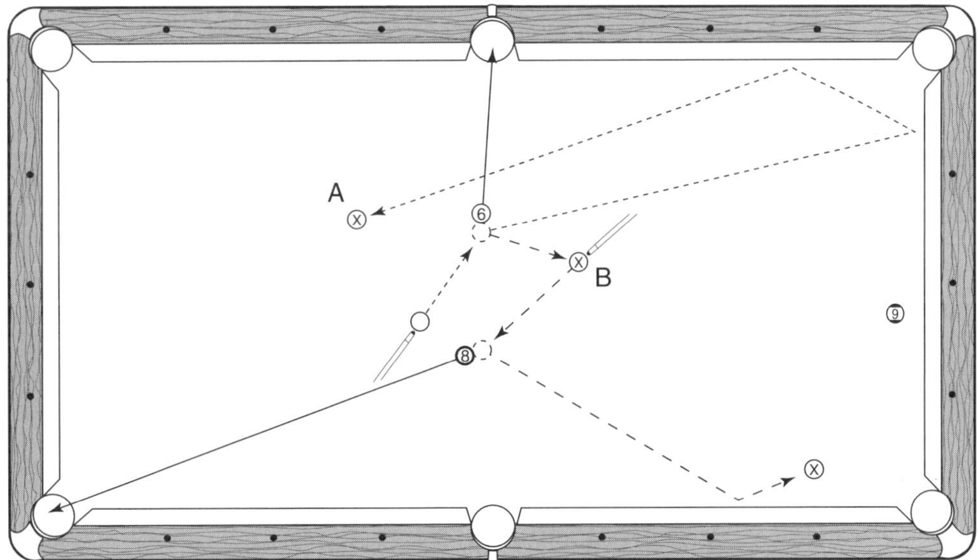

The pattern above is but another way of illustrating the concept in the previous section. You could send the cue ball two rails for a nice easy side pocket shot on the 8-ball at Position A. But why bother when you can drift the cue ball a foot over to Position B? This still gives you a relatively simple route from the 8-ball to the 9-ball.

The Easiest and Best Sequence

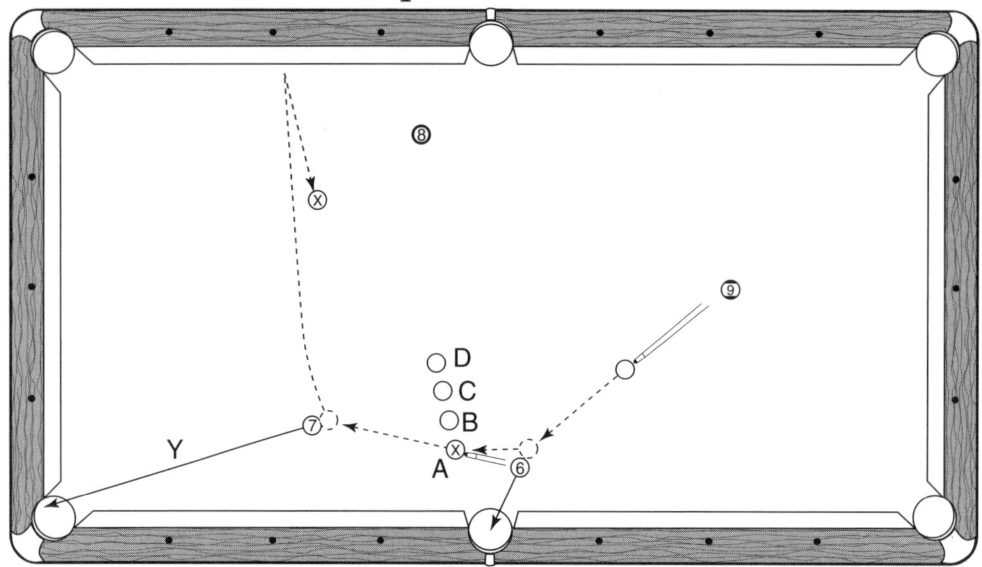

Johnny Archer was in the finals of the 1999 U.S. Open against Jeremy Jones when he came across this rather innocuous looking position. Even though this four-ball layout is a snap, it plays so easy for a top pro because they know the little details that keep things simple and that keep them out of trouble.

When playing the 6-ball, Archer chose to float the cue ball forward to Position A. This seemingly insignificant maneuver provided him with an angle on the 7-ball, which allowed him to draw across the table and out for the 8-ball. The rest of the run is a done deal.

Now let's consider some alternative routes from the 6-ball to the 7-ball. Position B is ok, but it requires you to float the cue ball to Position X with a soft draw stroke. You could also pound the cue ball to the top side rail and back out. Either of these routes could work, but neither is nearly as playable as the one from Position A.

The fun really begins if you were to send the cue ball to Position C when playing the 6-ball. One option is to follow down to Position Y for a tricky shot on the 8-ball into the side pocket. You could also play a stop shot on the 7-ball and send the cue ball three rails for shape on the 9-ball. With the cue ball in Position D (following the shot on the 6-ball) you could follow off the side rail and out to Position Y Another option is to power stun the cue ball off the rail and across to Position X for the 8-ball. Neither of these choices is very appealing.

The lesson: simplicity is often the result of paying close attention to the little things that make a big difference in pattern play.

The Right Choice is a One Railer

Excelling at two-rail position is vital to playing runout Nine Ball. Nevertheless, one rail position is used nearly 50% of the time by the pros because it enables them to exert maximum control over the cue ball.

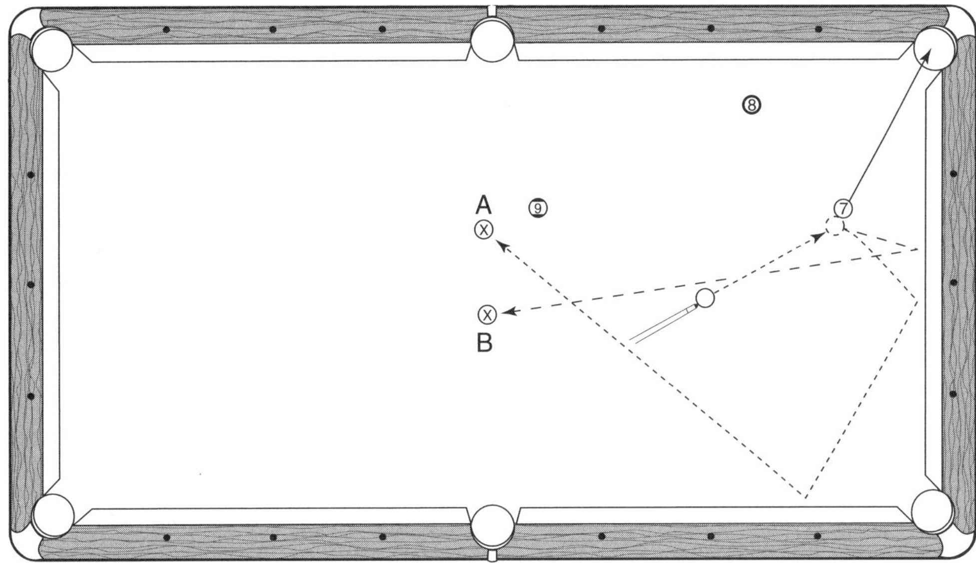

You could play two rails for position on the 8-ball, but if you overran your position zone, you would be hooked behind the 9-ball as shown by Position A. The one rail route to Position B for the 8-ball is much safer.

Shoot Easy Combos to Simplify Things

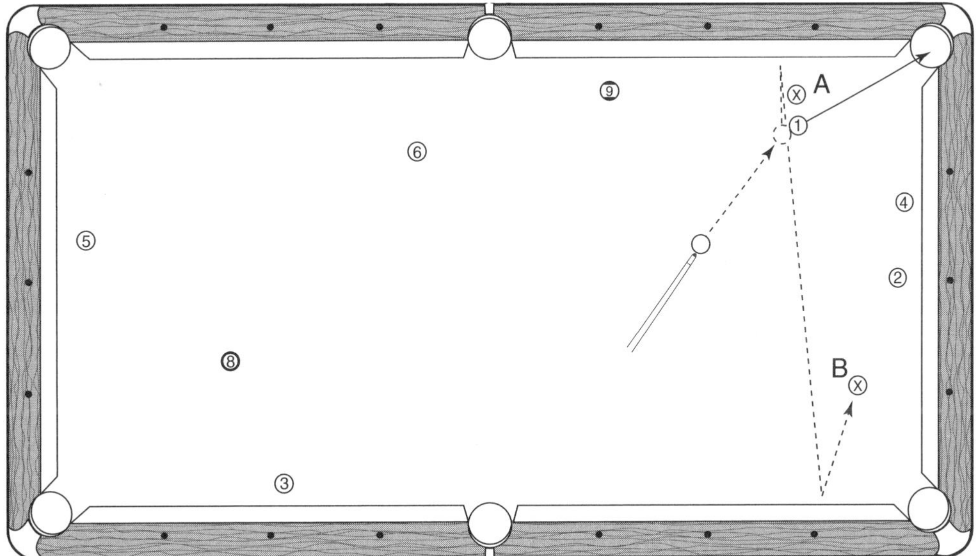

In this position, if you rolled to Position A after playing the 1-ball, you would have to bring the cue ball back down table for the 4-ball when playing the 3-ball. And when playing the 4-ball, you would have to send the cue ball to the opposite end of the table for the 5-ball. Both of these positional nightmares can be eliminated. Play the 2-4 combo from Position B after pocketing the 1-ball. The lesson: don't pass over easy combos when shooting them can greatly simplify the layout.

Pocket Choice

There are six pockets on a pool table, so you might as well make full use of all of them. Don't restrict yourself with theories that say you should avoid the side pocket. And by all means violate my principle #10 of position play that counsels you to play on the long side. The bottom line is this: use the best pocket for the shot at hand, no matter how foreign or offbeat that choice may seem to yourself or others.

Setting Up the Short Side

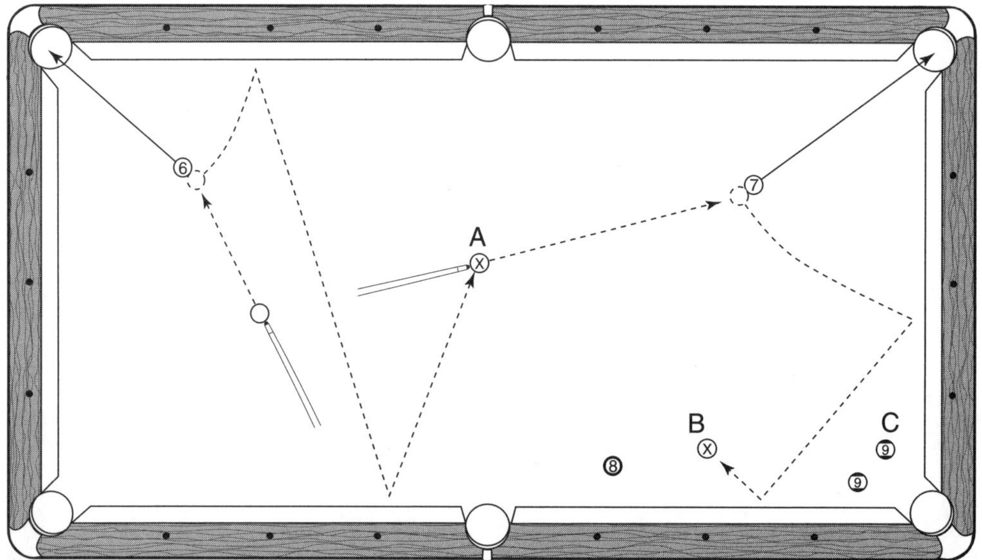

The 8-9 combo is not easy, but many players would go for it because the 9-ball is not far from the corner pocket. Rafael Martinez elected to pass on the combo and run out in the finals of the Sands Regency Open 15, 1994 against Efren Reyes. Martinez correctly surmised the percentages favored the run, providing he could get position on the short side of the 8-ball. The shot on the 6-ball was key as it set him up with the ideal angle on the 7-ball at Position A. A follow shot off the end rail resulted in perfect shape on the short side of the 8-ball at Position B.

As a final note, the best pattern would have been to play for Position B even if the 9-ball was at Position C.

Use All Six Pockets

Efren Reyes was doing battle with Francisco Bustamante in the semi-finals of the Sands Regency Open 29,1999 when he was confronted with this fascinating study in pattern play. Reyes could have followed standard operating procedure on the 5-ball, which calls for sending the cue ball between the 6 and 9-balls to Position A for the 6-ball. Reyes instead chose to exercise his creative powers by playing shape for the lower side pocket to Position B. By doing so, Reyes minimized the cue ball's traveling distance, which almost always guarantees better position.

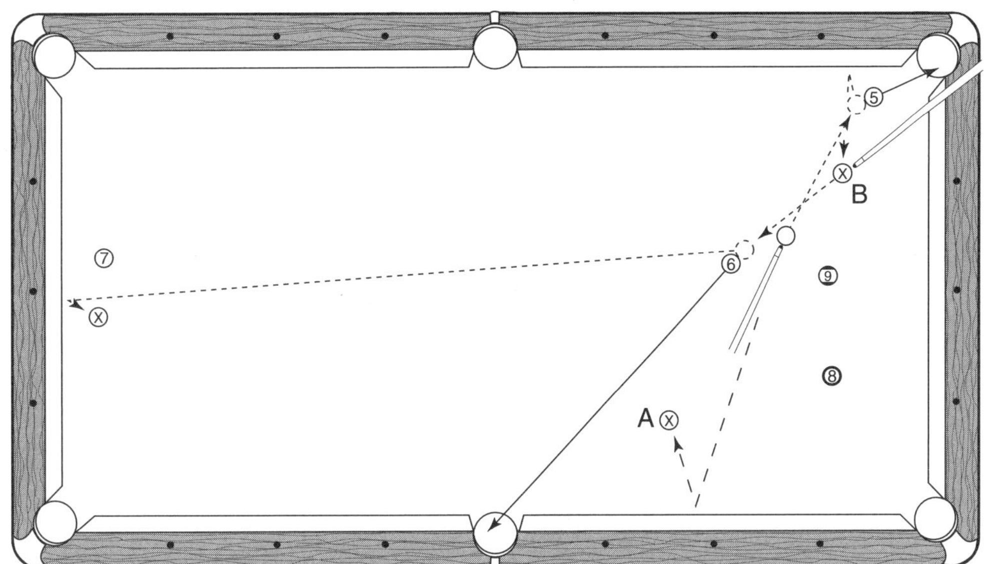

Multiple Pocket Shape

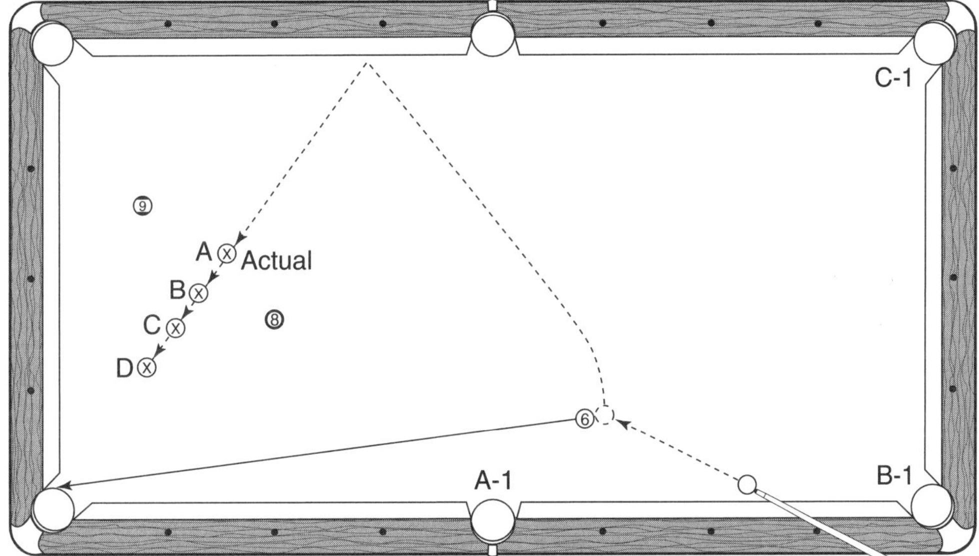

Tommy Kennedy was faced with the awkward position play above in the finals of the 1992 U.S. Open against Johnny Archer. Kennedy sent the cue ball across the table and down to Position A for straight in shape on the 8-ball into the side pocket A-1. If the cue ball had rolled to Position B, Kennedy could have shot the 8-ball into Pocket B-1. And if the cue ball had stopped at either Position C or D, he could have played the 8-ball into Pocket C-1.

When it is difficult to accurately predict the cue ball's rolling distance and its ending location, as in the example above, it is nice to have the luxury of playing position for several pockets at once.

Managing Risk and Avoiding Trouble

When you are in the process of planning your patterns, you must learn to carefully weigh the risks versus the potential rewards of any particular position route or series of routes. Should you play it safe, or go for the more aggressive route? Sometimes your choice is between which route to play, while at others the choice may be between a risky position route and a sure safety.

Weighing Risk and Reward

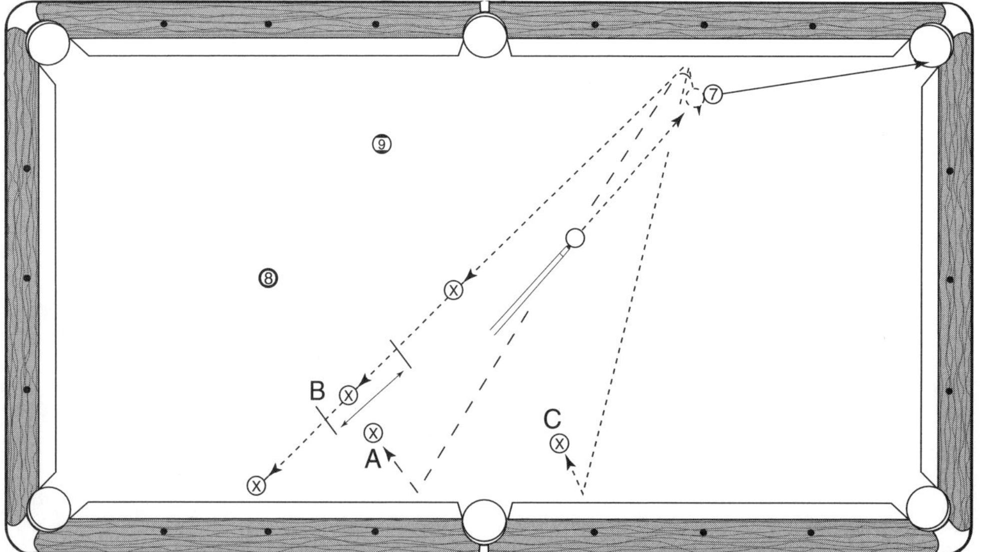

The last three balls are the crucial time of any rack of Nine Ball, and yet this is exactly the point at which many runouts break down because of poor planning or execution. The simple looking three ball run in the illustration should not pose any problems as long as you chose the correct sequence. The big key is avoiding a side pocket scratch. At the same time, however, you want to make the 8-ball as easy as possible.

Route A offers the best chance of having an easy shot on the 8-ball as the cue ball will be traveling down the line of the position zone after contacting the side rail. This route, however, brings the side pocket into play. Route B enables you to safely avoid scratching. The big risk here is speed control. If you come up short or long of the position zone you will have a tough shot on the 8-ball.

Route C eliminates the risks of the previous two shots. The safe route, however, leaves you with a longer shot on the 8-ball. Now you will have to send the cue ball to the end rail and back out for the 9-ball.

So what's the best choice? That may depend on your particular set of skills. A player with exceptional directional control who is not a great shotmaker might consider Route A. A player with a superb touch could opt for Route B, but this is probably the toughest of the three routes. A fine shotmaker is probably better off using Route C.

Going Near a Pocket for Shape

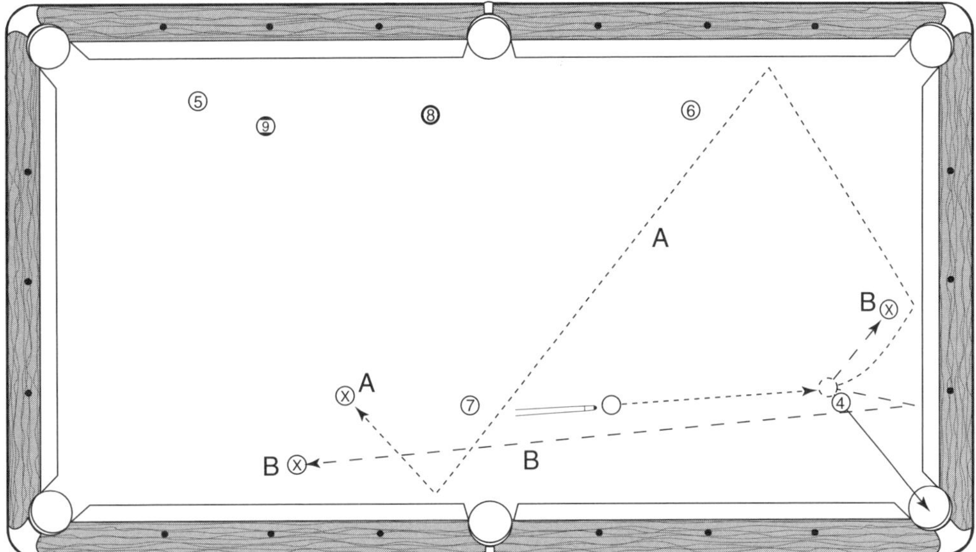

Route A is the only way from the 4-ball to the 5-ball, and it involves a high degree of risk. You'll need to thread the cue ball through an obstacle course while narrowly avoiding the side pocket. If you felt uncomfortable playing this shot, the better choice would be to play safe by banking the 4-ball down Route B to the other side of the 7-ball.

Balls Together Away From the Rail

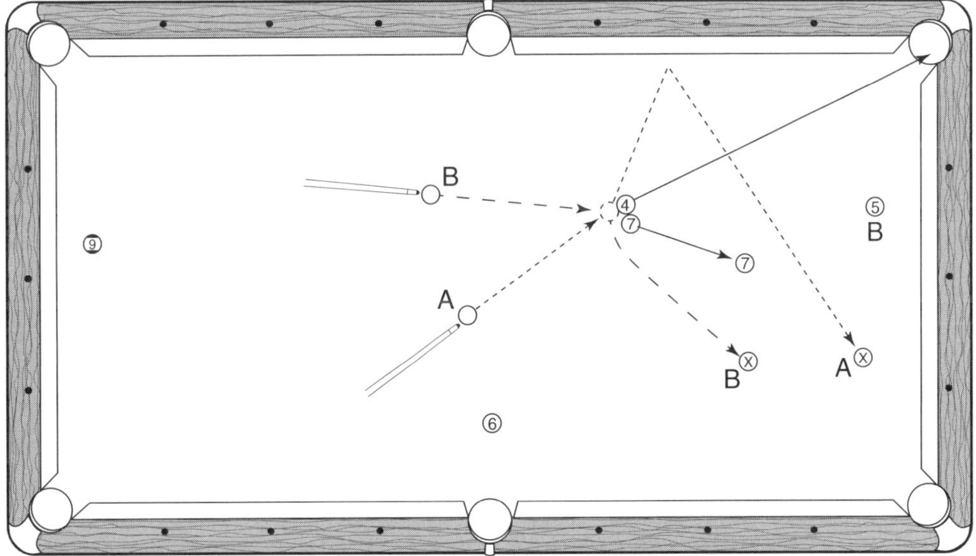

There is an element of risk when two balls are close together in the middle of the table. In is normally better to avoid the second ball (the 7-ball) by shooting away from it, as shown by Route A. If, however, you must play the 4-ball from Position B, you must carefully estimate the ending position of the cue ball and the second ball, especially if there is a chance it might get in the way of the next shot, as in the example.

Shape Versus Scratch

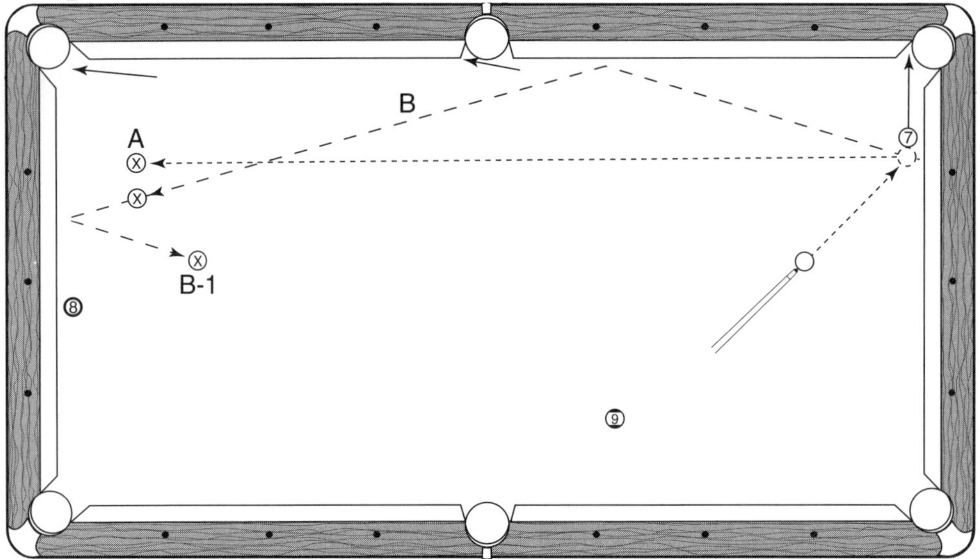

This position play is fraught with danger. There is a risk of scratching in the corner on Route A. Route B eliminates the scratch risk and replaces it with the risk of hitting the point and rebounding back towards the right end rail. You could also wind up without a shot on the 8-ball if the cue ball bounced out to B-1 In situations like this you must weigh each shot and chose the route you feel most certain you can execute.

Shape for a Safety

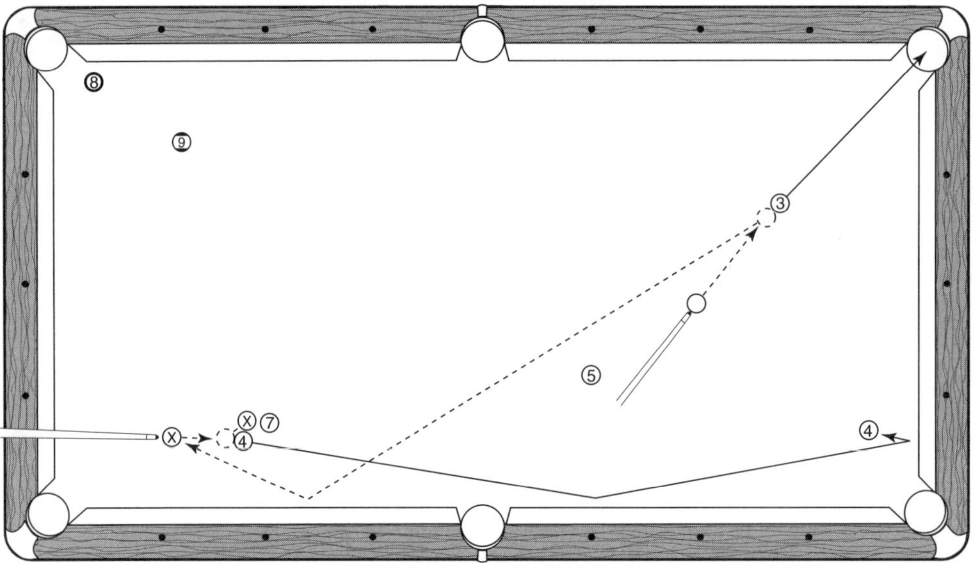

Tommy Kennedy was looking at a long draw shot into the 4-7 cluster in this action from the 1992 U.S Open against Johnny Archer. He chose to pass on the breakout and instead played position for the safety in the illustration. Kennedy won this game because of his low risk strategy.

Avoiding Trouble with the High % Route

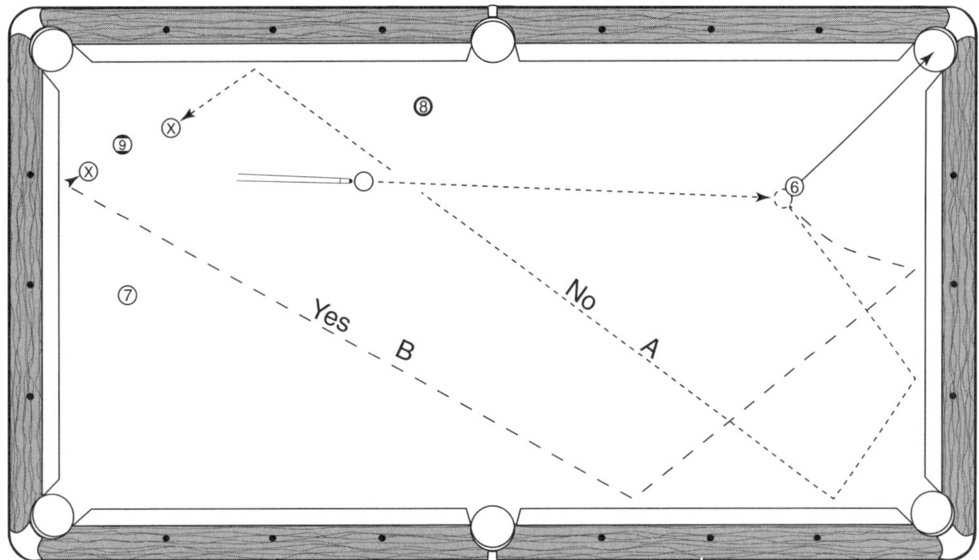

There is a natural inclination to use the three-rail route (Route A) to the 7-ball. If the shot is comes up short, you could hit the 8-ball end wind up in trouble. And is the cue ball hits too far down the side rail, it could end up behind the 9-ball. Francisco Bustamante eliminated these risks by using Route B in this match with Johnny Archer at the 1999 U.S. Open.

The Gap Past the Side Pocket

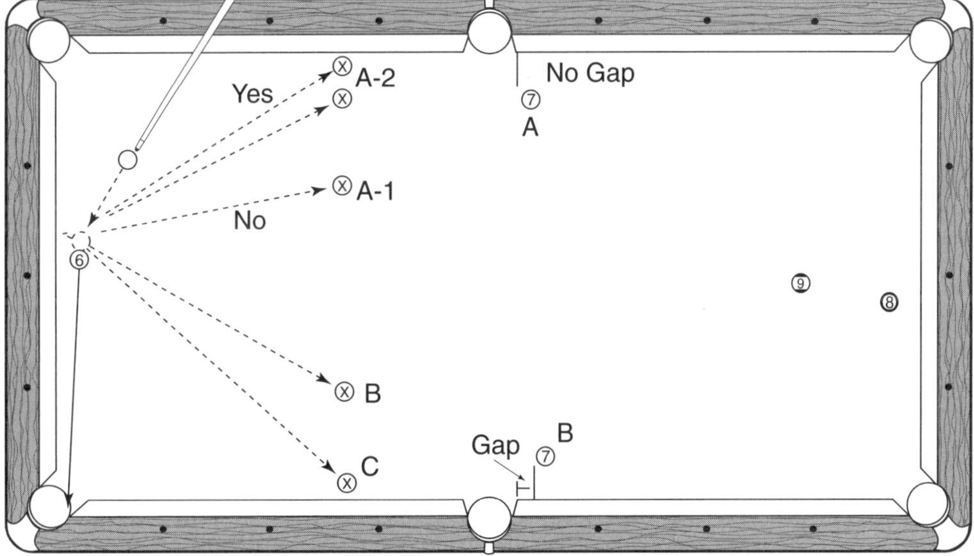

When a ball is near the side pocket you should check its position. If there is no gap, as in Position A, the risk of a scratch is almost certain if you get on the wrong side of the ball at A-1. A-2 is ok. Position B shows a gap, so now you can play to either side of the 7-ball down Route B or C and still get to the 8-ball.

Precision Pattern Play

At times the only solution to a run out is to play precision shape. If you can get on the next ball in a small zone, the run remains in tact. If you miss your shape by a few inches or less, this could easily result in a run out failure. Possible errors include scratching, getting hooked, or missing the correct cut angle. The big problem with many precision patterns is that a recovery route is usually not available. You either execute the shot exactly as planned or you suffer from a variety of possible consequences. The examples in this section show the degree of precision exemplified by some of the worlds leading professionals.

Precision Pattern Play - Varner

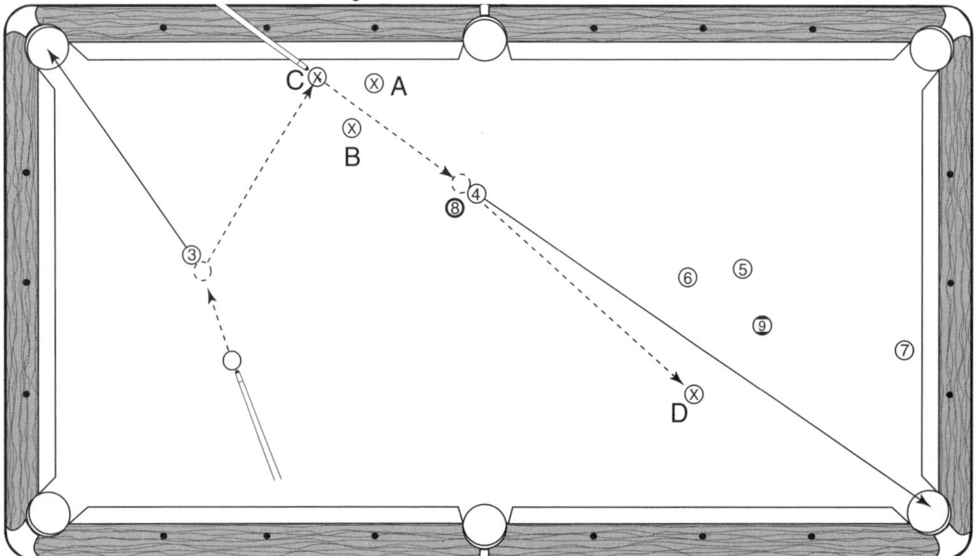

Nick Varner was locked in a tense battle with Buddy Hall at the Sands Regency Open 15, 1992 when he pulled off this precision play in the illustration. The big challenge was getting to the 5-ball, which was nestled amongst the 6 and 9-balls. The lower right corner pocket was the only logical choice for the 4-ball. Playing the 4-ball in this pocket meant that Varner had to leave himself with an almost perfectly straight in shot on the 4-ball so he could then get position on the 5-ball. If the cue ball stopped at Position A, it would run into the 8-ball on the next shot. Varner also would not be able to get to the 5-ball with the cue ball in Position B.

The solution was to play for a dead straight in shot on the 4-ball, which is one of the hardest things to do in pool. Varner was up to the task as stun followed the ball over 2' to Position C. He then played a follow shot to Position D and ran out. There were two big keys to this precision run out: 1) identifying the need for a straight in shot; 2) perfect execution.

Top Flite Planning and Execution

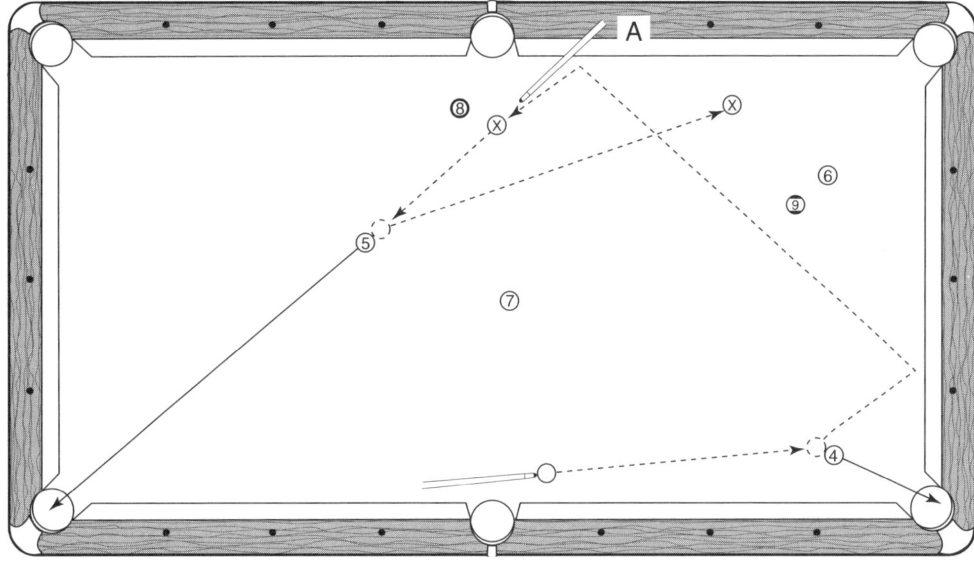

Buddy Hall's showed his mastery of position and pattern play in his duel with Efren Reyes at the 2000 U.S. Open. Before playing the 4-ball, Hall walked over to Position A to determine the position he needed on the 5-ball to get to the 6-ball (three balls at a time). He then played a perfect two-rail route that resulted in near straight in shape on the 5-ball. This was followed by a precision long-range draw shot for the 6-ball. Bravo!!

Precision Short Side Shape

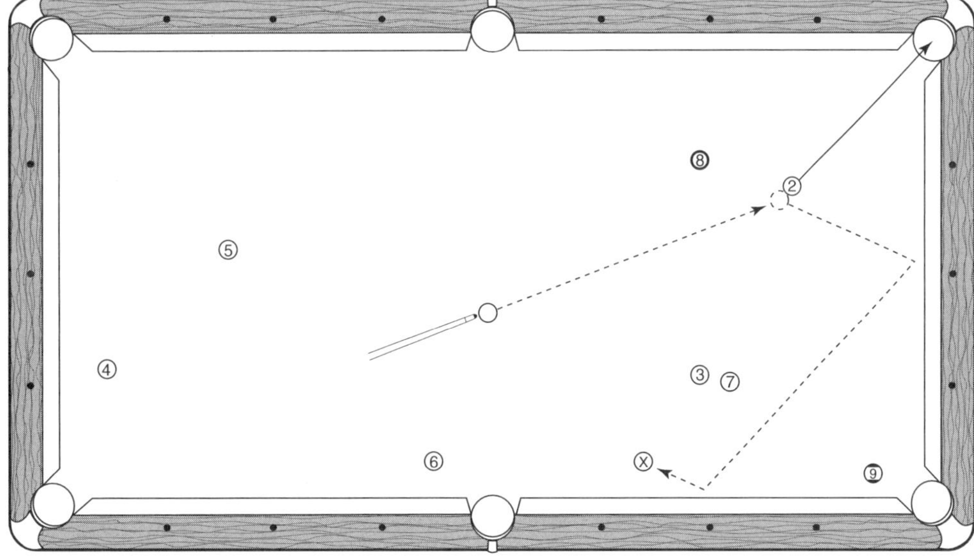

Japanese star Takeshi Okumura was engaged in the finals of the 2000 U.S. Open with Earl Strickland when he found himself in the position above. The only place the 3-ball would go was the upper right corner pocket. Okumura displayed exceptional touch in sending the cue ball two-rails to the short side for pinpoint shape in the 3-ball.

Across and Out to a Small Zone

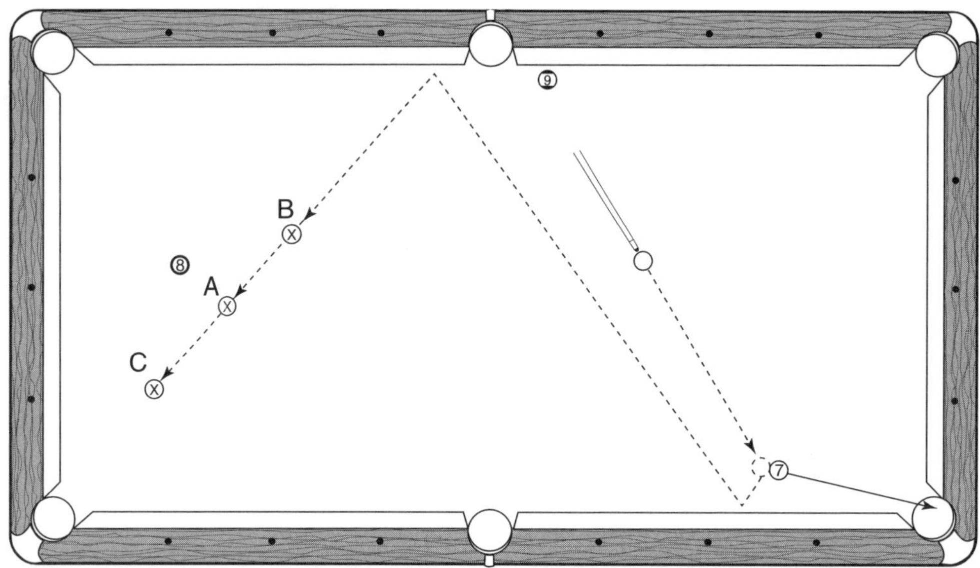

Francisco Bustamante had no choice but to play the otherworldly position route from the 7-ball to the 8-ball in this action with Efren Reyes at the Sands Regency Open 29, 1999 He narrowly avoided a side pocket scratch while crossing the shape zone to Position A. Notice the difficult shot he would have had if the cue ball had stopped at either Position B or C.

Setting Up a Precision Follow Shot

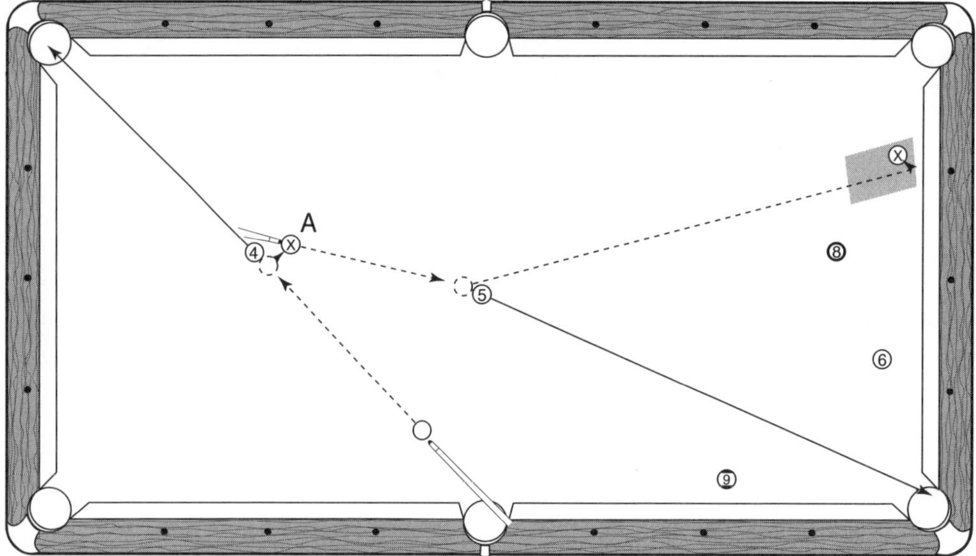

Ralf Souquet was after his first major title in the U.S. in this finals action against Efren Reyes at the Sands Regency Open 27, 1998. The big key was position on the 6-ball. Souquet prepared for the 6-ball in advance by setting up the ideal angle on the 5-ball with a stop shot on the 4-ball. From Position A, he demonstrated expert speed control as the cue ball drifted lazily down near the end rail for shape on the 6-ball.

Ultra Precise One- Railer

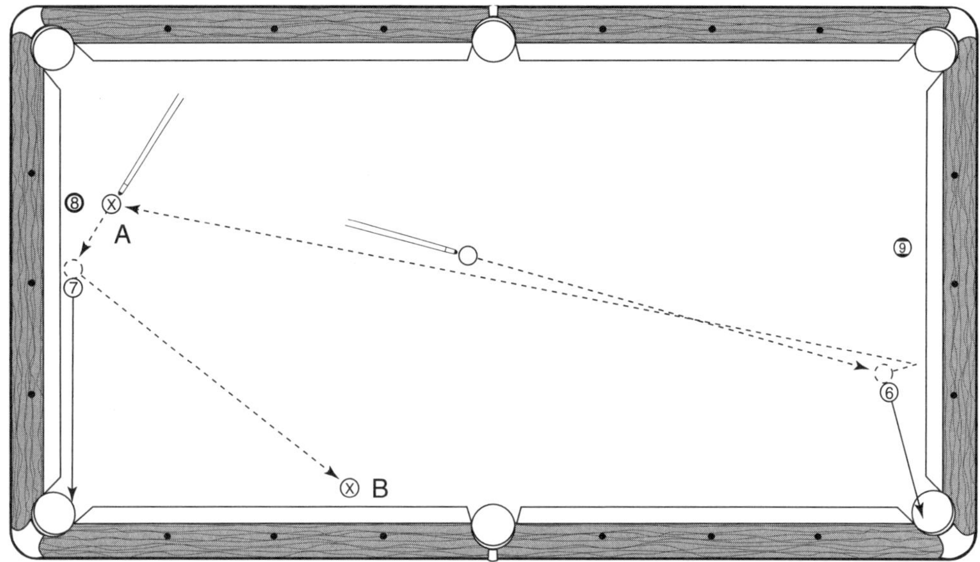

One of the toughest patterns occurs when two balls are close together on the same end rail. Mika Immonen answered the challenge as shown by this exceptional position play from the 6-ball to the 7-ball. The cue ball stopped at Position A, allowing Immonen to play the 8-ball in the opposite corner from Position B. If the cue ball had stopped an inch short of A, he would have had to go up the table and back for the 8-ball. This wonder shot took place at the 1998 U.S. Open against Jim Rempe.

Draw Control

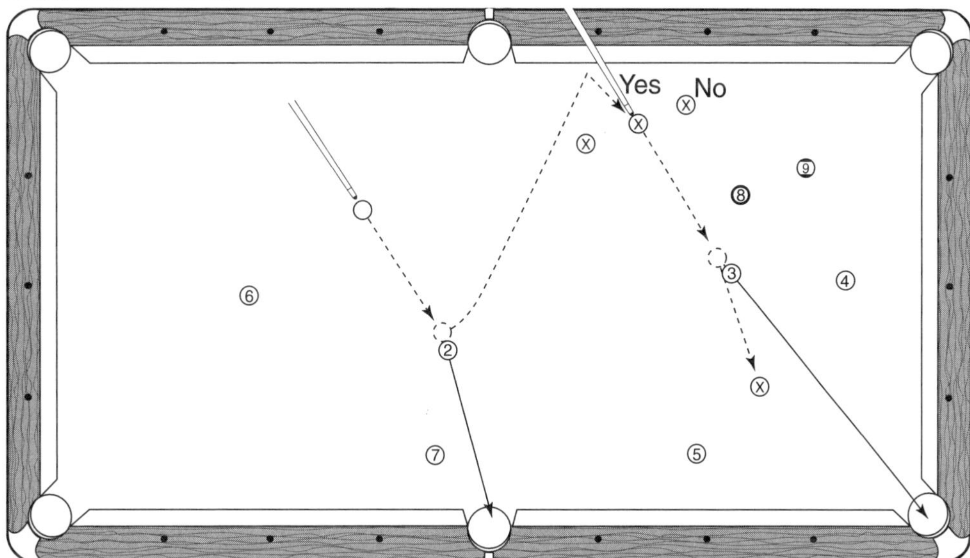

Kim Davenport brought the cue ball to the side rail and out for perfect position on the 3-ball in his match with Shannon Daulton at the 1999 U.S. Open. This kind of precision using draw is the hallmark of a very fine player.

Improving the Layout by Moving a Ball

Normally it is not a good idea to run into balls when playing position as the cue ball can be knocked of course, resulting in a scratch or a hook. At times, however, you can significantly improve a layout by hitting a ball with little or no risk. And sometimes, as we'll see in a moment, going for the hit is the best move even if it entails a fair amount of danger.

Optional and Mandatory Layout Improvement

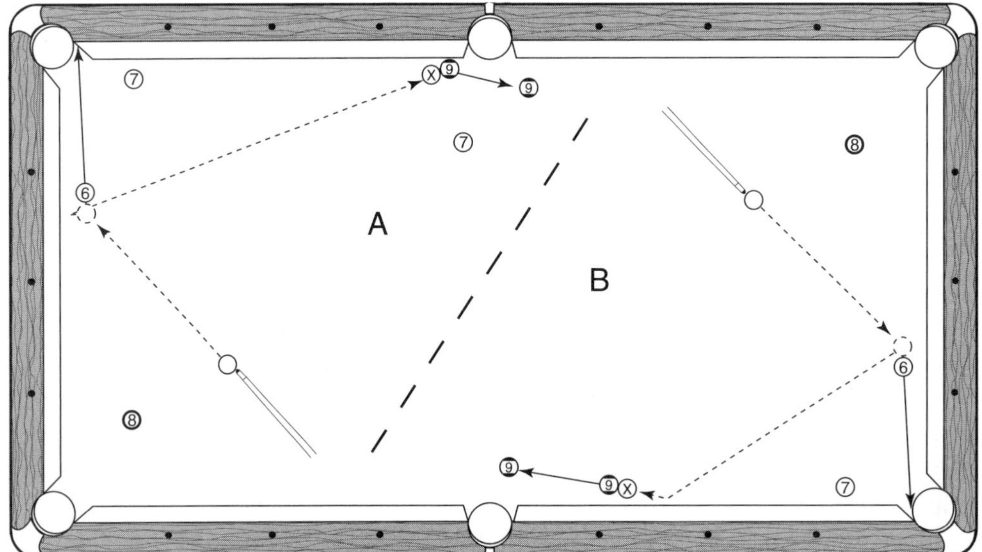

One of the most troublesome positions is a ball that's frozen to the rail near a side pocket. In Part A you really have little choice but to knock the 9-ball off the side rail unless you want to subject yourself to a very difficult shot on the 9-ball. Follow with a quarter tip of right english will send the cue ball into the 9-ball as shown. There was little risk to this crafty maneuver since shape on the 7-ball is almost guaranteed, and because it is impossible to scratch in the side pocket.

The 9-ball is in a much easier location in Part B, so it is not mandatory that you bump it from its present location. Nevertheless, you have the opportunity to make the run virtually dogproof by knocking the 9-ball in front of the side pocket. This shot eliminates a possible side pocket scratch when playing shape on the 9-ball. If the pockets are very tight, you will appreciate not having to send the 9-ball 3' down the rail to the pocket. Once again, there is little risk to this shot.

Looking Ahead

Smart Nine-Ball players identify the possible stumbling blocks to their run outs well in advance. The key in this layout is getting from the 7-ball to the 8-ball. While shape on the 8-ball is possible, it will not be easy thanks to the 9-ball, which is next to the 7-ball.

Planning ahead can enable you to easily eliminate this potentially big problem. A 5" draw shot on the 2-ball gives you a slight angle on the 4-

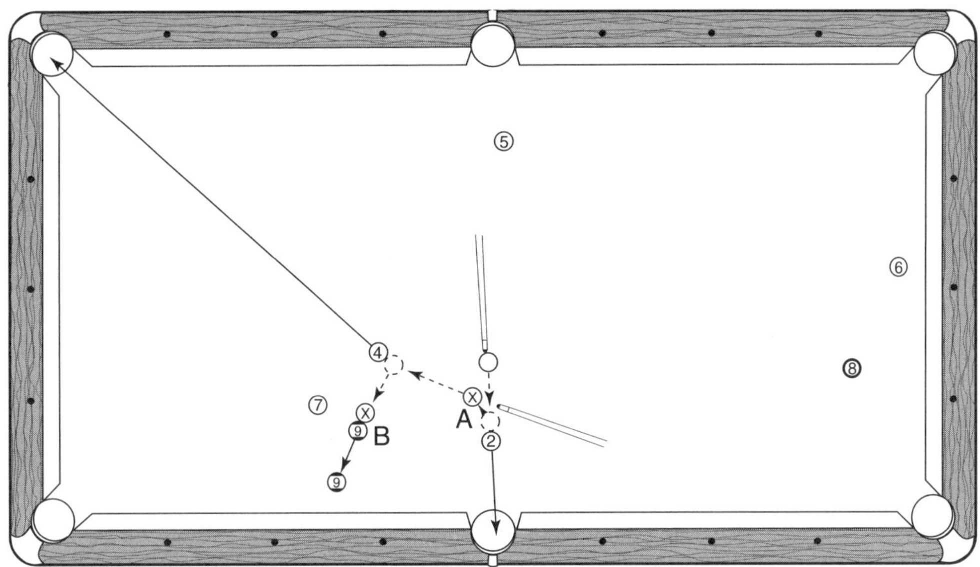

ball. With the cue ball in Position A, you can use a soft draw shot to bump the 9-ball away from the 7-ball, clearing out space to play the 7-ball. Getting from the 4-ball to the 5-ball is no problem with the cue ball in Position B. Once again, moving a ball carried almost no risk but offered a huge benefit.

Getting a Ball off the Rail

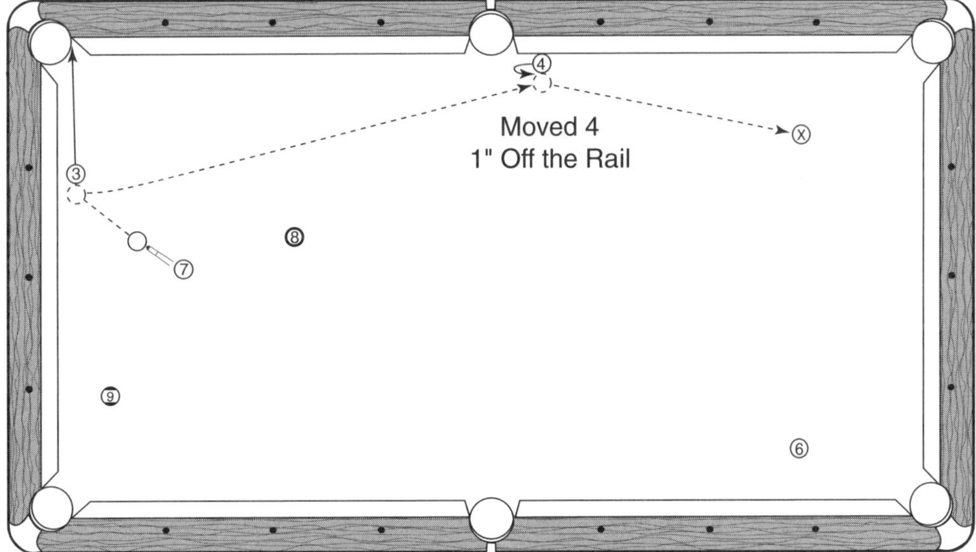

Alex Pagulayan was locked in combat with Ismael Paez at the 2000 World 9-Ball Championships, when he came across this incredibly difficult layout. Pagulayan was jacked up over the 7-ball, which is a challenge by itself. Adding to the difficulty was the 4-ball, which was frozen to the side rail near the side pocket. He chose to play the high risk, high reward shot in the illustration. Pagulayan's effort resulted in a true masterpiece.

End of Rack Pattern Play

Running a full rack is not easy no matter how well you play. Furthermore, I feel comfortable in saying that the vast majority of game ending runouts between amateur players commence with only 3-5 balls on the table. No matter what your level of play, however, end of rack pattern play is crucial to your success.

When you get to the final 3-5 balls, the congestion factor has typically been removed, leaving a clear path to the 9-ball. You run out when you are supposed to or you don't, simple as that. In this section, we'll cover but a few of the zillions of possible end of rack patterns to give you a feel for how the game should be played at this crucial stage. But first it's time for a pop test.

End of Game Run Out %'s

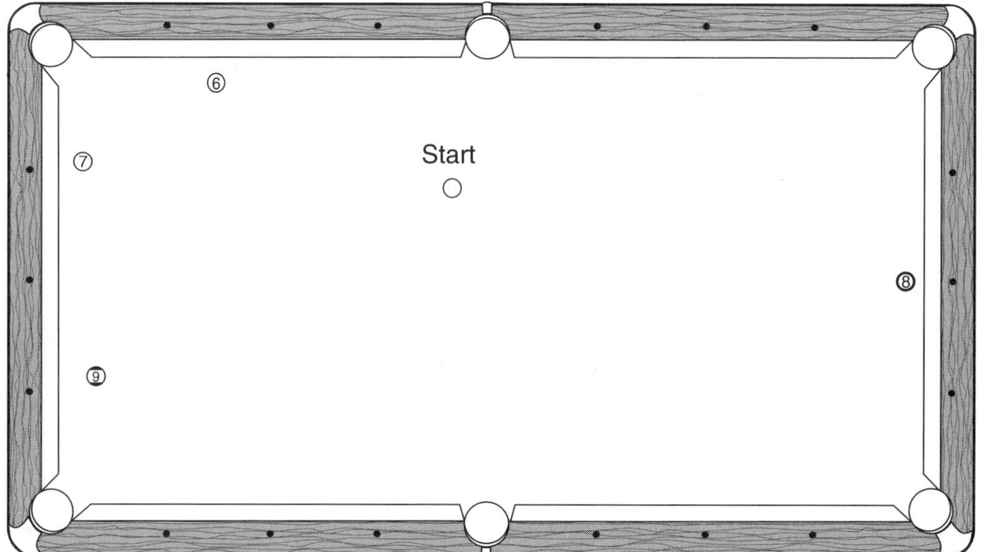

Here's a pop quiz that is designed to test your level of skill at running out in the end game. Place the balls on the table as shown and run out. All done? Did you run out? While this pattern is certainly not the most difficult you will encounter, it is typical of the kind of layouts that amateurs fail to convert all too often. I would estimate that a C Player would run out 30-50% of the time while a B Player would get out on 80-90% of their attempts. An A Player should be expected to run this table 95+% of the timc.

The 9-Ball Determines the Correct Route

Three-ball pattern play is especially crucial in the later stages of a rack when the game is on the line. This is the time to carefully plot the pattern that will enable you to arrive at the 9-ball in the simplest and most efficient manner possible. When playing the 7-ball (page 205), ask yourself what position on the 8-ball is best for getting to the 9-ball? When the 9-ball is in Position A, send the cue ball across the table to A-1. Now

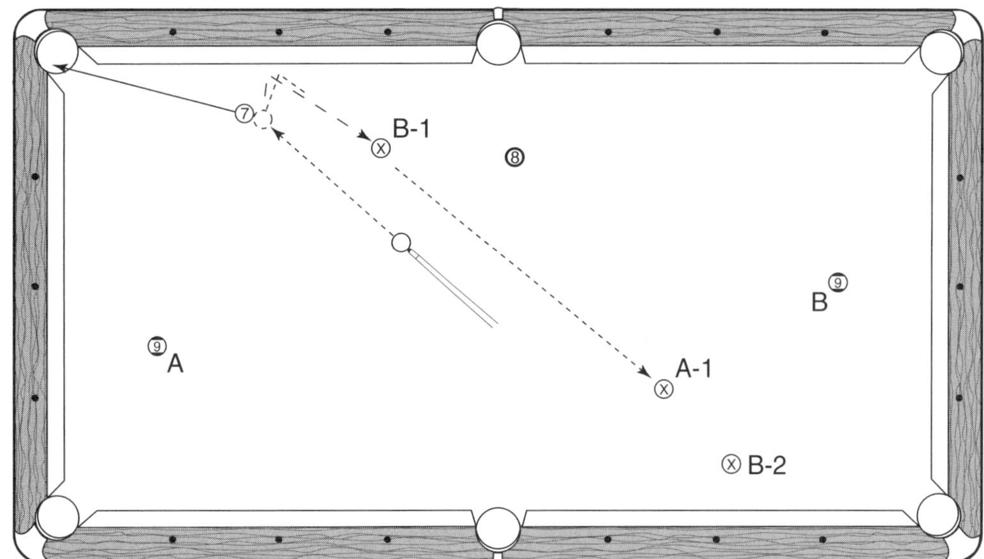

all it takes is a soft follow shot for shape on the 9-ball. The 9-ball has been moved to Position B, which changes things considerably. Now the percentages favor drawing back to Position B-1 so you can play the 8-ball in the upper right corner pocket. A stun/follow shot on the 8-ball will give you excellent position on the 9-ball at B-2.

When to Play for a Cut on the 9-Ball

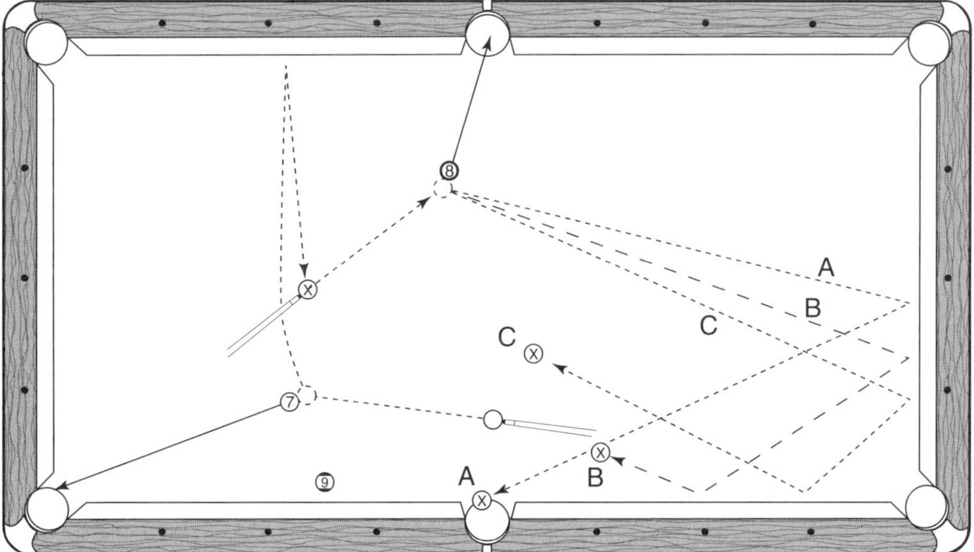

Most players favor a near straight in shot on the 9-ball, but sometimes playing position for a small cut angle puts the game in jeopardy. The 7-ball has been played perfectly, setting up a very workable angle on the 8-ball. If you tried to get straight in on the 9-ball by using Route A, you could easily scratch in the side. Route B gives you a reasonably large margin for error. If you made the mistake of applying too much draw and the cue ball traveled down Route C, you would still have an easy shot on the 9-ball.

End to End on the Last Three Balls

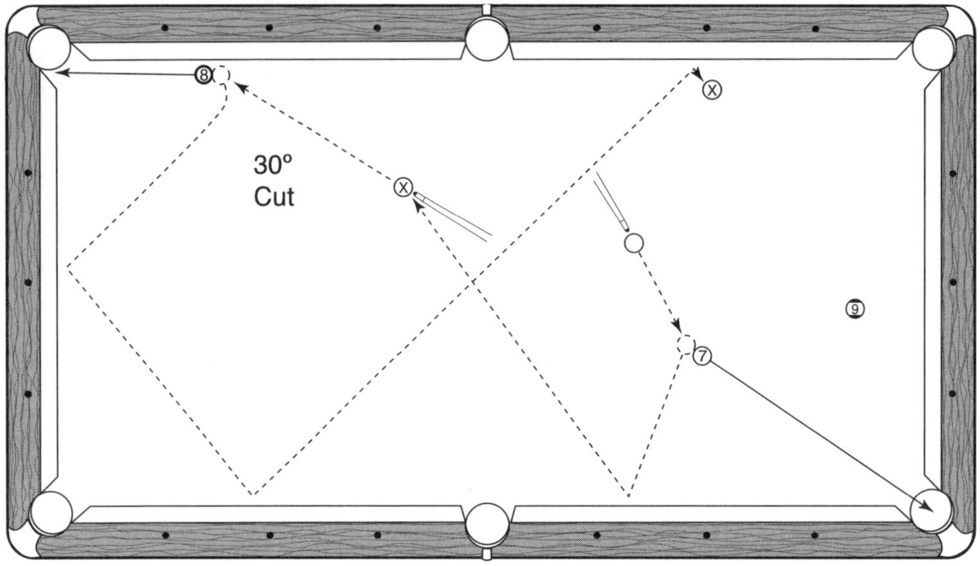

When the balls are lying tough you may be faced with anything but a roadmap runout to the 9-ball. This happens. Difficult end of rack patterns also appear regularly among amateurs as a result of their opponent's errors. So the next time you feel tempted to bemoan your fate when your opponent leaves you a tough shot after blowing an easy end of game runout, just be thankful you have a shot and a chance at winning.

Efren Reyes had no choice except to play the exacting route to the 9-ball shown above in this match with Johnny Archer at the 2000 U.S. Open. Reyes used the 7-ball to set up a 30-degrees cut angle on the 8-ball. This angle is just about perfect for playing three-rail position with inside (left) english. Reyes used a medium hard stroke on the 8-ball.

The 8 and 9-Balls are on the Same Rail

When the 8 and 9-balls are close together on the same rail, an alarm should go off alerting you that you are facing a testy situation. When playing the 6-ball, the big question is whether to draw to Position A or Position B for the 7-ball. With the cue ball in Position A, you can draw across the table and down to Position A-1 for the 8-ball, effectively ending the game. This route is very risky, however, as you could easily scratch or get hooked behind the 9-ball.

With the cue ball in Position B, a long distance draw shot to B-1 would give you ideal shape on the 8-ball. Route B, like Route A, is loaded with danger. If you drew too far back, you would be hooked behind the 9-ball. And if the cue ball stopped at B-2, you would have to play a kill shot or send the cue ball to the opposite end rail and back. Sometimes, as in the example above, there is no easy solution to an end of rack position. Good planning and great execution, as you've heard before, are the keys. And if often pays to go with the shot you know best.

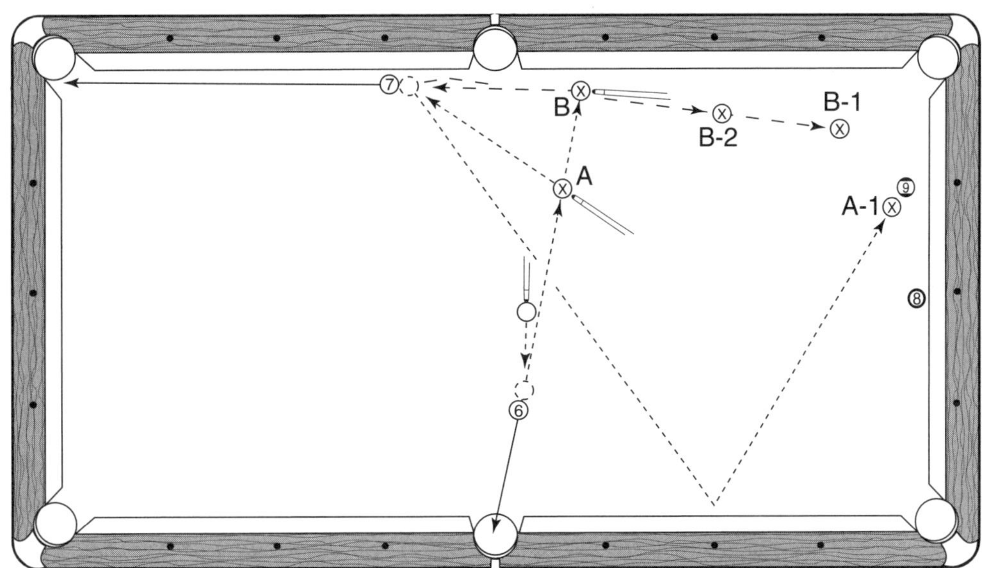

End of Rack Pattern

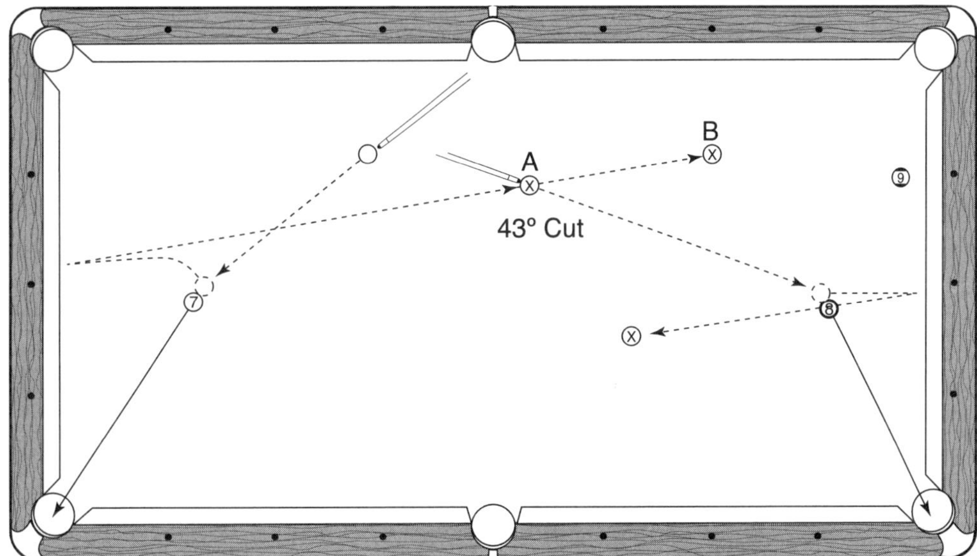

Keith McCready, who is widely known for his role in The Color of Money, was in a close match with Nick Varner, at the Sands Regency Open 12, 1990, when he came across this end of rack layout. Even great players like McCready make mistakes in their end of rack pattern play. McCready came up short at Position A when playing the 7-ball, which is completely understandable since it is difficult to control the speed on this rather awkward follow shot.

Position B would have been ideal. McCready still got out thanks to this impressive recovery route on the 8-ball, which required a soft stroke, and the skillful use of inside english. The lesson: it sure helps to have an arsenal of recovery routes at your disposal in the end game as they can enable you to save your run when you play what I call 50% shape.

Sending the Cue Ball to Center Table

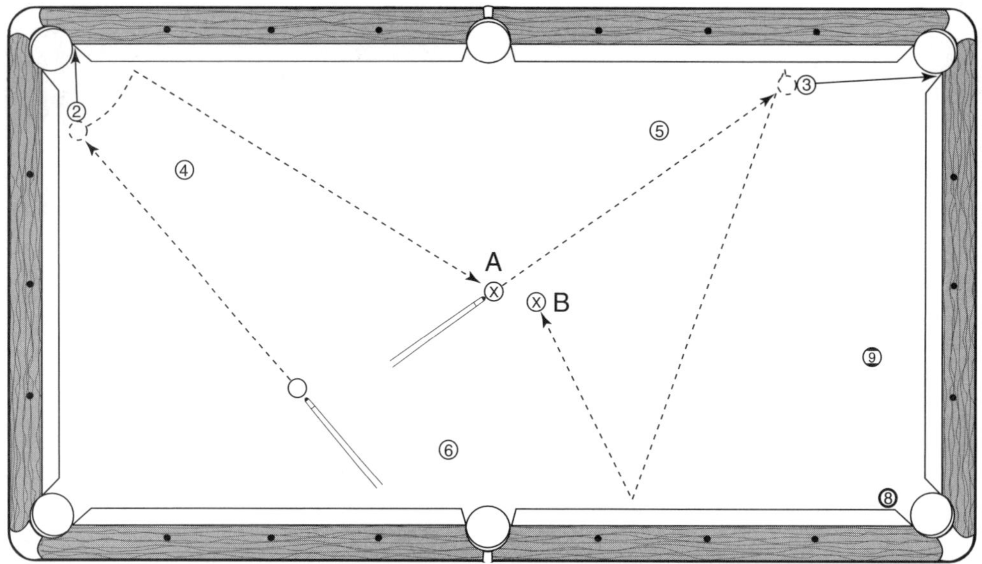

The center portion of the table is certainly a much used haven for the cue ball in Nine-Ball, especially when you consider that 1) the majority of the balls are less than a diamond from the rails after the break and 2) it is generally easier when playing Nine-Ball to send the cue ball to a rail and out for position. That said, I couldn't agree less with those who counsel you to return the cue ball to the center whenever possible. I advise that you play position in the center portion of the table only when the next ball dictates that it is the best place for the cue ball, period.

Kim Davenport demonstrated how to use the center against Shannon Daulton on his way to a 4th place finish at the 1999 U. S. Open. The two-rail route to the 3-ball sent the cue ball to Position A. This set up a crossing route to the 4-ball which once again resulted in ideal shape at Position B in nearly the same spot in the middle of the table.

Side Versus Corner Pocket

Some contend that you should play to the corners whenever possible while others favor the side pockets. In general, the average player is suckered into using the sides too often because they make pocketing some shots exceptionally easy. The downside is that improper use of the side pockets will force you into playing long and dangerous position routes, on far too many occasions. Let's take a look at the three ball pattern on the top of the next page. If you sent the cue ball down Route A, you would have good shape on the 8-ball that allows you to easily proceed down table to the 9-ball from the positions shown. Route A adheres to Principle # 12, which advises you to play down the line shape when possible.

Despite the advantages of corner pocket position, many players in this situation will succumb to the lure of the side pocket. Notice that you only have a short distance in which to land the cue ball. If you come up short or long, you'll have a tough time getting from the 8-ball to the 9-ball.

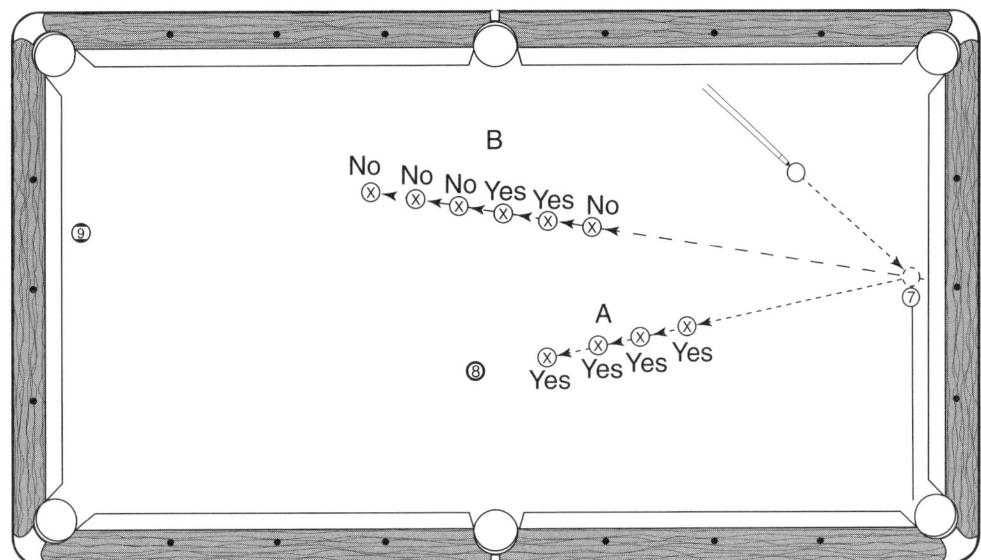

Side Versus Corner

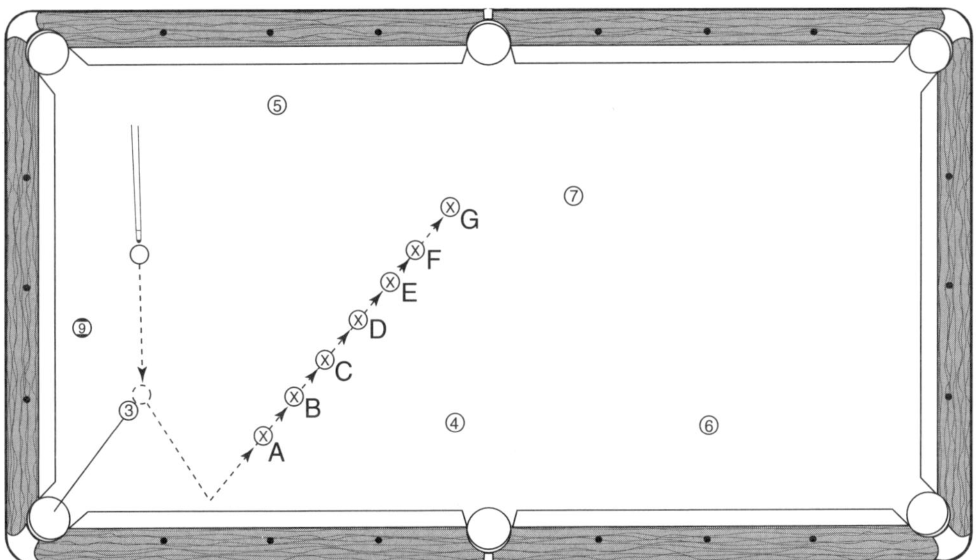

In this example, I would like for you to consider the many possible position routes from the 4-ball to the 5-ball after the 3-ball has been played. Ask yourself these questions:

- Do you like Position A for the corner and, if so, why?
- Should you play to the side or corner from B and C? How would you get to the 5-ball?
- Positions D-G are played in the side pocket. How would you get from the 4-ball to the 5-ball on each of them?

Now for my recommendation: I feel Position A is best because it allows you to float the cue ball to the middle of the table for a cut shot on the 5-ball. This will, in turn, make it easy to get on the 6-ball.

Patterning Balls in the Middle

Playing correct position on balls in the central area of the table is one the more difficult maneuvers in Nine-Ball. The diagram below shows the boundaries for the trouble zone. There are two big problems with balls in this zone: 1) the long distance the cue ball must travel to a rail, which makes cue ball control difficult; 2) the need to keep your cut angles relatively shallow. As a rule of thumb, you are almost always better off avoiding a backcut on balls in this trouble zone.

Ball in the Middle

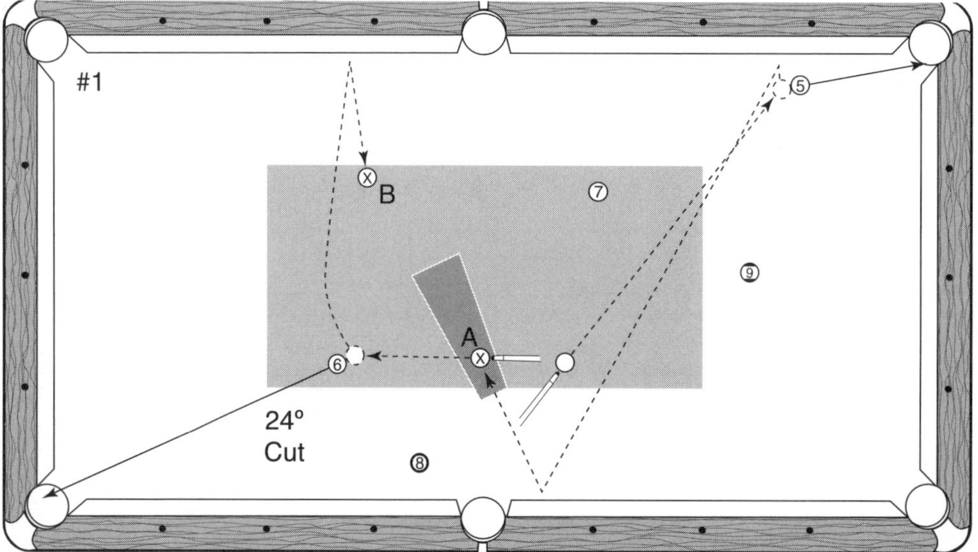

Jim Rempe gave a clinic on how to play balls in the dangerous middle with this runout that took place at the 1999 U.S. Open against Francisco Bustamante. In diagram #1, Rempe set up a perfect angle on the 6-ball with his across the table and out shot on the 5-ball. Rempe could have worked the cue ball into position for the 7-ball from anywhere within zone, but the cue ball came in for a perfect landing at Position A. The 24-degree cut angle allowed Rempe to exert maximum control when sending the cue ball across the table and out to Position B for the 7-ball.

Rempe ended up with a 26-degree cut angle on the 7-ball, which was also stationed in the danger zone. From here he floated the cue ball to the rail and out for position on the 8-ball. While this sequence was certainly acceptable, Rempe probably would have preferred that the cue ball had stopped at Position A. This would have lead to a shallower cut angle on the 8-ball, possibly at Position B. The thin cut on the 8-ball forced Rempe to send the cue ball across the table and back for the 9-ball, which he accomplished with an uncanny degree of accuracy.

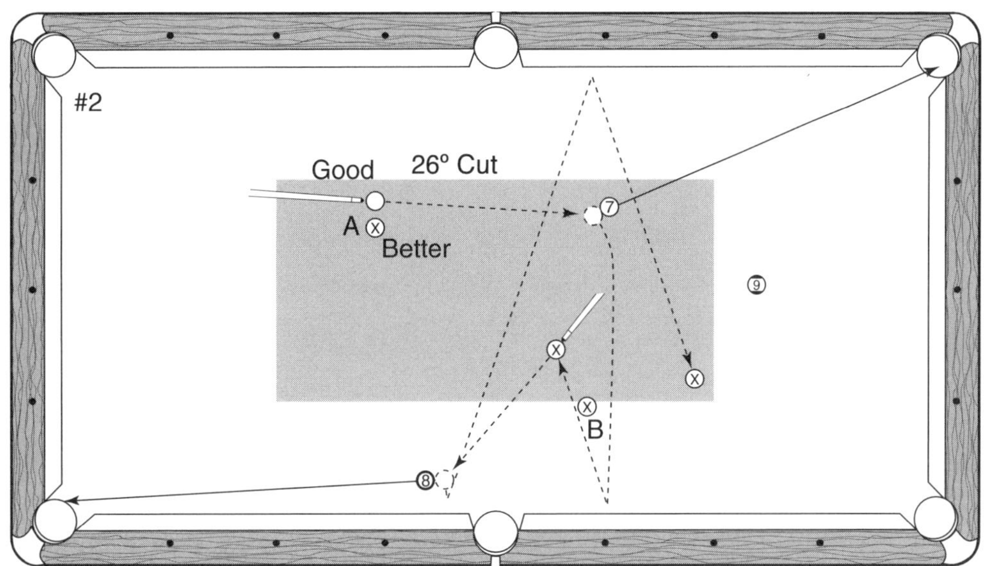

Shaping a Ball in the Middle of the Table

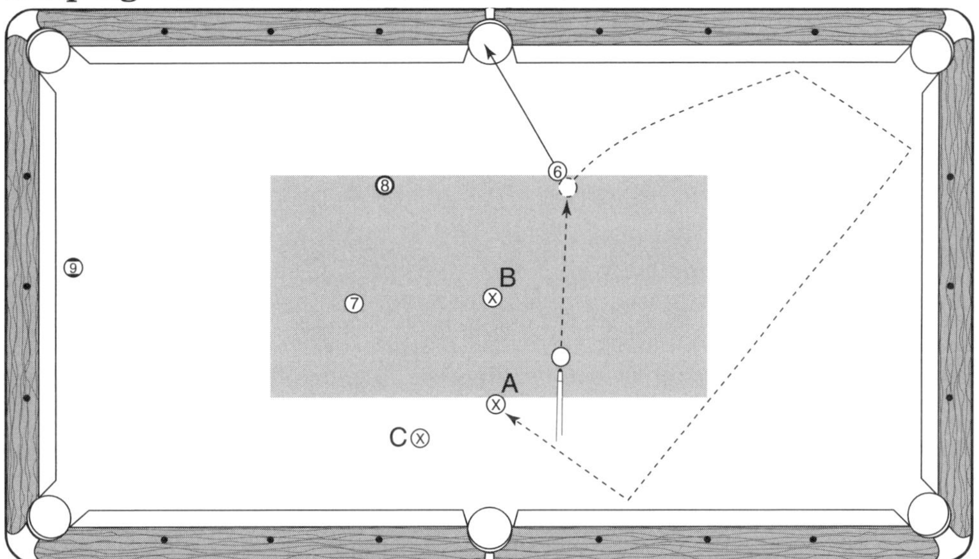

Efren Reyes grabbed a 9-8 advantage over Johnny Archer in the semifinals of the 1995 U.S. Open, thanks in part to his planning for a ball in the middle of the table. Reyes used a two-rail route to play down the line shape on the 7-ball. From Position A, Reyes had no trouble getting to the 8-ball. Now imagine for a moment what problems he might have encountered if the cue ball had stopped at either Position B or C.

The big lesson: when playing shape on a ball in the middle, you are much better off playing down the line shape whenever possible because of the especially urgent need to control the cut angle on the next ball.

Two Consecutive Balls on the Same Rail

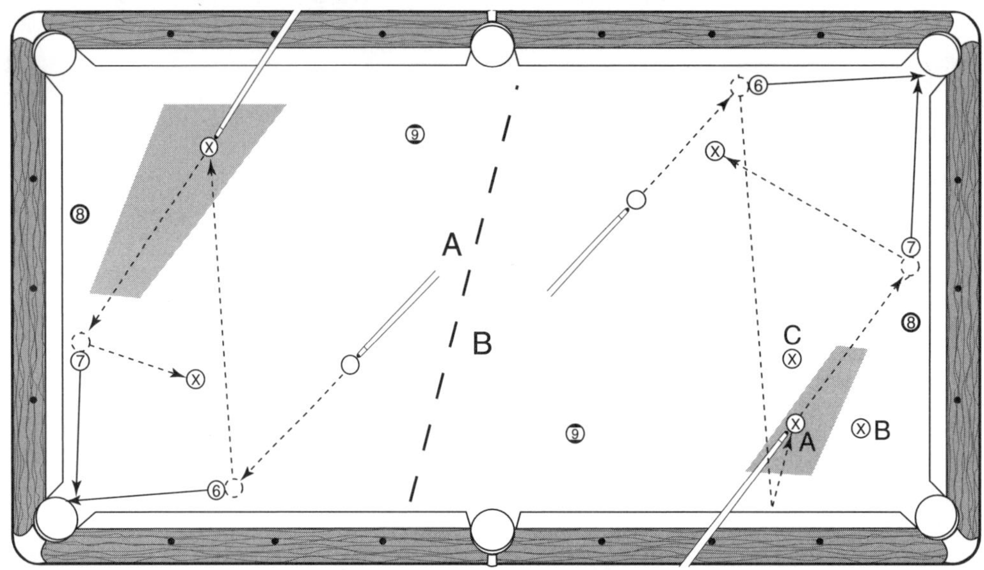

In Part A, the 7 and 8-balls are on the same end rail. The position zone is quite large, however, thanks to the distance between the two balls. The main objective is to leave a shallow cut angle on the first ball on the rail (the 7-ball) without getting hooked behind the second ball (the 8-ball).

The position zone in this example was accessed by playing a soft follow shot on the 6-ball with a quarter tip of inside (right) english. A small cut angle on the first ball on the rail ensures that you won't have a thin cut after the cue ball bounces off the rail. A lag shot on the 7-ball with a quarter tip of inside english put the cue ball in good position for the 8-ball.

The 7 and 8-ball are 7" closer together in Part B. As a result, the position zone for the 7-ball has shrunk dramatically. With the cue ball in Position A (after the 6-ball) you will be able to get on the 8-ball by using a soft stroke with a half tip of inside english as shown. The cue ball in Position B is behind the 8-ball. This mistake happens when you try for an overly shallow cut angle and miss the mark. The sharp cut angle on the 7-ball with the cue ball in Position C forces you to send whitey to the far end rail and back. While this pattern is not easy, it is often the best or only way to handle two ball that are close together on the same rail.

Two Consecutive Balls on the Same Side Rail (1)

A stop shot on the 5-ball in Position A will leave the cue ball in the middle of a position zone at A-1. Now you can gently roll the 6-ball into the corner and the cue ball will stop near the rail for the 7-ball into the far corner.

The 5-ball in Position B requires a totally different approach. The play is to draw into the sizeable position zone in the center portion of the table. From Position B-1 you have a 50-degree cut angle, which should enable you to send the cue ball across and back to where the 6-ball now rests, for the 7-ball into the upper right corner pocket. The gap between

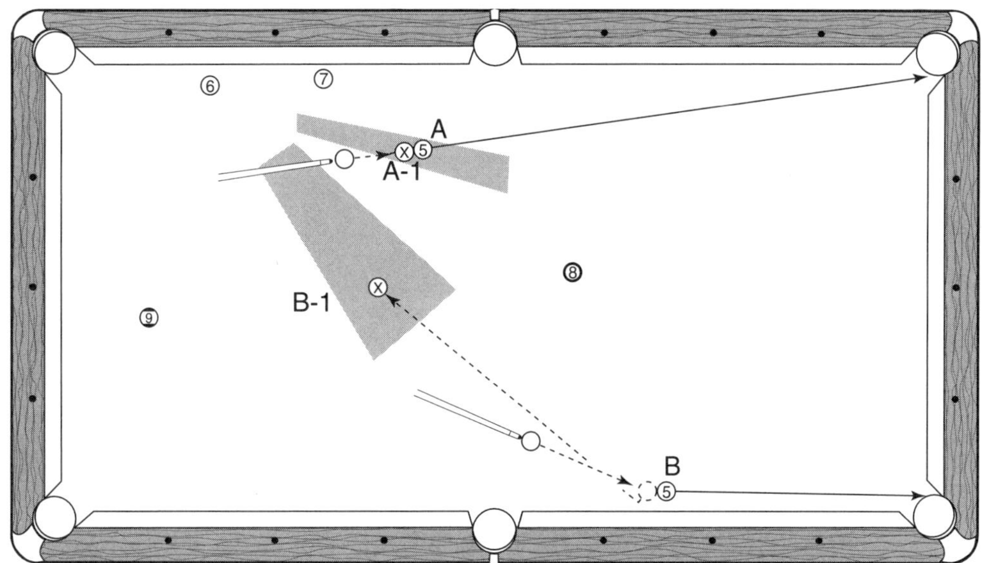

the two position zones is a no man's land where your cut angle is neither sharp enough nor shallow enough for easy access to the 7-ball.

Two Consecutive Balls on the Same Side Rail (2)

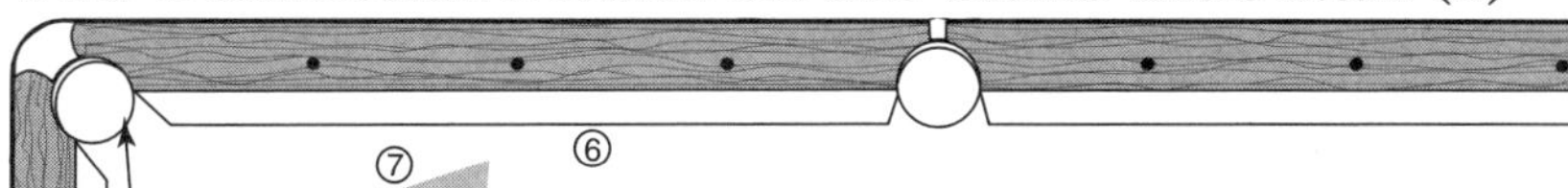

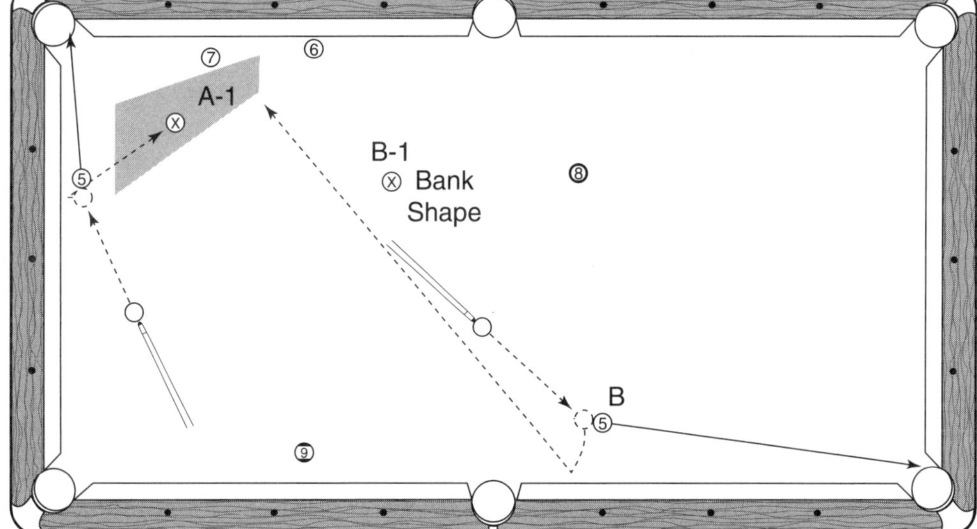

You've got double trouble because the first ball (the 6-ball) is now on the other side of the second ball (the 7-ball). With the 5-ball in Position A, you could follow to A-1. This long tough shot requires you to send the cue ball across and back for the 7-ball. You could also attempt to hit the 6-ball into a better location when playing the 5-ball.

You could try hitting the side rail at or just above the 7-ball with the 5-ball in Position B. This takes phenomenal speed and directional control. Another approach is to cinch bank shape by sending the cue ball to B-1. Now all of your eggs are in the bank basket, which isn't a bad idea if banks are one of your strong suits.

Either Side of the Ball Can Work

On the majority of most position plays you are clearly much better off with the cue ball on one side of the object ball versus the other. At times however, you will be able to easily play position on the next ball from either side of the object ball.

Either Side Works Just Fine

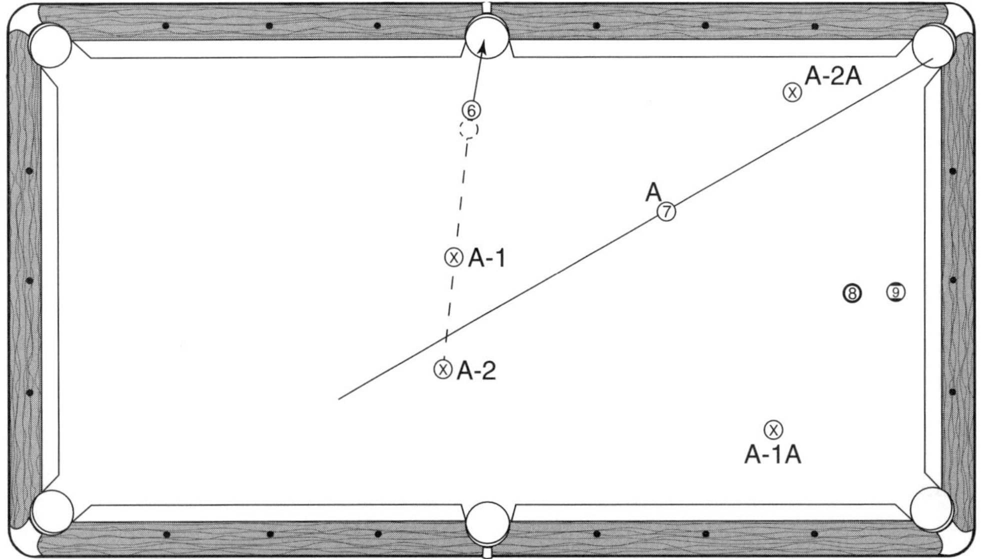

You will need to draw back for position on the 7-ball after playing the 6-ball into the side pocket. If the cue ball stops at A-1, you could play shape on the 8-ball at A-1A. And if the cue ball came to rest at A-2, you could play a follow shot to A-2A. In this case, there is really no distinct advantage to playing from either side. Your decision for this pattern should be based solely on personal preference: do you feel more comfortable playing the route to A-1A or the one to A-2A?

One Side Is Better

When you are afforded the luxury of playing to either side, you should still exercise your option to swing the odds slightly in your favor. Choose the better side, when doing so can increase your chances of running out by as little as 2%, much less 10-20% or more. The 8 and 9-balls are in the same positions as in the example above. On the next page, the 7-ball is now at the opposite end of the table. You could certainly play shape on the 8-ball from either side.

Position A is ideal for playing three-rail shape to A-1. You could also send the cue ball to the long side of the 8-ball from Position B for shape at B-1. (Those of you with a sharp eye will have noticed that the position zone for the 8-ball is slightly larger on the top half of the table). When playing the route to B-1, it is much easier to lose the cue ball, which could result in a scratch into the upper right corner pocket. So while both routes

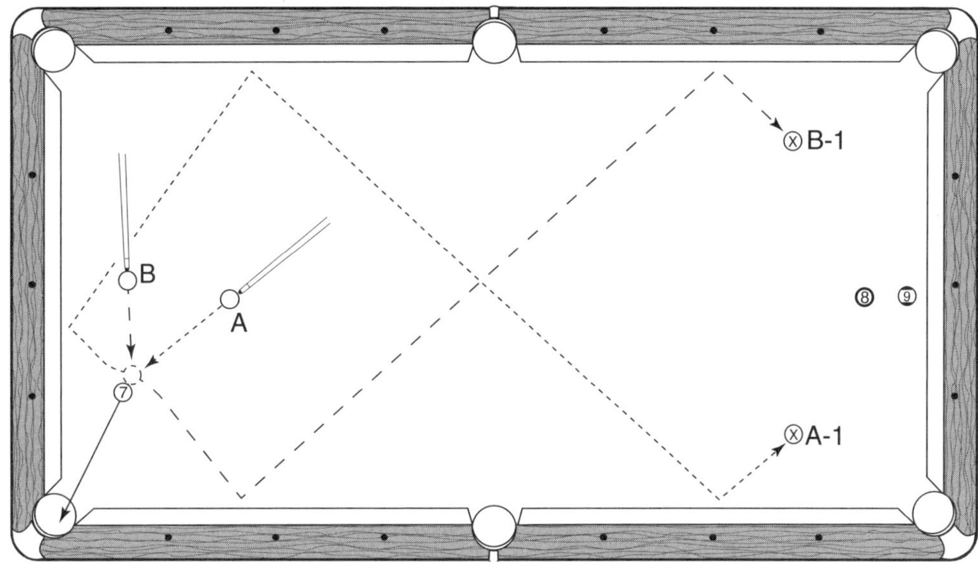

will work, the route to A-1 appears to be the better choice because it reduces the chances of scratching. I suggest you try them both to see what works better for you.

End Rail Position

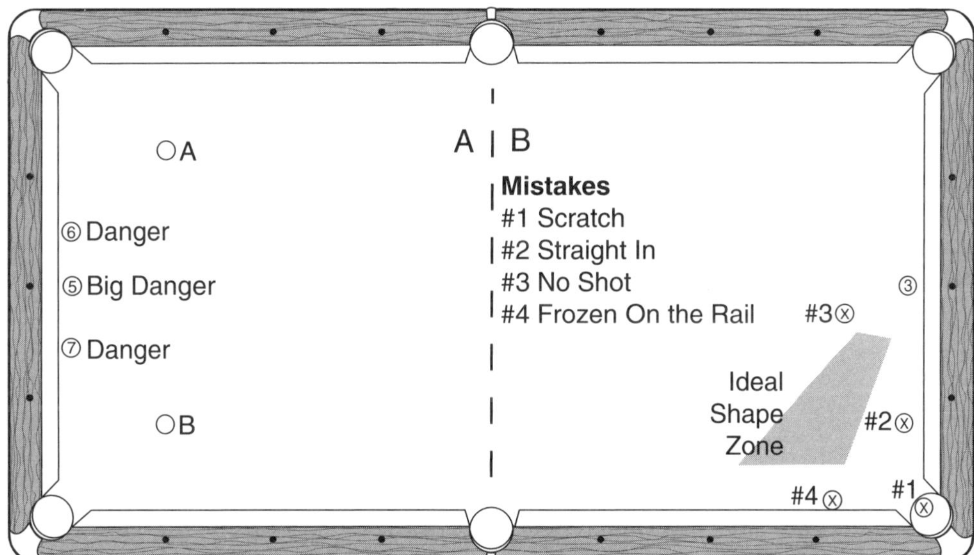

When a ball is on either end rail, you should proceed to it with great care. In Part A, the shape zone is small on either of a ball when it is opposite the middle diamond, as shown by the 5-ball. When the object ball favors one side or the other, you should play position on the long side if possible. Cue ball A is in good position for the 7-ball while Cue Ball B is ideal for the 6-ball. When you must play to the short side of a ball on the end rail, you've got to be extremely precise. Part B shows the ideal shape zone for the 3-ball. Notice all of the mistakes that could lead in run out failure if you miss the rather small position zone by a few inches.

End Rail Position (2)

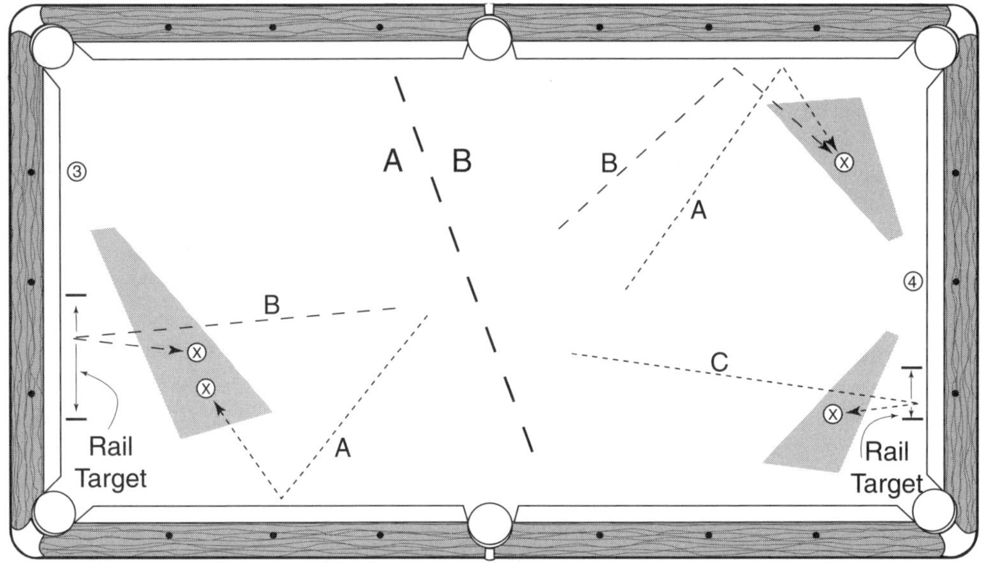

This illustration shows two methods for playing shape on balls on the end rail. In Part A, the 3-ball is opposite the diamond closest to the upper left corner pocket, which makes shape on the long side preferable.. Route A is better as it allows you to play down the line shape through the heart of the position zone. If this route is not possible or practical, then you will have to play across the zone down Route B. Most players find it easier to bounce off the rail and back into the zone as shown. Be sure to set your rail target a safe distance from the object ball and the corner pocket.

The position zone for the 4-ball, which is opposite the middle diamond in Part B, is the same size on either side. Route A is best as it takes the cue ball down the middle of the position zone. If the cue ball approaches the zone at a sharper angle along Route B, your cut angle will change a little more when it travels across the zone. Route C is more exacting as the cue ball will be traveling across the zone. Set your rail target with care and play to have the cue ball bounce off the rail into the zone.

Setting Up for a Bank

I've been preaching throughout the book that Nine-Ball is a game of percentages, and normally the percentages favor avoiding bank shots. But Nine Ball is a game loaded with exceptions to the rules. At times you should purposefully play for bank shape when there is no other viable alternative. And there will be other occasions when a bank can save your run after you've missed position.

Bank Shape Zones

The 9-ball is frozen to the rail, which rules out playing shape on an 8-9 combo. And it is nearly impossible to get position on the 8-ball for the upper left corner pocket. To finish off this rack, you really have no choice

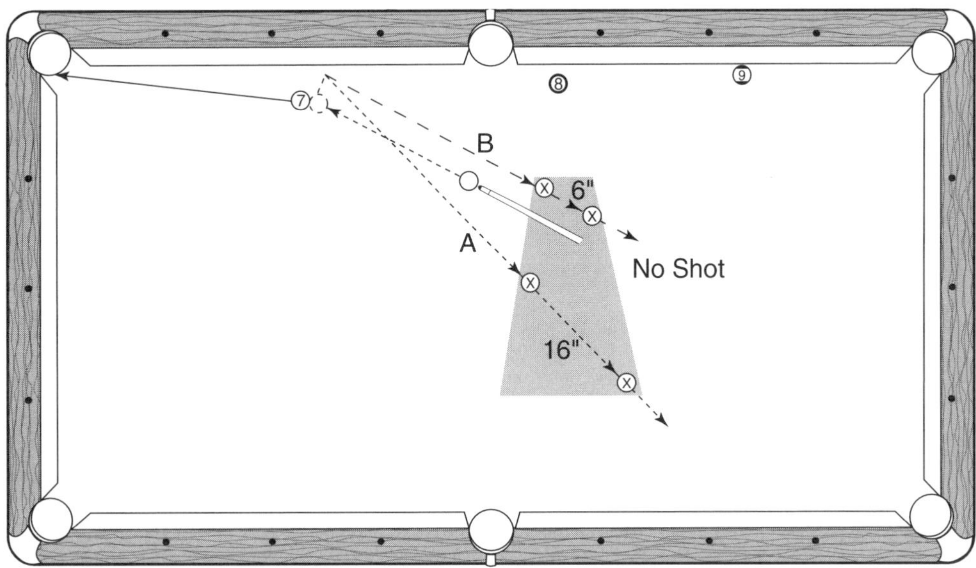

except to play position for a crosside bank on the 8-ball.

The diagram illustrates the ideal position zone for a bank shot on the 8-ball. The position route from the 7-ball to the 8-ball requires that you cross through the position zone. Principle #13 of position play advises you to send the cue ball across the wide part of the position zone when you must enter it at an angle. Notice that the zone is 10" longer on Route A compared to Route B. If you stroke the shot too firmly and roll past the zone, the bank will become impossible due to a double kiss.

Playing for a Bank

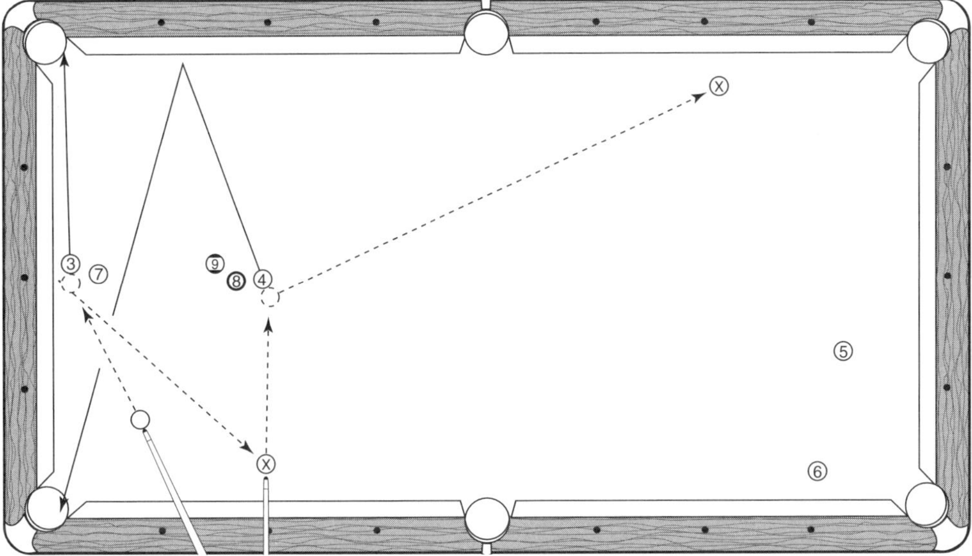

German sharpshooter Oliver Ortmann played bank shape on the 4-ball in a match with Fong-Pang Chao at the 2000 World Pool Championships. While this may appear to have been a risky shot, the 4-ball would have probaply ended up behind the 8 and 9-balls if he had missed the shot.

Miss Position then Play a Bank

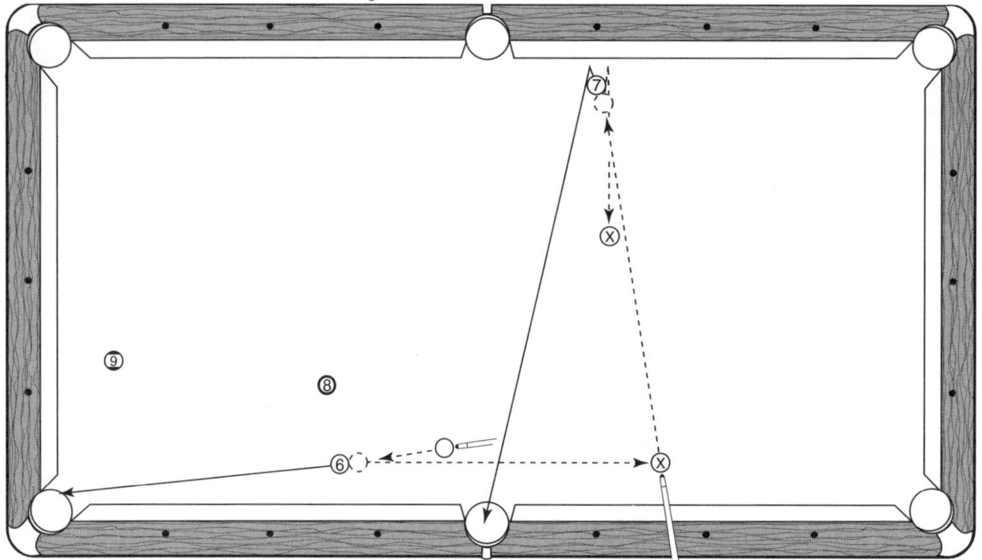

Ismael Paez was locked in an emotion packed semi-final duel with Earl Strickland, at the 2000 World 9-Ball Championships, when he missed position on the 6-ball. After quickly surveying the damage, Paez resorted to Plan B, which called for bank shape on the 7-ball. He controlled the speed perfectly on the 6-ball, setting up a cross side bank. He proceeded to run out on his was to staging an upset. Paez eventually finished in 2nd place.

CHAPTER 7

HOW TO RUN OUT

"Just do what you have to do."
Mika Immonen

When you survey the table as your turn begins, you probably have a good idea of whether or not the rack is the type you can run. In the beginning, your runs may typically last 2-4 balls, and these will come only on the easier layouts. As your skill rises, you will begin to approach more and more racks with the confidence that this is a layout you can handle. In time, you will find yourself running 5-6 balls regularly. Your first run of a full rack is a major milestone for any aspiring Nine Ball player. And should your game progress to the advanced (B) level or above, you will begin to occasionally experience the thrill of running the challenging types of layouts that belong on a highlight reel.

In fact, there is nothing much more satisfying in Nine Ball than those moments you spend waiting to break while you to bask in the glory of a well-executed run out. We're talking about the kind or run out that you know, your opponent knows, and any spectators who happen to be in attendance know, is a first class work of art.

When you get home from the poolroom, I recommend playing your run outs over again in your mind as you lie in bed waiting to fall asleep. This will of course be an enjoyable experience, but reliving your best runs can also help instill confidence and ingrain the patterns that were successful. Your personal highlight reel will also help set the stage for repeat performances in matches to come. In addition, you may preprogram your mind for a pleasurable dream in which you perform feats of cue magic on your way to winning an important title.

The Run Out Game Plan

Position Play (chapter 3) is how you get on the next ball. This includes the route, the target zone, and measures to reduce risk.
Patterns (chapter 6) are recognizable sequences of shots that tend to repeat themselves.
Run Outs (this chapter) are the end result of stringing position plays and patterns together.

In Chapter 3, I covered the position routes that can take the cue ball from Point A to B. Position plays are the building blocks of patterns. Chapter 6 focused on the patterns that appear most commonly in Nine Ball. As you'll recall, these are sequences of shots that typically cover 2-4 balls. The final step to running a complete rack is to recognize the various patterns within a rack and the routes that make up those patterns, and to be able to connect one pattern with the next.

A complete layout usually has 2-3 recognizable patterns within it. Each rack will open with a particular type of pattern. As that pattern is completed, the last ball of one pattern is quite often the first ball of the next pattern. Connecting balls smooth the transition from pattern to pattern. They are part of the prior and subsequent pattern. At the end of a rack, the last three balls are often connect the dots runs because any problems or congestion have been eliminated.

When a succession of patterns is played correctly, the cue ball's movement seems easy and effortless. When cue ball movement is superb, the game flows. It looks like a succession of easy shots. It looks right. The patterns make sense. It is not unduly difficult or complicated. Good pattern play and superbly executed run outs are perhaps best described by the run outs themselves. When you see a player like Buddy Hall making it look s-o-o-o easy, you'll know what I'm talking about.

The Importance of Shotmaking in Running Out

Shotmaking is an important ingredient in Nine Ball no matter what your level of play. Amateurs, for example, will need to make difficult shots on a regular basis due to less than perfect position and because of their opponent's misses.

Professionals, who play near perfect shape, must still pocket their share of challenging shots. In a study I conducted of 500 games of pro Nine Ball, I rated the difficulty of every position play. The toughest shots were rated A's. In over 25% of the games, the pros used an "A" to ignite a run. In fully 41% of their runouts required at least one "A" rated shot. Finally, during 22% of their games, an "A" was needed to sustain a run that was already in progress.

Starting and Maintaining a Run Out

The most important shot in a run is often the first ball. Unless you have an easy shot, you must make a challenging shot and play acceptable position. From that point, the goal is to stay in line until the end. This is done by identifying the correct pattern, playing good position, and by tying the patterns together with a connecting ball. On a many racks, the key shot may come somewhere in the middle of the rack. This could be a challenging position play or difficult shot that presents a hurdle that must be crossed. Another big key is the ability to close the deal. When you get to the last 2-3 balls, you have to be able to finish the job.

You need to constantly evaluate the effectiveness of your position plays. Ideally on most of your shots, the cue ball will land in your position zone. If the cue ball has strayed from its chosen course, you may have to rethink your pattern. Perhaps a recovery route may be available. If, however, you miss your position zone entirely, you may have to abandon your run and play safe. The table below summarizes the five possible results of any position play.

The 5 Step Position Grading System

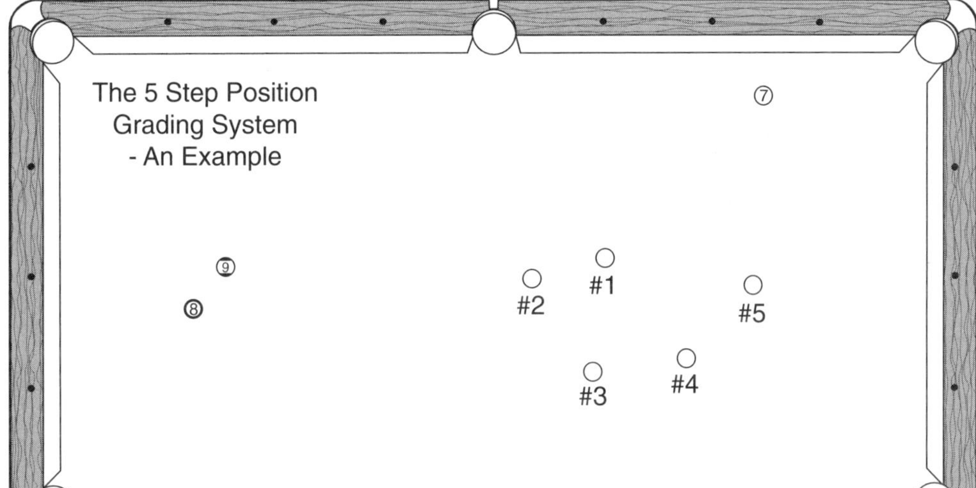

1 – Perfect. It will be as easy as possible to get on the next ball. You may even be able to do a little extra on this shot.

2 – Excellent. While not absolutely perfect, this is the grade of position that pros regularly shoot for. This is where the vast majority of well executed shots land. You can continue your run as planned.

3 – Fair. Workable position. You'll need to play a modest recovery route to get on the next ball.

4 – Poor. Only an excellent shot will enable you to continue your run. A safety may very well be your best choice.

5 – Terrible. You've missed position entirely. It's time for a safety. Hopefully you're not hooked.

Run Outs of the Champions Shot by Shot

In the remainder of the chapter I'll take you through several run outs by some of the worlds best players in tournament competition. In most instances, you'll discover that their cue ball control and pattern play was near perfect. However, there were times when even players at this level missed the ideal zone and had to play a recovery route or spectacular shot. As you proceed through the run outs, you should pay special attention to those position plays and patterns that have you saying "So that's how its done." Remember, every shot is either a learning or a confirming experience.

A Double Hill Thriller

Johnny Archer put on a spirited defense of his 1999 U.S. Open title at the 2000 U.S. Open before eventually finishing in the 7-8th position. One of his victories was at the expense of Efren "The Magician" Reyes. Archer captured the double hill thriller 11-10 with the run we're about to examine.

Diagram #1

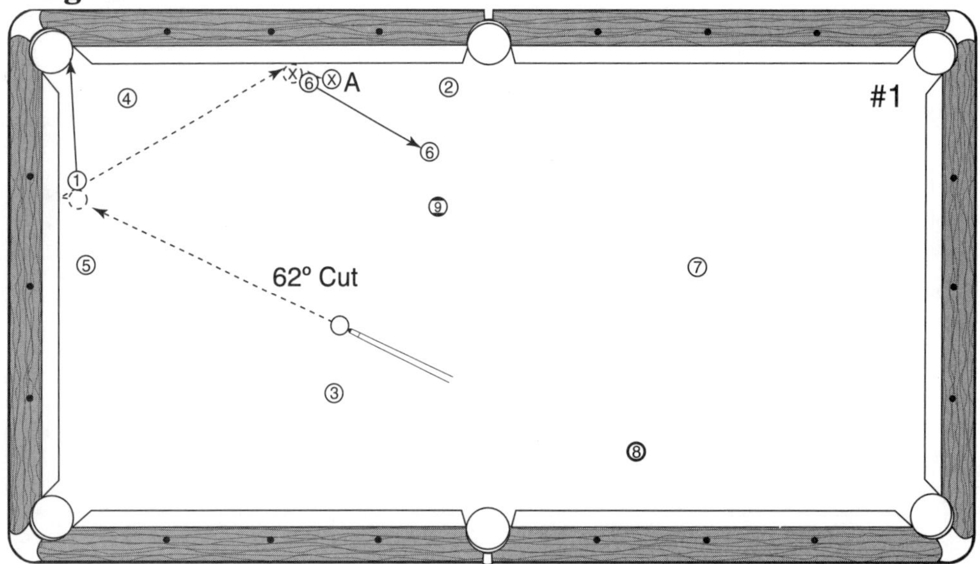

Archer was faced with a 62-degree cut on the 1-ball, which required a medium speed of stroke. He could not stop the cue ball in time to play the 2-ball in the side without some help. Archer applied inside (right) english to the cue ball and sent it on at precise route into the 6-ball. The cue ball drifted forward to Position A for ideal shape on the 2-ball. This shot would normally have been the big key to the run except for an error that Archer made later in the rack.

Diagram #2

Pattern 1 Archer's next goal was to take care of business on the far left side of the table. A soft draw shot on the 2-ball sent the cue ball to Position A for perfect shape on the 3-ball. While you normally like to play for an angle in Nine Ball, the 3-ball was best played with a stop shot.

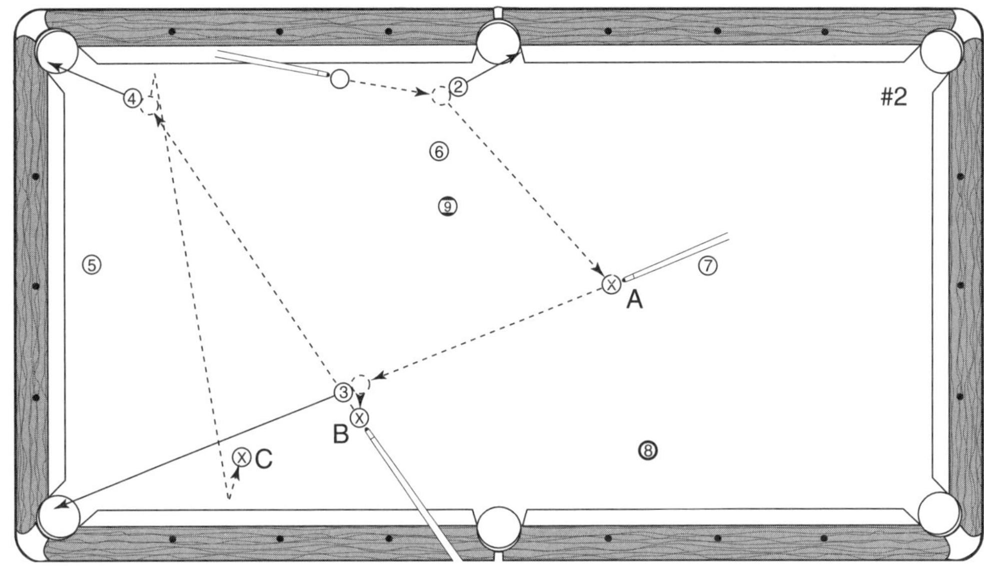

From Position B, Archer had no trouble sending the cue ball across and out to Position C for excellent shape on the 5-ball.

Diagram #3

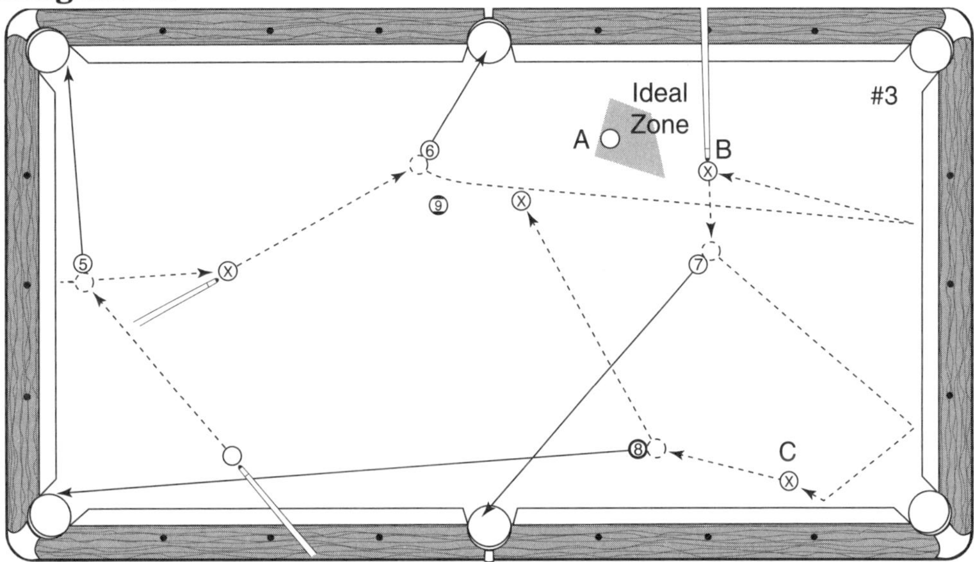

Pattern 2 The last ball of one pattern often serves as the first ball of the next pattern. In this case, the 5-ball was used to set up perfect shape on the 6-ball. Good shape on the 6-ball was vital because the 7-ball was in troublesome location in the middle portion of the table. After playing the 6-ball, Archer would have like the cue ball at Position A but it stopped short at Position B. After taking some time to get mentally prepared for the 7-ball, Archer played an excellent recovery route to Position C for the 8-ball. The 8-ball was played with a soft stroke for position on the 9-ball.

Reyes In Route to a Double Hill Thriller

Efren Reyes grabbed a 9-7 lead with the textbook run out below during his epic battle with Earl Strickland in the finals of the Sands Regency Open 21, June, 1995. Reyes eventually won the match 13-12 thanks to the kick shot that was heard throughout the pool world.

Diagram 1

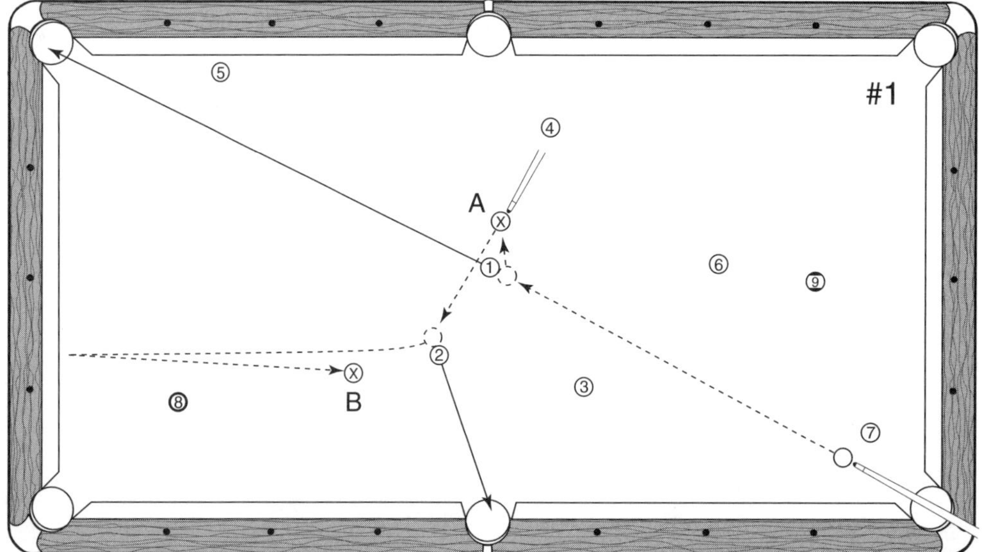

Reyes skills as a shotmaker were put to the test on this nearly straight in shot along the diagonal of the table. He speared it in the heart of the pocket and was no doubt glad to have a playable shot from Position A. The 1-ball proved to be the key to the rack, otherwise known as the "out shot".

Pattern 1 The next order of business was a pesky 48-degree cut shot on the 2-ball. Reyes used a medium soft draw stroke to send the cue ball off the end rail and out to Position B for near perfect shape on the 3-ball. Playing the first two balls superbly enabled Reyes to assume complete control of the rack, which he maintained until the last ball.

Diagram 2

Pattern 1 (cont.) Reyes played a soft draw shot on the 3-ball, which allowed the cue ball to drift sideways to Position A for the 4-ball. This shot completed the first pattern. In this phase, Reyes was able to clear the balls in the middle of the table, which is seldom an easy task. He also set up the correct angle for a critical position play on the 4-ball.

Pattern 2 Reyes next big goal was to play the 4 and 5-balls in a way that would lead to acceptable position on the 6-ball, which was in a potentially troublesome location near the spot. A soft follow shot with inside (left) english pulled the cue ball out to Position B, leaving Reyes with a 15-degree cut angle on the 5-ball. This was just what he needed to draw across and back down the table to Position C for the 6-ball.

If the angle had been a little shallower, he would have had to use a hard stroke when playing the 5-ball, which would have made distance and

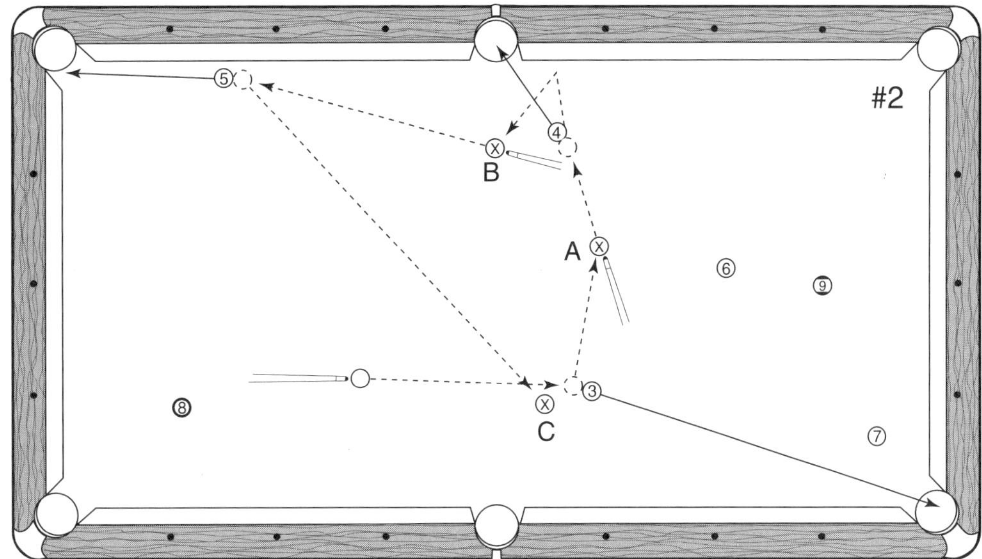

directional control much more difficult. An overly steep angle on the 5-ball would have brought a side pocket scratch into play. Seemingly insignificant shots like the 4-ball are often a big key to maintaining a run.

Diagram 3

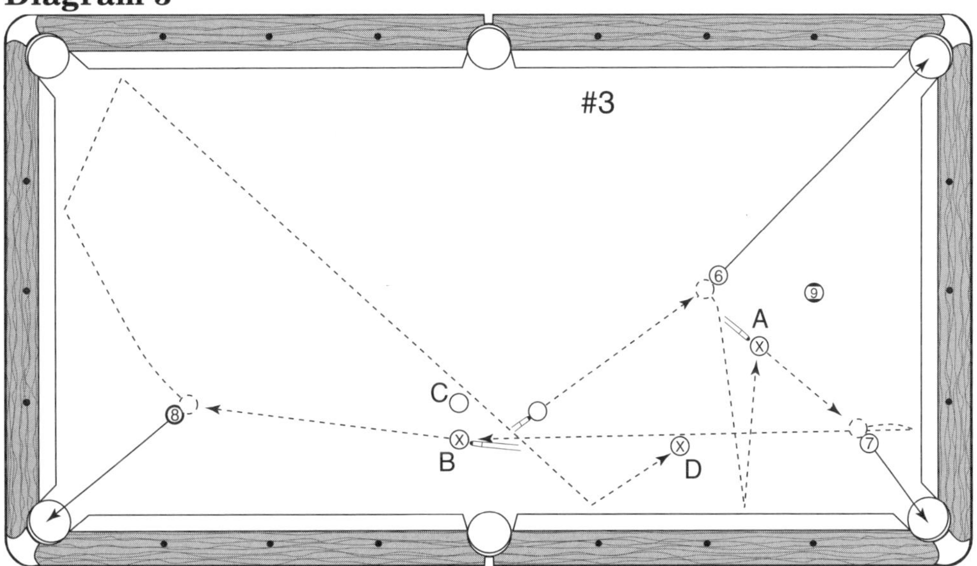

Pattern 3 The rest of the rack is a classic exhibition in how to maintain an iron grasp on a run. Reyes went on to complete the kind of rack that you know you are supposed to run, but somehow find a way not to. Reyes powered the cue ball to the side rail and out for excellent position on the 7-ball at Position A. Reyes then sent the cue ball to Position B using follow and a bit of inside english. Keen students of position play could debate the merits of playing three-rail position on the 9-ball from Position B versus Position C. Reyes used a natural three-rail route to get perfect on the 9-ball at Position D. Case dismissed.

Hall Captures His Second U.S. Open

BCA Hall of Fame Member Buddy Hall clinched his second U.S. Open in 1998 by a score of 11-5 over a surprisingly strong Tang Hoa with this gutsy run out. Hall, who is widely respected for his pinpoint position play and well conceived patterns, was able to over come some minor errors on a couple of very demanding position routes to complete his run to the title.

Diagram 1

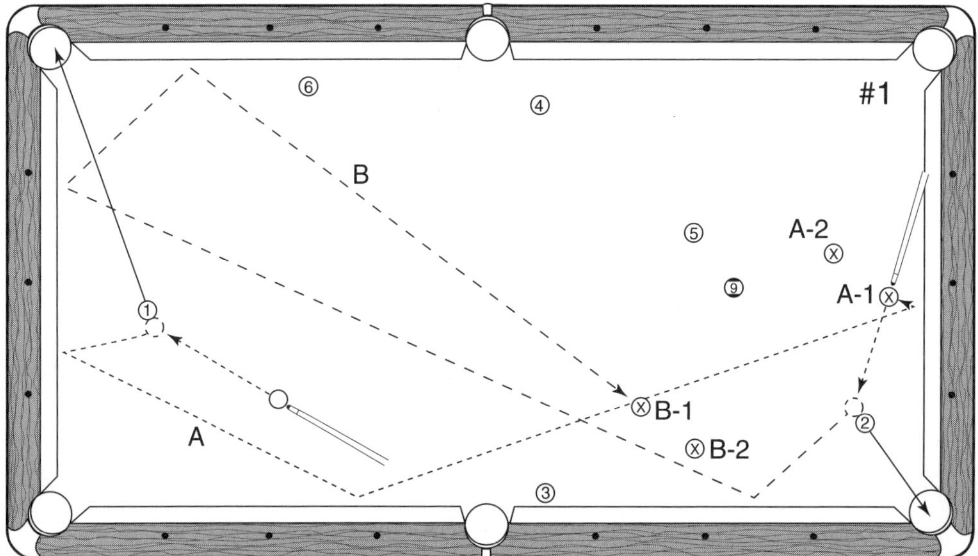

Pattern 1 Hall's goal was to use the first two balls to get good position on the 3-ball, which was on the rail near the side pocket. Hall's first shot was a difficult three-rail route (Route A) off the side rail and down table to the far end rail. The cue ball bounced softy off the last rail, coming to rest at Position A-1. If the cue ball had continued to Position A-2, the next few shots would have been much simpler. In pool, however, if you don't get what you want, you must at least get what you need. With the cue ball in Position A-1, Hall was forced to send the cue ball on an excursion around the table down Route B. The cue ball ran out of gas 15' after its journey began at Position B-1, a maddening 7" short of perfect. Position B-2.would have been ideal.

Diagram 2

Pattern 2 Those seven missing inches would have spelled the end of the run for most players, but not for a champion like Buddy Hall. He merely sliced the 3-ball into the distant corner pocket and deftly maneuvered the cue ball into perfect position at Position A. If the cue ball had rolled a few inches more to Position A-1, Hall would have been hooked.

Patterning the 3 and 4-balls correctly enabled Hall to obtain the shape he needed on the 5-ball. Hall once again showed phenomenal speed control on the 4-ball by drawing the cue ball across table to Position B for the 5-ball. Notice that the cue ball ended up a few precious inches past the straight in line to the pocket on the 5-ball.

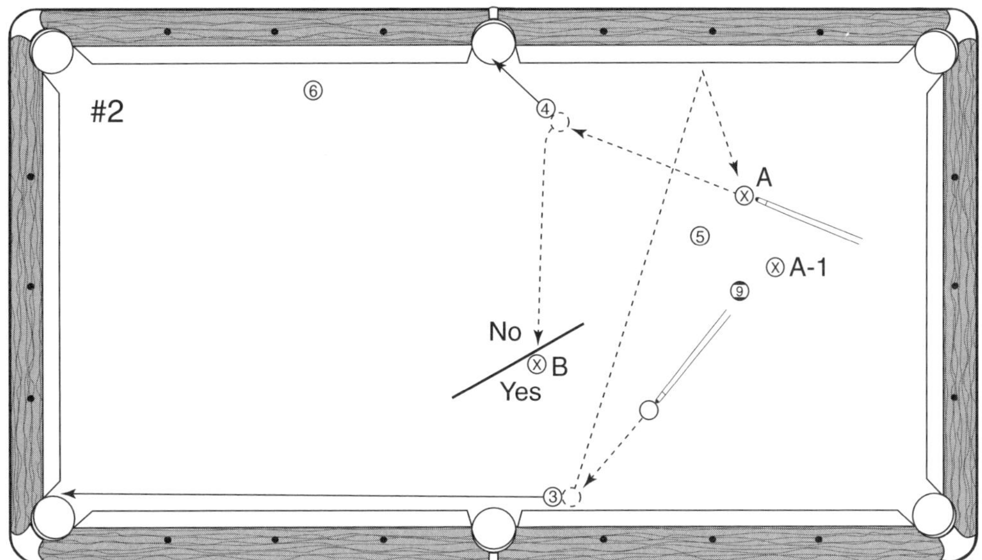

Diagram 3

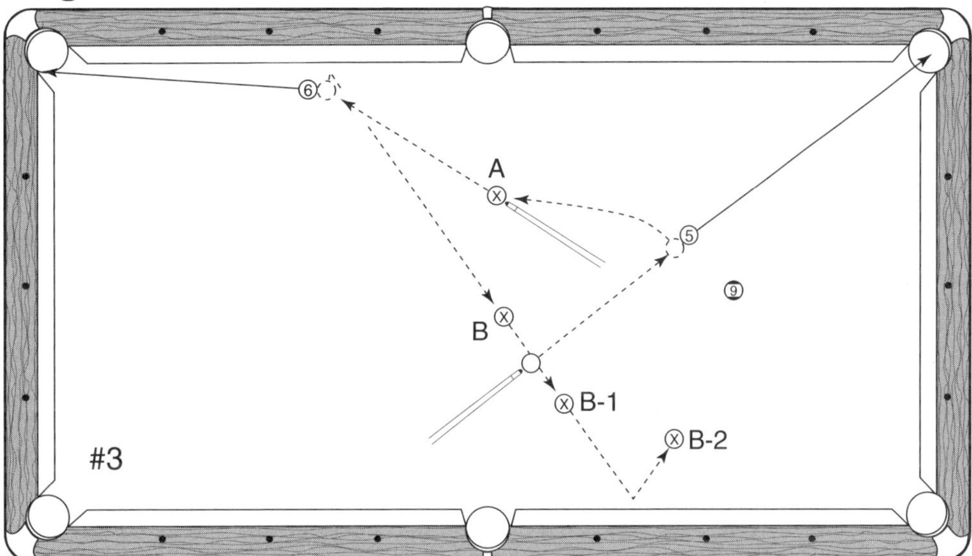

Pattern 3 The 4-ball served as the connecting ball to the end game pattern in this illustration. Hall used a stun/draw shot to force the cue ball over and back to Position A. This left him with a 28-degree cut angle on the 6-ball, which was perfect for sending the cue ball across and down the table for the 9-ball.

Hall had a huge margin for error when playing position on the 9-ball. Anywhere between B-1 and B-2 would have been ideal, except for the rail. For some reason, however, Hall stroked the 6-ball a little too softly, leaving himself with a 45-degree cross table cut on the 9-ball at Position B. Hall was unfazed by this slight miscalculation as he cleanly pocketed the 9-ball to the thunderous applause of the crowd.

Souquet's First Big Title In America

Germany's Ralf Souquet was still in search of his first major title in America at The Sands Regency Open 27, June, 1998. His quest for the crown would not be an easy one as his opponent in the finals was Efren Reyes. Souquet used precision position play and his unusually focused style of play to come out on top in a three set marathon, 6-2, 2-6, 6-2. The run out below clinched the title. Souquet would go on to capture the 2000 U.S. Open 14.1 tile against a field of the games finest Straight Pool players.

Diagram #1

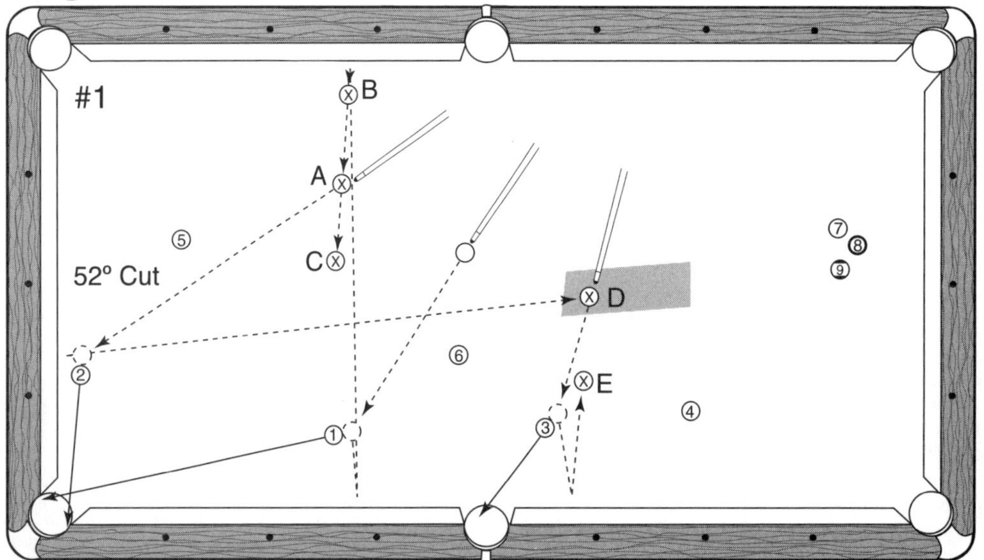

Pattern 1 Souquet's objective in the first pattern was to get position on the 2-ball that would allow him to play side pocket shape on the 3-ball. After pocketing the 1-ball, the cue ball rolled to Position A. Mission accomplished. If the cue ball had stopped at Position B, he would have been snookered behind the 5-ball. If the cue ball had come to rest at Position C, Souquet could have used this angle to send the cue ball down table into the 7,8, and 9-balls. We'll see in a few moments, however, that it is not always necessary to separate clusters. When playing the 2-ball, Souquet could have been in a bit of trouble if the cue ball had stopped a few inches short of Position D. Note that the cue ball landed in the front portion of the position zone. Souquet softly stroked the cue ball to Position E for the 4-ball.

Diagram #2

Pattern 2 The 4-ball was the first ball in a three-ball sequence that was designed to set up position for the last three balls. Souquet could have played a draw shot to Position A for short side shape on the 5-ball. He instead chose to cinch shape by drawing back about 20" to Position B. From here he played two-rail shape for the 6-ball at Position C. These shot vividly illustrated Souquet's very direct and efficient style of play. The plot is now thickening.

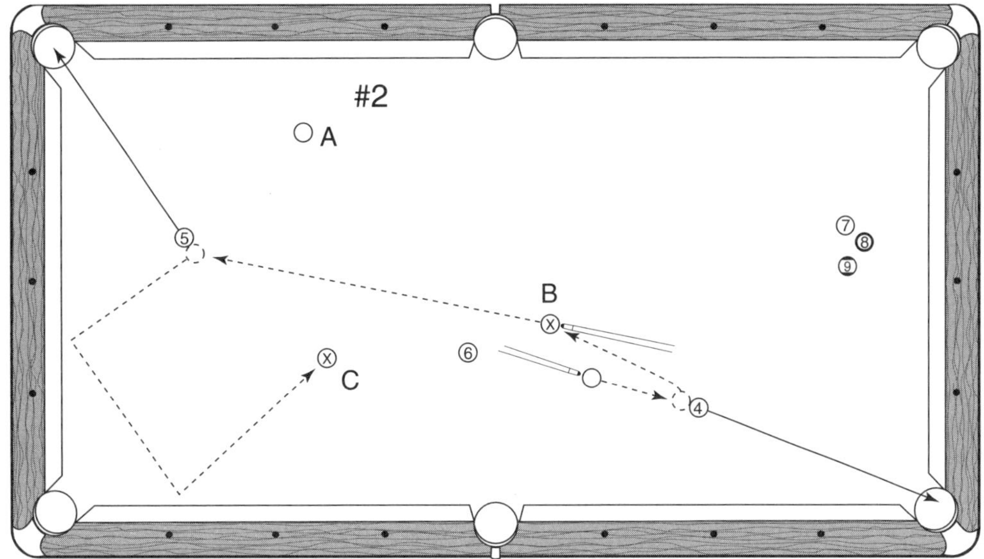

Diagram #3

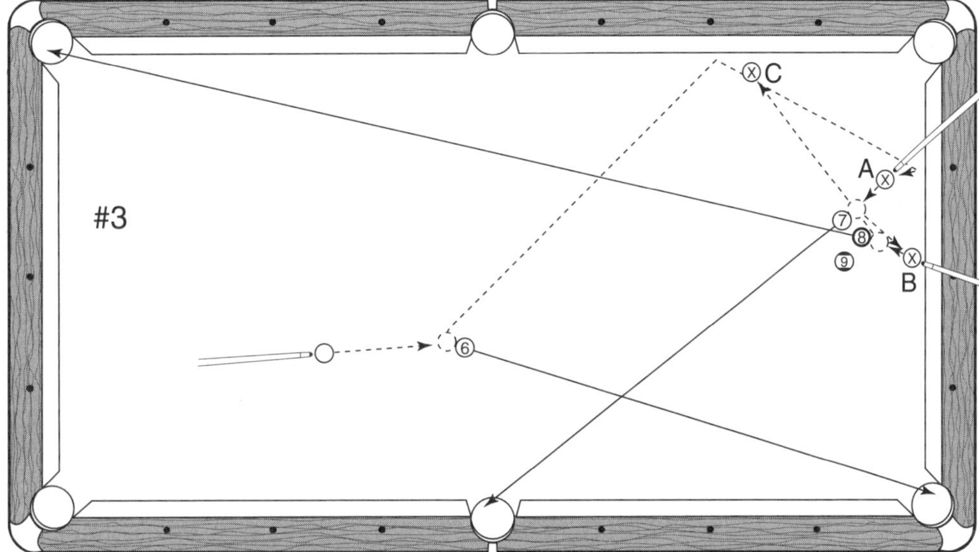

Pattern 3 The 7, 8, and 9-balls are obviously the key to this rack. When balls are clustered this close together, your best bet could be to either break them, or try to pocket them as they lie. We saw earlier that Souquet had a chance to break the three balls off the 2-ball. Now were about to witness the work of a master of the cue ball. The 6-ball is used to connect the previous pattern to the one for the last three balls. Souquet played a two rail follow shot with perfect speed control to Position A for the 7-ball. He then used a surgeon's touch to slide over to Position B for the 8-ball. A follow shot to Position C left Souquet with an easy shot at the 9-ball and his first big championship on U.S. soil.

Sigel Shows Off His Run Out Power

BCA Hall of Fame Member Mike Sigel, perhaps the best pure run out artist to ever play Nine Ball, took an early 2-1 lead in a tense duel with Earl Strickland before succumbing 11-13 at the Sands Regency Open 17, June, 1993.

Diagram #1

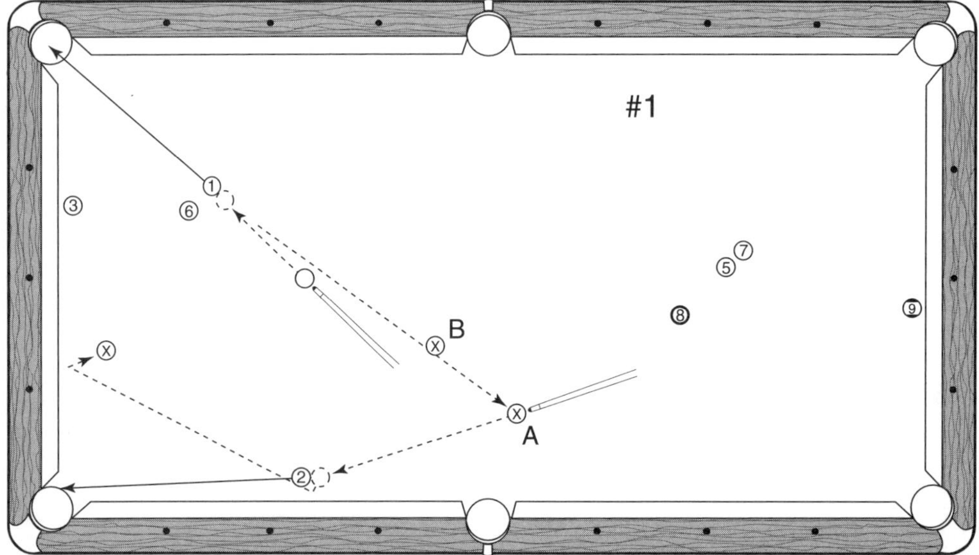

Pattern 1 Sigel's first task was to play the 1, 2 and 3-balls at this end of the table and get set for the 5-ball, which was at the opposite end of the table adjacent to the spot. He drew back perfectly on the 1-ball to Position A, leaving a slight cut angle on the 2-ball. While this shot looks easy on paper, pinpoint draw speed control is one of the toughest position plays in pool. If the cue ball had stopped short at Position B, Sigel would have been forced to cross the table and back for the 3-ball, which would have greatly complicated matters. Sigel used a soft two rail follow shot to send the cue ball to Position C for the 3-ball, completing the first phase of his run.

Diagram #2

Pattern 2 The preliminaries are now complete and its time for the fun to begin. With the cue ball in Position A, Sigel's only choice was to play a difficult two-rail draw shot to the 5-ball. Speed control was a major challenge for three reasons: 1) The shot required a hard stroke; 2) the cue ball would be crossing the line of the position zone; 3) the 5-ball is in the middle portion of the table, far from a rail. Sigel struck the shot crisply, but the cue ball unfortunately overran the ideal shape zone, stopping at Position B. Sigel's shotmaking skills paid off as he sliced in a testy 59-degree cut on the 5-ball, sending the cue ball off the 8-ball and up table for the 6-ball. When you are playing a difficult recovery route, sometimes all you can do is make the ball and hope for the best.

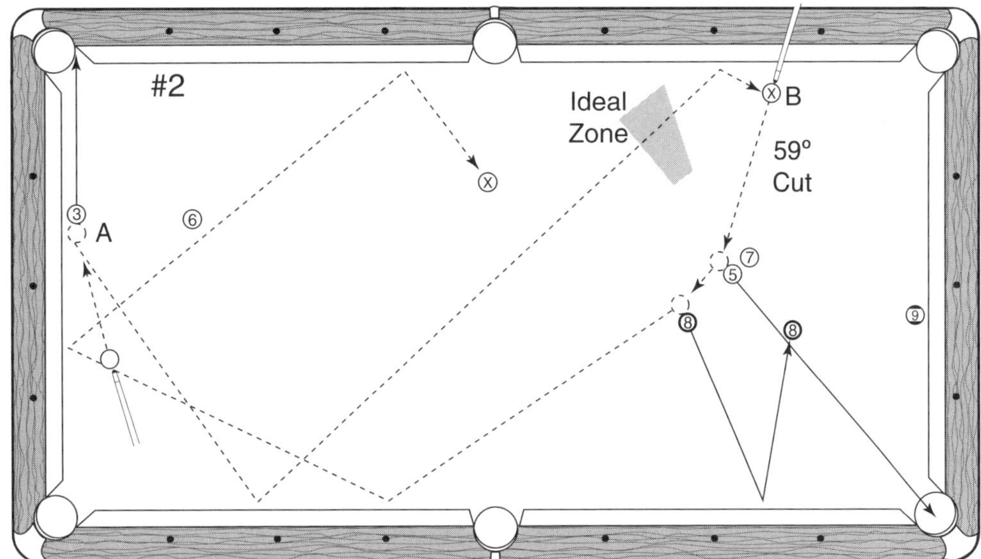

Diagram 3

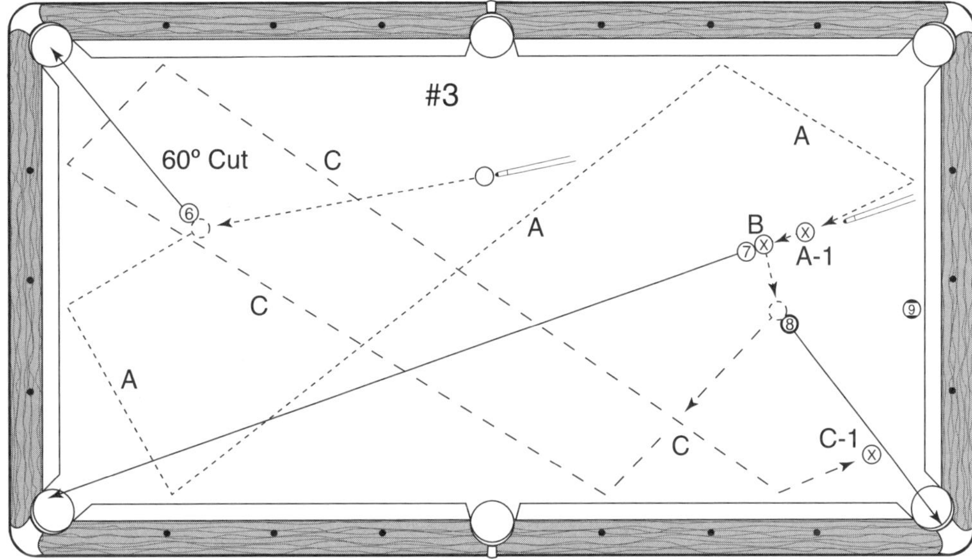

Pattern 3 Sigel was feeling the force of the Domino Effect, in which one missed position zone can lead to a series of difficult shots, thanks to his position on the 5-ball. The thin cut on the 6-ball prevented Sigel from playing the 7-ball in the upper right corner pocket, He improvised nicely by propelling the cue ball on a four-rail journey down Route A to the short side of the 7-ball at Position A-1. Perhaps Sigel was suffering from the post great shot letdown syndrome because, for some reason, he failed to send the cue ball far enough up table while shooting the 7-ball. If the cue ball had rolled a few inches past Position B, Sigel could have played a soft follow shot on the 8-ball for shape on the 9-ball. From Position B, however, he had to launch the cue ball on a recovery route that took whitey on an around the world journey down Route C. This storybook run had a happy ending when the cue ball cruised to a halt at Position C-1.

Guts, Determination, and Superior Shotmaking

Nick Varner climbed to the hill at 10-5 thanks to the run out below. He then withstood Johnny Archer's closing rush to win the match 11-9 in the finals of the Sands Regency Open 23, June, 1996. Varner, who is known for his solid all around game, coolness under fire and precision cue ball control, can also put down the tough gamewinning shots when they are called for.

Diagram 1

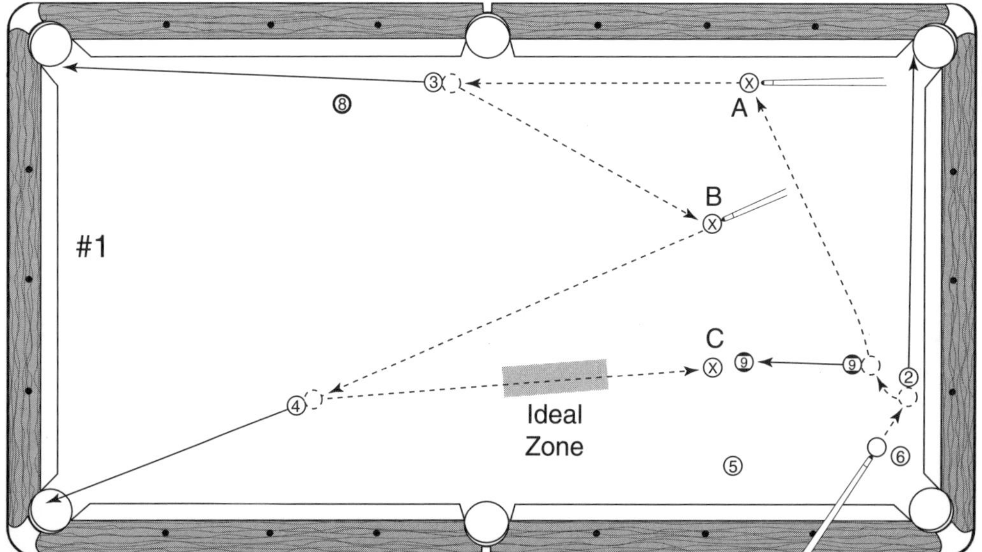

Varner was perhaps hoping to miss the 9-ball entirely when he played the 2-ball with a soft stroke and inside (left) english. In any event, the cue ball bumped into the 9-ball before continuing to Position A.

Pattern 1 Varner wound up with acceptable position on the 3-ball. His next task was to play a sequence of shots that would enable him to get good position on the 6-ball. A powerhouse draw shot on the 3-ball brought the cue ball back to Position B. Varner was then faced with a long shot on the 4-ball. He was fortunate to have a slight cut angle on the 4-ball, as this makes a long draw shot play just a little easier.

When you are stroking exceptionally well, the cue ball will sometimes run further than when you use your "average" stroke. This will cause you to overshoot your position zone. Varner was certainly in top form, as evidenced by his draw shot on the 3-ball, which perhaps explains why he drew well past the ideal shape zone to Position C when playing the 4-ball. In any event, he was now looking at a tough bank on the 5-ball, rather than a simple position play from the ideal zone.

Diagram 2

Varner was able to pocket the bank on the 5-ball thanks to his shotmaking skills and his Kentucky upbringing, where bank pool is the game of choice for a large part of the pool playing populace. The cue ball relocated well up table to Position X. A routine run out is now turning into quite an adventure.

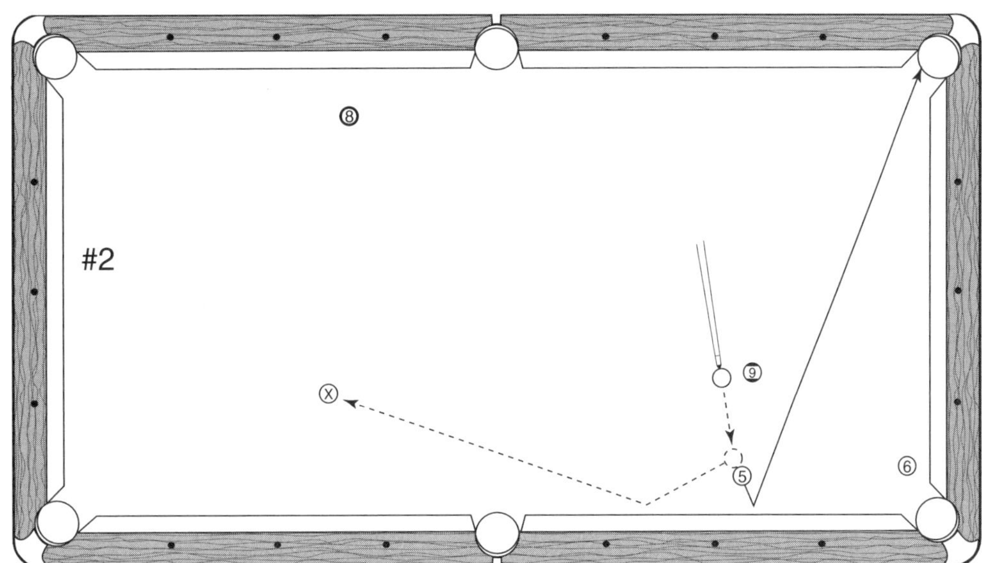

Diagram 3

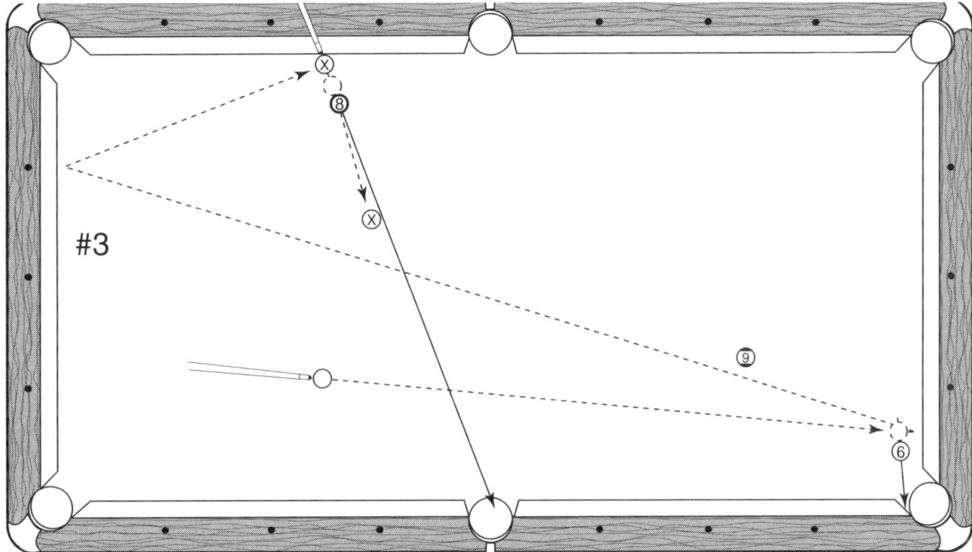

Even though the 6-ball was a long distance 80-degree cut, making the ball was not overly difficult. Getting position on the 8-ball was a whole other matter. Varner needed to hit the 6-ball thinly enough so the cue ball would not run into the 9-ball after rebounding from the end rail. At the same time, he had to chart a course to the 8-ball. When you are playing a long range cut like this, you are doing a good job if you can avoid outright disaster and wind up with a reasonably makeable shot. On shots like this, you must also accept that at least a little luck is involved. Varner's shot on the 6-ball was mostly skill, but he was also quite fortunate to end up with a straight in shot on the 8-ball. He of course took full advantage of his "luck" by running out the rest of the game.

Strickland's Firepower Wins 4th U.S. Open

From the opening bell of the 1997 U.S. Open finals to the very last rack, Earl Strickland wowed the crowd with a dead stroke performance that showcased The Pearl's many offensive weapons. The result was an impressive 11-3 win over the legendary Efren Reyes, which gave Strickland his 4th title in this event.

Diagram 1

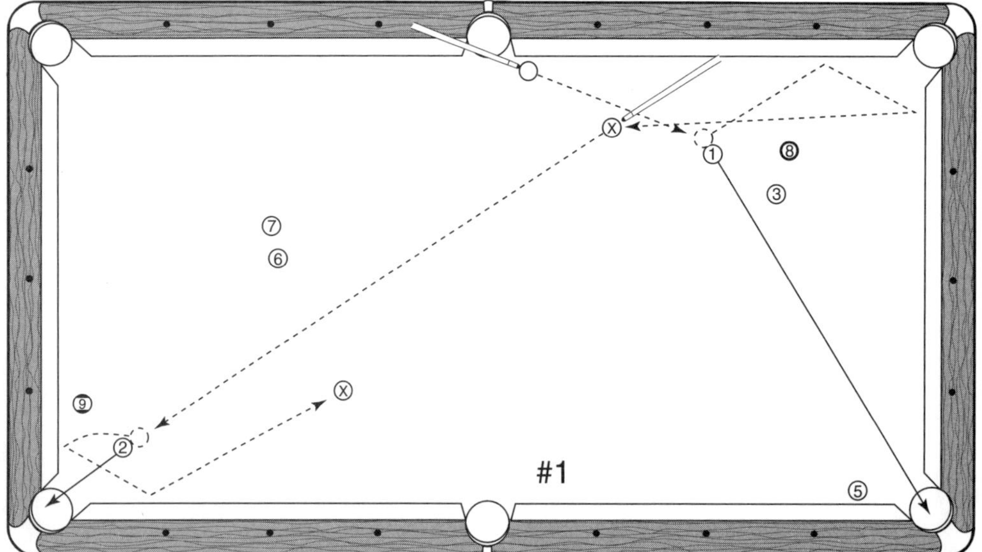

Pattern 1 Strickland's first order of business was a tricky cross table cut on the 1-ball. Strickland employed the seldom-used tactic of reversing the cue ball off the end rail with outside (left) english. This unusual use of english enabled him to avoid running into the 3 and 8-balls. His main objective was to stay out of trouble and get something to work with on the 2-ball, even if it had to be played from long range. The 2-ball was played with straight follow. The goal was to avoid hitting the 9-ball while sending the cue ball far enough down the table so that the 3-ball was a reasonably simple shot.

Diagram 2

Pattern 2 The next big hurdle was to get position on the 6-ball, which appeared to be the key to this rack, at least for now. Balls in the middle portion of the table, as we've discussed before, are often a major stumbling block. Strickland showed superb cue ball control and accuracy in pocketing the 3-ball and sending the cue ball off the end rail to Position A. The 30-degree cut angle was just what he needed to send the cue ball across the width of the table. Strickland played the 5-ball with low right english, which resulted in perfect shape on the 6-ball at Position B. Notice that the cue ball hit the rail below the side pocket, giving Strickland a comfortable margin for error.

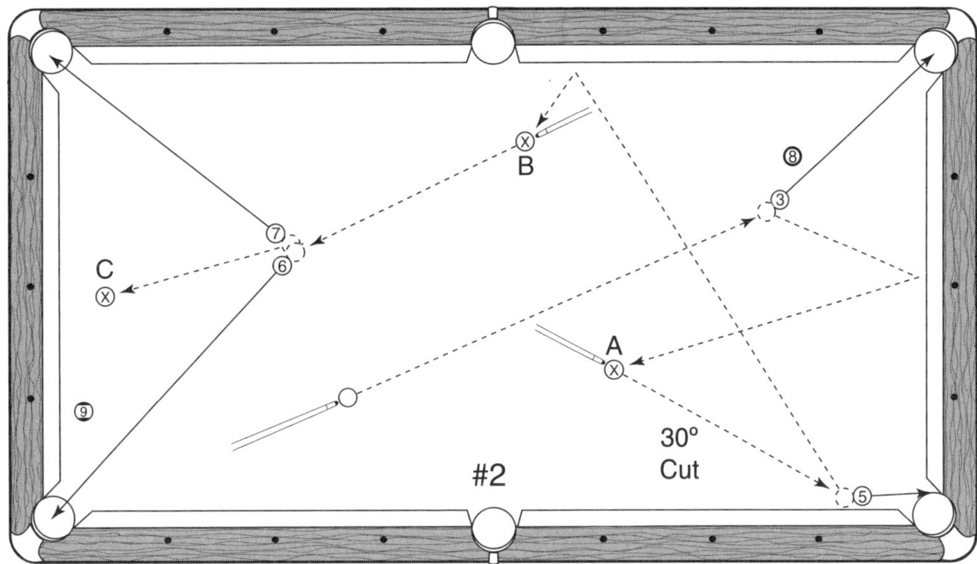

The 6-ball was meant to be the last ball of this sequence, but the 7-ball also fell while Strickland was pocketing the 6-ball. It is hard to say whether or not he was planning on both balls going at once. However, judging from the cue ball's ending location at Position C, it is a good guess that Strickland was planning on shooting the 7-ball into the upper left corner pocket.

Diagram 3

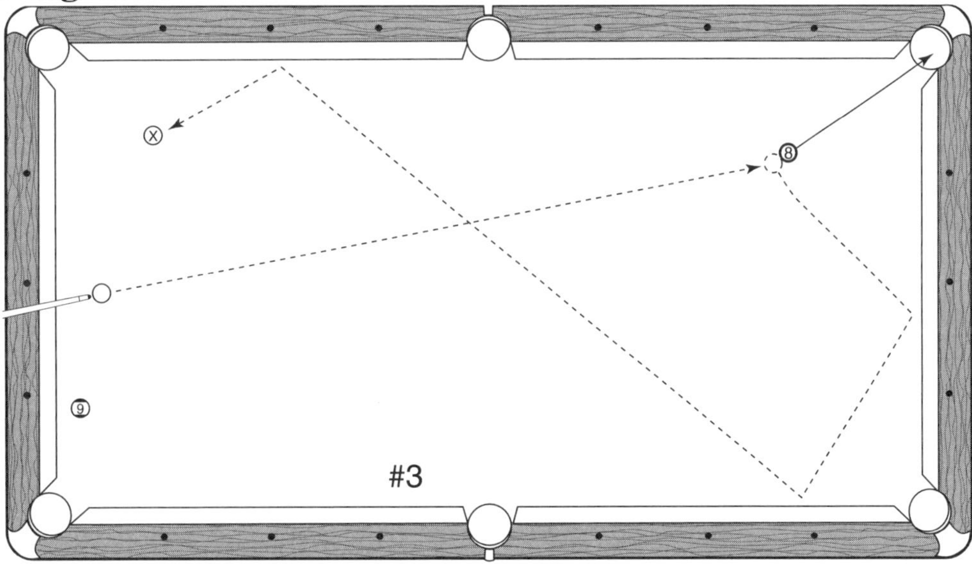

When it looks like two balls might go on one shot, and one of them is supposed to be your next shot, you should plan for shape on the third ball if possible. And, of course, when you are Earl Strickland, shape is anytime you can see the ball. Strickland's fireworks show effectively ended with this bombshell on the 8-ball. He jacked up and hit the cue ball at warp speed (over 12 MPH by my calculations), which resulted in the textbook three-rail route to the 9-ball.

Precision at Long Range

Even though Earl Strickland would prevail by an 11-5 margin, those in attendance were given plenty of evidence as to how Japan's Takeshi Okumura earned his spot in the finals of the 2000 U.S. Open in a huge field of 286 players. The run out you're about to have the pleasure of studying is one of the finest I've ever witnessed, especially when you consider that the balls seem to fighting Okumura through the entire encounter.

Diagram 1

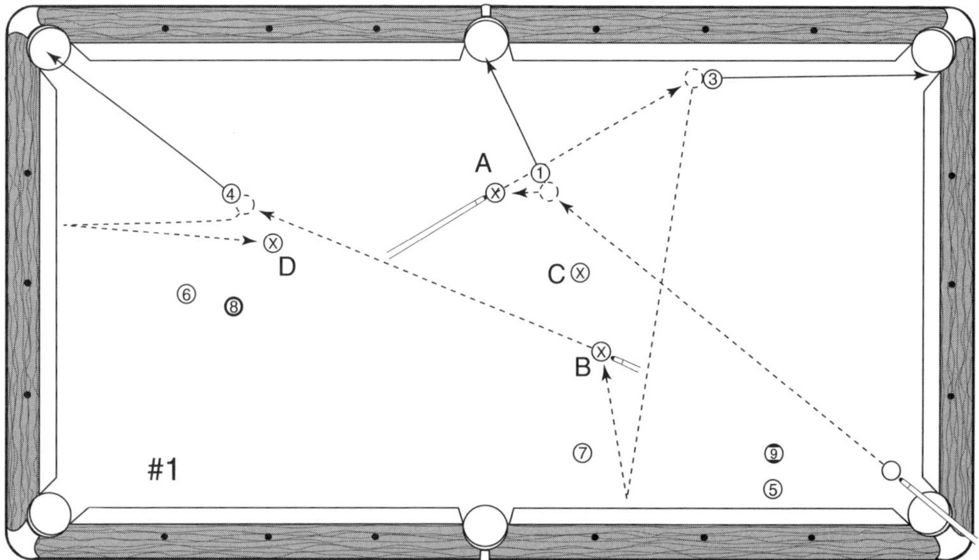

Pattern 1 The first three balls set the tone for the entire rack. When playing the first two balls, the goal was to end up with the ideal angle on the 4-ball. Okumura began with a soft follow shot on the 1-ball, which is never easy from a half table length away. This gave him a 29-degree cut angle on the 3-ball from Position A. He then pocketed the 3-ball and sent the cue ball across the table and out to Position B. Perfect!! If the cue ball had ventured to Position C, he would have lost shape on the 5-ball when playing the 4-ball thanks to the 6-ball. And if he had under hit the 3-ball, he could have been hooked behind the 7-ball. Okumura's precision play continued with his one-rail route on the 4-ball, which sent the cue ball to Position D.

Diagram 2

Pattern 2 The 4-ball ended the first pattern and at the same time acted as a connecting ball to phase two. With the cue ball in Position A, Okumura was is good shape for the 5-ball. He then played a draw shot across the table to Position B. Okumura wanted to send the cue ball far back up table as possible without risking a side pocket scratch. Mission accomplished. Okumura would perhaps have preferred the cue ball to be a little further off the rail, but the shot was very playable from Position B.

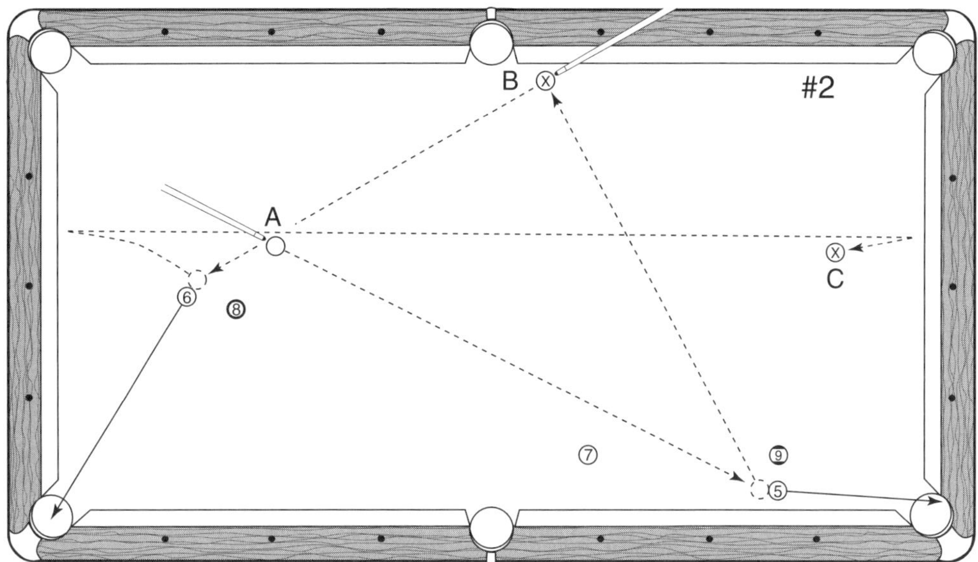

A follow shot on the 6-ball propelled the cue ball the length of the table to Position C for shape on the 7-ball. The 6-ball was the last shot of this pattern and the first one of the final pattern of this beautiful run out.

Diagram 3

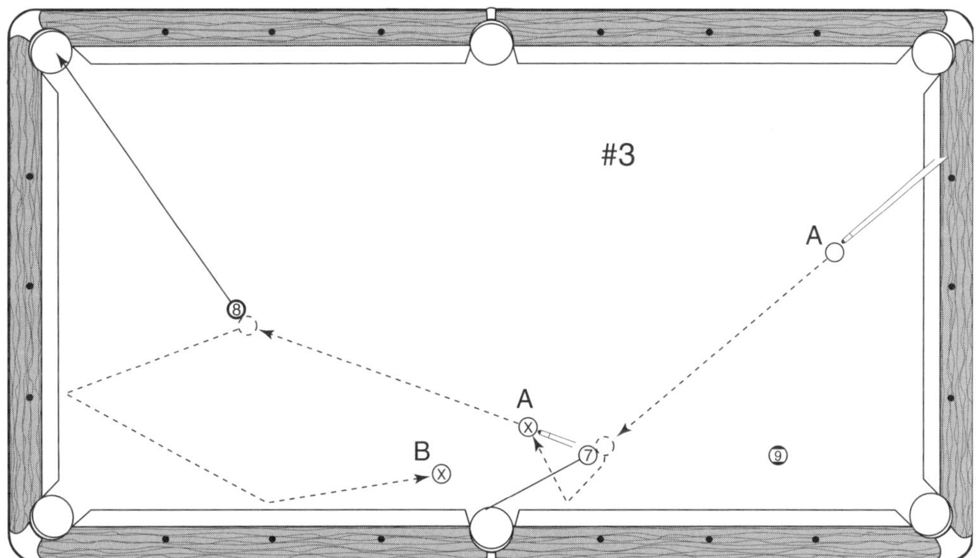

Pattern 3 The 6-ball was the first ball of the end of rack pattern. The 7-ball was played with great care, as should be done when the ball is approaching the side pocket from a sharp angle. Okumura used a medium soft follow stroke to send the cue ball to Position A for the 8-ball. A natural two-rail route to Position B gave him ideal position for concluding this masterpiece of position and pattern play.

Rempe's Mastery of the Cue Ball

Jim Rempe was up against a very formidable opponent in Francisco Bustamante at the 1999 U.S. Open when he approached the table with a chance to close out the match. Rempe put on a clinic in cue ball control to emerge with an 11-7 win while on his way to a strong 5-6th place finish.

Diagram 1

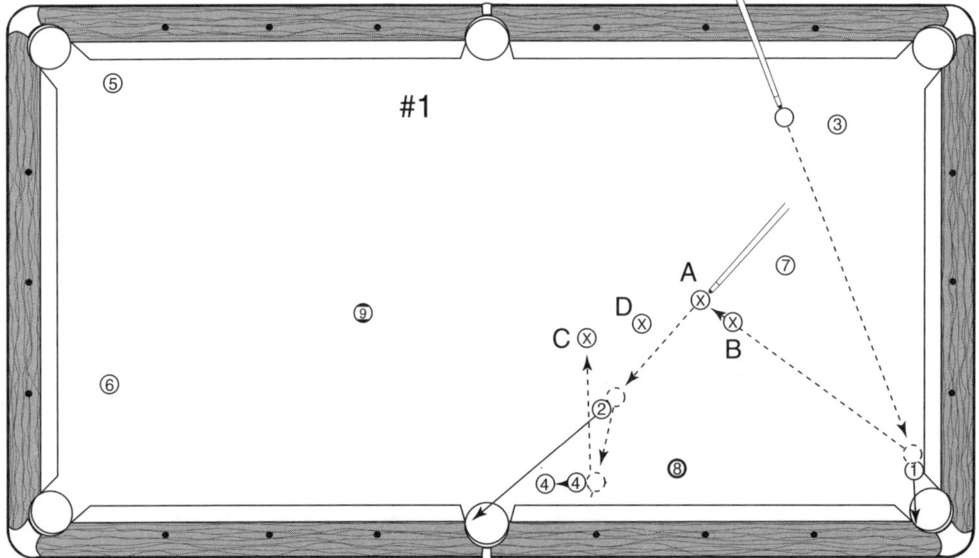

Pattern 1 The objective in the first phase of the rack was to stay out of trouble while preparing for the pesky 4-ball, which was stationed in a difficult spot high up on the side rail. It is hard to quibble with Rempe's shot on the 1-ball, as it took a fine touch with draw to send the cue ball to Position A. Position B, however, would have been perfect, as it would have enabled Rempe to slide over to Position D for excellent position on 3-ball., Rempe tried to knock the 4-ball in front of the side when playing the 2-ball, which would have greatly simplified matters. However, the 4-ball failed to cooperate, as it traveled only a few inches.

Diagram 2

Pattern 1 (conclusion) Rempe only had a small angle on the 3-ball, so he was required to pound the cue ball off the rail and across the table for position on the 4-ball. The pound shot is a recovery route, with which there is a tendency to come up short of the ideal zone. In this case, the cue ball halted at Position A, 8" short of ideal shape at Position B.

Pattern 2 The first step in the next pattern was getting from the 4-ball to the 5 and 6-balls near the far left side of the table. Rempe sliced in the 52-degree cut on the 4-ball and used a two-rail crossing route to perfection, sending the cue ball to Position C. He then played a follow shot on the 5-ball, sending the cue ball across the table and out for excellent shape on the 6-ball at Position D.

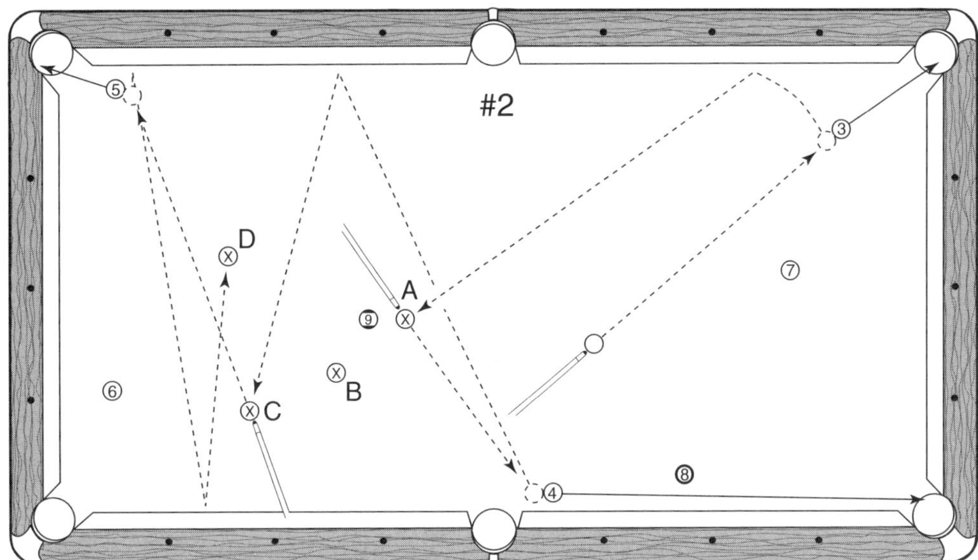

Diagram 3

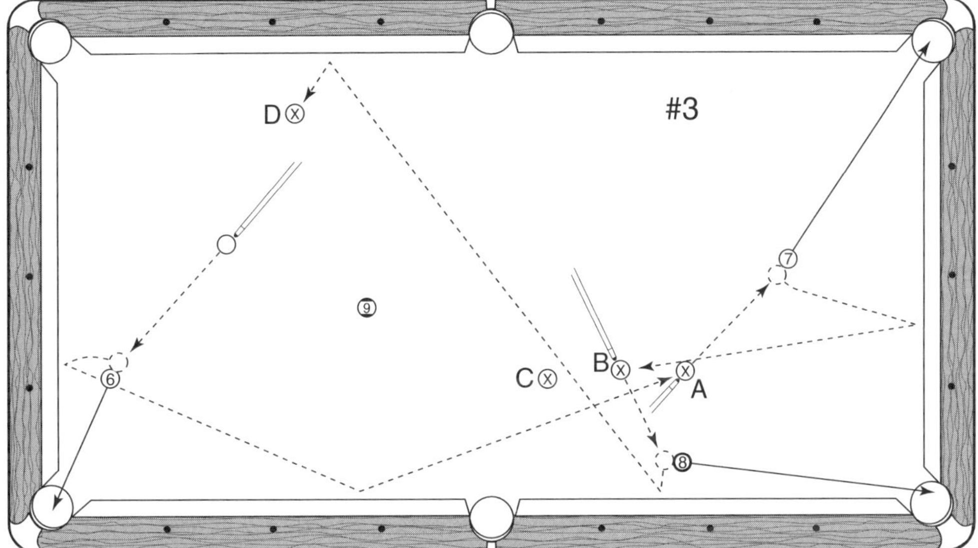

Pattern 3 The 6-ball was the connecting ball to the final pattern of the rack. Rempe used follow with inside (left) english to send the cue ball two-rails to Position A for the 7-ball. Rempe is an acknowledged master a one-rail position play. Nevertheless, he came up short at Position B when playing shape on the 8-ball, which is the tendency on a shallow angled cut shots. If the cue ball had rolled a few inches farther to Position C, shape from the 8-ball to the 9-ball would have been considerably easier. Rempe was up to the task as he played a superb two-rail route across and down the table to Position D for an easy shot on the 9-ball.

Throughout the entire rack, Rempe played good enough position to keep his run in tact. On the few occasions where he missed the ideal position zone by a few inches, he was able to get quickly back in line with a well-played recovery route.

Learn From Observing the Best

Your powers of observation are a big asset in developing your game and your run out power. The lessons which we covered in the previous series of run outs are summarized below.

A Double Hill Thriller

1-ball Bumping balls for shape may be the only way to contain the cue ball.
3-ball Know when to play straight in shape.
6-ball Shaping balls in the middle is tough.

Reyes In Route to Double Hill Thriller

1-ball Bear down and cinch the out shot.
2-ball The second shot often gets you completely in line.
4-ball Little shots are big. Use them to get the perfect angle on the next ball.
8-ball Natural shape is a winner.

Hall Captures His Second U.S. Open

1-ball The cue ball often dies off the last rail on long distance position routes.
2-ball Speed control is a major challenge on around the world routes.
5-ball The right side principle is critical in many situations.
9-ball Make the darn ball even if you're not happy with your shape.

Souquet's First Big Title In America

1-ball Set up the correct angle without getting hooked.
2-ball Barely reaching the position zone is often good enough.
6-ball The short side is available from even the most unlikely places.
7 and 8-ball Recognize when you must play precision shape.

Sigel Shows Off His Run Out Power

1-ball Draw speed control is a major weapon.
5-ball Great shotmaking can overcome many mistakes.
6-ball Imagination and skill can create incredible position routes.

Guts, Determination, and Superior Shotmaking

3-ball You have to accept what the table gives you.
4-ball When you are in great stroke, the cue ball may overrun your zone.
5-ball Bank shots can save a run.
6-ball Sometimes you must play for lucky shape.

Strickland's Firepower Wins Fourth U.S. Open

1-ball Reversing the cue ball with outside english is unusual but effective.
5-ball Shaping balls in the middle is a necessary skill.
6 and 7-balls You need to be prepared for the third ball if you make two at once.

Precision at Long Range

1-ball Soft follow shots are a vital weapon.
3-ball When you must play perfect shape, you must simply rise to the occasion.
5-ball Playing within the limitations of the shot is a winner.

Rempe's Mastery of the Cue Ball

3-ball Controlling the cue ball with a very hard stroke on a small cut angle is an important recovery shot.
4-ball Thin cut crossing routes are a valuable tool.
7-ball You must guard against coming up short on shallow one-rail position plays.

CHAPTER 8

CLUSTER MANAGEMENT

"If you go close to a ball you can get behind, bad things can and often will happen."
Grady Mathews

Cluster busting is the art and science of separating those annoying little groups of balls that could keep you from executing picture perfect run outs. Every cluster offers you the opportunity to exercise either your offensive or defensive prowess. Sound cluster management will enable you to run racks that a less knowledgeable opponent will stall out on. In addition, many clusters give you the chance to lock your opponent up tight with a killer safety.

Sound cluster management can help you to avoid costly blunders at critical junctures in a game of Nine Ball. The secret lies in intelligently appraising the table and then precisely executing your plan. This approach runs counter to the caveman like tactics of simply blasting away and hoping for a good roll.

Unfortunately, far too many players blast into clusters while operating on the theory that "might" could make "right". The skilled practitioner, however, approaches clusters with the care and precision of a diamond cutter. They realize that one false move can easily spell disaster.

Cluster Management

There are several things to consider that can influence how you handle the various clusters you'll encounter. These include:

- How the table is playing. If you are comfortable with your ability to control the cue ball off the cushions, you may go for a break out that you might not otherwise play.
- Your style of play will dictate your strategy. Aggressive players will go for some breaks outs where more defensive minded types would play a safety.

- Every cluster break carries with it a certain risk/reward ratio. Smart players weigh the odds before making a decision to play a break shot or a safety.
- Your opponent's game will at times influence your decision. For example, you might play a safe against an opponent who kicks poorly rather than attempt a break out.
- When assessing the table you need to ask; 1) Do you really have a cluster that needs breaking; 2) When can you break the cluster; 3) How can you break it.
- You goals for a cluster break could be: 1) To run out 2) To set up a safety; 3) Either of the above, depending on the outcome of the breakout.

Reading Clusters

Breaking clusters involves carefully weighing the risks and rewards. The lists below gives you the go signs and the pitfalls to breaking high-risk clusters. Keep these tips in mind as you evaluate clusters and you will soon develop an eye for the clusters you should break and those that require a defensive approach.

High % Breakouts

- The table is open near the cluster, which means there is little or no chance of getting hooked.
- The cluster is not close to a pocket and/or the cue ball will not be traveling toward a pocket after contact, which eliminates the risk of scratching.
- The tangent line of the shot points to the cluster (No draw or follow is needed), which enables you to control the path of the cue ball with great accuracy.
- The cue ball will be traveling a short distance into the cluster, which means that you will 1) not miss it; 2) could hit it exactly where intended.
- Precise contact with the cluster allows you to predict where the balls in the cluster are going to relocate.
- You can play shape on a ball that's not in the cluster. This ball is preferably close to a pocket and away from other balls.
- The cluster can be hit softly, which lessens or eliminates the possibility of the balls rolling to undesirable locations.
- The cue balls path is highly predictable, even if it's going to travel a long distance to the cluster.
- The balls in the cluster only need be bumped lightly to achieve favorable positioning.
- Options are available after the break out: 1) you can continue the run; 2) you have a safety available.
- The penalty for missing the break out is not substantial.

Low % Breakouts

- The balls are wedged against the rail, which could lead to a double kiss or a hook.
- There is a long traveling distance to the cluster, which increases the chances of failing to separate the balls.
- You could easily get hooked by a ball or balls that are stationed close by.
- A precise hit on the cluster is not likely, which increases the chances of not gaining favorable position.
- You could easily scratch after contacting the cluster.
- Good position is not likely despite a successful breakout.
- You must finesse the cue ball extraordinarily well to break the balls.
- The penalty for missing the cluster is very high, which translates into a poor risk/reward ratio.

Avoid High Risk Cluster Busting

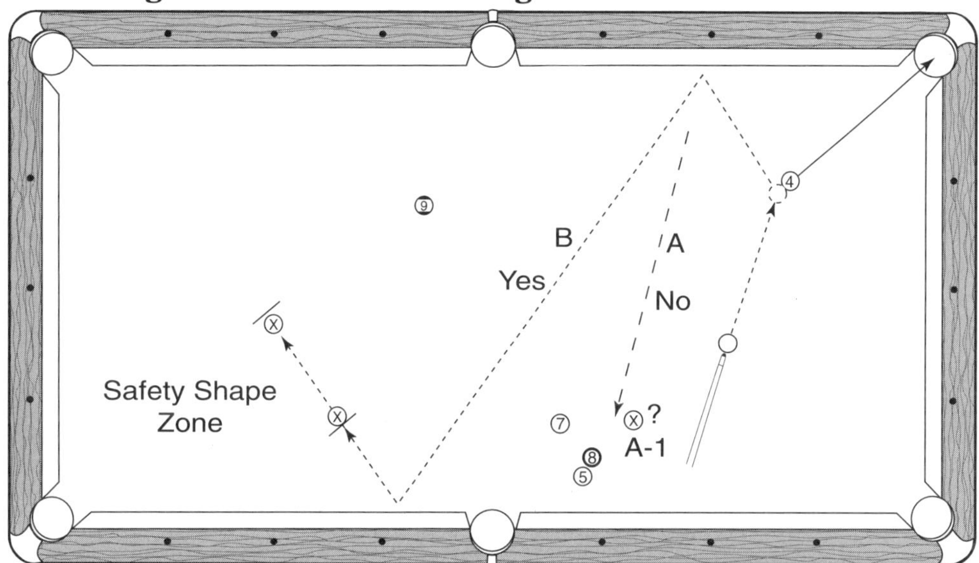

You could opt for the break out by following Route A into the cluster. Even if you are successful at separating the 8 and 5-balls, a good shot on the 5-ball is not guaranteed. At this distance, it's also quite possible that you could miss the cluster with the cue ball stopping at A-1. In this position, you would have to kick at the 5-ball. If you apply too little inside english, you could scratch in the side pocket. A much better choice is to pass on breaking the cluster and instead play past the side pocket to the safety zone. From this position a softly hit stop shot using draw will leave your opponent hooked behind the 8-ball. The lesson: Some clusters should be broken as part of a safety, not as part of a run out. This is especially true when the distance to the cluster is great, as in our example.

Controlling the Path to the Cluster

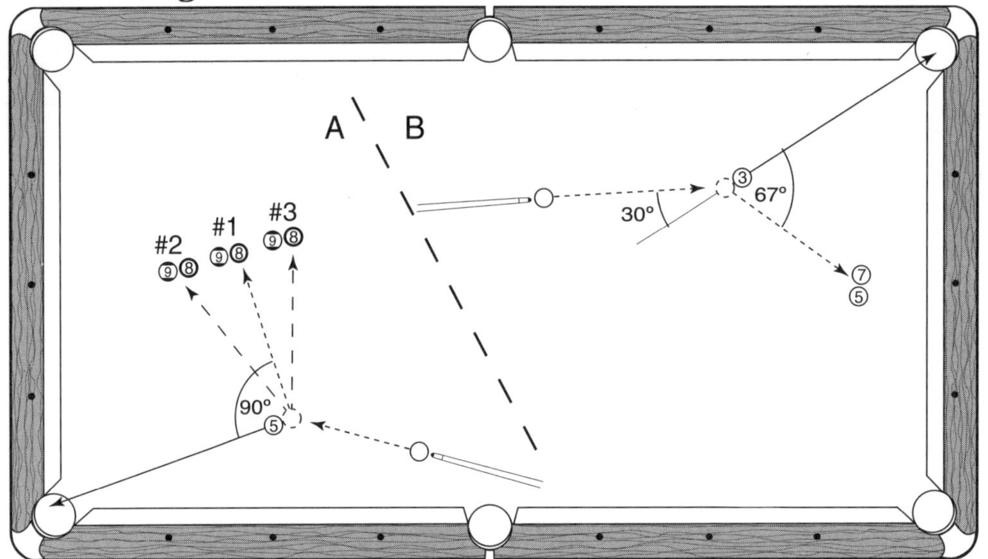

A reasonably short distance from the object ball to the cluster combined with a stun shot can enable you to break clusters with great precision. If the tangent line points directly at the cluster, a stun shot can be used to send the cue ball directly into the cluster. This is shown in Part A with the 8 and 9-balls in Position A. When the cluster is a little above the tangent line, as with the 8 and 9-balls in Position B, then you will need to use draw. If the cluster is positioned below the 90-degree line, as shown by the 8 and 9-balls in Position C, use a medium firm stroke with a touch of follow.

At times the position of the balls will allow you to play a soft follow shot to hit the cluster with precision. This occurs when the cue ball's path of departure following contact is lined directly at the cluster. In Part B, a 30-degree cut angle means the cue ball will depart at a 67-degree angle when hit with a soft follow stroke, The cue ball will roll directly into the 5-7 cluster. Soft cluster breaks like this are almost always best as they allow you to exert maximum control over both the cue ball and the ball(s).

Timing a Break Is Critical

The 6-8-9 cluster must be broken at some point, but the big question is when? You could pocket the 1-ball and bust the cluster right away. However, there's a very good chance the cue ball could wind up behind one of the balls leaving you with no direct shot on the 2-ball in Position A. A far wiser course is to first clear the 1, 2 and 3 balls. The cue ball should then be positioned near Position B for a cut shot on the 4-ball. The cluster can now be easily broken and, more importantly, a shot on the next ball (the 5-ball) is virtually guaranteed.

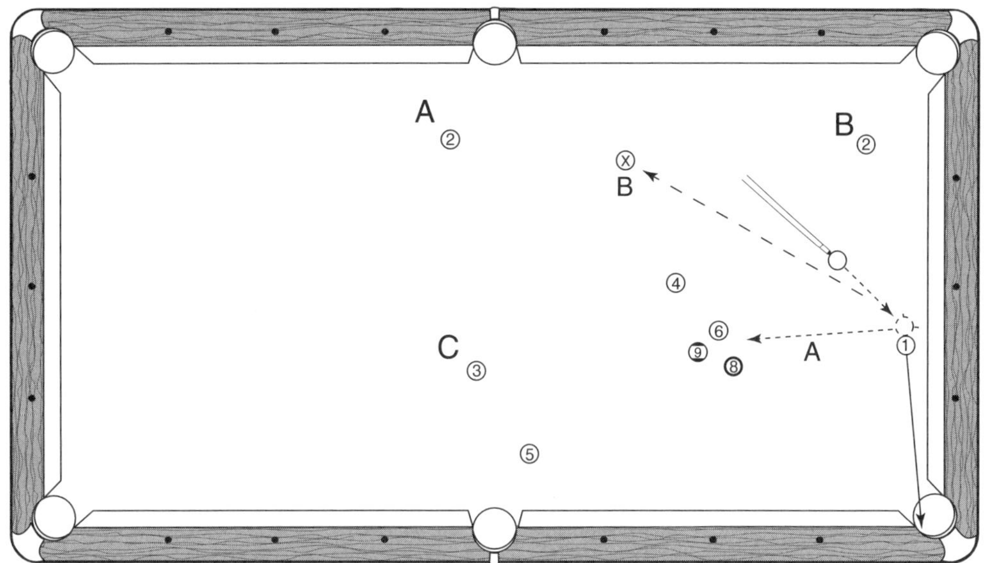

Now let's return to our original position on the 1-ball. If the 2-ball was in Position C, you would be smart to immediately break the 6-8-9 cluster when playing the 1-ball because you would almost certainly have an open shot on the 2-ball.

The Ideal Cluster Busting Scenario

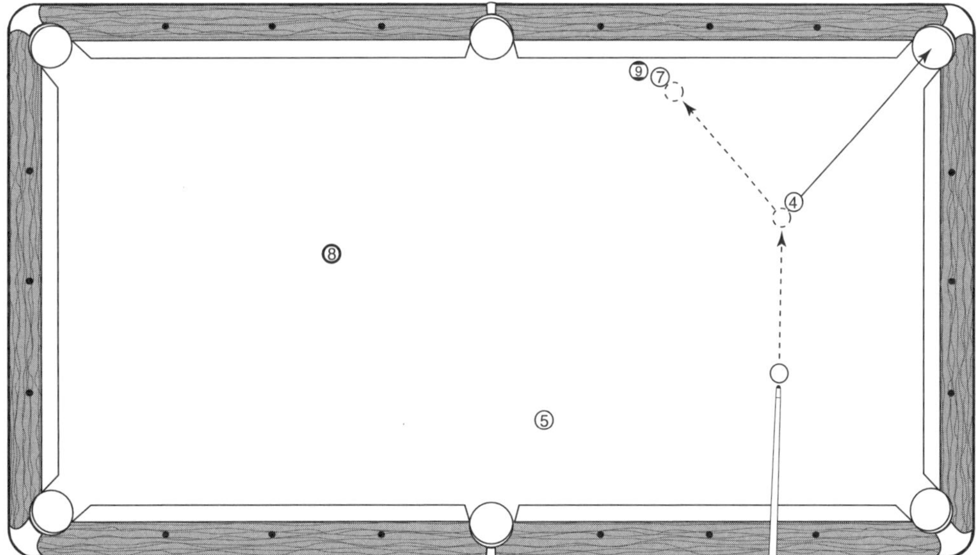

This shows the ideal scenario for breaking a cluster. The shot on the 4-ball is very easy, so you're not likely to miss. But by all means don't make the mistake of looking up prematurely to see if you've broken the cluster. The short distance to the cluster helps you to hit the 7-ball precisely where intended. The chances of getting hooked are almost nil. Finally, you should have an easy shot on the 5-ball, which is in front of the opposite side pocket.

Use Ball in Hand to Break Clusters

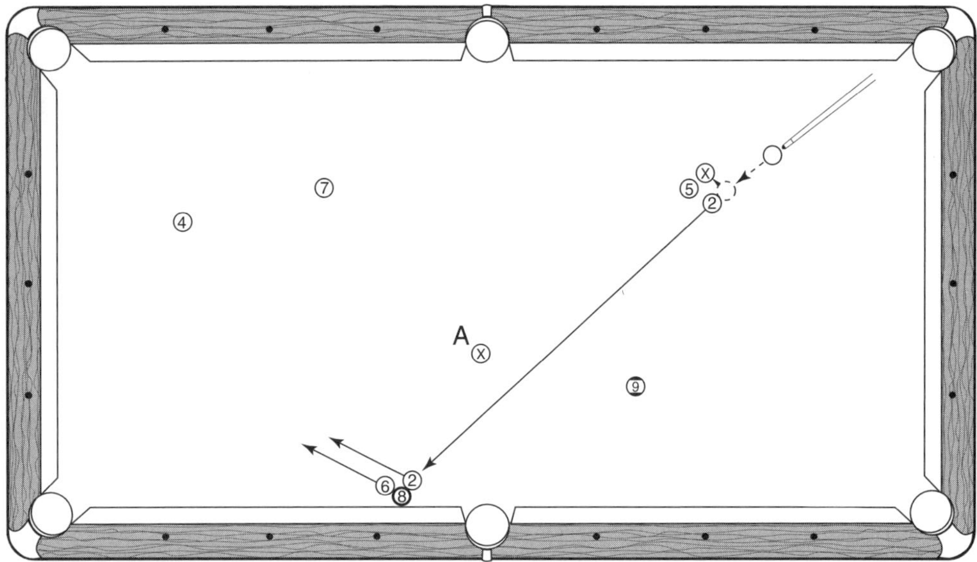

You could play the 2-ball with ball in hand and send the cue ball to Position A for a cluster breaking shot on the 4-ball. After playing the 4-ball, you might wind up with a shot on the 5-ball. You could also end up behind the 6-ball. The high percentage play is to shoot the 2-ball directly into the cluster and pin the cue ball behind the 5-ball. You now have an excellent chance of running out after your opponent plays a kick shot.

Breaking a Cluster with BIH

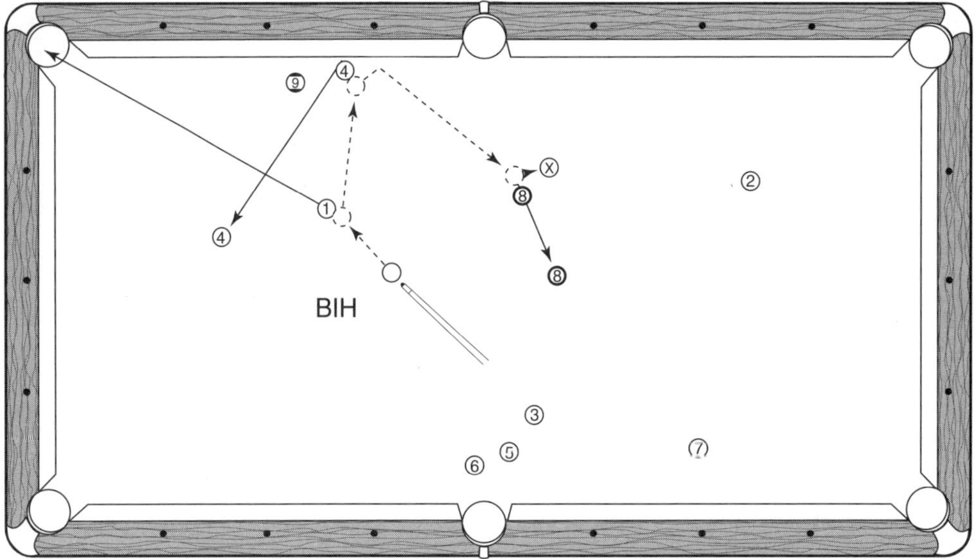

Francisco Bustamante showed excellent cue ball control when breaking this cluster against Earl Strickland at the 1992 Bicycle Club Invitational.. With ball in hand, he placed the cue ball in a position that allowed him to roll the cue ball into the right side of the 4-ball, separating it from the 9-ball. The cue ball then rolled to Position X for shape on the 2-ball.

How to Break a Cluster

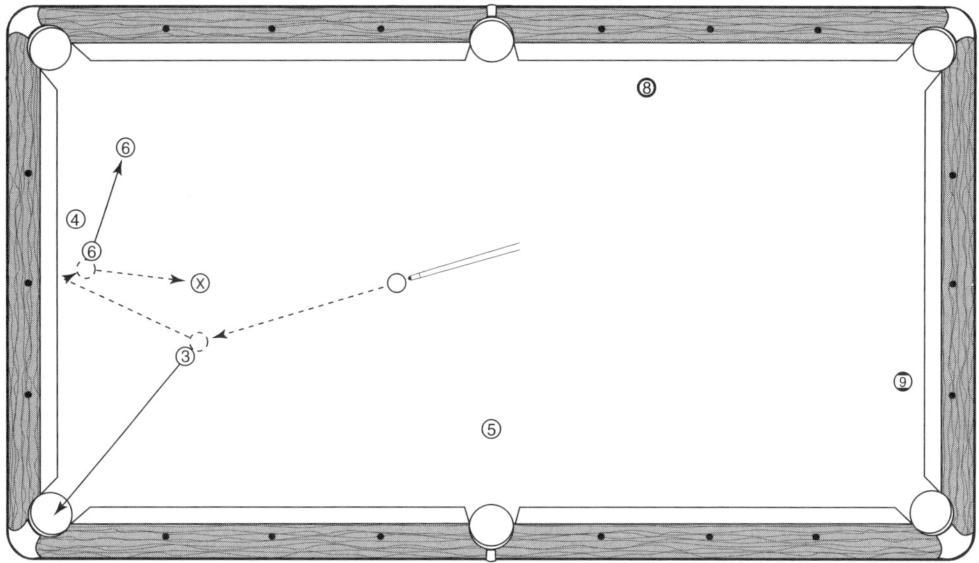

Finnish star Mika Immonen played this precise cluster break against Jim Rempe at the 1998 U.S. Open. A soft follow shot sent the cue ball off the end rail and into the right side of the 6-ball, leaving Immonen with a relatively easy shot on the 4-ball. Hitting the correct side and amount of the 6-ball was a big key to this shot.

Precision Cluster Breaking

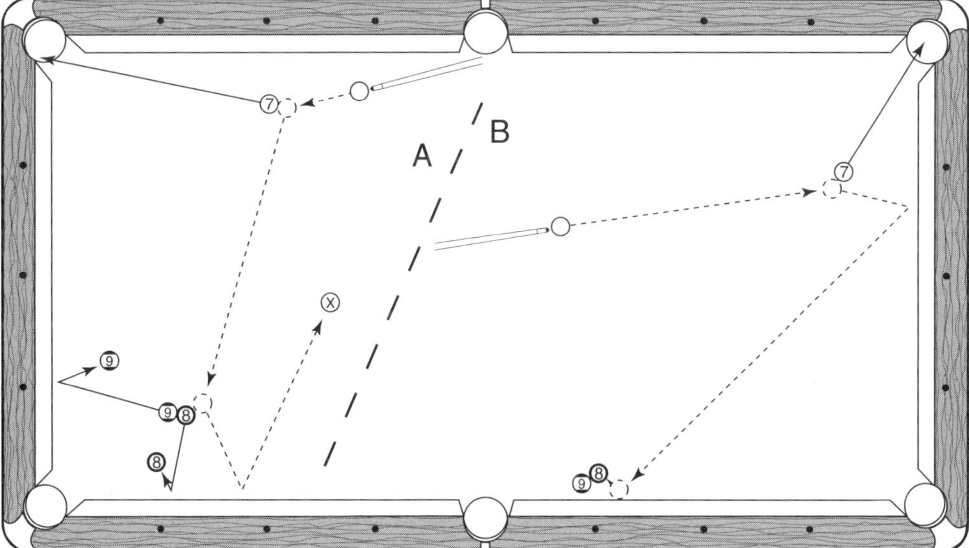

In Part A, controlling the path of the cue ball with the correct speed enables you to predict the contact point on the 8-ball, as well as the ending locations of the balls with accuracy. In Part B, this long-range cluster break is worth the risk if your cue ball control is above average. If the 8 and 9-balls were switched, there could be a post break shot hook.

Break a Cluster with a Safety

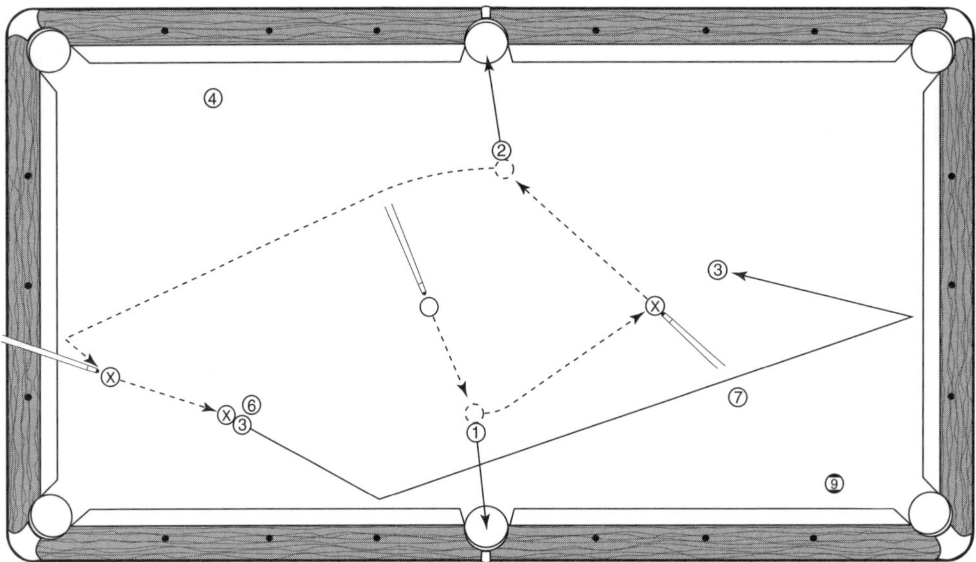

Earl Strickland won this game by playing shape for a safety rather than taking the chance of missing the cluster in a match with Cliff Joyner at the 1999 U.S. Open. The route to the safety zone and the cluster break were nearly identical. The safety zone was a couple of feet long, which gave Strickland a comfortable margin for error. At the same time, the penalty for missing the break was too severe to be worth the risk.

Use a Bank to Break a Cluster

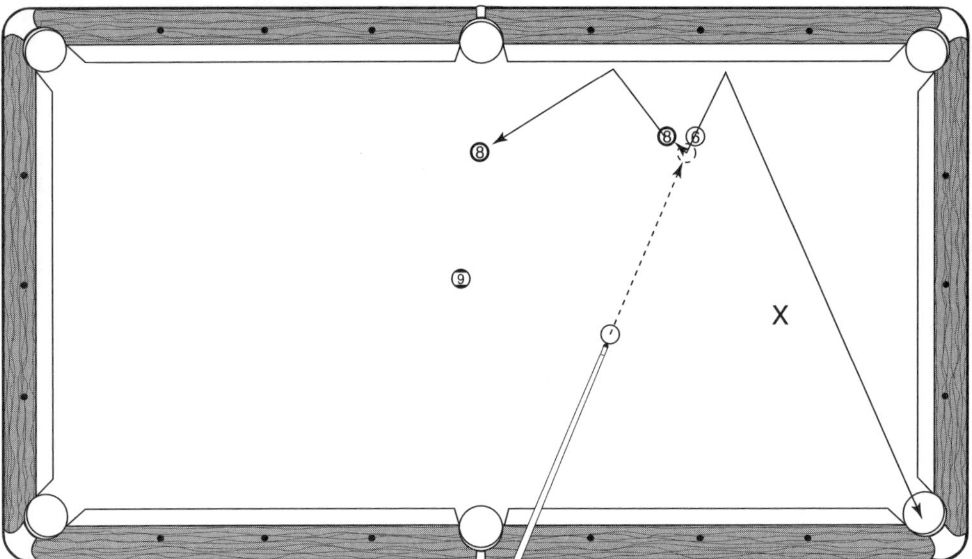

An offensive shot is often the best way to break a cluster. The 6-ball was hit with a hard stroke, which allowed it to be hit slightly to the left of center. This created a small cut angle, which enabled the cue ball to bump the 8-ball clear for a shot. This shot is preferred if you excel at bank shots. Other players might be better off playing shape for a safety at Position X.

CHAPTER 9

READING THE TABLE

"You have to be fairly intelligent when you're playing Nine Ball."
Bill Incardona

Reading the table is the skill of making sense out of the jumble of balls that makes up a typical layout in Nine Ball. As you improve at evaluating the table, your decision-making skills will come to be a big strategic weapon in your game. When you can consistently pick the right shot or course of action based on the position of the balls, you will have taken a huge step forward as a Nine Ball player. The end result is that you will make the most of your offensive opportunities while, at the same time, keeping your opponent's game in check with judicious use of defensive strategy. Basically, reading the table all boils down to determining whether the table is offering you a better opportunity for playing either offense or defense.

The Football Analogy

When a football team takes possession of the ball, they hope their drive will result in a score. When their drive stalls and they are facing 4th down and long yardage, they will almost always punt the ball, giving their opponent possession. Similarly, when your drive to the 9-ball begins with the first shot in a rack of Nine Ball, you are also hoping that you will score by eventually sinking the 9-ball. As in football, you should also give the ball away by playing safe or "punting" if you will, when your "drive" stalls, possibly due to missing position. Your "punt" in pool is designed to contain your opponent's offense. In pool, your defensive efforts may even keep your opponent from a clear-cut offensive opportunity. And yet, strangely enough, many pool players choose to go for it on pool's equivalent of fourth and 40, often when a safety is readily available.

The Stop Light Analogy

The stop light analogy is another way to help you accurately assess the potential of a rack. This analogy enables you to quickly assign a rack into one of the three categories below.

- **Green Light** There are no significant obstacles to running out, so it is all systems go. Now it's all about offense and execution.
- **Yellow Light** A run out is possible, but there are minor problems that must be solved. Perhaps there is a difficult shot or position play that must be executed with a high degree of accuracy.
- **Red Light** The rack has one or more problem areas that will almost certainly keep you from running out. Now it the time to look for a safety that can help you regain control of the table.

A Simplified Decision Matrix

When you are thinking pool like a pool player, the decision making process is automatic most of the time. Until you acquire enough experience, however, you may find it useful to employ this simplified decision making matrix.

#1 Do you have a reasonable offensive opportunity?

Yes. Continue below. No. Proceed to step #2.
A Does the layout indicate that a run out is possible?
B Is a combo, billiard or some other shot at winning available right away?
C Even if there is an offensive opportunity, is there a safety that gives you a better chance of winning than either of the above?

#2 Is there a good defensive opportunity?

Yes. Continue below. No. Proceed to step #3
A Consider your options for playing safe and chose the best one.
B If it is right after the break, should you push out?

#3 What options are there for avoiding a foul?

A Should you play a kick shot? Is there a safety built into the shot?
B Is a jump shot the best choice?
C Does an intentional foul give you the best chance of winning?

Know Your Game and Play Your Game

When playing Nine-Ball, there is no one strategic approach that will work with all players. Your unique set of skills determines when to play offense or defense. You can go a long way towards increasing your trips to the winner's circle by learning to play the highest percentage shot in all situations, always keeping your game in mind.

Don't let your ego or an unrealistic assessment of your skills cause you to shoot shots that aren't in your bag. You need to be realistic at all times about your chances of running out, playing a specific safety or making a combination on the 9-ball, to name just a few possibilities. As an example, amateur players should play many more safeties than pros because of positional errors and lack of shotmaking power.

Get to Know the Table

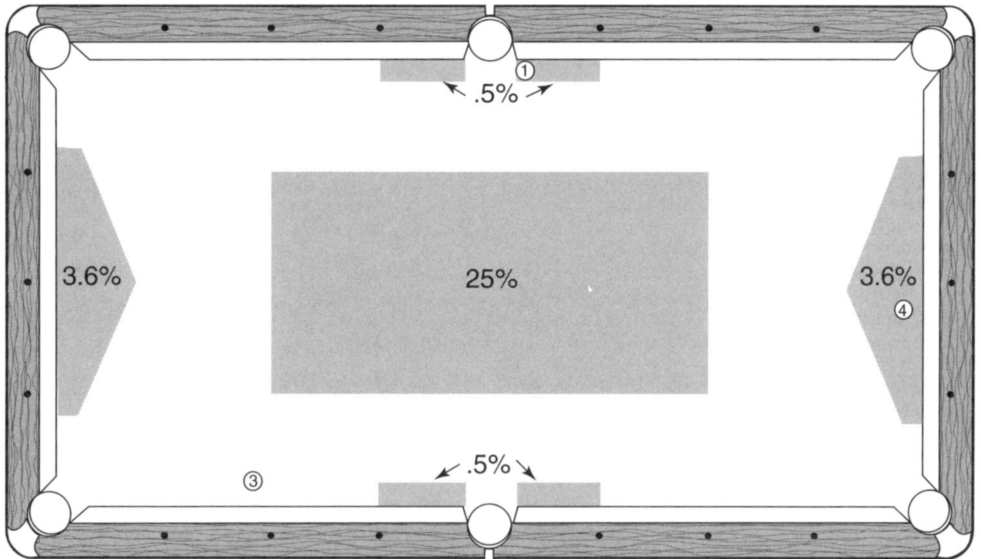

Since Nine Ball is a full table game, the balls will relocate after the break across the length of the table. A ball in almost any position could be in either an advantageous or poor location. It largely depends on the location of the other balls. As a general rule of thumb, however, there are certain ball positions that tend to cause more trouble than others.

The illustration highlights the acknowledged problem areas. The most troublesome position for a ball is high up on the side rail near the side pockets. The 1-ball, which is frozen to the rail right next to the side pocket, is in the spot that causes more headaches than any other single location. When you are inspecting the table after the break, look for balls that happen to reside in these problem zones, as they will have to be handled with care. Luckily enough, this trouble zone only occupies 2% of the table.

Balls that are located on or near either end rail also cause their share of problems. A ball in the end rail zone is most troublesome when you must play shape on it from the opposite end of the table, such as from the 3-ball to the 4-ball. You must also avoid getting straight in on balls in these zones. The two "end zones" occupy 7.2% of the table.

The center portion takes up 25% of the table. This zone causes problems with position because the cue ball must travel a long distance to the rail on cut shots, and because it is difficult to get the correct angle on balls in this area.

Where the Balls Tend to Locate

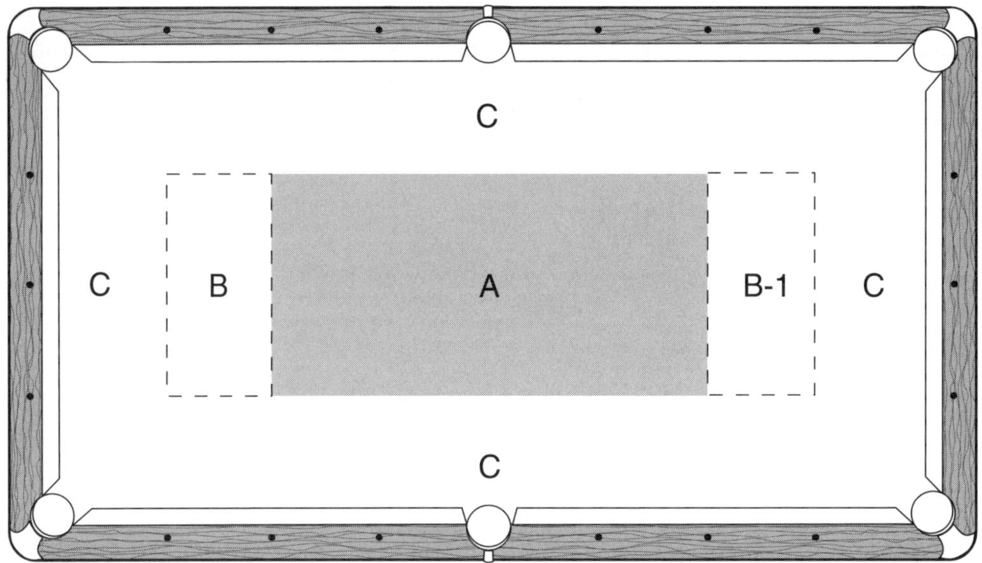

Ball location after the break is fundamental to reading the table. With that in mind, I conducted a brief study of 25 pro games to determine which sections of the table the balls were most likely to end up. The center portion of the table (A), as shown above, takes up 25% of the playing surface. Only 17.5% of the balls remaining on the table after the break ended up in this area. The two sections (B & B-1) at either end of the center make up 12.5% of the table, but are home to 13.5% of the balls after the break. This is not too surprising as Section B is where the balls are racked. Section C is composed of the playing surface that is within a diamond of the rail. This section covers 62.5% of the table, and yet 69.0% of the balls ended up there. This may be due to the fact that the balls tend to lose speed quickly as they strike the final cushion.

You may be asking yourself "how can I use this pocket billiard research"? Its real value is simply alerting you to the fact that the vast majority of shots are played with the object ball within a diamond of the rail. This may alert you to the special problems created by balls that end up close together near or on the rails. Knowing that most of the balls are near the rails should also be useful in planning your runouts. Balls near the rail are also useful for playing safe. Finally, an average of less than 1.5 balls per rack wind up in the center portion of the table, which is the ball location that creates problems with position play.

Reading the Table

When you are playing position, you are concerned with that one particular shot. And when you are playing a pattern, you must plan for a sequence of several balls. Reading the table takes things a step further as its purpose is to give you a realistic assessment of the rack as a whole, no matter when your turn begins. Part of your skill at reading the table is correctly assessing the type of rack you are facing. Some are roadmaps that say, "Please run me"; while others are ugly configurations that make you wish you could rerack the balls and start over again. Regardless of whatever the breaker (you or your opponent) and the Pool Gods dish out, you must learn to make the most of each and every rack.

How to Read the Table

While you are reading the table, you should be looking for things you can do, whether they be offensive or defensive in nature. This involves a realistic assessment of the layout and a high level of awareness of your unique skills. While you are reading the table, you should be weighing the risks and rewards of the layout. Then a decision must be made as to your course of action.

If you are wondering about your ability to read the table, your best measure are your results in competition. Are you making wise decisions that make things difficult for your opponent and that give you more than your share of offensive opportunities? Or are you making it easy for your opponent by playing low percentage shots or poor safeties that allow your opponent's to seize the advantage?

In the sections that follow, we'll cover numerous situations that come up repeatedly, where you have to read the table and make a decision as to your course of action. With enough experience, you will discover your options fall into three broad categories:

- The layout offers a clear-cut offensive opportunity.
- A defensive maneuver is obviously called for.
- You must weigh the situation before choosing to play either offense or defense.

There are common themes that run throughout a typical rack, as we'll see in the upcoming illustrations. Most racks, however, will present you with a special challenge or subtle nuance. It is essential that you learn to decipher the one or two special characteristics that must be handled in a specific way. Often a minute difference in a single ball's position can change the entire complexion of the rack. For example, a rack could offer the opportunity for a runout or a safety based on whether or not two balls are clustered or are even just 1/8" apart.

The Various Types of Layouts

There are zillions of positions the balls can take after the break shot. Nevertheless, there are some commonly recurring themes that appear on a regular basis. With enough experience you will be able to quickly size up the kind of layout you are up against. This will enable you to smoothly move into the next phase, which is selecting the correct offensive or defensive plan that maximizes your chances of winning the game.

TIP: While you are sitting in the chair waiting your turn or when watching other matches, "practice" reading the table. Keep asking what you would do if it was your turn, and evaluate the shooter's decisions.

The Roadmap (or Cosmo)

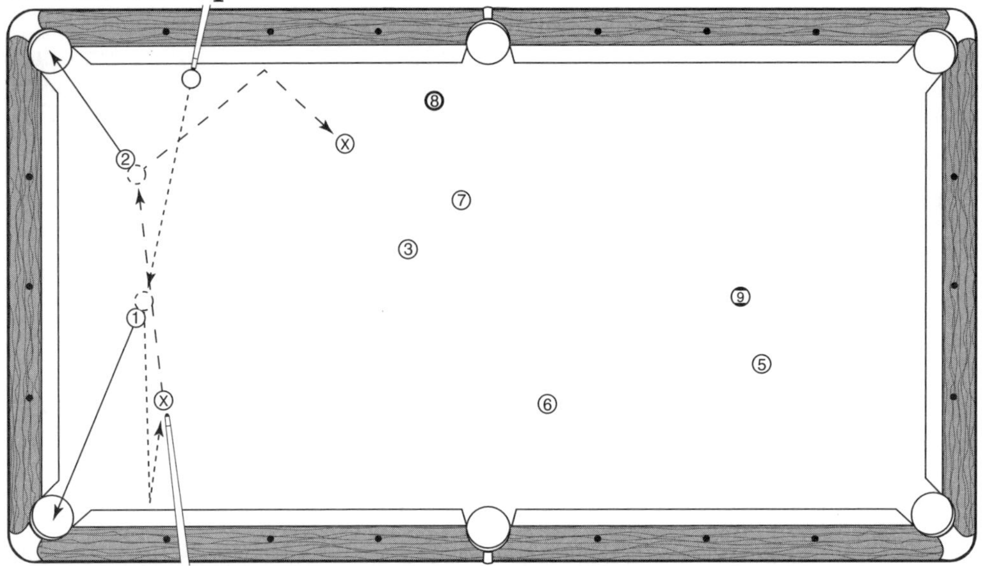

Nick Varner broke and ran this simple layout at the 1990 U.S. Open against Mike Sigel. There are no clusters and the balls are evenly spread. The big "problem" was getting on the 3-ball. Racks like this are known as "Connect the Dots" runs, "Roadmaps", or "Cosmos". Go for precision on these kinds of layouts, as this is a time to hone your position play.

Tough Racks that Appear Easy

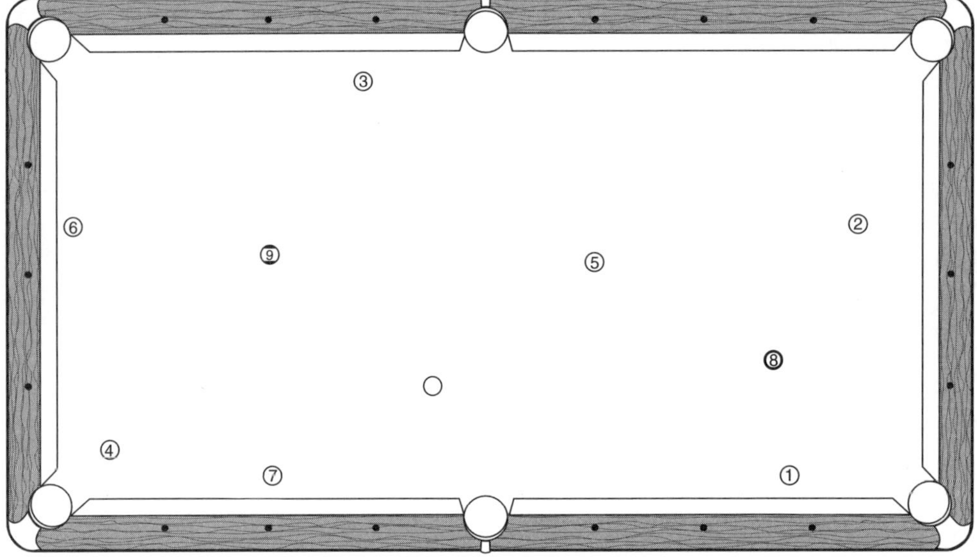

Even though the balls are spread evenly across the table, don't be lulled into a false sense of security. Always be on the look out for trouble. 1) You need an angle on the 2-ball, without getting hooked behind the 8-ball. 2) You need to avoid the 9-ball when playing position on the 4-ball. 3) Position on the 6-ball will not be easy. The lesson: proceed with caution because even simple looking racks can have their share of problems.

Precision Run Out is Possible

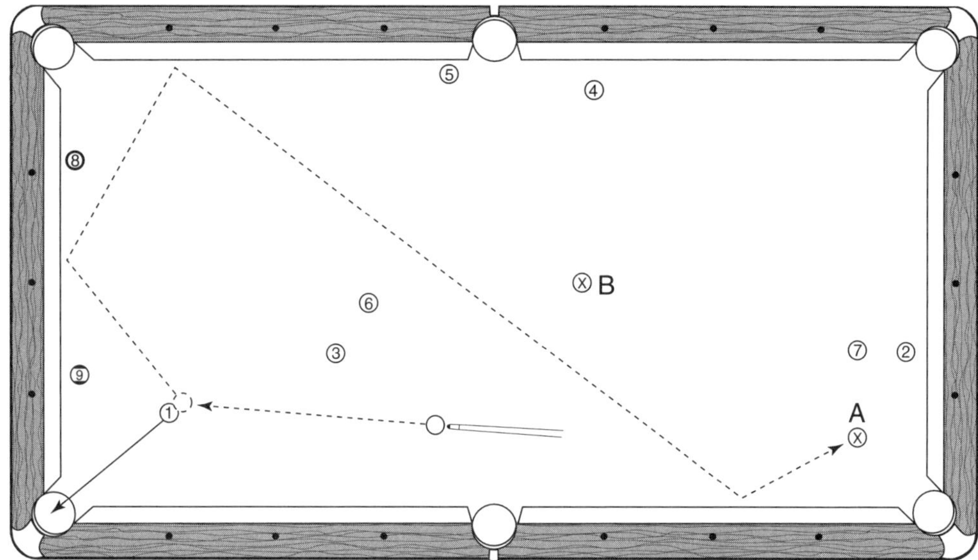

This type of rack can be run, providing you exercise pinpoint cue ball control, shot after shot. On the 1-ball, you must avoid scratching. You will also need an angle on the 2-ball at Position A so you can continue to Position B for the troublesome 3-ball. Try analyzing the rest of the rack with an eye towards the precise execution required for nearly every shot.

A Traveling Rack

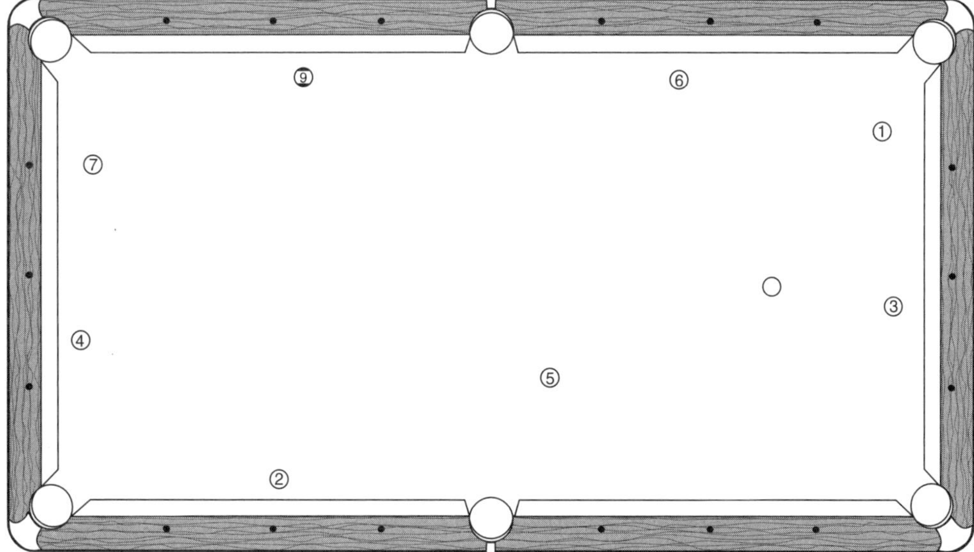

An opponent who knows how to gain separation by placing the balls in specific locations in the rack and/or the luck of the break can result in a traveling rack. Playing shape on the 2, 3, 4, and 7-balls is going to require that you exercise your skills at long distance cue ball control. If you read this rack correctly, you know that the correct cut angles on the key shots will be necessary to move the cue ball across and down the table.

A Tough Position Play

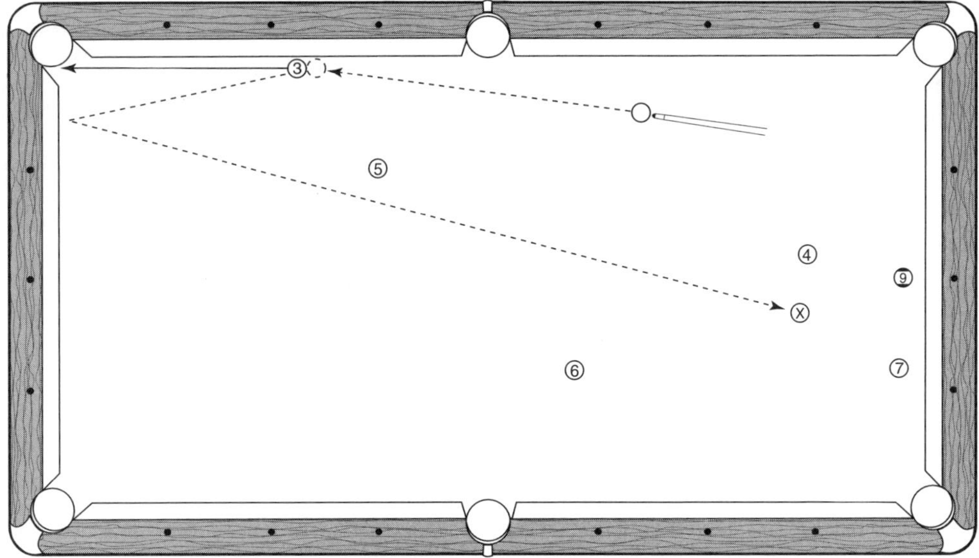

Francisco Bustamante was facing a long and difficult route from the 3-ball to the 4-ball late in a very close match with Efren Reyes at the Sands Regency Open 20, 1994. After surveying the table, he let loose with a very hard follow stroke, sending the cue ball two-rails and down the length of the table for excellent position on the 4-ball.

At times the key to running a rack is making a very difficult or unfamiliar position play like the one in the example above. If you are feeling very confident about your game, by all means give shots like this a go. Pulling off shots like this can boost your confidence while sending a message to your opponent that you came to play some pool.

If you have any doubts, however, about your ability to execute a shot like this, you may be better off playing safe. Remember, a good safety is certainly better than a less than confident stab at the ball.

The Out Shot

At times the outcome of a game rides a very difficult shot, which can ignite a run out. The idea is to pocket the ball and wind up with something with which you can work. Hopefully by the second ball you will have good shape and the rest will be easy. Jeanette Lee so ably demonstrated this concept while playing Robin Dodson at the 1994 U.S. Open with this long thin cut shot on the 5-ball.

Even though there were a couple of safeties available, she took an aggressive approach and went for the shot. Ms. Lee sliced in this off the rail table length 73-degree cut shot and sent the cue ball nearly 1.75 table lengths for position on the 6-ball. Wow!! Ms. Lee was rewarded with a run out. The lesson: on tough shots you must be completely 100% honest with yourself. Your decision to go for it or play safe is often based on the state of your game at that very moment, how you feel about your chances of making the shot, and the score of the match.

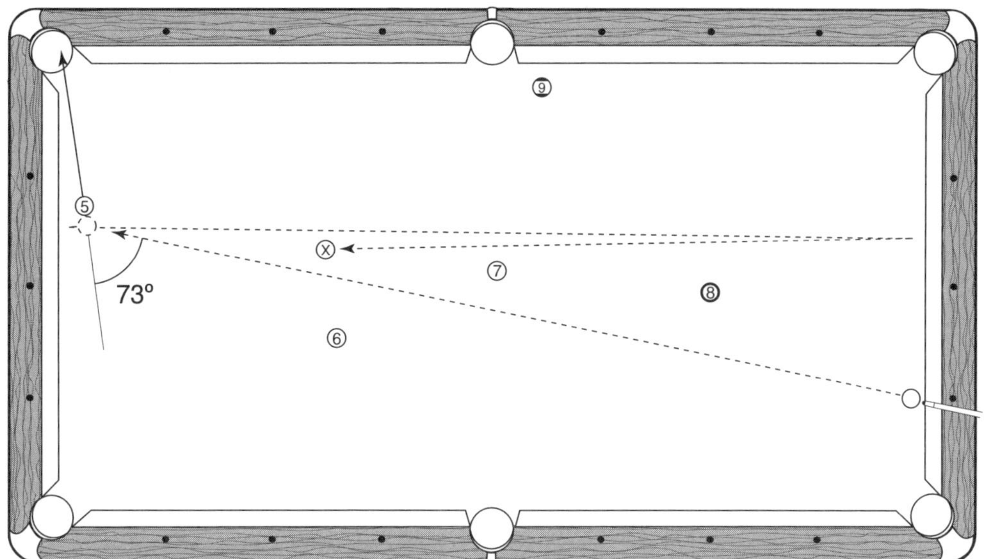

Short Rack Opportunities

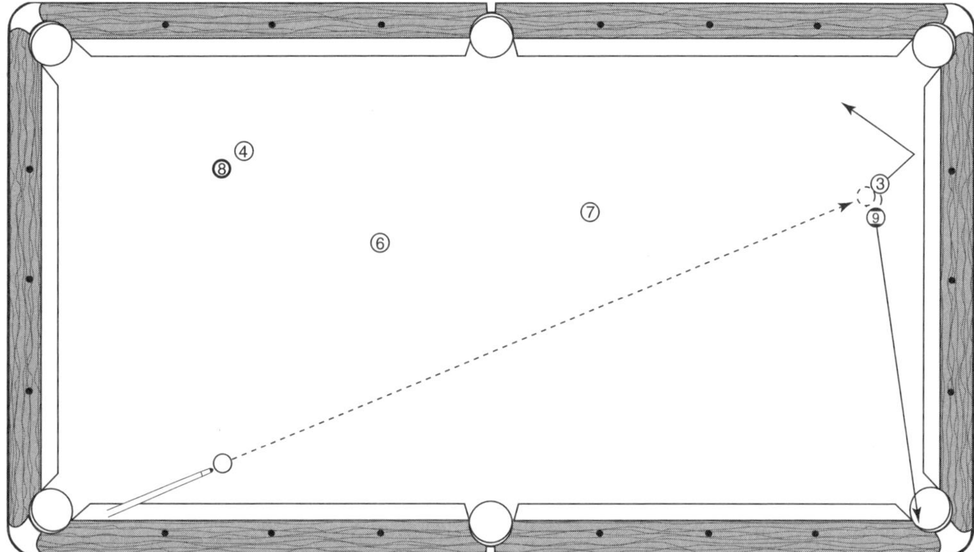

There is possibly nothing that can lift your spirits and demoralize your opponent more than a quick and easy win. I'm sure you know by now to keep a sharp eye out for high percentage combos, billiards and intelligent "cheese rides" that can bring instant victory. You should also, however, develop a sixth sense for the kind of offbeat shots that are lying dead, or near dead, but that are not the kind of shots you might normally come across. Kunihiko Takahashi spotted this backwards billiard on the 9-ball in a match with Chuck Altomare at the 1999 U.S. Open. The shot required an extremely hard stroke and a very full hit on the 3-ball. PS: Don't get bullied out of a shot like this by an opponent who calls "bad hit'. Explain that it is impossible to make the 9-ball straight in with a 100-degree cut angle!

Congestion Rules from the Start

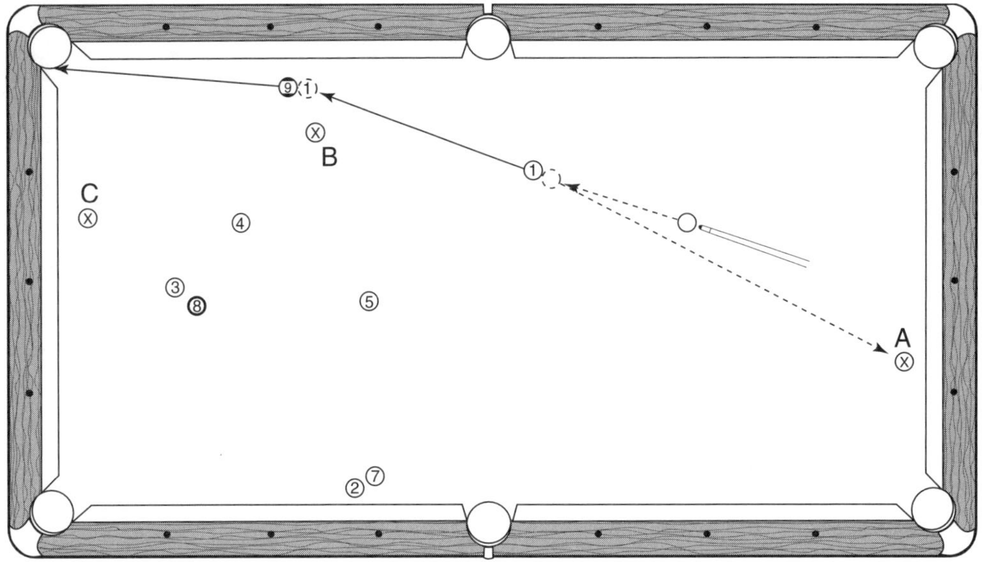

There is a common tendency to want to give up on "ugly looking" racks just to get them over with. You must remember, however, that every game counts just the same. So hang in there, play safe, massage the rack, and do whatever it takes to win. Patience is a game winning virtue in situations where anything but a nice easy run is available.

The layout in this example is the type that often results from a weak break, a poor hit on the 1-ball or an opponent who uses a soft defensive break, which is, of course, a cowardly tactic. The 2-ball is tied up on the side rail and there is no way to break it open on this shot. Furthermore, position on the 3-ball will not be easy (after the 2-7 cluster has been broken) because of the 4, 5, and 8-balls nearby. And finally, if you were to get on the 3-ball, it will be tough to follow this up with good shape the 4-ball.

When a rack can't be run, you should look for a shot on the 9-ball. In this case, the 1-9 combo is available. When playing a shot like this, try to build some defense into the shot. By drawing back to Position A, you will make things as tough as possible for your opponent in the likely event of a miss. Another option is to pass on the combo and play position for a safety. You could pocket the 1-ball and send the cue ball to Position B. From here you could break the 2-7 cluster and send the cue ball behind the 3-8 cluster or the 4-ball to Position C or thereabouts.

TIP: A poor break = congestion = opportunities to play safe

Whenever you are evaluating a layout where the balls are close together, don't automatically assume that the congestion factor will prevent a run out. In some cases, there will be room to make all the balls as long as you maintain exquisite control of the cue ball.

Congestion at the End

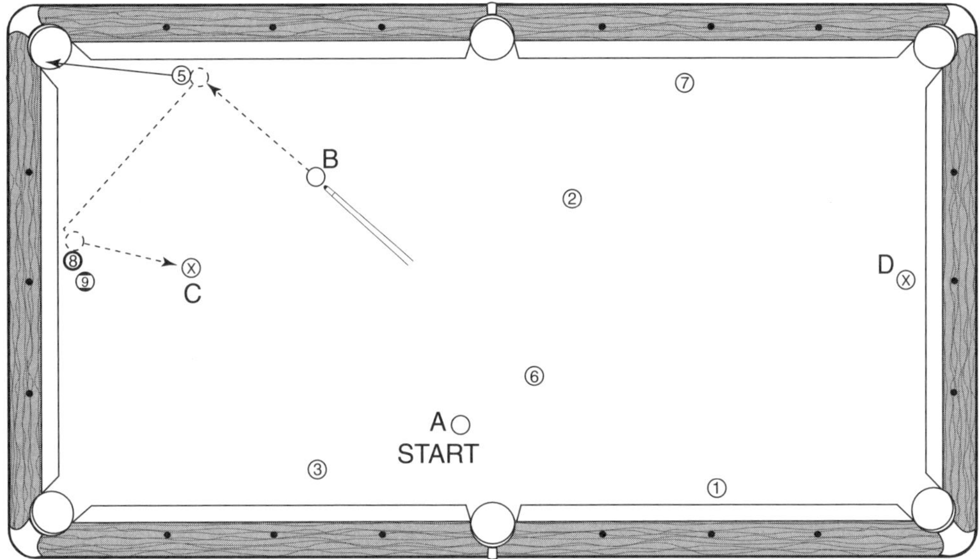

One of the most annoying layouts in Nine Ball occurs when the last two balls are tied up and in a position to thwart your efforts to run out. In the example, the 8 and 9-balls are clustered on the end rail. If you wish to run out, you will have to break this cluster. Timing is crucial, as you want to have a makeable shot after separating the balls. That pretty much rules out breaking the cluster after pocketing either the 2-ball or 3-ball. If you ran the first three balls and left the cue ball at Position B, you could break the 8-9 cluster and send the cue ball to Position C for the 6-ball. This would require near flawless execution.

Now back to our original position (A). Another choice is to simply run through to the 7-ball and play shape for a safety. The idea is to skim the right side of the 8-ball and break the cluster, sending the cue ball to somewhere around Position D.

The Improbable Dream

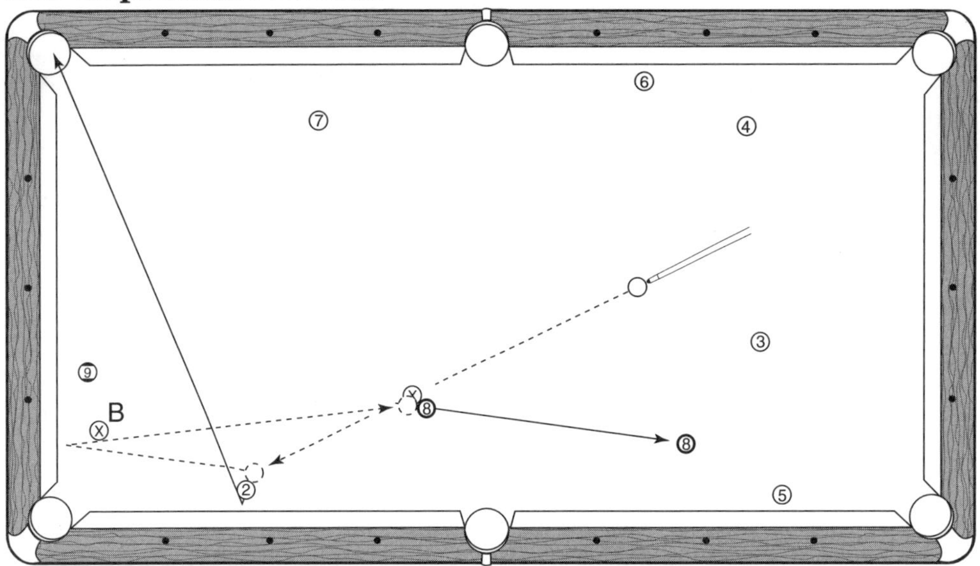

British sharpshooter Steve Davis took a commanding 10-5 lead over Kunihiko Takahashi by running the layout above on his way to an impressive 5-8th place finish at the 2000 World 9-Ball Championships. His first shot with the cue ball in Position A was a difficult crossover bank on the 2-ball. Next came a long 58-degree cut on the 3-ball followed by a table length shot on the 4-ball from Position B. Davis never was able to get completely in line during the entire run. This meant that he had to keep making one spectacular shot after another till the very end.

Davis's lack of position was not really due to poor position. Instead, he simply had encountered one of those racks where the balls were lying "funny". When this happens, you can still run out providing you keep making difficult shots with just enough position for the next shot. When you encounter a rack like this, don't despair. After all, racks like this give you the opportunity to showcase your shotmaking abilities.

As an afterthought, it occurred to me that the run out Davis played is the way many players who have not yet learned to control the cue ball proceed through nearly every rack. Don't you be one of them (but in the off chance you think you are, please see Chapter 3).

CHAPTER 10

PUSH OUT STRATEGY

"Any time there is indecision (after a push out) you know you have done your job."
Bill Incardona

The player who has possession of the table immediately after the balls have been broken may be faced with a hook, a very tough shot or some other difficult situation. At this point, they have the option to pass on the shot and instead play a push out. The shooter must inform their opponent they are going to push out. A legal push out is any shot in which the cue ball does not scratch or knock any ball off the table. The most commonly played push out involves rolling the cue ball a few inches, often without it hitting a rail or contacting another ball. When playing a push out, however, the cue ball can hit any other balls or pocket any ball on the table (if the 9-ball is pocketed, it is obviously respotted).

Once a push out has been played, their opponent has the option of taking the shot or letting the pusher shoot. A push out is not considered to be an intentional foul, so the player who pushes out is not on a foul, even if the second player accepts the shot. Once a push out has been played, the "regular" rules of Nine Ball apply for the remainder of the game.

The table below should be useful to newcomers to Nine-Ball who are unfamiliar with the timing for playing a push out.

Your Push Out Opportunities Come When:
- You've made a ball on the break.
- Your opponent hasn't made a ball on the break.

Your Opponents Push Out Opportunities Come When:
- You haven't made a ball on the break.
- Your opponent has made a ball on the break.

Professionals Use of the Push Out

Professional players view push outs as a necessary evil. Their dislike of push outs stems from the fact that they are usually at a disadvantage since their opponent will: 1) take the push if there is something good to work with or 2) refuse the push if the pusher has left a low percentage shot. The push out at the pro level is a fascinating study into the thinking of each player's decision-making process since push outs test a player's shotmaking, safety play, and knowledge of their opponent's capabilities.

In a study I conducted of 500 games of top caliber professional players, the pusher won 41.9% of the 43 games that featured a pushout. Their opponent (who made the decision to receive or reject the push out) won 58.1% of the time.

When they have to push out, the pros are hoping for close to 50/50 odds of winning the game, but as my study reveals, they fall short of this goal. The pushers knows their opponent also knows the moves and they are not likely to "pull something over" on them. If a pro gives their opponent a slight advantage by making the shot or safety opportunity just a bit too easy, their opponent will shoot. And if they push to a position that is a hair too difficult, they are going to have to shoot.

The Push Out is a Valuable Strategic Weapon

The push out is a highly strategic maneuver that involves sophisticated decision making by both players. The first player must decide how to push out, and their opponent must then decide whether to accept or reject the push out. When you push out, several good things can happen. Your opponent may:

- Fail to hook you on a safety opportunity.
- Let you play safe when they should have taken the push out.
- Go for a tough shot with no reward when they could have played safe.

Amateur players should use the push out much more often than the pros for several reasons:

- You or your opponent may exert less control of the cue ball on the break, which will lead to more hooks and tough shots.
- You or your opponents should pass on some of the tough shots, safeties or kicks the pros play at the start of a rack.
- Your opponents won't respond to the push out nearly as well as a pro who has all the shots and knows all the moves.

You can vary the degree of difficulty of the shots you leave your opponent to match your opponent's skills and tendencies. On the next page are some possible weaknesses in your opponent's game that you can exploit with a savvy push out strategy. Your opponent is a:

- Poor shotmaker who shoots at everything. Strategy: give them tempting shots that are out of their comfort zone.
- Poor safety player. Strategy: Give them opportunities to play safes that they can't execute, but that you can.
- Susceptible to a bluff. Strategy: Push out to a position that makes them think they must shoot, but that really offers little.
- Foolish risk taker. Strategy: Push out to very low percentage shots and combos and other shots on the 9-ball.

Common Errors

There are a host of strategic blunders that must be avoided when pushing out. These include:

- Pushing to easy shots that your opponent will take and make.
- Pushing to easy safeties that your opponent will play, leaving you hooked.
- Pushing to your weaknesses. Your opponent may pass the shot back to you if they feel your odds of success are far less than theirs.
- Pushing to your opponent's strengths. You can avoid this mistake by paying attention to your opponent's game.
- Pushing to sure sellouts.
- Thinking that distance alone makes a push out acceptable.

The 40-60 Rule of Push Outs

The objective when pushing out against a smart player is to gain a slight advantage over your opponent. In the long run, you cannot expect to win control of the table more than 50-60% of the time when playing against a knowledgeable opponent. When your pushout leaves your opponent an easy shot or safe, you lose. The same goes when you pushout to an overly difficult shot or safety. When pushing out, look for the middle ground where you and your opponent have a 40-60% chance of winning control of the table.

The matrix below shows the probable results for push outs that leave your opponent with a shot or safety in any of five levels of difficulty. You should always avoid pushing out to levels 1 and 5. You may get away with playing a pushout in levels 2 or 4 if your opponent is a poor strategist. Against a smart opponent, most of your pushouts should be confined to level 3.

Push Out Decision Making Matrix

Difficulty	Who Shoots	Probable outcome	Strategy
1 Very tough	You'll have to shoot	A loss is very likely	Very poor
2 Tough	Hope your opp. Takes	Odds favor non-shooter	Bluff/Poor
3 Average	Favors neither player	Game is up for grabs	Realistic
4 Easy	Hope you get to shoot	Odds favor shooter	Bluff/Poor
5 Very easy	Opponent will shoot	A loss is very likely	Very poor

Developing a Winning Push Out Game

Shots

- Master a number of the long distance safeties that you can push out to, or that you are likely to encounter after a push out.
- Learn to pocket at least two or three different types of difficult shots that you can make after a push out. These could include: jump shots, shots off the rail, jacked up shots, etc. The goal is to create a situation where it is heads you win (if you must shoot) and tails you win (if your opponent shoots).
- Execution is always the key. You must be able to execute what you leave yourself, or what you chose to accept from your opponent.

Your Push Out

- Custom tailor your strategy to your opponent's game. The better they play, the tougher you must make things, and vice versa.
- You should expect your opponent to take your push outs most of the time.
- Bluffing can be used effectively against lesser players providing you don't over do it.

Your Opponent's Push Out

- Most of the time you should accept your opponent's push outs.
- If you fall into a pattern of accepting or rejecting certain shots, your opponent will use this against you.

Strategy

- When you are the shooter after a push out, you should be looking to play safe most of the time against above average players. C Players can fire away against other C Players since their games are not usually won or lost until the last 3-4 balls.
- Distance is a key element in push out strategy. Most of the shots and safeties you will push to or consider accepting will be the longer and tougher versions of the shots that routinely appear throughout the rest of the game.
- Use your creativity to keep your opponent guessing.
- Consider strategies for dealing effectively with additional money balls when you are either getting or giving up weight.

Strategy Against Lower Level Opponents

- Accept their push outs and play a devastating hook.
- Let them sell out if you sense they don't really know what to do or they have left themselves in a jam.

Strategy Against Better Players

- Realize that they could be bluffing. Ask yourself if they have really left a reasonable shot or safe? If not, pass.
- They will test you to see what you know, or don't know.
- Think through a reasonable solution and give it your best.
- If you pass, take note of what they do. Learn from your experiences so you'll know what to do next time a similar situation arises.

Basics of Cue Ball Control

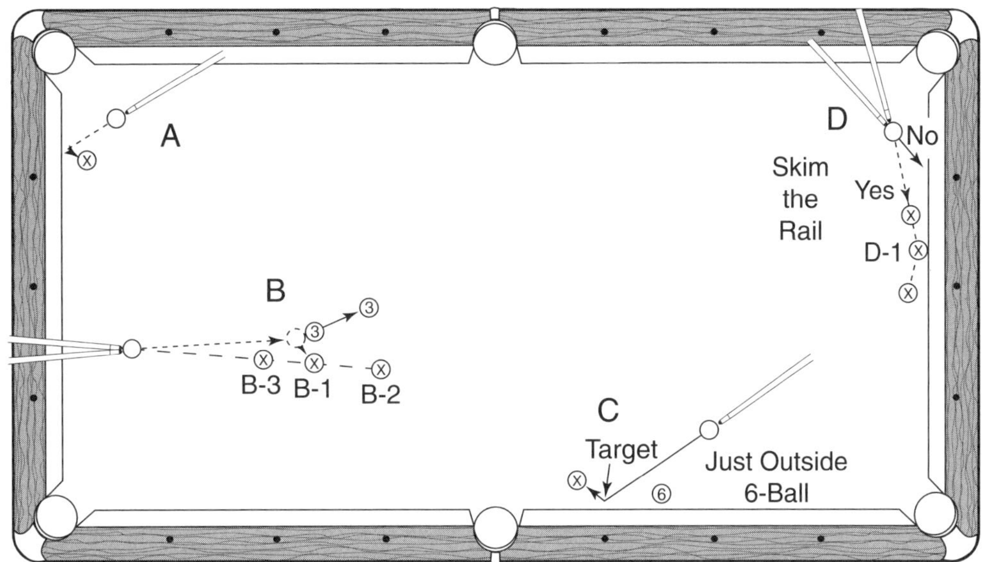

One of the most valuable skills in the push out game is the ability to softly roll the cue ball a short distance to within a couple of inches or less of perfection. This is easier said than done. Not convinced? Set up the cue ball a diamond or two from a rail and try to lag it softy so it dies on the rail. If you can stop the cue ball less than 2.25" from the rail (the diameter of a ball), you have a reasonably soft touch. If the cue ball comes to rest within an inch or less, you have a great touch that you can use to pinpoint your pushouts. A soft touch will enable you do things like:

- Leaving the ball frozen to the rail.
- Leaving the cue ball an inch off the rail (if that is your objective);
- Positioning the cue ball so your opponent is hooked by a precise amount for the purposes of regulating the difficulty of a jump shot.
- Precisely regulating the length of a shot.
- Exposing the edge of a ball for a curve shot or safety.

Position A shows a push out where the goal is to leave the cue ball an inch off the rail so you can elevate easier for a jump shot.

In Position B, the objective is to wind up at B-1. You could accomplish this by rolling straight ahead. If the cue ball rolled to B-2, your opponent would have an easier response. And if the cue ball came up short at B-3, the shot may be too tough. The easiest way to control the cue ball in this situation is to contact part of the 3-ball and let is kill the cue ball so it stops where intended.

You can use other balls or the diamonds on the rail as targets for the cue ball's route. In Position C, the cue ball was sent a quarter inch past the outside edge of the 6-ball. In Position D, the objective is to leave the cue ball close to the rail. This is accomplished by skimming the rail, which gives you the longest target.

Shoot Don't Push

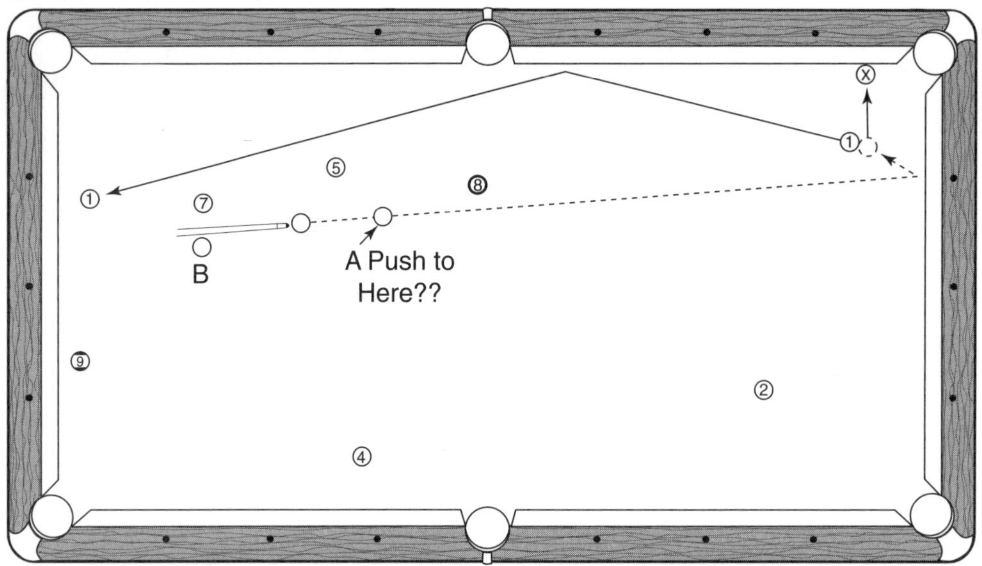

The 1-ball is in front of the pocket so you can't push to a shot. If your opponent passes on all hooks, you could roll up a little further to Position A as shown to make the kick safety a little easier. Against a skilled kicker you could push to Position B in the hopes they will take the shot and sell out. In many cases, however, the best choice is to avoid a push and play the kick safety in the illustration, especially against A Players and above.

Leave Two Tough Shots

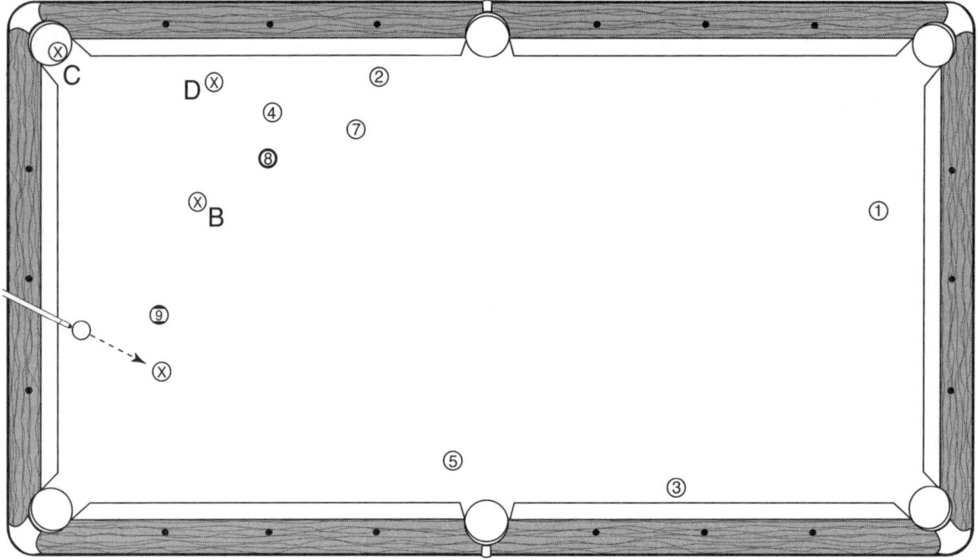

It pays to know when you should tempt your opponent with a makeable shot. The hard part is making the ball and getting shape. The possible positive outcomes are A) they miss the 1-ball; B) they make the ball and get hooked; C) they scratch. If they make the ball and the cue ball stops at Position D, they'll still have trouble getting out, but they could play safe.

Bank or Cut – What's Your Preference?

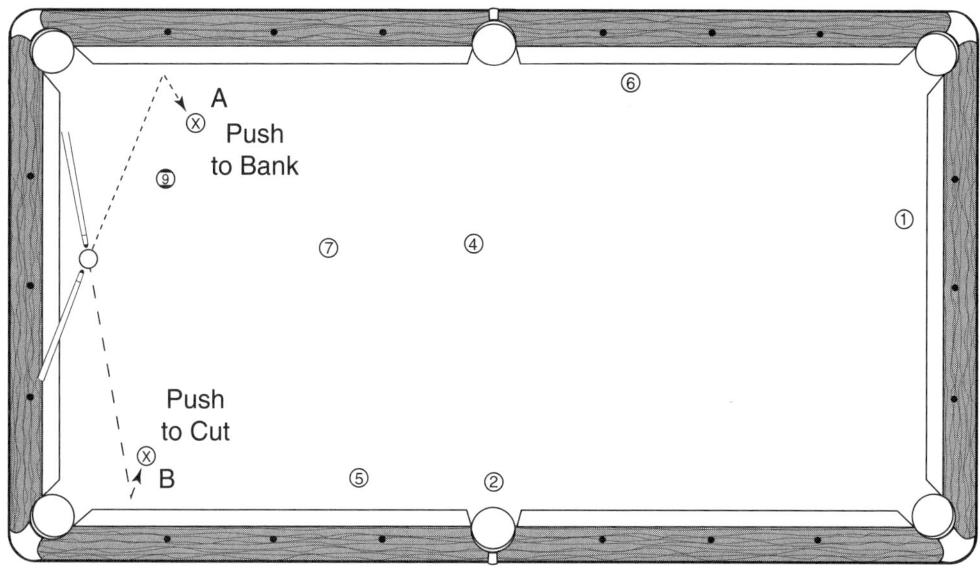

When a good safety is not available, push to a tough shot you can make, and that your opponent is likely to miss. If you are good at banking and your opponent isn't, you'd be wise to push to Position A. Push to Position B, if cut shots are your strong suit and your opponent is weak in this department. Make sure there is always a reward for making a tough shot such as: 1) keeping your opponent from winning; 2) good position on the next ball; 3) position for a safety.

When to Kick at a Pocket Hanger

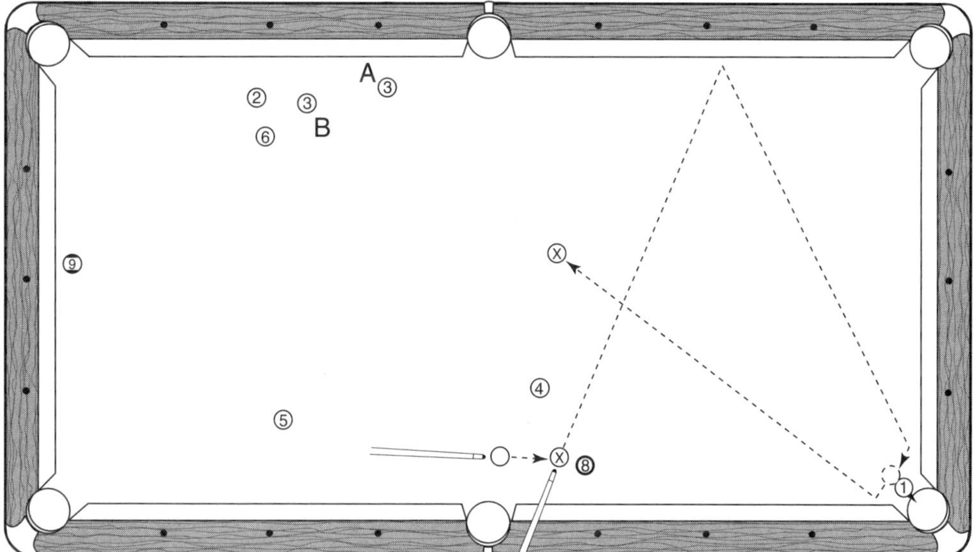

Your opponent has just played a push out, tempting you with a pocket hanger kick shot. You should go for it if the 3-ball is in Position A, but not if the 3-ball is in Position B. You must always consider any decision to accept or reject a push out within the context of the entire layout.

Accept Free Shots

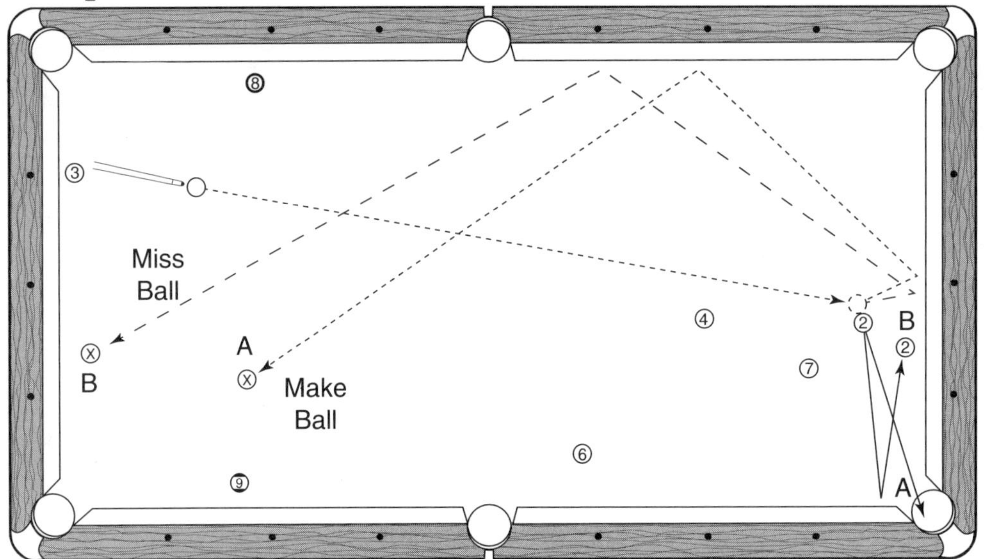

You should take full advantage your opponent's failure to build a penalty for missing into a push out. You have a free shot on the 2-ball. If you slice in the 2-ball, the cue ball will stop at Position A with excellent shape on the 3-ball. And if you overcut the 2-ball, the cue ball will stop at Position B, while the 2-ball will be stationed behind the 4 and 7-balls.

Get It Close to the Rail

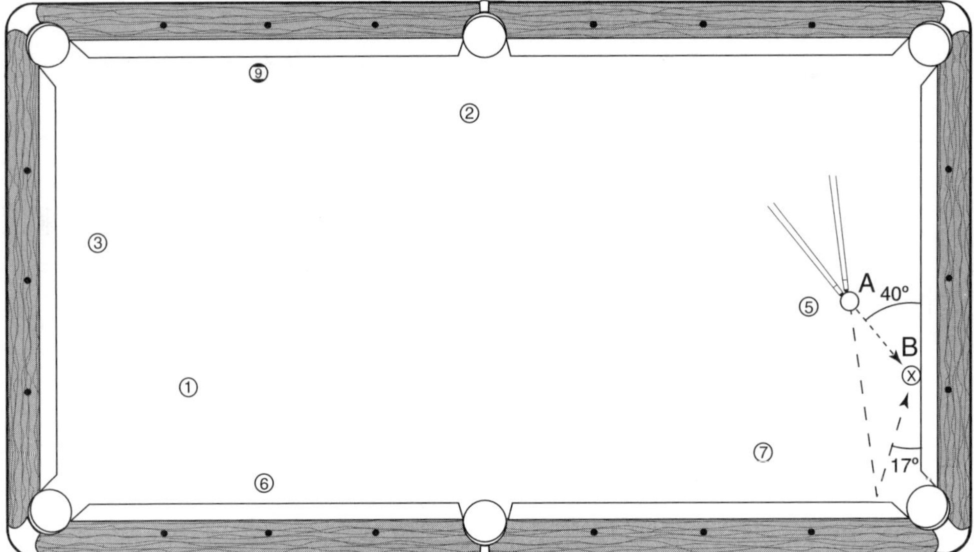

If you like jump shots, you could try pushing to Position A. Another choice is to freeze the cue ball on the end rail, leaving a long tough rail shot. You have a better chance of leaving the ball on or very close to the rail by sending it to the side rail and out rather than shooting directly at the rail.

Push to an Uncertain Hook

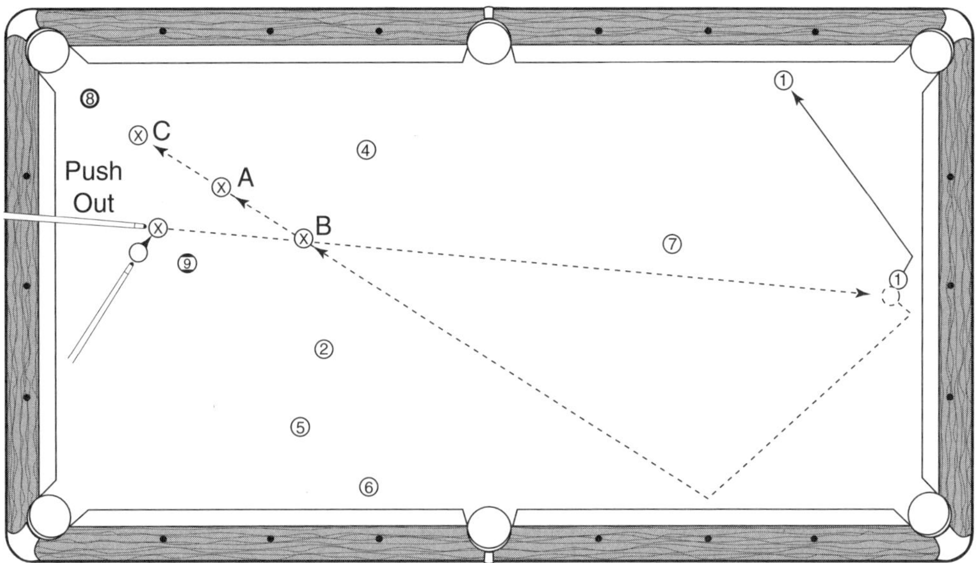

If you are playing a savvy opponent who knows the moves, hopefully you can beat them by setting up situations where execution is the key. Wager your skills against theirs. The 4-ball is a big ball, which can serve as a blocker. However, a hook is still uncertain. Position A is a hook while Position B is a sell out. Position C leaves your opponent a tough shot.

Sucker Shot versus Smart Safety

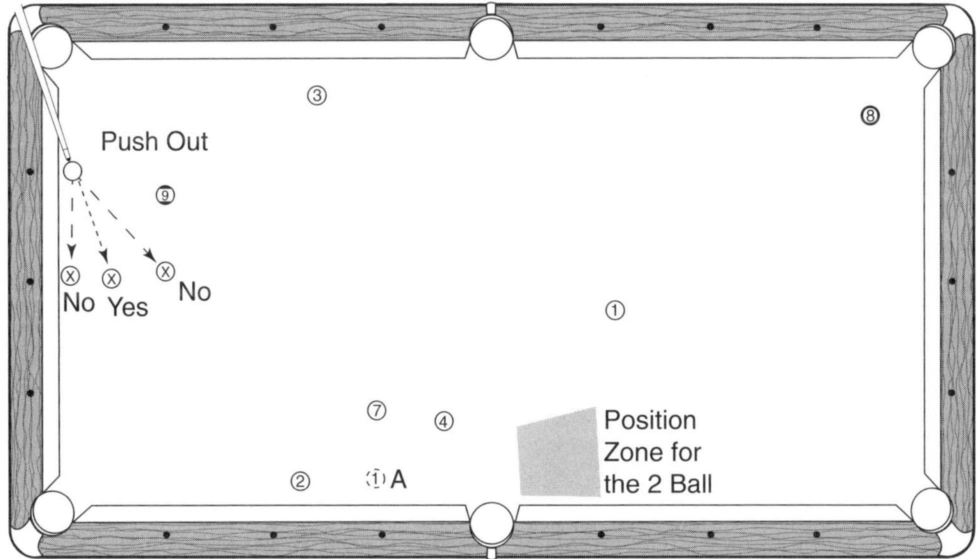

You can take advantage of an overly aggressive opponent by offering them tempting bait as shown. Make it hard for them to get on the next ball. Note getting from the 2-ball to the 3-ball is not easy. Play a safety if they pass on the shot by banking the 1-ball to Position A. If your opponent plays the safety, you will have to reevaluate your strategy. Perhaps your opponent plays a little smarter than you think they do.

Combo in the Lowest Numbered Ball

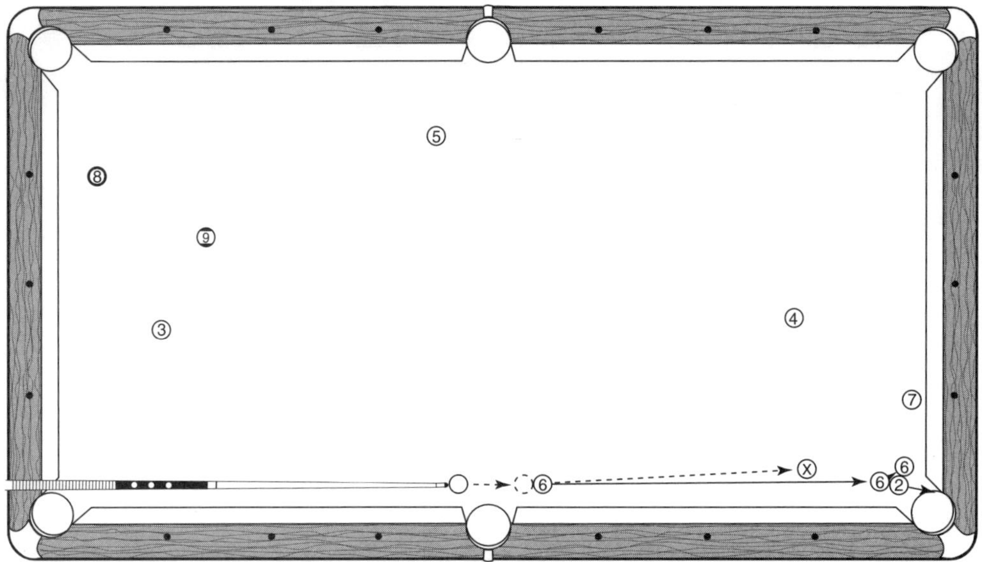

Many players do not know that the rules allow you to pocket the lowest numbered ball on a push out, and that it does not respot. The 2-ball is near the pocket, but even if you could make the kick shot, you would not be rewarded with a shot on the 3-ball. The move is to combo in the 2-ball and send the cue ball to Position X. Now either you or your opponent will have a long and challenging safety on the 3-ball.

Make the Run Much Tougher

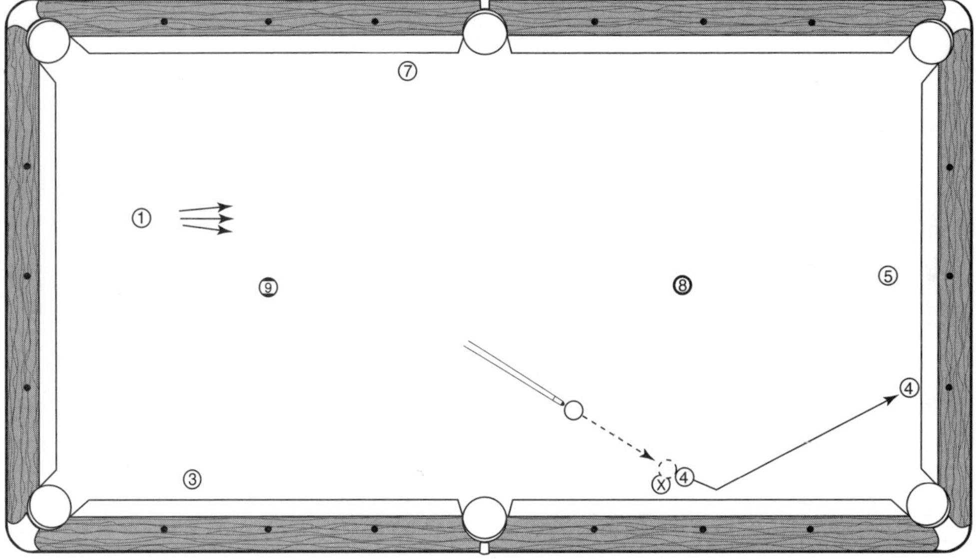

It is often a good idea to make the layout more difficult, especially when there is not a good place to push to a potential safety. A soft and accurate bank on the 4-ball will send it to the end rail opposite the 5-ball. Now it will be very difficult for your opponent to run out even if you leave a shot after they make you kick at the 1-ball.

Pocket a 9-Ball in the Jaws

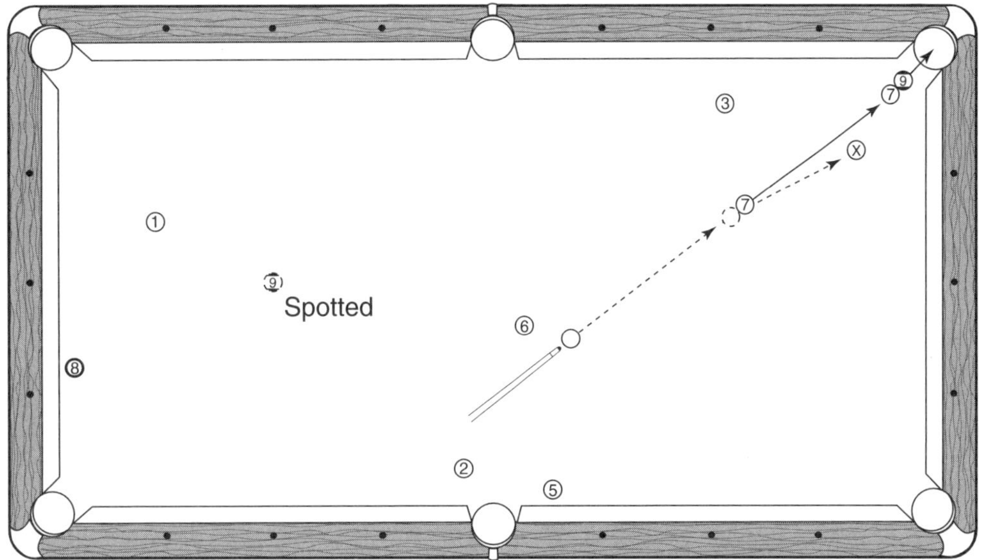

No player ever likes for his opponent to win a game without at least some kind of struggle, but this can happen when the 9-ball ends up in the jaws after the break. Play the 7-9 combo and send the cue ball to Position X, leaving a tough shot or safety. The 9-ball is then respotted.

Tying Balls Up

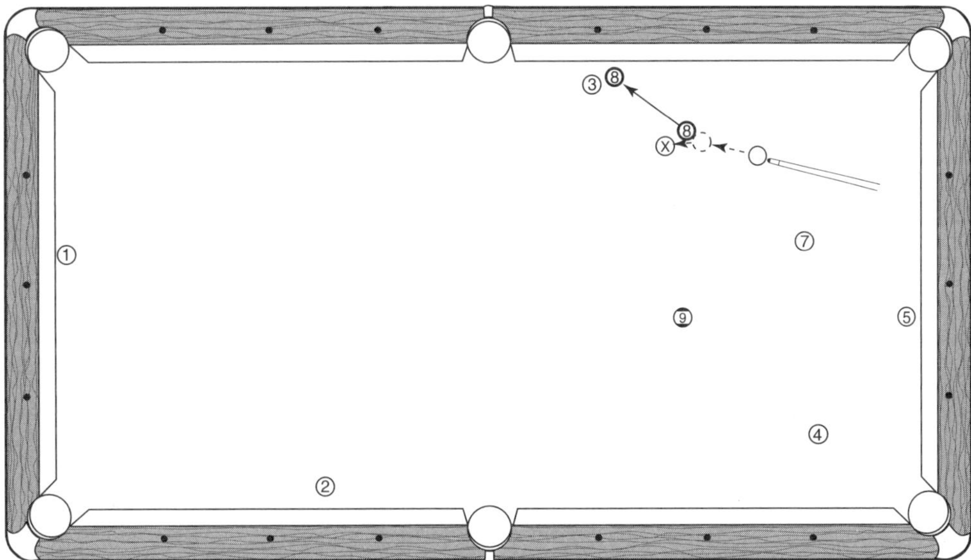

A safety will not be easy at this range with the 1-ball frozen to the end rail. If you push out, you must assume your opponent is going to let you shoot. So before you play a safety that could easily leave a shot, gently roll the 8-ball up next to the 3-ball when you push out. Now it will be hard for your opponent to run out even if you leave them a shot on the 1-ball after your safety.

The Beginner's Big Mistake

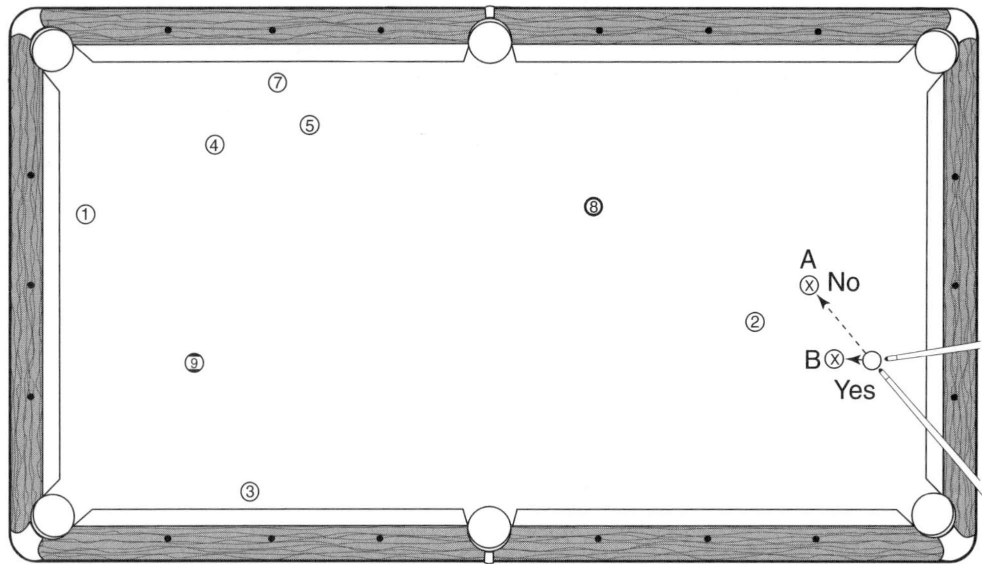

New players to the safety game often think that distance alone makes a good push out. Pushing to Position A gives your opponent an easy hook behind the 4, 5 and 7-balls. A better choice is to push to Position B, which is a moderately difficult kick safety.

Pushing to a Semi-Easy Hook Opportunity

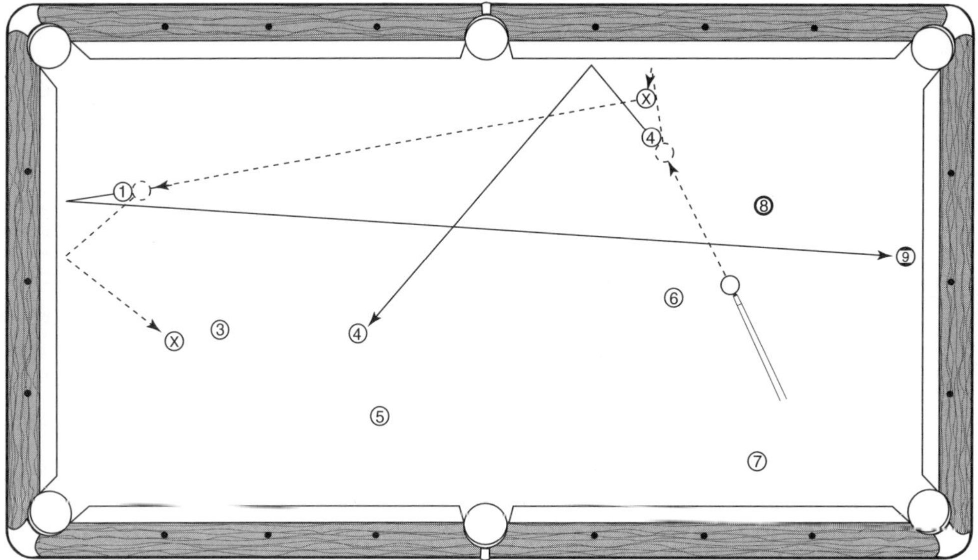

When pushing out, you must carefully consider your opponent's skills and chances for hooking you. Cliff Joyner played this push out against Earl Strickland at the 1999 U.S. Open. Strickland hooked Joyner, who then promptly kicked in the 9-ball! The lesson: a good safety doesn't always guarantee a win.

Be Wary of the Congestion Factor

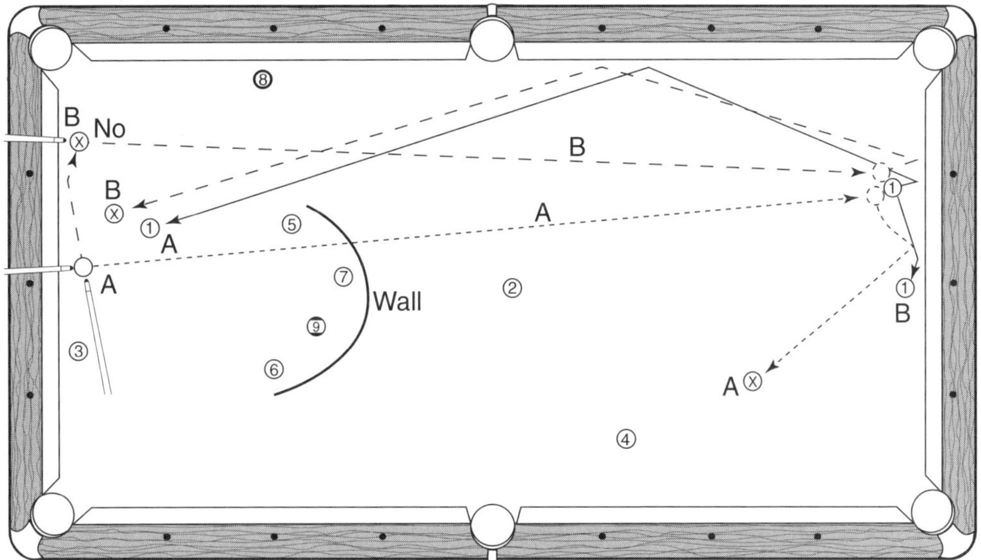

Congested racks can create ample safety opportunities, so you must be very careful not to push out to a situation where your opponent can hook you from long range. In the example, you should take advantage of the wall of blockers (the 5, 6, 7 and 9-balls) by playing Safety A. If you pushed out to Position B, your opponent has the opportunity to play Safety B.

A Bluff Could Lead to a Mental Mistake

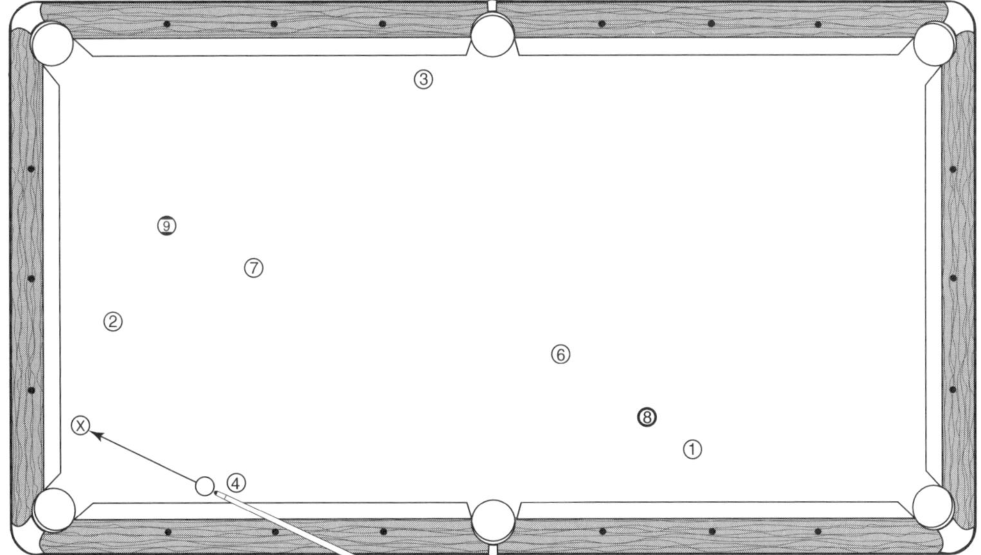

A push out to Position X will leave your opponent with a tough shot on the 1-ball (good) with even tougher shape on the 2-ball (good). In this position, many players get confused and make a mental error. They might overestimate their game and try the monster shot on the 1-ball. Or they could fear your game and feel they must shoot. The lesson: let them think their way into an error.

Push Out to a Better Kick Shot

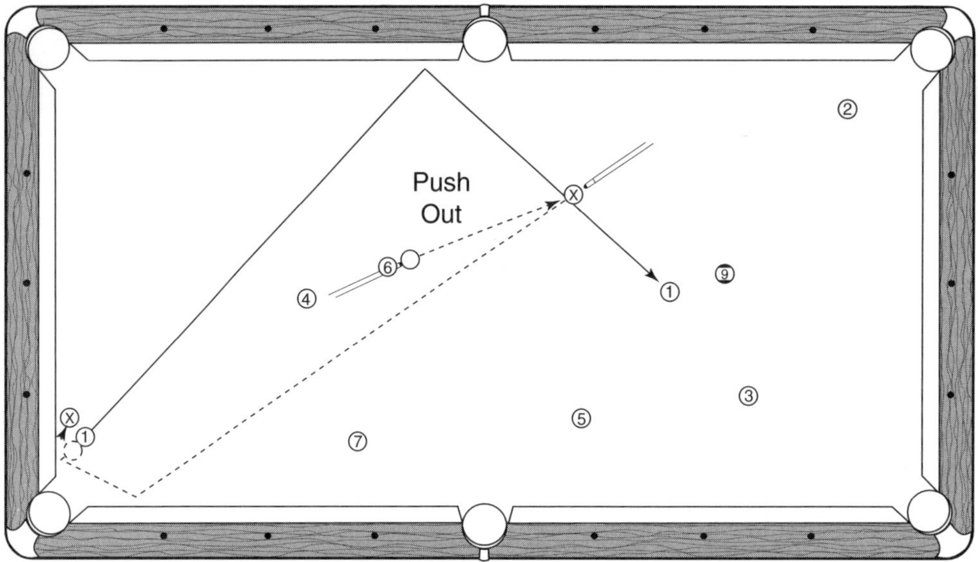

Johnny Archer played this push and kick sequence against Jeremy Jones in the finals of the 1999 U.S. Open. His strategy was to push out to an easier kick, but not such an easy kick that Jones would want to play it. What made Archer's shot possible was 1) seeing it in the first place; 2) rolling the cue ball 18" down the table to the perfect spot; 3) executing the kick shot to near perfection.

Combining Elements of a Push Out

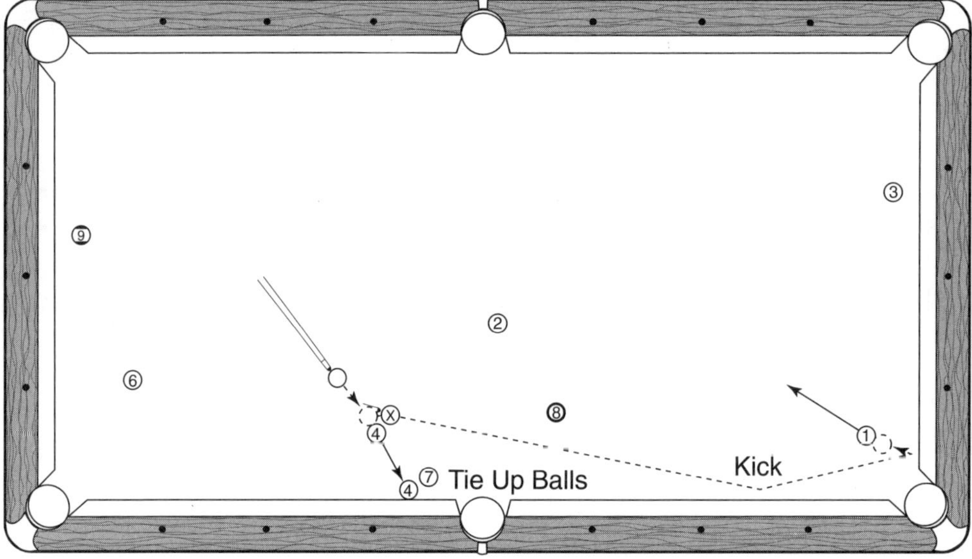

You should be on the look out for chances to combine several elements to create a winning push out. In this position, the 1-ball is in front of the pocket, which means that you must push to a kick or jump shot. Because the kick could leave a shot, you might as well tie up the 4 and 7-balls before kicking at the 1-ball.

Jump or Kick?

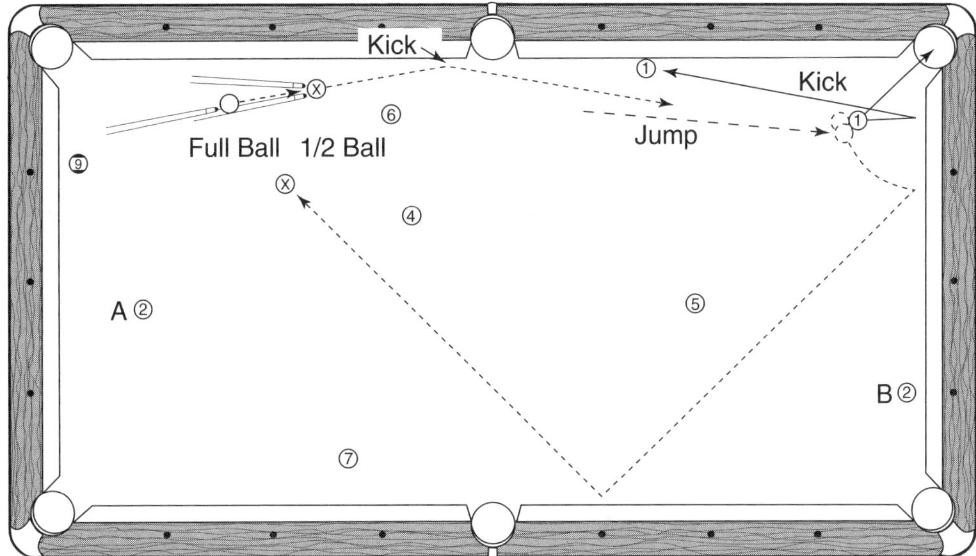

If you are skilled at jump shots and your opponent isn't, pushing out to a jump shot can be another of those deals where you win if you shoot and they lose if they shoot But if jumping isn't your strong suit, tempt your jump shooting opponents with a jump shots that could result in a foul. You should also build a playable kick shot into the push out.

In the example, the cue ball is directly behind the 6-ball. In this position, even a skilled jump shooter might pass on this shot. A push to Position X would be a:

- Poor strategy if your opponent is a good jump shooter and the 2-ball is in Position A.
- Good strategy if your opponent is a good jump shooter but the 2-ball is in Position B, which makes position on the 2-ball difficult.
- Good strategy in any case if your opponent is a poor jump shooter but loves to pull out the fancy jump cue, thinks they are the jump king, and always plays them.
- Good strategy if your opponent is the conservative type who passes on these kind of push outs, you are a good jump shooter, and the 2-ball is in Position A.
- Good strategy if your opponent dislikes jump shots, but thinks they are the second Efren Reyes and plays kick shots that offer little chance of success.
- Poor strategy if your opponent is a skilled kicker who can hit the proper side of the 1-ball if they miss, sending the 1-ball up the side rail as shown, leaving you with a tough safety.

This exercise shows that there is not always a pat answer as to what is the ideal strategy on a push out. In order for you to make the best choice, both you and your opponent's skills must be carefully weighed.

Cluster Balls Past Your Money Ball

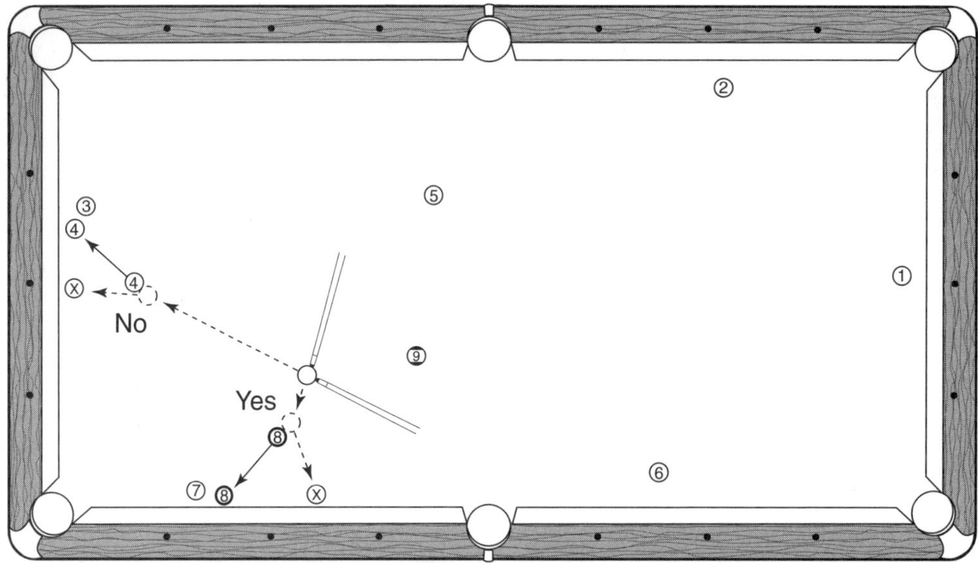

You can employ the strategy of tying up balls, which we discussed earlier, with great effect when you are being spotted the 7-ball or more. The strategy is to tie up the balls past your money ball, making it more difficult for your opponent to run out while leaving the balls you must make in the clear. In the example you are getting the 6-ball. When pushing out, the move is tie up the 7 and 8-balls, not the 3 and 4-balls.

Get Your Money Ball in Front of a Pocket

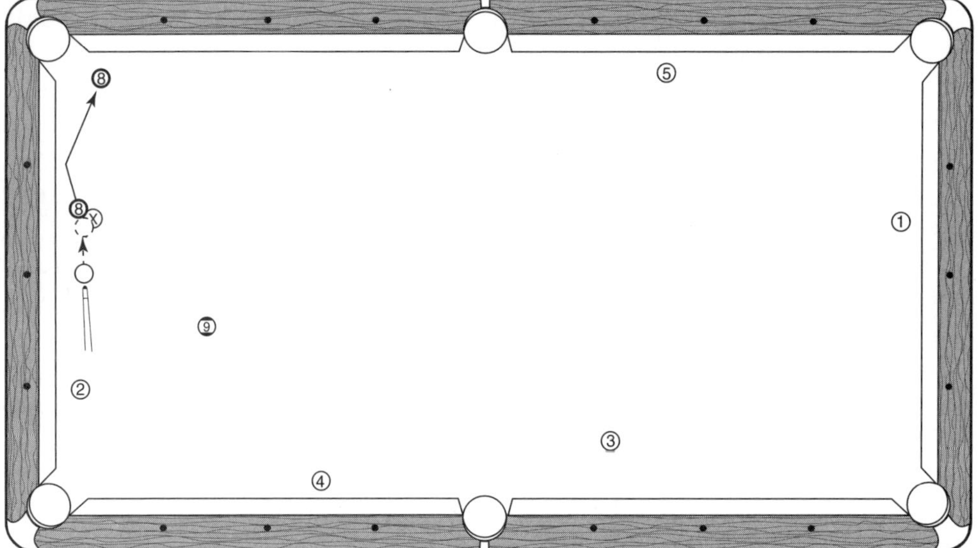

When you are receiving a spot, you can force your opponent's hand when pushing out by bumping a money ball close enough to the pocket that they must think long and hard about letting you shoot. By bumping the 8-ball in front of the pocket, you have set up a winning bank combo that your opponent will hate to shoot, and that he will dislike having you shoot.

CHAPTER 11

SAFETY PLAY

"Now if I'm playing good and thinking correctly I like my opponent to really have to work for even the semblance of a good shot."
Grady Mathews

A golfer who is facing a 270 yard carry over water to the green is better off laying up short rather than trying for the putting surface. The golfer is playing the percentages while trying to avoid a disaster. Strangely enough, however, pool players facing similarly long odds will try heroic shots that have close to zero odds of success.

I suspect that pool players are a little more foolhardy than other sportsmen because the penalty for failure does not seem as great, nor is it as obvious. After all, when you miss, you get to sit down and sip on your favorite beverage for a while. If, however, your goal is to win at Nine-Ball, you simply must avoid taking unrealistic chances, especially when a solid safety is readily available.

You must be willing to give up the table and play safe, which may go against the grain of many readers. Those of you who dislike playing defense must understand that if you develop a strong safety game you will get the table back quickly enough. When you are faced with an option between a safe and a shot, take a moment to coldly calculate the odds. If the situation clearly suggests that a safety is the better choice, you must quell your urge to fire away and instead send the cue ball snugly behind a well-positioned blocker.

Mindset for Safety Play

If you are gravitating to Nine-Ball from the world of Eight-Ball, you may be accustomed to playing with people who look down on safety play. To be successful at Nine-Ball, you will need to adopt a new mindset towards defense. If your opponents cry that you are playing dirty pool, you should take it as a compliment that your safety skills are improving. Besides, in today's world of pool, knowledgeable opponents will say nothing, or good shot, when you lock them up tight because they know it's all part of the game. And they'll most certainly return the favor as soon as the opportunity presents itself.

In Nine-Ball, safeties are commonly used by players of all levels of skill, so you might as well join them in making full use of these defensive maneuvers. After adopting a mindset for safety play you will quickly begin to see how your new found defensive skills give you a chance to ignite your offense. In most situations where there is a choice between a safe and a hard shot, the skill required to play the safety is far less demanding. And yet a well played safety can go just as far, if not farther, towards helping you win a game than the most heroic of super shots.

Good safety play will help you win the battle for control of the table. In addition, an airtight safety game can frustrate and demoralize your opponent. For many of you, the ability to consistently recognize and execute a few basic safeties can alone make you 10-20% better almost overnight.

Safety battles are like tennis rallies or pitcher/batter duels. They can be decided on one shot, or they may last several turns. You should look forward to these encounters, especially if you are the superior defensive player.

Defensive Goals

When playing offense, the object is crystal clear: make the ball and play good shape. When playing safe, there are many possible objectives, which are largely determined by the position of the balls and your skill at defense. Possible safety objectives include:

- Hiding the cue ball behind a blocker.
- Leaving a long and difficult shot or safety.
- Separating a cluster while hooking your opponent.
- Setting up a combo on the 9-ball.

You will see these objectives met over and over again as we proceed through the diagrams in this chapter. The safeties in the illustrations will appear in your games. When they do, you will know what objectives can be sought by each type of defensive opportunity.

Rating the Quality of Your Safeties

The very best of your safeties will give your opponent little or no chance to hit the next ball, which, of course, means you will return to the table with ball in hand. The worst safeties provide your opponent with an easy shot or chance to hook you the way you wished you had hooked them in the first place. The results of your safeties will largely speak for themselves.

The Spectrum of Safeties

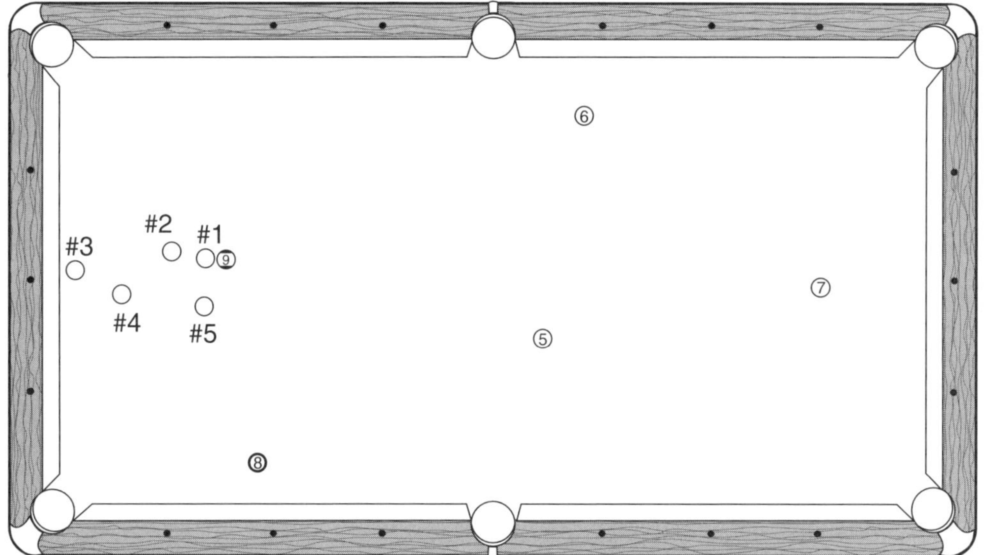

The illustration shows five cue ball locations that are a result of an attempt to play safe. They are graded on the Spectrum of Safeties, which appears below.

1 Excellent - You get ball in hand on your next turn.

2 Good - Your opponent is hooked but has a fair chance of hitting the ball. However, the odds are good that they will leave you a shot or an easy safety with which you can lock them up tight.

3 Average - Your opponent may be hooked with reasonably good chance to hit the ball and quite possibly return the favor. They may also have a clear shot at the ball which gives them a fair shot at making a tough shot or hooking you with a well played safety. The outcome of the game is basically a 50/50 bet with a so-so safety.

4 Poor - Your opponent is the favorite to win the game thanks to a below average quality safety.

5 Awful - The lowest quality safeties immediately make your opponent the heavy favorite to win the game. A poor safety has about the same effect as missing a shot that leaves an easy run out for your opponent.

The spectrum of safeties above will help you evaluate the quality of your safeties. If most of your safeties rate a level 1 or 2, you are playing solid defense. Accu-Stats considers a 3-5 as a mistake when computing their performance average. If your appraisal of your safety play indicates that the majority result in a level 3 or below, you have discovered an area of your game that can provide you with some substantial and immediate improvement. Some steps for improving your safety play include:

- Raising your ability to execute the safeties you choose to play.
- Learning to recognize additional opportunities to play safe.
- Exercising your imagination when a defensive maneuver is not obvious at first glance.

Skills for Excelling at Safety Play

Mastering the Basics

Cue ball control is the foundation for good safety play, just as it is when playing position on offense. You must be able to send the cue ball along the correct path at the required speed so it will arrive at its predetermined destination. In the discussion that follows we'll discuss the many skills that can enable you to control the cue ball and that can provide the foundation for a solid safety game.

Hitting the Object Ball the Correct Thickness

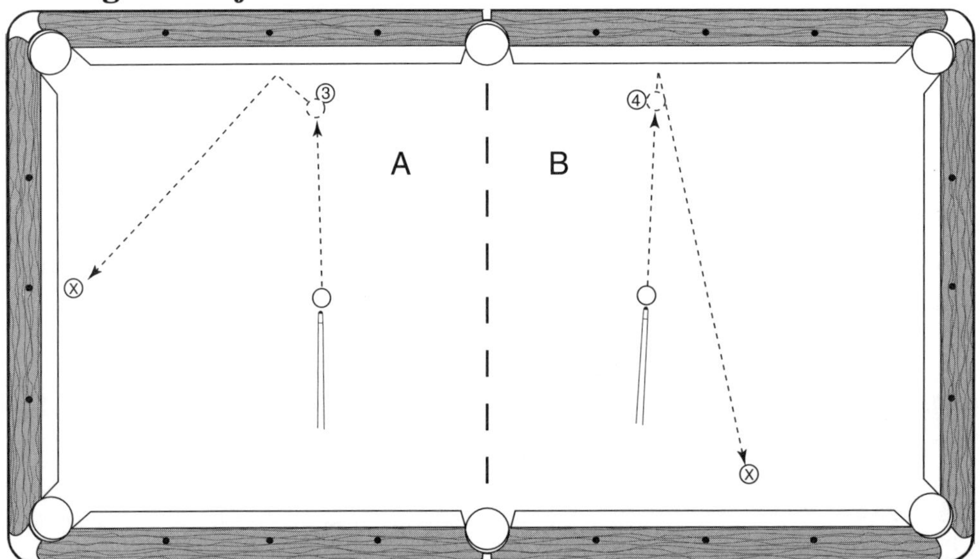

You can exert great control over the cue ball's direction and rolling distance by hitting the correct amount of the object ball. Part A of the diagram shows the path the cue ball would take after a half ball hit on the 3-ball. In Part B, a thin hit on the 4-ball will produce the route shown. It is often suggested that you look at the object ball as a pie that can be cut into several sized pieces. The recommended sizes come in the following increments: full, 3/4, 2/3, 1/2, 1/3, 1/4, 1/8, and 1/16 (for those with great vision). If you can master the cue ball's path after it contacts various amounts of the object ball, you will be able to access a variety of safety zones with the skill of a first rate pool surgeon.

Controlling the Cue Ball's Path off the Rails

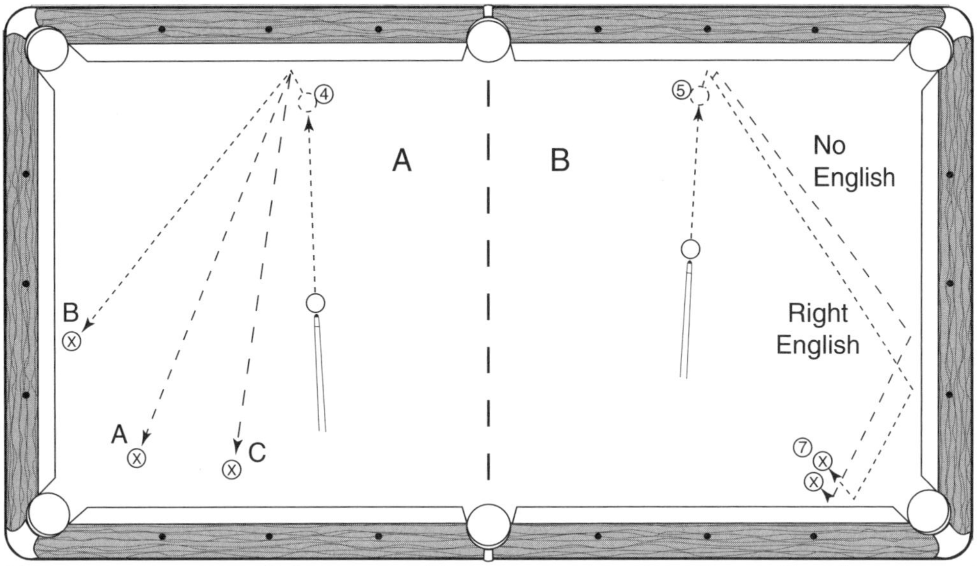

The proper use english can enable you to pinpoint the ending location of the cue ball after it has contacted one or more rails. In Part A, Route A shows the cue ball's path after a thin hit on the 4-ball using no english. When you apply outside english (left in this position) the cue ball will rebound at a significantly wider angle as shown by Route B. Outside english is commonly used on off the rail safeties to better control the cue ball's direction and rolling distance. Keep in mind, however, that this kind of shot requires a fine touch. A common mistake is to apply too much english, which causes the cue ball to overrun the safety zone.

Inside english (right in this example) is demonstrated by Route C. Notice how the cue ball's path is somewhat narrower compared to when no english was used. Inside english slows down the cue ball, so you must guard against hitting this type of shot too softly.

Part B demonstrates a familiar three rail safety. Most players find it easier to control the speed and distance on this shot by hitting the object ball (the 5-ball) thinner with half tip of right english. The alternative is to hit the 5-ball a bit fuller with a slightly firmer stroke, which will send the cue ball down the a slightly different path to behind the 7-ball.

The Angle of Departure

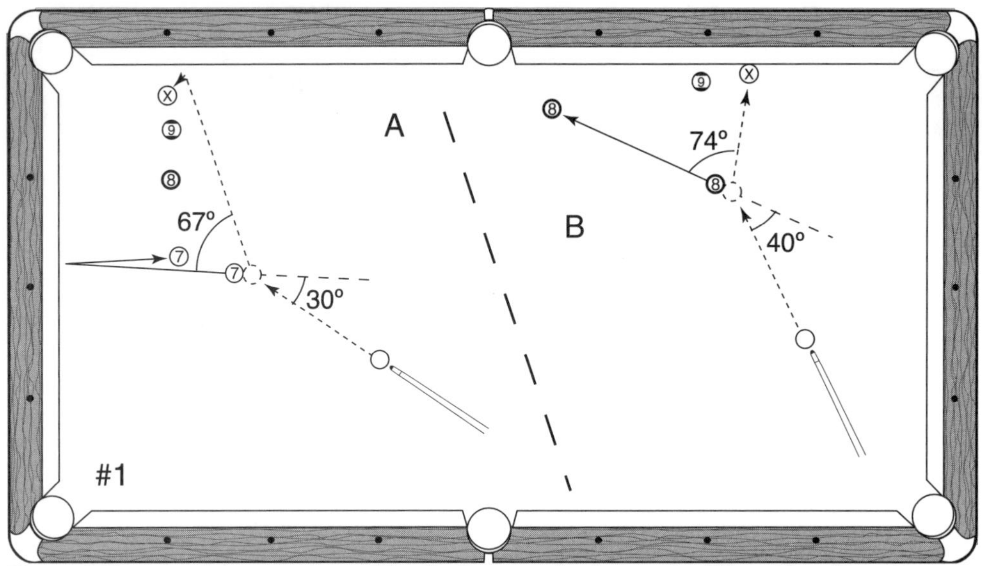

One of the most accurate methods for precisely controlling the direction on safeties is to employ the angle of departure. On cut shots hit with a very soft follow stroke, the cue ball will only follow the tangent line for a very brief instant (too short to show on the illustration) before it straightens out and then follows a path that corresponds to the cut angle. In Part A of Diagram #1, the 7-ball was cut at a 30-degree angle. This leads to a 67-degree angle of departure. The cue ball will predictably follow the path shown and snuggle up behind the 9-ball. Part B shows a 40-degree cut on the 8-ball. This corresponds to a 74-degree angle of departure. On this commonly played safety, a fine touch was required to keep the cue ball from bouncing too far off the rail.

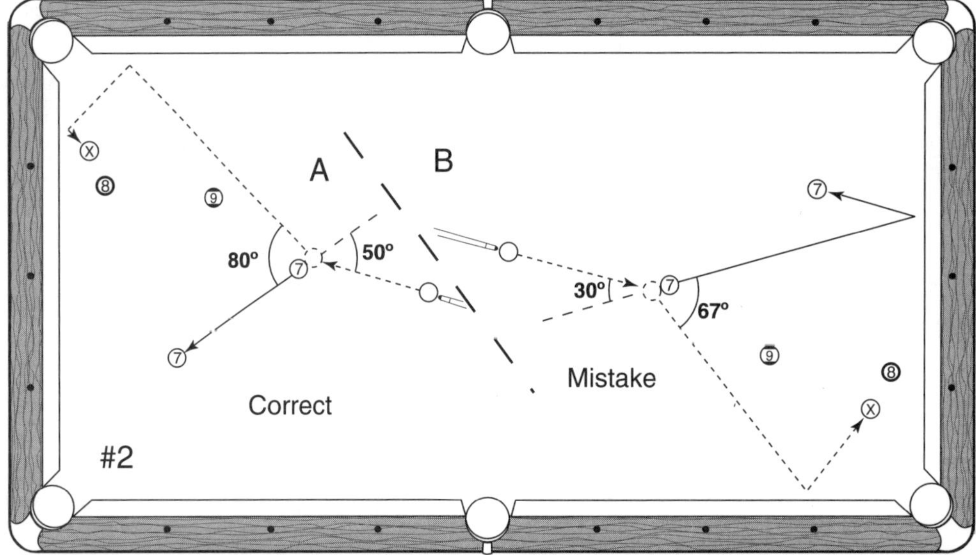

When using the angle of departure, keep in mind that you can adjust the cut angle on the object ball to match the desired path for the cue ball.

In Part A of Diagram #2, the correct cut angle of 50 degrees enabled the cue ball to travel two rails to behind the 8-ball. Part B shows a very common mistake in safety play: a too full hit on the 7-ball (30-degree cut) , which resulted in an overly shallow angle of departure. The safety failed to result in a hook as intended.

Angles of Departure

Cut angle	Angle of departure	Cut angle	Angle of departure
10	33	30	67
15	25	40	74
20	33	50	80

The Thin Hit

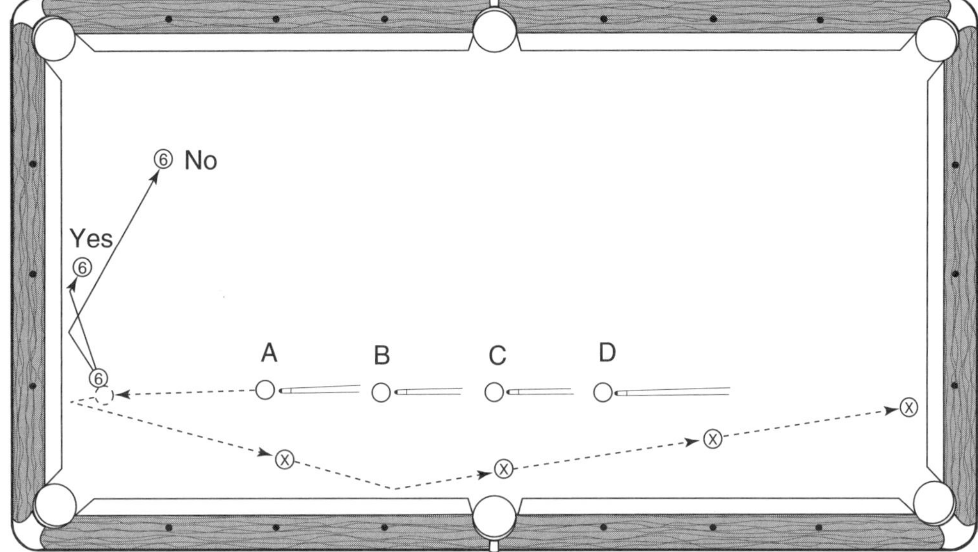

The ability to hit the object ball thinly is an extremely valuable skill in Nine-Ball. It can enable you to play tight safeties. Thin hits can also bail you out of a jam when your opponent has left a considerable distance between the cue ball and object ball. There are two common mistakes when playing these safeties: hitting the ball too fully for fear that you might miss it entirely, and trying to hit the ball so thin that you miss it entirely.

To cure these maladies and gain mastery of this skill, practice thin hits similar to the ones shown in the diagram below. Start with the cue ball at Position A and work your way back to Position D or beyond. Shoot the cue ball at different speeds so it lands in the four positions shown. Observe the ending location of the object ball. The idea is too hit it as thin as possible so that it stays near the end rail. A too full hit on the object ball will result in the error in the illustration. There are two main purposes to this drill: 1) improve your skill at thin hits, 2) to gain an understanding of the practical limits of this shot, taking into consideration your unique level of ability.

Draw Control

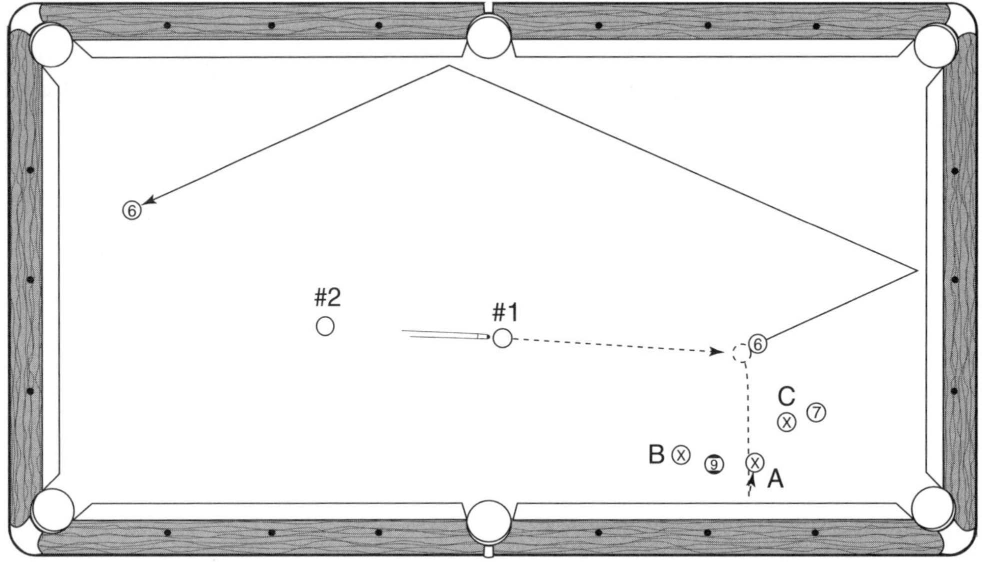

Sending the cue ball a long distance with draw takes great control and requires a high speed of stroke, which could propel the object ball to an unfavorable location. Because of this, on most draw shot safeties you will use a relatively soft draw stroke to send the cue ball a short distance to a position behind a blocker. On most safeties using draw, you will be making a nearly full hit on the object ball while having the cue ball drift sideways behind a blocker, as shown with the cue ball in Position #1 in the illustration above. When this safety is played correctly, the cue ball will nestle in behind the 9-ball. If you hit the 6-ball too fully, the cue ball would end up around Position B, leaving your opponent with a direct hit or shot at the 6-ball. And if you were to hit the 6-ball too thinly, the cue ball would end up around Position C, again exposing a shot. I suggest that you be watchful for both of these kinds of errors.

With the cue ball in Position #2, you have a longer distance to object ball. To play this shot, you will need to use a drag draw shot. This requires a very low hit on the cue ball with a medium firm stroke. Don't become discouraged if you have trouble at first with the drag draw shot. This is an advanced safety that takes time to master completely.

Safety Skills Inventory

You have to arm yourself with a broad range of skills if your goal is to develop an airtight safety game. I suggest you make a copy of the list of skills below. Rate yourself from 1-10. The safeties in the 1-4 range require your immediate attention. Those that fall into the 5-7 range need work as time is available, while those in the 8-10 category are the safeties that can win you games right now. Take your list to the poolroom and practice the areas where you are weak. The idea is to establish a plan for systematically building your skills in all key departments.

__Hit the object ball the correct thickness
__Control the cue ball's path off the rails without english
__Control the cue ball's path off the rails with english
__The angle of departure
__The thin hit
__Draw control
__Drag draw shots
__A soft touch
__A very soft touch
__Stop the cue ball dead in its tracks
__Float the cue ball a short distance with a firm stroke
__Control over the object ball's path when required
__Send the cue ball through traffic to the chosen destination
__Kicks shots

Knowing When to Play Safe

The next prerequisite for good safety play is the talent for knowing when you should play one. In some cases a safety is obviously the best play. In others instances, however, you must carefully weigh the odds between going for a run and turning the table over to your opponent. You should consider playing safe when:

- You have no shot.
- You have a very difficult shot.
- You have a makeable shot, but can't get position.
- You can improve a layout by separating a cluster or sending a ball to a more advantageous location.
- You can set up an easy combo on the 9-ball.
- You have a safety readily available.

Safety Over a Shot

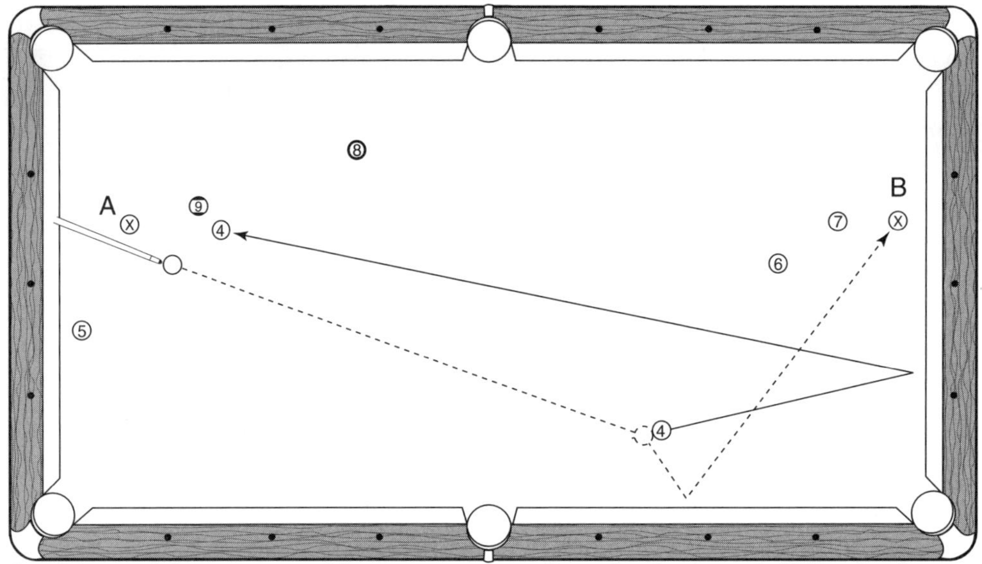

In this position, you could attempt to pocket the long and difficult shot on the 4-ball and draw back to Position A for the 5-ball.. On the 1-10 scale, this is probably at least an 8. If you were to miss, a loss is very likely. The high percentage play is to bank the 4-ball to the opposite end of the table while sending the cue ball to Position B. You will encounter abundant opportunities to play safeties that can enable you to avoid difficult shots that, even if pocketed, will likely lead nowhere. So many players, however, are so offensive minded that they fail to capitalize on chances to lock up their opponent.

Selecting the Best Safety

The ideal safeties are easy to execute, and that result in a hook or difficult kick shot. The worst safeties are those that are tough to execute and yet have a good chance of resulting in a sell out. In the real world, most safeties fall somewhere in between. This means that you will need to carefully weigh the risks and rewards of each option in much the same way that you go about evaluating various position routes.

In the position above, the 7-8 combo is a difficult shot, which makes a safety the logical choice. Part A shows a safety that is easy to execute. A 2/3 full hit will send the cue ball and 7-ball to the positions shown, resulting in a hook. In this position, your opponent should not have too much trouble hitting the 7-ball by kicking off the end rail. If they make a good shot or get lucky, they could send the 7-ball to the opposite end rail and leave you with a tough shot or safety. This safety is easy to execute, but has only a moderate reward.

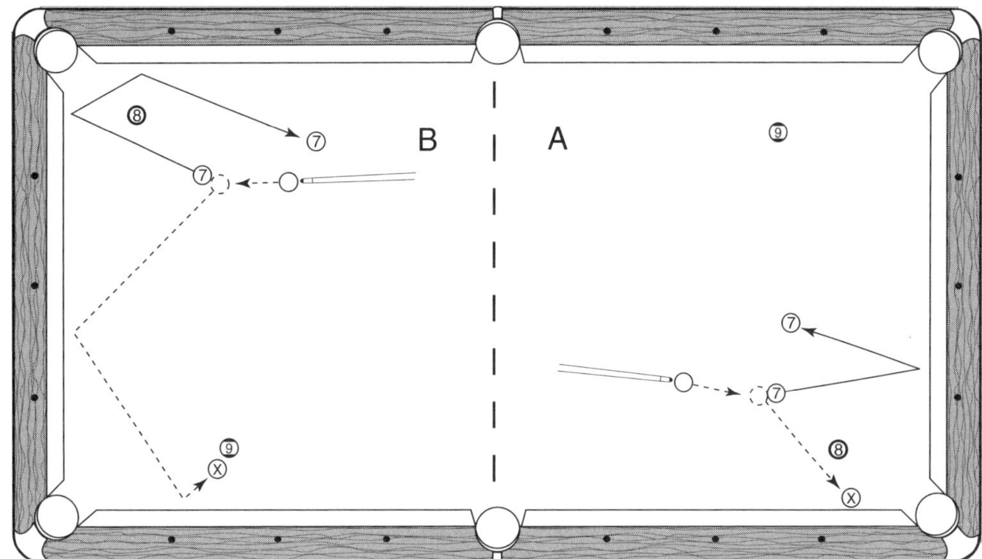

The balls are in the same relative positions in Part B. This time the play was to send the cue ball two-rails over behind the 9-ball. Now your opponent is faced with a much tougher kick on the 7-ball. And even if they hit the 7-ball by kicking off the end rail, a sellout is very likely. The safety in Part B was more difficult to execute than the one in Part A, but it also carried with it a much higher reward.

Which Safety is the Better Choice?

Some of the factors that could influence your decision include:

- Your skill at playing safe. Can you execute the safe in Part B a high percentage of the time? If so, go for it.
- Your opponent's skill at kicking. If your opponent has a poor kicking game, then the safe in Part A may be better. But if they are highly skilled at the kicking game, then you need to make things tough on them by playing the safe in Part B, even if you are not 100% sure that it will result in a hook.
- The score of the match. If both of you need one game, you may pick the easier safe, for example, rather than risk the match on the high risk/high reward safe in Part B.

When you are considering playing a particular safety in competition, the key questions are:

- Do you really know the safe?
- Can you execute it a reasonably high percentage of the time?
- Are you confident that you can execute it under pressure?
- What is your opponent's expected response?
- Is the safety the high percentage choice, all things considered?

TIP: Don't delay the inevitable hook. Know when to take a chance.

Basic Hook Safeties

The most fundamental goal of safety play is to leave an obstacle between the cue ball and the lowest numbered ball. Once you are sure that a prospective safety can meet this fundamental goal, then it is time to consider other possible objectives that can make your opponent's task of avoiding a foul even tougher.

Hitting the Hook Zone

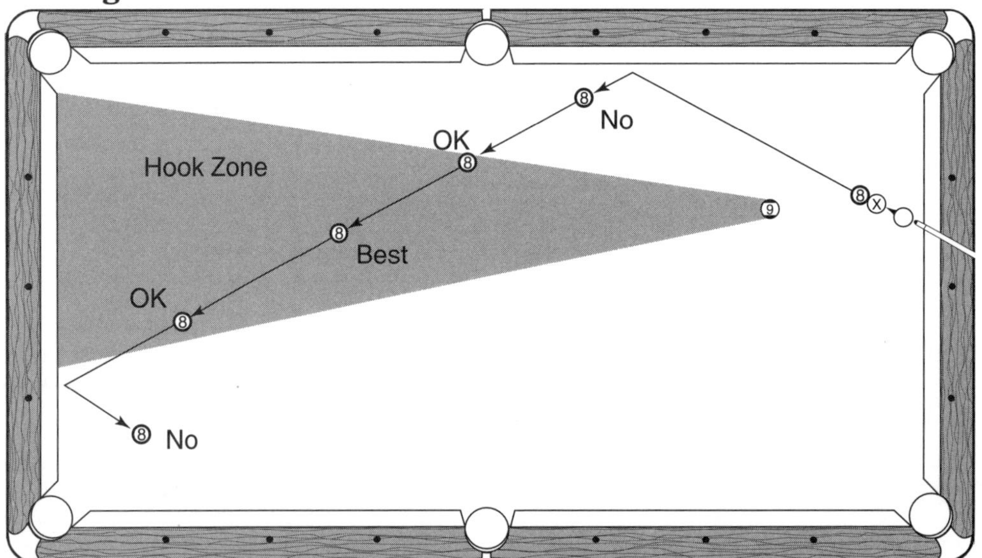

Missing position on the 8-ball could result in the common end game position shown in the diagram above. Since you have no reasonable shot at the 8-ball, it's time to play safe. A stop shot on the 8-ball at the proper speed will leave the cue ball and 8-ball on opposite sides of the 9- ball.

A hook zone is the area of the table where the object ball is shielded from direct contact by the cue ball. The diagram shows the 8-ball in three locations within the hook zone. If the object ball rests in the hook zone, then your opponent will have to play a jump, kick, or curve shot in order to make contact.

One of the beauties of a stop shot safety is that you know exactly where the cue ball will reside, assuming you execute the shot correctly. Any time you can predict the cue ball's resting spot with 100% accuracy, you can also determine the exact location and size of the hook zone.

In this example, sending the 8-ball into the hook zone should not be too difficult since it is over 3' long. Try to send the 8-ball into the middle of the zone as this will give you about a 20-inch margin for error on either side of the bulls-eye. If you hit the 8-ball with too little force, it will stop short of the zone, and that if you strike it too hard, it will leak out of the opposite end of the hook zone.

This safety is the high percentage play. In amateur competition, this safe will win most games, especially if your opponent is not very skilled at kick, curve, or jump shots. Advanced players and professionals dislike leaving the game up for grabs, even when the odds are in their favor. In this position, an A Player may choose to cut the 8-ball slightly left of center with a stun-follow stroke. The idea is to float the cue ball up against the 9-ball. If successful, this would eliminate the jump shot. It would also force their opponents to kick two rails for the 8-ball, which is significantly more difficult than a one-rail kick. The "floater" safety should be mastered in practice before you use it in serious competition. Remember, a well-executed safety of "average" difficulty is normally much better than a "hero" safety that backfires.

Hitting the Hook Zone (2)

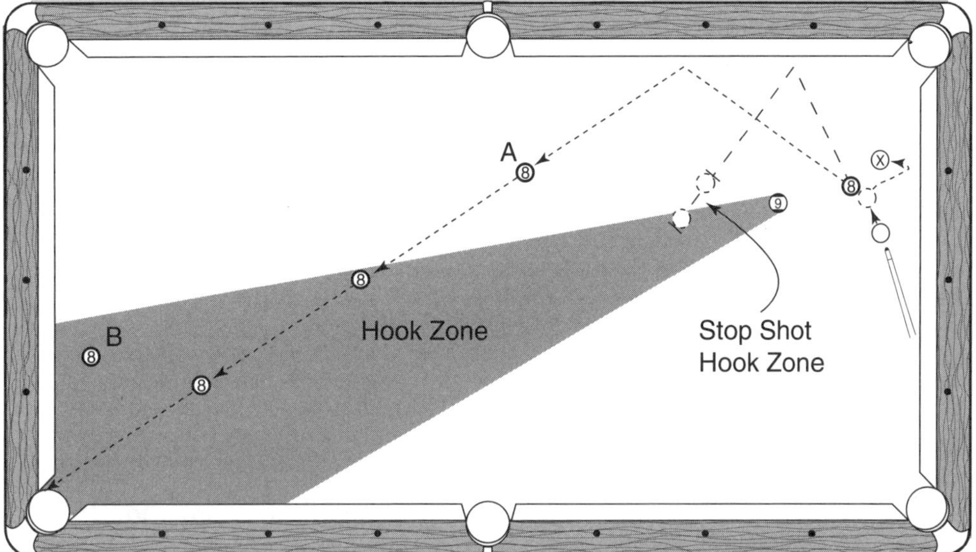

The 8 and 9-balls are in identical locations as in the previous illustration while the he cue ball has been moved a scant 2 1/4 inches towards the bottom side rail. This small difference makes a huge difference in how this safe is played. A straight on stop shot is no longer feasible because the hook zone is only about 5" long. To consistently hit this tiny target would require a superhuman touch.

The better choice is to cut the 8-ball on the right side with draw. This shot will give you a much wider hook zone, similar to the one in the previous illustration The difficulties with this safety are calculating how much of the 8-ball to hit and using the correct speed of stroke. If you hit the 8-ball too easily, for example, it will stop short of the hook zone near Position A, leaving your opponent with a shot. When you are cutting the object ball with draw, your hook zone cannot be as precisely defined as with a stop shot. This suggests that you not attempt to send the 8-ball too far down the hook zone (to Position B, for example) as the thinner hit on the 8-ball would make it even more difficult to control the cue ball.

Eliminating Options

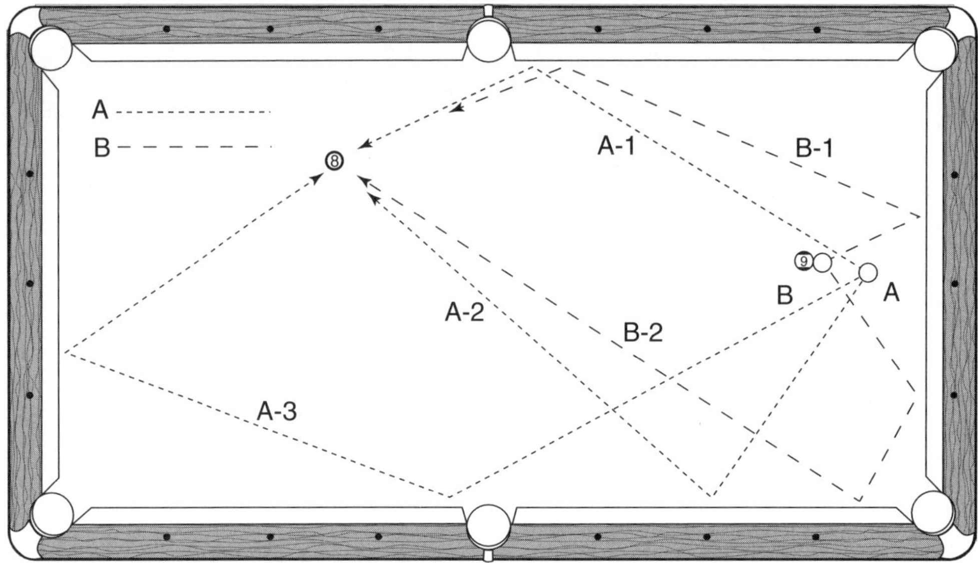

Your best bet when playing safe is to eliminate as many of your opponents options for replying to the safety as possible. This illustration dramatizes the difference between a so-so safety and a "pro" safety. With the cue ball 5" from the blocker (the 9-ball) in Position A, your opponent can hit the 8-ball without much trouble by sending the cue ball down Route A-1. If this safety had appeared earlier in the game and Route A-1 was not available because of a blocker, your opponent would have a significantly more difficult kick down Route A-2. Route A-3 is another possibility.

With the cue ball snuggly up against the 9-ball in Position B, your opponent's chances of hitting the 8-ball have been drastically reduced. Options A-1, A-2, and A-3 have been eliminated. Now he must choose between a 2-rail kick off the short rail down Route B-1, or the equally challenging 2 rail kick along Route B-2. I would rate an average player's chances of hitting the 8-ball from Position A at about 80%. With whitey in Position B the odds are only about 20-30%. The lessons: a few inches can make a huge difference to the quality of your safeties. Leave the cue ball close to the blocker and your odds go way up.

Block the Natural Kick Route

Another way to make life difficult for your opponent is to cut off the natural kick route. This will force them to play a much lower percentage kick route to avoid the obstructer. The 8-ball is positioned along the natural one-rail kick route to the 7-ball. If your opponent chooses Route A, they will have to open the rebound angle by over 20 degrees with a liberal dosage of outside (left) english. It is difficult to regulate large amounts of english properly, which in this cases reduces your opponent's chances of hitting the 7-ball.

Your opponent's other choice is to send the cue ball down Route B on the opposite side of the 8-ball. Reverse (right) english or a hard stroke

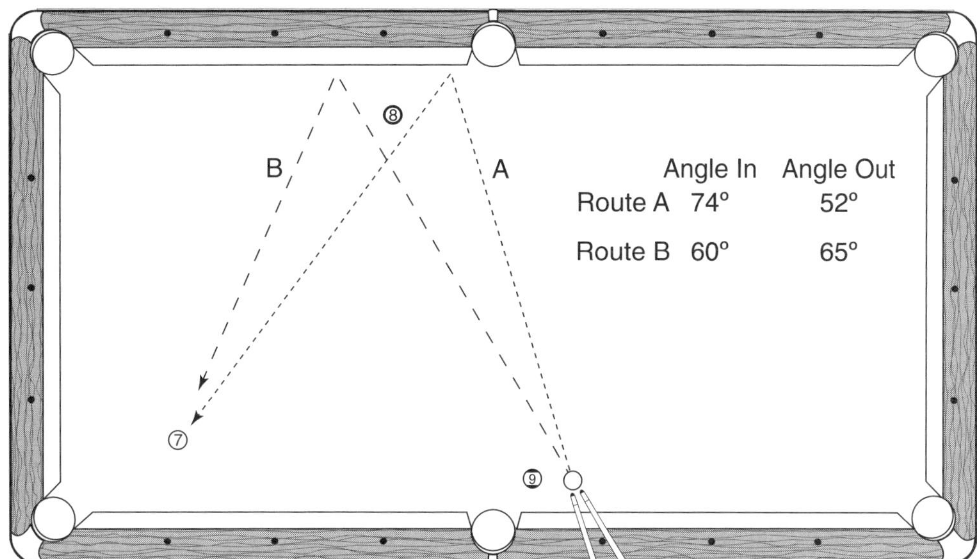

is needed to contact the 7-ball. Most players have even more trouble hitting the object ball when they have to reduce the rebound angle, as with Route B. When playing safe, if you must chose between cutting off one route or the other, it is usually better to eliminate the route that enables them to use outside english.

Hooking Behind the "Big Ball"

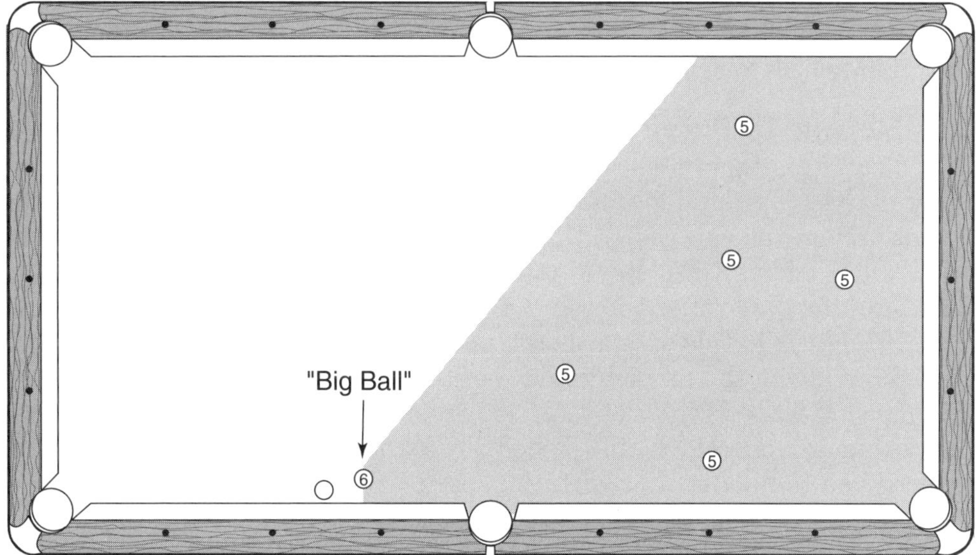

When a blocker is stationed within a ball's width or less of the rail, it is said to be in the "Big Ball" position. Blockers in this position are very effective at shielding the cue ball from the object ball in a large area of the table. Observe that the 5-ball is blocked no matter where it rests within the hook zone thanks to the cue ball's location behind the "big" 6-ball.

Basic Hook

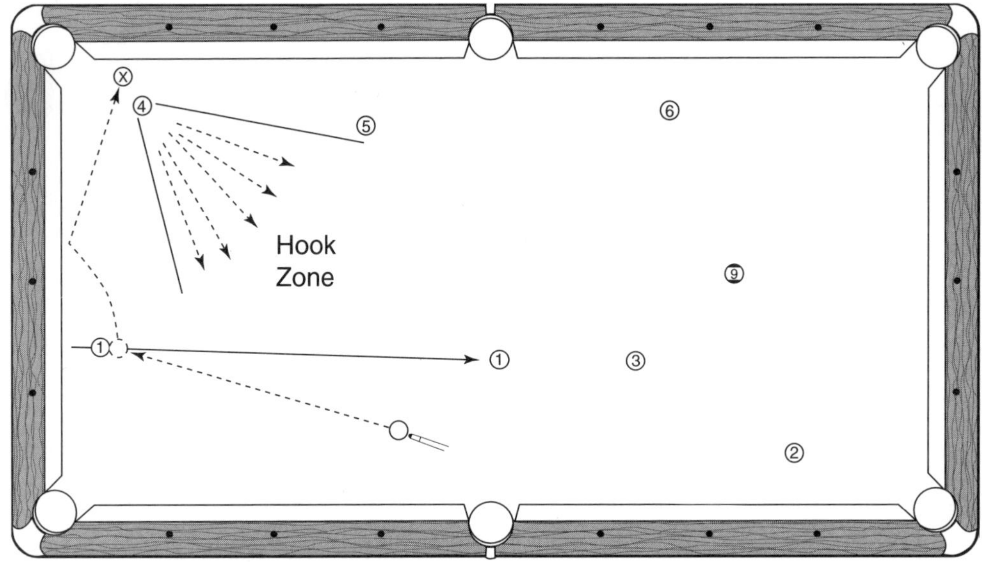

One of the most basic yet effective safeties is to bank a ball down the table while using follow and a soft touch to position the cue ball behind a nearby blocker. Mike Sigel, otherwise known as Captain Hook for his defensive skills, executed this simple but lethal safety to perfection against Nick Varner at the 1990 U.S. Open. Nearly the entire table is blocked from Varner's view. When playing this safety, a nearly full hit makes it easier to control the speed of the cue ball. This is especially important for those players who dislike using soft stroke. The 1-ball was banked directly up the table, which also makes it easy to control its ending location.

Off the Side Rail and Down Table

In the early stages of a game when the balls are spread across the table, there may be a grouping of balls that offers an attractive opportunity for a hook. When you can couple this with distance, you have the makings of a powerful safety. Efren Reyes took advantage of these circumstances to play the safety shown at the top of the next page at the 2000 U.S. Open.

The keys to this safe are both speed and direction. Direction is controlled by hitting the correct amount of the 1-ball and by running english. When you must send the cue ball a long distance off one or more rails, english helps in controlling the speed. The correct application of english enables you to hit the shot with the speed with which you are most comfortable. To fully appreciate the strength of this safety, I suggest you now put yourself in Johnny Archer's position (Reyes's opponent). How would you go about hitting the 1-ball?

TIP: The best route to the object ball after an opponent's safety may be to send the cue ball back along the same route it just traveled to the hook zone. In the example, it leads almost exactly to the 1-ball's new location!

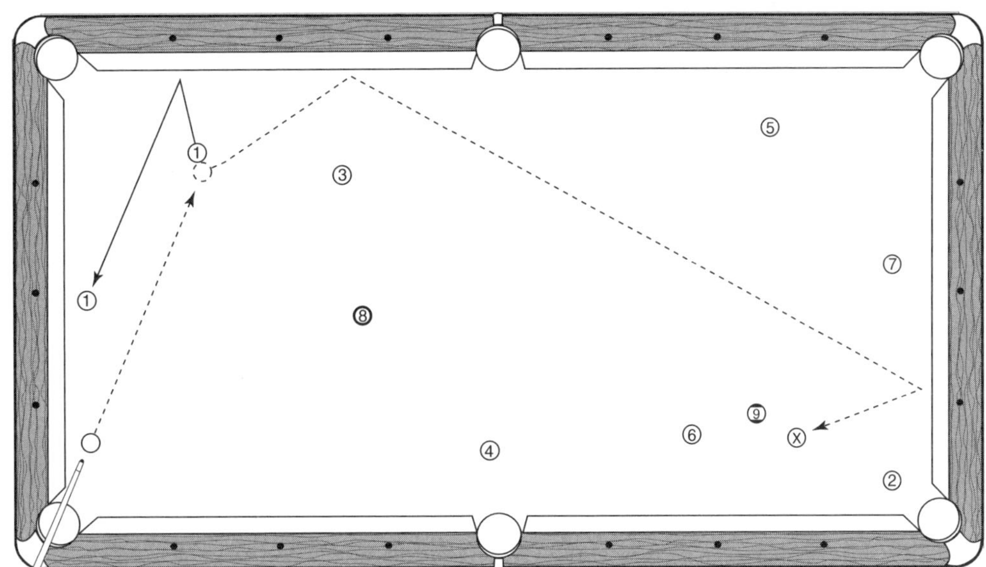

Multiple Ball Hook Safeties

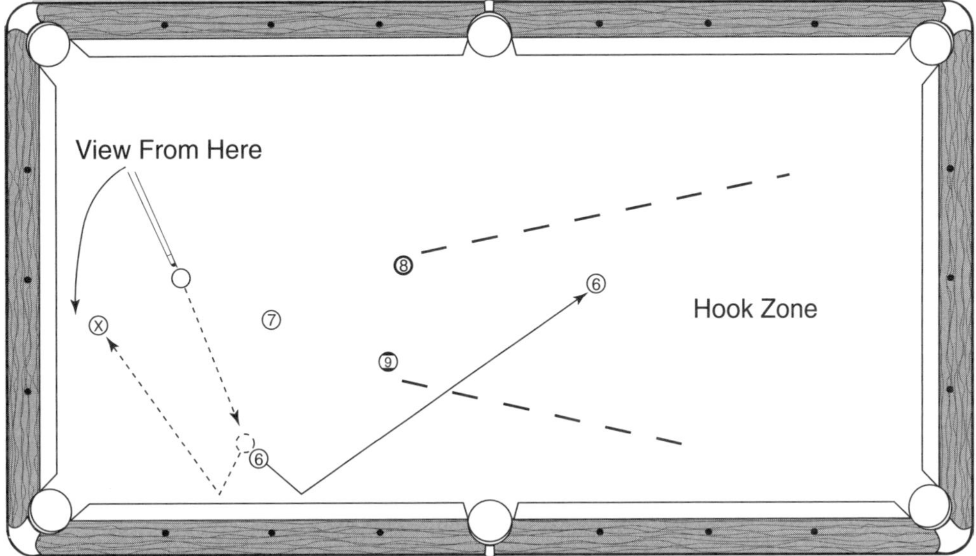

A number of balls may block a large portion of the table, even though they are not necessarily in close proximity. In this position, the safety is not difficult, yet very effective thanks to the location of the potential blockers. The key is to walk over to where you think you would like to send the cue ball. Then look up table to see if there are any gaps between the balls. In this case, the 7, 8 and 9-balls provide a solid wall of protection.

Risk Versus Reward

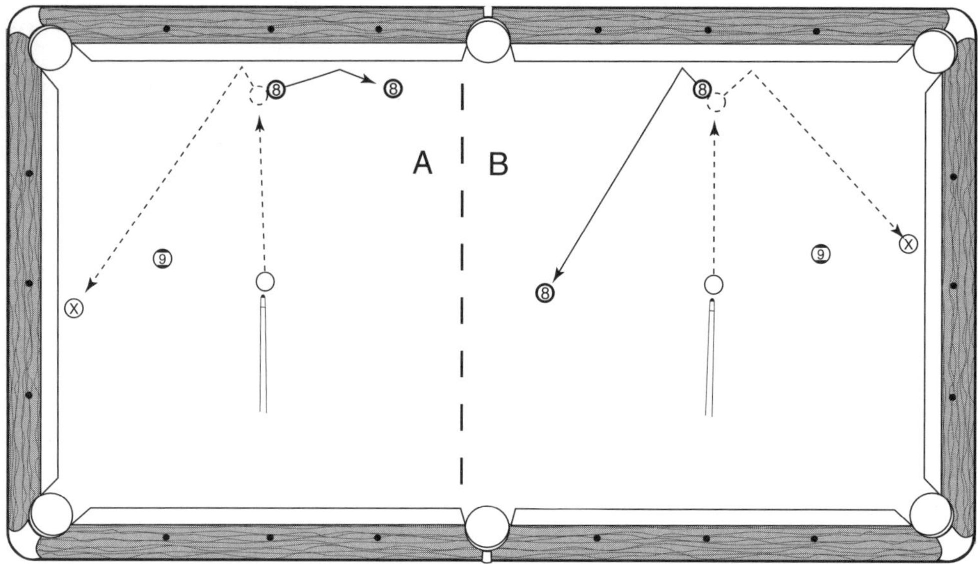

The risk of a safety is very often commensurate with the reward. In Part A, you should be able to hook your opponent behind the 9-ball. A thin hit on the 8-ball with a little left english will work. The keys to this commonly used safety are speed control and hitting the correct amount of the object ball so that it follows the path shown. This safe is not difficult because it is easy to predict the 8-ball's ending location near the side rail. It is always easier to control the cue ball on a safety when you don't have to worry much about the object ball.

The balls are in the same relative positions in Part B. This time a decision was made to hit the 8-ball more fully. The 8-ball traveled to the middle of the table. In this position, your opponent is faced with a much tougher kick shot than in Part A The tradeoff for leaving your opponent with a tougher kick is that this safety is much more difficult to execute. The big key on this safe was in matching the speed of stroke with the fullness of the hit on the 8- ball.

Multi Rail Hook Safeties

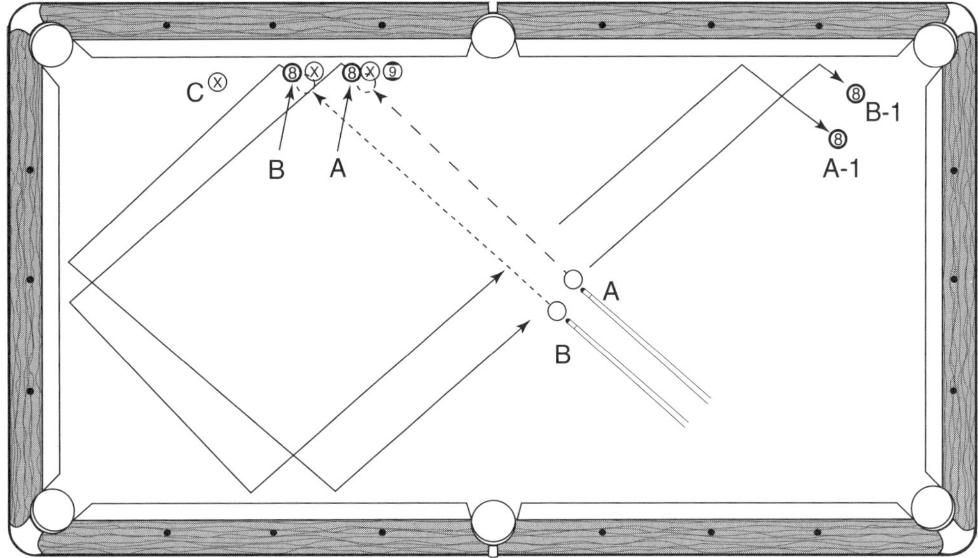

The 8-ball will not go in the upper left corner pocket when the 8 and 9-balls are close together, as shown by the 8-ball in Position A. You could play a bank into the lower left corner pocket, but this shot would require a very hard stroke and/or inside english. In this situation the odds favor the three-rail safety down Route A. Use a firm stroke and hit the cue ball a small fraction below center. You should also aim just a hair to the right on the 8-ball as this will cause the cue ball to drift up against the 9-ball as shown. The cue ball will travel 3 or 4 rails to at or near Position A-1.

Now let's assume the 8-ball is about 6" further down the rail in Position B. With the balls in this position, you could attempt to run out by sending the cue ball across the table and back to Position C. However, this is a difficult shot that requires near perfect speed control. A more conservative approach is to play a stop shot while banking the cue ball three-rails to Position B-1. Hit the 8-ball just a shade on the right side so the cue ball will stop closer to the cushion. This subtle move dramatically increases the size of the hook zone and also makes the kick much tougher. The Lesson: Never overlook the chance to do the little extras that make a safety so much more effective, especially when you can do them with little or no risk.

All levels of players should play the safety with the 8-ball in Position A. With the 8-ball in Position B, the correct decision could vary depending on the situation, how your are playing, and your skill as well as that of your opponent. If you are a C Player, the safety is probably the best choice. B Players may go for the run out if they are playing particularly well, or they might pass on the shot if they are out of stroke. An A Player may feel that his best chance of winning against another A Player who excels at the kicking game is to go for the run rather than leaving the game up for grabs, even if the odds are in his favor.

Controlling the Right Ball is Key

The success of any safety depends on controlling either the cue ball, object ball or possibly even both balls. If you are able to master a variety of cue ball routes across and around the table, you will be able to access blockers and play killer safeties from countless positions. This takes care of the cue ball.

You may be unaware of how far the object ball has the potential to roll when pocketing a shot since its rolling speed is abruptly halted when it enters the pocket. When playing certain safeties, however, controlling the rolling distance and direction of the object ball is the big key to the success of the shot.

The most challenging safeties require you to control both the cue ball and the object ball in order for the shot to be successful. These shots tend to confuse many players because of the need to control the ending location of two balls. You can solve this problem by fixing in your mind exactly what you must do with each ball prior to assuming your stance. The final step is to decide how you want to hit the cue ball (draw, follow, english) and at what speed. Once you get over the shot, your thoughts should be focused on aiming and executing the shot as well as possible.

Airtight Safety

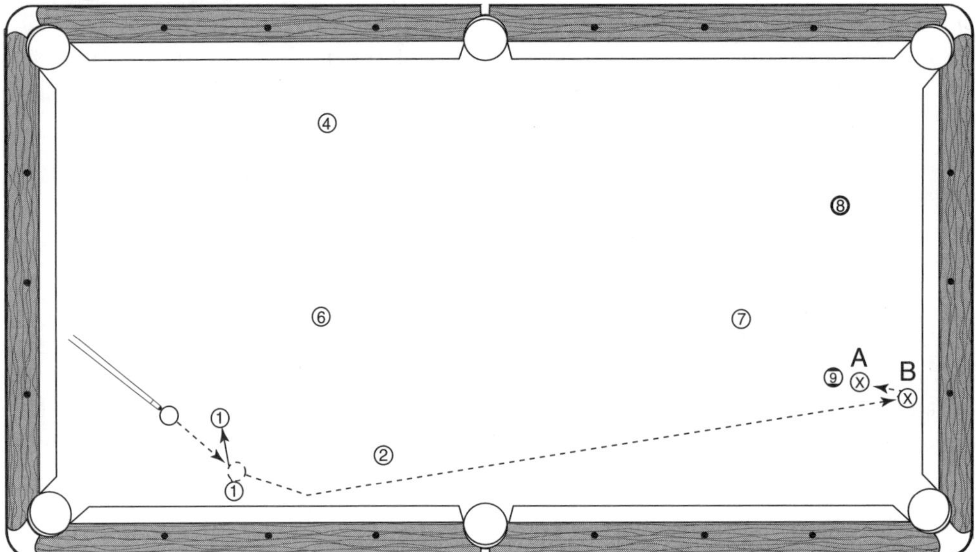

Steve Mizerak put on a clinic in safety play on his way to a 13-10 victory over Earl Strickland at the 1994 U.S. Open. Mizerak, the 1978 U.S. Open Champion, would go on to record a very respectable 9-12 finish. One of his gems was this precision two-rail safety, in which the cue ball came to rest behind the 9-ball at Position A. The keys to this type of safety are a thin hit and superb speed control. If the cue ball had stopped 6” short of A at

Position B, Strickland would have had a clear shot at the 1-ball. Mizerak was able to pull this shot off in part because of his skill at Straight Pool, which teaches you how to finesse the cue ball.

Controlling the Cue Ball at Long Range

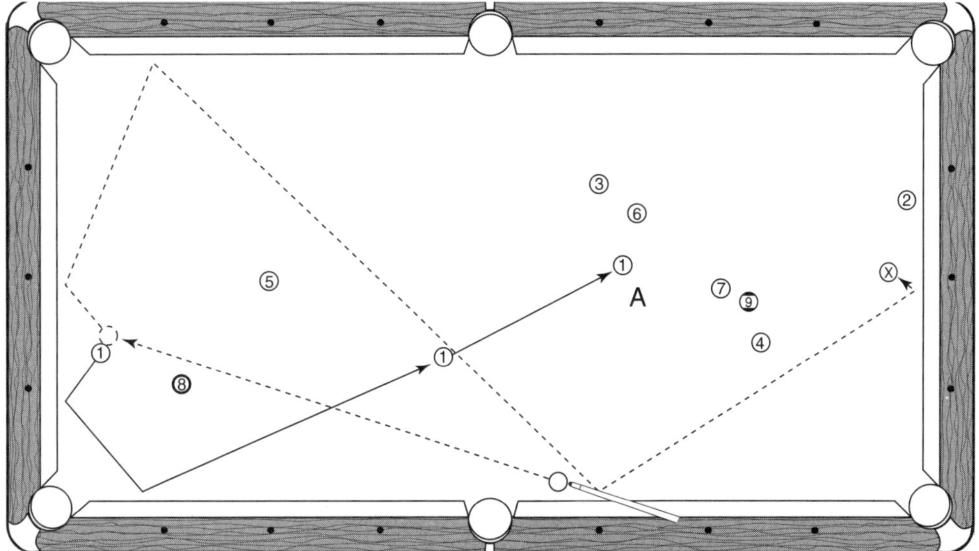

This creative safety was executed to perfection by Keith McCready in a match against Nick Varner at the Sands Regency 12 Open in 1990.A firm stroke with a full tip of right english helped propel the cue ball four rails to behind the wall off blockers at the opposite end of the table. Even though the 1-ball traveled two rails to the middle of the table, the shot was still under complete control thanks to the precise routing of the cue ball. The 1-ball could have continued up to Position A before it would have no longer been blocked. The secret to this shot was in properly routing the cue ball. Speed control on the cue ball was not overly critical due to the wide coverage provided by the wall of blockers.

Beware of the Returning Object Ball

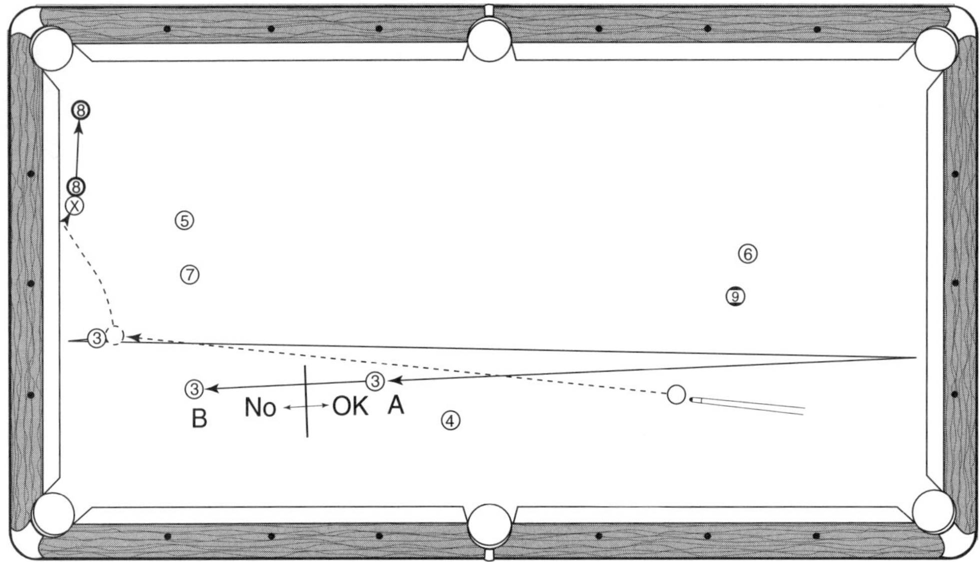

The idea is to bank the 3-ball down the table while leaving the cue ball behind the 5 and 7-balls. The 8-ball is helpful in containing the cue ball as shown. The cue ball's ending location on this safety is very predictable. The key to the shot is banking the 3-ball at the correct speed so that is stops on the opposite side of the blockers. Position A is ok. If you failed to control the object ball's rolling distance, it could wind up at Position B, leaving your opponent with an easy return safety.

Control Both On a Billiard

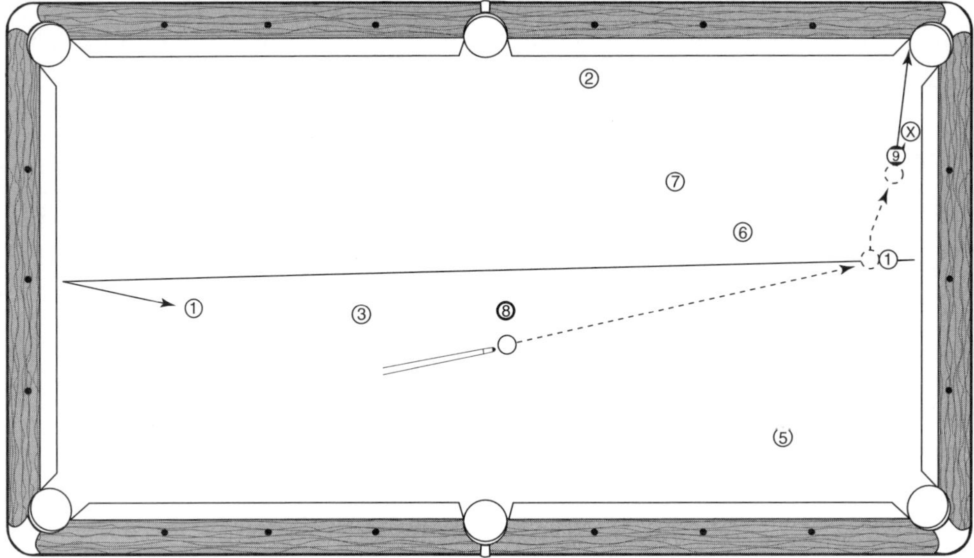

Tony Robles opened his match with Jose Garcia at the 1998 U.S. Open with this exacting billiard on the 9-ball. The cue ball was nearly four feet from the 1-ball, which meant that Robles would have to exert superb speed control for the 9-ball to be struck fully. In addition, he had to contact just the right amount of the 1-ball, which in this case meant hitting it 2/3 full. That takes care of the cue ball.

Robles also built a safety into the shot by deftly controlling the path of the 1-ball safely past the 6, 8, and 3-balls. The 7-ball wound up as a blocker, separating the cue ball and the 1-ball. The big key to this shot was controlling the cue ball, but Robles control of the 1-ball should not be overlooked. Even if he had missed the billiard, the chances were good that Garcia would have been hooked. At worst, he would have been facing a long tough shot or safety on the 1-ball.

Don't Accidentally Make a Bank

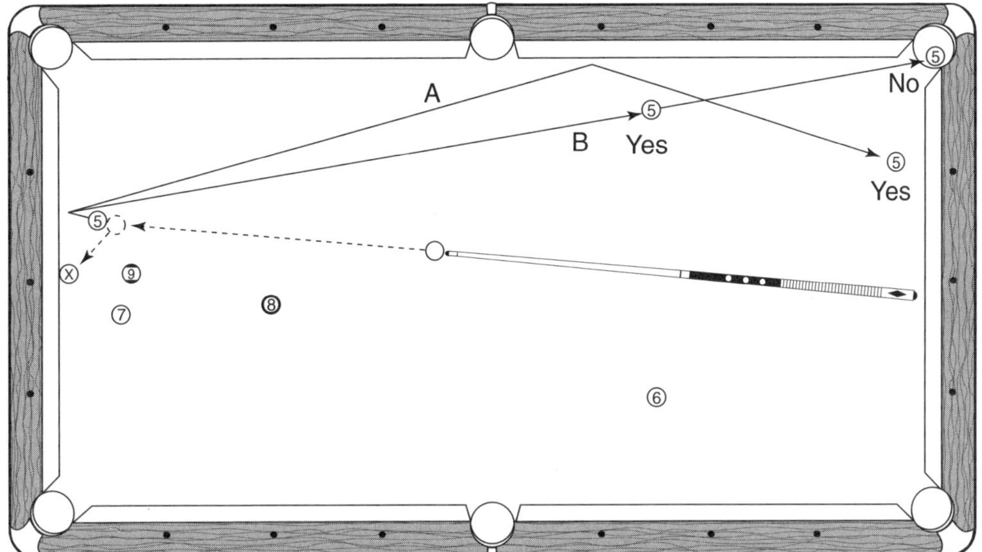

One of the biggest mistakes in safety play is to play a safe on yourself. by accidentally pocketing a ball. The goal is to bank the 5-ball at least 1.5 diamonds past the side pocket. This eliminates the possibility of leaving your opponent a direct hit or shot at the 5-ball. If you were to hit the shot a little too hard, you might make the 5-ball. You can avoid this disaster by aiming to hit the side rail on Route A, or by banking the 5-ball with good speed control down Route B.

Control Both Balls

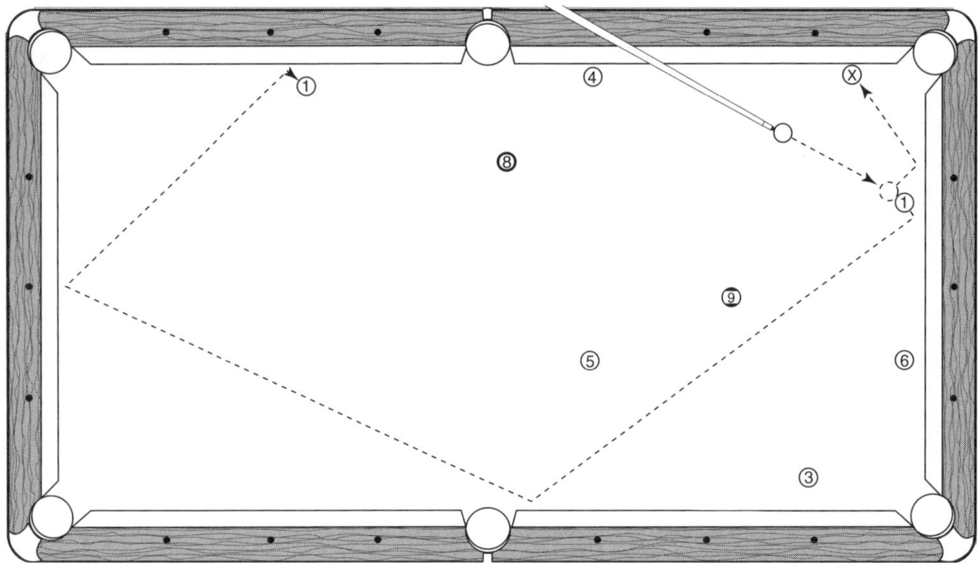

George SanSouci chose this aggressive safety in his match against Earl Strickland at the 2000 U.S. Open. His reward for executing it successfully was winning this game. The 1-ball traveled 12.5' to the upper side rail with perfect speed. At the same time, SanSouci exercised great control of the cue ball by sending it a short distance to the top rail with a hard stroke, which is a difficult assignment. Luck played about a 2% role in this safety as SanSouci carefully plotted the course of both balls and executed the shot to perfection.

Thin Hit Across Table

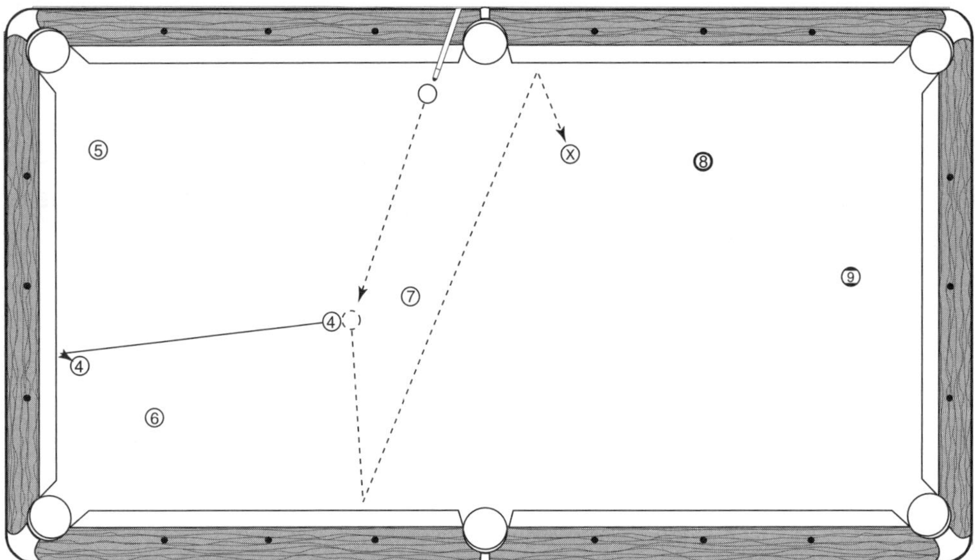

The safety in this diagram does not look overly impressive at first glance as it did not even result in a hook. Nevertheless, Steve Mizerak used it to win this game against Earl Strickland. Mizerak's first concern was to leave the 4-ball near the end rail, which he accomplished with near perfect speed control on the object ball.. While it was difficult to gauge the exact rolling distance of the cue ball, Mizerak was able send it down the table far enough to leave a 64-degree cut shot.

While Strickland would be expected to make this shot most of the time, at this particular moment Mizerak correctly sensed that his conservative style had pulled Strickland out of his rhythm, making a miss more likely, which is exactly what happened. Sharp-eyed readers may have already noticed getting to the 5-ball would not be easy even if Strickland had pocketed the 4-ball. The success of this safety rested partly in its execution and partly in Mizerak's ability to sense a temporary weakness in his supremely talented opponent.

An Effective Long Distance Safety

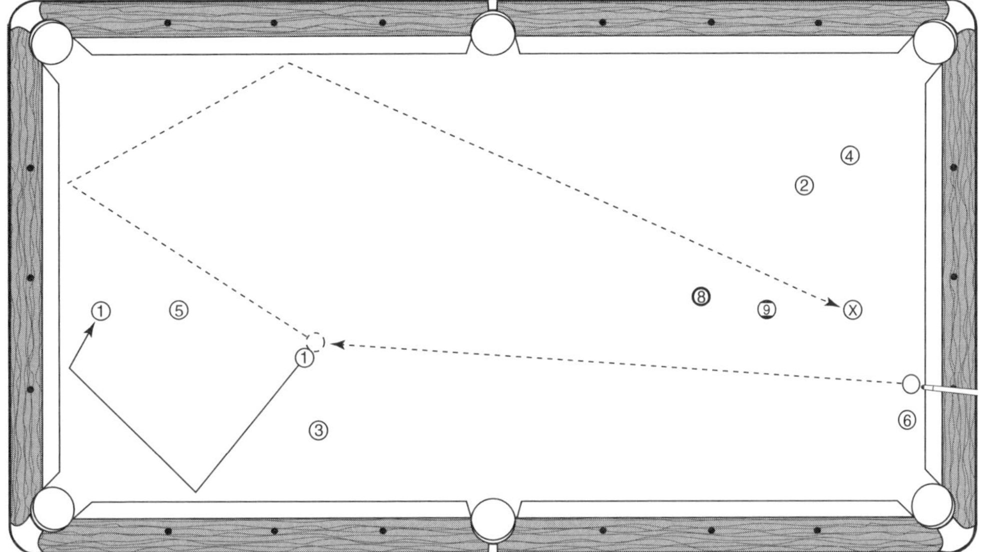

Two-Time World Nine Ball Champion Robin Dodson played this beautiful long distance safety against Jeanette Lee at the 1994 U.S. Open. The cue ball and the object ball each came to rest behind blockers. If Ms. Dodson had miss hit the shot ever so slightly, a sellout would most likely have resulted. The degree of difficulty of this safety was heightened by the cue ball's initial position close to the end rail. You will have countless opportunities to play safeties like this, so keep this particular shot in mind.

Using Available Blockers

A ball or group of balls has the potential to be a hiding place for the cue ball. It all depends on their location and whether or not you can send the cue ball behind them with an acceptably high rate of success. When you are surveying the table for possible hook safeties, ask yourself what ball(s) you can possibly employ as blockers, and how you would go about leaving the cue ball and object ball on opposite sides of the defenders. Once you have determined a safety is available, take a moment extra to see if there is a little step or two that can improve its effectiveness.

Using Available Blockers

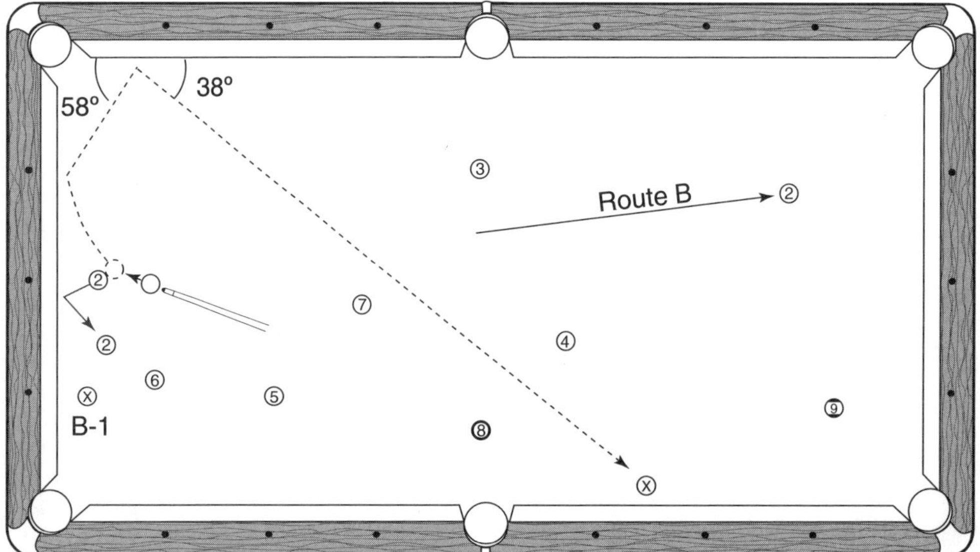

Efren Reyes played this safety in route to a victory in the semi-finals over Francisco Bustamante at the Sands Regency Open 29 in 1999. The big clue as to the availability of this safety was that the balls, although widely scattered, were almost all on the same side of the table. Reyes's ability to control the cue ball off two rails with outside english enabled him to thread the needle through the blockers to the opposite end of the table. Observe that the cue ball entered the second rail at 58-degrees and departed at only 38-degrees. The angle out was much shallower, thanks to the english. Your ability to use english to control the cue ball's path can enable you to send the cue ball behind blockers that other players would b crash into.

If you were in this position and didn't mind using the mechanical bridge, you could bank the 2-ball down Route B while sending the cue ball to B-1.

Window Free

Takeshi Okumura played this safety in the finals of the 2000 U. S. Open. Even though the cue ball was a table length from the 1-ball, this was not a difficult safety thanks to the line of widely spaced blockers strewn along

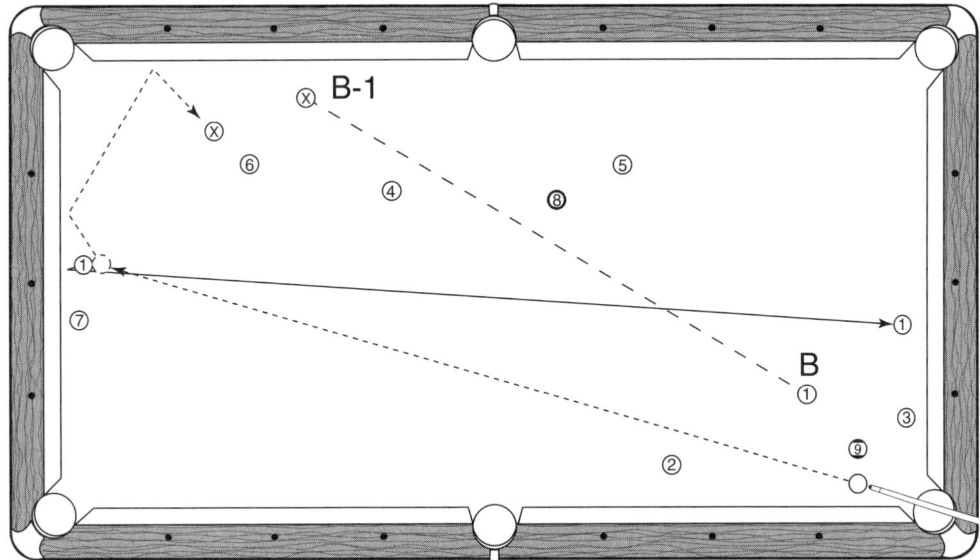

the topside of the table. When preparing a safety with widely spaced blockers, walk over to the area where you wish to send the cue ball. Walking is good exercise, and it will enable you to determine if there is a potential window between the balls that could result in a direct line to the object ball. If Okumura had hit the 1-ball too far to the right, the 1-ball could have ended up at Position B and the cue ball at B-1, leaving a 1-9 combination.

Banking Past a Big Ball

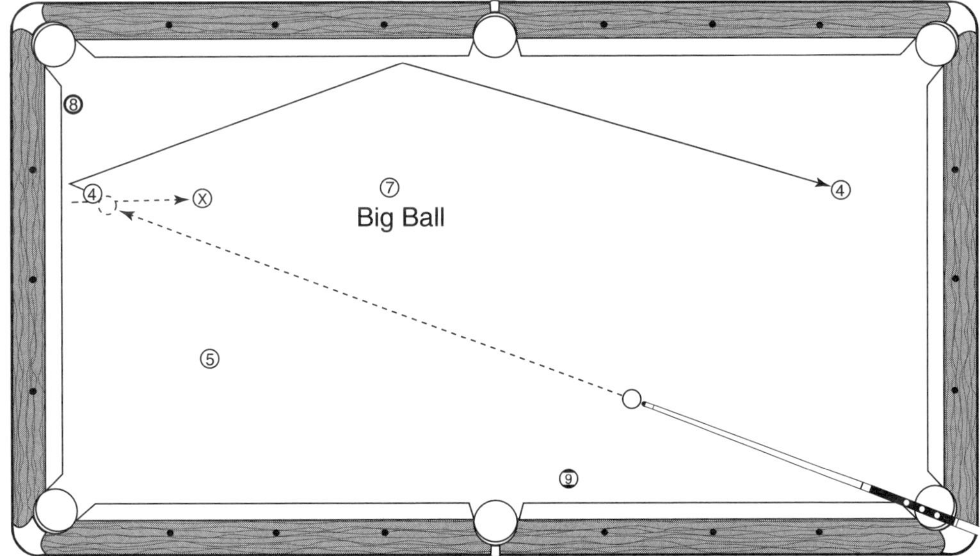

A solitary ball in the middle of the table, can effectively shield the object ball from direct contact. In this illustration, the 7-ball is a big ball as it has the potential to obscure a large portion of the right side of the table. The key is an accurate hit on the 4-ball. It must be struck just a hair left of center with follow so it will not veer to either side of the 7-ball.

Soft Follow Shot Safeties

One of the big benefits of playing safeties with a soft follow stroke is that they allow you to control the cue ball with great precision. This can enable you to play killer safeties with seemingly little effort on your part. The big keys to these kind of safeties are a soft touch and knowing exactly where you must hit the object ball to send the cue ball where required.

Lock'em Up Tight

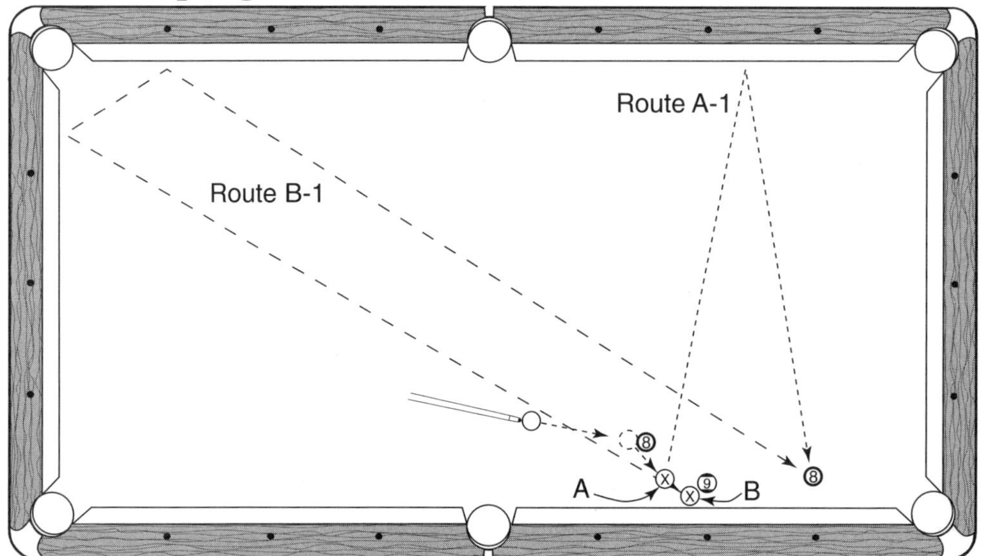

You could play the 8-9 combo, but it's a very difficult shot. The safety is a much better percentage play. The safe is quite easy because the 9-ball, which is slightly less than a ball's width from the rail, can provide you with a big hook zone.

When it comes to safety play in the "short game", there are plain old average safeties, and then there are the you've-got them-in-jail safeties that astronomically raise your chances of winning. An average safety would leave your opponent with an easy one-rail kick at the 8-ball down Route A-l. Your opponent should have no problem hitting the 8-ball. What's more, he might make the 8-ball or leave you with a tough shot or safety.

If you were to leave the cue ball in Position B, you will have increased the difficulty of the kick shot by a factor of at least five. Your opponent must kick 2 rails into the 8-ball down Route B-1. Those extra 3" made a huge difference in the effectiveness of this soft touch safety. Chalk one up for the player with a well-developed sense of touch.

Super Soft Hit Safety

The rather mundane looking safety in the illustration at the top of the next page is, in reality, one of the finest safeties ever played. Nick Varner was clinging to a 10-9 lead in a race to 11 against Johnny Archer in the finals of the Sands Regency Open 23, 1996, when he was confronted with a possible table length combo on the 8-9. After much deliberation, Varner

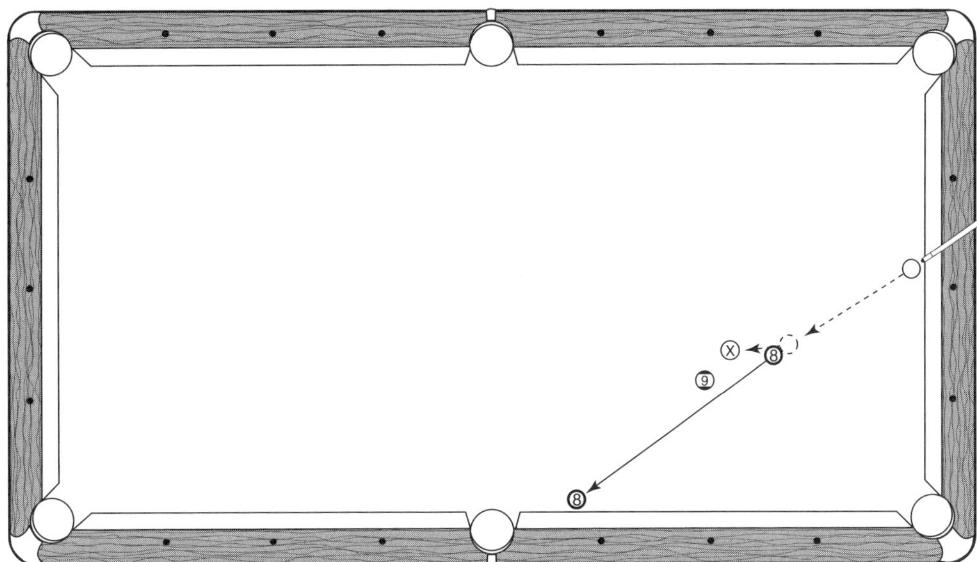

chose to slow roll the cue ball into a near full hit on the 8-ball. He used an extremely soft stroke, which clocked in at approximately 1 MPH). His speed control was otherworldly as the 8-ball caressed the rail and stopped less than a quarter inch after contact. Meanwhile, the cue ball crawled up behind the 9-ball. Archer missed the hit and Varner won the title. The two big secrets to this safety were perfect speed control and hitting the correct position of the 8-ball. Much, much, much easier said than done!!!

A Finesse Follow Shot Safety

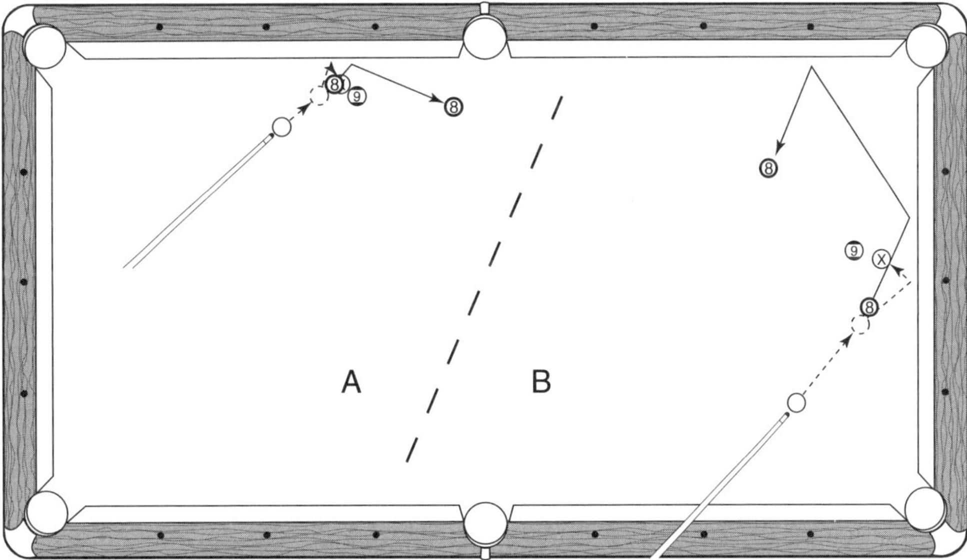

In Part A, you need to cut the 8-ball a hair to the left using a very soft follow stroke. The cue ball will come directly off the rail instead of following around the 9-ball, which would leave your opponent a shot. The concept is the same in Part B, only this time you must hit the 8-ball a little thinner with a soft follow stroke.

Inside English Kill Shot Safety

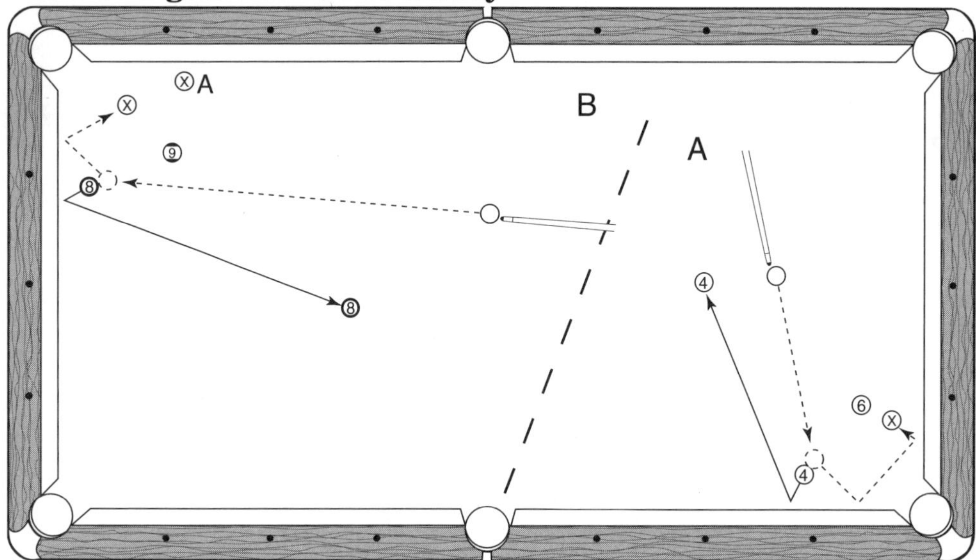

Controlling the cue balls speed is not always easy even though it will only be traveling a about a foot or less to a position behind a blocker. When a couple of inches or so can spell the difference between a hook and a hit, you need the best possible techniques working in your favor. One of the most effective means for putting the breaks on the cue ball is inside english in combination with a soft follow shot. In Part A, you can confidently bank the 4-ball out to the middle of the table because the left english will kill the cue ball's speed as it strikes the two rails as shown.

In Part B, inside english makes it much easier to contain the roll of the cue ball after it has struck the end rail. Even so, this safety still requires a soft touch and just the right hit on the 8-ball or the cue ball could possibly leak out to Position A.

Finesse Draw Safeties

Most players find it more difficult to control speed on position plays when using draw as opposed to follow. The same holds true when using draw on safeties. But if you are able to master finesse draw safeties, you can create and execute safeties that help put games on your side of the wire. To play finesse draw safeties, you need to master a stroke that is both authoritative and soft. You can't baby a finesse draw shot or the draw won't take properly. And you can't use too much speed or you'll lose control of the object ball.

Soft Draw Hook Safety

Robin Dodson played the safety at the top of the next page in a match with Jeanette Lee at the 1994 U.S. Open. The 1-ball traveled about 6' while the cue ball slid over behind the 7-ball after contact. The shot was played with a soft stroke with a full tip of draw. The secret to the shot

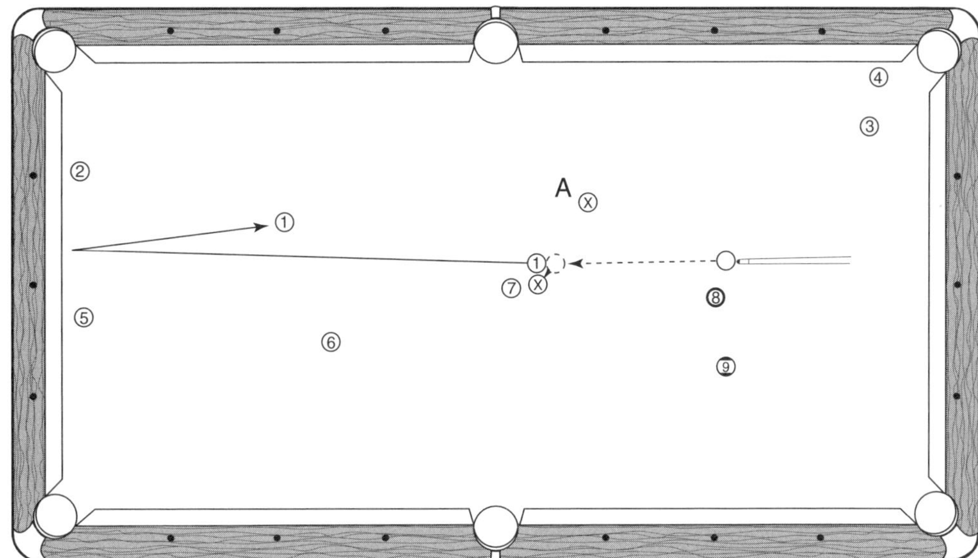

was a perfect hit with the perfect speed. The cue ball was hit hard enough so that the draw spin would hold the cue ball in place and keep it from rolling forward. And yet, at the same time, the speed needed to be soft enough so that the 1-ball would not come back down table to somewhere around Position A.

Draw Spin Finesse Safety

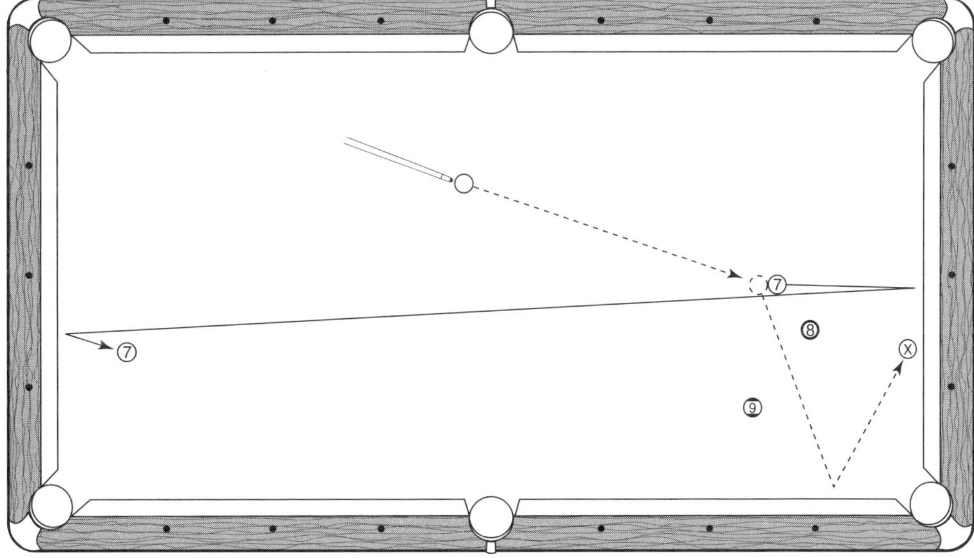

The 8-ball is blocking the 7-ball and the 7-9 combo is out of the question with the cue ball past the side pocket. In this position, a draw/spin safety is in order. Use a medium soft stroke and a tip of draw. Also use a half tip of inside (left) english, which will turn the cue ball off the side rail and down behind the 8-ball. The purpose of the draw is to hold the line of the cue ball to the side rail and to keep it from scratching in the corner pocket.

Thin Hit Safeties

Thin hit safeties are yet another of the weapons that can add real power to your safety game. The challenge in these safeties is hitting just a small slice of the object ball without missing it entirely. To play thin hit safeties effectively you must be comfortable stroking at the lowest ranges of the Spectrum of Speed (see page 138). A dose of english can also be instrumental in sending the cue ball to a precise ending location.

Thin Hit at Short Range

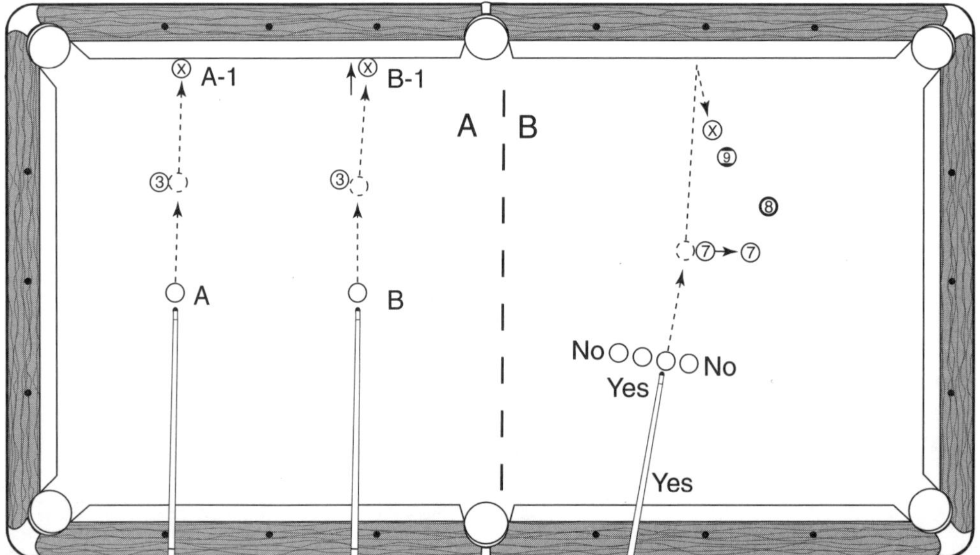

One of the big challenges in playing thin hit safeties is to calculate how much the cue ball will be diverted from its original path by a thin hit on the object ball. In Part A, if you were able to brush the 3-ball as thinly as possible with cue ball A, the 3-ball would barely move and the cue ball would continue on its initial line direction to A-1. The 3-ball and cue ball are in the same relative places in Position B. This time the 3-ball was still hit very thinly, but noticeably greater than before. Observe how the cue ball was diverted 2" to the right of its initial line of direction to B-1. While this is a seemingly small amount, when you are playing precision safeties to extra small target zones, an inch or two can make all of the difference in the results of the safety.

The safety in Part B shows how the ability to hit the object ball thinly with good speed and english can produce a lethal safety. Small differences in the location of the balls will determine whether or not a safety is "on" or "off". In the example, the safety is a go from an area about 5" wide.

Frozen Ball Safety

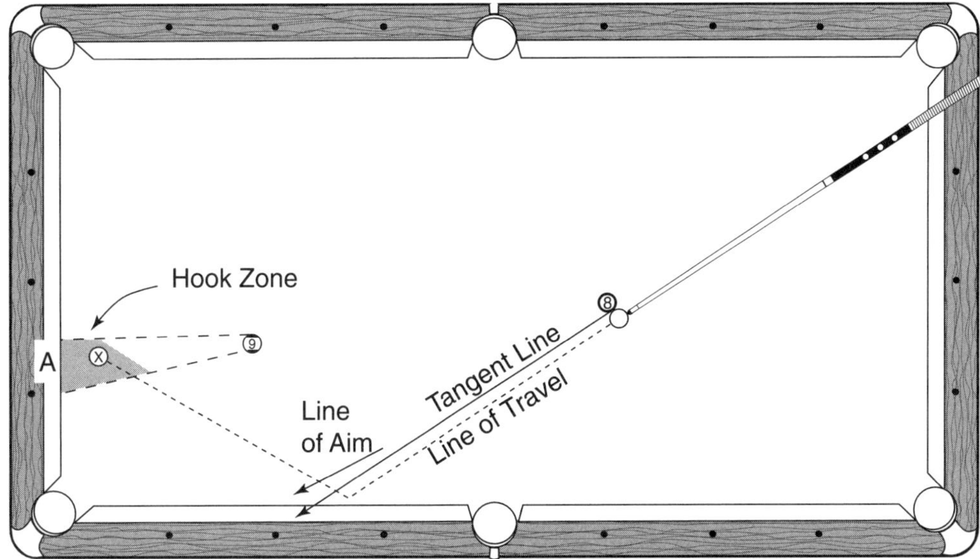

The cue ball is frozen against the 8-ball and there is no practical offensive shot. There is, however, a devilish little safety thanks to the position of the 9-ball. The idea is to brush the 8-ball while moving it as little as possible. The 8-ball is not going to move more than an inch if the shot is hit correctly. Since you can predict the 8-balls ending location with great accuracy, this allows you to establish the boundaries of the hook zone behind the 9-ball. Before playing the shot, walk over to Position A to calculate exactly where the hook zone lies.

To establish your point of aim, draw a tangent line between the cue ball and 8-ball. Locate the point where it intersects with the rail as shown. When playing the shot, aim a couple of inches inside this line, This will guarantee that you hit the 8-ball. This maneuver should be carried out in full view of your opponent so you can explain exactly why the shot was a legal safety, if necessary. The cue ball ended up in the hook zone in the example using straight follow. You could use english if needed to send the cue ball along a slightly shallower path to a position behind the blocker.

Ball in Hand Thin Hit Safety

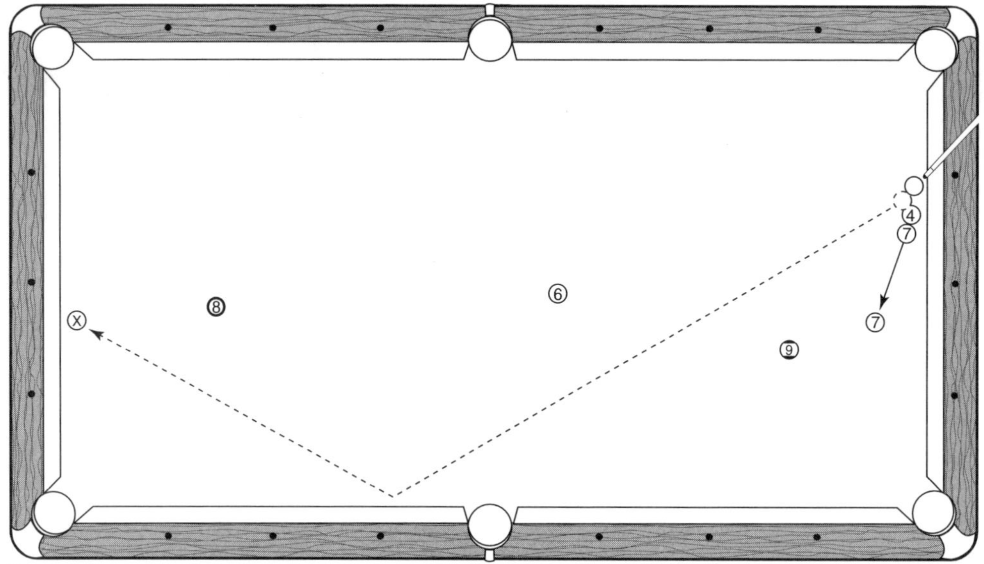

Its quite possible for you to have ball in hand and no shot because the balls are clustered together. This can also happen after your opponent has purposefully tied up the balls with an intentional foul. When in this position, don't bemoan the fact that you don't have a roadmap runout to the 9-ball. Instead, look for a route to a blocker. Also try to separate the balls in as constructively as possible. In the example, the play is to hit the 4-ball thinly enough so you can control the cue ball's path to behind the 6 and 8-balls, which will server as blockers. Another important goal is to clearly separate the 4 and 7-balls. If your opponent fouls again, you can use a second ball in hand to position yourself for a runout.

Thin Hit Safety or Bank Shot?

The 9-ball is the only ball left in the position above, which occurs with great frequency in games between amateurs. You could play a thin hit safety or go for the gusto with a table length bank shot. The decision is largely based on the position of the balls, but could also rest on the various skills of the two players. With the cue ball in Position A the long rail bank is not overly difficult. If you are confident in your banking and wish to avoid a safety battle against a crafty opponent, you may be wise to go for the bank. However, a thin hit safety is an easy shot from here and could be the better choice if your opponent is a poor safety player.

With the cue ball in Position B, the bank may be the better choice unless you posses the eye of an eagle. Position C is the mirror image of Positions A and B. Now a thin hit safety is probably best as it is not too difficult from this distance.

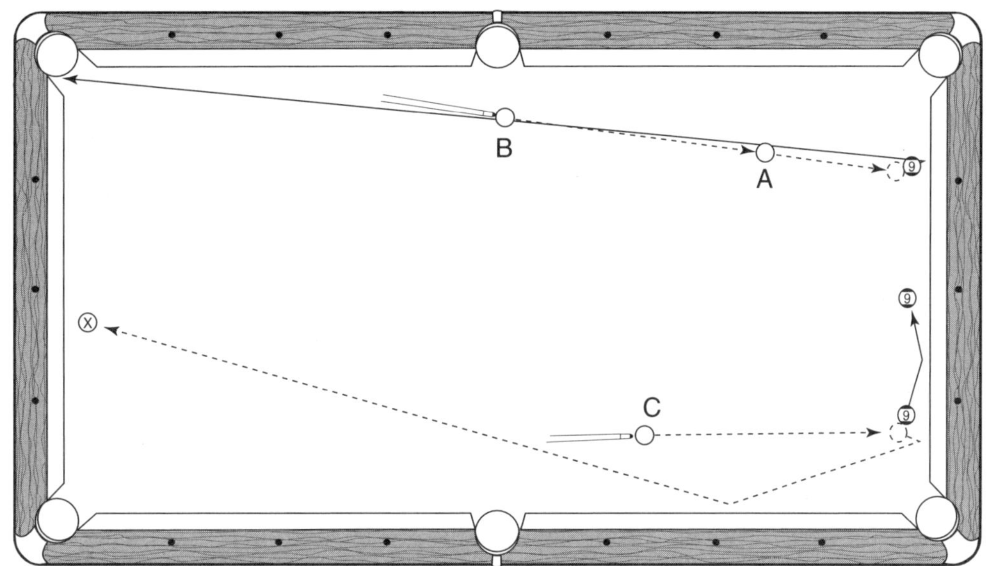

Perfect Speed Avoids Possible Scratch

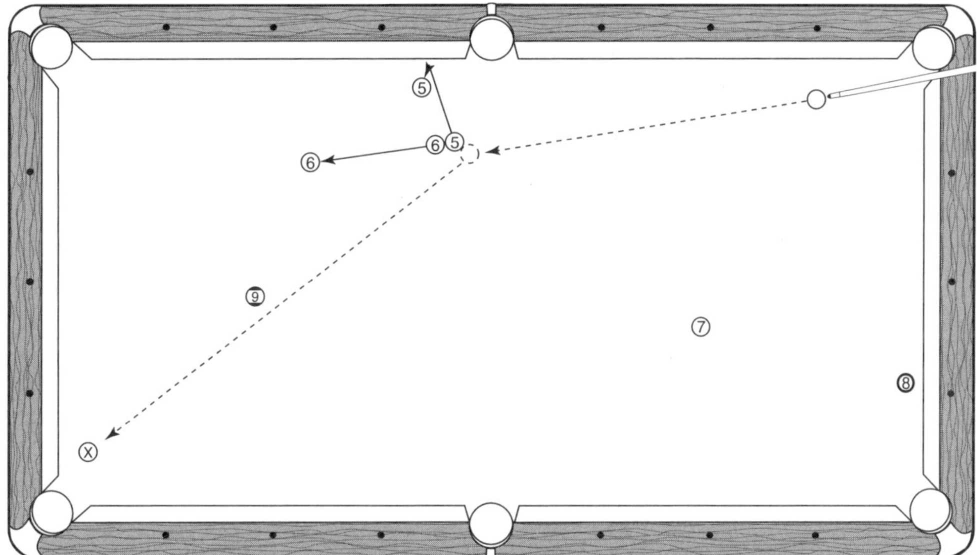

In today's modern safety warfare, distance is often used as a strategic weapon to leave you with the toughest shot or safety possible. Ewa Laurance, the 1991 U.S Open champion, was confronted with a long-range safety in against Robin Dodson in the finals of the 1992 U.S. Open. The 6-ball was instrumental in controlling the 5-ball. Ms .Laurance hit the shot at the perfect speed as the 5-ball made it to the rail with a little room to spare while the cue ball stopped inches short of a near scratch. I suspect that she knew a scratch was possible, but she had enough confidence in her speed control to send the cue ball in the direction of the pocket, knowing full well that it would fall short.

Crossover Bank Safeties

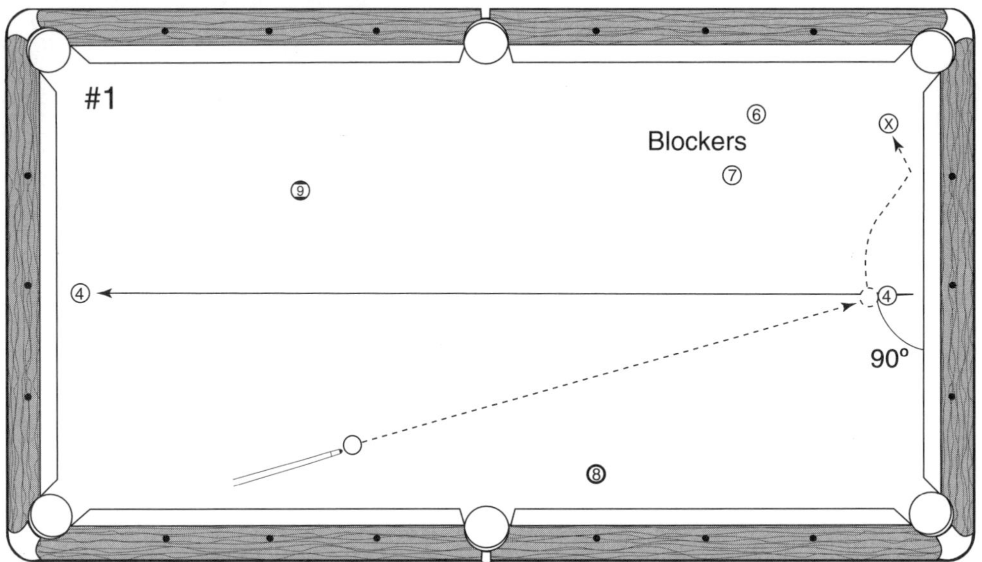

One of the most commonly used safety maneuvers is to bank a ball down the table while the cue ball crosses over the path of the rebounding object ball. Diagram #1 gives an example of a long distance crossover safety. The 4-ball is banked straight down the table while the cue ball crosses over and behind a wall of blockers. It is much easier to control both the cue ball and the object ball when you bank the ball at a 90-degree angle to the end rail. When you know the exact line the object ball will be traveling, you can concentrate on speed of stroke. If the speed is right, the 4-ball will arrive near or at the opposite end rail. In addition, the cue ball will arrive safely at its destination without the worry of a scratch or double kiss. This safety left your opponent with a table length two-rail kick shot.

The safety in diagram #1 can also be very effective in the end game. Let's assume that the 4-ball is the 9-ball and the other balls are no longer on the table. You could play a thin cut or bank on the 9-ball, but either of these shots could easily be missed. If you are not confident in your ability to pocket the shot, play a crossover bank safety and leave your opponent in a similar predicament. They may sellout going for the shot or by playing a poor safety. Keep in mind, if you are playing a knowledgeable player, they could return the favor. If so, at least you gave them the opportunity to screw up. In addition, they also showed you a little more of their knowledge of safety play. Getting a read on your opponent's game is important, especially at the amateur level.

Diagram #2 at the top of the next page shows an advanced version of the crossover bank safety. If you were to bank the 9-ball straight back down the table, you might leave a cut shot if your speed is off slightly. With the 9-ball a few inches off the rail you can cut the 9-ball a little to the left and still avoid a double kiss.

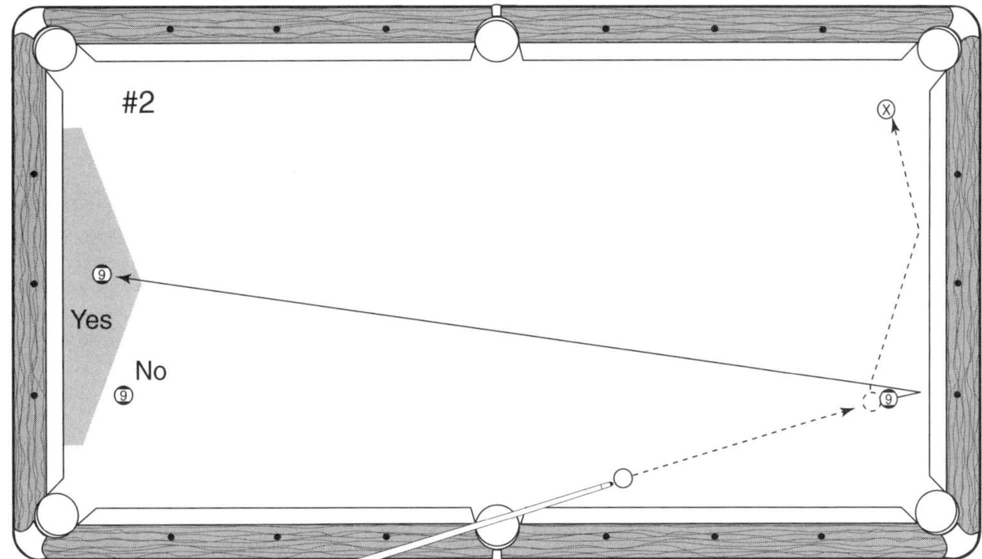

The zone shows the target for the object ball on crossover bank safeties. When the ball you are banking is about a diamond or more from the rail, you must guard against scratching. Since most crossover bank safeties are played with a medium soft follow stroke, the path of the cue ball after contact is very predictable. The only reason for scratching is a lack of knowledge about the cue ball's path after contact. This problem can quickly be eliminated with a few minutes of practice.

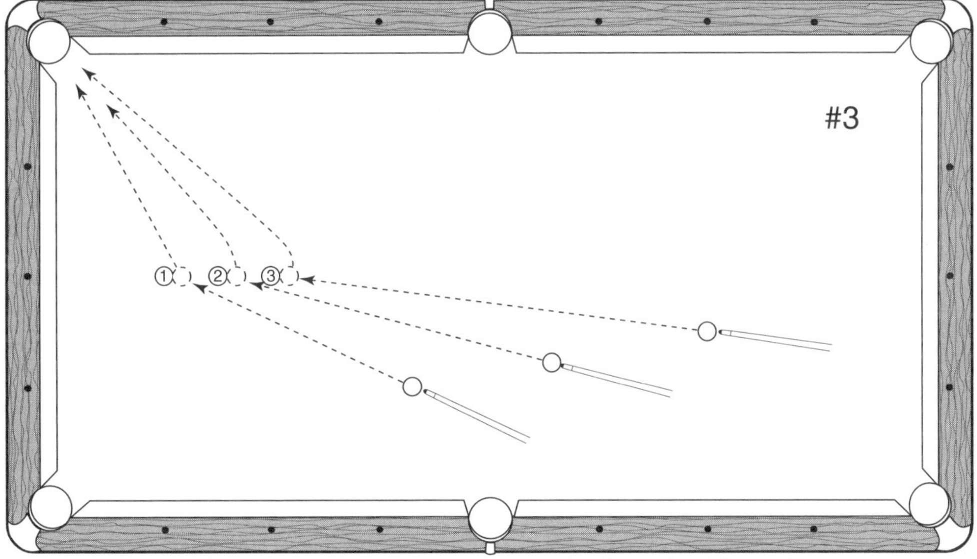

Set up the 3 balls in Diagram #3 in turn, with the 1-ball first. Shoot crossover safeties starting with the cue ball in the corresponding position, which is a dead or near dead scratch. Then adjust the cue ball's position in small increments to both the left and right. This exercise will teach you what a scratch crossover scratch shot looks like, and how to avoid scratching.

Safes with a Carom

When the balls are lying a little funny, you may wonder how to go about playing safe. At times like this, it pays to be creative and draw upon your knowledge of a variety of shots, any one of which can be employed to construct an effective safety. One such concept is the carom safety. A carom safety consists of shooting the lowest numbered ball off another ball so that it will continue to a safe location.

A Carom Safety

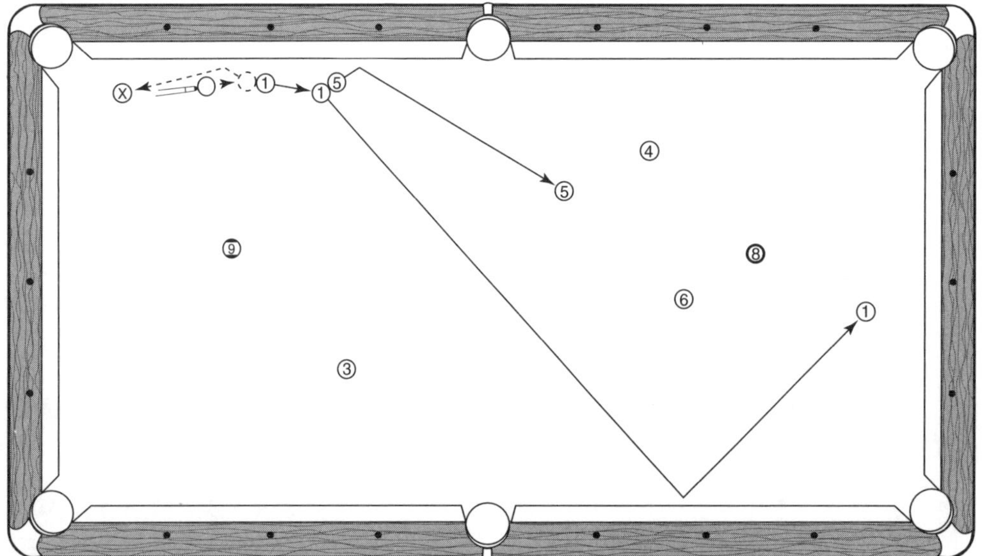

You could hit the 1-ball thinly on the right side and send the cue ball to the other end of the table. The problem with this safety is that you run the risk of scratching. A better choice is to carom the 1-ball into the 5-ball and draw back to Position X. The 1-ball should bounce off the side rail and behind the blockers up table. The big key is to calculate how much of the 5-ball must be hit to get the 1-ball started on the correct line. In this case, about a 1/3 hit on the 5-ball was required. As a word of caution, you should only attempt this safety when the cue ball and the other two balls are in a relatively straight line. Otherwise, aiming is quite difficult.

A "Dead" Carom Bank Safety

The 5-ball is frozen to the 8-ball, which is a familiar position for playing a carom into a pocket. In this position, you can use the highly predictable path of the 5-ball to play a deadly carom safety. The preshot planning process indicates that the 5-ball will follow the path shown in the illustration to behind the row of blockers. As long as the 5-ball is struck between 2/3 and 1/2 full, it should have the correct speed to stop behind the blockers. The key is to hit the correct amount of 5-ball with draw and enough speed so the cue ball ends up at Position X.

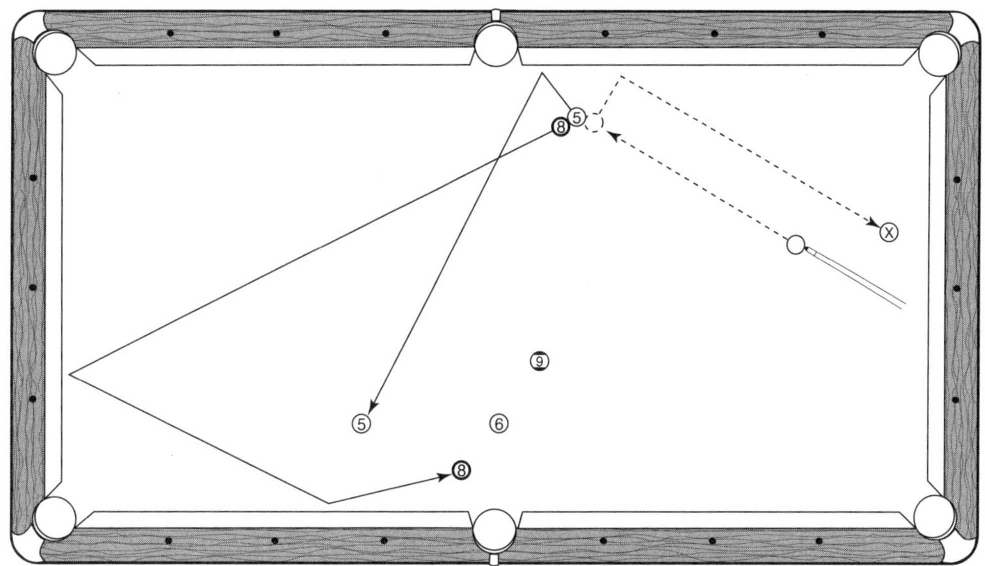

Carom Safety at Long Range

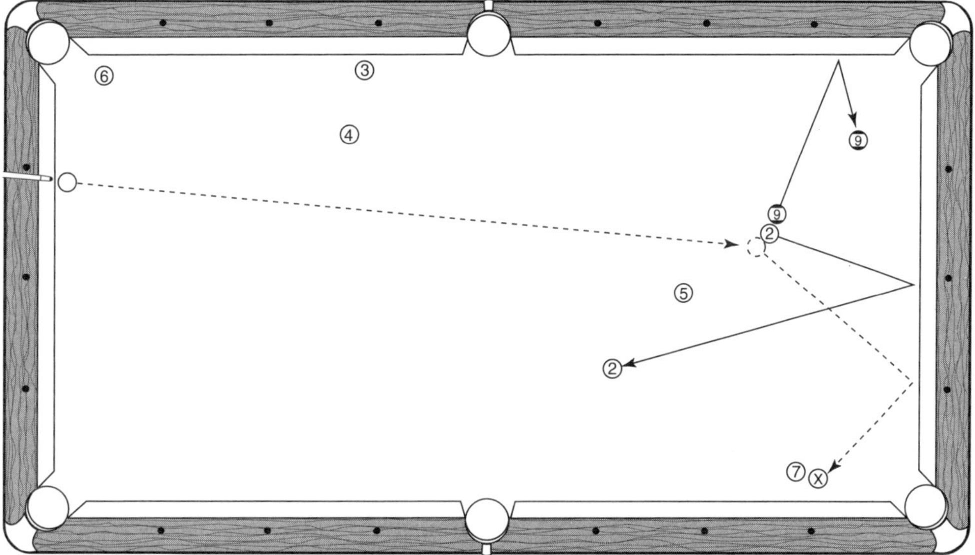

Kunihiko Takahashi of Japan was in a jam when he stepped to the table facing this puzzler at the 1999 U.S. Open. The solution was a creative and very well executed carom safety. The 2-ball hit only a small portion of the 9-ball, which allowed it to retain much of the force of impact with the cue ball. This enabled the 2-ball to roll three diamonds up table after contacting the end rail. The cue ball contacted the 2-ball perfectly, so that it would continue to behind the 7-ball. The big secret to this safety was Takahashi's extensive knowledge of how the balls interact, something that come largely with experience, a sharp eye, and a good memory.

Kick Safeties

On most kick shots the outcome is somewhat uncertain. At times, however, you can play a kick shot safety that has a very high probability of success. In this section we'll cover a few of the most commonly played kick safeties. For a more complete discussion of kick shots, please refer to Chapter 12.

Two Rail Kick Safety

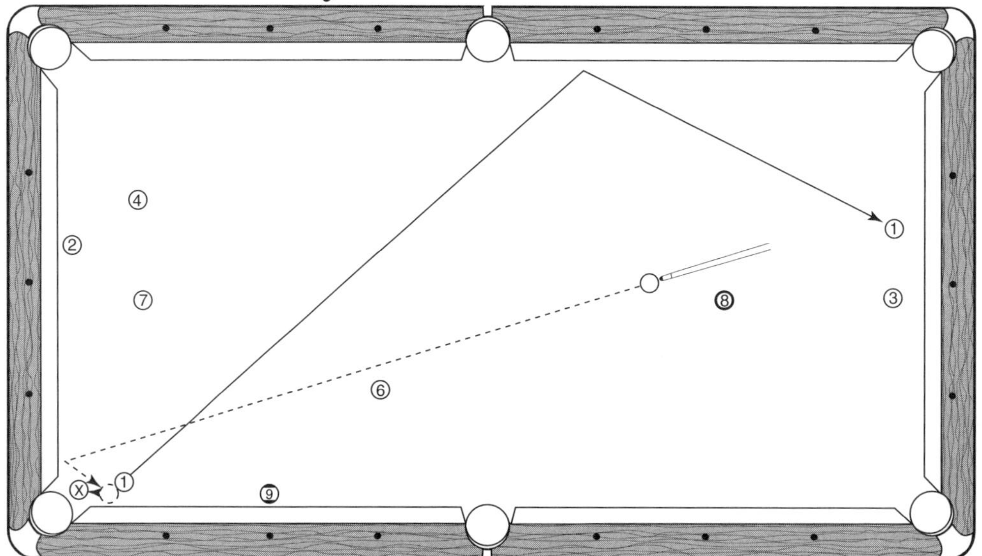

Nick Varner was hooked on the 1-ball after the break in his match against Keith McCready at the Sands Regency Open 12, 1990. Since there was no place to push out except for a jump shot, Varner elected to play the two-rail kick safety in the illustration. He walked over to Position A to get a preview of the cue ball's position at contact and to determine the initial direction of the 1-ball. He then used a medium speed follow stroke to execute a kick safety to perfection. This shot not too difficult because of the 1-ball's position less than a ball's width from the rail, which allowed Varner to predict contact with confidence. The Lesson: whenever you are kicking at a ball that's is close to the rail, you often have the opportunity to play a kick safety.

Short Rail Kick and Stick

There is nothing but open spaces on the left side of the table. The last thing you want to do is kick softly at the 4-ball while just trying to make a good hit. Instead, you must hit the 4-ball firmly to drive it down table, hopefully behind any of the blockers in the middle of the table. The shot is played with a hard draw stroke and an eighth of a tip of reverse english. which will cause the cue ball to stop dead upon contact This shot is not too difficult because of the 4-ball is only a few inches from the rail. If the 4-ball was just another inch or two further from the cushion, the degree of difficulty would rise dramatically.

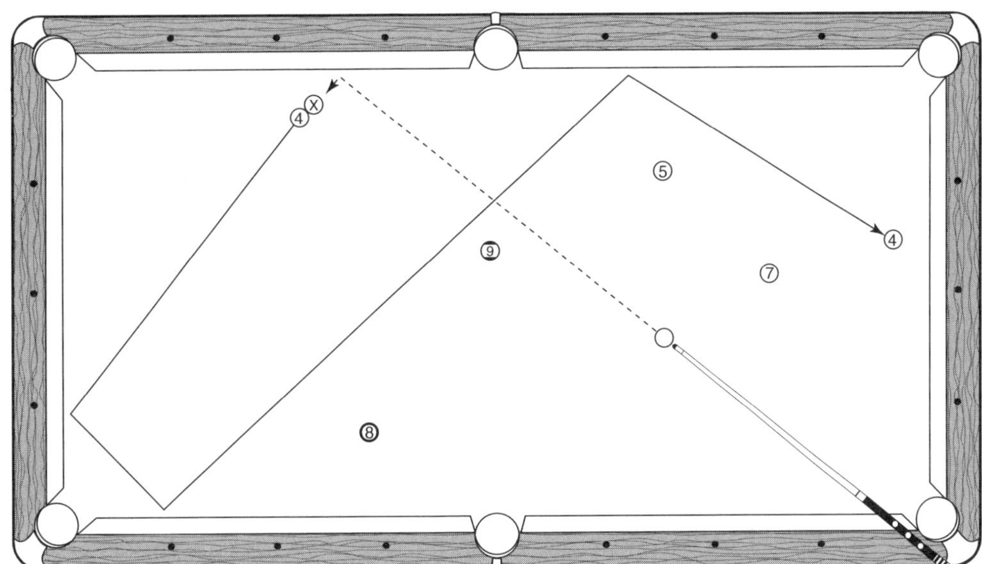

Thin Hit Kick Shot

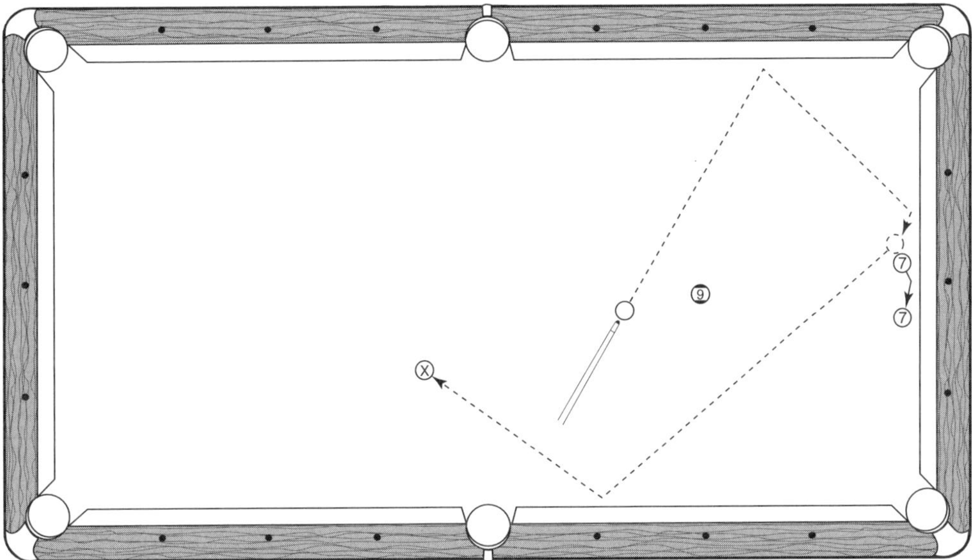

When presented with this kick shot, you have three choices: you can try to pocket the 7-ball in the lower right corner pocket, blast into the 7-ball and try to drive it up table, or you can play the two rail thin hit safety shown in the diagram. The kick to pocket is a low risk shot that could easily result in a sellout. The blast and hope is a good choice if your kicking game is only average. The soft kick safety is for advanced players who are skilled at kicking.

There is not a large margin for error on this safety but it is still much larger than on the kick shot to pocket the ball. It is important that you use a soft stroke on this shot, but the key to this shot is hitting the 7-ball thin enough that you don't knock it in front of the pocket. And you certainly don't want to bail out in the other direction and miss the ball altogether, which is a common mistake on this shot.

Missing Safe (1/2 Safe, 1/2 Shot)

While missing is certainly not a pleasing thought for most pool players, the realities of pool dictate that you at times must allow for a miss when playing shots with a high degree of difficulty. If you plan for the possibility of missing, you give yourself two chances to win the game: with the shot or a safety. The 1/2 shot/ 1/2 safeties (also commonly known as Two Way Shots) that we'll be covering feature shots on the 9-ball, even though they can be used at any time during the game. Nevertheless, amateur players will find them particularly valuable during the end game when only 1-3 balls remain on the table.

Overcut to Miss Safe

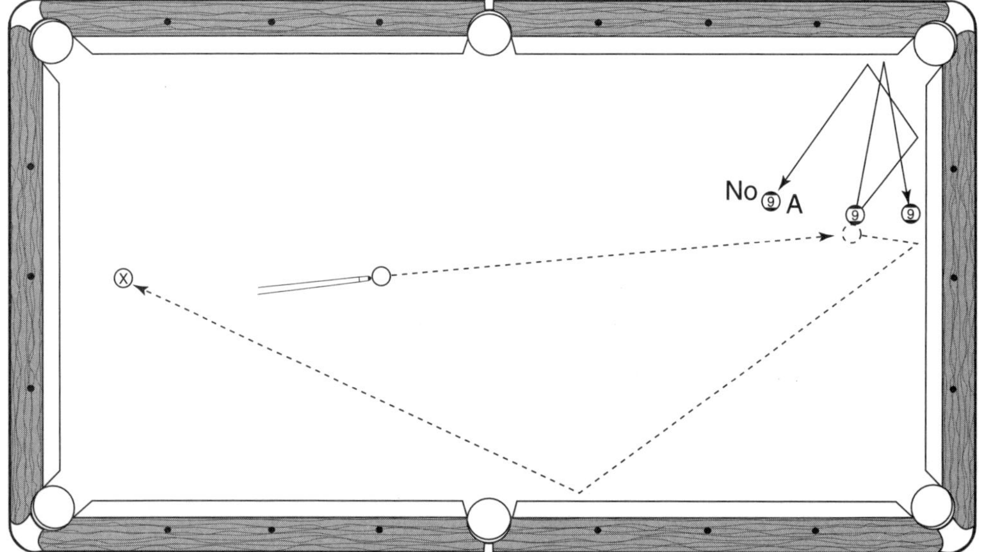

Let's suppose you missed shape or your opponent left you thin long tough cut shot on the 9-ball. It would be great if you could fan this 62-degree cut shots like this on command. You can stack the percentages in your favor, by aiming to miss the shot just a shade above the pocket as shown. If you hit the shot as planned, you'll leave your opponent in a bind. If you cut the shot more than you planned, you should still leave him safe. And if you undercut the shot, the 9-ball will disappear into the pocket! In other words, it's heads you win, tails you win! If you play to make the 9-ball and fail to cut the shot enough, which is a common mistake on thin cut shots, the 9-ball would rebound two rails to Position A, leaving your opponent with a shot.

Miss Short Rail Banks on the Pro Side

This 20-degree backcut short rail bank is not difficult as banks go. Still, it is not a sure thing. Your best bet is to aim to miss slightly in the hopes that you might "miss" the ball into the pocket. When you miss this bank above the pocket and the 9-ball stops at Position A, you are said to have missed it on the "pro side". A miss on the amateur side would leave the 9-ball at Position B.

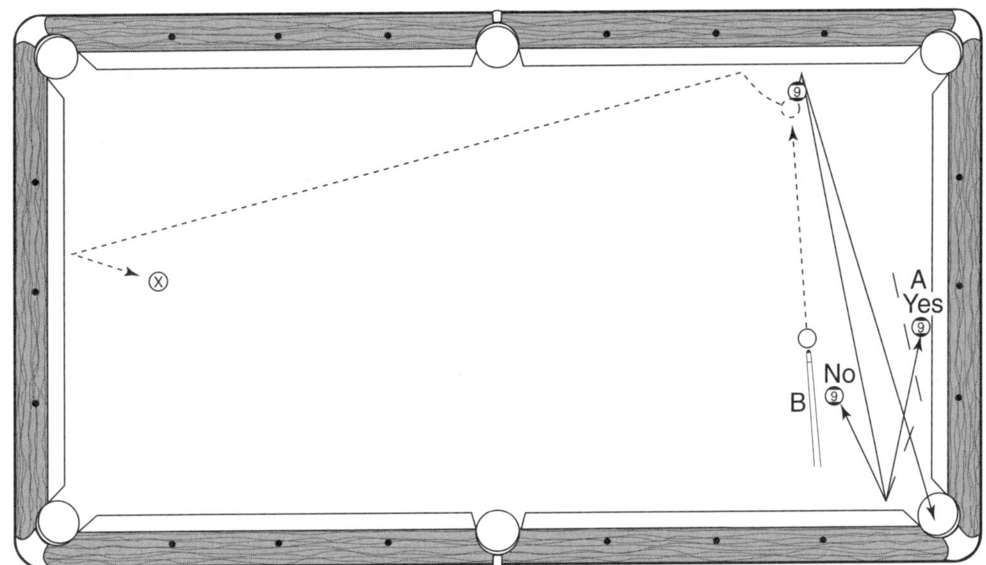

Cross Side Bank Safeties

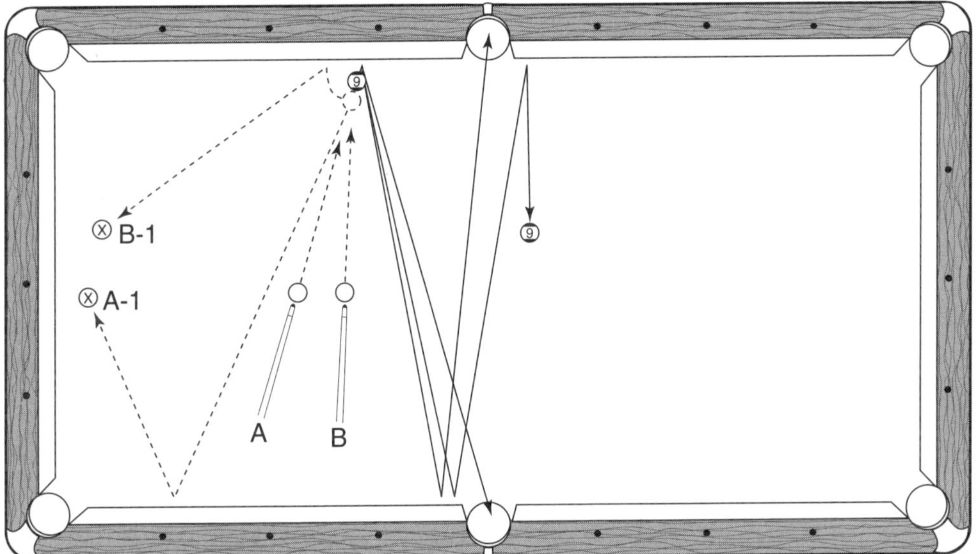

This bank is the kind you should expect to make a vast majority of the time. If you are uncomfortable with the rails or your bank shots are way off the mark, you can build a safety component into the shot. With the cue ball in Position A use a hard draw stroke to pull it back to A-1. When the cue ball is in Position B, use a hard stun/follow stroke to send it to Position B-1.

If you play this bank a little short of the side pocket, you give yourself three chances to win: 1) bank it straight in; 2) make it in the opposite side pocket; 3) leave a tough shot that your opponent could easily miss.

Cross Side Safety Bank

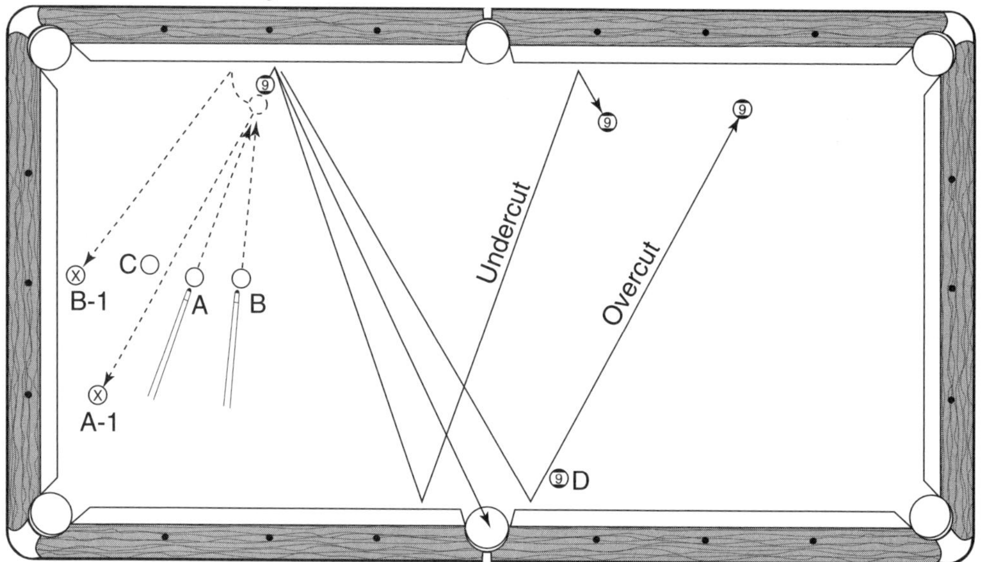

OOn certain banks you should shoot for the pocket even if you will leave your opponent a shot if you miss. Most players at the C level or better would make the bank upwards of 40-50% of the time while pros might make it on 80% of their attempts. Your primary goal is to pocket the ball. A secondary objective is to make your opponents shot as difficult as possible should you miss. On this bank, the 9-ball will land much closer to the middle of the table if you undercut the shot. This is preferable to missing long because you overcut the shot.

Another step you can take to make things tough is to get the cue ball to the end rail if possible. From Position A you should draw back to A-1. With the cue ball in Position B, a follow shot will send it to B-1.

When the cue ball is too far to the left, such as at Position C, you can no longer play safe by sending the cue ball to the end rail. You could, however, play the bank with a soft draw stroke and a half tip or more of inside english. Your goal is to make the ball or miss to the far side of the side pocket. If you do miss, you want the cue ball on the top rail and the 9-ball at Position D, leaving your opponent with a tough shot or safety.

Missing Long Rail Banks on the Pro Side

The diagram at the top of the next page shows a long rail bank. Many players mistakenly fear long rail bank shots because they feel they almost always result in a sell out when missed. Such is not the case if you play them to miss on the pro side. In the illustration, notice the cue ball has taken residence on the bottom side rail. This one indication that the shot was hit with the proper speed. The biggest factor in leaving a missed long rail bank safe is the location of the object ball. The 9-ball in Position A gives your opponent a relatively tough cut shot. Position B is even better as it gives your opponent no reasonable chance to win the game with this shot. The 9-ball in Position C is a sell-out, which occurred because the bank was overcut.

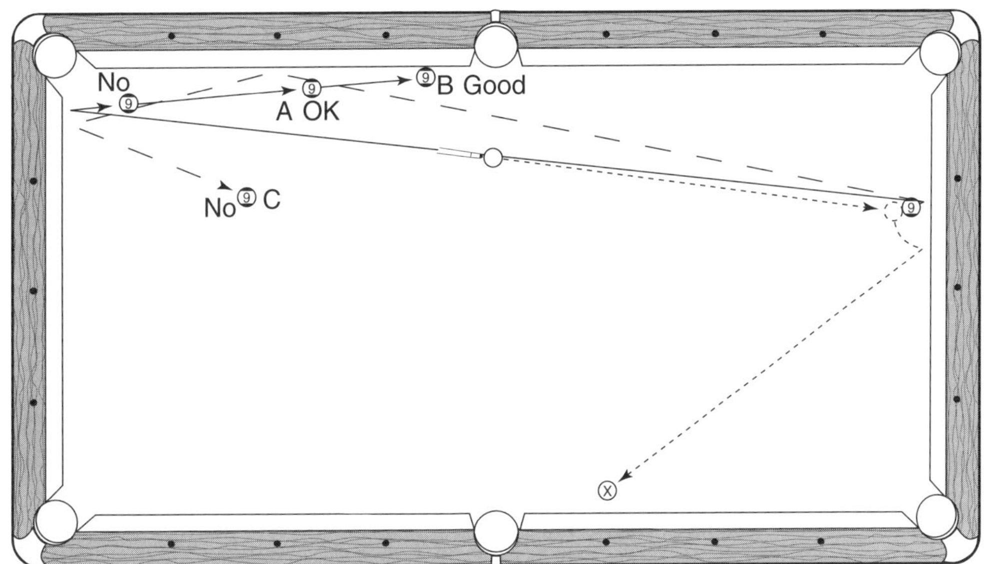

Leave a Tough Shot after a Bank

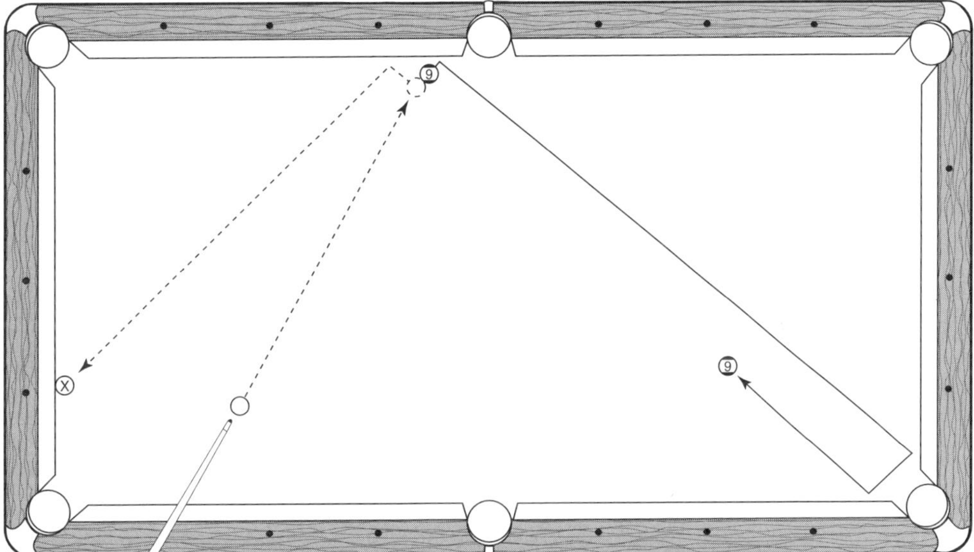

We've seen in previous sections that superb control of the cue ball swing the odds in your favor, even after a missed shot. Now we'll advance that concept to the final degree with this offensive/defensive shot, which was played by Johnny Archer in a match against Nick Varner at the 1991 World Championships. Varner had just missed the 9-ball and left Archer in a jam. Archer's response was to go for a difficult cross table bank, which he missed by a couple of inches. Even though he failed to pocket the ball, he did two things that kept him in the game: 1) he hit the bank with enough speed that it exited the vicinity of the corner pocket; 2) he exercised exceptional distance and directional control over the cue ball, which ended up frozen to the rail. Varner missed the ensuing shot but eventually won the game and the match.

End Game

The end game starts when there are three or less balls on the table. A very high percentage of games between amateurs players are won and lost due to missed shots and positional errors during the end game. Once a game gets down to the last three balls, there seems to be an impulse to go for it, among most players. This is a time, however, when games can be won with smart safeties rather than spectacular shots no matter what your level of play.

Long Distance End Game Warfare

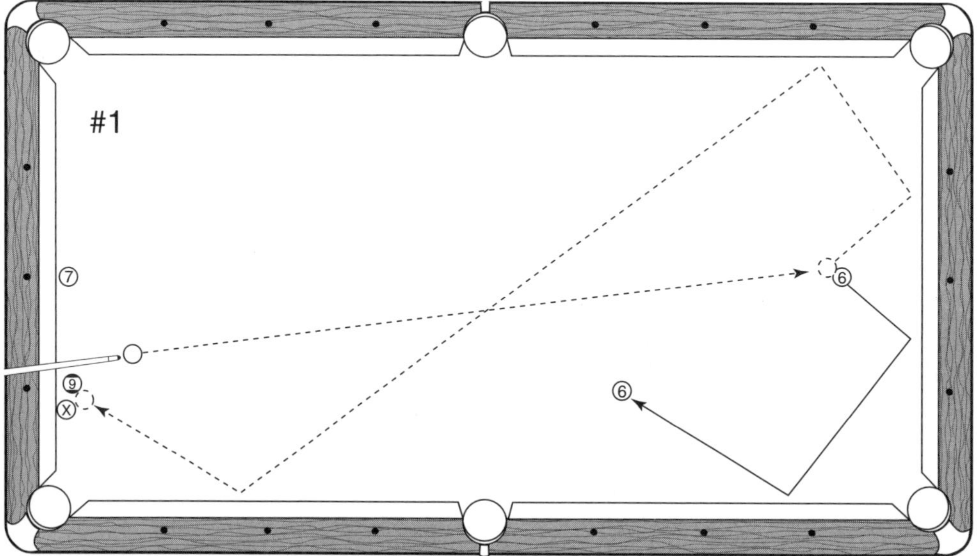

Even pro players are not immune from end game safety play. Shannon Daulton, who was pitted against Kim Davenport at the 1999 U.S. Open, was faced with what appeared to be a do or die shot on the 6-ball in Diagram #1. Rather than take a flyer on the 6-ball, he purposefully left Davenport the difficult shot shown in the diagram. Daulton felt confident of his chances of returning to the table because running the last three balls in this position would be an incredibly difficult chore for any player including Davenport. Daulton showed his knowledge of safety play by seeing a safety that is not obvious to most until after it has been played. His execution was perfect as he left the cue ball snuggled up against the end rail.

Davenport's response to the previous safety is displayed in the diagram #2 on the next page. He also failed to take the bait and instead played a crafty two-rail bank safety that left the 6-ball near one end rail and the cue ball close to the other. This game of cat and mouse would continue another four innings before Davenport came out on top. Davenport went on to finish in 4th place in the event.

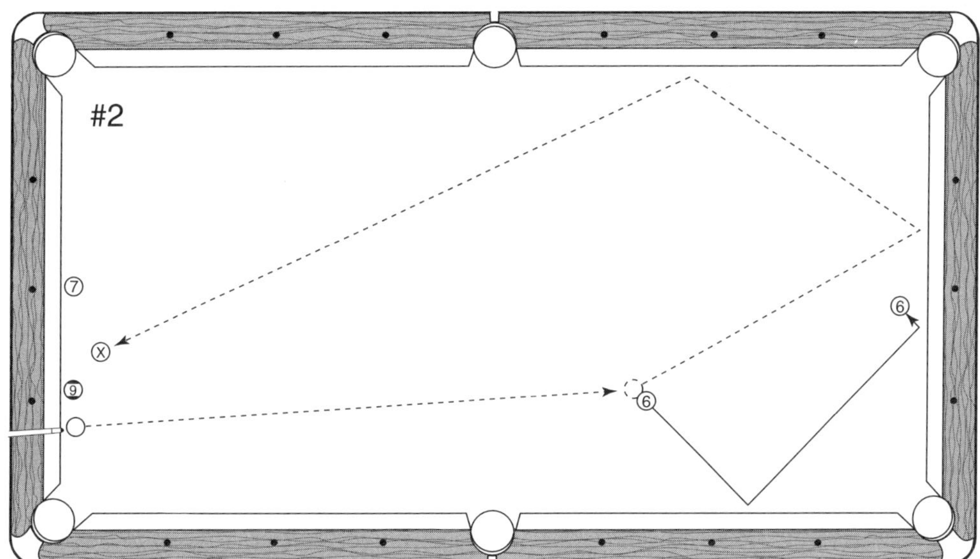

Two End Game Bank Safeties

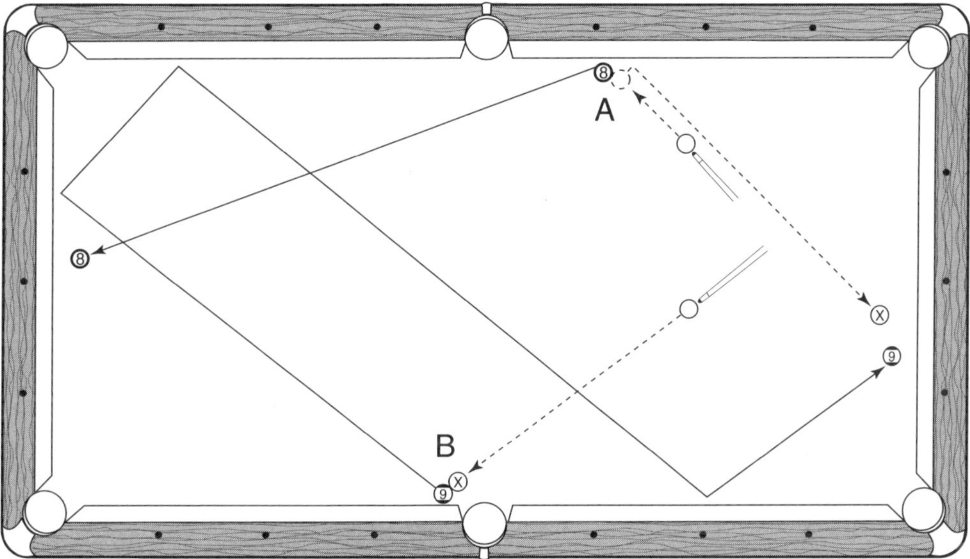

The illustration shows two end game safeties. You could attempt to end the game in Position A by playing a 48-degree cut past the point of the side pocket. A more conservative approach is to bank the 9-ball down table. Now your opponent is forced to beat you, which is better than just handing over the game, which almost certainly would have happened had you missed the cut shot.

In Position B there is no offensive shot, but the balls are lying perfectly for a four-rail safety. This shot must be hit squarely with a very hard stroke. It is nearly impossible to hit this shot too hard because the 9-ball will slow down quickly after hitting the 4th rail. When you are in a tough spot at the end of a game, take a moment and let your creative juices flow. Perhaps you'll discover a bank safety like these that can turn the odds back in your favor.

Strategic Safeties

On many occasions you will face a very makeable shot that the little voice, that urges to run out, leads you into playing. At the same time, however, there may be a maneuver that can improve your overall odds of winning the game. When you have ball in hand or are facing a shot where it will be tough to get on the next ball, your best bet may be a strategic safety.

Pass on a Shot that Leads Nowhere

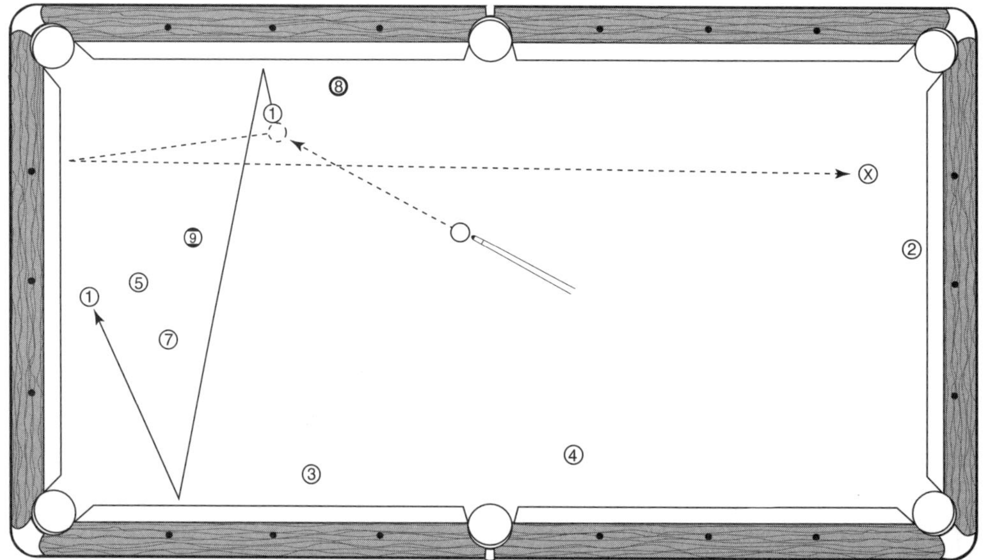

Pocketing the 1-ball is no problem, but getting to the 2-ball is a huge problem, thanks to the 8-ball. Even though shape is impossible on the 2-ball, many players will pocket the 1-ball and then stop to consider the 2-ball. This is an especially common error among amateur players.

When you are faced with a simple shot that leads nowhere, your decision should be whether to play safe right away or pocket the ball and then play safe. In our example, I would recommend passing on the shot and playing safe right now. The safety in the illustration leaves your opponent with a very difficult response. If you chose to first pocket the 1-ball, it would be hard to get close to the 2-ball to play an effective safety. Besides, if you pass on the first ball and play safe, your opponent will have one more ball to make if you leave a shot.

Pass on Shot, Hook at Long Range

Earl Strickland, one of the straightest shooter's ever to play the game, was faced with a long cross table shot on the 2-ball in a match against Efren Reyes at the Sands Regency Open 21, 1995. In a post match interview Strickland confided that he was a little off his game. Perhaps that's why he chose to play a safety against Reyes, even though Reyes has the best kicking game in pool. The Lesson: If a world champion can pass on an open shot, even if it would lead to shape on the next ball, so

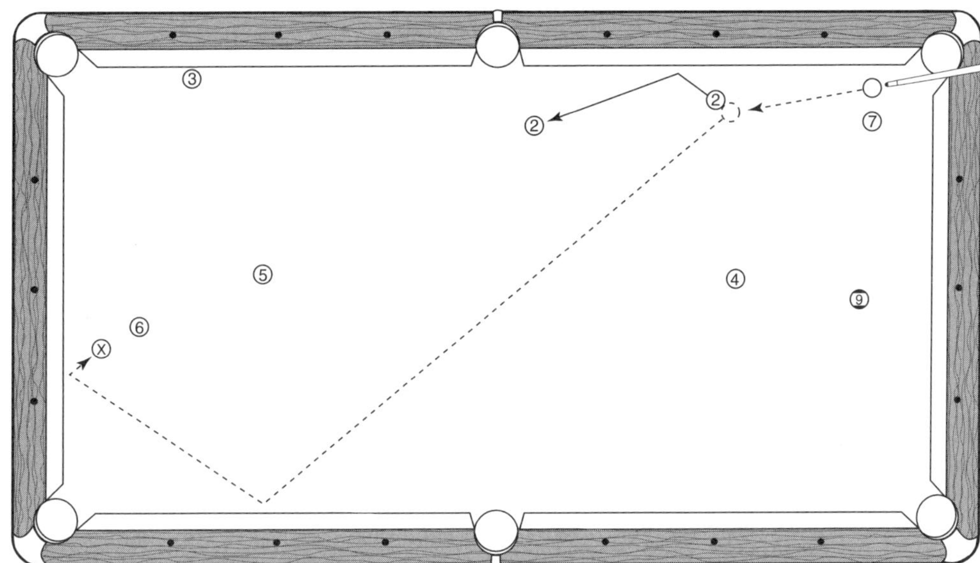

should you. Amateur players would be wise to consider playing a safety like this at all times if: 1) they are not particularly straight shooter's; 2) their opponent has a poor kicking game.

Pass on Shot for Sure Safe

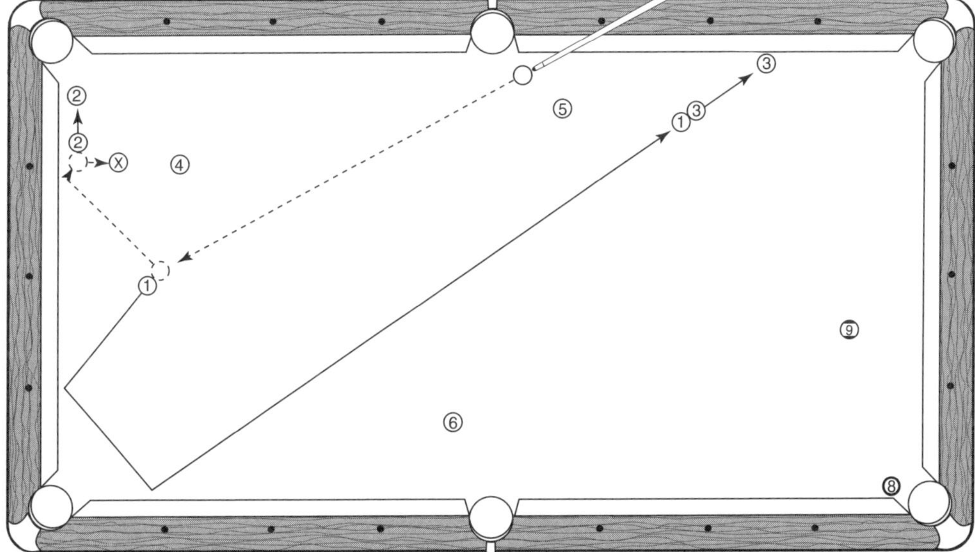

After making a ball on the break, Kim Davenport was confronted with a slow inside english position play off the rail on the 1-ball.. He decided against running out and instead played safe. A nearly full hit on the 1-ball with a medium hard stroke enabled him to slide the cue ball behind the 4-ball. The 2-ball helped to hold the cue ball in place. Davenport subsequently ran out on his next turn in this match that took place at the 1999 U.S. Open. Once again, if passing on an open shot is good enough for the pros, it is a strategy all players should consider.

Simplify the Rack with Ball In Hand

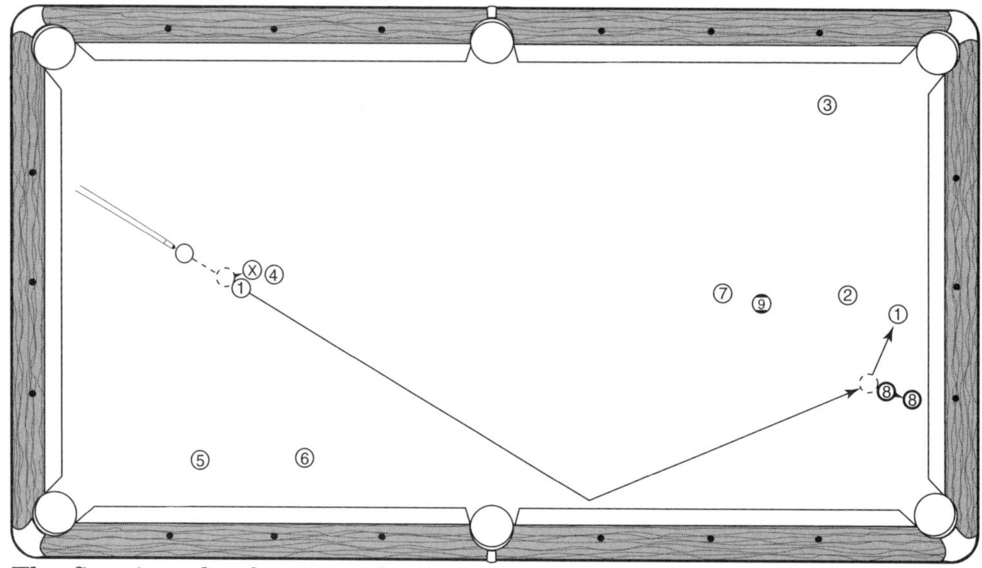

The first impulse for most players when awarded ball in hand is to set up a combo on the 9-ball or try to run out. Many times, however, it is better to delay gratification until the next turn by playing safe. Ball in hand allows you to get close to your work and exercise great control over the cue ball. This in turn can enable you to achieve a strategic objective while locking your opponent up tight.

Steve Mizerak employed this tactic by taking ball in hand and hooking his opponent behind the 4-ball. In doing so he accomplished his main objective of getting the 1-ball close to the 2-ball. He then ran out after Earl Strickland missed the hit on a difficult kick shot. This action took place at the 1994 U.S. Open.

Set Up Combo on the 9-Ball

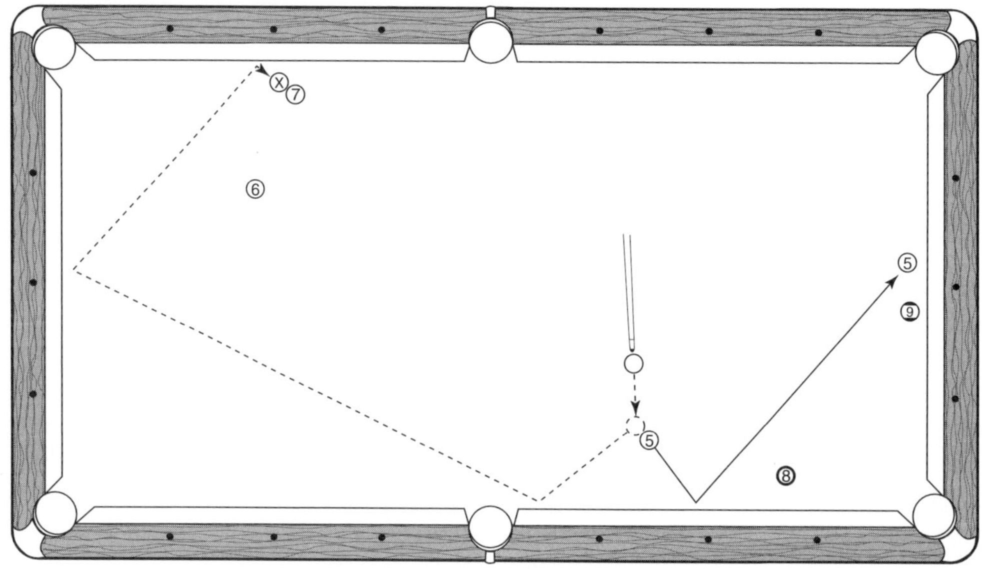

Steve Mizerak once again showed his expertise in the safety game at the 1994 U. S. Open as he tied up his opponent while setting up an easy 5-9 combo. On his next turn he was well rewarded for this strategic maneuver and his exquisite cue ball control with an easy win. The big key to this safety was routing the cue ball with perfect speed up next to the 7-ball. As a byproduct, the 5-ball ended up in perfect position for an easy combo. Mizerak would still have had a simple run with ball in hand even if the 5-ball had stopped short of the position in the diagram.

Leave Shots Your Opponent Doesn't Like

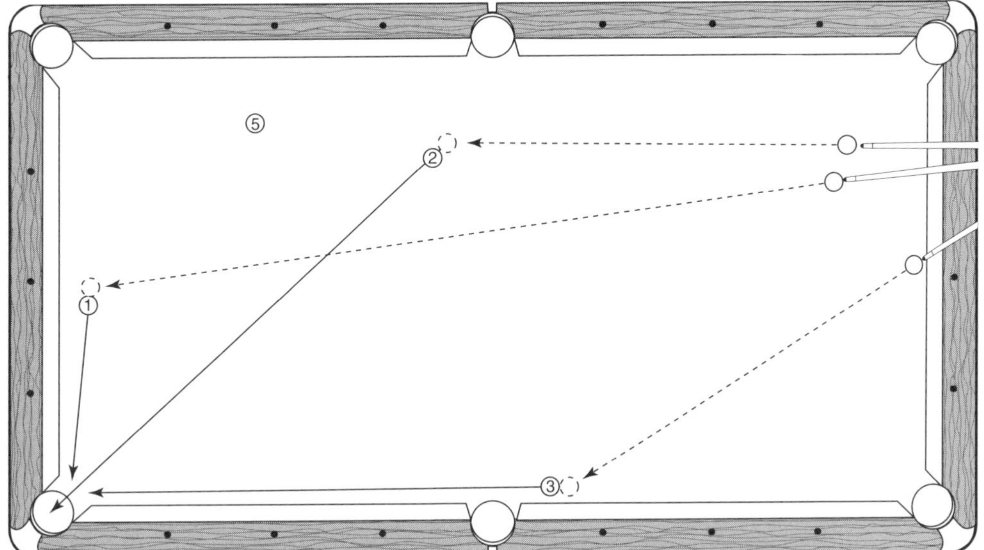

You don't have to always hide the cue ball to play an effective safety. Thin cuts, banks, shots off the rail and long distance shots can pose a problem for any player, much less an amateur who is not a particularly straight shooter. Leaving a tough shot at the right time is really based on your knowledge of the inherent difficulty of the shot and on your knowledge of your opponent's game and their tendencies. The proper timing for leaving tough shots can be influenced by the pressure of a particular situation. A big factor is your opponent's ability to respond to the challenge and pocket difficult shots while under the heat.

The illustration shows three of the zillions of tough shots that can bring out the worst in your opponent's game. The 1-ball is a table length 76-degree cut shot. If this shot was on the 9-ball, it would plenty tough. Should your opponent have to make this and play shape on anything but a hanger, then the odds of them getting out rise greatly. The cut angle on the 3-ball is a modest 30 degrees. However this shot is a monster thanks to the cue ball's position on the end rail. The 5-ball prevents the 2-ball from being played in the upper left corner pocket. This 41-degree cut angle is a very tough shot because of the distance factor and due to the unfamiliarity of cross table cuts, which are seldom played.

Creative Safety Play

After you have played Nine-Ball and studied the safety game for a while, you will have developed an arsenal of weapons that should enable you to handle 95% of the situations that require a safety. Your knowledge of the safety game and of how the balls interact with one another will, at times, be put to the test when you come across a position far from routine. Take a few extra moments under these circumstances to see if you can conjure up a creative solution rather than just throwing the outcome of the game up for grabs.

Imagination Creates a Winning Safety

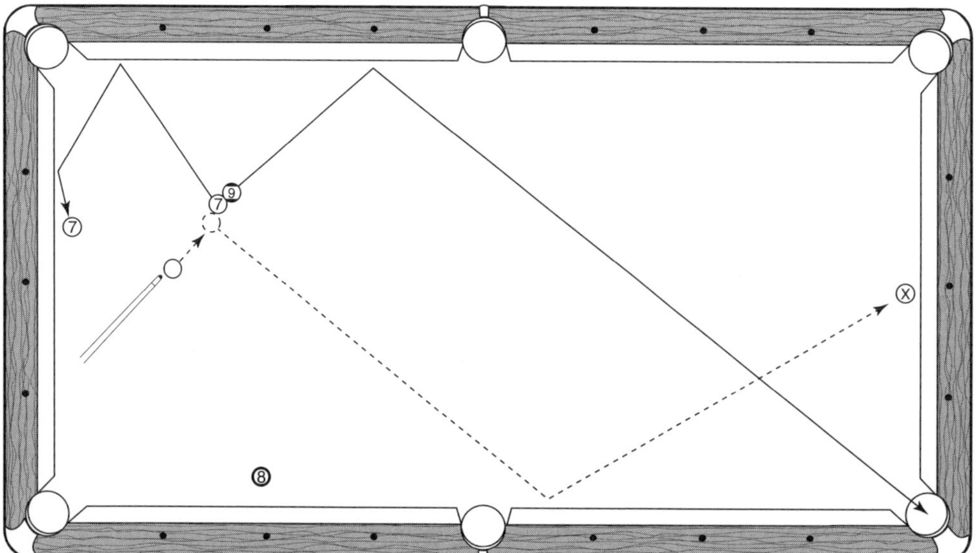

After missing position on the 7-ball (badly I might add) I was faced with this rather bleak looking position. After much inspection, I came to the realization that the 7-ball could be caromed off the 9-ball to the end rail as shown. Since the shot had to be struck rather firmly, the problem was in controlling the cue ball so it would not return back down the table . My creative solution was to go against my instincts and play a draw shot with inside english. This neutralized the cue balls speed and sent it along the path shown to the opposite end rail. The 9-ball continued into the lower right hand corner pocket. My opponent immediately cried about my luck, but good luck is often your reward when you execute a shot exactly as planned.

Grady's Near Masterpiece

Grady Matthews was faced with the rather daunting task of computing a safety, thanks to a little luck on a kick shot by Buddy Hall at the Sands Regency Open 15, 1992. Mathews drew on his extensive knowledge of Nine-Ball and the cue games in general and composed the safety in the diagram. The 3-ball traveled about 18' to the middle of the table while the cue ball rolled to a stop a long distance from the 3-ball. As matters would

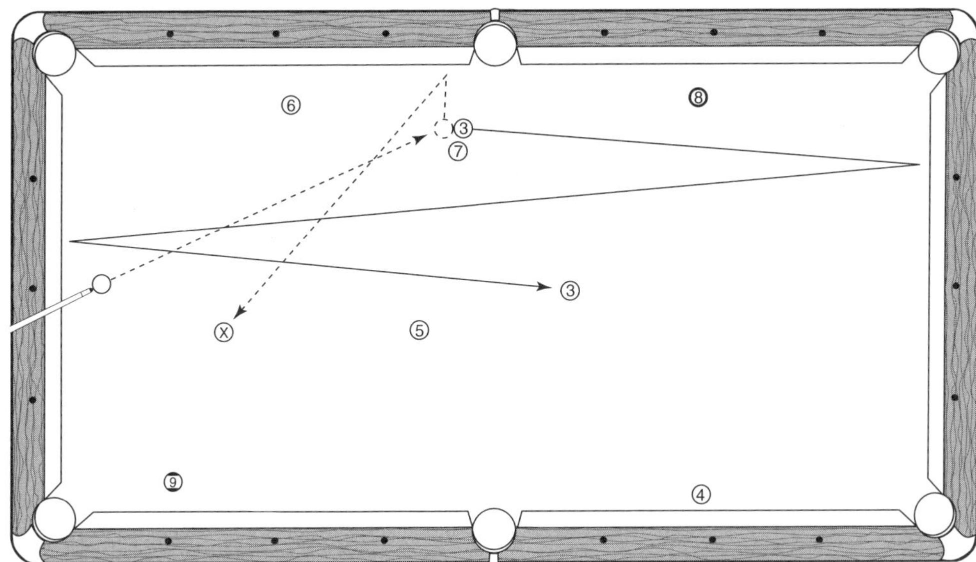

have it, Mathews' safety came up 2" short. Hall pocketed the 3-ball and ran out. Still this was a great safety that probably would have won the game for Mathews from 99.9% of all other pool players on the planet.

Jump and Hook

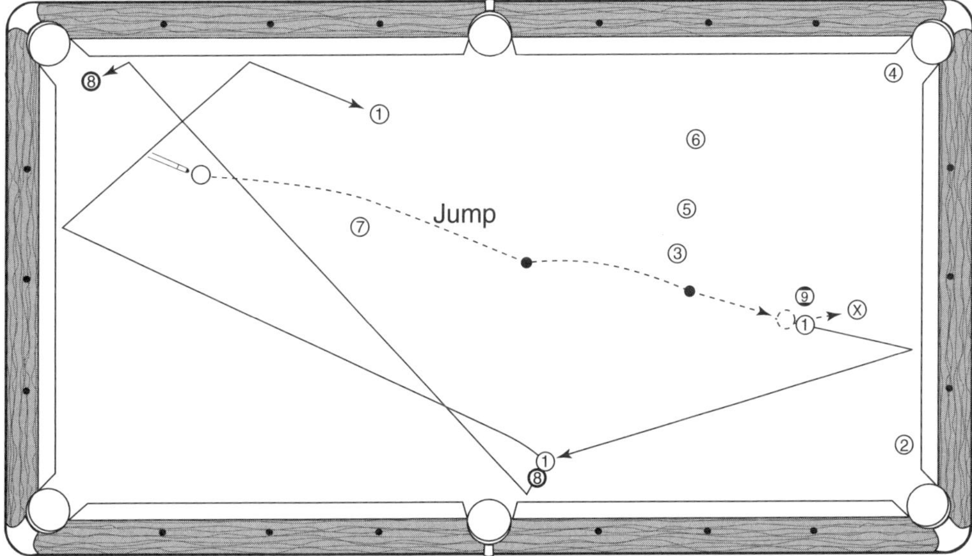

Loree Jon Jones left Allison Fisher hooked behind the 7-ball in a match at the 1999 WPBA Prescott Resort Classic. The 8-ball blocked the natural kick route to the 1-ball while the 2-ball took away the two-rail path. Ms. Fisher could have aimed below the 8-ball at the third diamond and played a kick shot with a hard stroke and draw, but the hit was very difficult. Her creative solution was to jack up her cue to 60-degrees elevation and sending the cue ball skyward. The cue ball hopped twice, struck the 1-ball solidly, driving it up the table. Meanwhile the cue ball drifted to a stop behind a row of blockers.

Rail First Safety

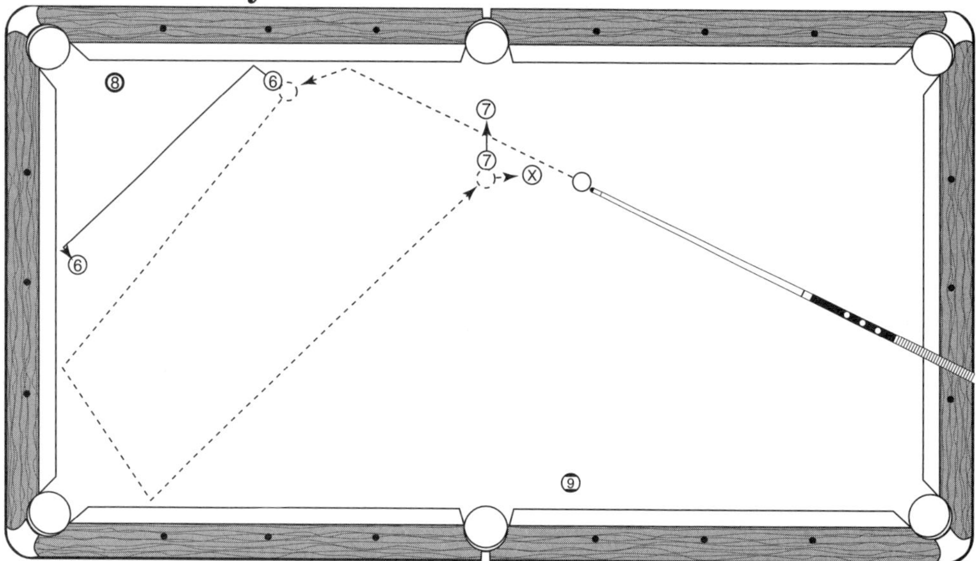

Keith McCready played this creative safety against Nick Varner at the Sands Regency Open 12, 1990. Rather than slugging at the kick shot, McCready played a finesse safety by hitting the 6-ball thinly after contacting the top side rail. Running english (left) was used to accelerate the cue ball off the second and third rails.

Use a Second Ball as a Stopper

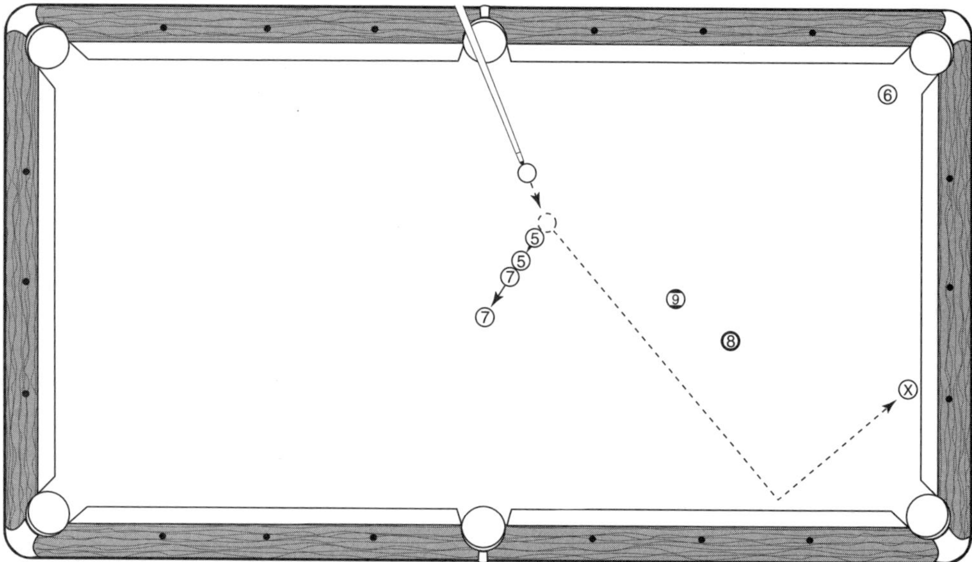

You have to be at least somewhat concerned with the object ball's ending location while attempting to hook your opponent on most safeties. Such is not the case when you have a stopper to hold the object ball in place after it has been struck by the cue ball. In the example, you can concentrate your energies on sending the cue ball to Position X, which is on the opposite side of the 8 and 9-balls.

CHAPTER 12

THE KICKING GAME

"I get more satisfaction out of a great kick shot than I do out of running the table."
Allison Fisher

A kick shot is played by banking the cue ball off one or more cushions before contact is made with the lowest numbered ball. Kick shots can appear for any of the following reasons: you are hooked after the break; your opponent got lucky after a miss; as a result of your opponent's safety; when you make a mistake playing position and hook yourself. Since you are going to be constantly facing kick shots, it follows that a strong kicking game is a most necessary skill in Nine-Ball.

Your opponent receives ball in hand after you have committed a foul. When playing a kick shot, you must hit the lowest numbered ball and drive either an object ball or cue ball to a rail. Failure to do so is a foul and results in ball in hand for your opponent. This rule encourages safety play. In fact, I am now seeing good to excellent safeties from amateur players at the "C" (average) level and above.

If your kicking skills are not up to par, your opponent's will take advantage of this deficiency and hit you with a barrage of safeties. After all, why should they take a chance on a moderately risky shot when they feel quite certain a safety will result in ball in hand? Hopefully this discussion has motivated you to hone your kicking game skills. If not, you'll discover the incentive after losing enough matches to players who are beating you with hook safeties, even though you are superior to them in most of the other areas of skill.

There is no getting around the luck factor that is an inherent part of all but the easiest of kick shots. This seems to disturb many players. When faced with a kick shot, those with a negative attitude towards kicking will bemoan their fate, and proceed to play the shot in a halfhearted manner. When you come up against one of these types, you've got the green light to play safety after safety.

Your Attitude Towards Kicking

I suggest that you adopt an attitude of positive expectancy when preparing to play a kick shot. If you plan wisely and execute the shot to the best of your ability, good things will happen enough of the time to make your efforts well worth it. There is a certain fascination that should accompany every kick shot. I like to think of them much like a golfer who is preparing to attempt a putt outside of the "gimme" range. The golfer knows they may not make the putt, especially if it is a 30 footer, for example. But that doesn't stop them from giving the putt their very best effort. Similarly, you should approach kick shots with the same attitude: plan the shot as best you can, give it a good go, and be pleasantly surprised when the shot turns out the way you want it to.

You must convince yourself that a kick shot is not punishment handed down by the Pool Gods. Enjoy the challenge of kicking. Try, really try, to make something good happen. Don't just go through the motions while possibly expecting the worst.

When you execute a devastating kick shot in response to your opponent's safety or lucky leave, the effect can be devastating. After all, they were probably expecting your effort to result in ball in hand. Act as though you expected to lock them up. This tactic could unnerve your opponent, who may begin to wonder how he can beat someone who kicks like Efren Reyes.

The #1 Basic Requirement

The #1 basic of the kicking game is that you acquire the ability to consistently make contact with the object ball. If you can at least hit the ball and drive either it or the cue ball to a rail without scratching, you have given yourself a chance for something good to happen. From this point forward, skill in the kicking game becomes increasingly complex. Some of the extras that add depth to your kicking game includes: kicking with the proper speed; kicking to hit a certain side of the ball; and kicking to meet a specific strategic objective.

"You can't get lucky if you miss it." **Pat Fleming**

The Possible Outcome – How You View a Kick Shot

Kick shots come in all sizes and degrees of difficulty. Kick shots almost always carry a much more uncertain outcome than do shots in which you are aiming directly at a ball. Because of this, you must often incorporate your feelings about the possible outcome of the shot into the planning process. Your perception of the difficulty of the kick often plays a big part in your feelings about the possible outcome of the shot.

A Game Plan for the Kicking Game

The ideas below should be instrumental in helping you to develop a solid approach to the kicking game. The game plan is based on playing the percentages as much as possible, as opposed to just slugging away.

Build a Solid Foundation

Construct a solid foundation by mastering the basic concepts and kick routes that you will most often encounter.

Your Style

You can play most kick routes without using english. Nevertheless, many players feel more comfortable applying a little running english to most of their kick shots.

Your Goals Can Change

New players should have a goal of hitting the ball. As your skills progress, you can adopt more sophisticated goals and strategies.

The Conditions

The playing conditions have a large effect on the kicking game. With enough experience and attention to detail, you will learn how to quickly adjust to the table you are playing on.

Early Versus Late Game Strategy

Kick battles are most common early in the game when blockers abound. You will most likely have to adopt a different approach to kicking in the later stages of a rack.

The Main Objective

Your main objective should be to play a safety on most kick shots unless the object ball is directly in front of a pocket.

Kicking Battles

Kick/safety battles can last several innings. Be mentally prepared to battle long and hard for control of the table.

Speed Control is Crucial

Speed control is a valuable asset in the kicking game. Don't just blast away and hope for the best. There will, however be rare occasions when the power blast and pray approach is your best choice.

Play the Percentages

There are few certainties when playing kick shots. The idea is to stack the odds as much as possible in your favor.

Basics of Kicking

The Importance of Speed Control

There are two main components to a kick shot: the route and speed of stroke. This sounds like the requirements for playing position doesn't it? When playing a kick shot, hitting the ball and avoiding a foul is almost always not good enough by itself. For a kick shot to be a success, it must meet a specific strategic objective. This is accomplished with the hit on the object ball and the speed with which the shot is played. Later in the chapter there are examples of kick shots that range from a very soft stroke (a 2 on the Spectrum of Speed) all the way to kick shots hit with an extremely hard stroke (a 9 on the Spectrum of Speed).

Adjusting for Speed and the Table

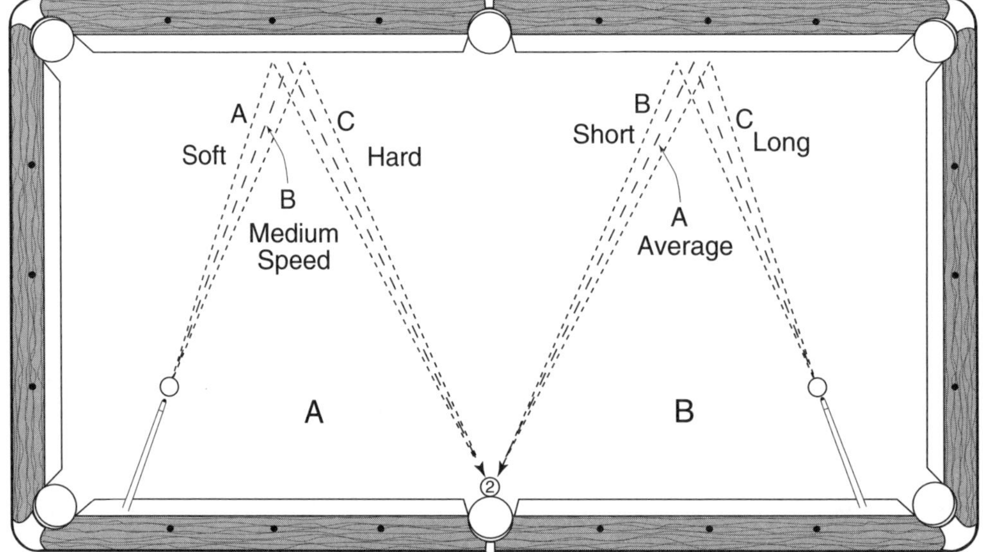

The speed with which you play a kick shot has a significant impact on the cue ball's rebound angle. Part A shows the cue ball's rebound path when it is hit with three very different speeds of stroke. A soft stroke will send the cue ball into the rail and out towards the 2-ball down Path A. The cue ball will rebound at a sharper angle when hit with a medium speed of stroke, which is shown by Path B. The sharpest rebound angle is created by a hard stroke, which leads to Path C. Even though the goal is to hit the 2-ball with each kick shot, the point of aim on the rails must accommodate each speed of stroke.

You must make similar adjustments when playing on unfamiliar tables. In Part B, Path A shows your "average" table. If a table banks "short", that means your kick shot will travel down a path beneath that which you expected. You must compensate for this by aiming further down the rail, as shown by Path B. A table plays "long" if the cue ball rebounds at a shallower angle than normal. In this case, you need to adjust your aim to hit the first rail closer than usual. Path C demonstrates how to compensate for a table that plays long.

Combining Adjustments

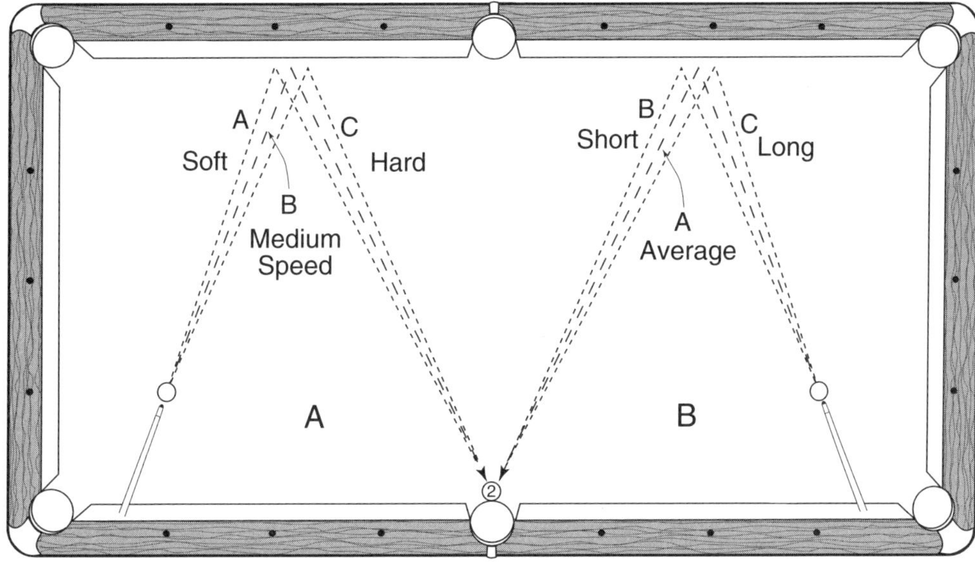

So far we've talked about how to make a single adjustment for speed of stroke and the table. In the real world of kicking, you will very often be called upon to make multiple adjustments. Sometimes these adjustments may cancel each other out. For example, if a table plays long, you can offset this with a hard stroke. And if a table plays short, you could cancel this by using a softer stroke than normal.

Most of the time, however, you may not have the luxury of matching the speed of stroke to the table. For example, even if a table plays short, it might not be practical to use a soft stroke on a kick shot. Remember, you are almost always better off playing a kick shot at the speed that the shots calls for. If a table plays short and the kick calls for a hard stroke, for example, you must aim well past the normal point of aim to compensate adequately for both the table and the hard stroke. This is shown by Part A of the diagram above. The aiming equation is reversed in Part B. When a table plays long and you are using a soft stroke, you will have to aim much further towards the near side of the rail to allow properly for both the table and the soft stroke.

How to Adjust to the Table

Shot Requirements	Table Plays	Do This
Hard stroke	Long	Aim normally (Cancel out)
Hard stroke	Short	Aim very long
Soft stroke	Long	Aim short
Soft stroke	Short	Aim normally (Cancel out)
Medium stroke	Long	Aim short
Medium stroke	Short	Aim long

English Pick Up

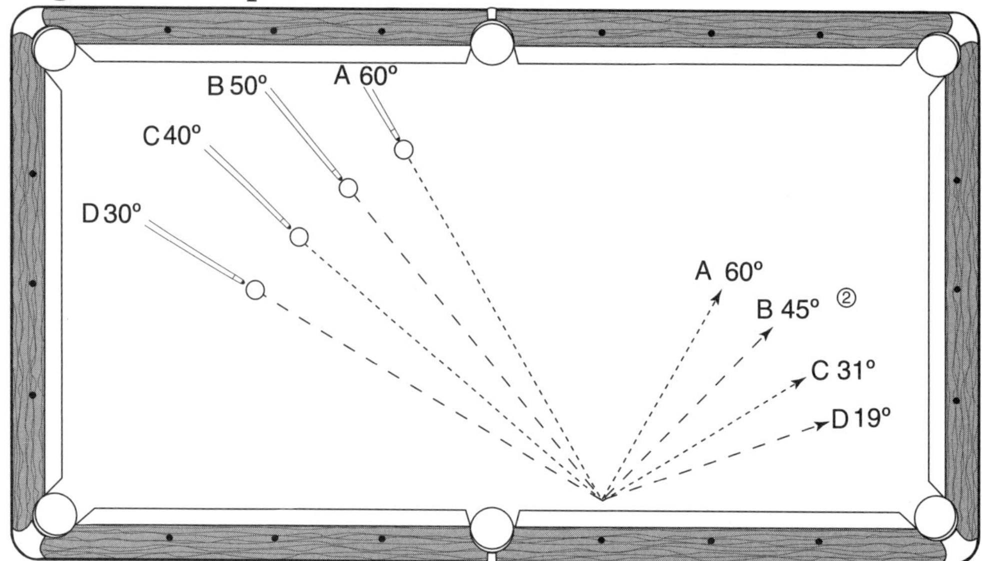

The angle of incidence equals the angle of reflection is a fancy way of saying that the cue ball will rebound from the rail at the same angle at which it entered the rail. While this is certainly true some of the time, on most occasions there will be a small to large difference in the two angles.

When the cue ball enters the rail at a 60-degree angle down Route A, it will rebound at the same angle when shot with a medium speed. When the entrance angle dips below 60-degrees, the cue ball starts to rebound at a shallower angle. The cue ball on Route B entered the rail at 50-degrees and exited at only 45-degrees, thanks to a slight pick up of english off the side rail. In Route C the cue ball entered at 40-degrees and exited at only 31-degrees. And finally, the cue ball on Route D entered at 30-degrees and departed at only 19-degrees.

English pick up off the side rail is one of the main reasons why so many players have trouble kicking at balls in the middle of the table. The tendency is to miss on the far side of the ball because of the failure to adjust for the natural opening of the rebound angle. In the example, a player kicking down Route C at the 2-ball would have a tendency to miss to the ball on the far side.

Testing a Table

Before you begin a match, take a just a few moments to run some tests that can inform you of how a table is playing. You'll certainly want to run these tests on unfamiliar equipment, but also consider conducting them on the table(s) you play on regularly as conditions do change thanks to humidity, temperature and the aging of the cloth.

Illustration #1 shows a couple of kick routes that can alert you to the current playing conditions. Route A is a very common three-rail kick route that was played with a medium speed and a half tip of follow.

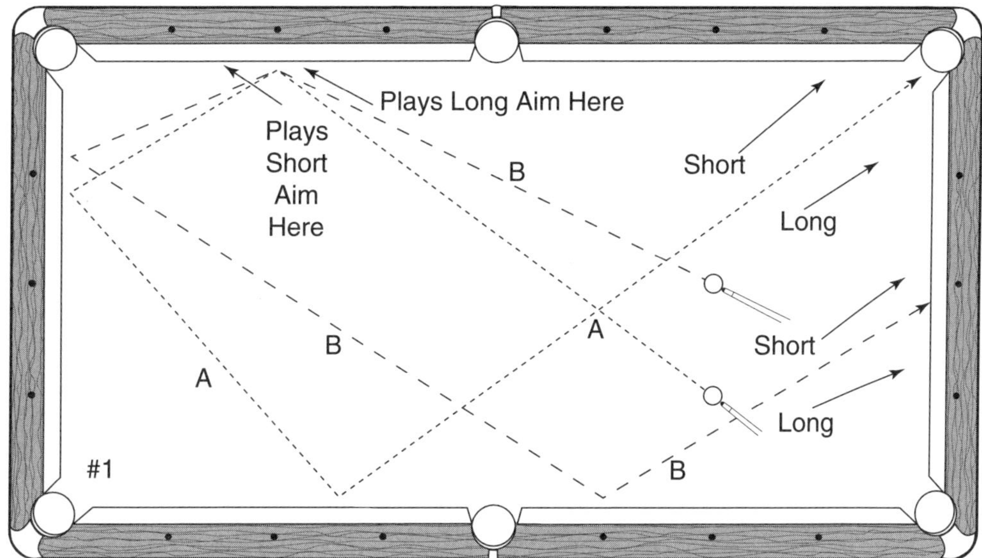

No english was used. The cue ball will head directly toward the corner pocket on an “average” table. If the table is playing short, the cue ball will strike the side rail. And if the table is playing long, it will hit the end rail. If the table is playing either long or short, adjust your point of aim and try the kick again. Keep adjusting until you make the ball.

Route B is played with a medium speed and half tip of follow. The cue ball should strike the third rail a few inches from the middle diamond. If the cue ball hits to either side, make the necessary adjustment and try again until you are hitting the target on the rail.

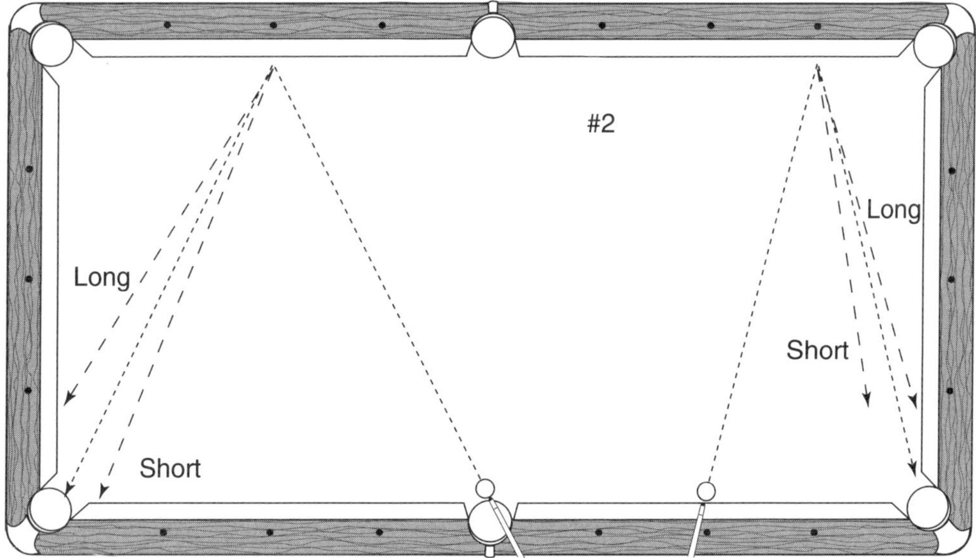

Illustration #2 gives you some additional tests that will only take a few moments, but that could make the difference between winning and losing.

The ABC's of Kicking Targets

You need to be realistic about your current level of skill when planning your kick shots An accurate assessment of your level of proficiency can help you make better decisions and be useful in managing your expectations. The first step is to rate your current level of skill at the kicking game using the ABC rating scale. Remember, an A Player is a expert player, a B Player is at the intermediate (advanced) level, and a C Player is an average player. When you are playing competitively, set your targets based on your level of skill and the degree of difficulty of the kick shot you are about to play.

Targeting Based of Your Skill and the Degree of Difficulty

Easy to Hit (But not a pocket hanger)

- **C** players go for three quarters hit on the correct side.
- **B** players go for a half ball hit on the correct side.
- **A** players go for the pocket or a precise safety. Hit the desired frac tion of a ball.

Medium Difficult to Hit

- **C** players go for a hit the easiest route possible.
- **B** players go for a side of the ball.
- **A** players go for a half ball hit or less on the correct side.

Hard to Hit

- **C** players go for the hit.
- **B** players go for the hit.
- **A** players can slightly favor one side of the ball.

Very Hard to Hit

- **C** players consider other options, such as tying up balls or moving money balls away from the pocket.
- **B** players go for the hit or consider other options.
- **A** players go for hitting the ball or, in extreme cases, playing an intentional foul while tying up some balls.

Kicking to Hit

The Triangle Method

The triangle method gives you a reliable measuring tool for calculating where to aim on the rail to hit the object ball. The method works best when the rebound angle is above 60-degrees. In Part A, the cue ball entered and exited the rail at 70-degrees along a path straight to the 4-ball. The contact point on the rail was set by using the diamonds to create the triangle in the illustration.

Start by estimating a contact point on the opposite side rail. Then draw line C-D. Now hold your cue over the middle of the cue ball with the tip pointing at the estimated contact point on the opposite rail. Now you measure Distance A between the cue's contact point on the bottom rail and Point D. Now duplicate this distance on the opposite side of Point D. This will give you the point where the right side of the triangle contacts the bottom rail (B-1). Now hold your cue from B-1 to the estimated contact point

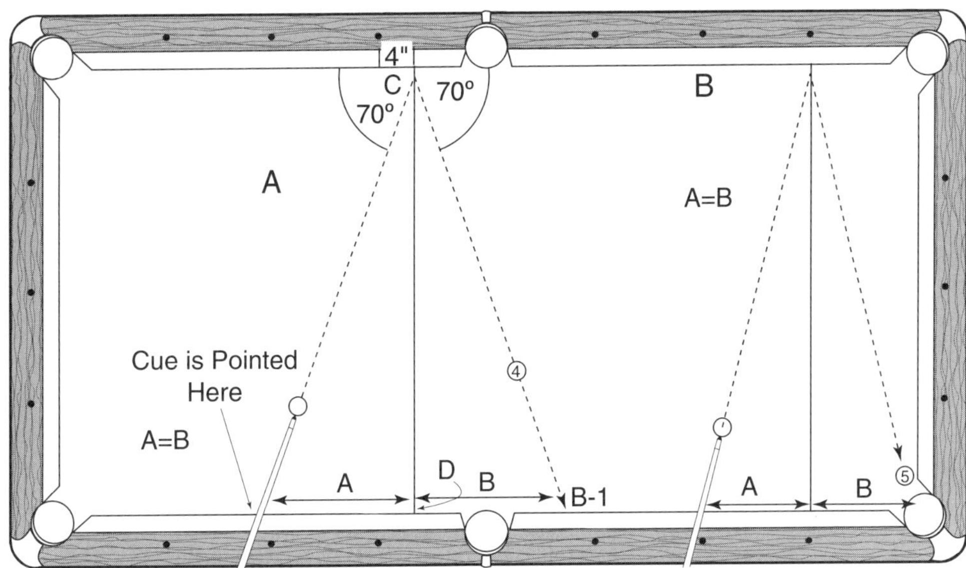

at C. If the object ball is under your cue, you have the correct point of aim. You will usually not be far off with your original guesstimate, in which case a small adjustment to the point of aim is all that is necessary to establish the correct contact point with the rail.

The Dominant Rail

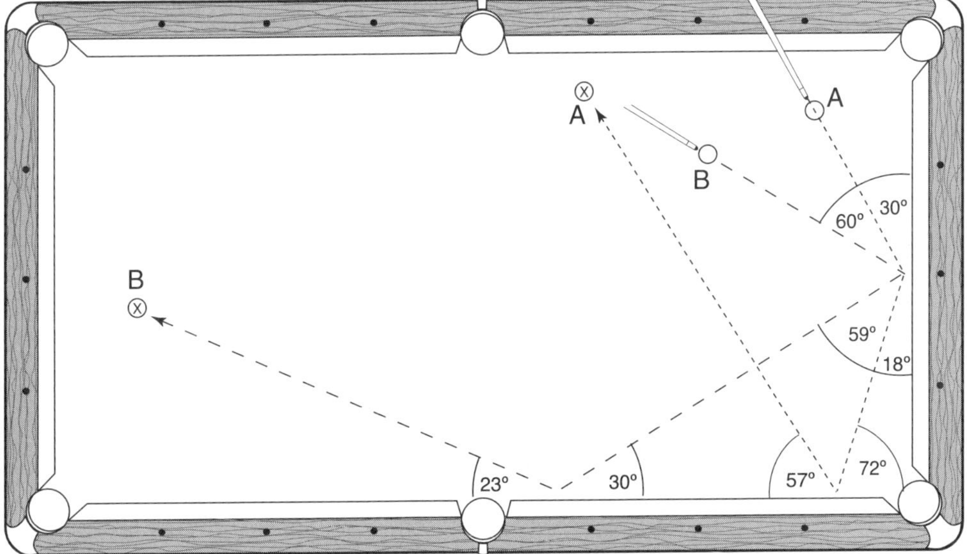

When a kick route covers two rails, either the first or second rail will dominate the cue ball's path. When the cue ball was sent into the rail at 30-degrees (Route A) it rebounded off the first rail at 18-degrees. It then entered the second rail at 72-degrees and exited at 57-degrees. The second rail exerted a slightly greater influence on the path of the cue ball. When the cue ball entered the first rail at 60-degrees, it exited at 59-degrees. The dominant rail was the second rail as the cue ball entered it at 30- degrees and rebounded at only 23-degrees.

Kicking Past Obstructers

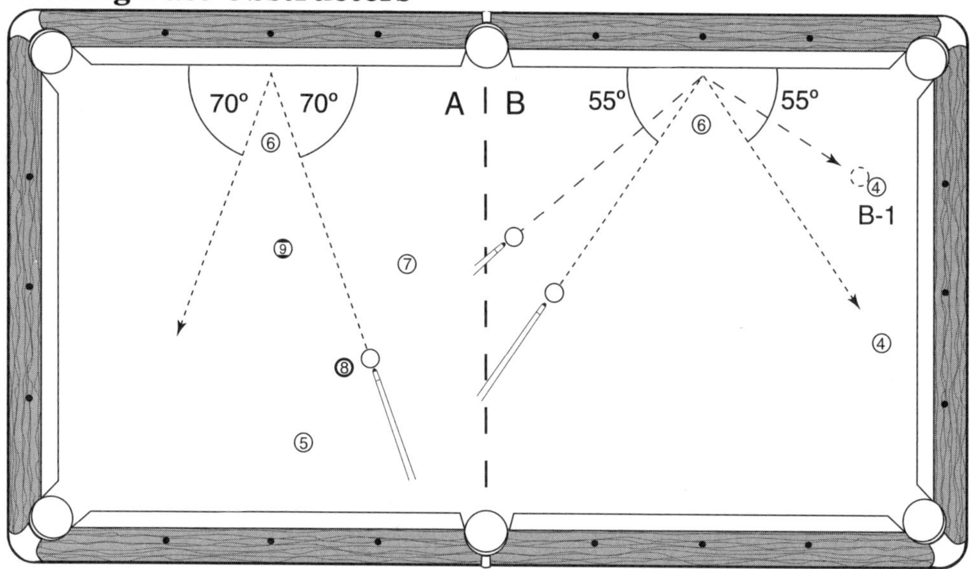

In Part A, your only route to the 4-ball is past the 6-ball. When an obstructer is 7" from the rail, you can enter and exit at a 70-degree angle or less without hitting it. In Part B, the obstructer (the 6-ball) is only 4" from the rail. Now you need an entrance angle of 55-degrees or less to clear the 6-ball. The 4-ball using Route A was hit with follow. If you have a little room to spare, you can aim wide of the obstructer and spin past it with outside english. This as shown by Route B to the 4-ball at B-1.

Two or Three Rails is Often Better than One

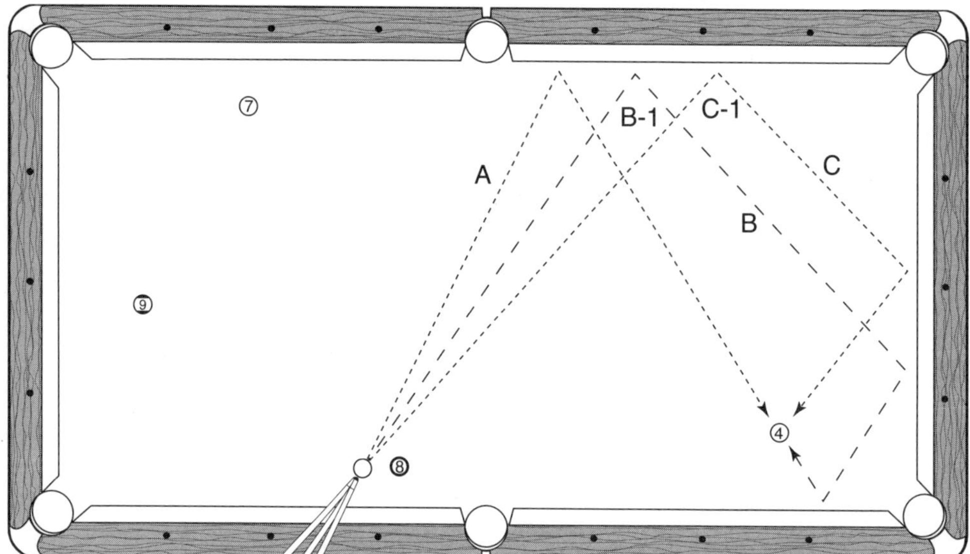

The 4-ball is several inches from the rail. You could easily miss the 4-ball when using Route A. Even if you hit the 4-ball, a sell out is likely. A better choice is Route B, which takes the cue ball two rails into the 4-ball. Route C also gives you a great chance of hitting the ball.

Aim at the Big Ball

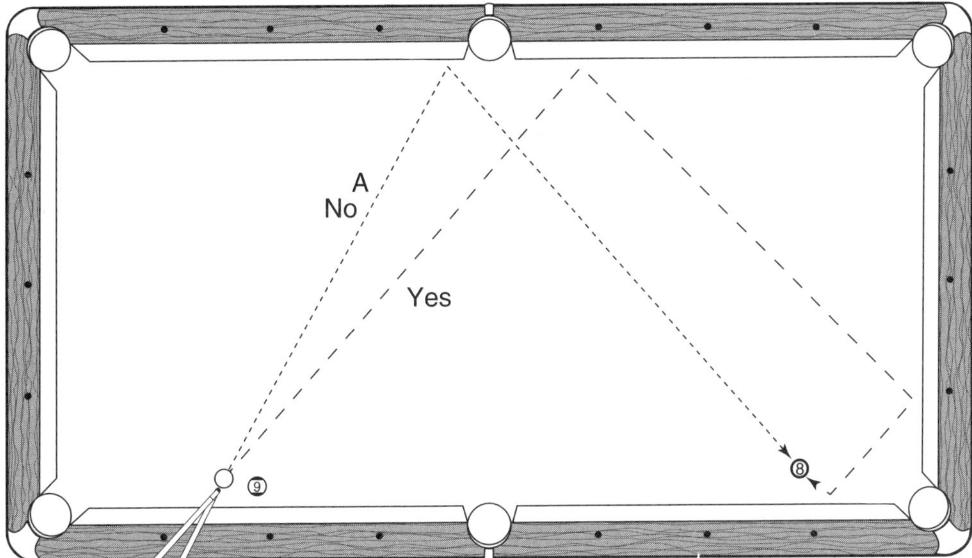

The one-rail route to the 8-ball seems the easier and more direct, but it is loaded with danger. You could scratch by squeezing the cue ball between the 8-ball and the rail, or by hitting the 8-ball slightly left of full. This route may also result in both balls remaining at the right side of the table. The high percentage play is to kick two-rails for the 8-ball. Hitting the 8-ball is almost guaranteed. In addition, you could drive the 8-ball to the opposite end of the table, making things much tougher for your opponent.

Long Distance End Rail Kicks

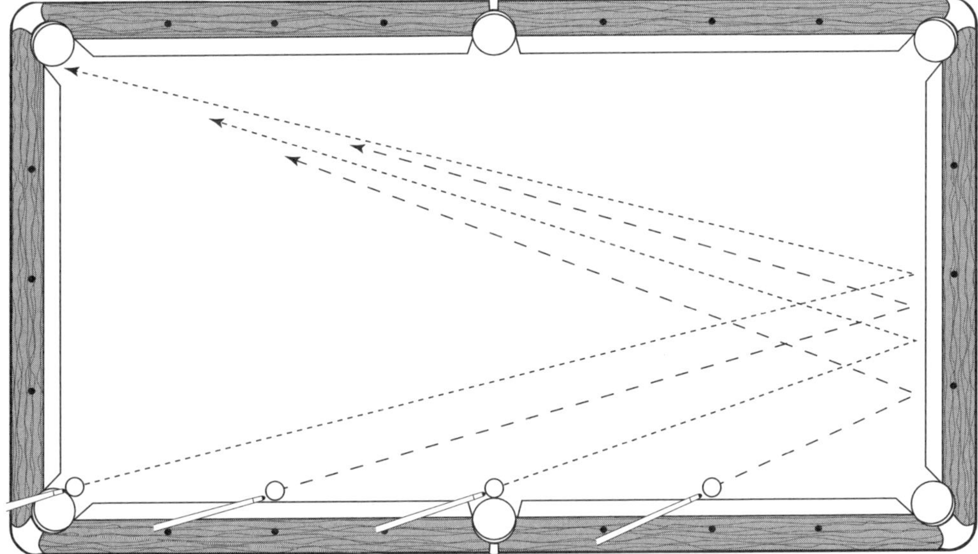

The cue ball is entering the rail at a fairly steep angle in each of the four positions shown, which means the exit angle off the end rail is very predictable. These kick routes should be useful in hitting or pocketing balls near the upper left corner pocket.

The Side Pocket Gap

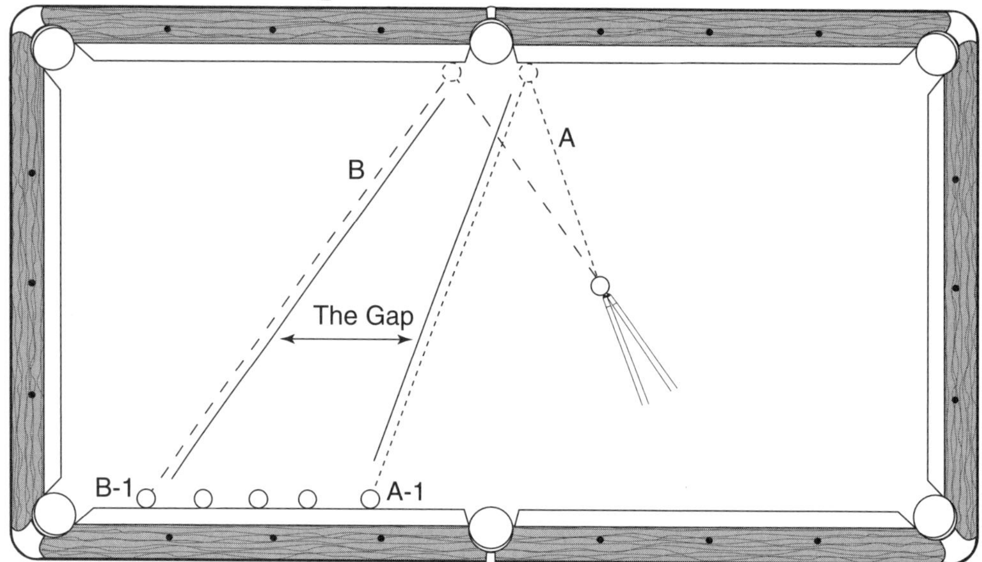

Three cushion players don't know how good they have it, not having to contend with obstructions like pockets, unlike us poor pool players. So be it. Either side pocket can block your kick shots off the side rails. The 5.5" wide side pocket effectively removes about an 8.75" wide target zone from the side rail. This comes from adding up 5.5" for the pocket, a half inch on either side for a margin for error, and 1.13" on either side for the radius of the cue ball.

The diagram illustrates the effect that the missing chunk of the rail exerts on kick shots. Kicking to the top rail along Route A results in contact with the bottom side rail at A-1. Kicking down Route B on the opposite side of the side pocket leads to contact with the bottom side rail at B-1. On both of these shots, 1/2 tip of follow was used with a medium hard stroke. A line drawn down the inner edge of the cue ball that connects where it strikes each side rail gives you the boundaries for the gap. You would miss contact with any ball located within the gap if you played a kick shot with a half tip of follow and a medium hard stroke.

If the ball you must hit resides within the gap, you will need to adjust the route to access the gap by: varying the speed of your stroke; applying english; using draw or follow, or some combination of the adjustments above. I suggest you play Routes A and B, each time marking the position where they hit the side rail. Then place several target balls along the bottom side rail. Try to hit them from either side of the side pocket. This will teach you much about effects of english and how to alter the cue ball's path off the rail.

Corner Pocket Gaps

Since you can't kick all the way into the corner because of the pocket, you will have to allow for the gap created by the pocket. You can only kick so close to the corner pocket before you start flirting with the point of the

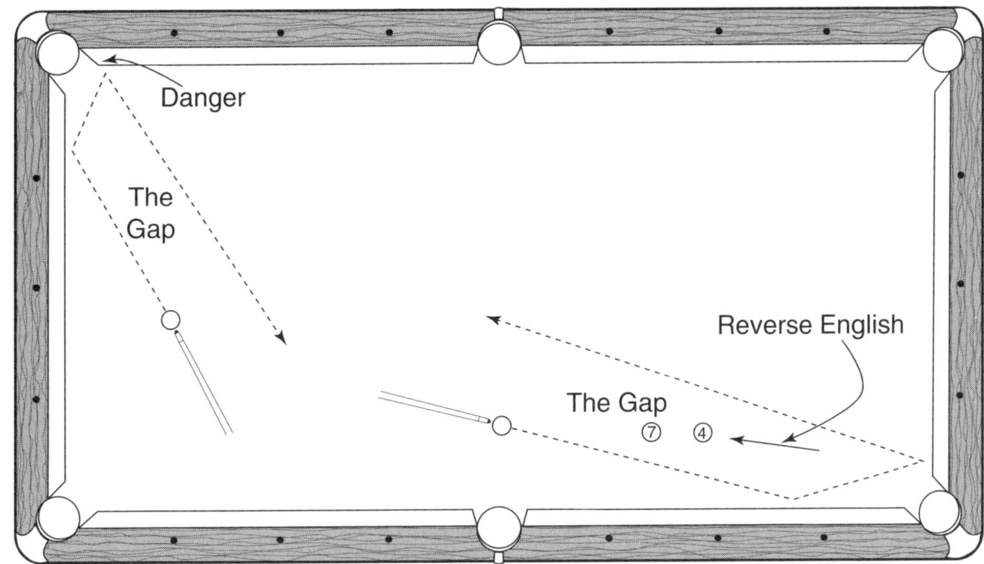

pocket adjacent to the second rail. Let's say you needed to hit the 4-ball and the end rail was your only choice. You would have to use right (reverse) english. Reverse (inside) english kick shots are extremely difficult to regulate, and take a lot of practice to master.

"The Shot Heard Around the Pool World"

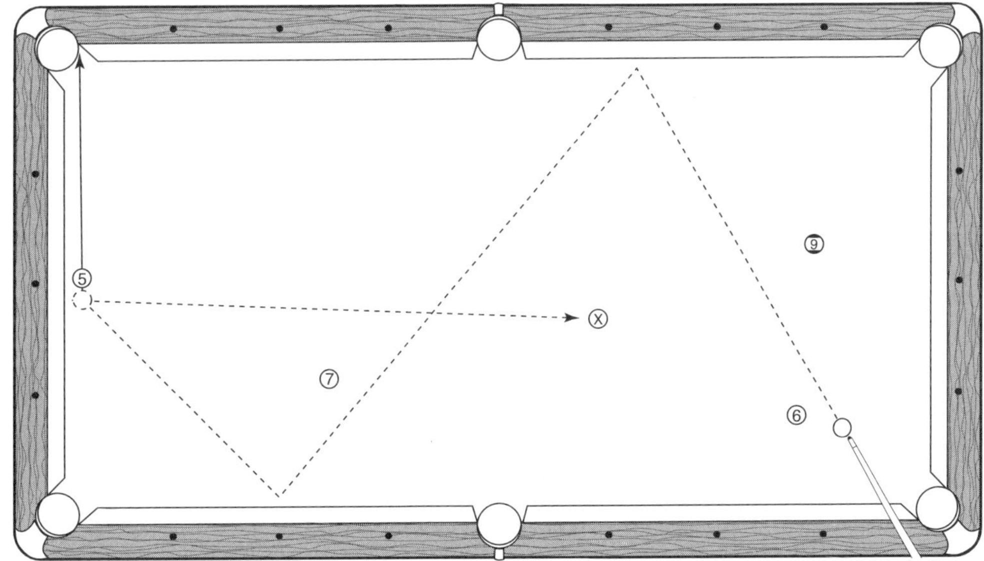

The final match of the Sands Regency Open 21, 1996 was tied at 12 in a race to 13 between Efren Reyes and Earl Strickland when Reyes inadvertently hooked himself. After a few moments of contemplation, he uncorked a monster "Z" shaped kick shot, making the 5-ball. He then ran out for the title. The moral: never give up, cause you never know what might happen if you make a good hit.

> *"I can't think of a greater shot and I've made millions of them."*
> **Earl Strickland**

Kick to Separate the Balls

The Big Ball Ensures a Hit

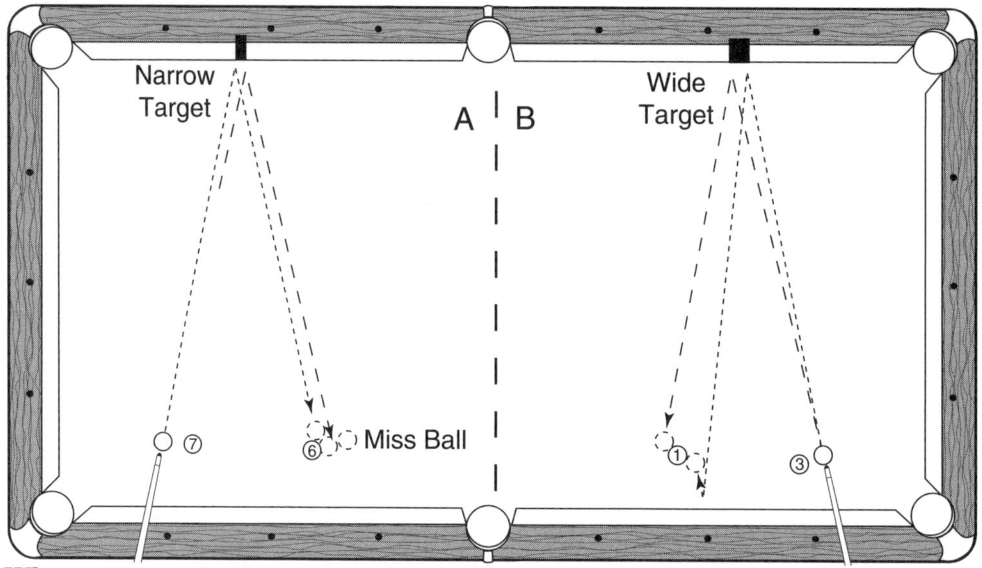

When you are in the early stages of learning the kicking game, you want to ensure that you make contact with the object ball. Experienced players with a relatively sound kicking game may also chose to go for a sure hit on certain occasions when they are:

- In a match with a player of their caliber for strategic purposes.
- Playing a less skilled opponent who is not much of a threat to run out, except with ball in hand.
- To avoid having their opponent line up a combo or ride a money ball with ball in hand.

In Part A, if you are highly skilled at the kicking game, you could kick for the outside edge of the 6-ball. If you are successful in hitting the 6-ball, you could drive it towards the left end rail while the cue ball relocates to the opposite end of the table. The penalty for missing is ball in hand.

The balls are in the same relative positions in Part B. Notice how your target on the rail is much wider when you are playing to either hit the ball first or to go to the bottom side rail before making contact. Use a hard stroke on this kick to make sure the object ball (or cue ball) strikes a rail if the cue ball hits the second rail before contacting the object ball.

Separate the Balls

Quite often the goal is to put distance between the cue ball and object ball by sending each ball to the opposite ends of the table. This shot requires a bit of a gamble, but less than the kick shot in Part A of the previous illustration. Aim for full contact with the object ball. Hopefully your aim

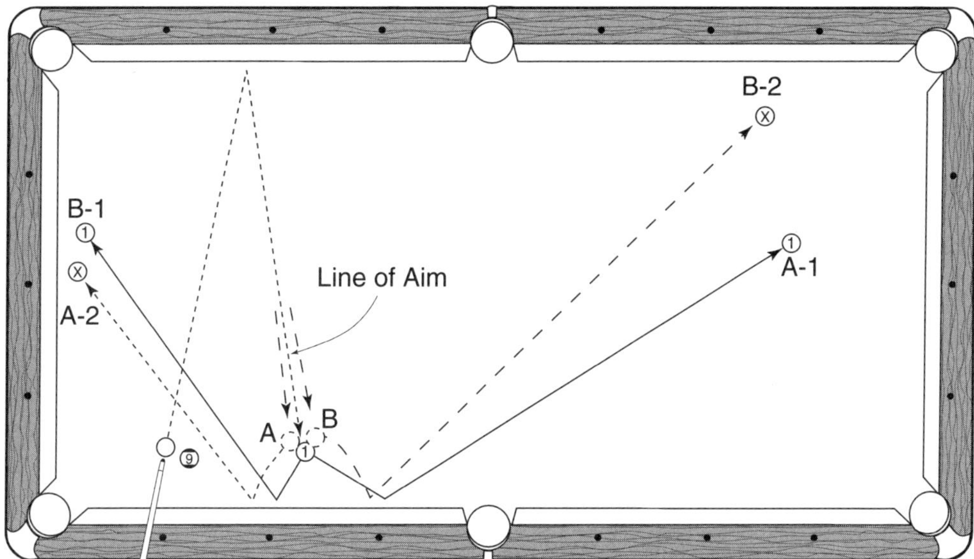

will be slightly off in either direction. If you kick down Route A and hit the lower half of the 1-ball, it will travel to A-1 while the cue ball relocates to A-2. If you "miss" down Route B to the upper side of the 1-ball, it will rebound to B-1 while the cue ball rolls down table to B-2.

Separate the Balls

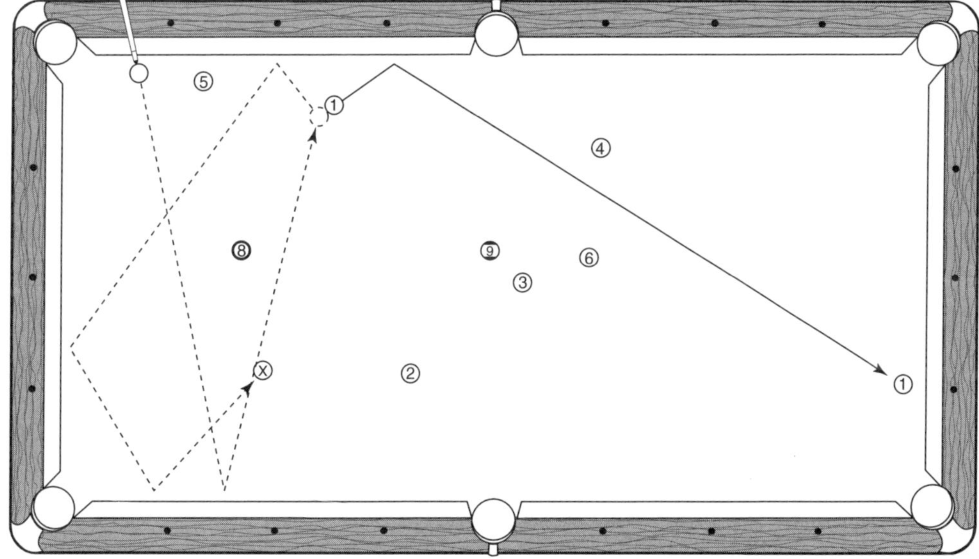

Jim Rempe was in a bind when he stepped to the table during his match with Francisco Bustamante at the 1999 U.S. Open. Rempe rifled the cue ball across table and back into the left side of the 1-ball, sending it to the opposite end rail. The cue ball traveled three-rails to behind the 2-ball. Rempe won this game and eventually the match on his way to a very respectable 5th place finish.

Kick to Hook

Kicking at Balls Near a Rail

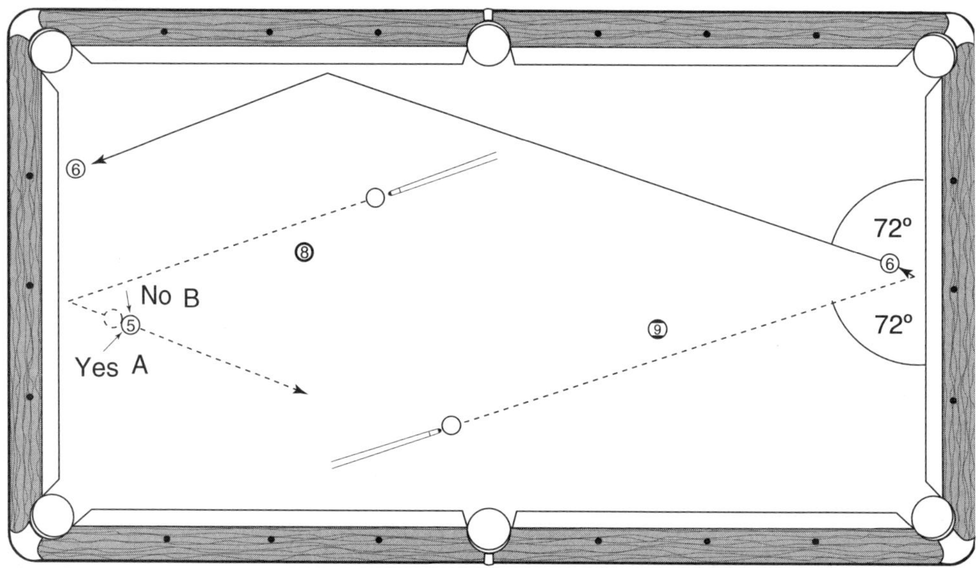

The diagram shows a kick shot where the odds are stacked heavily in your favor. Here's the situation: the 6-ball is close to the rail; you have room to go in behind it; your angle of attack is quite steep, which makes hitting the ball fully a cinch. Use a medium hard follow stroke. The follow turns into draw when the cue ball bounces off the rail, stopping the cue ball dead. The 6-ball will travel to the other end of the table, leaving your opponent in worse shape than he left you with his safety. Be sure not to push out to this useless hook unless you are playing a novice who hasn't leaned that being hooked in this position is usually an advantage!

When the ball you are kicking for is this close to the rail, the obstructing ball will always be adjacent to your line of aim. You can use the obstructer as an aide in establishing your line of aim.

The 5-ball is just a couple of inches further from the rail, but this short distance significantly raises the degree of difficulty of this kick safety. Now you must aim with great care. Since this kick is not a sure thing, you may wish to favor Side A of the 5-ball as this usually avoids a complete sell out. If the cue ball hits Side B, an unfavorable result is much more likely.

Kick and Stick

Nick Varner was stuck behind the 4-ball in a match with Mike Sigel at the 1990 U.S. Open when he played the outstanding kick and stick shot in the illustration on the next page. Varner's aim was perfect as he hit the 1-ball square on the nose. At this angle, a hard draw stroke was used to stop the cue ball dead. Varner unfortunately hit the shot a little too good as the 1-ball crawled just past the blockers. Sigel made the cut shot into the upper left corner pocket and ran out. The lesson: sometimes our best is very good, but just not quite good enough under the circumstances.

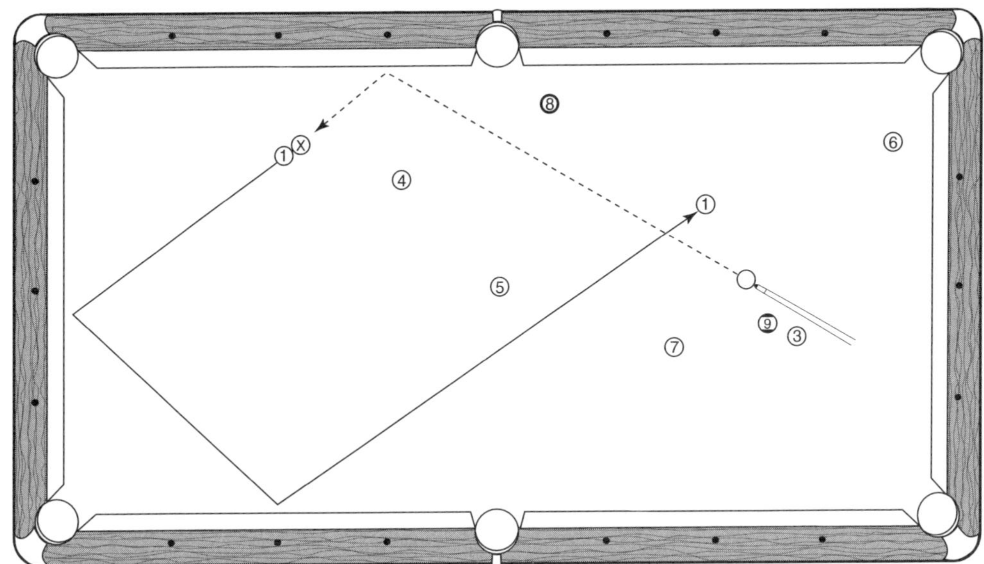

Two Rail Stick and Hook at High Speed

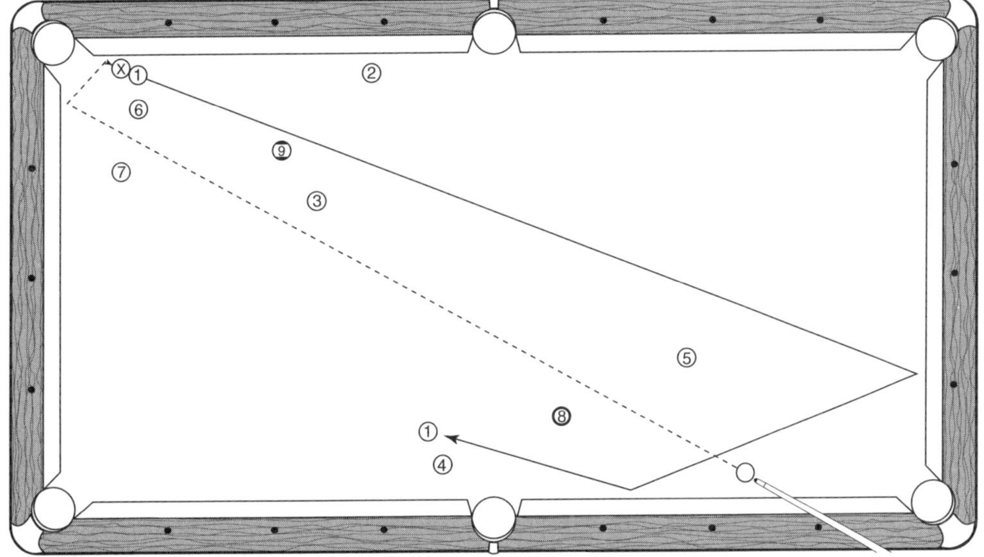

Efren Reyes used this kick and stick shot to grab a 3-1 lead over Nick Varner on his way to winning the finals of the 1994 U.S. Open. Reyes loaded up the cue ball with topspin and used a hard stroke to send the cue ball two-rails in behind the 1-ball. The cue ball remained motionless behind the 6-ball while the 1-ball scurried around the table before coming to rest.

A Soft Hit Kick Safety

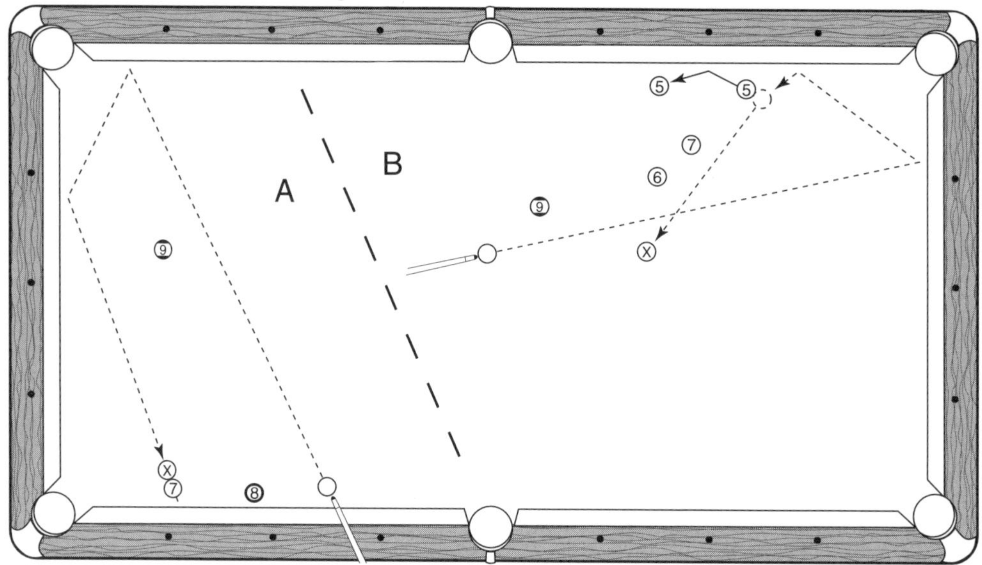

The shot in Part A calls for a very soft stroke and a near perfect two-rail route. The goal is to bump the 7-ball to the rail. This kind of kick is for advanced players who have a fine touch and excellent directional control. The two-rail route to the edge of the 5-ball is played with left english and a soft stroke. It is designed to take advantage of the blockers nearby.

Kick and Hook One-Rail

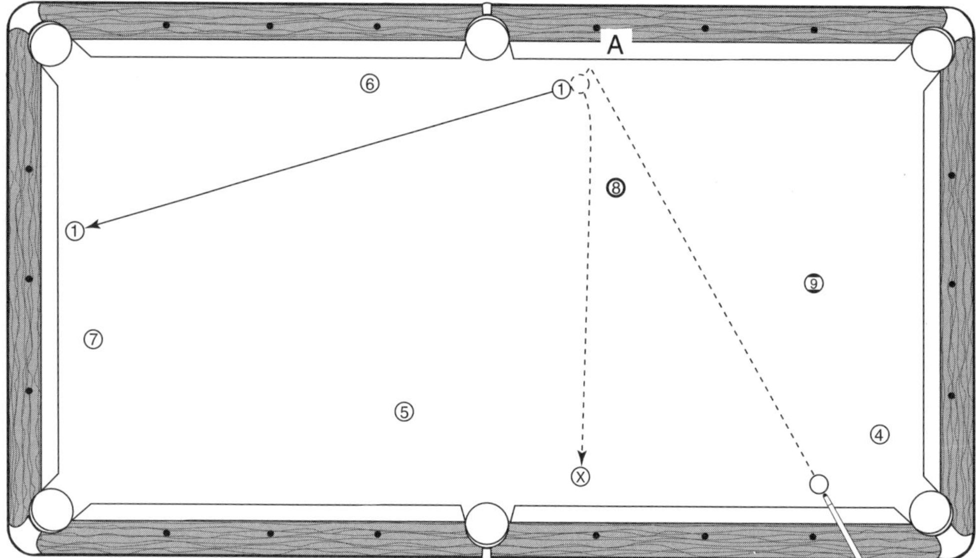

Efren Reyes and Johnny Archer went double-hill at the Sands Regency Open 23, 1996. The final game was a tense 13-inning duel that included this precision one-rail kick by Reyes. The big key was hitting the correct portion of the 1-ball. When the ball you are kicking for is close to the rail, you can hit the ball with great accuracy. I suggest that you walk over to Point A to determine the desired contact point on kick shots like this.

Kick and Hook

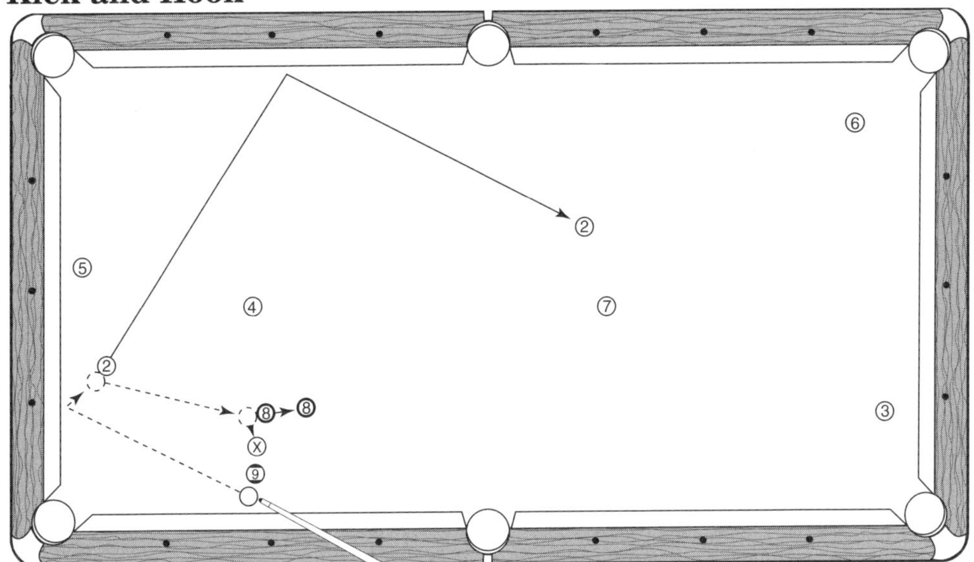

Buddy Hall played this masterful kick against Earl Strickland at the Sands Regency Open 12, 1990. Hall jacked up, applied right english, and sent the cue ball into near full contact with the 2-ball. The 2-ball headed down table while the cue ball nestled in behind the 8-ball. The big key was regulating the english so the 2-ball could be hit about 80% full.

A Perfect Kick and Hook

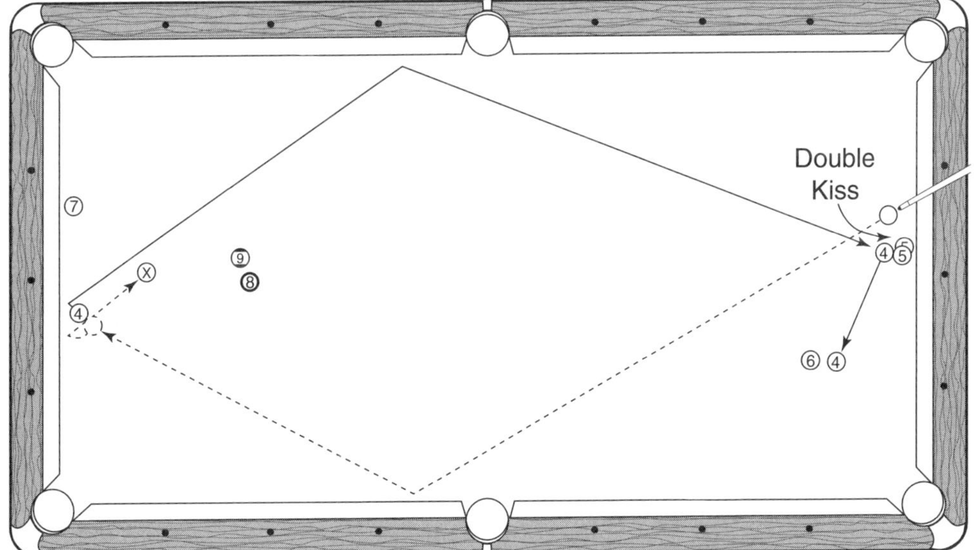

Corey Deuel was up against Fong-Pang Chao at the 2000 World 9-Ball Championships when he came across this long thin hit on the 4-ball. Deuel chose instead to play a powerful one-rail kick shot. The result was this mind-boggling kick/safety. The shot was played with a very hard stroke. Notice how the cue ball arched forward and to the left behind the blockers after making perfect contact with the 4-ball.

Kick to Pocket

Tough, But Easier than it Looks

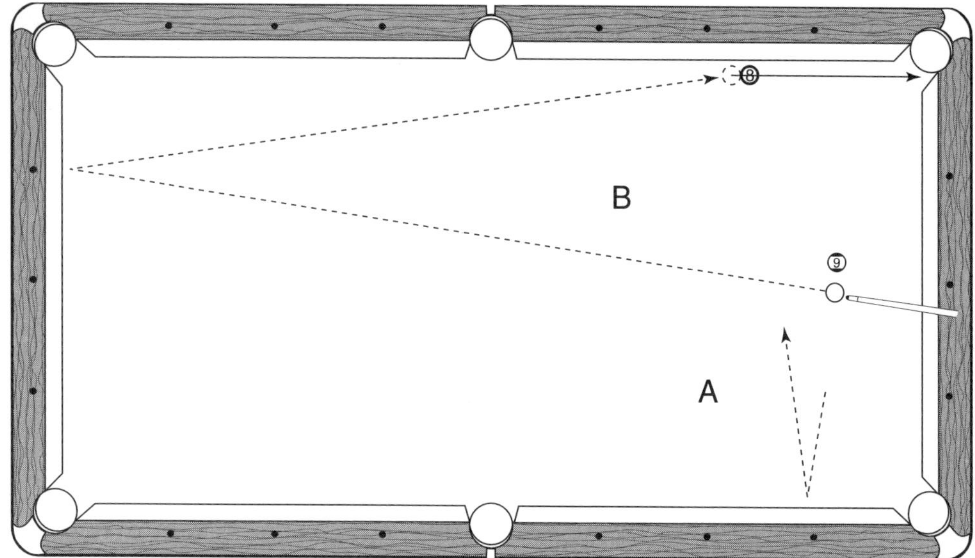

On most kick shots, your objectives are to hit the ball and leave your opponent tough. Occasionally, however, either the kick to pocket is not difficult or you have no choice except to go for the pocket. In this end game position, you could kick down Route A, but a sell out is likely. Route B at least gives you a chance to win the game. This shot is not quite as difficult as it looks because the 8-ball is slightly off the rail.

Ride the 9-Ball

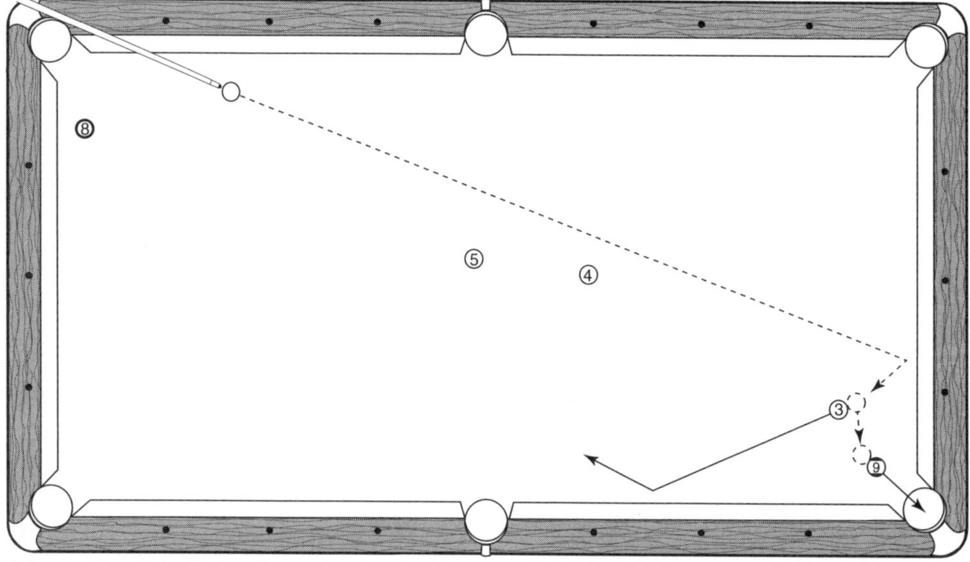

When the 9-ball is close to the ball you must hit, there may be a chance to ride the money. Earl Strickland was in the finals of the 2000 U.S. Open against Takeshi Okumura when he employed this tactic. Strickland used a very hard stroke which produced this spectacular kick/billiard.

Kick to Pocket off the Side Rail

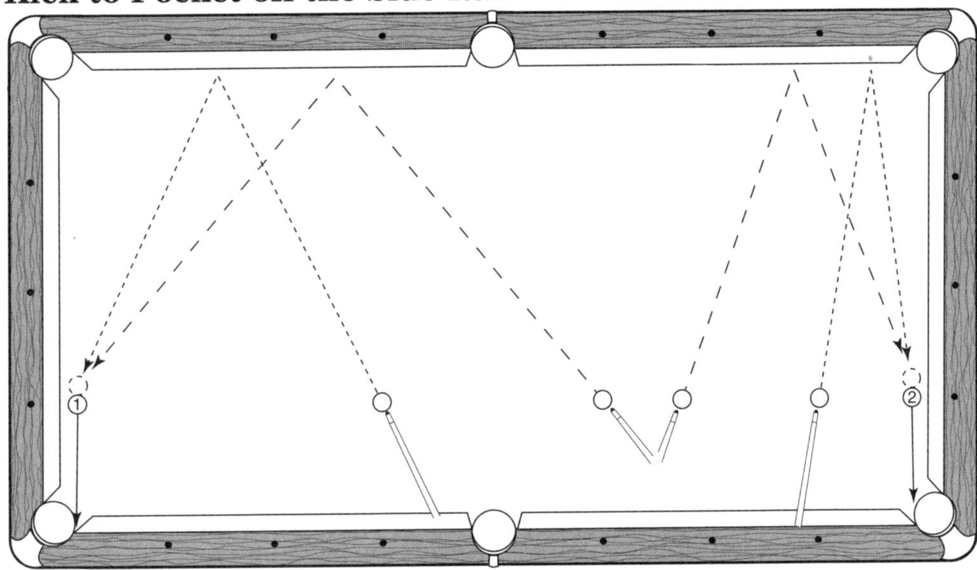

When the object ball is close to the rail and within a diamond of the pocket, your chances of pocketing the shot are reasonably good. You can pocket these shots: 1) with a perfect hit; 2) by going rail first; 3) by hitting the gap; 4) hitting the ball slightly above and cheating the pocket. The diagram shows four possible shots. You may have to adjust your aim slightly to allow for the table on which you are playing. Since these kicks go in quite often, you should also play for position on the next ball.

Skill Lets You Get Lucky Sometimes

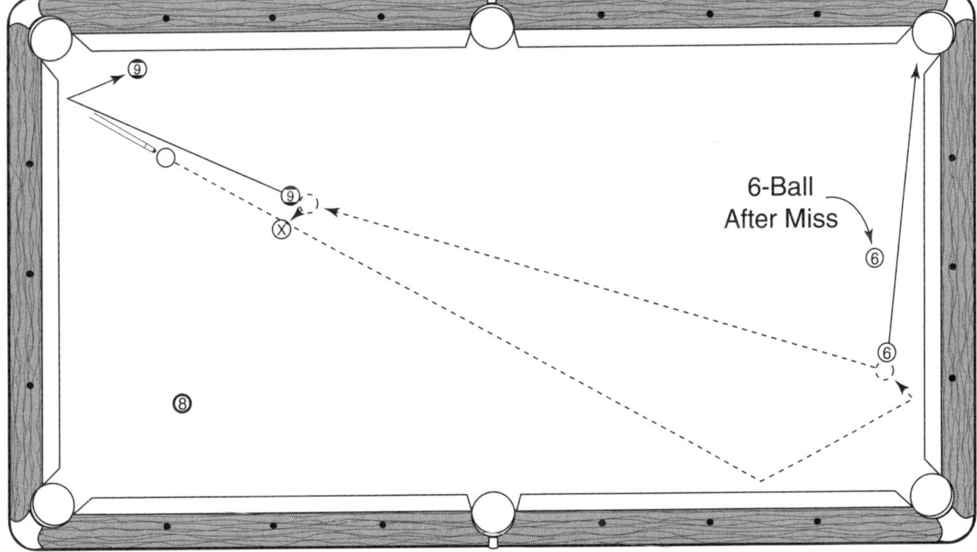

Efren Reyes was in the semifinals of the 1994 U.S. Open against Johnny Archer when he was looking at this challenging kick shot. Reyes skill enables him to "get lucky" at times, as shown by this kick shot. If Reyes had missed, he would have likely left Archer a table length bank shot.

Creative Tactics

Creative Use of Spin Plus Great Execution

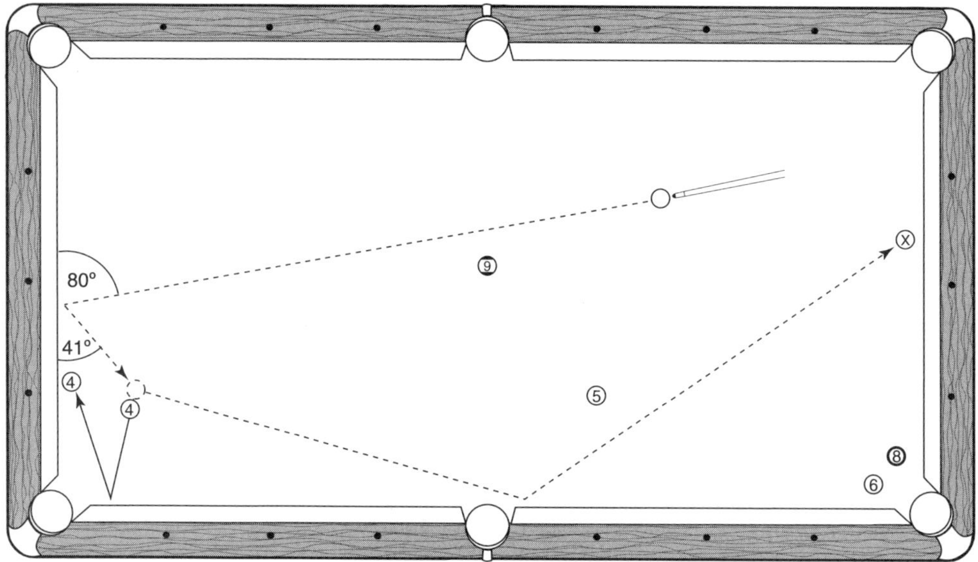

Johnny Archer was in the finals of the Sands Regency Open 22, 1995 against Rodney Morris when he was confronted with this potential sell out. Archer pondered the situation for several moments while devising this ultra precise kick safety. The shot required a medium soft stroke and a tip of left english. The 4-ball was hit very thinly while the cue ball grazed the point of the side pocket and continued to Position X.

Draw Bender

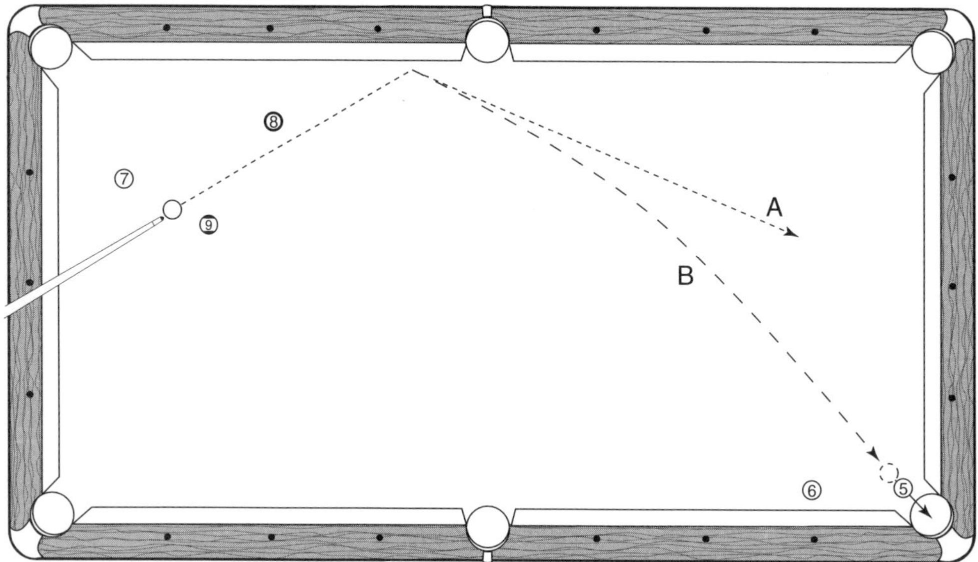

All of the standard kick routes have been cut off. Path A shows the cue ball's line of travel if you used follow, which certainly won't work. In addition, you can't alter the cue ball's path enough to hit the 5-ball with inside english. The solution is to use a hard draw stroke. The cue ball will bend as it comes off the rail, resulting in Path B.

Jump/Kick and Hook

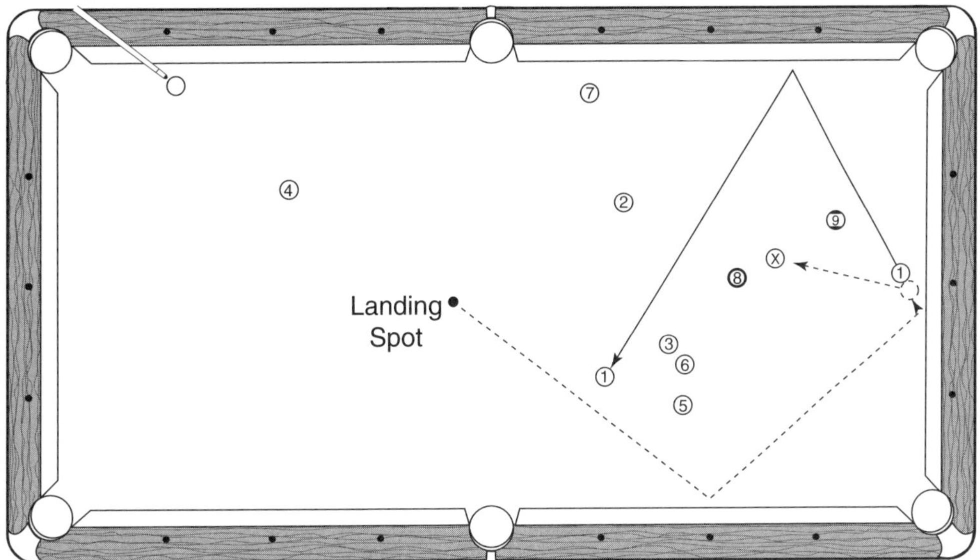

The ideal kick route to the 1-ball was blocked, but Jim Rempe had the solution: jump the 4-ball. This allowed him to play the kick safety in the illustration. The big keys were Rempe's imagination and the long landing strip, which lowered the risk of the cue ball jumping the table. This shot took place in a match with Mika Immonen at the 1998 U.S. Open.

Curve Kick Shot

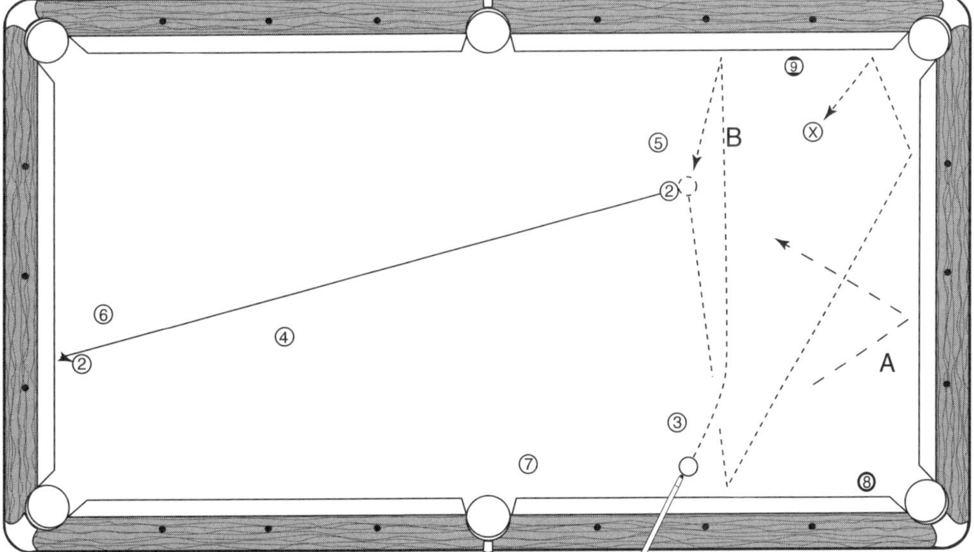

Sometimes the best, or only way to make contact on a kick shot is with a curve/kick shot. Efren Reyes was in combat with Kim Davenport at the 1995 Pro Tour Championship when he was faced with a kick shot on the 2-ball. Reyes could have chosen Route A, but he would have been kicking to the open side of the table. Instead, he played a curve/kick shot down Route B, which left Davenport with a long tough shot on the 2-ball.

Kicking Errors

Don't Kick Softy to an Open Area of the Table

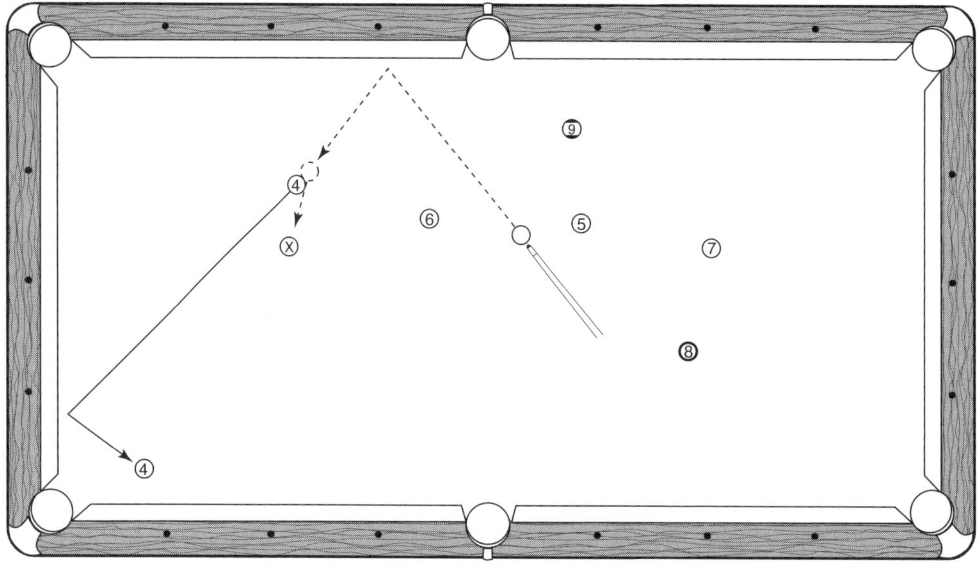

It is a mistake to kick softly at a ball that is sitting by itself at one end of the table as shown in the illustration. While a player who commits this kind of blunder may have every intention of pocketing the ball, the odds say that the shot will be missed and a sellout will result. The lesson: hit a solitary ball hard and try to drive it to the other end of the table.

Avoid Scratching

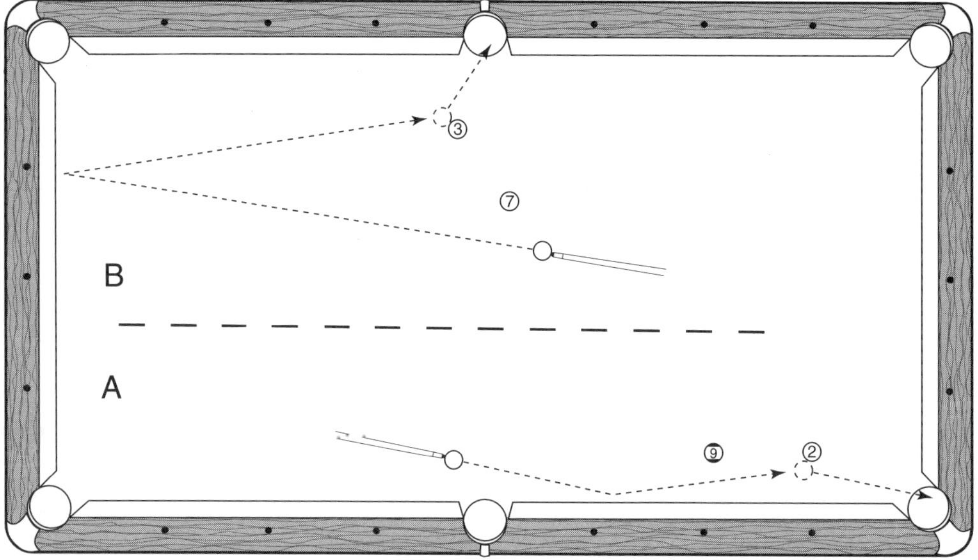

When the object ball is several inches or more from the pocket, the risk of scratching can still be high when the cue ball is approaching from certain directions. In Part A, the 2-ball is several inches from the rail, and yet a scratch is very likely if the cue ball hits too far down the rail. A scratch is very likely if you hit the left side of the 3-ball in Part B.

Using the Wrong Speed

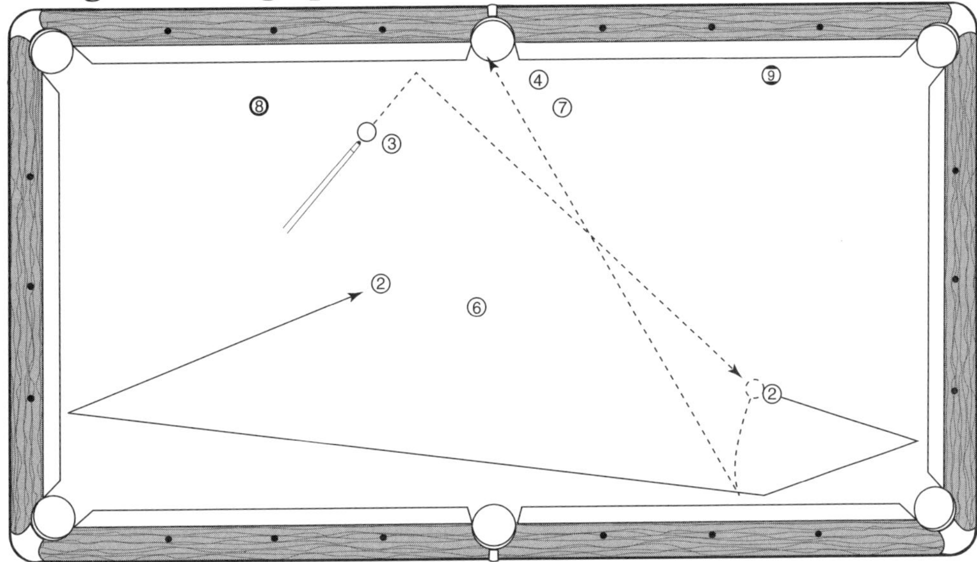

Kunihiko Takahashi made a full hit on the 2-ball, but used excessive force as shown by the 2-ball, which rebounded three diamonds off the end rail, and by the cue ball, which traveled across table and into the side pocket. When playing kick shots, you must always take care too match your speed of stroke to the requirement of the shot. This shot took place in the 1999 U.S. Open in a match with Chuck Altomare.

A Common Scratch on a Kick

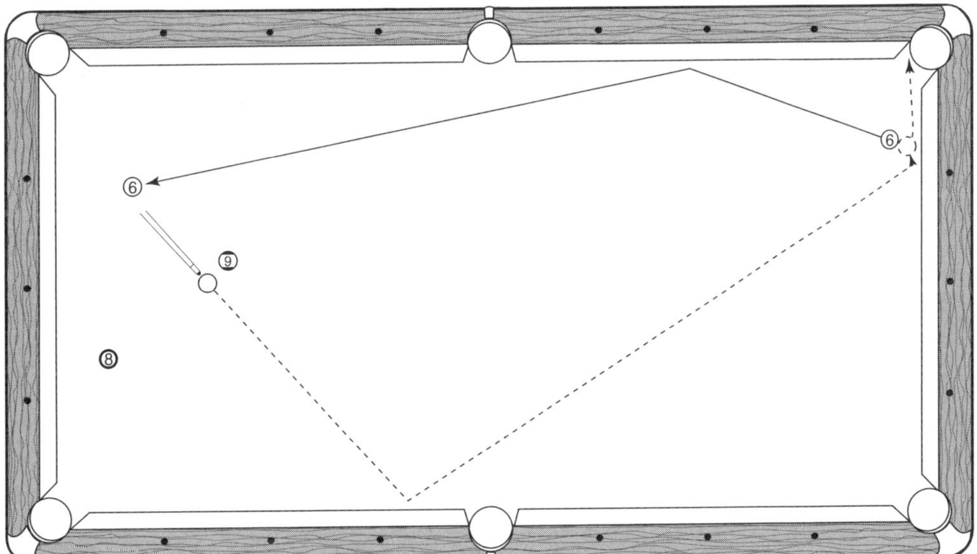

On a great many kick shots you must turn the cue ball loose, which increases the risk of scratching. It may hearten you to know that a world champion committed the error in the diagram. His mistake was contacting the far side of the object ball when it was only a little more than a ball's width from the rail.

Be Wary of the Point (1)

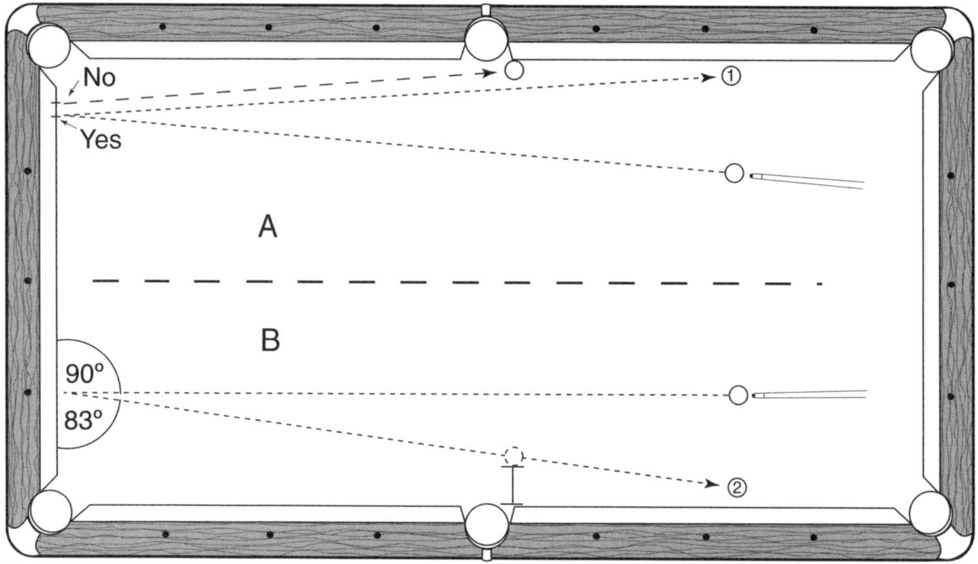

It is particularly annoying when the cue ball bounces off the point of the side pocket as this gives your opponent ball in hand. Hitting the point eliminates any chance of something good happening had you at least hit the ball. In Part A, the cue ball was sent a scant 1" off line, but this was enough to send it into the point. If you are skilled at regulating english, you can avoid the point by aiming wide of the corner pocket and using a quarter tip of left english, as shown in Part B.

Be Wary of the Point (2)

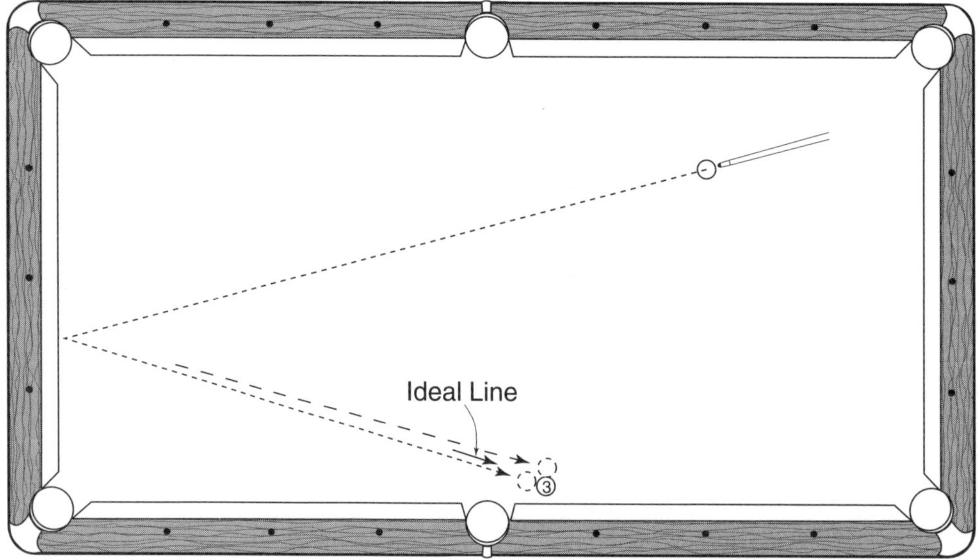

In this example, the object ball is right next to the side pocket. To avoid hitting the point, you should aim for a half ball hit on the object ball. This will give you a small margin of error against hitting the point and missing the ball entirely.

Hitting the Wrong Side

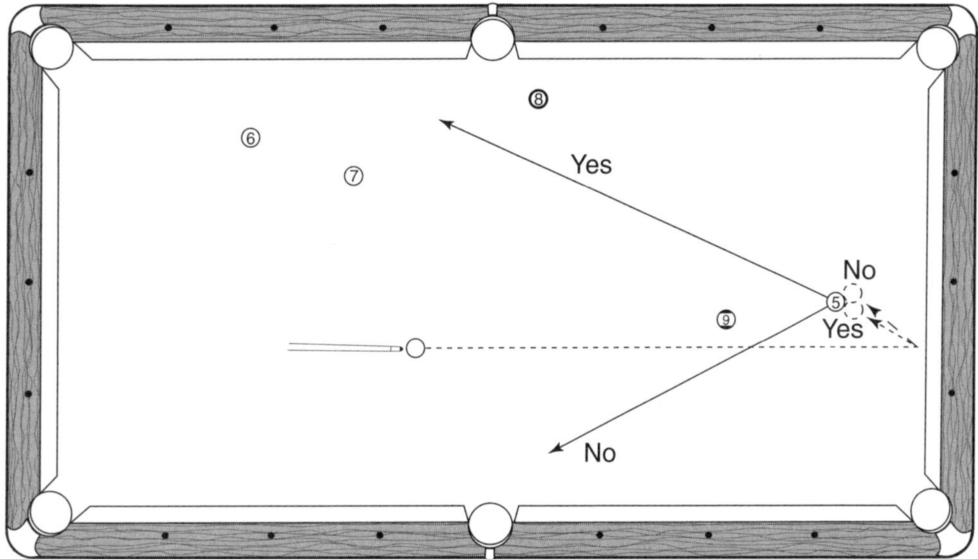

When you must use english to hit the object ball, you need to exercise great care or you could easily wind up hitting the wrong side of the ball. Left english is required to spin the cue ball off the end rail into the 5-ball. If the 5-ball is hit on the correct side, it will head towards the blockers. If too much spin is used, the 5-ball will be struck on the wrong side, sending it towards the open end of the table.

A Sure Safety Beats a Suckers Kick Shot

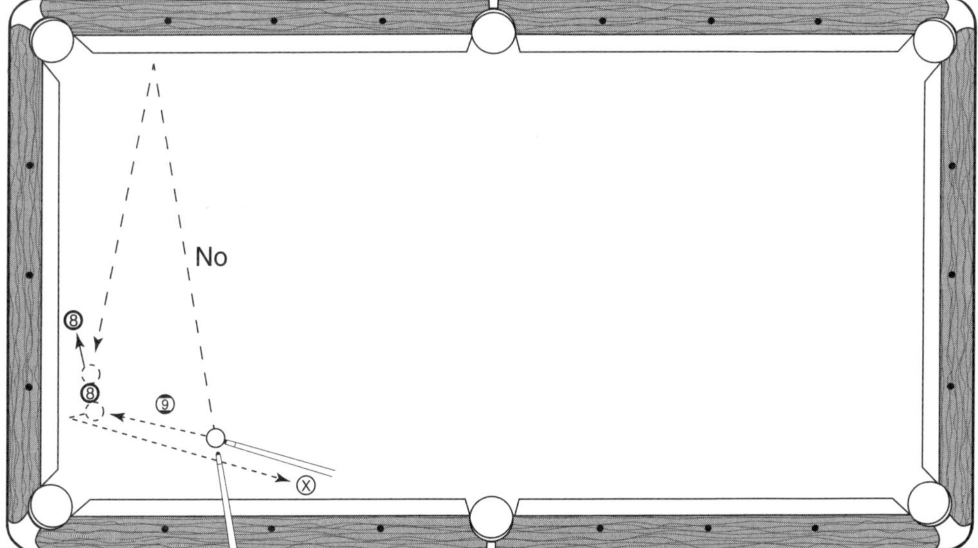

It is a colossal blunder to kick to make a ball that is near the end rail when the ball is much more than a quarter inch from the cushion. Even though the shot looks like it shouldn't be too difficult, I would guess it is missed at least 90% of the time, if not more. The smart play is to skim the object ball and go for a safety.

Short Distance to the First Rail

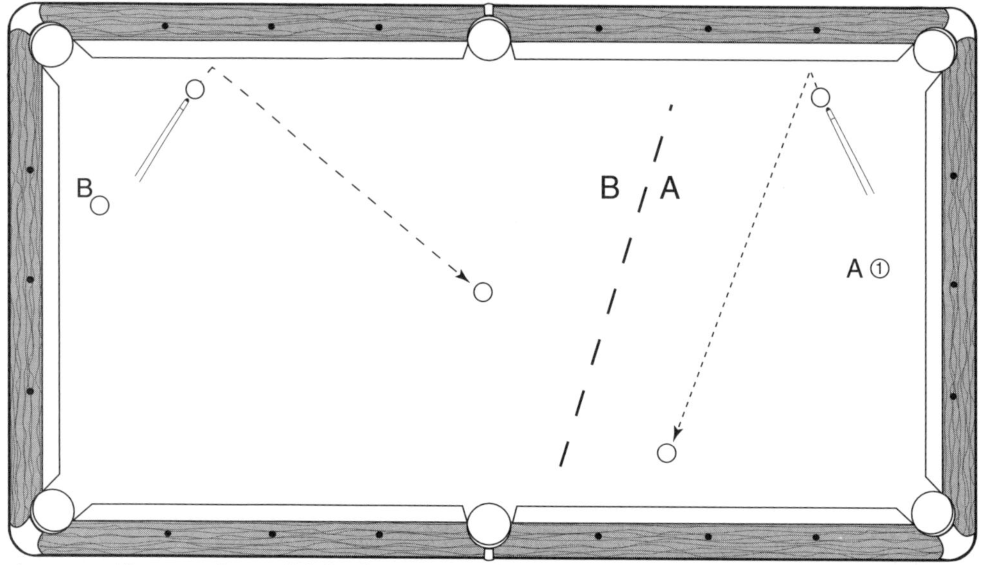

Among the toughest kick shots are those that have a very short distance to the first rail. In Part A, the cue ball will only travel about 2" before hitting the cushion. Even though the rebound angle is fairly sharp, this kick is tough to judge. The problems are magnified in Part B because of the shallower rebound angle. When playing these kick shots, avoid english unless it is necessary. And when aiming, try visualizing the route as if the cue ball was further from the rail, such as at Positions A or B.

Trying to Hit Balls Thinly and Missing Altogether

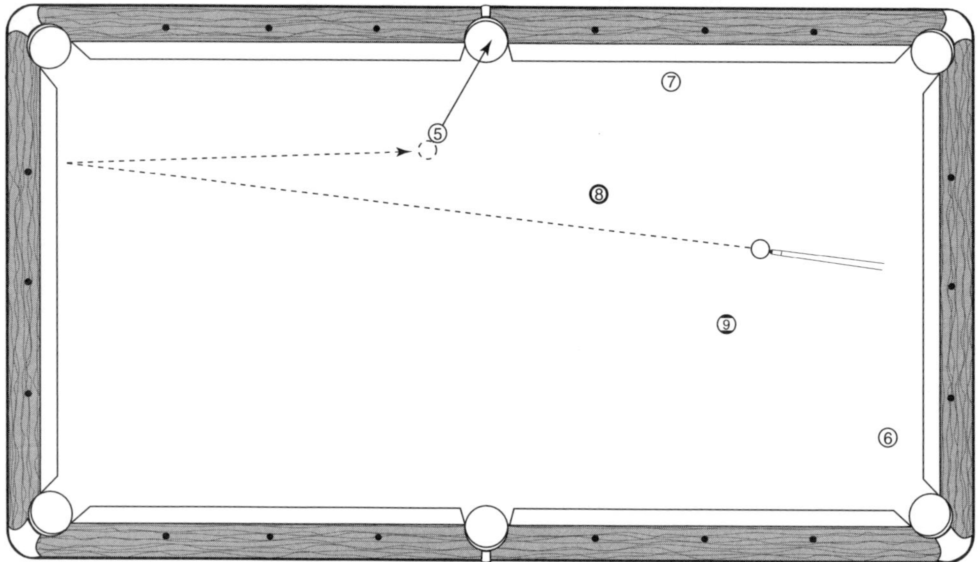

You could try to kick/cut the 5-ball into the side pocket, but this requires a very thin hit on the 5-ball. Although the reward could be substantial, the risk of missing a thin hit far out weighs it. The correct shot is to go for a solid hit on the 5-ball and hope for a hook.

CHAPTER 13

THE ABC'S OF STRATEGY

"It's all a game of percentages."
Jim Rempe

Nine Ball is a very demanding game as it requires a level of shotmaking and position play unlike any of the other popular pool games. The big difference in players skills leads to much larger variances in how certain shots should be played. In this regard, Nine-Ball is really a lot like other sports where there are significant differences in the skill sets of even the very best performers. For example, legendary golfer Jack Nicklaus was able to play long shots, with a high trajectory, to distant greens other pros couldn't match At the same time, however, he often lost shots to competitors who had stronger short games. In pool, Philippine superstar Efren Reyes is known for his strong kicking game and position play. But he loses ground to competitors with more powerful break shots.

There are very few players who have complete mastery of every facet of pool. So there is a good chance your game may be strong where your opponent's is weak, and vice versa. So don't let your admiration of their areas of expertise lead you into thinking you can't win. Instead, adopt strategies that enable you to take full advantage of your skills, and to exploit your opponent's weaknesses.

To maximize your strategic decision-making, you need to make a realistic appraisal of your game. This means identifying your strengths and weaknesses. When competing, this self-knowledge will help you to make the most of your strong points while minimizing the impact of your weak spots. You may dislike admitting your weaknesses, but it is mandatory if winning is your goal. That doesn't mean your weaknesses need be permanent. In fact, I recommend you systematically eliminate your weak spots in practice, one by one.

In today's world of pool, players of all levels of skill are likely to wind up facing each other in tournament play, leagues, or even for a friendly wager. Blind draw tournaments, handicapped leagues and negotiated money games result in a player often matching up against a C Player one moment, an A Player in their very next match.

Since all opponents are not created even close to equal, it follows that you should adjust your strategy to match the level of your opponent's game. The changes in strategy can be quite subtle when an A Player is playing an A-.Player. There will be a major change in tactics when a B+ Player faces a C Player, as compared to the strategy he should employ against another B+ Player.

Rating Your Game and Testing Your Skill

You may be well aware of how you stand compared to other pool players in your region. You may even have a ranking or handicap as a result of your participation in a local or national league, or from competing in a series of tournaments. One of the big problems with pool, however, is that not all ranking systems are created equal. A "C" Player in one region could be a B- in another area of the country, or even across town. Or an 8 might be a 6 somewhere else.

In the discussion that follows, I am making no attempt to create a universal rating system. Instead, I'm simply suggesting that the number of racks or balls you regularly run in Nine Ball is a reasonably accurate indicator of your current level of play. Later in the chapter I will present strategies that are based on how you rate yourself (A, B, or C) against the criteria below, regardless of your rating in your league or poolroom.

Measuring Your Ability By the # of Racks Run

The number of balls or racks you can break and run on when you are playing reasonably well is a good indicator of your level skill. Because of the particularly challenging nature of the game, it is difficult to exceed your norm by any significant figure just as it is not likely that a 90 shooter in golf will break 80. Your lifetime best, while not necessarily an accurate of an indicator of present level of skill, does give you a good idea of your potential.

How to Measure a Run

I'm going to spend a moment discussing how you can measure your runs in Nine-Ball because I believe the ability to do so can be helpful in gauging your current level of play. The method for measuring the number of racks you've run is quite crude compared to how they are measured in Straight Pool, in which your run is a precise number. There are several reasons measuring runs in Nine-Ball is somewhat imprecise:

- Runs can start with part of a rack.
- You can break in the 9-ball.
- You can make the 9-ball in a variety of shots at any part of the game.

Since this gauge is meant to be a measure of your skill, I suggest you not count 9-balls on the break as part of your best run. A run of fi of a rack is about 4-5 balls or more. If your run starts on the 4-ball and continues through that rack and the entire next rack (you break and run) that would be a run of 1fi racks. If your run had started on the 2-ball and continued through that rack and two more complete racks, that would be a run of three racks. You do not get credit on your run for any balls you make that do not lead to the completion of the rack. For example, let's say you started a match by breaking and running the first rack and you continued through to the 7-ball of the next rack before missing. That would only count as a run of one rack, not 1fi racks.

Your Typical Good Runs

A typical good run doesn't occur every day, but on most days, providing you play for at least a couple of hours.

C Player Your best daily runs usually are 5-7 balls, most of which are routine shots. You seldom break and run a complete rack. When you do run a complete rack, it is usually an easy layout with no problems. An average run is 3-4 balls

B Player You can occasionally break and run out. You will occasionally run two racks if the balls are lying well An average run is 5-6 balls.

A Player You run one to two racks quite often. A typical run is 7-8 balls. Runs of three or more come a lot less often than most otherwise knowledgeable observers would have you come to believe. An "A" Player's ability to run three racks is a very perceptible dividing line between pretty good players (B-B+) and really good players (A- and above). To run three or more racks with any regularity, you need:

- A great break.
- Excellent cue ball control.
- The ability to consistently make tough shots to continue your run.

Personal Bests

The personal bests do not include 9-balls on the break. It is also debatable whether or not they should include quick wins that come by a combo, billiard or some other shot on the 9-ball at the beginning of a rack. Remember, the main purpose of this gauge and the one above is to give you an accurate measure of your ability as a player.

C Player 1-2 racks

B Player 2-3 racks

A Player 4-5+ racks (this also hold true for a professional)

The Three Phases of a Rack

Your strategy for playing a rack depends on the number of balls left on the table, the challenges and opportunities the layout presents, and your and your opponent's level of skill. As a matter of convenience, I have broken the rack into three phases. The number of balls in the first two phases depends on the number of balls that went in on the break. The last phase almost always consists of three balls, since it is nearly impossible to make seven or more balls on the break.

Length of the Phases

Balls on the break	**0**	**1**	**2**	**3**	**4**	**5**	**6**
Beginning	3	2	1	0	0	0	0
Middle	3	3	3	3	2	1	0
End	3	3	3	3	3	3	3

The composition of the layout may go through many changes as you progress through a rack. Please understand that there will be plenty of exceptions to these rules thanks to the fact that no two racks of Nine Ball are exactly alike.

Phase 1: The Beginning

When playing the first three balls, the key to running out is to avoid the obstacles that seem to be everywhere. When 7-9 balls are on the table you have ample opportunities to play safe. The first phase is also a time for taking shots on the 9-ball or other money balls, if you are getting spotted, providing they have little risk of costing you the game should you miss. The game is still young for C Players. B Players may or may not have an opportunity to win at in this phase, depending on the difficulty of the layout. A large majority of games between A Players are decided in the first if not the second phase.

Phase 2: The Middle

This is the phase where the outcome of the game is decided in a vast majority of games between B Players. Most games between A Players that have not been decided in Phase 1 are settled in Phase 2. In games between C Players, the game may or may not yet be on the line. It all depends on the difficulty of the layout.

Phase 3: The End

By the time a game between A Players reaches Phase 3, it has in most cases already been decided. Games between B Players should have been decided at this point, but executional errors often put the game up for grabs. A very high percentage of racks are won and lost by C Players in Phase 3. It's sort of like watching a 50% free thrower: the ball might go in, but it could just as easily be missed.

The ABC's of Strategy

A game of Nine Ball takes on a much different complexion for players of varying levels of skill. The following sections provide strategic guidelines for the three broad categories of players discussed earlier. Each section emphasizes strategies for playing those in your category. The sections also give you some basic guidelines for competing with those in the other categories as well. You need only read the section that applies to the group you will be competing against. However, I recommend that serious students also read the tactics that players in other skill groups will employ against you. For example, a C Player who is about to play a B Player should read the section called C Players vs. B Players. Serious competitors, however, would be wise to read the section titled B Players vs. C Players to gain a better understanding of the tactics your opponent will be employing against you.

No matter what your level of play, you need to view your limitations realistically if you wish to have a chance of competing successfully. Remember, winning at Nine Ball largely depends on managing your game. That means making the most of what you've got, not trying world beater shots that you saw Earl or Efren make in Championship play.

Strategies for All Levels of Players

Quick and Easy Wins Nine Ball is unique in that it offers the opportunity for quick and relatively easy wins via combos, billiards and other specialty shots. Most players find it difficult to resist the opportunity to "ride the nine or money." Nevertheless, you must make intelligent use of this tactic no matter what your level of shill. You should, of course, keep an eye out for easy wins, as these are a quick tonic to your psyche. They can also demoralize your opponent. Also keep in mind that there is often a high penalty for missing these shots. Remember, it's a game of percentages.

The Break I'll repeat a rule that holds for all opponents in Nine-Ball: Don't scratch on the break!!! After a foul on the break good players will run out or play safe and lesser players will ride the 9-ball or any other balls if they are receiving weight.

Racking Money Balls If you are receiving a spot, rack your money balls in the row behind the 1-ball. The same holds true when you are racking for someone who is receiving an extra money ball or two. Racking the money balls in this position lessens their chances of going on the break.

Strategies for C Players

C Player vs. C Player

The ebb and flow of games between C Players is truly astounding. At any moment, anything can and does happen.. You may receive a gift at any time, or be the beneficiary of your opponent's generosity. You should learn to manage your expectations and try to stay on an even keel, which is not always easy given the unpredictable nature of these contests. When all is said and done, your ability to manage your emotions and the ability to make shots while not testing your limitations in Phase 3, are the largest determinants of success and failure.

Weight It is very difficult for a C Player to give another C Player a spot. So think twice before giving weight to a fellow C Player, but almost always be grateful for a ball spot, even if it is only the last two.

Intimidation Don't make the mistake of overestimating your opponent's play due to an impressive shot or two. Recognize that you have a great chance of winning since your opponent will give you many chances to win most games.

Expect Mistakes Don't worry about having to play perfect pool.
The Rolls C Players have been known to literally torture one another with the luck factor, which plays a significant role in many games. Realize that many of the good rolls are neutralized by poor play, and by the abundant opportunities to win that are present in most games.
Phase 1 You should be looking for ways to make the 9-ball, especially if you are playing another C Player. Ride the money with ball in hand, especially if you can play safe.
Target Practice Unless the entire rack is lying easy, realize that that the first three balls are largely target practice to get you in stroke for the later phases when the game is on the line.
Shotmaking The primary weapon is shotmaking. It pays to know your shotmaking capabilities and those of your opponent, for it is mostly good or poor shots (as opposed to position plays) that decide games.
Run Out Range The game may be within your run out range with 4-6 balls on the table. It depends on the layout and on how you are playing at that particular moment. In this phase, you may continue to play position with the idea of running out, but you don't want to run 2-3 balls, miss and hand the table over to your opponent with three easy balls to run.
End Game Errors Be prepared for tough shots and safeties in the end game as a result of your opponent's errors.
Safeties "Average" safeties can lead to ball in hand in many instances thanks to your opponent's lack of advanced kicking skills. Emphasize safeties starting with the last five balls, and especially when the game gets down to the last three balls or less. The "smarts" can give you a huge advantage when playing another C Player. And don't forget that safeties usually have a larger margin for error than do shots, which makes them often easier to execute under end of game pressure.
Kick Shots Emphasize hitting the ball. Don't get too fancy trying to skim the edge as you don't want to give your opponent a chance to ride the 9-ball with ball in hand.
Jump Shots Unless you have made it a point to learn the mechanics of the jump shot, they can do more harm than good. You might consider jumping only when a kick is next to impossible or you only have the edge of the ball to hurdle.
Running Out Once you have decided the rack is within your run out range, try to keep things as simple as possible when playing shape.
Don't Be a Hero Don't give away games by attempting difficult runs on the last three balls. Play safe and let your opponent beat themselves.

C Player vs. B Players

Unless the format favors upsets or you are receiving weight, realize that you are a fairly substantial underdog going into the match. You may still have a chance to score an upset if you have a great day, get a few rolls, and your opponent is off their game. Relax and enjoy the opportunity to play a better player. And try to learn from them while in your seat.

Ride the Money You should be looking for ways to make any money balls against B Players early in Phase 1, and possibly in Phase 2 if the layout is difficult and a run out is not likely.

Safety Play safeties early in the game when the layout easy. Even if you can't run out, you have to keep them from running out, so play the first safety of the game if possible. Play safe in Phase 3 in situations where you might normally go for a low percentage shot.

Unnerve Them C Players have a unique style that can be rather unnerving to better players who have forgotten their modus operandi or are not used to it. Your go for the gusto, riding the money and shotmaking style of play may completely throw a B Player off guard and have them mumbling to themselves.

Make it Tough B Players can run out, but usually when 5-6 balls or less remain. Tie up balls, and do what is necessary to keep them from running out until the game gets to your range.

Spot Balls B Players seldom give a C Player more than one extra money ball. You must be conscious of its position while looking for ways to make it out of rotation.

Tie Up Balls If you are receiving a spot, tie up balls past the spot. For example, if your opponent is giving you the 7-ball, try to tie up the 8 and 9-balls. This can prevent them from running out should you miss the 7-ball later in the game.

Time of Possession You will spend less time at the table than when playing a C Player. Try to offset the tendency to grow cold by strictly following your routine and playing every shot to the best of your ability.

C Player vs. A Player

When two players with a large gap in skill compete, the outcome almost always depends on how the better player is playing. Unless you are receiving a huge spot and your opponent is having a bad day, you must look at matches with A Players as learning experiences. So enjoy watching good pool, and see if some of their game might rub off on you.

Ride the Money You should be looking for ways to make the money balls against A Players early in the game when a run out is less likely, especially if you are getting multiple wild balls. When you can move two or three at a time and one is lined up at least somewhat towards a pocket, let'em rip!!

The Break It is often your best chance if you are receiving weight. If you make a ball on the break (but not a money ball), immediately scour the table for a possible way to pocket a money ball either on the first shot, or within a couple of shots. Also look for a shot on the cash when your opponent fails to make a ball.

Set Up Money Balls When you have nothing better to do, try moving your money balls to places where you can make them with a combo or some other shot on the cash while playing safe.

Tie Up Balls If you are receiving a big spot, tie up balls past the spot. If your opponent is giving you the 6-ball, try to tie up the 7 and 8-balls, or the 8 and 9-ball, for example. This could prevent them from running out later in the game.
Safety Play You should play more safeties at all times during the game in an attempt to thwart your opponent's offense. You will likely lose most battles, but you can't let this frustrate you.
Pushouts Be cautious when evaluating an A Player's pushout. They will offer bait or play safes you don't see. It is usually better to take the shot than let the A Player shoot. When you push out, make it as tough as possible. Don't push out to easy safeties.
The Chair Don't be surprised if you spend upwards of 70-80% of your time in your chair. Don't become too frustrated if you play less than your best, because you will spend plenty of time cooling off in the your seat.
Move Balls The 7, 8, or 9-balls should be moved to a location that will make running out much tougher. Do this when a kick is likely to be missed or on push outs. Hopefully the A Player will then miss at the end of the rack when it is within your run out range.

Strategies for B Players

B Player vs. B Players

You and your opponent are perfectly capable of shooting some very fine pool, and are thus very dangerous and unpredictable. You could easily wind being paired against a B Player who looks like a C Player one minute and an A Player one rack later. You must understand that their play averages out to the B level over the long haul. Contests between B Players are often decided by who is on their game and/or by who can sustain a higher level of play than normal through an entire set.
Know the Gaps B Players have many well-developed skills as well as several gaps in their arsenal. Play around your opponent's strengths and force them to do the things that hate doing, which could be shooting long shots or short rail kick shots, for example.
Intimidation Your opponent is very capable of playing fine pool. Don't let their great pool lead you into thinking you don't have a chance, as they most likely will cool off soon enough.
The Rolls In a short race, the rolls could definitely favor one player to a great degree. However, there are enough innings in B Player matches that the outcome is most closely tied to who is playing better pool. So don't fret about luck and stick to making the most of what you have to work with.
Pace of Play You must guard against conforming to your opponents pace of play, whether it is faster or slower than your normal tempo. If you are up against a slow player, you must avoid letting them take you out of your game, even though you will be spending more time in the chair.
Weight There is enough difference between B Players that upper level B Players can give other B Players a single ball spot, such as the 8-ball. If you are giving or getting weight, you must plan accordingly.

The Score Avoid losing confidence, at those critical junctures, when your opponent has jumped into a lead of 2-3 games and is playing well; especially, if you made a poor shot or two that helped get him started.
Push Outs You can gain an edge with your skill in a particular area, such as in hiding the cue ball on long distance safeties.
Safety Play This is an area of skill where the B Player, with a significant advantage, can pick up a large percentage of the games that are up for grabs. If that describes your game, take full advantage of your skill. If not, get to work on bringing your safeties up to par.
Kick Shots This is another of the critical areas of skill that can separate one B Player from another, especially when you consider that relatively strong safety play is a common characteristic of many B Players.
Jump Shots There is a wide range of skill on jump shots. You should quickly asses you opponent's ability to play jump shots as this may alter your strategy when playing safe or pushing out.
Phase 1 A low percentage of racks are run in this phase unless the balls are lying well. Play safeties and use ball in hand to improve difficult layouts.
Ride the Money Consider combos or other shots on the 9-ball when the rack is lying tough and the opportunity presents itself, especially if a safety is built into the shot. If you are getting a ball spot, take a shot on it when it has a good chance of going and a miss won't cost you the game.
Phase 2 This is winning time for most B Players as the rack is now well within your runout range. Tighten up your safety play and initiate the safety battle, as this is the critical juncture in the battle for control of the table.
Run Outs You will win a very high percentage of matches against fellow B Players by simply running out the last 3-6+ balls when you know you are fully capable of doing so.
The Last Three Positional errors may force you to abandon a run. If you are confronted with a tough shot or a relatively easy safety, play safe!
The End Game You may wind up facing a tough shot or safety in the end game as a result of an opponents error. So be prepared to come with a big shot or creative safety when the game is in Phase 3.

B Player vs. C Player

You are the prohibitive favorite, providing the match is being played even up and the contest is sufficiently long to neutralize the luck factor. The three main things that could cause you trouble are: failure to close out easy racks, dealing with odd ball leaves at the end of the game, and rides on any extra money ball if a ball spot is being given.
Phase 1 This is a dangerous phase because you may not be able to run out, meanwhile your opponent may realize this and take shots at the 9-

ball and the spot balls, if any. You goal is to navigate your way through this phase, and possibly the early part of Phase 2, until it is run out time.
Main Goal Your will accomplish your main objective of winning by playing smart pool. Save the heroics for matches with B and A Players. Manage the rack until you get into your run out range.
Lucky Shots Don't let your opponent's occasional lucky shots on a money ball demoralize you. Understand that they play these shots as a part of their strategy because they can't run out like you can.
Stay Focused It could be easy to become complacent against a weaker opponent. If you allow this to happen and start playing down to their level, you could find yourself in danger of losing the match.
Push Outs You can gain a significant advantage by outfoxing a C Player with push outs. Offer shots and safeties that you can execute, but that they can't, or that they don't recognize.
Safety Play Play lots of safeties throughout the game whenever you have even the slightest doubt about making a shot. Your main objective on safeties is to hook your opponent, since there is a good chance they will miss hitting the kick shot.
Money Balls If you are giving up an extra money ball or two, you must be very conscious of their position, especially in the first two phases when C Players like to take them for a ride.

B Player vs. A Player

You should relish your role as an underdog. While an upset is not likely in a long race, one could happen with a handicap or in a short race format. Let your confidence soar and let your best game come out. You have a chance to realize a whole new level of play by playing well against an A Player. Even if you don't come out on top, you may score a moral victory by keeping things close and, in the process, discover you are a better player than you give yourself credit for being. Your overall level of skill can make life difficult for an A Player if you are having an especially good day and/or they are off their game. Most of all, enjoy the match and learn during it. That way you will always end up a winner.
The Break Really bear down on the break, because it gives you a chance to win without having to wrest control of the table from an A Player.
Kick Shots You may have to gamble a little bit here on accomplishing a tougher objective than normal, such as hitting a side of the ball, because a "normal" kick could leave too easy of a response.
Push Outs Be wary of what your opponent offers you, as A Players are good at bluffing. But don't be afraid to go for a shot or safety if you feel your opponent has a good chance of taking control of the table. When you push out, make sure you don't leave a safety, even when pushing from long range.
Phase 1 This is a crucial stage as you can easily lose the rack due to your opponent's skill at running out. Unless the rack is lying easy, play tight and wait for you opportunity to get out. If you are getting the 7-ball or more, you can go for the win from the start.

Run Outs Play safeties until the rack is solidly in your run out range. You want to avoid failing on heroic run out attempts as this could leave an easy run for your opponent. When you have a high percentage run out, execute each shot to the best of your ability. Remember, against A Players, execution is key.

Safeties Try to limit your opponent's responses by sending the cue ball up closer to the blockers than usual. Generally it is better to hide the cue ball instead of the object ball, because if your opponent kicks the object solidly you will probably be snookered.

Strategies for A Players

A Player vs. A Player

When you are playing a fellow A Player, the primary items that determine the winner include: the break, execution, attitude, and adaptability to the conditions. With top players, Nine-Ball is largely about executing what you already know to near perfection. As long as you stay in line, your position plays and shotmaking requirements become somewhat repetitious. Then it all comes down to execution. In sum, you must take charge of the table and run out over and over again.

You should be psyched to give a very good performance, but understand that both of you will make mistakes. Even the pros make mistakes as shown by Accu-Stats Video Productions, which rates the performance of top pros at major tournaments. In 44 rated matches at the U.S Open, from 1998-2000, the winners and losers (88 total) averaged .841. That translates into about 3 mistakes every 20 shots. Bear in mind, however, that these are the best players competing against the best under pressure on tough tables.

The Score In most encounters between A Players you will have a chance to fire back, even if your opponent jumps to a lead of several games in the early going, so remain patient and get mentally prepared to make the most of your opportunities. In a short race format, make every effort to jump out ahead, especially if you are an habitual slow starter.

Pace of Play You most likely have a well-rehearsed routine that keeps you from falling into the trap of mimicking your opponents pace of play. Nevertheless, you need to guard against going cold or hurrying your shots when you return to the table against a slow playing opponent.

The Rolls Most matches between A Players are decided in far less innings than those between less skilled players, which creates less opportunities for the breaks to completely even out. As a result, the impact of a few rolls in either players favor is magnified. You must not get upset if the Pool Gods seem to be conspiring against you. Make the most of what you are given to work with.

Intimidation You may derive an edge from your reputation. If your opponent is favored, you still have an excellent chance of winning. Relax and enjoy your role as a spoiler. Realize also that he may also feel pressure to win against someone he feels he is supposed to beat. Either player may also be subjected to the forces of intimidation during the course of the match due to their opponent's fine play.

Safety Play The best safeties lead to ball in hand or a difficult kick. The rest will leave the outcome very much in doubt. So you must be prepared to gamble a little when appropriate when playing safe in an attempt to nail down a winner. You must also take into account your opponent's ability to jump their way out of a hook.

Kick Shots The first rule is to hit the ball. But you must go well beyond that against a fellow A Player. Your goals for a kick shot (make ball, safety, leave long shot, etc.) should be directly correlated to the difficulty of the shot and the layout.

Jump Shots Even though the games of A Players are well rounded, this is one area where you will still find some major differences in skill. Examine the area where they keep their cues to see if they have a jump cue in waiting. Try to make an accurate assessment as to their ability to use it when they play their first couple of jump shots.

Phases 1 and 2 The great majority of racks are decided in Phase 1 and a lesser amount in Phase 2. Be prepared to run out or to play a killer safety.

Target Practice The last three balls (Phase 3) are the easiest part of the rack because the obstructions are gone and the balls are almost never close together. The last three balls of your runouts are really not much more then target practice. Focus, execute, do what you know how to do, get the job done, be a closer. These are the thoughts of a top player at the end of a rack. There will be some exceptions when the layout is tough.

The Break The break is often the single biggest factor in determining the outcome among upper level players. Monitor your break and adapt quickly to the table by changing positions and speeds if necessary. Pay attention to your opponent's break and consider copying it if it is working particularly well. And be sure to conduct periodic rack inspections.

Battle for Control You must battle hard for every chance to ignite your offense against a skilled player. Don't expect to have anything handed to you, but be grateful when it happens.

Push Outs Never underestimate the knowledge of a fellow A Player by pushing out to situations that are either too easy (they'll shoot) or too difficult (you'll have to shoot) if at all possible.

Neutralize Your Opponent's Strengths Your fellow A Players game is most likely very well rounded. However, he may count on a couple of areas to win a game here and there. Discover these as quickly as possible (unless you already know his game) and deny him the opportunity to beat you with his strengths.

A Player vs. B Player

Your strategy should closely resemble that which you use against an A Player. B Players can be very dangerous when they catch a couple of rolls and their best game kicks into gear. While you are a substantial favorite, even when giving up a spot (within reason, of course), you cannot afford to play in a haphazard manner. Don't, by all means, play down to your opponent's level as that is a sure recipe for an upset.

Time of Possession You should play well, since you should be doing anywhere from 60-70%+ of the shooting. And, of course, your advantage in table time could weaken your opponent's game.

Avoid Frustration You must be on guard against frustration if you fall behind a player you feel you should beat easily. B Players can and do run out, especially when things are working in their favor. You must also put your ego aside and not worry about the potential consequences (embarrassment) should you suffer an upset.

Their Strong Suit B's usually have a strong shot or two which they love playing, such as the jump shot. They think theses shots give them an edge, and they are willing to shoot with little hesitation. If they are really strong in a particular area, you must deny them the opportunity to use it. But if they think they are Sky King, the cue ball will often descend on the poolroom floor; so, give them all the jump shots they can handle.

Money Balls You will most likely be giving up one or more balls as a handicap. You must therefore manage their position on the table to minimize or eliminate any easy wins. You want to make your opponent earn everything.

Phase 1 Play a B Player tough from the start, like you would an A Player, because they are always a threat to beat you in any game if given a chance. Try to break up trouble when playing safe.

Phase 2 This is the segment of the rack where you must nail down the game if the layout in Phase 1 was not conducive to a run out.

An Off Day You should not worry about beating a B Player when your game is off, as long as you make use of your knowledge of strategy and tactics.

Safety Play A fair number of games against a B Player will feature a turnover in Phase 3. This will lead to the judicious use of safety play. Safeties in Phase 3 are now about using distance, freezing the cue ball on the rail, creativity, and controlling both balls. There are several cagey maneuvers pros and top amateurs use to avoid selling out when less knowledgeable players will go for the most heroic and/or foolish of shots.

A Player vs. C Player

If you are playing a C Player even up in anything longer than a race to two, you should virtually never lose. Most match ups between these two disparate levels involves a handicap, often substantial, which can put the outcome in doubt. Still, it is one of the laws of pool that the better play will usually win as long as the weight is within reason and the match is sufficiently long to neutralize the rolls factor.

The Basic Strategy When an A Player is playing a C Player with no ball spot (although there could be games on the wire), the object is to avoid losing the game with a stupid mistake on the last 3-4 balls.

Time of Possession You will get 70-80% of the table time, so you should get in great stroke providing you don't get complacent.

The Luck Factor A Players, who give up big spots, must get used to the C's apparent advantage in the luck department. Sure they will win some games by smashing the balls around the table, but they will lose even more when these shots fail to produce.

Manage the "Money Balls" You will almost certainly be giving away some kind of handicap. If this is in the form of an extra money ball or two (or three), you must be careful to eliminate your opponent's chances for short rack victories. Again, this line of thinking may be foreign to A Players who mostly play opponents at their level.

Kick Shots Reduce your goals when kicking on all but the easiest kicks. Just make sure to avoid giving your opponent ball in hand as the last thing you want is to have them take dead aim on one or more money balls.

Break Clusters On pushouts you want to separate balls in the later phases of the rack that can keep you from running out.

When to Gamble You can take some chances on combos or tough run outs in the early stages when the game is out of their run out range.

The Last 3-6 Balls Your strategy in this phase is more about avoiding losing than about beating your opponent. You should win even when giving up a handicap, providing you play your game and play smart. You needn't take the aggressive approach that must be used against A Players.

Phase 3 Concentrate on tightening up your act as the game reaches the mid point. This is the time where you want to take control and eliminate any chance of losing. Let the C Player beat himself in the end game.

Strange Happenings in Phase 3 If you are playing a C Player without a ball spot (which could happen in a tournament where games are given on the wire) and they are shooting in the end game, you are in for a unique experience if you are used to playing only A Players. Be prepared for long distance shots, safeties and a wide assortment of goodies you'll seldom encounter in the world of precision run outs.

Big Ball Spots When you are giving away a multiple ball spot, you must play tight from the start, since your opponent's end game starts a lot sooner than yours.

Safeties Use your safeties to control the game. In many cases, you can play safe to larger zones if your opponent is especially poor at kicking.

Ball In Hand You may use it to play a shot at the 9-ball when a safety is built into the shot in a situation where you might normally try to run out.

Avoid the Barrage If you are giving away a big spot (the world), you must learn to withstand an occasional barrage when it seems like one of your opponent's money balls can't stay out of the pocket. You've got to suck it up, fade their barrage, and be prepared to assume command once again.

CHAPTER 14

COMPETITIVE NINE BALL

"Your mind is the biggest thing in all of sports. I think some players have it and others don't."
Johnny Archer

What draws so many to Nine Ball is the highly competitive nature of the game. Every few minutes a fresh new game begins, bringing with it the possibility of victory. The game has skyrocketed in popularity as Nine Ball players today, at almost every level, have more opportunities to compete than every before as the number of leagues and tournaments has proliferated throughout the land. And, of course, a few players on occasion are still known to enjoy a friendly wager one-on-one.

To compete successfully at Nine Ball, you've got to relish the opportunity to do battle with a skilled opponent. You've got to love the pressure of matching skills, shots and strategies against a worthy competitor who may very well be your superior in many facets of the game. When you are up against a tough opponent, you must wage a war in the battle for intimidation. You give yourself the best chance to gain the upper hand by letting your cue do the talking. When you are competing at Nine Ball, your ability to get lost in the game is largely what can enable you to emerge in the winner's circle. Your talent for playing one shot at a time and a strong will to win are mandatory operating equipment.

Your mental strength will be tested on several occasions during the course of any contest. A bad roll, a poor shot or some fine play by your opponent could cause you to doubt your ability to win. At times like this, you must show the quality that pool players refer to as "heart". You must right your ship, rekindle your fighting spirit, and signal to your opponent via your play that you are a force to be reckoned with until the finish line. And when you are ahead, you must demonstrate a killer instinct and be able to close out a match, especially one that goes double hill.

"It's not how good you play but how good your opponent plays on you."
Jim Rempe, voicing a quote he attributed to Irving Crane

Intimidation – The Mental Side of Nine-Ball

When two players compete, one player usually has an edge in the mind game over the other. One player usually feels some degree of intimidation while the other feels they are the better player, or that this is their time to win. The intimidation factor becomes quite obvious when you see a relative unknown compete against a great player.

While competing your emphasis should naturally be on making the most of your opportunities during a match, and on playing each shot to the best of your ability. A big part of the win/loss equation, however, also falls on the quality of your opponent's game. That's why there is so much truth to Rempe's quote above. If you are the type of player who seems to put others in top gear, then your intimidation factor is rather low. This of course makes winning that much tougher. On the other hand, if you are the kind of player who turns opponent's arms to stone, you have a huge built in advantage going into every match.

I want to emphasize any advantage you gain in the intimidation department should come from your game, your confident demeanor and other positives factors that combine to elevate the fear factor in others. You should not try to intimidate your opponent's with a poor attitude or tactics that go beyond the boundaries of good sportsmanship. In short, you can be a consummate sportsman and still intimidate the hell out of your opponents. Perfect examples are: Johnny Archer, Efren Reyes and Allison Fisher.

The quest to acquire the intimidation factor creates a fascinating paradox: part of you wants to play against a formidable opponent who motivates you to play your best; the other part wants your opponent to make mistakes so you can get to the table and runout. All things considered, perhaps the ideal scenario is to play someone whose game you respect. This will motivate you to play your best. You want them to play well, but with just enough mistakes so that you can win after an exciting and memorable contest. While blowouts are nice, your sweetest victories will be the close encounters with skilled opponents where you emerge victorious.

Qualities that Opponents Find Intimidating

Part of winning at pool is doing all of the little and not so little things that intimidate your opponent into thinking they can't win. There are many elements of your game other than blatant sharking that can signal to your opponent that you are a force to be reckoned with. These could include:

Style of Play

Most players have at least a few opponents whose style of play grates on them like chalk on a blackboard. Their opponent's style intimidates them or throws them off their game. That's one of the reasons why some very fine players have a problem with certain opponents.

Fast and Flashy Players

Fast and flashy players will intimidate some opponents, especially if this is combined with superior shotmaking. This form of intimidation usually works well on less experienced players who are unaware of the many benefits that come from playing a fast player. If fast players intimidate you, you can take the cure by remembering that they are more prone to making errors. In addition, you have to spend less time waiting for your turn, which should help keep you sharp.

Cold and Methodical

Emotionless and methodical players are among the most intimidating. They take their time, plan each shot carefully, make few mistakes and keep you waiting in your chair for longer periods of time. In addition, they almost never show any signs of mental weakness. The best way to combat these types it to take your time (but not too much time),bear down on every shot, and really get into the match rather than fussing in your chair between turns.

TIP: Whether you are a fast or slow player, you should never change your tempo to match that of your opponent. Play at your ideal speed and your ideal rhythm.

Your Arsenal of Skills

Most players seem to be, at least, a little intimidated by an opponent who is particularly skilled at one facet of the game, especially if this area is a weak spot in their game. This even happens at the pro level. As an example, Earl Strickland intimidates other pros with his shotmaking and run out power. Johnny Archer's break can be more than a little disconcerting, while Efren Reyes ability to kick his way out of trouble is a source of frustration to almost everyone who plays him.

A Single Shot

A single shot can signal to your opponent that you have come to play and that you are a force to be reckoned with. In many cases, a big shot can turn a match around or give a player momentum that carries through to the end of the match. If you are on the receiving end of a potentially intimidating shot, remind yourself that it takes much more than a single shot to win or lose the match. Enjoy your opponent's great play and let it draw you deeper into the match.

A Picture Perfect Run Out

Knowledgeable opponents will be most impressed by picture perfect run outs in which you control the cue ball perfectly from start to finish. A well executed run out means that your opponent has had the dubious pleasure of watching you play perfect pool for several minutes. The impact of a well-executed run or two can have a lasting impact. Your opponent will start thinking that every time they miss, they will severely punished.

Your Reputation as a Player

Your name often precedes you in competition, as does that of your next opponent. Tournament players are known to scour the board to see who they are going to play next, and possibly in future rounds, should they keep on winning. If they see your name, what do you think they would be thinking? And what are your thoughts when you know you are going to be playing a very fine player?

If your opponent views you as a tough match, the advantage can be worth a couple of games in a race, especially if you back it up with a strong start. On the other hand, if you are looked as an easy match, you need to make a statement early in the match that you have come to play.

You can gain an instant reputation and a degree of respect by knocking off a fine player or two. If you have just beaten an excellent player, chances are your next opponent will know who you beat and possibly by how much. This could instill an element of doubt in their mind as to the outcome of their upcoming match with you.

Your Mental Strength

Your opponents will be looking at more than just your game for signs that you can be beaten. They will appraise your composure when you are behind, your ability to deal with bad rolls, and your demeanor following a poor shot. They will also take notice of how you respond to their good play. Any weakness in these areas will signal to your opponent that your mental game is less than rock solid, and that it can be further weakened. This will give your opponent additional confidence that they can win, which of course is one of the last things you want to have happen.

The best antidote for intimidation is experience in pressure situations. In the early going, you can and should expect to take your lumps as you learn how to deal with the many scenarios that you will encounter. Over time you learn how to view each event in a way that only contributes to the well being of your game. With enough seasoning and a positive outlook towards the learning process, there will come a day when there will be little, if anything, that your opponent does (within the boundaries of acceptable sportsmanship) that will cause your mental game to weaken appreciably.

The Battle for Intimidation

There are several possible mindsets at work as you and your opponent are set to begin a match. And as the match wears on, confidence levels can rise and fall because of either player's performance. In most cases, one player will gain an edge over the other, if not in the beginning, then by the time the match is in the later stages. Broadly speaking, there are five possible levels of intimidation.

Levels of Intimidation – the Spectrum

1 Your Opponent is Very Intimidated.

You are the heavy favorite and both you and your opponent know it. Still, you should focus on playing your best game as insurance against what would be a tough to swallow loss. You want to avoid playing down to the other player's level, which might give them a shot at an upset.

2 Your Opponent is Somewhat Intimidated.

With your mind in Level 2, you know you are the favorite, which should give you confidence. You must not become overconfident or take your opponent for granted as this could lead to an upset.

3 There is Mutual Respect and Little or No Intimidation

Level 3 can lead to your best game, as you know you must really play your best. As the match wears on, one player may emerge with the edge as the other feels the pressure of trailing, missed shots, bad rolls, or their opponent's fine play.

4 You are Somewhat Intimidated.

With your mind in Level 4, you still have a chance, but you have your work cut out. You are the underdog, but you have enough confidence to know you at least have a chance. If things go your way, you could wind up gaining an edge in the mental game over your opponent.

5 You are Very Intimidated.

The highest level of intimidation usually occurs when you know going into a match that your opponent is the overwhelming favorite. You could also find yourself in level 5 if you totally break down during a match. When your mind is in level 5, defeat is almost guaranteed. You are ready to roll over and play dead. You have all but conceded the match to your opponent. Respect for a superior player's game has turned into mind numbing fear. Under these conditions, you really have nothing to lose, so you might as well lighten up, enjoy your role as the underdog, and give it your best shot.

Nine Ball is a Battle of Skill Sets

When competing at Nine Ball, it is your break, position play, shotmaking, safeties and kick shots versus those of your opponent. Whenever you do something well, there is a chance your opponent is thinking they can't match your superior skill in that area. If you continually bombard your opponent with a wide array of shots that clearly demonstrate your skill in several parts of the game, there is a good chance they could break down and mentally concede the match even though there are several games to be played.

Your opponent may be an outstanding shotmaker, play pinpoint position or posses a powerhouse break shot. Even so, you should not be overly impressed with any one element of your opponent's game, especially if you are confident in your areas of expertise. Remember, whatever you give up in one area, such as the break, you may more than make up for with superior skills in another area, such as your pattern play.

TIP: Don't be overly impressed with any one facet of your opponent's game. They can only beat you by doing several things well.

Scouting Your Opponent

You can improve your chances of winning by gaining an understanding of the kind of player you are going to be up against. This information is intended to help you establish a game plan for winning, and for developing a healthy respect for their game. Information can be acquired from variety of sources including:

- Your knowledge from previous encounters.
- Watching them compete against other players.
- A scouting report from a knowledgeable friend.
- Observing their play during your match.

Below are samples of the kinds of information that can give an edge:

Intelligence Report #1

"He can't kick but he can jump like Earl".

Action Strategy: Play tight safeties.

Intelligence Report #2

"Misses long pressure shots at the end of the game."

Action Strategy: You can push out to a long shot at the end of a match as long as there is no safety available.

Intelligence Report #3

"Has a weak break that leaves the balls in the foot end of the table".

Action Strategy: Be prepared to play a defensive game.

The Mini-Max Strategy

You should make every effort to fine-tune your strategy. A realistic assessment of your skills as well as those of your opponent will accomplish this. The goal is to be able to maximize the impact of your strengths while minimizing the damage of your weaknesses. At the same time, you want to minimize your opponent's ability to use their strengths and make them play the shots they dislike playing. I call this the Mini-Max Strategy, which should make it easy to recall this approach to playing strategic Nine Ball.

The Mini-Max Strategy

- Maximize your strengths.
- Minimize the impact of your weaknesses.
- Minimize the impact of your opponent's strengths.
- Maximize the damage of their weaknesses.

Your Kicking is:

- Good: Try to hit the proper side of the ball with the proper speed and go for the pocket when a reasonable opportunity presents itself. Consider kicking instead of pushing out when hooked after the break.
- Poor: Aim for the center of the ball. Try to avoid giving up ball in hand. Hit harder to try to separate the balls. Try to "make something happen."

Opponent's Kicking is:

- Good: Play the tightest safeties you can to reduce their possible responses. Be more inclined to take riskier shots than to leave them with easy to hit kicks with which they can easily turn the tables.
- Poor: Play safeties much more often instead of going for run outs.

Your Safety Play is:

- Good: Play more safeties that have an excellent chance of leading to ball in hand rather than always trying to run out.
- Poor: You should go for the run out more often. Be aggressive with your offense.

Opponent's Safety Play is:

- Good: You should try to avoid safety battles. You should take the shot much more often when your opponent pushes out..
- Poor: You must be prepared to execute the tough shots, easy kicks and return safeties they leave you with. Initiate safety battles.This kind of player specializes in non-safe safeties.

Your Shotmaking is:

- Good: You can afford to play further from the object ball to give yourself a bigger zone for the correct angle.
- Poor: You will need to play closer to the object ball. You must also concentrate on pattern play and on getting the best angle possible on each shot.

Opponent's Shotmaking is:

- Good: You must be careful what you leave him on a pushout. You must also play two-way shots that are a half shot, half safety.
- Poor: You can tempt your opponent on pushouts with shots you can make and they can't (dependant on their skill at safeties). You can also play more offensively on tough racks when they have a shot or two that will likely prevent your opponent from running out if you miss.

Your Position and Pattern Play is:

- Good: You can attempt to runout much more often.
- Poor: You should play more safeties. Be patient. Try to rearrange the rack if possible. Avoid giving a stronger opponent a chance to exercise their skills.

Opponent's Position and Pattern Play is:

- Good: Avoid attempting low risk runouts that leave the table with a relatively easy run out. Try to learn what you can about the game and the table from their game.
- Poor: Play more aggressively in the early stages of a typical rack, and in the middle stages of difficult layouts since you have little fear they will run out if you were to miss.

Your Break is:

- Good: Look forward to breaking the balls. Try to take full advantage of this critical area of strength.
- Bad: Realize that you can still win by skillfully executing the other parts of your game the way you are capable of doing. Make certain you get good racks. Play smart pushouts.

Opponent's Break is:

- Good: Understand that even the best breakers often run in streaks. Be ready to run out if they hit a cold spell where the balls aren't falling. (Slip them a slug periodically – just joking.)
- Bad: Be prepared to seize the initiative at the start of the game. Be prepared to deal with clusters and obstacles at the break end of the table.

The Score – All About that Most Vital Statistic

The score seems to have an inordinately large impact on the play of many players. Some players play well with the lead and the confidence that it engenders. Players who fall in this category are quick starters. If you let them jump out to an early lead, they can be hard to catch. Some players who get out in front early make the mistake playing too cautiously in an often futile attempt to protect what they feel is their match. Players who adopt this mindset often are in for a rude awakening when the rolls turn and/or their opponent's game kicks into gear.

In the other camp are the self-styled slow starters, who seem too like the thrill of coming from behind. While their ability to play excellent pool from arrears is quite admirable, as a practical matter, it makes no sense, especially if they are playing against a seasoned competitor. With the short race format used in most leagues and tournaments, you are simply asking too much of yourself if you have to consistently overcome 2-3+ game deficits.

If you feel you belong to either the frontrunners or the comeback artists, then you have just discovered a part of your mental game that needs work. Quick starters need to keep playing with the same aggressiveness they have shown in the beginning clear through to the end. They must also know their limitations, so as not to throw away the match due to recklessness or running out of fuel. Slow starters must quell this urge to spot their opponents an early lead. Slow starters need to warm up properly before a match, shake off the early match jitters, and start playing their game from the start.. Your ultimate goal is to play your best game under any circumstance, no matter what the score.

> *"You cannot let the score affect how you play the game."*
> **Johnny Archer**

Categories of Games

There are five basic categories of games, which are listed below.

1 The games you figure to win and you do win.
2 The games you are supposed to win and you lose. You give them away.
3 The games your opponent figures to win and he does win.
4 The games your opponent is supposed to win and they lose. Your opponent gives them away.
5 The games that are up for grabs.

In the ideal scenario, you would always win the games you are supposed to (the 1's), and more than your share of the games that are up for the grabs (the 5's). And you would never give away "sure" wins (2's). At the same time, your cause is aided by an opponent who gives away games (4's), thanks perhaps to the pressure you apply with your fine play.

When analyzing your matches, you will discover those games that could be added or subtracted from your total if you and your opponent had performed up to expectations. Your analysis should also include the games that were up for grabs. It is important to recognize what shot or series of events lead to you either winning or losing those games. Your analysis can serve as a valuable learning tool.

Accessing Your Top Gear and Closing a Match

The mantra that is a religion many instructors, myself included, is that you should play one shot at a time and give each and every shot your best. Your games and matches are a collection of these individual shots. In the real world, however, you will experience periodic fluctuations in your level of concentration, which affect ability to execute. The end result is a level of play that is at least occasionally less than your best.

The great champions in all sports recognize these fluctuations, but they also know when and how to shift into top gear when a game or match is on the line. Joe Montana was famous for his ability to rally his team to victory late in the 4th quarter. Jack Nicklaus was known for his ability to play his best golf while others around him were folding like lawn chairs. In pool, Mike Sigel was the best at playing under the heat as shown by his astounding record in the finals while accumulating over 100 professional victories.

Perhaps you are wondering why these athletes didn't give a 4th quarter or "back 9 on Sunday" kind of effort to the whole contest? A sustained end-of-contest kind of effort is simply not possible. Top athletes know that their intensity varies from time to time. They also know they can consciously turn up their game on command. They know there is a top gear that is available and they can access it when the time is right. When the game is on the line, winners can:

- Call on the special powers.
- Put their game into overdrive
- Beat the percentages.
- Get the job done.
- Run out for the cash.

The ability to close out a match should not be taken lightly. It is one thing to win the last couple of games against a weaker opponent when you have a big lead. Closing out a match is a completely different matter when you are on the hill and your opponent is running racks and is threatening to pass you at the finish line.

One of my favorite lines in the movie *The Hustler* comes when Bert Gordon (George C. Scott) counsels Fast Eddie (Paul Newman) after a losing a big lead (and his money) that "The game isn't like football. Nobody pays you for yardage". Fast Eddie lacked Minnesota Fats' ability to close the deal. He learned, however, and won a rematch later in the movie.

The ability to close (win!) comes from putting yourself in the position often enough that you gain experience in dealing with the pressure. Eventually you will be able to maintain the style of play and the momentum that took you close to the goal all of the way to the winner's circle. You will come to trust your game to the point where you can execute the way you know you can when the match is on the line.

> *"You don't get any consolation for having a big lead and losing."*
> **Johnny Archer**

Rolls, Mistakes and Great Shots

The rolls is pool lingo for the luck factor, both good and bad. Nine Ball is a completely fair game in the long but at times excruciatingly unfair in the course of a race to 5, 7 or 11 games. The Pool Gods simply do not dole out the rolls evenly in the short run, but over the long haul they are eminently just. It may not seem that way, however, because most players seem to filter out their own good rolls; and can recite every one of their bad rolls, or their opponent's good rolls.

No one has yet conducted an in depth scientific study of the rolls to determine how they are dispersed throughout a typical match. Still, it is safe to assume that the rolls play a substantial role in deciding the outcome of the short races (6 or less games) that are popular in weekly tournaments throughout the country. In longer races, such as to nine or more games, you have a much better chance of overcoming a disadvantage in the rolls department by out playing your opponent.

The rolls can provide your opponent with an advantage from which you cannot recover if you focus your energy on bemoaning your fate. If you choose to fight back, you may prevail in spite of a deficit in the rolls department.

Each bad roll can be counteracted by eliminating a mistake or by making a great shot. Let's assume that your opponent lead in the rolls by a margin of 6-3 in a race to nine games. It is possible for you to have won if they failed to take advantage of their good fortune by making mistakes. You could also have come out on top by making fewer errors than normal, or by making a great shot or two.

The table below shows five possible ways in which the rolls may be dispersed over a relatively short session.

1 The rolls greatly favor you.
2 The rolls are slightly in your favor.
3 The rolls are about even.
4 The rolls slightly favor your opponent.
5 The rolls greatly favor your opponent.

When the rolls fall into category #1, the Pool Gods have decided to shine on you for a while. When everything is going your way, winning is made easier, providing you don't get complacent. However, you shouldn't count on this lasting forever. And you will certainly have a much tougher time beating your opponent when the rolls are heavily stacked in their favor (category #5). This condition in which the rolls are lopsided in one players favor can last throughout an entire match. In most instances, however, the rolls fall into categories 2-4. When they are about even or when one player holds a slight advantage, both players usually have a chance at winning.

"The balls will not stay loyal to any one person." **Bill Incardona**

Developing the Killer Instinct

If you play the same people regularly, you may tend to play well against some opponents and slack off against others. You may, for example, lighten up against people you like or against friends who you happen to draw in a tournament. Remember, however, that playing less than your best takes away from their victory. In addition, your opponent may be aware that you are playing well beneath your ability, and this will rob them of the satisfaction they would have received by beating you at your best.

You may also lighten up because you feel bad that your opponent is not getting to play much, if at all. If this is the case, you need to be reminded that pool is inherently the most selfish sport yet devised by man. The whole idea is to stay at the table for as long as possible, and to deny your opponents the opportunity to shoot. You simply can't afford to feel guilty because you are doing most, if not all of the shooting. If you play the nice guy once too often, your opponent may take advantage of your generosity by winning the match.

In short, you've got to develop a killer instinct. You've got to want the table all for yourself. You have to take great pleasure in running out and playing the kind of safeties that give you ball in hand so you can run out all over again. You cannot feel bad because your opponent, who came to play pool, has instead turned into a spectator. Rest assured that as you move up the competitive ladder, you will encounter more and more opponents who have trained themselves to think precisely in this manner.

Men and Women in Today's World of Pool

Men tend to be highly competitive by nature, thanks to the hunter instinct that dates back to our beginnings, and our to upbringing that emphasizes sports. Men, by nature, have a killer instinct. Men dislike losing even if it is to their best friend. Furthermore, since pool is really an enlightened form of hand-to-hand combat, the game only serves to magnify men's competitive instincts to an extremely high level. It is me versus you, survival of the fittest, and may the better man win.

The majority of women who are new to pool may not, in most cases, have the same competitive drive as men players. Some women may even feel bad for their opponent when they conclude a winning match. As women gain experience and their games improve, they learn to become much more competitive, but this process can take many years to unfold.

Women who are new to competition may compete with men who they know at a local poolroom or tavern. Initially this is a non-threatening environment when playing the men. Competing against another women as a beginner may bring additional pressure, however, especially if the men are watching the contest.

As a woman player starts working on her game and improves, she becomes more competitive and the desire to win grows. When a female player begins to play in important ladies events, that may last 2-3 days or longer, the expectations rise, along with the pressure to do well. When a woman player enters this phase, her competitive mindset is becoming closer to that of male players.

A big issue for many female players I've talked to is that they tend to have a problem keeping their mind on the table because they are so used to multitasking in their lives. This often makes it difficult for them to completely put aside everything else that is going on in their life in order to focus exclusively on their pool game for an extended period of time.

Men and Women Competing Together

The sizeable gap between the number of men and women in pool has been closing for many years now as pool has become even more respectable and as the number of leagues and tournaments has proliferated. A high percentage of competitive events now encourage participation by both sexes, which of course means that more and more men and women will be facing each other at the table. These mixed gender match-ups have a tendency to bring forth issues that are not present in matches involving competitors of a single sex.

Let's face it, most men don't want to lose to a women. Period. The male player has their big fat ego on the line when playing a woman. They hate the thought of being teased by their buddies after losing to "a girl". This thinking may have been understandable 20-30 years ago when there were few women in the game and fewer still who could be classified as C Players (using the same standards as for the men) or above.

The times are changing as the quality of women's pool has risen dramatically. Want proof? Just tune in to the ladies playing on TV. Allison Fisher, the dominant women's player in the 1990's, scored a near perfect .970, according to the Accu-Stats scoring system, in a match with Loree Jon Jones at the 1999 WPBA Prescott Resort Classic, a score seldom matched by the best male players. BCA Hall of Fame member Jean Balukas beat several of the best male players at Nine Ball and Straight Pool, which was her best game.

While the number of highly skilled women players is still far below the men, they are gaining ground. Nowadays it should come as much less of a surprise when a male player encounters a female who plays well enough to beat them in tournament or league competition. Since winning is still the name of the game, I would, therefore, advise my male counterparts to put aside this ego thing. Start viewing women who play pool as pool players. Give them the respect they deserve. And don't be too surprised if they play well and beat you on occasion.

Women who have attained sufficient skill to compete with men in amateur events may still view their male opponents as the favorites. This can certainly take some of the pressure off of these mixed gender encounters if you approach them with low expectations. This mindset may enable you to play well for part of a match, but the pressure always appears at the end, which can sabotage your efforts. I suggest that women players, who have built a reasonably solid game, should go into any contest with the attitude that you are going to play your game and you are playing to win. Learn to view yourself as a very capable pool player who has every right to expect to win.

Tournaments

Types of Tournaments

Nine Ball has exploded in popularity to the point where you can compete in a tournament seven days a week if you live anywhere close to a major metropolitan area. Weekly tournaments are one of the greatest bargains in pool. They allow you to compete against a wide variety of players, gain valuable experience, and possibly win prize money for entry fees that typically range from $5-$20. In short, there is a tournament for every pocketbook and level of skill. There are several types of weekly events:

- Open events in which players of all levels are welcome to compete.
- Handicapped events that are open to all levels of play.
- Restricted events that only allow players up to a certain level of skill, such as B Players and below.

If you are a C Player, your entry fee will be accepted almost anywhere you go. Most, but not all, events are also open to B Players. A Players may will often be required to give substantial handicaps, if they are even allowed to compete. In recent years, however, there has been a substantial growth in the number of regional tours that cater to advanced players (see the appendix for details). The entry fees for regional event usually range from $30-$100. These are still a great deal as they allow upper level players to compete, for substantial prize money, with talented opposition in fields that may occasionally feature several top pros.

Prize money, at most events, usually depends on the number of entrants. Some tournaments will subtract a green fee, which is only fair considering table time is usually included in the price of your entry. Some of the most popular events are those in which the house actually adds money to the pot. At most billiard room tournaments you will usually have at least an hour of free practice time, which only sweetens an already great deal.

You will most likely be paired against players of all levels of skill over the course of a few tournaments. In some open events, A, B, and C Players will be competing with one another, with or without handicaps. If you are new to Nine Ball, open tournaments give you a chance to play better players for much less than it would "cost" if you played them in a money game. And if the event is handicapped, you could learn from your opposition while winning at the same time. What could be better?

Manage Your Expectations

When playing in tournaments, it is wise to manage your expectations. Do your best to win at all times against better players and accept loses as learning experiences. Against players at your level, you will be provided an opportunity to improve upon your ability to play under pressure. As I mentioned in an earlier section, your ability to close out a match is one of the most important lessons you can learn in pool.

How to Win a Tournament

The best player does not always win a tournament, otherwise they wouldn't continue to hold them. While skill is important, there are a host of variables that enter into the win/loss equation that are largely out of any players hands. When top pros win, they will almost always acknowledge the roll that luck played in their victory. On the way to winning, there are usually at least one or two close matches that very easily could have gone the other way. For example, Corey Deuel completed the monumental task of capturing eleven matches in a row (including 10 in a row on the losers side) on his way to winning the 2001 BCA Championship. One match went double hill match while two others were decided by scores of 11-9.

I suggest that you make every effort to play your best pool in every event you enter. When you play great pool, however, don't be surprised if the Pool Gods seem to conspire against you somewhere along the way. They may, in fact rob, you of a title you feel should have been yours based on your level of play. You should recognize, however, that you might win from time to time with less than your best game.

The items listed below are a sampling of the many factors that can aid in your march to a title. Your mental approach and game are in your control. The other factors are in the lap of the Pool Gods.

- You play great pool.
- You beat the players you are supposed to beat.
- You pull off an upset or two.
- You never give up.
- You receive a bye in your first round.
- The best players are on the other side of the chart.
- You face a series of easy matches at the start, which help put you in stroke.
- Players that you would have trouble beating lose to players who you can beat, even though you aren't the favorite.
- You get great rolls match after match.
- Your opponents get terrible rolls.
- The tournament format encourages upsets. Single elimination, short races.
- You win a match or two despite a sub par effort.

Single Elimination

In single elimination tournaments, your task is crystal clear: keep winning or you're out. You must be prepared to play one match right after another. Do you like odds? If so, the following calculation may be of interest: if you play in a 32 player field and you are a 70% favorite to win each match, your odds of winning a single elimination event are 1 in 5.9 tries. In a 64 player field, your chances would drop to a win in every 8.5 tries.

Double Elimination

The winner's side of a double elimination bracket is the high percentage route to victory. On the winner's side you must cope with a steady diet of players who are on their game and who are feeling good about themselves as a result of their recent victories. Your matches will attract more and more attention and you will have to deal with the intimidation factor as you will no doubt come across some very fine players. While on the winner's side, you should also devise a routine for spending the often vast amounts of time that separate your matches. Three obvious choices are; rest, the practice room, and scouting future opponents.

Take heart if and when you are deposited on to the left side of the flow chart, especially if this happens a lot sooner that you anticipated. A good attitude and some solid play can take you a long way on the "losers" side. You could be up against players who are off their game or who are disheartened to be on loser's side. Many, in fact, probably will have one foot out the door when you face them.

The loser's side is no place for complacency as your survival in the tournament is at stake. Since you must play more matches, you will have a chance to get in stroke and adapt to the conditions. Your quest will be aided if you are in good shape, both physically and mentally. You will need every edge, as your matches will only get tougher as you continue your winning ways.

Preparing for a Big Tournament

The goal of your pre-tournament preparations is to bring your game to a peak just prior to the start of the event. With the proper preparations, you can expect to arrive at the tournament with complete confidence in your game. The time to begin your preparations is largely an individual matter that is related to the importance of the event, your available time and how much practice is required to get your game in top form.

Solitary Practice

- Spend some time practicing and evaluating your technique.
- Work with your instructor to correct any flaws.
- Use practice drills to get in stroke and stay in stroke.
- Trusting practice should be emphasized as the tournament nears. You should be too concerned with your mechanics as you are hopefully in the groove.

Competing to Get Ready

- Only play Nine Ball, because you need to have your shotmaking particularly sharp.
- Play easy games so you can practice running out.
- Play practice races that are the same length as the tournament for a friendly sum against people at your level or higher.
- Simulate tournament conditions as closely as possible.
- Compete in local events to build your immunity to pressure.

Mental

- Visualize yourself playing great pool and executing one fine shot after another. Imagine the surroundings as vividly as possible.
- Establish a goal of where you would like to finish, taking into account a realistic appraisal of the competition.
- Set goals that will ensure you have a rewarding experience no matter what happens. These could include: learning from your mistakes and from watching and talking to good players, meeting new people, and, most importantly, having fun.

Practical Matters

- Make all preparations well in advance, especially if you are traveling out of town. This includes: hotels, travel, and things to be taken care of before you leave home.
- Make sure you have packed all of the accessories that are important to your success. Make a checklist for your equipment and accessories. This could include: shapers, tappers, cleaners, towels, bridge heads, chalk holders, gloves, cue holders, etc.

At the Site

- Plan to arrive early so you will be relaxed and well rested.
- Follow a healthy regime. Eat properly, not too heavy, and don't abuse alcohol.
- Practice so you can get used to the conditions. Test the tables and make any refinements in your strategy.
- Tell yourself you like the conditions if possible. If the conditions are not ideal, let your opponents be bothered them, not you.
- Consider the distractions and other challenging elements. Be prepared to deal with them to eliminate excuses for losing.

Before Each Match

- Know when you will be playing and be ready.
- Give yourself enough time to warm up properly before each match (20-30 minutes) on the practice tables and/or the table on which you'll be playing.
- Follow a routine that enables you to concentrate 100% on playing great pool.
- Don't let prematch nerves be a source of concern. A little anxiety shows you're up for the contest. All players feel it.

Money Games

I'm going to begin the topic of playing pool for money by stating that is a part of the game that provides enjoyment for countless participants, and it will always be for as long as the game is played. Playing for money is an accepted practice at golf clubs across America. In addition, casino gambling, lotteries, and wagering on football, basketball and other sports is a source of pleasure for millions. It would be a case of sheer hypocrisy to expect pool players to be held to standards higher that those who participate in America's other mainstream activities.

As for the big money games of the pros, it continues to be a shame that these incredibly skilled performers must supplement their meager earnings in tournaments by gambling. I believe that most if not all of them would not feel the need to play for money if tournament prize money was even 10% of what golfers play for.

Handicapping

Nine Ball is played for money far more than any other pool game. The game provides fast action, as the average game lasts about 4-5 minutes. In addition, it is an easy game to handicap. When you are making a game, chances are good that you will either be giving or getting a handicap. Handicaps are referred to as a spot, or weight.

In a perfect world, the object of the pre-match negotiations would be to arrive at a game in which each player has a 50% chance of winning. In the real world of pool, this seldom happens. One player just wants to play and is not overly concerned with winning. Their opponent, on the other hand, won't usually play unless they are the favorite, often the heavy favorite. Particularly skilled negotiators are known to win upwards of 80% of the time. And then there are those players who grossly overestimate their skills and/or underestimate their opponent's games. They are lucky if they walk away with the cash 20% of the time. You can broadly lump those who play for money into three categories:

The Winners. Their games and/or negotiating enable them to win at least 70% of their encounters.
The Sportsmen. They win roughly 40-60% of the time. They like winning, but they like playing and the action even more.
The Losers. They would like to win, but they come out on the short end most of the time, due to poor negotiating skills and poor play.

If you are a philanthropist, have money to burn, and don't mind losing, you will find plenty of people in a poolroom who will be more than happy to relieve you of your funds. Should you wish to make pool a money making enterprise, or if you want to at least avoid being labeled a sucker, then you will need to hone your negotiating skills. Classes are in session daily at many rooms across the land. Before you wager your dough, I suggest you listen in on the conversations of some of the more articulate poolroom attorneys. Listen to the lines and the responses. Pretty soon you'll have an answer to every objection. The skills you learn can also prepare you for a career as a used car salesman.

Since pool players are known to have short memories, I suggest that you reach a complete understanding with your opponent, on all of the critical aspects of your negotiations, so that you avoid any disagreements. There are many components to the negotiating process, the most important of which are discussed below.

Spotting
You can have a field day calculating the many possible spots in Nine Ball. In fact, some of the most adroit game makers derive a large part of their advantage from skillfully manipulating the various elements below to arrive their winning edge. They know which bargaining chips, such as the break or a game on the wire, hold special appeal to a certain audience. They also know better than to give up multiple wild balls to someone who incessantly rides the money.

Wild Ball This is an additional game ball for the player being spotted. When a player is getting the wild 8-ball, for example, they win anytime the 8-ball is pocketed on a legal shot, just as they would with the 9-ball. Other common wild ball spots are the wild 7-ball and the wild 6-ball.
Called Balls - The concept is the same as for the wild ball discussed above except that you have to call the pocket in which you are playing the ball. This greatly reduces your chance of winning with a slop shot.
Multiple Wild Balls – When one player is significantly better than the other, the lesser player may receive two or more wild balls or called balls. For example, an A Player might spot a B Player the call 7-ball and wild 8-ball. In fact, the possible combinations are endless. If you are giving multiple wild balls, don't let them count on the break.
The Last Two - The game is over when the player receiving this spot makes the ball before the 9-ball, when the 9-ball is the only other ball on the table. This spot basically eliminates the need to play shape on and pocket the 9-ball. This spot can be extended to the last three, etc. This spot is amongst the smallest that a B or A Player can give another. However, the last two is a huge spot for one C Player to give to another, since their games are largely decided on the last few balls.
Games on the Wire - Let's assume two players are racing to 9 games. If Players A gave Player B a two game head start, Player B would be said to be getting two games on the wire. This spot is commonly used in tournaments instead of the ball spots discussed above because it is less confusing and reduces misunderstandings.
The Breaks - One player may have the privilege of breaking every rack while his opponent is assigned the duties of rack boy. Stronger players use this spot as a big bargaining chip to entice players of far less ability into playing. The stronger player in confident that his opponent cannot often win from the break, and that he will be able to quickly take control of the table after the break. The breaks are often given in combination with a wild or called ball, in an attempt to create an even game.
Combination Spots
Spots can be combined in a thousand or more ways. Here are just a very few samples:

- The 8-ball and the breaks.
- The called 7-ball and the last two.
- The last three and the breaks.
- The wild 6-ball and a game on the wire.

Format

A big part of your negotiations also centers on the format. The most common format today is a race to x number of games. The most common lengths are to 5, 7, 9 or 11 games. Below are some tips for choosing the length that gives you the best chance of winning.

- Slow starters should bargain for long races.
- Fast starters should request short races.
- The better player should extend the race, while the lesser player should try to keep the sets as short as possible.
- The player giving weight should extend the races, while the player receiving weight should make them as short as possible.
- The larger the wager, the longer the set should be.
- The length you use should also be a function of the time available and how many sets you want to play.

Many players prefer to play sessions that are over only when one player gets a specified number of games ahead of the other. For example, in a five ahead set, a player could win by taking the first five games. If the players are evenly matched, they could battle back and forth for hours before one player pulls five games ahead. Another format is to pay after every game. This format allows for the greatest flexibility in changing the wager, the spot and the length of time that you are going to play.

Money Management

When you are playing poolroom regulars and friends for friendly wagers, money management is not as nearly as much of an issue as it is for those who wager large sums. Nevertheless, you can increase your enjoyment by following sound principles of money management.

Let's assume you have $100 of fun money in your budget for wagering at pool (after groceries, the rent, etc.). The last thing you should do is bet it all on one game the moment you enter the poolroom. Instead, divide your stake into a sufficiently large number of units, or barrels. If you were going to play someone by the game, you might be wise to play for $10 per game. Your opponent would have to get 10 games ahead before you were out of funds, which is not easy unless you are in a bad game or are suffering from extremely poor play.. If you were going to play races to 9 games, for example, you should play for $50 per set. This would enable you to make a comeback in a second set should lose the first set.

The amount you wager is a very personal matter. Most players are content playing for nominal sums. For them the game is of primary importance. Those who feel they must bet large sums to get a charge out of pool are really gamblers first, and pool players second. In summary, there is no single answer for how much you should wager. A $100 is a small fortune to some, while to others it is tip money. Your pocket book and your common sense will hopefully enable you to wager sensibly.

When negotiating the game, the amount of the wager is but another bargaining chip. For example, if your opponent wants to play for an amount higher than you've been discussing, you may agree only if they reduce (or increase) the spot, lengthen (or shorten) the set, or agree to play on a different table. When you are selecting a table, be sure it is one you like. Also be sure that it isn't the table on which your opponent practices for eight hours daily and on which he plays like a world-beater.

The Rules

You should briefly discuss the rules just to make sure you and your opponent are in agreement. Primary topics include the three-foul rule, who will act as a referee on close hits, and cue ball and/or object ball fouls. For a more complete discussion of the rules, please see the appendix.

Time

You can save yourself much grief by setting a firm time limit before play begins. If you happen to be winning when your quitting time arrives, your opponent cannot insist that you keep playing until the room closes. Perhaps my favorite phrase is "You've got to give me a chance to get my money back." Well guess what, when you're ahead and the money is in your pocket, whose money is it? Remind your opponent of your agreement and tell them you'll be glad to play them again on another day.

Backers

You will have truly moved up in the rankings when someone else is willing to finance your money games. The typical split of the winnings is 50/50. The backer assumes all losses. Treat your backers like kings and try to make games where you have an excellent chance of winning. And never, ever commit the dastardly act of losing on purpose (dumping, doing business). If the word gets around that you dumped a match, you will lose your backer, and your reputation will go straight down the tubes.

Hustles and Shark Moves

Whole books and tapes have been devoted to the subject of relieving your "opponent" of their cash as quickly and efficiently as possible. They cover the usual gamut of strategies, including the stall, every hustler's favorite. You begin the stall by playing well beneath your ability until you have your unsuspecting opponent believing they have a chance. Once the bet is to your liking, balls start finding the pockets and you emerge with the cash. If trickery and deceit is your thing, you may wish to purchase guides on this subject. Better yet, why not spend your time and energy perfecting your game so you can win with your newfound skills.

The Collection Department

When you are playing friends and regulars for nominal stakes, you needn't worry too much about getting paid. Even if you're opponent "forgot their wallet", or their spouse "emptied out the ATM", they most likely will pay you soon enough rather than have you hounding them. If you insist on gambling with strangers and/or for big stakes, then you must take precautionary measures. At a minimum, you should insist on getting paid after every game or fifth game (if you are playing by the game) or at the end of every set. In the world of high stakes play, it is standard operating procedure for the money to be posted prior to beginning play. In fact, if the wager is sufficiently high and/or trust is low, a neutral third party is often compensated for holding the money.

You should be aware of how your game can be affected playing on the "owsies". When you are not going to be paid right away, there is a tendency to let down. This is fueled by the feeling many players have that they don't want to have to worry about collecting a debt some time in the future.

League Play

League pool has exploded in popularity because this format combines the rugged individualism of pool with the highly social nature of pool players, many of whom grew up playing team sports. While Eight Ball was initially the game of choice for league pool, Nine Ball is catching up fast.

Many league players view league night as an enjoyable night away from home that gives them a chance to socialize with others who share a common interest, enjoy a beverage or two, and shoot a few games of pool. That is all fine and dandy. This section, however, is for those who are out to win and to grow as pool players. The suggestions below have been adapted from my book, *A Mind For Pool,* which gives a more detailed overview of how to compete successfully in league pool.

An Introduction

A typical league season lasts anywhere from 10-30 weeks. It is comprised of a series of home and away matches between teams of 4-5 players plus substitutes. Women are making their presence felt in competitive pool, and this is certainly true in league pool, where many leagues and teams are comprised of both sexes.

You will gain the most from your experience by playing in a league that most closely mirrors your level of play. In leagues that use a handicap system, this is not an issue. As a matter of fact, I encourage newer players to compete in handicap leagues as a way of learning from better players. You should also choose your home poolroom or tavern with care. Make sure it is a place in which you feel comfortable playing, and that it has an owner who supports league pool.

Your Team

You need more than a collection of bodies on league night to be a competitive force in league pool. The best teams are put together by the recruiting efforts of the team's captain. The captain should have a clear objective of the kind of player that he feels would make a good teammate

The captain will naturally want to recruit the best player's he can, unless it is a handicap league. Team chemistry is one of the most important ingredients for success, and for having a good time. Teammates have to be able to get along over the course of a long season. Team captains, who want to construct a winning squad, must put some effort into the selection process, rather than simply rounding up a group of friends. They should pick those who share their commitment to the team and who are nuts about pool. If you don't want the captains job, you should look for a team and a captain who are serious about winning and who are supportive of each other's efforts.

Team captains derive a certain pleasure from their role as leaders. In exchange, they must take care of the mundane details, such as collecting money, arranging for substitutes and record keeping. Their teammates should show their appreciation for their captain's efforts by showing up on time, playing hard, and maintaining a good attitude at all times.

Team Goals

Before the season starts, the team should get together to establish their goals for the season, and to devise a plan for reaching them. The captain should put the goals on paper, make copies, and distribute them to his teammates prior to the first match. Email can also be used for this and in many other ways to keep teammates in touch with one another. Some possible goals include:

- Contend of fist place.
- Improve on last year's performance.
- Win the league title.
- Beat the top teams or an arch rival.
- Qualify for the nationals.
- Help each other improve.
- Learn to play as a team.
- Compete successfully in the nationals.
- Have fun.

Individual Goals

Team goals must always come first, but there are some individual goals worth striving for. You and your teammates must not, however, be at odds with one another should you be competing for the same honors. Some possible individual goals include:

- Improve your game.
- Increase your winning % over last season.
- Become skilled at coaching and instructing your teammates.
- Win the league MVP.
- Win or at least play very well in a season ending tournament.

League Night

You should try to arrive at least 30 minutes to an hour before the start of play. You will reduce your captains stress level and give yourself time to a get in stroke and get used to the tables. Your team can share thoughts on how the table(s) is playing. In addition, you may spot a flaw in a teammates game that can easily be corrected prior to the start of play. The whole team should also meet briefly to discuss the other team, especially if you know their players from previous encounters. This session can help to refine your strategy and to arrange your line up.

Before play starts, the captain or some other team member should devise a motivating statement, which can set the tone for the evenings play. Be creative, since the same line may lose its effect if used week after week. Your motivation could come from wanting to beat the #1 team, keep a winning streak alive, or to secure a place in the nationals. Before each game, one or more teammates should make a positive comment to the person who is about to play.

In one on one play, you only have one person to worry about. In league play there could be upwards of 10-20 people crowded around the table. Under these conditions it may be too much to expect 100% peace and quiet. League pool offers a stern test of your powers of concentration. It is futile to keep quieting the crowd, so it is best to stick to business unless the other team is blatantly sharking you on shot after shot.

Some leagues permit coaching on at least one shot during each game. These sessions can help your team win and serve to educate the player. Your coach should be very knowledgeable, an excellent communicator, and be familiar with the other players games. Mid game advisory sessions should be fast and effective. If they become drawn out lectures, they can extend the matches well into the night while boring everyone to tears. A dissertation on pool can also disrupt your player's rhythm.

After each game is over, your team should congratulate the winners, which signals to the other team that your squad is united in a common cause. Losing players should be consoled and encouraged about their game.

It is pointless to criticize a player for a mistake while their match is in progress. If, however, a player is missing due to an obvious flaw, he should be reminded of the proper cure prior to his next turn. The time for evaluating mistakes in position, strategy, or shot selection is after a match is over. Any criticism should be offered in the most constructive manner possible. This objective is most easily met if you and your teammates have a stated goal of trying to improve each other's games.

Hopefully your teammates are still around at the end, especially if your match comes last. After the match is over, it is a good idea to hold a brief meeting to discuss what went right and wrong, what you can learn, and any plans for next week, including any practice sessions in between matches.

CHAPTER 15

PRACTICING NINE BALL

"I've picked every weakness out and worked on them until they matched the rest of my game."
Jeanette Lee

Every one of the great players you've witnessed on videos, TV, or in live action running racks with apparent ease and pocketing unbelievable shots have put in long hours at the practice table developing and refining their skills. Although you may lack the time or inclination to practice as much as the pros, your game will nevertheless benefit from at least a few hours of practice every week.

If you are really serious about improving your game, you'll make time for practice. A practice routine that is enjoyable and productive will have you to looking forward with enthusiasm to your sessions, rather than viewing practice as some form of torture. Don't forget that when you are practicing you are stroking and hitting pool balls – how bad can that be?

To improve in the critical areas of skill, you need closely spaced repetitions of the same shot. This enables you to make the corrections needed and really learn the shot. This obviously can't take place in a match.

As you enter your matches, hopefully you will hold several competitive advantages over your opponents, which give you the winning edge. Well, any advantages you posses are largely acquired in practice. No practice equals few, if any advantages, simple as that. And if your practice sessions are also superior, you can build your storehouse of skills more quickly, which provide you with your competitive advantages.

In short, if your practice sessions are different and better than your fellow competitor's, it will certainly show in your performances. So let's get to work on your game, starting with a complete evaluation of your skills.

Rating Your Game in the Key Competencies

Your Nine-Ball game is the sum total of your skills in a wide range of critical competencies. You can compete successfully at certain levels with only a modest level of skill in a few key areas. An average player, for example, who is a skilled shotmaker, and who has mastered a few basic safeties, can compete very successfully against players at his level. As you move up the ladder, however, you must begin to fill in the gaps in all key areas of skill. Your opponent's will take advantage of gaps in your game which, of course, will result in lost games and matches.

You can take a big step towards improving your game by conducting a skills inventory of your game. I suggest you use the 1-10 scale. If you wish to add precision to your rankings, you can fill in the gaps between whole numbers with decimal points. You should be as objective as possible. If you are not sure how you rate in certain areas, have a knowledgeable friend or instructor evaluate your game.

You can use a simplified or detailed approach to rating your game. For example, you can rate yourself in the overall category of shotmaking with the complete understanding there are many different shots that make up this area of skill. You can add precision to your evaluation by breaking the major categories into subcategories, which will enable you to pinpoint very specific areas for improvement. While this is a more painstaking approach, it will lead to significantly better results.

The list below should help get you started. You can amend it as needed. While the items below could be broken down even further, there is a practical limit to what you can evaluate and practice regularly or as needed.

Champions Checklist

Fundamentals
__Grip
__Stance
__Bridge
__Stroke
__Aim
__Preshot routine
Basic Shotmaking
__Cut shots
__Thin cut shots
__Off the rail
__The long green
__Jacked up over a ball
Specialty Shots
__Banks – short rail
__Banks – long rail
__Caroms
__Billiards
__Combinations
__Curve shots
The Break
__Power break
__Control break
__Adaptability to the table
Kick Shots
__Basic routes
__Using english
__Using speed
Position Play
__Basics: stop, draw and follow
__No rail routes
__1-rail routes
__2-rail routes
__3-rail routes
__4-rail routes
__Use of outside english
__Use of inside english
Pattern Play
__Basic 3 ball patterns
__Advanced patterns
Safety Skills
__Full hit safeties
__Thin hit safeties
__Control of the cue ball
__Control of the object ball
__Knowledge of a variety of safeties
__Imagination
Push out
__Strategy
__Skills
__The Lag for Break

Once you have completed your inventory you will have a blue print for developing your game. You will know your strengths and those areas which fall well below the rest of your game. You should systematically go to work on any glaring deficiencies in the key competencies with practice. At the same time, you should also work on refining your strengths and on keeping them honed to a fine edge. In the final analysis, developing and keeping a variety of skills at an acceptably high level is really like a juggling act. The goal is to keep as many balls (skills) as high up in the air as possible.

A Sample Comparison of Skills

Skill	**Position**	**ShotM.**	**Patterns**	**Safeties**	**Break**
Pro	9.8	9.2	9.6	9.3	9.4
A	8.6	9.0	8.3	9.2	8.1
B	7.1	8.3	7.0	6.6	8.4
C	4.8	6.0	3.6	2.8	3.4
Your Game	?	?	?	?	?

The table above is a sample of what a broad based skills inventory might look like for players of various levels of skill. Our mythical pro rates a 9.2 or better in all areas, which is what you would expect from a top player. At his level, this player may win his share of matches and compete very successfully, but shotmaking, which is his biggest weakness, may be the one thing that could keep him from the winner's circle.

The A Player has a solid game. His safety play is his biggest weapon while his comparatively weak break offers room for substantial improvement.

Our B Player shows consistent skill for his level of competition in all areas except his safety play. Poor safeties could be costing him games against opponents he would otherwise be beating.

The C Player's skills leave room for much improvement in all areas. Like many average players, this player has learned to pocket balls first, which shows by his 6.0 rating in shotmaking. This player needs to go to work right away on his safeties (2.8) and pattern play (4.8). The break can wait until his other skills are more fully developed.

The rather simplistic analysis above is designed to give you an idea of the process of evaluating your game. No matter what your level of play the goal is to develop a solid, consistent game with no glaring weaknesses. Balance is the key. Still, no matter how well you play, chances are you will always have certain areas in which you excel Your strengths should be exploited to the fullest in competition. While competing, you need to minimize the impact of your weak points until such time as you can eliminate them in practice.

Practice Environment

I suggest you choose your practice environment wisely. When you want to really focus on specific areas of your game and you do not wish to be interrupted, you should practice in quiet surroundings. This could be on your home table or at the poolroom during the afternoons. If you are using devices, such as the donuts (hole reinforcements), and you wish to practice without feeling self-conscious, choose off hours at the poolroom. If you wish to simulate game conditions, you may opt to practice in noisy surroundings. Practicing in a loud, noisy and crowded environment will teach you how to tune out distractions, which will most certainly be present on a busy league night or during a tournament. This kind of environment may be best for using the suggestions for practicing with a friend that appear later in the chapter.

There are perfectly valid reasons for spending most of your practice time on the same table, and for switching tables, rooms and conditions periodically. When you practice on the same table, it is easier to measure your progress. You can set up identical drills and routines and compare results from one session to the next. Because you feel comfortable with the conditions, playing on the same table can help boost your confidence.

In the real world of competitive pool, conditions do change, often radically. Therefore, you need to develop the skill of adapting to strange conditions if you are to compete successfully away from home.

Increase Your Awareness

When playing or practicing, keep your awareness level running high. This should be the case no matter what the occasion or results from the most recent series of shots or games. A high level of awareness will help you to confirm the things you are doing correctly. Reinforcing the positive builds repetition and confidence. Awareness is also instrumental in turning poor shots into learning experiences. As you play, tune into things like:

- Visualizing a successful shot before you play it.
- The feel of the tip at contact.
- Your cueing (where you strike the cue ball).
- The feel of your stroke.
- The roll of a well struck shot.
- The cue ball's route to the position zone.
- The speed of the table.
- How english takes off the rails.
- The sound of the ball hitting the pocket.

Solitary Practice

The majority of your practice time should be spent by yourself. Spend this time wisely and the dividends to your game will be substantial. There are countless ways that you can structure each session. Since there are so many things to be worked on, practice should always be both enjoyable and educational. To get the most from your sessions I suggest you follow these suggestions:

- Practice regularly and for at least 1-3 hours at a time.
- Prepare an agenda for each session.
- Develop a series of short and long-term goals. These could include improvements in your fundamentals, mastering certain position routes and developing your safeties, for example.
- Keep a journal. It could include results from your drills, new discoveries and things to work on in future sessions.
- Practice as long as you remain enthusiastic. Before your desire slips, start practicing something else or end your session.
- Frequent practice is best, especially for newer players. Lengthy but infrequent sessions don't work nearly as well.
- Resist the temptation to "play" during practice. Be disciplined.
- Intermediate and advanced players should practice under a variety of conditions.
- Have a knowledgeable friend or instructor watch your game.
- Use the donuts to mark the position of the cue ball and the object ball so you can repeat the same shots exactly as before.
- Practice components of your game that your opponents probably ignore in their sessions, such as safeties, kick shots and the break.

How to Structure Each Session

I suggest you follow a practice routine that works for you. The ideas below should be helpful in designing a highly effective practice routine. Each session should be made up of a few core elements. Beyond these, you should custom tailor your sessions to meet both your short and long term goals.

• The Start

At the beginning of your sessions, take at least 10 minutes to get your stroke in the groove and to build your confidence. There is little point in immediately working on the tough assignments until you are loose and confident. There are countless ways to loosen up. One very effective technique is to shoot easy shots first so you can build your confidence and experience success at pocketing ball after ball. Gradually increase the difficulty as you loosen up and your stroke starts to feel relaxed and fluid.

• The Heart of Your Session

After your warm ups, it is time to work on your specific agenda for this session. This part of your session could include things that you wish to work on in every session to keep in tune such as:

- Shotmaking drills where you keep track of your pocketing percentages.
- Certain fundamentals, perhaps with a practice device.
- Basic position routes that you wish to master.
- Safety skills.
- Your break shot.
- The kicking game.

"Every time I go to the table (in practice) I really focus on my technique." **Allison Fisher**

"You have to maintain your strengths too." **Allison Fisher**

• Specific Items for that Session

Since it is impossible to work on everything at each session, you must build certain skills one by one. At each session you may wish to pick out a specific skill, shot, position play or some other item from the checklist above that you wish to emphasize. In one session you may spend 20-30 minutes (or even more) on banks shot while at the next session you may spend the same amount of time working on your shots off the rail.

• Trusting Practice

In the later stages of your session, you are entitled to engage in practice that most closely resembles how you would play in competition as a reward for your hard work. When you are playing at your best in competition, you should be playing with a sense of freedom and trust in your game. The idea is to break loose and let your best game out while playing largely on instinct.

• End Strongly

I always end each session by shooting a long straight in stop shot diagonally across the table. I want the last shot to leave a positive impression. If you stay down and execute this shot perfectly you will feel your stroke at its best, and you will see the object ball split the pocket while the cue ball stops dead in its tracks. I suggest that you use this shot or some other technique that will help you leave the table in a great frame of mind.

Practice Tips for Solitary Sessions

There is a lot of room for varying your agenda and techniques within the heart of your practice session. Any or all of the ideas below can be of value in adding variety to your practice sessions, and to expanding your skills.

• Work on Your Weak Spots

Any time you are playing in a friendly match or in serious competition, make a note of any errors or shots that are consistently giving you trouble. Then go to work at systematically removing these weak spots in upcoming practice sessions.

• Expand Your Skills

In a particular session try devoting a major part of the post warm up period to a particular segment of the game. For example, a session may consist of an hour or two of nothing but safeties. During this session you could start with the most basic safeties and work your way up to the most difficult versions. Push the envelope. After all, practice is a time to learn the limits of each shot as well as the extent of your capabilities.

• Take Extra Shots

While you are practicing running racks of Nine-Ball, you may find that your stroke is slightly off kilter. If so, take a few moments between games to shoot few shots to get back in tune. Replay a missed shot (or position play) during a run until you are satisfied with the result before continuing on with the rest of the rack.

• Give Yourself a Head Start

Some of your solitary practice should be spent running racks from the break, which enables you to work on your break and runouts. After the break, separate clusters so you can practice running out. Give yourself ball in hand to get started, but don't necessarily put the cue ball in a position where you have a simple shot on the first ball. Instead, set up an out shot where you have a 40-70% chance of making the ball. This kind of shot will help to simulate game conditions where you quite often must make a challenging shot on the first ball to ignite your run.

• Experiment With Your Pace of Play

Try experimenting with your pace of play during the trusting segment of your session, which was discussed above. All players have a natural pace from which they should not deviate greatly. Nevertheless, if you are a very fast player who is prone to making silly mistakes you should try a little slower and more methodical pace. Slow paced players have a tendency to suffer from paralysis of the stroke due to analysis. If this is the case with your game, you could benefit from a faster tempo.

• Fundamentals
While you are practicing specific shots, patterns, or other non-fundamental aspects of your game, you may sense from time to time that something doesn't quite feel right with your technique. At times like this, take a moment to check your fundamentals. On your next couple of strokes, you should look for any of the flaws that you know have a tendency to creep into your game, such as jumping or twisting your wrist at contact.

• Play the Ghost
Another popular practice technique for advanced players is to play the ghost. Here's how it's done: break open a rack and give yourself ball in hand. After several attempts, perhaps over several sessions, you will begin to get an accurate measure of your run out percentage. This information gives you a fairly reliable gauge against which you can measure your progress. Less skilled players who seldom run out can keep an average of the number of balls made after the break.

The ABC's of Practicing with a Partner

Regular practice sessions with a partner can be extremely productive. The ideal practice partner should share your devotion to improving their game, and not look at practice as a social event. They should also respect your time by showing up promptly for your sessions. Possible candidates include your pool playing friends, family members, teammates, your coach and anyone with whom you can conduct some serious and productive sessions.

There is no reason why you can't have more than one practice partner. As a matter of fact, there is something that can be gained from practicing with players of varying levels of skill. Let's consider a sampling of the ways that players of all abilities can benefit from practicing with one another:

A Players and C Players
The A Player will get lots of practice on hard shots, position plays and safeties because C Players are always leaving open but tough shots. The A Players suggestions on technique may also open the door to something that can help the C Player's game. The C Player will gain from observing the excellent play of the A Player, tips on all aspects of the game, and from his answers to their questions.

A Players and B Players
The A Player can act as a mentor for the B Player who is looking to refine their game. The B Player's knowledge of the game and of the A Players technique (after a couple of sessions) should enable him to detect when a recurring flaw is starting to creep into the A Players game.

A Player and A Player or B Player and B Player
When either of these two knowledgeable players practice, there should be a mutual exchange on new ideas and information that can help each others games. In addition, each is well qualified to monitor the others technique, which can be of great value in avoiding slumps.

B Player and C Player

A "B" Player will benefit from getting to shoot the majority of the time when playing with a C Player, which will help him hone his skills. The C Player can gain from observation and from asking lots of questions. The B Player can also offer suggestions on fundamentals and on basic position play, safeties, and pattern play.

C Player and C Player

Players at this level will share the table equally, which will give each player ample time to work on their game. Players at this level can help each other by sharing suggestions on technique or position as long as they are well aware of their competencies as well as the areas where their lack of knowledge could result in passing along misinformation. If they are unable to objectively evaluate the areas where they are knowledgeable enough to be of help, then a qualified instructor should be enlisted to provide this information.

How to Practice with Your Partner

The techniques below will help you gain maximum value from your practice session. I suggest you and your partner(s) give each a try and then use those which are the most enjoyable and productive.

• Analyze the Game as You Play

While playing a game, when you are uncertain of a position route, put the donuts underneath the cue ball and object ball before playing the shot. Before attempting the shot, analyze with your partner how to play it. Make it a policy that you can interrupt each other as long as the player shooting has not begun there preshot routine. Carefully observe how the first shot turns out. If you like the results but aren't sure how you got them, you can replay the shot now or after the game is over. You can take the same approach to shots that are unsuccessful: shoot them now if doing so doesn't disturb the layout, or try the shot after the game is over..

• Watch Your Partner's Game

One of the benefits of practicing regularly with another player is that you get to know each other's games. This will allow you to monitor each other's fundamentals. It can also enable you to watch for other negative tendencies such as overrunning position (due to shooting too hard), sloppy safety play, and missing with inside english, just to name a few of the many possibilities. If you and your partner are ultra dedicated to helping each other, you may wish to record these tendencies in a journal.

• Concede Easy Outs

A and B players can create more opportunities to practice the skills that win the battle for control of the table and the game by conceding the easy 1-3 or even 4 ball run outs. Once the rack has been clearly decided (let's assume a 90%+ probability of a run out) stop play and rack the balls. This will save you time for extra break shots, safeties, shotmaking and safety practice.

• Better Player vs. a Much Weaker Player

When either player is much better than the other, their can be a decided imbalance in the number of shots each gets to shoot when playing a game. This can be rectified by letting the weaker player finish out easy runs. The stronger player will get practice doing the things that win games in the early going while the weaker player gets needed practice on running the last 3-4 balls, where most of his games are decided, when he is playing opponents of his caliber.

• Alternating Shots

You can get a good feel for your partner's game by alternating shots because you have to shoot what they leave you. This can enable the more knowledgeable player to offer even better advice on how the shot should have been played. On alternate shots, the stronger player gets to practice harder shots and demanding position plays left by the other player while the weaker player gets more shots within their range of ability. In addition, the weaker player gets to experience firsthand what good shape looks like. In fact, the light bulbs may go off when they step to the table with excellent position on a shot that is nowhere close to how they would have played it.

• Customize Your Practice

Another way to customize your game playing practice is to trade off skills. For example, An A Player could play all of the break shots, because the break is so important to a player at his level. In exchange, the C Player gets ball in hand once the rack reaches the 6-ball or 7-ball no matter who is at the table, since position and pattern play at this stage is a big area for improvement.

Put your imagination to work to create a barter system for exchanging any shot or skill at any time during a game when both you and your partner agree that one player really needs work on that area while the other has it pretty well mastered.

• Play Sets Like You Are in Tournament Competition

Play races to as many games as you and your partner normally encounter in tournament or money games. Put something on the set that will encourage both of you to bear down and give the contest your very best. Bragging rights may suffice for some. For others, a nominal wager of $2-$5 or table time should work. But please don't confuse this with gambling and some of the negatives that can unfortunately accompany this activity. Remember you are friends and practice partners first and foremost.

• B vs. B In Practice

If you and your partner are both B Players, then a lot of your games are decided by the player who has the ability that day to consistently run the last 5-6 balls. To get as much run out practice as possible, break the balls and remove as many of the lowest numbered balls as necessary so that 5-6 balls are on the table.

• Sharking

When you and your partner are competing in the real world, you will quite often have to deal with opponents who employ gamesmanship or sharking tactics, whether intentional or not. You must be prepared for these tactics so you can quickly brush them aside and go about your business. You and your partner should at times engage in a little shark warfare just so you know what to expect, and so you can become hardened to the point where these tactics have virtually zero effect on your game.

Having a Teacher, Coach or Mentor

You can eliminate much trial and error and speed your progress by enlisting the services of a knowledgeable pool person. In addition, a qualified teacher, coach or mentor can help you learn things the right way at the start. This will save you the time and trouble of relearning the game because several bad habits have taken root. I suggest you choose your teacher wisely. Make sure the chemistry is right, they are well qualified, and they are sincerely interested in you and your game. If you have any doubts as to the value of a qualified teacher, mentor, or coach, listen to the words of 1990's Player of the Decade Johnny Archer on fellow pro and friend Jay Swanson:

"I can't begin to tell you how much he (Jay Swanson) helped my game. There wouldn't be enough time on the tape. He was a very smart player."
Johnny Archer

Tips for Being a Great Student

- Show enthusiasm, as this will motivate your instructor.
- Keep an open mind to new ideas, especially in the weakest areas of your game.
- Your pool game will take time to develop, so remain patient.
- Develop a plan with your instructor and stick to it.
- Keep your mind on the business at hand.
- Ask good questions, and remember there are no bad questions.
- When something doesn't feel right, let your instructor know.
- Practice between each lesson.
- Show up on time for your lesson.

Practicing Your Fundamentals

Practice Drills For Your Stroke

A fundamentally sound and consistent stroke is at the heart of any player's game. In this section there are a number of drills and tips that will help you to hone your technique and put you in excellent stroke for your next match.

5 Donuts in a Row

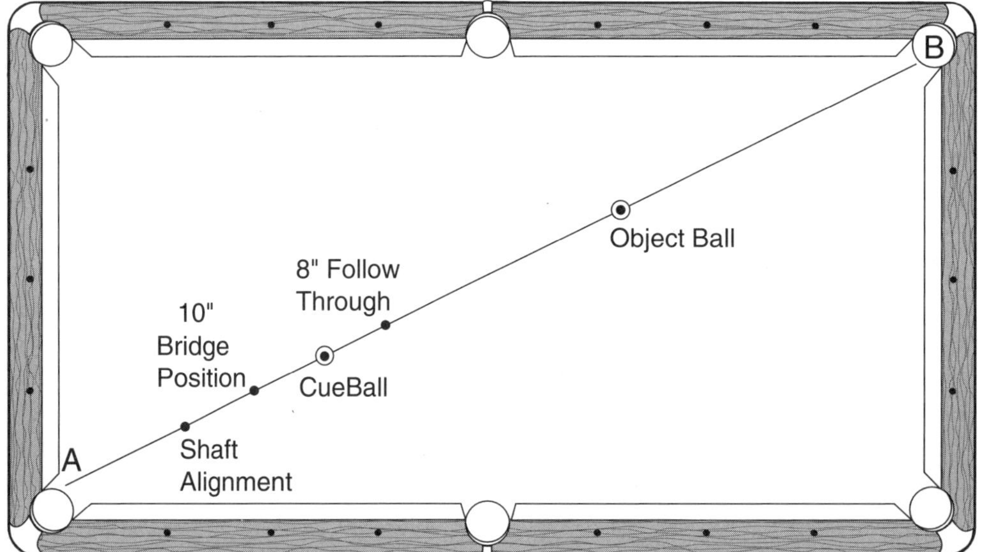

You can attain a perfect set up for a very useful stroke drill by stretching a piece of string or dental floss from Points A to B as shown in the illustration. Place a donut underneath the string opposite the third diamond up from Point B as shown. The second donut goes underneath the string at a point 2.5 diamonds up from Point A. So far you have prepared the positions for the cue ball and object ball. Now comes the part of the set up for you to exercise some freedom in positioning the donuts in accordance with your unique fundamentals. If your goal, for example, is to follow through 8" with a full, medium to medium hard stroke, place the third donut underneath the floss 8" past the cue ball's position. Now let's assume you wish to use a 10" bridge. Place the next donut 10" from the donut for the cue ball as shown. The final donut goes underneath the string about 10" from the donut for your bridge. Now remove the string, place the cue ball and object ball on the appropriate donuts and you're ready to go.

• Check Your Bridge

There are several valuable aspects to the drill. For starters, assume your stance and check your bridge to see if the distance you've set up is the length you really like to use. If not, make the adjustment in the position of the donut for the bridge and proceed to the next step.

• Check Your Alignment
Assume your stance once again and look down at the first donut. Your cue's shaft should completely obscure the donut from view. If not, your stick alignment needs to be corrected.

• Straighten Your Backstroke
Now lets assume your bridge is the length you desire and your set up is straight. Take several warm-up strokes while looking down through your cue at the first donut. It should remain out of view throughout your warm-up strokes. If not, then your stroke is wavering sideways on the backstroke. Keep stroking until you can make it track above the donut. If you do this drill repeatedly (20 or more warm-up strokes) you will begin to get the feel of a perfectly straight stroke. One of the beauties of this drill is that it gives you instantaneous feedback on the quality of your stroke.

• Play the Shot
The final step to the drill is to shoot the ball as a stop shot. Be sure to stay down and hold your follow through as if posing for a picture. There are three things to look for:

- The length of the follow through. Does the tip go to or beyond the final donut?
- The straightness of your stroke. Does the tip rest directly over the last donut?
- Is your cue level?

Cue Over the Diamond Drill

There is a very valuable part of the drill discussed above that you can practice without going to the trouble of setting up the donuts. Take your stance with the tip of your cue covering the foot spot and the shaft directly over the middle diamond on the end rail. Your cue should completely cover the middle diamond directly beneath it. Take several practice strokes while looking down at your cue. The diamond should remain out of view. If not, you are twisting your cue during your stroke. You can refine this drill by drawing a thick line the width of your shaft and about three inches long on a "post-it" note. Place the paper directly over the middle diamond in line with your cue. When you take your stance and stroke, even the slightest deviation from a perfect stroke will be readily apparent. The line on the paper should remain totally covered from set-up to follow-through.

After practicing this routine for ten-to-fifteen minutes, try alternating between the drill and shooting at object balls. About four-to-five shots each works well.

Shotmaking Practice

Accurate shotmaking is a must for playing Nine-Ball. No matter how well you can control the cue ball, you will still be required to make your share of thin cuts, long shots and all of the other challenging shots that the game demands. When playing competitively it is hard to know exactly how accurate you are on specific shots since you don't have a scorekeeper recording your percentages, like they do in basketball on free throws. You can, however, learn which shots you play well and those where you need work by practicing the exact same shots from session to session. Record your percentage of successes from each session, compare your results to previous practices and note your progress. Let's assume that the shotmaking portion of your practice consists of 10 different shots, each played 10 times. This totals 100 shots. You can compare your results in specific categories, as well as your overall rating from session to session.

Test Your Cut Shots

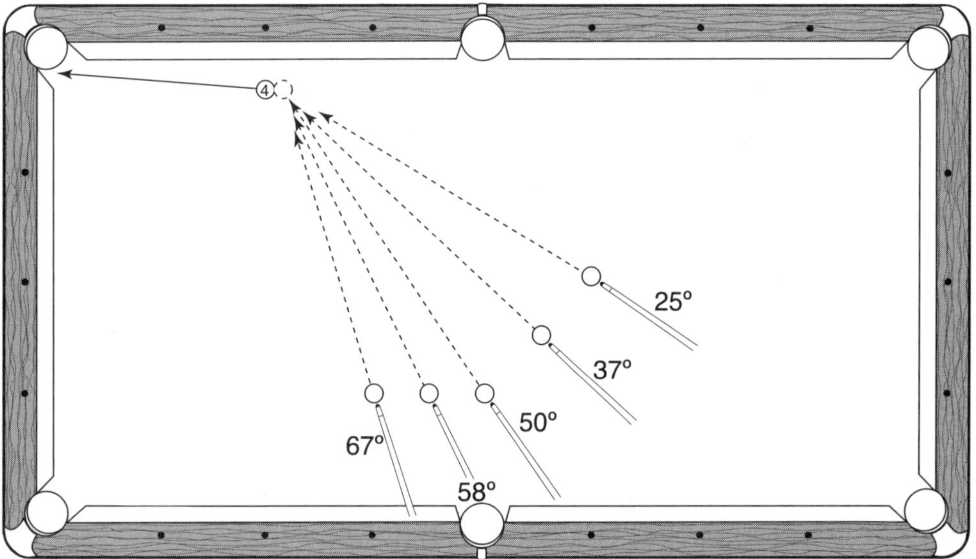

The diagram shows a practice exercise involving cut shots from 25-degrees to 67-degrees. Shoot each shot 5 or 10 times in each session, recording your results as you go. You may also try starting with either the thin cuts or the thicker cut shots. I suggest you use your imagination and knowledge of your game to set up the shots you want to work on for several sessions until you feel you have them mastered. Then pick out a new group of shots and go to work on them in the next series of practices.

The Long Green Practice Drill

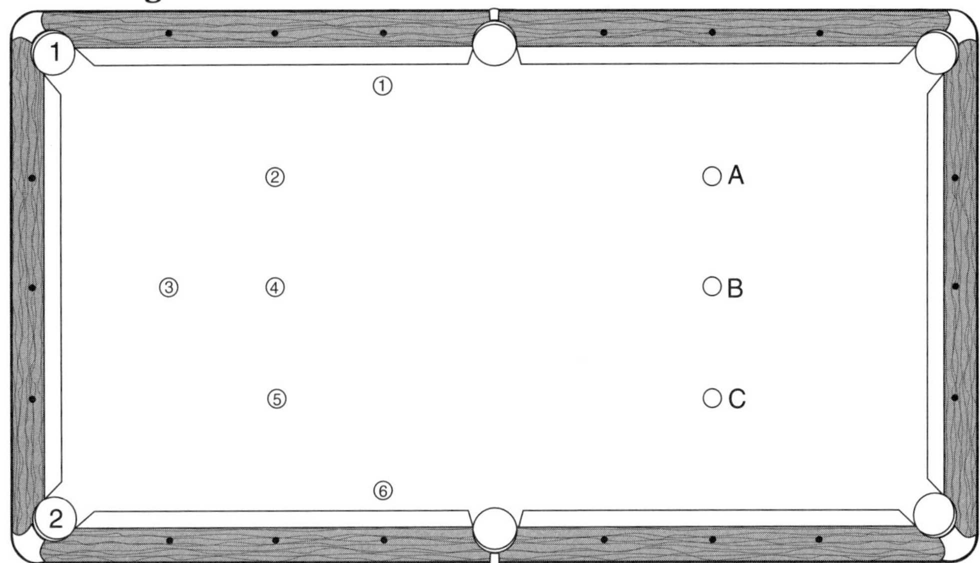

When all is said and done, proficiency at long green shots may be the single most important deciding factor in who wins at Nine-Ball. To play your best Nine-Ball, you've simply got to approach these shots with total confidence in your ability to put the ball in the pocket.

The cue balls and object balls in the diagram below are easy to set up as they are on the intersections of the diamonds, with the exception of the 1-ball and 6-ball, which are a half of a ball's width from the rail. When you first practice these shots, use the cueing and speed of stroke that are presented in the table below. Then try other speeds and other cueing options. Each shot has a mirror version so you can gain proficiency in pocketing in both directions.

Mirror shots are also useful in discovering flaws in your technique. You may consistently pocket a ball in one direction, but not in the other. Since the same shot (distance and cut angle) is not really the same because of the direction, you may feel comfortable cutting one way but not the other. A slight loss in confidence could cause you to jerk your stroke just enough to miss.

The cut angles of these shots range from 0 to 62-degrees.The number in parentheses indicates the pocket for each shot.

O.B.	Cue Ball A	O.B.	Cue Ball B	O.B.	Cue Ball C
1 Draw –	Medium hard (1)	1 Draw-	Medium hard (1)	1 Follow –	Medium hard (1)
2 Follow –	Medium (1)	2 Follow –	Medium hard (1)	2 Draw –	Medium (1)
3 Follow –	Medium (2)	3 Follow –	Medium (1 & 2)	3 Follow –	Medium (1)
4 Draw –	Hard (2)	4 Draw –	Hard (1 & 2)	4 Draw –	Hard (1)
5 Draw –	Medium (2)	5 Follow -	Medium hard (1)	5 Follow –	Medium (2)
6 Follow –	Medium hard (2)	6 Draw –	Medium hard (2)	6 Draw –	Medium hard (2)

Position Practice

Excellent shotmaking and good position play really feed off one another. If your position play is excellent, it takes a lot of the pressure off your shotmaking. And if your shotmaking is a strength of your game, you can get away with minor mistakes in position. That said, solid position play will add a degree of consistency to your game, like perhaps no other aspect of Nine-Ball. In this section are exercises that can significantly improve your cue ball control. They should, however, be augmented by practice on the position routes which were covered in Chapter 3, which discussed position routes for players of various levels of skill.

One-Rail Rebound Pathways

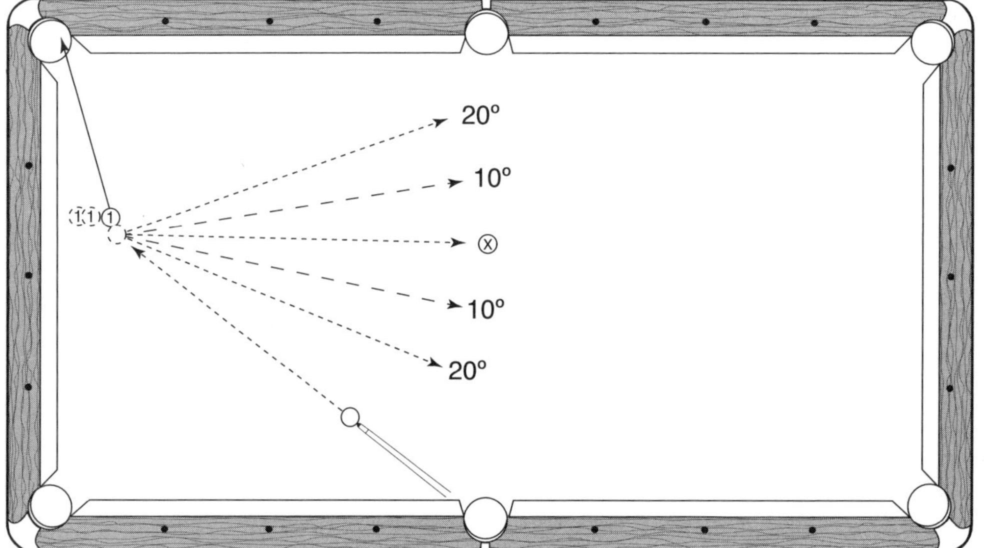

One-rail position is played on about 49% of all position plays by leading professionals, so that should be enough to convince you these position routes must be mastered. The drill above will increase your awareness of the cue ball's rebound path off one cushion and improve your speed control as well.

The 1-ball is placed 2 ball widths off the rail with a 40 degree cut angle. The other recommended positions for this drill are one ball's width and a half ball's width from the rail as shown. You should use cut angles of 20, 30, and 50 degrees. The goal is to learn to control both the distance and direction of cue ball. There are 5 basic directions as shown. Practice each variation until you can send the cue ball within a few inches of the directional line. This will teach you to use the correct english and cueing for each shot. You can learn speed control by setting up donuts a diamond apart along each route. Try to stop the cue ball as close as possible to each donut.

Soft Follow One-Rail

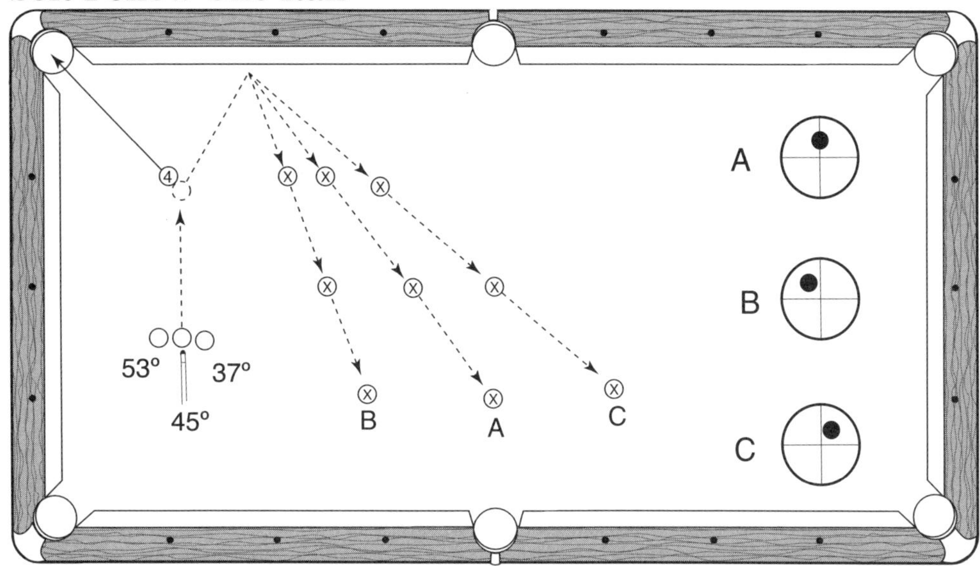

This one- rail position drill will improve your touch and speed control on soft follow shots. Play the shot at 45 degrees with straight follow, then follow with outside english, and using follow with inside english. Try to stop the cue ball at the three positions shown on each path. After playing it at a 45-degree cut angle, repeat the drill with cuts of 37 and 53 degrees. Notice the difference in the cue balls route and traveling distance.

Draw Off One Rail

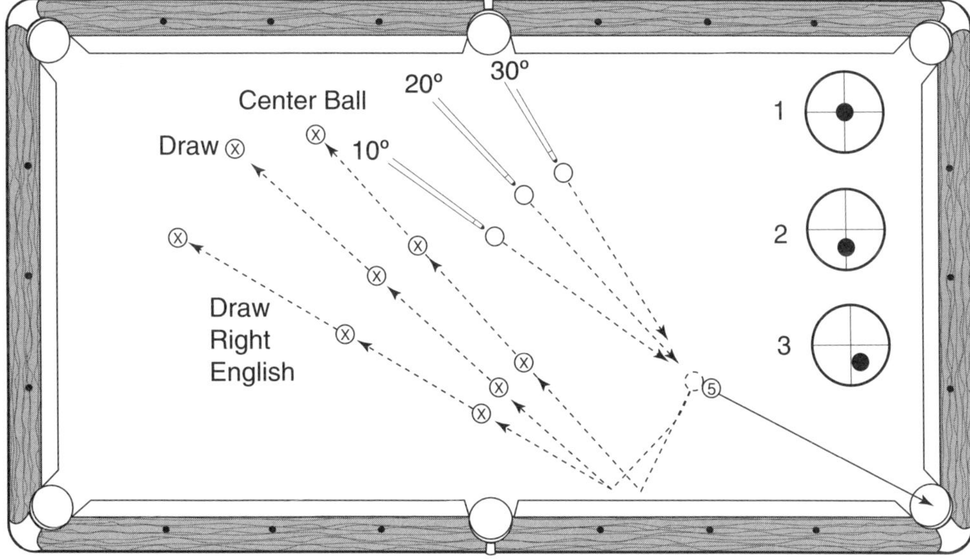

This drill will help you master several of the most common one-rail position routes. Repeat the routine three times using: 1) centerball; 2) 1 tip of draw; 3) 1 tip of draw with outside (right) english. Try to send the cue ball to the locations shown.

No-Rail Position

Stop Shot

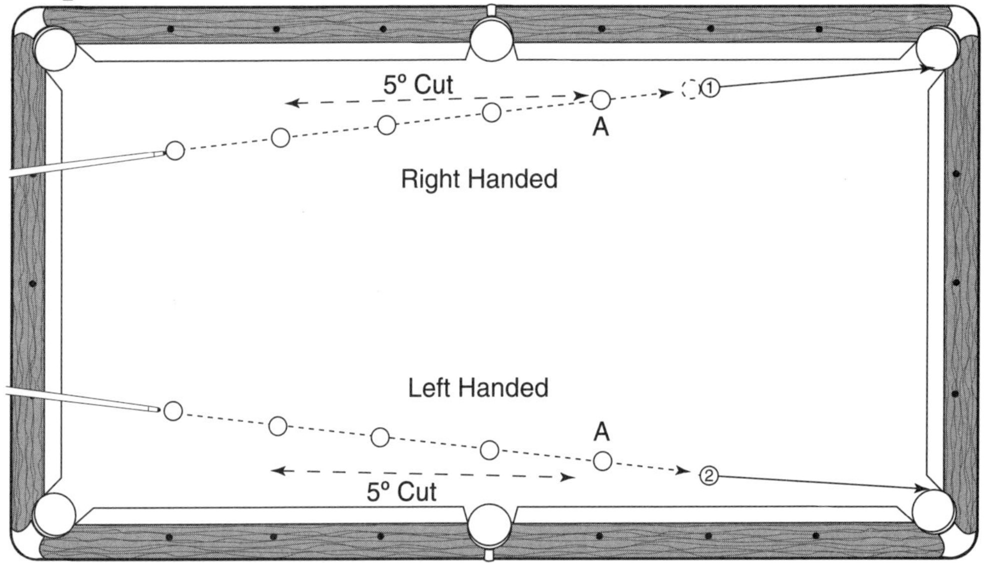

Second in importance to one-rail shape is the ability to control the cue ball without contacting a rail. According to my research, the pros play this kind of position on nearly 24% of their position plays. Some of the most common no-rail position plays include stop shots, soft follow shots, small angled draw shots, follow/stun and draw/stun.

The illustration demonstrates the stop shot, which is the foundation of position play. Begin with the cue ball a diamond from the object ball at Position A. Use a medium-firm stroke cueing in the dead center. As the distance increases, you will need to stroke the cue ball with draw, and at just the right speed in order to stop the cue ball in its tracks. Next, practice stop shots at a 5-degree cut angle. Pay special attention to how far the cue ball drifts sideways after contact with the object ball.

Follow Shots

Soft follow shots are especially useful for developing your speed control. With the cue ball and object ball lined up nearly straight-in at a 5-degree angle, practice getting shape at Position A, then Positions B, C, D, E and F. Stick with each ending location until you can consistently stop the cue ball near or on the target. The 5-degree angle was chosen because most soft follow shots (or any shot for that matter) are seldom lined up directly at the pocket. It is useful to become familiar with how much the cue ball veers to the opposite side of the line to the pocket after contact. A long shot forces you to shoot with both accuracy and touch.

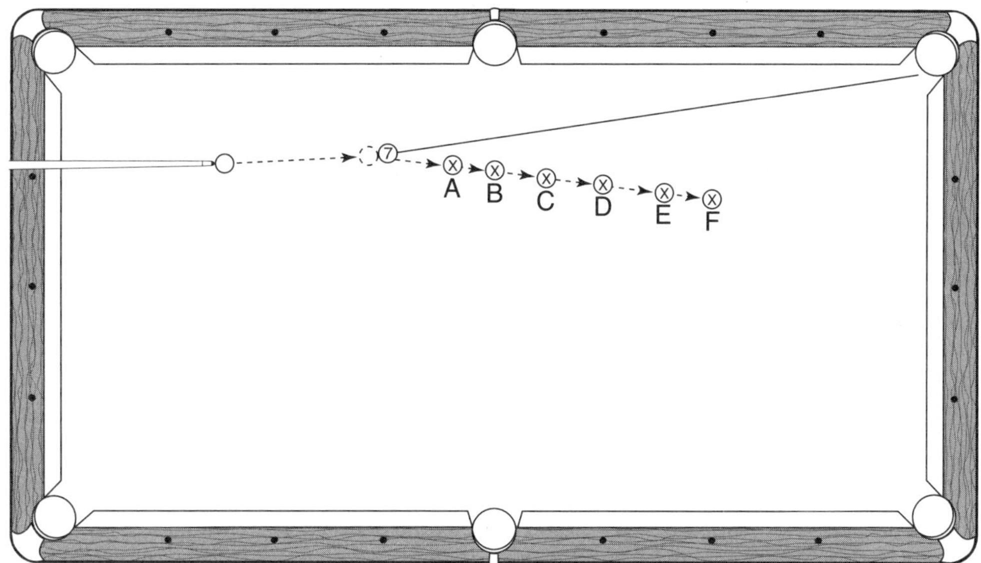

Progressive Draw

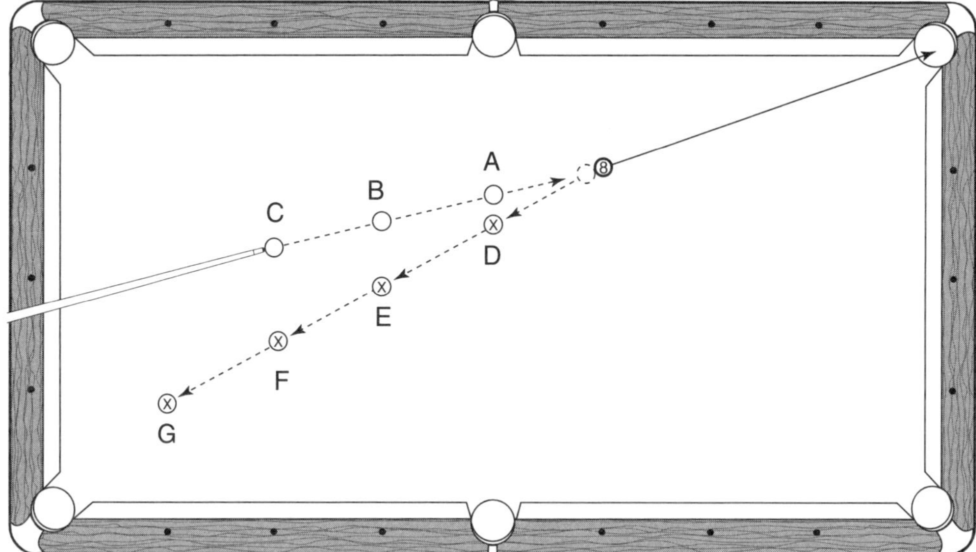

Progressive drills are especially useful for developing your draw stroke. The object ball is placed in the same position for each shot. Start with the cue ball in Position A. After drawing to Position D, the goal is to draw the cue ball a foot further back on each successive shot to Positions E, F and G. This takes expert technique and speed control. To generate decisive draw spin, be sure to strike the cue ball at least one tip below center. Use a smooth stroke and follow through completely. Avoid the temptation to overpower the cue ball, as that will produce excessive cue ball speed and minimal backspin. Once you have completed phase one, repeat the frill with the cue ball at Position B, and finally at Position C. A small cut angle of 5 degrees is recommended because it will teach you the widening path of the cue ball on draw shots.

Two-Rail Position

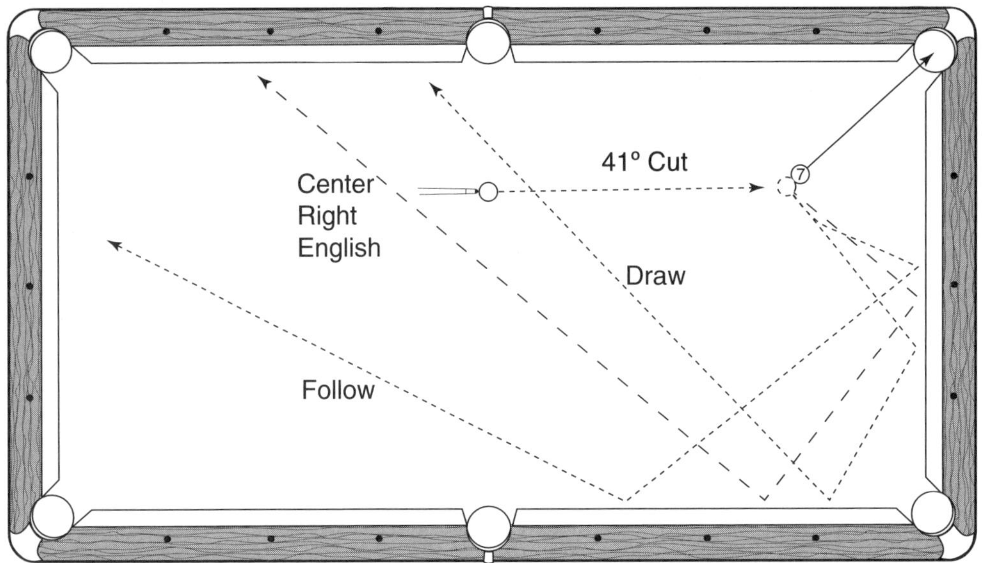

Professional players use two-rail position on 22% of all position plays, so skill at these routes is a must. In the illustration, the arrows after contact indicate various two-rail routes. In each case the route would technically turn into a three-rail route if the cue ball continued to the third rail. Most three-rail routes are basically extensions of two-rail position routes.

The 41-degree cut shot and slight variations of it are among the most commonly played two-rail position plays in Nine Ball. Notice the path taken by the cue ball when a tip of draw or a tip of follow were used. The wide gap between these two can be filled by a variety of speeds and cueing. The diagram shows another route using a center axis hit and right english that fills part of the gap. Set up the shot exactly as in the example and practice using different speeds and cueing. An hour or so practicing these routes should have a noticeable impact on your position play.

Across and Down the Table

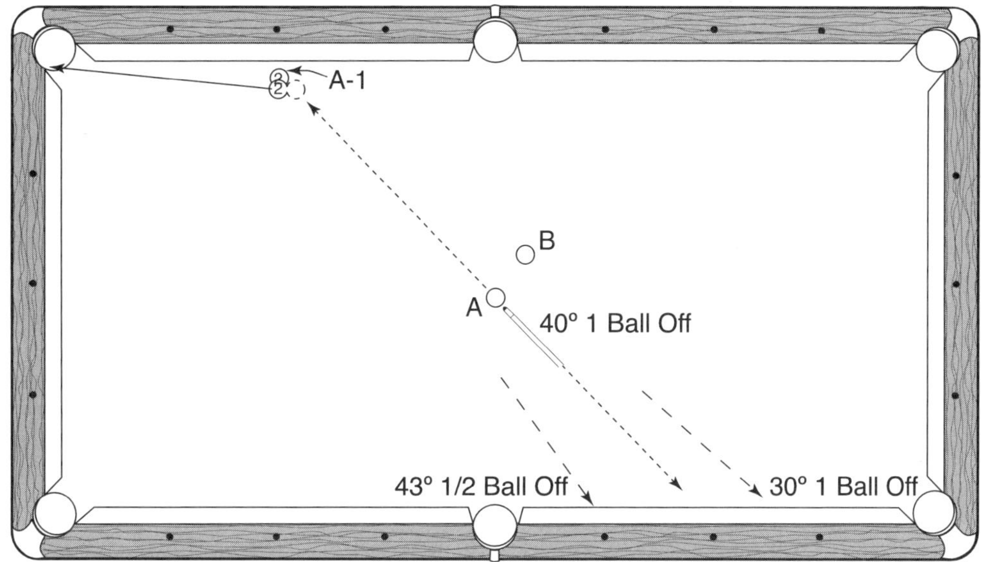

This drill will help you master a series of the most valuable and misplayed two-rail position routes in Nine Ball. The goal is to bring the cue ball safely past the side pocket and to the opposite end of the table on a cut shot with the object ball close to the rail.

The illustration shows a 40-degree cut with the 2-ball a ball's width off the rail and the cue ball at Position A. The arrow pointing at the bottom rail shows the expected path of return on a well stroke shot using draw with outside (right) english. Another arrow points towards the rail showing where the cue ball would hit with a 43 degree cut on the 2-ball when the 2-ball is a half of a ball's width off the rail at A-1.

With the cue ball in Position B at a cut angle of 30-degree (the 2-ball is 1 ball width off the rail), the cue ball would come back along the line of the directional arrow when hit with low right english. The key ingredient to these shots is a high quality spin draw stroke, not brute force. The following tips can help you to approximate the cue ball's route back across the table:

- The closer the object ball is to the rail, the sharper will be its rebound angle.
- You can come very close to estimating the cue ball's return path if you draw a line from the point where the cue ball will hit the first rail through the cue balls original position and on to the bottom rail. The cue ball will usually return at a little sharper angle than this directional line.

Hitting a Target Ball

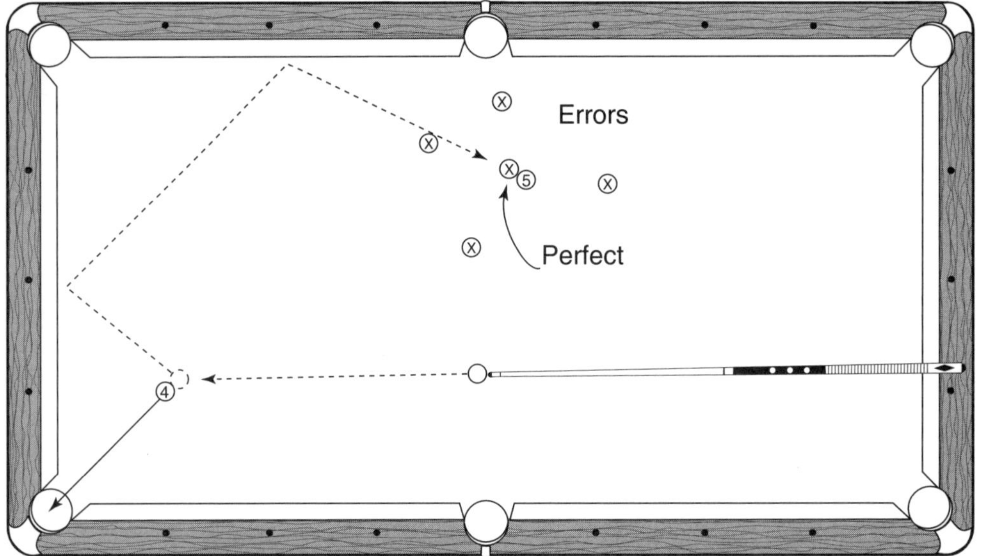

This drill will quickly illuminate any errors with your speed control or directional control. Set up a series of the most commonly used position plays, such as the two-rail route in the illustration above. Place an object ball in the exact spot where you would like to send the cue ball. The objective is to have the cue ball stop as close to the target ball as possible. A bull's eye would be a direct hit on the target ball just as the cue ball is about to stop. The diagram shows several possible errors to look for. These include poor direction, hitting the shot too easy, or using excessive force. Try playing each shot at least 8-10 times.

On almost every position play, there is a tendency to make the same kind of error over and over again. To cure this problem, place a donut where the cue ball stops after each shot. Your dispersion pattern will reveal your error tendencies. For example, if you are overrunning a shot consistently, you will need to remind yourself to use a softer stroke until you develop the right touch for the shot.

Avoid Obstructers

Your skill at position play largely depends on your ability to avoid obstructing balls on the cue ball's journey from point A to point B. When practicing a specific position route, try placing one or more object bails within two-to-three inches of the cue ball's pathway. This will teach you to route the cue ball like a pro! The illustration shows two of the many commonly used position routes where you must avoid crashing into another ball. The position of the obstructers in each case makes avoiding contact a challenge.

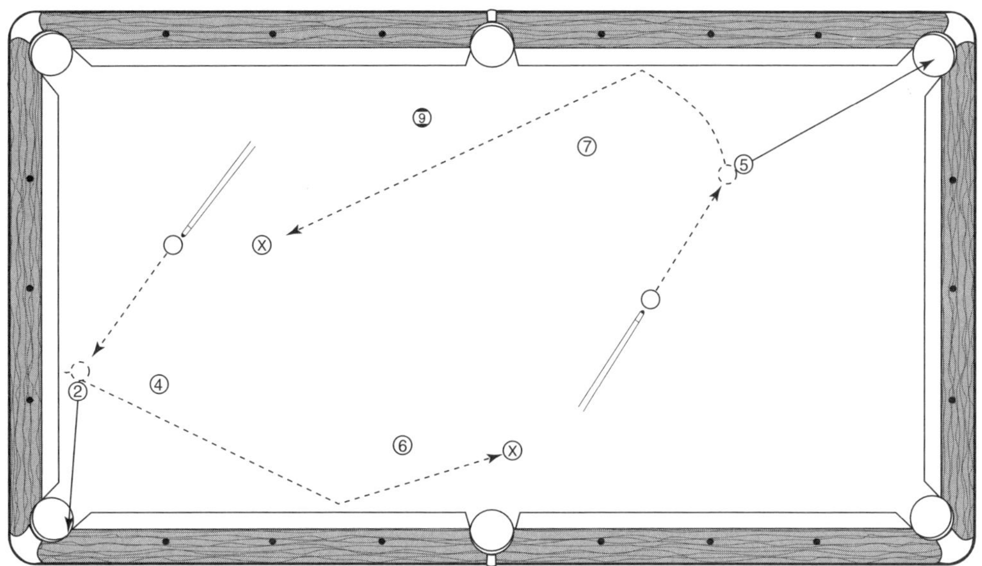

Opposites Add Variety

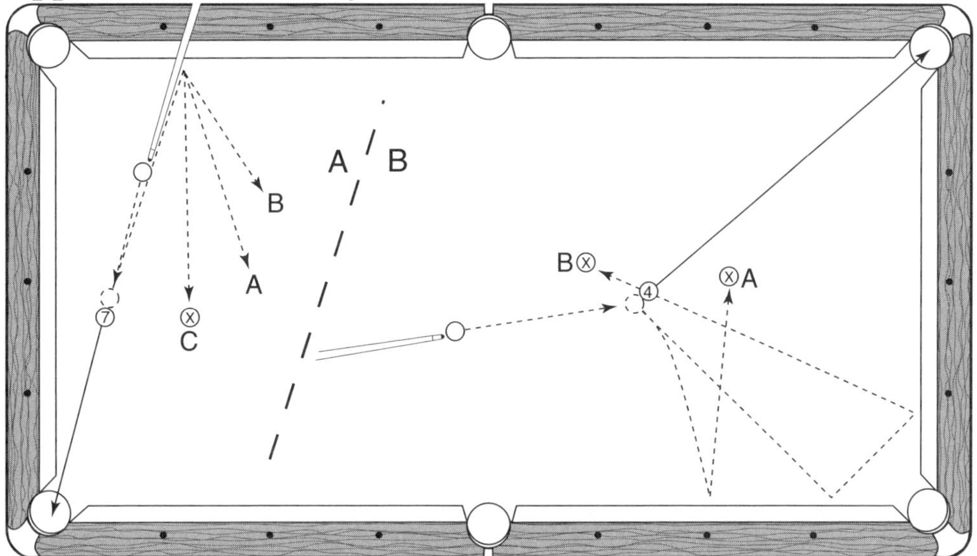

The nine principle contact points on the cue ball, along with the different speeds of stroke, combine to offer you a wide variety of position possibilities. You can expand your capabilities by playing a specific shot with center-ball, follow, draw, and then with both right and left english.

In Part A, the draw to the rail and back out shot is normally played with straight draw (Line A) or with draw and outside english (Line B). You can add another route to your arsenal by leaning to play it with draw and inside (left) english, which will sharpen the rebound angle, sending the cue ball down Line C. In Part B, the shot is usually played with draw, which will send the cue ball near Position A. Now try this position play with a center right english and a firm stroke. The cue ball will now travel down Route B.

Pattern Play

The position plays drills we've just covered as well as those that are in Chapter 3 are the building blocks for pattern play. If you can consistently play your routes correctly, you will be able to sting together several position plays into patterns that will enable you to run out regularly.

Build Your Run Out Power

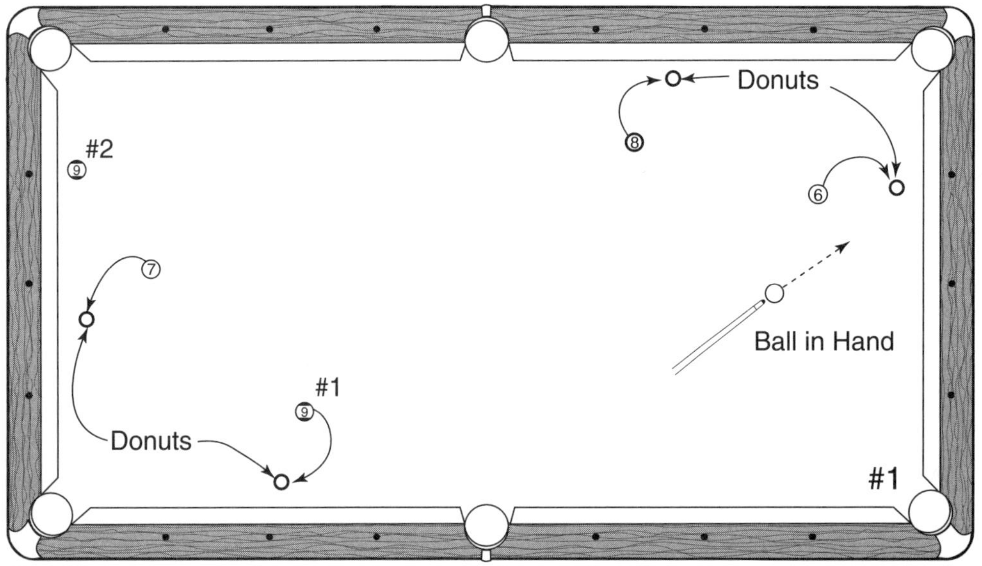

Our first pattern play exercise can help you build your run out power. Set up 3-5+ ball patterns with the donuts, such as the one in Diagram #1. Play the pattern over and over until you get it just right. This pattern requires that you excel at one-rail shape from end to end and from side to side. Take notice of which position plays give you trouble and make the necessary adjustments until you play them just right. Observe the position plays you have played correctly and internalize the results.

The next step is to move the location of one of the balls. Now play the pattern again. In the example the 9-ball, which was originally in Position #1, was moved to Position #2.

Keep moving one ball at a time to different positions, give yourself ball in hand, and try to run out. Be sure you cover some of the most troublesome locations. These would include:

- A ball frozen to the rail.
- A ball opposite the middle diamond on an end rail.
- A ball in the middle portion of the table.
- A ball near or on the rail near a side pocket.

For example, in Diagram #2, the 8-ball has been moved to the center of the table. Take a moment to evaluate the pattern and devise a plan for running out. After the 8-ball, was moved the 7-ball was in still in its original location at Position A. Now let's move the 7-ball to Position B. Again, notice how the complexion of the run changes.

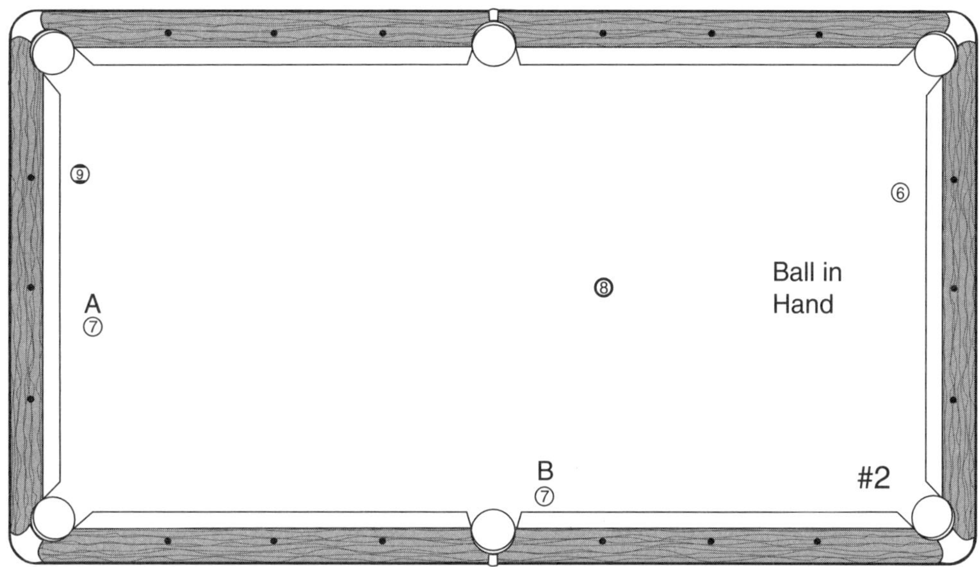

Use Cosmos to Build Concentration

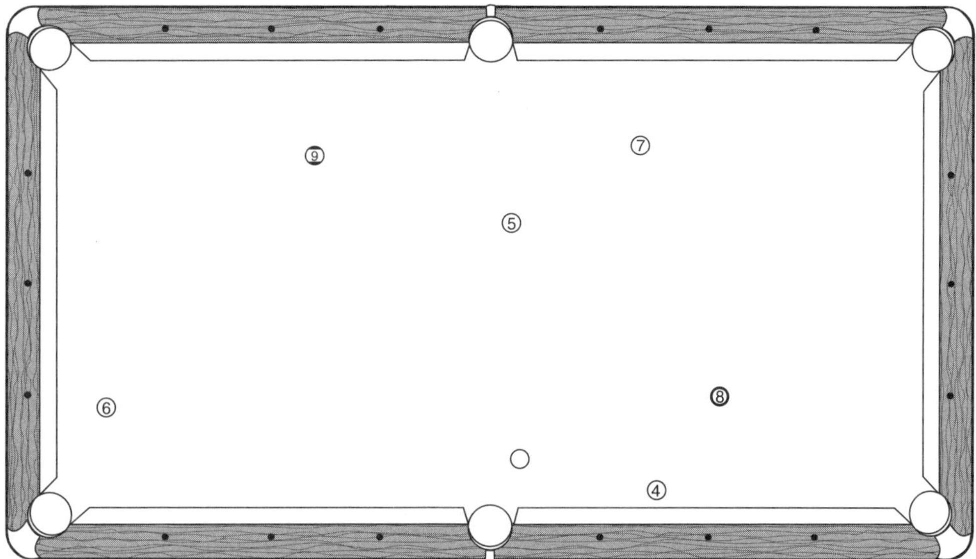

A cosmo is a layout or pattern so comparatively easy you have to commit a major blunder to not get out. But blunders can and do happen. To cure blunderitis, practice easy 5-6 ball run outs where none of the balls are in a difficult position. There is really nothing difficult to this layout. The shots are easy, and the routes are simple. And yet this is the kind of layout that amateurs fail to complete due to lack of planning or poor execution. The solution is to treat each shot and position play with the utmost of respect. Seek perfection when running a cosmo. This exercise in concentration will keep you from throwing away those games you "should have won." The discipline this exercise builds will also help you with tougher layouts.

Practice the Key Principles

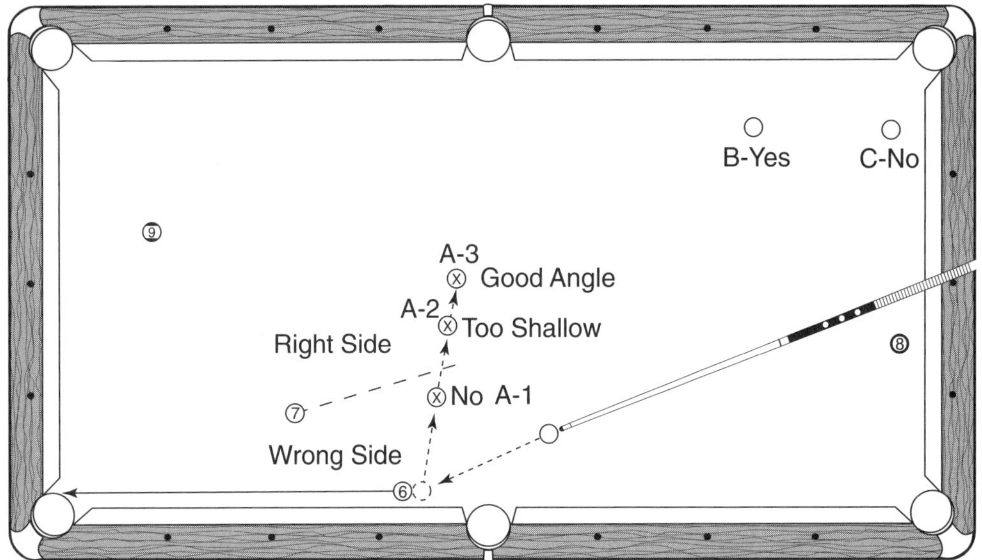

The Principles of Position Play discussed in chapter 5 are critical to playing patterns effectively. To run out consistently you have to know and be able to use the principles; and, easily and effectively incorporate the key ones into each position play. This does not happen overnight, but the learning has to start somewhere. I suggest you begin by incorporating these three principles into your planning process on each and every shot:

- Which side of the ball do I need to be on (Note: in some instances you may wish to have a straight in shot)?
- What angle do I need?
- How can I play 3 balls at a time?

Take as much time as needed while working on this exercise, even if it means you will be playing much slower than normal. Complete the planning process before your preshot routine, then play each shot. Don't worry if your execution is a little off. This is only natural as you are focusing more energy than normal on planning, which may disturb your natural rhythm. Eventually the planning process will become so natural to you that it will have no effect on your game.

The example should acquaint you with the thinking process. The cue ball is going to rebound off the rail after playing the 6-ball. But to where, and why? If it stops short of the dashed line you will have trouble getting to the 8-ball from the 7-ball. This would violate the need to play for three balls at a time, so Position A-1 must be the wrong side. If the cue ball traveled to the opposite side of the dashed line to A-2, it would be on the right side but with the wrong angle. Position A-3 is the winner as it is on the right side with enough angle to send the cue ball off the rail and down to Position B for the 8-ball.

When playing the 7-ball, you wouldn't want to send the cue ball to Position C, for this would violate the principle of playing for 3 balls at a time. With the cue ball at Position B, it will easy to get to the 9-ball. From Position C, however, it would take a monumental effort to get good position on the 9-ball.

A Useful Run Out Drill

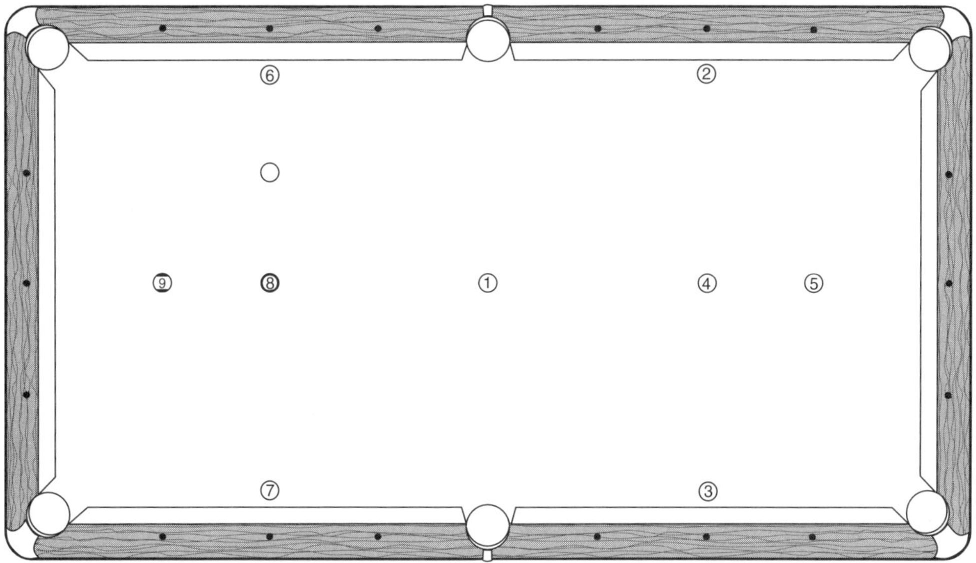

This drill is for advanced players courtesy of BCA Instructor Ed Smith of Califon Billiards in New Jersey. Start with cue ball in hand. The object balls next to the rails should be a quarter to a half inch off the rail. Run the balls in order as in Nine Ball. If you hit another ball, that is considered a miss and you must start over. After successfully completing the drill, alternate ball positions. For example, you could exchange the 4 and 8-balls or the 3 and 7-balls. A second and considerably more difficult version is to freeze the balls to the rails.

Additional Pattern Play Drills:

Center Axis Only

Practice running out while cueing only on the center axis. This will teach you the natural roll of the cue ball, lessen your dependence on english, and improve your shotmaking. As a variation, you can limit yourself to using english only once or twice per rack.

No Side Pockets

Improper use of the side pockets is a major problem for many players. You can help solve this problem by making it a rule that you can't shoot into the side pocket. This will teach you some new patterns and position routes.

Practice Drills For Safety Play

Smart safety play often leads to ball-in-hand or an easy shot, either of which can translate into victory. Safeties can also demoralize your opponent, which also increases your chances of success. This should provide you with enough incentive to develop this critical facet of the game, which so many neglect to practice.

Controlling Sideways Drift

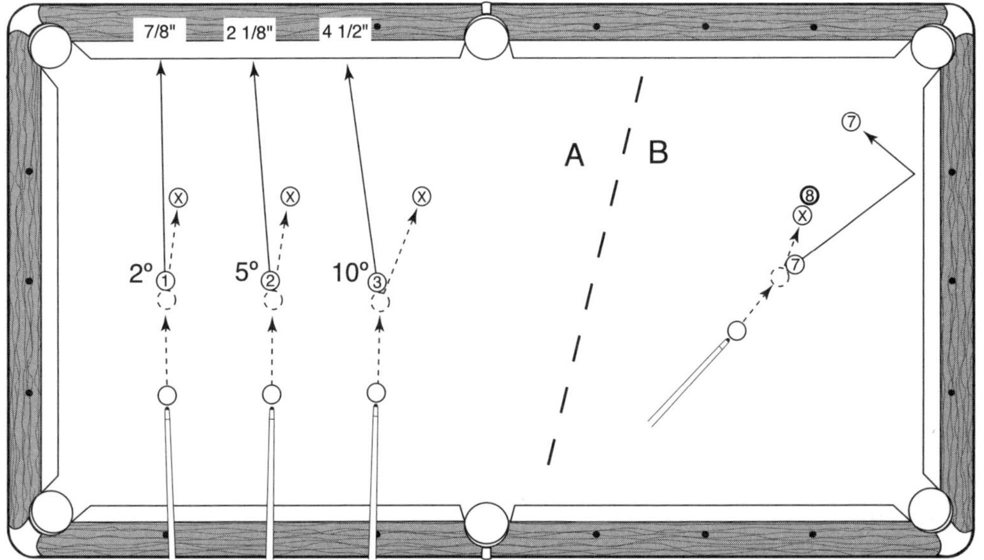

One big key to safety play is a delicate touch, which enables you to control the rolling distance of the cue ball with great precision. Another key ingredient is the knack for hitting just the right amount of the object ball so the cue ball follows the proper course.

Part A gives you a drill to help you discover how far the cue ball veers off to the side on soft follow shot safeties when you are hitting a little less than a whole object ball. Set up the cue ball and object ball in the locations shown. Place a marker, such as the edge of a piece of chalk, on the rail below each diamond at the distances shown. This will give you a precise point of aim for cut angles of 2, 5, and 10-degrees. Play a series of soft follow shots while trying to stop the cue ball various distances past the object ball's original location. Take notice of how far the cue ball veers off to the side, as well as the cue ball's ending position on each shot.

Part B shows a practical application of this safety. Set up a number of positions similar to the one in the illustration. Your initial goal is to send the object ball to the opposite side of the blocker. The advanced version of this safety calls for pinning the cue ball up against the blocker as shown.

Float and Hook

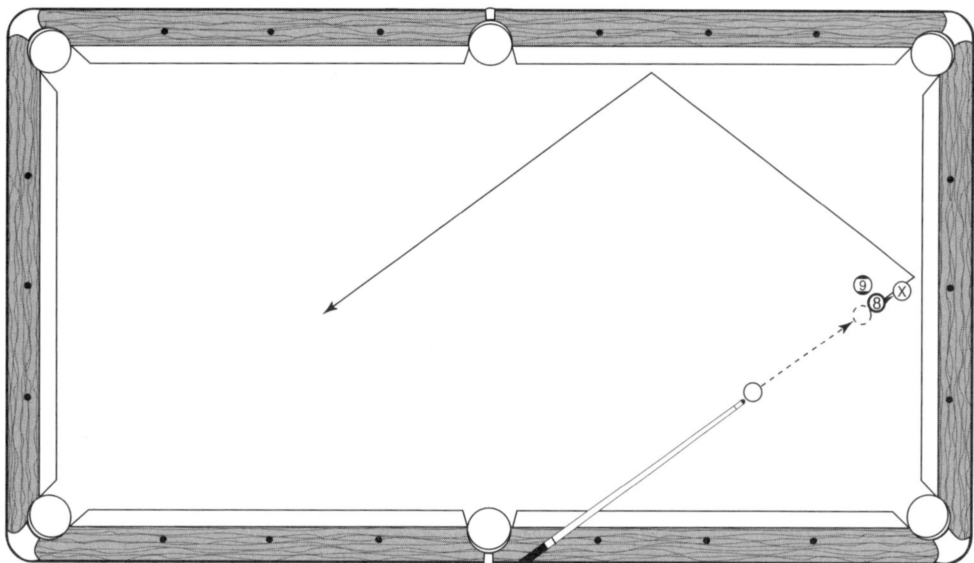

The ability to stroke the cue ball firmly and yet have it travel a very short distance forward after contacting the object bail is a valuable skill. In the example above, your goal is to send the object bail around the table and have the cue ball float forward behind the 9-ball. The trick is to stroke the cue ball firmly and just an eighth of a tip above center. Be sure to hit the 8-ball fully, as even the slightest bit of cut could eliminate the hook.

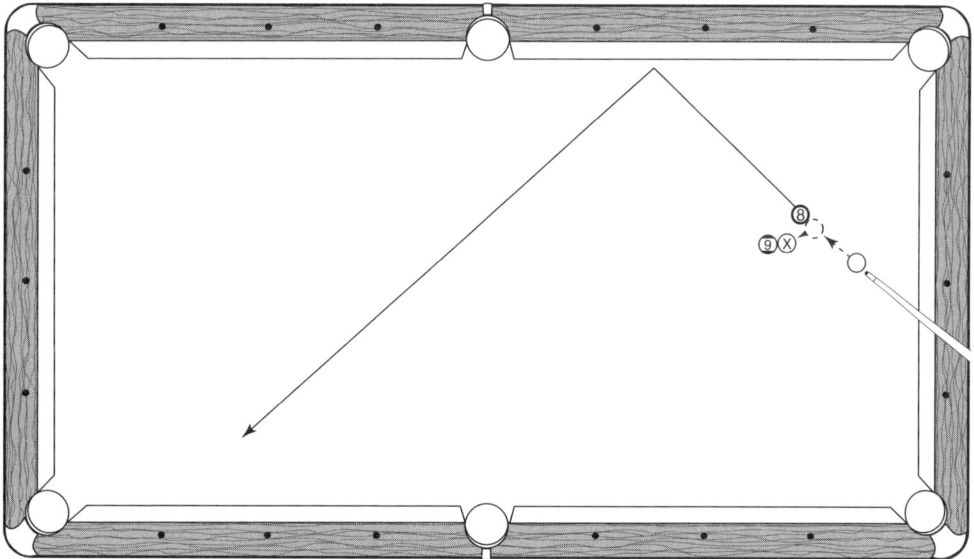

In the position above you want the cue ball to drift sideways and up against the 9-ball after sending the 8-ball up table. Use a medium stroke and strike the cue ball in the dead center. Aim an eighth of a tip left of center on the 8-ball. Try both of these drills from a variety of positions.

The Cue Ball's Route After Contact (1)

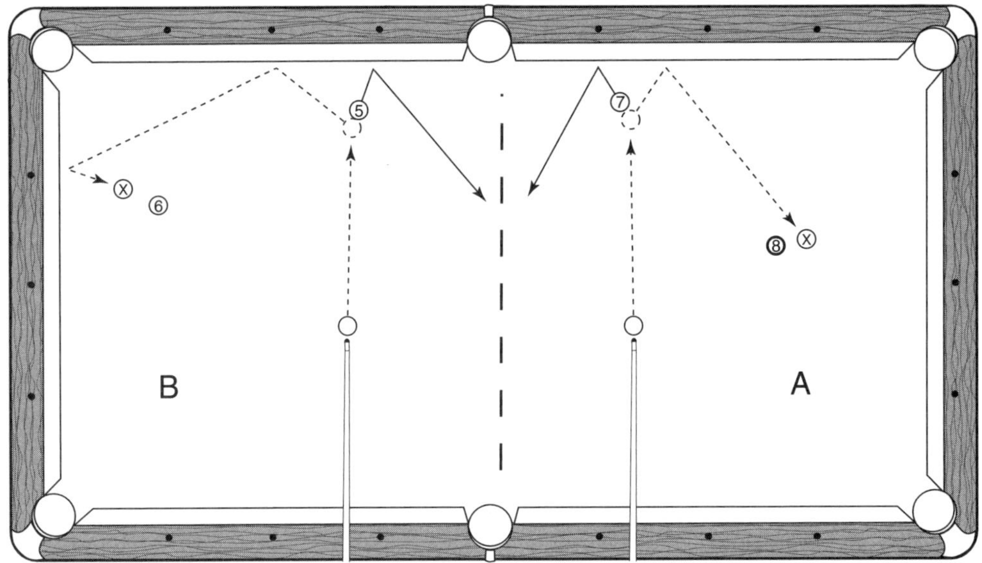

Playing safe is a lot like position play, only your target is a hook zone instead of a shape zone. Hook zones come in all sizes and shapes, but they tend to be quite a bit smaller than shape zones. You will need to perfect your routing skills if you intend to consistently hit the hook zones.

The drills in this section require expert cue ball control. You don't need to worry about the object ball as long as you take care of whitey. The cue ball and object ball are in the same relative positions in Parts A and B. In Part A, the goal is to cut the 7-ball just the right amount using follow so the cue ball bounces off the rail and rolls behind the 8-ball. Set up several variations of this drill by changing the hit on the object ball and the location of the hook ball.

In Part B, a soft draw shot with just the right speed and contact on the 5-ball will send the cue ball two rails in back of the 6-ball. Again, I suggest you set up several variations of this shot so you can master a variety of safety routes.

The Cue Ball's Route After Contact (2)

The drills in this illustration can further raise your routing skills. In Part A, a thin hit on the 5-ball with a soft stroke and follow will result in the pathways shown. Notice how english can significantly alter the cue ball's direction. Set the cue ball and object ball in the same locations and play several safeties using the three cueing options shown. Hit the same amount of the object ball each time. Then place a ball in a position behind which you would like to send the cue ball and practice playing hook safeties. Next, change the amount of contact on the object ball and repeat the drill.

Part B shows a medium range thin hit safety. Set up this shot and others like it and go for a hook behind the blocker. Speed control and directional control are both essential ingredients of this safety.

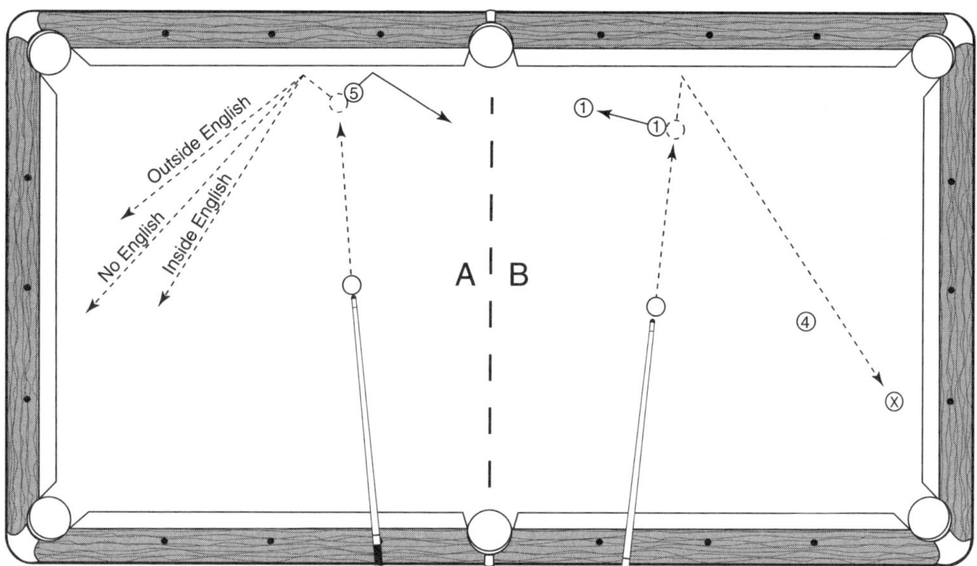

Long Distance Hook Safeties

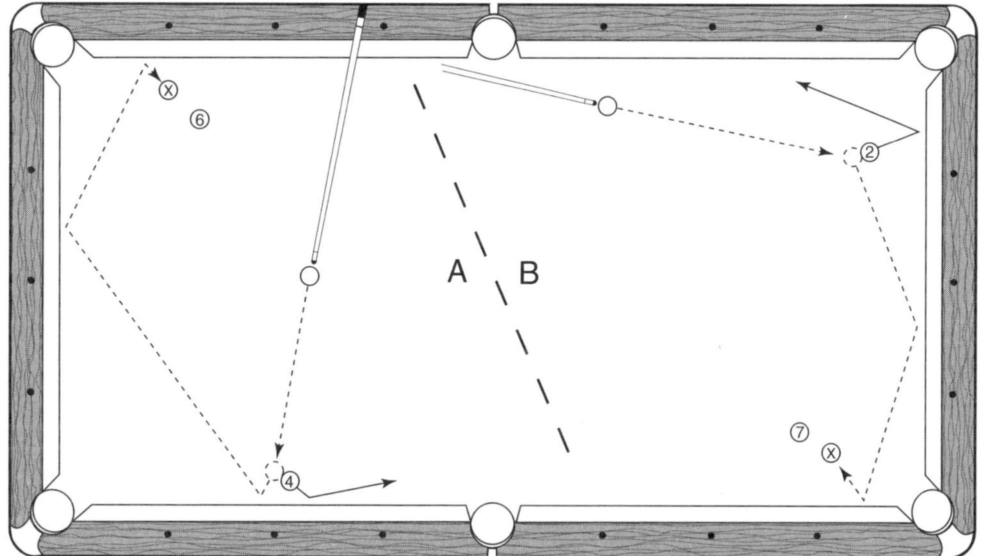

When the blocker is a long distance from the object ball, you must exercise exquisite control over both the direction and speed of the cue ball. Part A shows a typical three-rail route to a blocker using follow, outside english and superb speed control. Part B presents a tricky two-rail safe that requires draw, proper contact on the 2-ball, and great touch. These are the kind of safeties that appear in games over and over again in competition, which makes them of great value to your game. They are also the type that are misplayed simply because few players are willing to take the time and trouble to practice them.

Kicking Practice

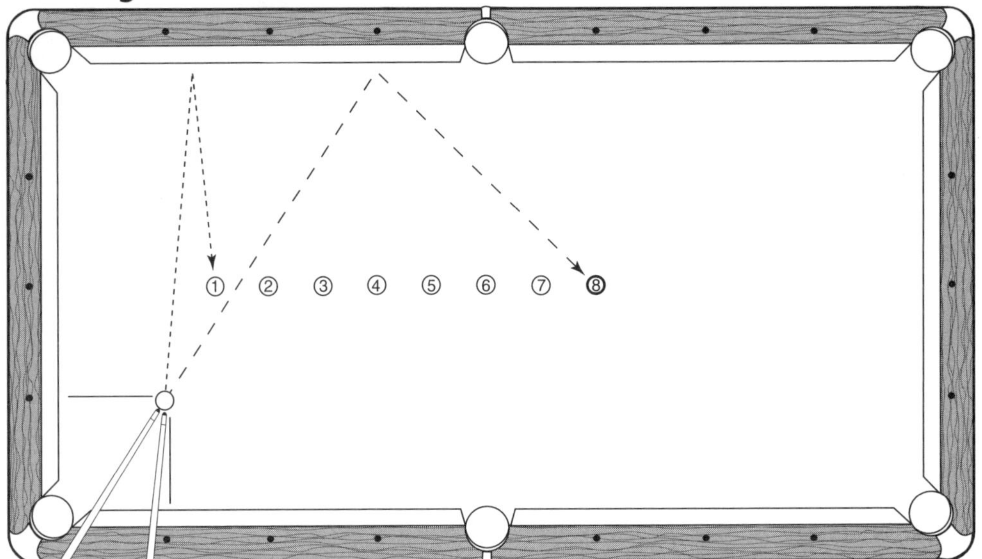

You can develop an eye for kick shots, much as you have done for aiming regular shots. It just takes practice. I suggest that you pick out several of the shots in the chapter on kicking as practice exercises. Another method to develop your skills is with a series of progressive drills. The drill in the illustration somewhat resembles one that players have used for practicing banks shots.

Place the cue ball and 1-ball where shown and kick for the 1-ball off the side rail. When you can hit it three times in a row, place a ball a half diamond further up the table in the position of the 2-ball. Once, again, when you have hit it three times in succession, proceed to the next ball. The kick shot to the 8-ball is one of the most troublesome in pool. If you can hit this on three consecutive shots, your kicking practice is really starting to pay off.

If you make this routine a regular part of your practice sessions, try keeping score to measure your progress. One way is to keep shooting each ball until you hit it. A perfect score would be an eight. Advanced players should keep shooting each one until you hit it three straight times. A perfect score would be 24 (3 x 8). You can add variety to the exercise by using difference speeds of stroke and by aiming for different sides of the ball.

Break Shot Practice

It is of primary importance that you strike the cue ball solidly on the break shot.. You can check the quality of contact by lining up the dot or circle on the cue ball in the exact position where you would like to hit it. Chalk up, play your break shot, and check the cue ball to see if you are hitting it on the bulls eye. If you are hitting it correctly and the cue ball is following past the rack or drawing back to far despite a solid hit on the 1-ball, you need to adjust your contact point in one direction or the other.

APPENDIX

Rules

The World Standardized Rules of Nine Ball below are excerpted from *Billiards: The Official Rules & Record Book 2001* published by the *Billiard Congress of America* (BCA).The General Rules of Pocket Billiards apply except when clearly contradicted by these additional rules. I suggest that you purchase the rulebook at your local retailer, or from the Billiard Congress of America, 4345 Beverly Street, Suite D, Colorado Springs, CO 80918. Ph: 719-264-8300.

The rules below are the official rules that have been adopted for competition. In certain instances, however, local rules may take precedence. Where appropriate, I have included local rules that are often used in informal competition, or are used by the local tournament director.

5.1 Object of the Game

Nine Ball is played with nine object balls numbered one through nine and a cue ball. On each shot, the first ball the cue ball contacts must be the lowest numbered ball on the table, but the balls need not be pocketed in order. If a player pockets any ball on a legal shot, he remains at the table for another shot, and continues until missing, committing a foul, or winning the game by pocketing the 9-ball. After a miss, the incoming player must shoot from the position left by the previous player, but after any foul the incoming player may start with the cue ball anywhere on the table. Players are not required to call any shot. A match ends when one of the players has won the required number of games.

Local Rules Some matches are handicapped by giving one of the players an extra ball (known as weight, or a spot) or more with which they can win the game. The player receiving a spot, such as the 7-ball, would win whenever the 7-ball is pocketed on a legal shot, just as they would with the 9-ball.

5.2 Racking the Balls

The object balls are racked in a diamond shape, with the 1-ball at the top of the diamond and on the foot spot, the 9-ball in the center of the diamond, and the other balls in random order, racked as tightly as possible. The game begins with cue ball in hand behind the head string.

Local Rules Some tournament directors may chose to rack all of the balls in the same positions every game, although this is not recommended. Spot balls are usually racked behind the 1-ball.

5.3 Order of Break

Winner of the lag has the option to break. In 9-ball, the winner of each game breaks in the next, unless specified by the tournament organizer. The following are common options that may be designated by tournament officials in advance: (a) Players alternate break. (b) Loser breaks. (c) Player trailing in game count breaks the next game.

Local Rules In numerous competitive events, the first break is decided by the toss of a coin. In some tournaments and money games, one player gets to break every game as their weight, or part of their weight.

5.4 Legal Break Shot

The rules governing the break shot are the same as for other shots except:
1. The breaker must strike the 1-ball first and either pocket a ball or drive at least four numbered balls to the rail.
2. If the cue ball is pocketed or driven off the table, or the requirements of the opening break are not met, it is a foul, and the incoming player has cue ball in hand anywhere on the table.
3. If on the break shot, the breaker causes an object ball to jump off the table, it is a foul and the incoming player has cue ball in hand anywhere on the table. The object ball is not respotted (*exception: if the object ball is the 9-ball, it is respotted*).

Local Rules If the breaker is giving weight, such as the 8-ball, and they make the 8-ball on the break and foul or knock the 8-ball off the table, which is also a foul, the 8-ball would be respotted.

5.5 Continuing Play

On the shot immediately following a legal break, the shooter may play a "push out". (See rule 5.6). If the breaker pockets one or more balls on a legal break, he continues to shoot until he misses, fouls, or wins the game. If the player misses or fouls, the other player begins an inning and shoots until missing, committing a foul, or winning. The game ends when the 9-ball is pocketed on a legal shot, or the game is forfeited for a serious infraction of the rules.

5.6 Push Out

The player who shoots the shot immediately after a legal break may play a push out in an attempt to move the cue ball into a better position for the option that follows. On a push out, the cue ball is not required to contact any object ball nor any rail, but all other foul rules still apply. The player must announce the intention of playing a push out before the shot, or the shot is considered to be a normal shot. Any ball pocketed on a push out does not count and remains pocketed except the 9-ball. Following a legal pushout, the incoming player is permitted to shoot from that position or to pass the shot back to the player who pushed out. A push out is not considered to be a foul as long as no rule (except rules 5.8 and 5.9) is violated. An illegal push out is penalized according to the type of foul committed. After a player scratches on the break shot, the incoming player cannot play a push out.

Local Rules If the player giving weight pockets the ball he is spotting his opponent on a pushout, that ball is respotted. If the player getting weight pockets his spot ball on a pushout, it remains pocketed.

5.7 Fouls

When a player commits a foul, he must relinquish his run at the table and no balls pocketed on the foul shot are respotted (*exception: if a pocketed ball is the 9-ball, it is respotted*). The incoming player is awarded ball in hand; prior to his first shot he may place the cue ball anywhere on the table. If a player commits several fouls on one shot, they are counted as only one foul.

Local Rules A tournament director or participants in a money game may elect to not play object ball fouls (otherwise know as cue ball fouls only).. If a ball is disturbed, the opponent has the option of replacing it as close to its original location or having it remain in its new location.

5.8 Bad Hit

If the first object ball contacted by the cue ball is not the lowest numbered ball on the table, the shot is a foul.

5.9 No Rail

If no object ball is pocketed, failure to drive the cue ball or any numbered ball to a rail after the cue ball contacts the object ball on is a foul.

5.10 In Hand

When the cue ball is in hand, the player may place the cue ball anywhere on the bed of the table, except in contact with an object ball. The player may continue to adjust the position of the cue ball until shooting.

5.11 Object Balls Jumped off the Table

An unpocketed ball is considered to be driven off the table if it comes to rest other than on the bed of the table. It is a foul to drive an object ball off the table. The jumped object ball(s) is not respotted (*exception: if a pocketed ball is the 9-ball, it is respotted*).and play continues.

Local Rules Balls that are being given as weight are respotted when knocked off the table by the player giving the weight.

5.12 Jump and Masse Shot Foul

If a match is not refereed, it will be considered a cue ball foul if during an attempt to jump, curve or masse, the impeding ball moves (*regardless of whether it was moved by a hand, cue stick follow-through or bridge*).

5.13 Three Consecutive Fouls

If a player fouls three consecutive times on three successive shots without making an intervening legal shot, the game is lost. The three fouls must occur in one game. The warning must be given between the second and third fouls. A player's inning begins when it is legal to take a shot and ends at the end of a shot on which he misses, fouls or wins, or when he fouls between shots.

5.14 End of Game

A game starts as soon as the cue ball crosses over the head string on the opening break. The 1-ball must be legally contacted on the break shot. The game ends at the end of a legal shot which pockets the 9-ball, or when a player forfeits the game as the result of a foul.

Local Rules A player receiving weight also wins when they make the ball they are receiving as a spot.

Glossary for Nine Ball

To be a complete player, you've got to know the lingo. The glossary contains the standard items you would expect to find, such as head string, draw shot and english. It also includes the many colorful terms that serious competitors and those who wager at pool use on a regular basis. I'm not encouraging you to become a pool hustler, but I believe that a working knowledge of the poolplayers lingo can add to your enjoyment of the game.

A

Across the Line A position play in which the cue ball is traveling across the position zone. It is very difficult to accomplish.

Action When a money game is in progress. Also refers to a money game.

Ahead Session A money game in which you win by getting a certain number of games ahead of your opponent.

Air Barrel When the losing player in a money game plays a final game or set even though he doesn't have the money to pay if he loses.

Area Shape An extra large position zone that is used to keep the cue ball out of trouble.

Around-the-World A position play in which the cue ball travels up and down the table off all four rails.

B

Back Cut When the cue ball is closer to the rail than object ball being played.

Backer One who finances a money game in exchange for a share of the winnings, if any.

Bad Hit Failure to hit the designated object ball first. It is a foul.

Balance Point The point where the cue is in balance, which is the point where 50% of the weight is in front and behind.

Ball in Hand A rule that allows a player to place the cue ball anywhere on the table (in Nine Ball) after his opponent has scratched or committed a foul.

Bank Pool A pool game where you only score when you pocket a bank shot.

Bank Shot A shot in which the object ball contacts one or more cushions before going into a pocket.

Bar Box Tavern sized tables. 3.5' x 7'. Coin operated.

Barking Using loud and/or abusive language in order to arouse a potential opponent's manly instincts so they will play you for money.

Barrel A gambling unit, ($20 equals 4 barrels at $5 per game).

Bear Down When you give a shot your 100% undivided attention. Playing with great determination.

Bed The playing surface of the table.

Behind the Line Any ball that's between the head string and the head rail.

Big Ball 1) An oversized cue ball that's used on some bar tables. 2) A ball that is easy to hit on kick shots because it is near a rail. 3) A ball that blocks a direst hit on a large portion of the table

Big Table A 4.5' x 9' table.

Billiard A shot in which the cue ball glances off one ball before driving another ball into the pocket.

Body English Twisting and turning the arms and/or body in an attempt to influence the shot.

Brazilians When a player is a game they have little or no chance of losing.

Break (The) The first shot of the game.

Break Out Separating a cluster.

Bridge Using the front hand to support the shaft of the cue. Also refers to mechanical bridge.

Bridge Hand For a righthanded player it's their left hand. Vive versa for lefties.

Broken Down A player who is mentally defeated before the contest is over.

Bumping A delicate shot that sends a ball a short distance to a more advantageous location.

Bust A wide-open break shot.

Busted A gambler who has lost all of their money.

Bye When a player, through the luck of the draw, advances to the next round without having to play an opponent.

C

Calcutta Selling players at a tournament through an auction to create a separate prize fund for the spectators.

Call The act of designating a specific pocket for a shot.

Called Ball The designated shot.

Call the Hit A referee or neutral party judges whether a hit is good or a foul (bad hit).

Called Pocket The designated pocket for a shot. On rare occasions, local rules may call for the shooter to designate the pocket for the Nine-Ball

Carom A shot in which the object ball glances off another ball on its way to the pocket.

Chalk A small cube with a tacky substance that is applied regularly to the cue tip to help prevent miscues.

Cheating the Pocket. Shooting the object ball into either side of the pocket.

Chirping When a player converses with the crowd in an animated manner.

Choke Up Shot A shooting technique for playing hard to reach shots.

Cheese (The) A money ball in Nine Ball.

Choke To miss a shot or play poorly because of the pressure.

Cinch To place all or nearly all of your attention on making the ball with little consideration to the positional requirements of the shot.

Cling The momentary contact of the cue ball and the object ball. It can vary slightly depending on the condition of the balls.

Close the Angle When the cue ball rebounds off the cushion at a greater angle than the angle of approach.

Closed Bridge A bridge with a loop for the cue, formed by connecting the tips of the thumb and index finger to the middle finger.

Cluster A group of object balls that are touching or are very close together.

Combination A shot that involves two or more object balls. Two ball combinations in which the first ball drives the second into the pocket are the most common.

Combo (See combination).

Come Up Dry When you fail to make a ball on the break.

Complementary Angles A cut shot with an angle that makes it ideal for playing position on the next shot.

Connecting Ball A straight-in shot which, when played with a stop shot, leaves you with a straight-in shot on the next ball.

Contact Induced Throw Friction between the cue ball and object ball on cut shots that alters the path of the object ball.

Contact Point The spot on the object ball that the cue ball must hit to make the shot.

Corner Hooked When the cue ball is deep in the jaws and it's path to the object ball is blocked.

Cross-Corner A bank shot into the opposite corner pocket.

Cross-Side A bank shot into the opposite side pocket.

Crutch (See mechanical bridge).

Cue The stick with which you shoot.

Cue Ball The all white ball which you shoot with the cue.

Curve What happens when you hit down on the cue ball with english.

Cushion The raised surface that surrounds the edge of the playing surface.

Cut Break A control break in which the cue ball glances off the side of the 1-ball and then goes to the side rail and out.

Cut Shot Any shot that has an angle to it.

Dead Combination A combination shot that's lined up to the pocket which virtually can't be missed.

D

Dead Punch (See dead stroke.)

Dead Shot A shot that's lined up to the pocket. A shot that can't be missed.

Dead Stroke When a pool player is playing at peak levels and his stroke is on automatic pilot. When a player is in the zone.

Deflection Hitting the cue ball with english, which causes it to take off to the opposite side of the english.

Diamonds Markings along the top of the rails that are useful in calculating bank shots and kick shots and as targets for position routes..

Dime A thousand dollars or ten dollars.

Dirty Pool The practice of using underhanded tactics.

Dogged It When a player misses because of pressure (choking).

Dog Proofing Playing a layout in such a manner that your success is virtually guaranteed.

Domino Effect (The) When one seemingly little mistake can cause your whole pattern to begin to unravel.

Double Elimination A tournament in which a player must lose twice to be eliminated.

Double Hit Hitting the cue ball two or more times in succession. It's a foul.

Double Kiss When the cue ball strikes an object ball two times in one shot.

Down the Line Shape A principle for playing position that ensures that you will have position

Draw(the) Used to determine the pairings at a tournament.

Draw Shot Hitting the cue ball below center and applying backspin.
Draw/Stun Shot A shot that is part draw and part stun.
Duck 1) A very easy shot. 2) Play a safety.
Dump The crime of losing a money game on purpose which is being financed by a backer. The two players then split the winnings. Also known as doing business.
Dutch Doubles A format in which teams are comprised of a male and female player that alternate shots.

E

Eight Ball A game in which each player shoots either the solids or stripes. When their group is pocketed the 8-ball is the gamewinning shot.
Elevated Bridge Raising the palm of the bridge hand off the table so you can shoot over an obstructing ball.
End Rail Either the head rail or the foot rail.
English Side spin that results from stroking the cue ball on either side of its vertical axis.
Even-up 1) Paying an outstanding dept. 2) Playing a money game with no spot or weight.

F

Fade It The ability to handle adversity and continue to play well.
Fan It In To make a very thin cut.
Feather Shot A very thin cut shot.
Ferrule The hard white piece of plastic or ivory at the end of the shaft to which the tip is attached.
Fish Somebody who loses money a very high percentage of the time they gamble.
Float the Cue Ball A shot that sends the cue ball a short distance after either a firm or soft stroke.
Floating Follow A shot in which the cue ball rolls slowly forward after being hit with a firm stroke.
Flow Chart It is used to keep track of the progress of a tournament.
Flush A gambler or player who has a big bankroll.
Follow Top spin that causes the cue ball to roll forward after contacting the object ball. It's applied by striking the cue ball above the horizontal axis (above center).
Follow/Stun Shot A shot that is part follow and part stun.
Follow Through The final phase of the stroke. Extending the cue tip past the cue ball's original location.
Foot of the Table The end of the table on which the balls are racked.
Foot Rail The rail at the end of the table where the balls are racked.
Foot Spot The spot on the table that's on the middle of the foot string. It's where the head ball of a rack is located and where balls are spotted.
Foot String An imaginary line that crosses the table two diamonds up from the foot rail. It goes directly over the foot spot.
Force Follow Hitting the cue ball extra hard above center creating lots of top spin.
Force Shot Making the cue ball travel a good distance sideways when the cut angle is shallow.
Foul Scratching or not meeting the legal requirements of a legal shot or legal safety.
Frame A player's turn at the table.
Free Shot A shot that does not hurt a players chances of winning a game if he misses. If the shot is missed the opponent is left safe.
Free Wheeling Very close to dead stroke. When a player is loose and confident, partly due to their opponent's poor play.
Freeze out When two player agree to play for a specific sum of money. This establishes a minimum amount that either player can win or lose.
Freeze up the money Putting up the money for a freeze out in a neutral location (such as above the light) or giving it to a neutral party.
Front runner A player who plays well with a lead.
Frozen Ball A ball that is in contact with another ball or a cushion.
Full Ball Sending the cue ball into 100% contact with the object ball.

G

Gear A player may have several levels of play to their game. Their "top gear" is their best game.
Getting Down When two players agree to a serious money match.
Getting In Line A demanding shot that puts the cue ball into good position for the next shot.
Good Hit When the cue ball makes contact first with the intended object ball.
Go Off Losing a lot of money, possibly all of a player's bankroll.

H

Hanger A ball that's sitting in the lip of the pocket.
Head of the Table The end of the table from which you play the opening break shot.
Head Rail The rail between the two corner pockets on the end of the table at which you break.
Head String An imaginary line that runs across the table two diamonds up from the head rail.
Heart The quality of mental toughness. The ability to come through in the clutch. All great players have it.
Heat (the) Playing competitive pool under pressure. Feeling the pressure.
Hit (the) The sensation a player feels from using a particular cue.
Hold-up English Spin that sharpens the cue ball's rebound off the cushion. It also slows the cue ball down.
Hold-up A technique that retards the roll of the cue ball.
Hooked When another object ball is blocking the cue ball's direct access to the designated object ball.
Hook Zone An area of the table where the object ball is blocked from a direct hit by the cue ball.
Hot Seat The winner of the winner's bracket in a double elimination tournament. They are guaranteed no worse than second place.
House Cue A one-piece cue provided by the establishment.
House Pro The resident pro whose duties usually include giving lessons and running tournaments.
House Rack (See slug.)
House Rules A set of local rules which you are expected to follow.
Hug the Rail When a ball frozen to the cushion remains frozen as it rolls towards the pocket.
Hustle Conning an opponent into playing a money game when he has little or no chance of winning.

I

In Jail When the cue ball is in a position where your opponent has neither a shot nor a safety. Pool's equivalent of checkmate.
Inning A player's turn at the table.
Inside English Applying sidespin on the same side of the cue ball as the direction of the cut shot.
Intentional Foul A strategic maneuver in which you deliberately give your opponent ball in hand.

J

Jack-it-up The act of raising the bet in a money game.
Jacked Up When you must raise your bridge to shoot over an obstructing ball. Raising the backhand and shooting a draw shot when the cue ball is near a rail.
Jam Up When a player is shooting very well. A very good player's game.
Jawed When the object ball barely misses and comes to rest in the pocket opening.
Jaws The area of the playing surface that is inside the edges of the pocket.
Jelly Roll A sum of money that is paid to a someone who has helped another to win money. This could include setting up a game or letting the player use your cue.
Joint The midsection of the cue that holds the shaft and butt together.
Jump Shot A downward stroke that causes the cue ball to leave the bed of the table and sail over obstructing balls.
Jumped Ball An obstructing ball that's been cleared.

K

Key Ball A shot in Nine-Ball that largely determines whether a run will be successful.
Kick Shot Shooting the cue ball into one or more cushions before contacting the object ball.
Kill Shot A type of draw shot that checks the cue ball's roll after it rebounds off the cushion. Sometimes english is also used with the draw.
Kiss When the object ball glances off another ball.
Kitchen The area of the playing surface between the head string and the head rail. It's the area from which you break.
Knock The act of dispensing information that ruins a players chances of getting a game.

L

Lady's Aide (See mechanical bridge).
Lag A very soft stroke. Easing the ball into the pocket.
Lag for the Break At the start of a match each player simultaneously rolls the cue ball down the table and back. The player whose ball stops closest to the head rail wins and gets to break the first rack.

Lamb Killer A player who specializes in beating less skillful players for money.
Leave The position of the balls that one player receives as a result of another's shot.
Lemonading The art of stalling or playing less than your best in the hopes of raising the wager.
Let Your Stroke Out Shooting one or more shots with a full, loose and free stroke.
Liking it When you are in a money game that you believe you can win.
Line The word on how well a stranger plays.
Lock A game that is so one-sided that the better player has little if any chance of winning.
Locksmith A player who specializes in making games where he is the heavy favorite.
Long When a bank shot misses to the far side of the pocket. Also when a player runs the cue ball past the ideal position zone.
Long Green (the) Long shots on a big table that are considered difficult.
Long Rail Bank A table length bank shot.
Long Side Shape When the cue ball is positioned so you can shoot to the closer pocket.
Long String An imaginary line that runs down the middle of the table. Balls are spotted along the long string, starting at the foot spot.

M

Mark (a) Somebody who loses money a very high percentage of the time they gamble.
Masse' A shot in which the cue ball curves radically as a result of a nearly vertical stroke on the side of the cue ball.
Match A contest between two players.
Matching Up The negotiations that precede a money game.
Mechanical Bridge A long handled implement with an attachment that has several ridges in which the cue is placed. It is used for shots that can't otherwise be reached.
Miscue What occurs when the tip fails to stick properly on the cue ball at impact.
Miss A shot that fails to go into the pocket.
Money Ball A ball that, when pocketed, results in victory.
Move A strategic maneuver.
Mushroom When a tip spreads out and become wider than it's original shape.

N

Nap The degree to which parts of the cloth rise above the rest of the playing surface.
Natural Position Shape that results from allowing the cue ball to roll without using English.
Nine Ball A pool game played in rotation with balls 1-9. The first player to sink the 9-ball wins.
Nip Draw A special draw stroke in which you use a short punch-like stroke.
Nit A player who always wants a lock and bets low even though he is a good player.
Nut Artist Someone who plays only when they have a game they can't lose.
Nuts (the) A money game in which you have little or no chance of losing.

O

Object Ball The ball at which you are shooting.
Off Angle When you have played position on the wrong side of the object ball
On the Hill When you are one game away from winning the match.
On the Break Making the money ball on the first shot (the break shot) of the game.
On the Snap (See on the break.)
Open Bridge A bridge formed by laying the hand flat on the table and placing the cue in a vee formed by the thumb and index finger.
Open the Angle English that causes the cue ball to rebound from the cushion at less of an angle than the angle of approach.
Opening Break (The) The very first shot of a match.
Open Your Nose In a money game the losing player continues to play and lose more money. A loss, however, is not a certainty.
Out of Line 1) When you fail to play ideal position. 2) When a player's behavior is unacceptable. 3) When you have made a money game that is going to be very tough to win.
Out of Stroke When a player is off their game and their stroke does not feel right.
Out Shot A difficult shot that, if made, should result in victory even though there are several balls that still must be pocketed.
Outside English Applying sidespin on the cue ball opposite the side the object ball is being cut to the pocket.
Overdrive Follow A technique for applying extra follow to the cue ball. It is used for breaking clusters.

Over Cut Missing a shot because the object ball was hit too thinly.

P

Parking When the cue ball comes to straight back to the center of the table on a break shot. It happens on well struck break shots.
Pattern Play Playing the balls in a specific order and/or a certain style of playing position.
Pinch 1) Using inside english to make a bank shot that could not otherwise be pocketed. 2) Using a kill draw stroke to minimize the sideways movement of the cue ball on a small angled cut shot.
Plan B Resorting to a different shot or pattern as a result of a shot not being executed exactly as intended.
Player A person who plays very well, especially under competitive conditions.
Pocket Billiards The formal name for pool.
Pocket Speed Hitting a shot with just enough force so that the object ball drops with a few inches to spare.
Pocket Speed Plus Hitting a shot with a little more force than is necessary to send it to the pocket to avoid a roll off.
Point (the) The sharp edge where the pocket ends and the rail begins.
Pool Games that are played on a rectangular table with six pockets, a cue ball and several colored balls.
Pool Detective A person who makes a point to know various players games and who passes that information on to others. He is regularly guilty of killing off action.
Pool Gods Mythical characters who control the rolls and the luck factor in each contest. It is not wise to upset them.
Position Where the cue ball is located in relation to the next shot.
Position Zone An area of the table in which the cue ball is well placed for the next shot.
Post up (See freeze up.)
Pound Shot A shot that uses a very hard stroke to send the cue ball off a cushion when the cut angle is very shallow.
Pounding the Ball The act of using a pound shot.
Process of Elimination Planning A technique for planning patterns which involves sifting through your options and eliminating the least likely choices until you arrive at the best choice for playing the shot.
Proposition Offering a wager on an unusual and/or very difficult shot that the person offering the wager knows very well. It can also be an offer to play a variation of a regular pool game.
Pro Side (the) The act of missing a shot to the side of the pocket that minimizes your opponents chances for winning or at least avoids a complete sell out..
Push Out The option to send the cue ball anywhere on the table on the first shot after the break without incurring a foul.

R

Race A match that's decided by the first player to win a specific number of games (i.e., a race to seven games).
Rack 1) A triangular shaped object that is used to put the balls in place at the start of a the game and for each new rack. 2) The position of the balls once they've been placed in position and the rack had been removed. 3) The position of the balls after the break.
Rake (See mechanical bridge).
Rail The raised surface that surrounds the playing surface. It includes the cushions.
Rail Bird A spectator at a competitive game.
Rail Bridge A bridge that's formed by placing the bridge hand on the rail.
Rail Shot When the cue ball is frozen to the cushion or is very close to it.
Rail Target A spot on the rail that is chosen as a place where you want the cue ball to hit.
Rain Table Playing under extremely humid conditions, which affects the rails and speed of the table.
Recovery Position A challenging position play that is used to get back in line after playing poor position.
Regulation Sized Table A 4fi' x9' sized table.
Reverse English Sidespin that causes the cue ball to rebound off the cushion at a sharper angle than the approach angle.
Riding the Cash Hitting the lowest numbered ball first with a powerful stroke and sending the ball into a money ball. The object is to make the money ball with a lucky shot.
Riding the Cheese A forceful shot at a money ball that is largely dependent on luck to be successful.
Ring Game A money game of Nine Ball with three or more players, all competing against one another.

Road Player A hustler or skillful player who travels around the country playing pool for money.
Rock The cue ball.
Roll Off When an irregularity in the table or a not perfectly level playing surface causes a slow moving object ball to roll off line.
Roll Out See push out.
Rolls The breaks of the game. There are good rolls and bad rolls.
Rotation A pool game that uses all fifteen balls. They are played in order, 1 through 15.
Run The number of balls made on any particular turn.
Run Out Making several ball in succession to win the game.
Run Out Player A player who runs out with great regularity.
Running English English that opens up the rebound angle and adds speed to the cue ball
Run the Rack Breaking and running the entire rack.

S

Safety A defensive maneuver that's designed to leave your opponent with a tough shot or safety, or perhaps no shot at all.
Safety Zones A place on the table where your opponent cannot pocket a ball.
Saver A deal between two players at a tournament in which they share each others winnings. The percentage is negotiated.
Sawbuck Ten dollars.
Score 1) How a match stands at any time. 2) An amount that is won in a money game.
Scotch Doubles A format in which two players alternate shots.
Scratch When the cue ball disappears into any of the six pockets.
Scratch Shot A shot in which a scratch is very likely or is unavoidable.
Sell Out A poor shot that results in a loss of the game.
Session A lengthy money game.
Set A single race. One race that is a part of a series of races, such as 2 out of 3 sets for the match. It could also refer to playing under the ahead format.
Shape (See position).
Shark A tactic that's designed to distract or throw an opponent off their game. A player who hustles pool.
Sharking The act of using shark tactics.
Shim Thin slices of wood that are placed in the pocket openings to tighten the pockets.
Shooting the Lights Out When you are shooting very straight and playing perfect pool.
Short A bank shot that misses on the near side of the pocket. When the cue ball fails to reach the intended location for good position.
Short Side Shape Playing position for the more distant pocket.
Short Stop A very capable and experienced player who is just a couple of notches below the very best.
Shot Clock A timer that is used to restrict the length of time players can take on a shot. It is used mostly at major pro tournaments.
Short Rack A game that is won with a combo, billiard, 9-ball on the break or other shot so that there are several balls on the table when the game is over.
Short Rail Bank A bank across the width of the table.
Shotmaker A very straight shooter who emphasizes making balls over playing position.
Sideboards When a ball that is near a pocket makes a shot play much easier.
Side Rail The rails that run along the length of the table.
Side Rail Break Shot A break shot where the object ball is close to or on the rail.
Skid When the cue ball and object ball maintain contact for a fraction of a second longer than normal. This almost always results in the shot being under cut. Skids can also happen on straight or nearly straight in follow shots that are hit with a soft stroke.
Skimming Balls Rolling the cue ball very softly off the edge of an object ball. It is a defensive measure.
Single Elimination A format for tournament play in which you are eliminated after one loss.
Slate The hard playing surface that rests under the cloth.
Slop Shot A lucky shot that involves little or no skill.
Slug A rack in which there are gaps between the balls. It is given by unscrupulous players to neutralize their opponent's break.
Snatch See draw shot.
Sneaky Pete A two piece cue that looks like a house cue. Hustlers often use it.
Snookered When the cue ball rests behind a ball which blocks a direct hit on the designated ball.
Snow Slang for the cue ball.
Specialty Shots Combinations, billiards, caroms and some banks are the three most commonly played specialty shots.
Spectrum of Speed A 1-10 scale used for measuring the various speeds of stroke.
Speed The level of a persons game.

Speed Control The ability to control the cue ball's rolling distance. Good speed control is essential for playing good position.
Speed of Stroke The force that you apply to the cue ball.
Spin Your Rock Applying English to the cue ball.
Spot A location on the table. The foot spot and the head spot.
Spot Up Placing a ball on the foot spot. Usually it occurs after a money ball has been pocketed and a foul had been committed.
Squatted (See parking).
Squirt (See deflection).
Staking A person who is financing a money game.
Stakehorse A person who finances money games.
Stall Playing less than your best in the hopes that you can raise the bet.
Stance The position that you take for a shot.
Stealing When a player is in a money game which they have little or no chance of losing.
Steering When a knowledgeable pool person advises another on who to play for money and on who to avoid playing.
Stick It Stopping the cue ball dead in its racks upon contact with the object ball.
Stiffed When the winning player in a money game fails to collect the wager.
Stone Slang for the cue ball.
Stop Shot (See stick it)
Straight In Refers to a shot where the cue ball and object ball are lined up directly at the pocket.
Straight Pool Also known as 14.1. A game played to a designated number of points. A point is scored for each ball pocketed.
Stroke The swing of the arm, wrist and hand that propels the cue through the cue ball.
Stun Shot A firmly hit shot in which the cue ball slides across the cloth.
Sweat Watching a pool game. For example, sweating the action.
Sweater A person who is watching a pool game.
Sweet Spot (The) The position for the cue ball that yields the most balls on the break.

T

Table Leaks (The) A table on which it is easy to make balls on the break.
Table Roll (See roll off).
Thin Cut A shot in which very little of the cue ball contacts the object ball.
Throw Friction between the object ball and cue ball that changes the path of the object ball.. English can cause throw, as can contact.
Ticky When an object ball hits one rail, then hits an object ball, and then goes on to accomplish some worthy objective.
Time Shot A lucky shot in which the balls roll around the table in a series of collisions before the object ball is pocketed.
Tip The small round leather item that is attached to the ferrule. Also refers to how much English is used on a particular shot.
Trap When a player is engaged in a losing game.
Triangle Another term for the device used to rack the ball. The area in which the balls are racked.
Through Traffic Skillfully maneuvering the cue ball past a number of potentially obstructing balls.
Two Piece Cue A cue that has a joint in the middle.
Two Way Shots A shot that gives you the luxury of playing position and a safety at the same time.
2.25" Rule (The) It states that everything about a shot can and very often does change within the space of 2.25".

U-W

Under Cut Missing a shot because the object ball was hit too fully.
Warm Up Strokes A series of movements of the arm, hand and wrist that prepares the shooter for the final stroke.
Weight A handicap that one player gives another in a money game.
Whitey Slang for the cue ball.
Wild Ball A ball that a player is receiving as a spot that does not have to be called.
Window A gap between two closely spaced balls which exposes the object ball to a direct hit
Wing Ball The two balls that are on either side of the rack in Nine Ball.
Wire (on the) 1) A string above the table with beads or balls for keeping score. 2) A spot that consists of games, as in 1 on the wire in a race to 9.
Woofing See barking.
World (The) A huge spot or handicap.

A Nine Ball Players Cue Case

Nine Ball players today are using several cues, which has lead to the growth in sales of large cue cases, which can accommodate 2-3 cues and several shafts. The larger cases have big pockets, which can hold the wide range of accessories that have become necessary operating equipment. Perhaps you already own a cue case that can accommodate the items from the list below that are vital to your game. If not, before you purchase a new case, I suggest that you assemble the items from the list below you want to have available when you play, and then see if they fit in the case you are considering for purchase. Keep in mind that three cues is the maximum number permitted in competition according to BCA rules.

Regular Cue – One or two shafts.

Jump Cue – Make sure it meets the legal minimum of 40".

Break Cue – This cue typically features a slightly larger tip, which flat, but rounded at the edges. Break cues typically weigh about 19 ounces.

Jump/Break Cue – This is a break cue in which you can quickly unscrew about 1/3 off the end to quickly turn it into a jump cue.

Joint Protectors – These screw on to the end of the butt and shaft to protect your cue.

Cue Holder – Today's Nine Ball player typically uses 2-3 cues, and may also carry their own mechanical bridge. These items can be held securely in place with devices that are affixed to the edge of a table (not the pool table) next to where you are playing.

Chalk – Carry a couple of pieces in your case just in case you wind up playing in a place where there is nothing but a few worn pieces available.

Chalk Holders – You can avoid having to hunt down chalk or the games that some opponents like to play with the chalk. In addition, you can use pieces that are broken in just the way you like them.

Gloves – If you use a glove, consider carrying two in case something happens to the one you are wearing.

Powder – If you use powder, you probably have a difficult time playing without it, so you should make sure to carry your own container.

Sandpaper – Some players like to use a fine grade of to clean their cue.

Cleaners and Conditioners – They are extremely useful in removing chalk and dirt from your shaft, which of course enables the cue to slide smoothly through your bridge.

Towel Wipe down the cue regularly to prevent build up of chalk, which gets into the pores and creates unwanted friction. You may also consider carrying a towel to clean the balls.

Shaper – There are numerous devices on the market for restoring your tip to the proper curvature.

Tapper – They open the pores on your tip so they will hold chalk better.

Tip Repair – Extra tips, holders, and adhesives.

Rulebook - A copy can help settle any disputes regarding the rules.

Glasses for Pool – These are glasses with high rims that are made for shooting pool.

Bridge Head – The quality of mechanical bridges varies from place to place, so you may wish to carry a bridge head that can be attached to the end of a in just a few seconds.

Cue Ball – Since the cue ball gets the most use, you can ensure that the most important ball is in great condition by carrying your own cue ball.

Training Devices – There are a variety of balls with markings on them that are valuable practice devices. Aiming trainers are also available.

The Donuts – Be sure to include a package of donuts (hole reinforcements), which enable you to easily mark the position of the balls.

Pool Notebook – A small notebook in which you can record shots, strategies, and things to work on.

Bar Table Nine Ball

Nine Ball has long been a popular game on bar tables, but it is now being played more than ever before on the smaller tables thanks to the tremendous growth in the number of leagues and tournaments. The lessons in this book, which were all shown on a regulation sized table, also apply to Nine Ball on a bar table with but a few modifications.. Any differences in strategy are due primarily to the size of the table. Other factors which can also influence your strategy and shot selection include: pocket openings, type of cue ball, and the overall playing conditions.

There are three main categories of Nine Ball players: 1) those that play only on big tables; 2) those that play only on bar tables: 3) those that switch back and forth. This section is for categories 2 and 3. Those of you who switch back and forth have a special challenge, as you must be constantly adapting your strategy. When playing on a big table, the 5,000 square foot playing surface dictates that you emphasize execution. On a bar table, which measures 3,200 square inches, you must deal with the congestion factor.

Many big table players make the mistake of thinking there is nothing to playing on a bar table. They are often in for a rude awakening, once they discover that their big table style does not universally apply to the smaller table.

Fundamentals

Basic Strategy Even though you can be rather successful with a "bar stroke", that does not mean you should slack off on your fundamentals. You will must make shots of a reasonable degree of difficulty. In addition, everything is relative: if you only play on a bar table, what looks like a hanger to a big table player could be a long green shot to a bar table player.

The Congestion Factor The size of the table dictates that your will bridge closer to the rails. This means that your cue will tend to be slightly more elevated on a larger number of draw shots compared to a big table.

A Common Mistake: Many amateur bar table player's make the big mistake of placing their regular closed bridge on top of the rail. This leads to a mini jump shot, which creates the tendency to overcut the shot. Remember, you always want to keep your bridge as level as possible.

The Conditions

Basic Strategy: You will encounter a wider variety of playing conditions on bar tables due to: 1) Managements attention to the conditions varies much more in taverns than in pool rooms; 2) Smaller tables tend to harder to keep level than big tables; 3) differences in cue balls. As a bar player, you must be able to quickly adapt to the conditions. In addition, you cannot let less than perfect equipment affect your attitude. If your opponent starts complaining about the conditions, you can gain an edge in the mental game.

Lopsided Cue Balls At times you will encounter a weighted cue ball that has a disturbing tendency to do a semi-circle as it slows to a halt. You will need to allow for this when plotting your position and safety zones.

Obstructions You at time will need to be able to shoot with a short cue. Use a short stroke when obstructions force you to shoot with a short cue.

The Big Ball

The big cue ball is still used on many bar tables, although it is far less common than it was twenty years ago. If you have played on tables using a big ball, then you are already aware of the special challenge of shooting with the big ball. If not, the suggestions below will help you adapt more quickly to the big ball.

- Aim for a thinner hit on cut shots to compensate for the larger cue ball.
- Use a considerably more powerful draw stroke than normal when the cue ball is more than a couple of feet from the object ball.
- Avoid long draw shots when possible.
- You don't need to overpower the break as the big ball will do plenty of damage by itself. Play more of a controlled break.
- You can shoot with confidence because the cue ball holds it line of travel to the object ball better than a lighter and smaller regulation sized ball.
- Use very little english unless you shoot regularly with the big ball.
- The cue ball will have a tendency to run much further on follow shots.
- The cue ball's path off the tangent line will bend forward quicker on follow shots.

Position Play

Basic Strategy You can play to zones on a bar table at times because the shots are shorter and the pockets tend to be more forgiving. Easier. You must also be able to play pinpoint shape because of the congestion factor.

English Use english to refine the cue ball's route through traffic. You generally don't have to allow for as much deflection as on a big table because 1) the shots are shorter; 2) bar table cue balls tend to weigh more.

Area Shape Be sure to leave yourself a shot on a bar table by playing area shape as much as possible, providing it doesn't impact the quality of your position. This is an especially valuable tactic when you do not trust the roll of the table.

Cheat the Pockets There are many routes you can play on a bar table that are not as readily available on a big table, thanks to the fact that the corner pockets are quite generous.

Play More Corner Pocket Shape You should play more of your shots into the corner pockets than on a big table because: 1) bar table side pockets are smaller; 2) corner pocket position often improves the pattern.

Roll Offs Factor in any roll offs in planning your position routes and zones. You may need to hit the shot more firmly and go an extra rail to avoid the possibility of a roll off. You should also consider playing for smaller cut angles and using a firmer stroke if a table rolls off badly.

Scratching You must be acutely aware of the possibility of scratching in the corners when playing shape on balls on the end rail. This is especially true when you are playing short side shape to a ball on the end rail. You also need to factor the conditions into your routes to avoid scratching.

Pattern Play It tends to be very intricate on a bar table.

Cut Angles When the cue ball is rolling towards the position zone, the angle on the next ball can change very rapidly. You can offset this tendency by playing for a little longer shot.

Safety Play

Basic Strategy You can play tight defense on a bar table because of the closeness of the balls and the congestion factor.

Clusters Be sure to consider clusters as hiding places, especially when the balls are largely in the area of the rack.

Set Up Combos This is a very productive strategy when playing safe on a bar table, especially if you are getting weight.

Strategy

Basic Strategy Bar sized tables dictate that you play more offense on certain shots that you would pass on if playing on a big table. However, the congestion factor leads to more opportunities to play safe.

Offense You should go for shots on which you'd play safe on a big table.
Lucky Shots You should occasionally play to luck in a money ball early in the game when the odds are in your favor and your opponent likely won't run out if you miss. You should also take advantage of opportunities to ride several money balls when getting spotted.

Shotmaking
Basic Strategy You must be better at certain shots like combos and banks than you are on a big table because you are expected to make them on a bar table. In short, you must go for more shots. And you must be sure to make all of the shots you are supposed to make, so don't let up on the easy shots just because you are playing on a small table.
Banks You will have to play more long rail banks since there is less margin for error on skim the ball safeties.
Combos Proficiency at combos is a major weapon on bar tables, especially if you are a player who regularly receives weight.
Billiards The congestion factor will give you ample opportunity to play billiards.
Over a Ball You will have to use an elevated bridge quite often, so shooting over a ball is a necessary skill.
Jump Shots These shots carry a higher degree of risk than do jump shots on a big table because of: 1) the smaller landing areas; 2) cue balls that tend to be heavier; 3) thinner slate that makes it tougher to get the cue ball airborne.
Learn to shoot well over balls.
Side Pockets The side pockets are smaller, so you should avoid sharp angled cuts to the side pocket.
Rail Shots The cue ball is going to wind up on or very close to the rail much more often, so you must get used to using a rail bridge.

Push Outs
Use of Distance You must be very careful when using distance to make a push out difficult because your opponents will have more opportunities to either play an offensive shot, or to use congestion in the area of the rack.
Kick Shots When planning a push out, be sure to consider pushing to kick shoot.

Kicking
Strategy Can be precise with your kick shots since the distance to the object ball is not too great. Try to play strategic kick shots rather than just going for the hit.
Kick Routes You may have to play imaginative routes as it is easy for normal big table kicking lanes to be cut off by congestion.
Tie Up the Rack Pass on kick shots and tie up the rack if you are not playing the 3 foul rule and the kick shot is extremely difficult.

The Break
Racking The thicker cloth on some bar tables can make racking difficult, especially when there are several sets of pit marks. So be sure to conduct periodic inspection. You and your opponent should reach an agreement on what is an acceptable rack.
Solid Contact The short distance to the 1-ball should enable you to hit it squarely.
Soft Break Since you have a greater chance of making a ball on the break than on a big table, you should consider backing off on the speed and using a softer break for complete control.

Ring Games

A ring game is a Nine Ball game between three of more players. Ring games often spring up when there are a group of players who are seeking some relatively low stakes action or when the players have had no success at making a game between two players. Before play begins, the players must establish the amount of the wager and the order of play, which is by the luck of the draw. In some ring games, the 9-ball is the only money ball, while in others players are also paid for pocketing the 5-ball. A typical wager could be $1 on the 5-ball and $2 on the 9-ball. Sometimes a local rule is used in which the 9-ball is respotted if it is made out of rotation.

Ring games seem to bring out the best in some players whose games otherwise seem to lie dormant. In addition, many players will jump into a ring game with players who they would otherwise never play without a spot. If you are the best player, you should win in a ring game, but your success is far from guaranteed.

Ring Game Tips and Strategies

- Ring games with three players give you a chance to shoot almost as much as in a regular game, which enables you to stay sharp.
- While opinions vary, I believe a four handed game is best.
- Games with more than four players are a true test of your patience and ability to play when cold.
- You must be able to play your normal speed after waiting long periods for a chance to shoot.
- Safety play is not permitted in a ring game, You must make an honest attempt to hit the lowest numbered ball. If you fail to hit it, the next player usually has the option to shoot or make you shoot again. Rules vary, however, so this is not always the case.
- Combos, billiards and other specialty shots on the money ball are particularly valuable in a ring game. An offensive mindset is mandatory.
- A big break is a huge asset in a ring game.
- Ride your hot streaks for all they are worth, because dry spells are a way of life in ring games.
- When there is a player who is much worse than the others, be thankful if you are following him. And if you are not, insist that the order be changed periodically.
- If you are following the best player, or the one who is following the weakest player, you may face lots of full racks.
- Ring games can break up at any moment, so you must be prepared for the game to end, even if you are behind.
- It is easier to quit when ahead in a ring game because the losers can continue playing. In addition, no one person is directly responsible for your winnings. Still, quitting when you are far ahead in a game that is progress is not a popular maneuver.
- Avoid a game in which you are pitted against two partners or friends. In other words, don't get stuck in the middle.
- Players with very limited resources have been known to "take a shot" at a ring game.
- Don't be too upset if there is some good natured gamesmanship, as ring games are normally much more vocal than games between two players.

Where to Play Competitive Nine Ball

The leagues and tours below offer numerous opportunities to compete for the serious pool player.

League Pool

American Poolplayers Association (APA)
1000 Lake Saint Blvd., Suite 325
Lake Saint Louis, MO 63367
PH: 314-625-8611 or 800-3-RACKEM
Internet: www.poolplayers.com

Billiard Congress of America
4345 Beverly St. St. D
Colorado Springs, CO 80918
PH: 719-264-0900
Internet: www.bca-pool.com

Valley National 8-Ball Association (VNEA
333 Morton St.
Bay City, MI 48706
PH: 800-544-1346
Internet: www.vnea.com

The Association For P.O.O.L.
720 Jackson St., St. 205
Herndon, VA 20170
PH: 800-984-7665
Internet: tapleague.com

Tours

BCA All American Tour
4345 Beverly Street, Suite D
Colorado Springs, CO 80918
PH: 719-264-8300
Web: bca-pool.com

Joss Northeast 9-Ball Tour
PH: 518-356-7163
Web: azbilliards.com/josstour/
Contact: Mike Zuglan

Florida Pro Tour
Searing Inc.
4153 SW 47th Ave. St. 163
Davie, FL 33314
Attn: John Di Toro

Florida State Amateur 9-Ball Tour
P.O. Box 653
Kingsland, GA 31548
Contact: Tim and Kay Higgins

Planet Pool Promotions
10314 Naglee Road
Silver Spring, MD 20903
301-445-2233
Web: planet-pool.com
Email: tours@planet-pool.com

Southeast Open 9-Ball Tour
Tommy Kennedy
Ph: 912-576-2556

The Tri State Tour
616 5th Street
Carlstadt, NJ 07072
Contact: John Leyman,
201-804-4990
Todd Fleitman
908-352-5562
Web: tristate-tour.com
Email: jleyman@tristate-tour.com
Email: tfleitman@tristate-tour.com

The Viking Tour
1434 Parkhaven Rd.
Lakewood, OH 44107
Mike Janis 800-200-7665

Women's Regional Tours

ACW
12653 168th St.
Renton, WA 98058
Ph: 253-373-9999
Email: LindaC@acwtour.com
Web: acwpool.com

Arizona Women's Billiard Tour
Meiko Yamanobe
602-605-2165 pgr. or
Susan Williams
520-481-8994
Email: swcue@hotmail.com

Hunter Tour
Contact: Julie Stephenson
PH: 817-888-0081
Email: julies@onramp.net
Web: hunterclassics.com

Northeast Women's Tour (NEWT)
Ph: 732-280-7285
Contact: Micaela Dames
Web:
http://hometown.aol.com/newt9ball
Email: micaelamd@aol.com

Southeastern Amateur Ladies 9-Ball Tour (SEAL)
Contact: Marcia Manuel
Ph: 678-290-1888
Email: MarWPBA@aol.com
Web: azbilliards.com/seal/

Southern California Women's Billiard Tour
Contact: Mike Hurst
PH: 949-645-7180
Email: facets58@netzero.net

The Ladies Florida Tour
5803 NW 44th Ave.
Fort Lauderdale, FL 33195
Contact: Marcy Horowitz
Ph: 954-232-3373
Web: ladiesfloridatour.net
Email: getmarcy@aol.com

Western Women's Regional 9-Ball Tour
Contact: Julie Hunter
PH: 7775-882-5997
Email: cuepho9835@aol.com
Web: WWR9BALL.com

National Wheelchair Poolplayers Association (NWPA)
Ph: 702-437-6792 (MI)
Ph: 714-636-3371 (CA)
Email: chb@nwpainc.com
Web: nwpainc.com

National Pool Publications

The publications and web sites below do an excellent job of covering professional and amateur pool. Each has something special to offer the pool enthusiast.

Pool and Billiard Magazine
Ph: 888-766-5624
Web: poolmag.com
Email: poolmag@poolmag.com

Billiards Digest
Ph: 312-341-1110
Email: email@billiardsdigest.com
Web: billiardsdigest.com

The National Billiard News
Ph: 248-348-0053
Email: pool@mediaone.net

Professor-Q-Ball
Ph: 901-756-2594
Web: professorqball.com
Email: paul@professorqball.com

Chalk and Cue (Canada)
Ph: 905 –270-4264
Email: cnc@netcom.ca

Web Site to the Pros
AZBilliards.com

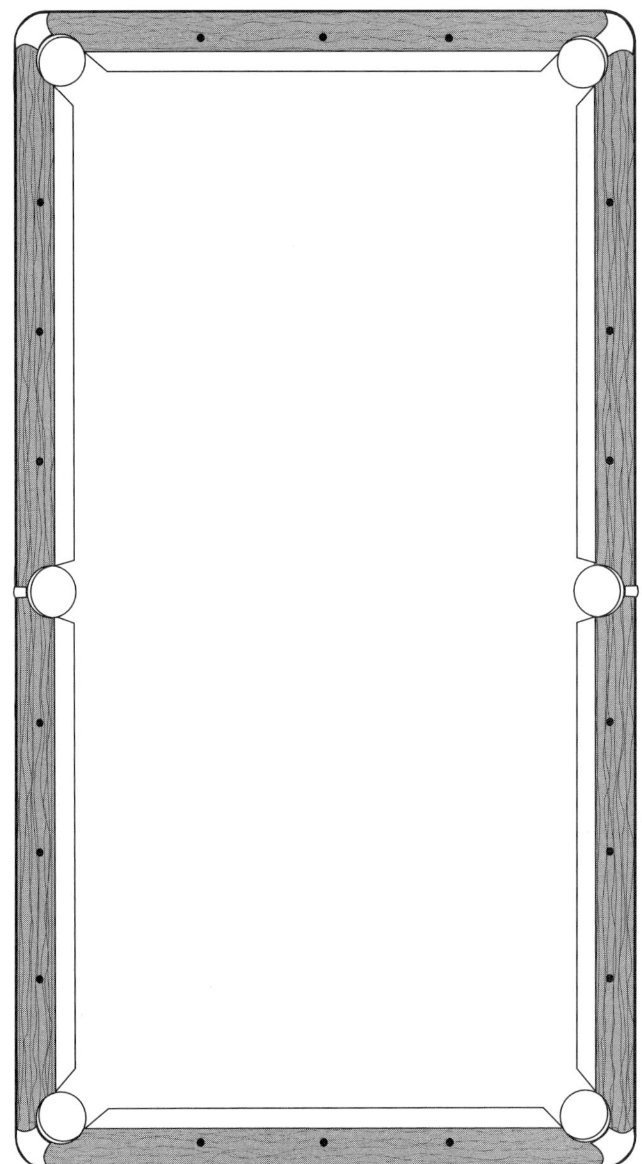

PHIL CAPELLE'S PLAY YOUR BEST NINE BALL

Notes

Top Nine Ball Players

Players in the BCA Hall of Fame

Luther Lassiter ("Wimpy") Many consider him to be the finest Nine Ball player ever. In the All Around Championships in Johnston City, IL, he won the Nine Ball title four times. Lassiter was one of the finest shotmakers to ever pick up a cue.

Mike Sigel ("Captain Hook") Won the U.S. Open in Nine Ball three times and a world's title. Sigel is a great all around player with over 100 pro titles. He is well known for superb cue ball control and shotmaking under pressure, and for having no weaknesses.

Nick Varner He is the only back-to-back winner of the U.S. Open, having won in 1989-1990. Varner was named Player of the Year four times. In 1989 he won an astounding 8 tournaments. Varner is a tough, rock solid competitor, with no weaknesses.

Buddy Hall ("The Rifleman") Hall is a two-time winner of the U.S. Open and is the owner of countless other Nine Ball titles. Hall has been named Player of the Year on three occasions. While he is a superb shotmaker, Hall is perhaps best known for his precise cue ball control and his pattern play.

Steve Mizerak ("The Miz") Mizerak won the 1978 U.S. Open in Nine Ball, to go with his U.S. Open titles in Straight Pool. He was also named Player of the Year. Mizerak has a silky smooth and powerful stroke and has excellent command of the table in all situations.

Top Nine Ball Players

Earl Strickland ("The Pearl") Strickland has captured a record five U.S. Open titles and has been named Player of the Year six times. In addition, Strickland has won several World Titles. He is an offensive machine who can intimidate any opponent when on a roll. He is also known for his powerful break, accurate shotmaking, and expert cue ball control.

Johnny Archer ("The Scorpion") Archer has been named Player of the Year four times in the 1990's, and was also player of the decade in the 1990's. Has perhaps the best break in Nine Ball, is a talented shotmaker, and posses a solid all around game. Twice world champion and a winner of the U.S. Open.

Efren Reyes ("The Magician") His one U.S. Open title was followed by three consecutive second place finishes. He won the inaugural Masters Title and also owns a World Championship. He has twice been named Player of the Year. The best kicker in pool, he plays pinpoint position, is extremely creative, and arguably the best all around player ever.

Jim Rempe ("King James") He captured numerous titles throughout the 1970's, more than any other player. Known for his expert position play, textbook stroke, and command of the table.

Allen Hopkins ("Young Hoppe") He is a solid all around player who excels at all of the major games. Hopkins is a two-time winner of the U.S. Open in Nine Ball, along with numerous titles in the other games.

Kim Davenport He is the winner of numerous professional events and has been named Player of the Year. Davenport is a tough competitor and an extremely accurate shotmaker under pressure.

Top Foreign Players

Americans have long dominated pool, but times are changing as Nine Ball has grown in popularity throughout the world. The following list highlights just a few of the many fine players from across the globe.

Fong Pang Chao, of Chinese Taipei known as "The Stoned Faced Killer", is a two-time World Champion and winner of the Challenge of Champions.

Francisco Bustamante is a native of the Philippines, who now lives in Germany. He has perhaps the most powerful break in pool. He has won numerous titles in the U.S. and has been named Player of the Year.

Jose Parica of the Philippines has won several pro titles in the U.S. and has been named Player of the Year. He is one of the best shotmakers in pool and a fearless competitor.

Takeshi Okumuru of Japan has a World Championship to his credit along with a runner-up finish in the U.S. Open. His position play and patterns are extremely precise.

Oliver Ortmann of Germany has won a World Championship in Nine Ball and is also holds several major Straight Pool titles. Ortmann plays fast and loose and is an incredibly gifted shotmaker.

Ralf Souquet has finished first and second in the World Championships. He also won the 2000 BCA U.S. Open in 14.1. Souquet is a true craftsman who excels at position play and control of the table.

Kunihiko Takahashi of Japan has won a World Championship. He has a very soft touch and plays excellent position.

Mika Immonen of Finland holds a World Championship, thanks to a solid stroke and flawless position play.

Top Women Nine Ball Players

Jean Balukas A member of the BCA Hall of Fame, Ms. Balukas was a great all around player who dominates women's pool until her retirement. She was named Player of the Year on five occasions. She won the U.S Open in Nine Ball three times in a period of four years. In Straight Pool she has recorded runs above 100 balls.

Allison Fisher Ms. Fisher has been named Player of the Year five consecutive times. She has won three World Championships, five National Championships and virtually every other major title. She excels at shotmaking, position play, and has near perfect mechanics. She also has a BCA U.S Open 14.1 title on her resume.

Loree Jon Jones She has been named Player in the Year on four occasions. Along the way she has captured U.S. Open, a World Championship, and a host of tour events. She has a textbook stroke and plays superb position.

Ewa Laurance A native of Sweden, she is a two-time winner of the U.S. Open and has won a World Championship. She has also been named Player of the Year. Nothing moves but her arm when stroking, which makes her a model of consistency.

Jeanette Lee "The Black Widow" has won numerous pro titles, including the U.S. Open, and has been named Player of the Year. She has a solid all around game and is also an excellent Straight Pool player, having run in excess of 100 balls.

Robin Dodson has earned a reputation for playing her best pool in the most lucrative events. She won back-to-back World Championships and has been named Player of the Year. She is an expert at safety play, but her biggest strengths are her shotmaking and her ability to play under pressure.

Foreign Players

The world wide growth of pool has led to the emergence of several find players who are becoming know to fans in the U.S. and throughout the world. England's Karen Corr, a deadly shotmaker, has won numerous titles on the WPBA. Gerda Hofstatter is a consistent top finisher who has won a World Championship. Shin-Mei Lie of Chinese Taipei has won a World Championship, as has Ireland's Julie Kelly. Helena Thornfeldt from Sweden and Jennifer Chen of Taiwan are two more solid performers on the WPBA.

Index of Players

Accu-Stats Video Productions

Pat Fleming

Pat Fleming is the founder of Accu-Stats Video Productions and the man who is largely responsible for the filming and production of the videos of the top pros in tournament action. I created numerous illustrations that appear throughout the book from the videos, which I trust you have enjoyed and found to be particularly instructive.

Pat Fleming, who was born in 1948, got hooked on pool at a very early age while playing on a toy table that his father had acquired. When he became a teenager, he started working part time at a local poolroom. One of the benefits was free table time. It was not long before Fleming was running over 100 balls. Fleming was attracted to pool because it was an individual sport, and one in which he was particularly gifted. He subsequently went on to compete successfully as a pro, with a best finish of third place at the 1981 World 14.1 Championship. During his career, Fleming recorded victories over most of the great players of his era, including Archer, Strickland, Sigel, Varner, Mizerak, Rempe, Hopkins and many others.

Although Fleming enjoyed some success as a pro, the business side of pool somehow managed to lure him just far enough from the table that he could film the action of his peers. In 1983 Fleming created Accu-Stats to measure the performance of the pros. At the time, Fleming had no idea that this would one day lead to the founding a video business devoted to pro pool.

He began recording matches on video in 1987 for the purpose of dissecting the matches to derive statistics for his Accu-Stats newsletter. The newsletter was a hit with many fans. In late 1987, Fleming began selling the videos to players, and eventually to fans of the sport. Since then, he has traveled to numerous tournaments annually, recording events in Nine Ball, Straight Pool, One Pocket, Banks, Three Cushion Billiards and other games. In the process he has created a library of tapes that is an invaluable resource for fans of the game.

When asked what he likes most about the business, Fleming replied, "I like the high profile of being so involved, and I cherish the preservation of the game through video." Of all the pros Fleming has taped, his two favorites are Jim Rempe, who he likes for his skill, composure and longevity, and Efren Reyes, who he admires for his skill, creativity and demeanor.

Fleming has constantly upgraded the production of the videos, adding cameras and graphics. He is aided by a team of enthusiastic people who share his love for the game. Fleming and his staff of Pete Fleming, Julian Robertson, Shaun Robertson, Dean Gupton and Merlyn Glodek use state-of-the-art equipment to produce tapes that are of a quality that rival the coverage of pool by the TV networks.

The Accu-Stats Scoring System

The Accu-Stats rating appears next to the players name on all Nine Ball matches that Accu-Stats has filmed from the 1998 U.S. Open. A players Accu-Stats rating is a measure of a player's total performance. The ratings take into account the critical areas of skill. There are five types of errors: Misses, Scratch on the Break, Bad Kick, Bad Safety, and Bad Position. To compute the "Total Performance Average", you take all of a players successful shots and divide them by the total shots played. For example, if a player pocketed 80 shots and made 20 errors, his average would be .800. If a player pockets 73 balls and makes only 3 errors, his average is .961. To win pro tournaments, you must average at least .875. To finish in the money, you should average .825. To be competitive in a pro event, you should average .800.

The .950 Club (Feature Started in 1998)

Accu-Stats started posting the scores of the matches it films in its catalog, starting with the U.S. Open in 1998. The pros have registered 11 matches with performance ratings above .950 out of 222 played (111 matches x 2 player). That computes to a less than 5% of matches played leads to a score in excess of .950. At the Derby City Classic, 7.1% of matches resulted in scores above .950, thanks in part to the race to seven format. Only 4.1% of matches to 9 or more resulted in scores above .950.

Nick Varner .977	2001 Masters 9-Ball Championships
Mika Immonen 1.000	2001 Derby City Classic III
Mika Immonen .983	2001 Derby City Classic III
Earl Strickland .957	2000 U.S. Open
George SanSouci .951	2000 Derby City Classic II
Earl Strickland .958	1999 U.S. Open
Allison Fisher .970	1999 WPBA Prescott
Shannon Daulton .963	1999 Derby City Classic
Jim Rempe .960	1999 American Seniors Open
Jim Rempe .951	1999 American Seniors Open
Jose Garcia.958	1998 U.S. Open

Duel of the .900's

Efren Reyes (.919) df. Ralf Souquet (.920) 13-10	2001 Masters
Evgeny Stalev (.918) df. Charlie Williams (.917), 7-6	2001 Derby City
Johnny Archer (.930) df. Rudolfo Luat (.902), 11-8	1999 U.S. Open
Johnny Archer (.938) df. Jeremy Jones (.901) 11-7	1999 U.S. Open
Mika Immonen (.934) df. Jim Rempe (.903) 11-10	1998 U.S. Open

The Commentators

You just have to hear these guys. After awhile you will think they are your best friends talking pool with you in your living room. The conversations and comments are insightful, knowledgeable, humorous, offbeat and totally unrehearsed.

Bill Incardona is the voice of Accu-Stats, having logged more hours on tape than any other commentator. He gets psyched up for every match, and has an intensity that is completely genuine. His is extremely knowledgeable, has a great rapport with his guests, calls it like he's sees it and isn't afraid to ruffle a few feathers.

Grady "The Professor" Mathews is his colorful side kick on many matches, but takes the lead on many more. He is very eloquent, knows pool and the world of pool, and has many entertaining stories to tell, which spice up his telecasts.

Guests in the booth include some of the best players in the world. Among those I particularly enjoy are: Nick Varner, Buddy Hall, Johnny Archer, Jim Rempe, Jay Helfert and Danny DiLiberto.

Classic Comments

Below is a sampling of the type of comments that you are likely to hear on the Accu-Stats videos from the lead commentators and their guests.

"It's that violin stroke that they play that sweet music with, that Earl doesn't like the sound of." **Bill Incardona** after Francisco Bustamante hooked Earl Strickland

"After the match I'll buy him dinner, but right now I want to see him scratch every time he gets to the table." **Bill Incardona** when playing Tony Ellin

"Sometimes it is hard for me to not think of how awesome and intimidating some players are. The upper echelon players demand respect when they are at the table. You feel their presence." **Bill Incardona**

"So give me a menu and let me order. I'll order a kick 2-cushion hook safety." **Bill Incardona** commenting on a lengthy safety battle

"I'm dogging it up here. And I very rarely dog it up here as I happen to be one of the best booth players in the country, maybe the world." **Bill Incardona** after a miscall

On Close Matches: "I love knowledge and ability, excitement; this is everything. This is the embodiment of championship pocket billiards." **Grady Matthews**

"The balls always know who is behind." **Grady Mathews**

"My toughest opponent is myself." **Johnny Archer**

"The whole thing in 9-ball is momentum." **Johnny Archer**

"I wouldn't go into my desperation mode before the other guy reaches the hill." **Nick Varner**

"They (the crowd) like to see the pain, they like to see the struggle, they like to see the suffering." **Nick Varner** on the crowds response to a hill-hill match

"If you have confidence that eliminates pressure." **Jim Rempe**

"His offense is so powerful that it just makes you shake when you watch him play sometimes. I have to play him, but he also has to play me." **Steve Mizerak** on playing Earl Strickland

"If you hit the cue ball in the center, none of these things (deflection, curve, throw) will happen." **Jeff Carter** on the virtues of center axis stroking.

"Sort of like killer bees from Brazil." **Tony Annigoni** on the arrival of the Philippinos

"On long shots you have to stay perfectly still. The only thing that should be moving is your cue." **Buddy Hall**

"I think that's what makes a great champion because he plays out of love." **Earl Strickland** after winning his 5th U.S. Open

"Great kickers make their luck." **Dave Maddux**

"I love these safety battles. It's like a chess match." **Jay Helfert**

"To stay focused. To realize that this is not a social event. This is not a tea party. You're here to play pool and make some money." **Jeanette Lee**

Recommended Matches

The Accu-Stats catalog lists over 300 videos of Nine Ball. The list below is some of my favorite videos. Pat Fleming's top 12 are marked with an asterisk (*). The list should help you to get started with building your collection. You and your friends may also have videos that you would like to recommend to one another. The commentators are listed below the players.

Two Legends at War - 1992
S15-05 Buddy Hall df. Nick Varner (SF) 13-12
Bill Incardona, Grady Mathews $32 150 Min.

Two Tough Shots Claim Win - 1992
S16-03 Earl Strickland df. Johnny Archer 13-12
Bill Incardona, Grady Mathews $24 102 Min.

Battle of the Giants – 1993*
S17-05 Earl Strickland df. Mike Sigel 13-11
Bill Incardona, Mark Wilson $24 100 Min

Straight Shooting Exhibition - 1993
189B-10 Mike Sigel df. Johnny Archer 11-10
Grady Mathews, Es Sheahan $24 111 Min.

Reyes First U.S. Open Title-1994
199B-15 Efren Reyes df. Nick Varner 9-6
Bill Incardona, Johnny Archer $22 85 Min.

A Red Hot Finish – 1994*
S20-02 Francisco Bustamante df. Efren Reyes 13-12
Grady Mathews, Buddy Hall $22 84 Min.

A Shocking End to a Classic Battle – 1994*
S20-15 Johnny Archer df. Rafael Martinez, (F) 15-14
Bill Incardona, Buddy Hall $28 130 Min.

"The Magician" at Work - 1995
95PC-03 Efren Reyes df. Kim Davenport (F) 11-9
Nick Varner, Buddy Hall, Tom Kelly $24 71 Min.

The Shot Head Around the Pool World- 1995*
S21-11 Efren Reyes df. Earl Strickland (F) 13-12
Bill Incardona, Jim Rempe $24 107 Min.

The Rocket over The Hurricane – 1995*
S22-10 Rodney Morris df. Tony Ellin 11-10
Bill Incardona, Tony Anigonni $24 105 Min.

Double Hill Thriller – 1996*
TB-12 Grady Mathews df. Bob Vanover 13-12
Buddy Hall, Danny DiLiberto $24 120 Min.

Titanic Final Game Caps Masterpiece – 1996*
S23-08 Johnny Archer df. Efren Reyes 11-10
Bill Incardona, Dave Maddux $24 111 Min.

Run Out City - 1996
S23-10 Nick Varner df. Johnny Archer (F) 11-9
Bill Incardona, Buddy Hall $32 150 Min.

The Pearl on a Roll - 1997
229B-14 Earl Strickland df. Efren Reyes (F) 11-3
Bill Incardona, Grady Mathews $20 65 Min.

Souquet's First Major Title in America – 1998*
S27-10 Ralf Souquet df. Efren Reyes (F) 6-2,2-6,6-2
Bill Incardona, Jay Helfert $32 160 Min.

Hall Gets Out From Everywhere - 1998
239B15 Buddy Hall df. Tang Hoa (F) 11-5
Nick Varner, Kim Davenport $28 126 Min.

"The Pain, the Suffering" – 1998*
239B13 Mika Immonen df. Jim Rempe 11-10
Nick Varner, Jay Helfert $28 132 Min.

Legends Run a Marathon – 1999*
SR99-07 Jim Rempe vs. Nick Varner (Mystery match)
Grady Mathews, Jerry Forsyth $36 178 Min.

Archer Wins the U.S. Open - 1999
249B13 Johnny Archer df, Jeremy Jones (F) 11-7
Grady Mathews, Nick Varner $34 145 Min.

The Scorpion Stings The Magician – 2000*
259B-01 Johnny Archer df. Efren Reyes 11-10
Bill Incardona, Grady Mathews $30 123 Min.

Earl Fires a .957 on Way to 5th Open - 2000
259B Earl Strickland df. George SanSouci 11-6
Bill Incardona, Mark Wilson $26 94 Min.

Immonen Plays Perfect (1.000) Pool - 2001
D3-9B7 Mika Immonen df. Johnny Archer 7-3
Bill Incardona, Danny DiLiberto $26 111 Min.
(Tape also includes John Pinegar df. John Hager, Jr.)

Duel of the .900's – 2001*
M1-13 Efren Reyes df. Ralf Souquet 13-9
Grady Mathews, Buddy Hall $26 95 Min.

Reyes Captures Inaugural Masters - 2001
M1-14 Efren Reyes df. Earl Strickland 13-10
Grady Mathews, Buddy Hall $26 95 Min.

Player Review Favorites
These tapes feature an analysis by either or both of the contestants that was taped and added to the tape after the match was filmed. You can learn much from hearing the player's analysis of their own game as they candidly describe both their good shots and their mistakes.

Parica in Dead Stroke – 1992
S15-03 Jose Parica df. Earl Strickland 13-5
Jose Parica, Bill Incardona $20 44 Min.

Voice of Accu-Stats Analyses His Game – 1992*
179B-02 Tony Ellin df. Bill Incardona 13-11
Bill Incardona, Bill Staton $24 109 Min.

Jeanette Lee on Winning at Pool – 1994*
199B-13 Jeanette Lee df. Robin Dodson 11-3
Jeanette Lee, Pat Fleming $20 66 Min.

The Miz and Billy Show - 1994
199B-05 Steve Mizerak df. Earl Strickland 13-10
Steve Mizerak, Bill Incardona $24 91 Min.

Archer Talks Pool – 1997*
229B-05 Johnny Archer df. Ismael Paez 11-7
Johnny Archer, Grady Mathews $22 86 Min.

Jose Garcia's Clinic on Position Play (.958) – 1998*
239B-09 Jose Garcia df. Tony Robles (PR) 11-4
Jose Garcia, Pat Fleming $20 55 Min.

How to Order Videos of the Pros

Accu-Stats Video Productions
P.O. Box 299
Bloomingdale, NJ 07403
PH: 1-800-828-0397
Email: Accu-Stats@accu-stats.com
Web: accu-stats.com

- Catalog – Lists 100's of tapes
- Best and most popular tapes are highlighted
- Discounts for multiple purchases

How To Learn from Watching Videos

Preshot Routines Each player follows a certain procedure prior to playing a shot. This includes evaluating the table and getting set over the shot. Look for players whose style most closely matches yours, and then see if there is something you can add to your favorite's routine.

Take Notes Keep a note pad handy for things you want to work on. Make diagram using the blank diagram on page 448.

Shotmaking Observe the pros method for playing such key shots as the break, kick shots, banks, billiards, and the jump shot.

Strategy Pay special attention to their pushouts and choice of safeties. Amateurs can gain much from improving their safety play.

Watch them Play Look for their pace of play, changes in momentum, and how the players react to mistakes and great shots by both themselves and their opponent. Observe how each player conducts themselves at the table.

Position Play I strongly advise you to play any position route that you wish to master in slow motion to learn the precise path of the cue ball.

Pattern Play Look for the flow, as each shot seems to naturally connect to the next one.

Commentators The commentators are all top players, so it pays to listen to their comments, criticisms, and words of advice.

Evaluate their Decisions Before each shot, ask yourself how you would play the shot. Then consider the commentators choices and observe what the player chose to do. This will train you to think about each shot, and you will learn how closely your thinking matches that of a top player.

Slow Motion If you are a super serious student of the game who loves watching videos, I suggest you purchase a VCR with enhanced special effects. Slow motion and frame advance help you to see the cue ball do things you could never see with the naked eye. This is especially important for learning the cue ball's true path after contact, and for how the cue ball reacts coming off the rails. Slow motion also enables you to hone in on your favorites mechanics. Slow motion can also teach you how a rack of Nine Ball comes apart on the break.

Rewind Make liberal use of the rewind button. Play over any parts that you didn't fully understand on the first viewing.

Time Log When you come to a part of the video that you will want to review at a future date, check your VCR's counter and write down the time it appears on the video.

About Phil Capelle

I remember waiting in line to cash a check at the student union at U.C. Berkeley when I gazed over at the double glass doors, which led to the campus poolroom. I suddenly felt the urge to go check out the happenings. Within moments I was checking out a rack of balls. Little did I know at the time, but I was about to embark on a journey in pool that has now lasted over 30 years, with no letup in sight.

Like most beginners, I was lucky to make a ball the first time out. I knew that help was needed if I was going to really "get into" the sport. A trip to the campus bookstore was in order. I discovered a copy of *Willie Mosconi on Pocket Billiards*. What a great roll! I improved dramatically almost overnight after reading his advice on the fundamentals. It proved to me that a little knowledge can take you quite a ways.

Thirty years later, I continue to learn new things every day about this endlessly fascinating and challenging game of pool. Much of what I discover about pool comes from teaching and watching others play. In the years ahead, I look forward to sharing my findings with you, and I hope they greatly help your enjoyment of pool.